A Companion to African Cinema

Wiley Blackwell Companions to National Cinemas

The Wiley Blackwell Companions to National Cinemas showcase the rich film heritages of various countries across the globe. Each volume sets the agenda for what is now known as world cinema whilst challenging Hollywood's lock on the popular and scholarly imagination. Whether exploring Spanish, German or Chinese film, or the broader traditions of Eastern Europe, Scandinavia, Australia, Latin America, and Africa, the 20–25 newly commissioned essays comprising each volume include coverage of the dominant themes of canonical, controversial, and contemporary films; stars, directors, and writers; key influences; reception; and historiography and scholarship. Written in a sophisticated and authoritative style by leading experts they will appeal to an international audience of scholars, students, and general readers.

Published:

A Companion to African Cinema, edited by Kenneth W. Harrow and Carmela Garritano

A Companion to Italian Cinema, edited by Frank Burke

A Companion to Latin American Cinema, edited by Maria M. Delgado, Stephen M. Hart, and Randal Johnson

A Companion to Russian Cinema, edited by Birgit Beumers

A Companion to Nordic Cinema, edited by Mette Hjort and Ursula Lindqvist

A Companion to Hong Kong Cinema, edited by Esther M. K. Cheung, Gina Marchetti, and Esther C.M. Yau

A Companion to Contemporary French Cinema, edited by Alistair Fox, Michel Marie, Raphaëlle Moine, and Hilary Radner

A Companion to Spanish Cinema, edited by Jo Labanyi and Tatjana Pavlović

A Companion to Chinese Cinema, edited by Yingjin Zhang

A Companion to East European Cinemas, edited by Anikó Imre

A Companion to German Cinema, edited by Terri Ginsberg & Andrea Mensch

Forthcoming:

A Companion to British and Irish Cinema, edited by John Hill

A Companion to Korean Cinema, edited by Jihoon Kim and Seung-hoon Jeong

A Companion to Indian Cinema, edited by Neepa Majumdar and Ranjani Mazumdar

A Companion to Australian Cinema, edited by Felicity Collins, Jane Landman, and Susan Bye

A Companion to Japanese Cinema, edited by David Desser

A Companion to
African Cinema

Edited by

Kenneth W. Harrow
Carmela Garritano

WILEY Blackwell

This edition first published 2019
© 2019 John Wiley & Sons, Inc.

The right of Kenneth W. Harrow and Carmela Garritano to be identified as the authors of the editorial material in this work has been asserted in accordance with law.

Registered Office(s)
John Wiley & Sons, Inc., 111 River Street, Hoboken, NJ 07030, USA

Editorial Office
The Atrium, Southern Gate, Chichester, West Sussex, PO19 8SQ, UK

For details of our global editorial offices, customer services, and more information about Wiley products visit us at www.wiley.com.

Wiley also publishes its books in a variety of electronic formats and by print-on-demand. Some content that appears in standard print versions of this book may not be available in other formats.

Library of Congress Cataloging-in-Publication Data

Names: Harrow, Kenneth W., editor. | Garritano, Carmela, 1968– editor.
Title: A companion to African cinema / edited by Kenneth W. Harrow, Carmela Garritano.
Description: Hoboken, NJ: Wiley-Blackwell, 2019. | Series: Wiley Blackwell companions to national cinemas | Includes bibliographical references and index.
Identifiers: LCCN 2018023725 (print) | LCCN 2018024153 (ebook) | ISBN 9781119100058 (Adobe PDF) | ISBN 9781119099857 (ePub) | ISBN 9781119100317 (hardcover)
Subjects: LCSH: Motion pictures–Africa–History and criticism.
Classification: LCC PN1993.5.A35 (ebook) | LCC PN1993.5.A35 C655 2018 (print) | DDC 791.43096–dc23
LC record available at https://lccn.loc.gov/2018023725

Cover Design: Wiley
Cover Image: © Nathan Meyer/EyeEm/Getty Images

Set in 11/13pt Dante by SPi Global, Pondicherry, India
Printed in Singapore by C.O.S. Printers Pte Ltd

10 9 8 7 6 5 4 3 2 1

Dedicated to our children and grandchildren
Mikołaj, Ayla, Evren, Felix, Lucille, Max, and Miriam

Contents

Notes on Contributors

Abdalla Uba Adamu is Professor of Media and Cultural Communication, Bayero University, Kano, Nigeria. He is currently the Vice-Chancellor, National Open University of Nigeria (NOUN). His research focus is on interfaces between African Islamicate cultures and contemporary popular culture. His recent publications include "Controversies and Restrictions of Visual Representation of Prophets in Northern Nigerian Popular Culture" (*Journal of African Media Studies*, 9(1): 17–31).

Moradewun Adejunmobi is Professor of African American and African Studies at the University of California, Davis. She is the author of two books: *J.J. Rabearivelo, Literature and Lingua Franca in Colonial Madagascar*, and *Vernacular Palaver: Imaginations of the Local and Non-Native Languages in West Africa*. Her research on Nigerian film, media, and performance has appeared in *Popular Communication*, *Cultural Critique*, *Black Camera* and *Cinema Journal* among others.

Akin Adesokan is Associate Professor of Comparative Literature, and of Cinema and Media Studies at the Media School at Indiana University, Bloomington. His books include *Roots in the Sky*, a novel; *Postcolonial Artists and Global Aesthetics*, a critical study; and *Celebrating D.O. Fagunwa: Aspects of African and World Literary History*, a co-edited volume on the work of Daniel Fagunwa, the pioneer Yoruba novelist. His writings have also appeared in *AGNI*, *Screen*, *Glänta*, *Social Dynamics*, *African Affairs*, *Black Camera*, *Research in African Literatures*, *Frame*, and *Textual Practice*, as well as in numerous edited volumes. He is a Contributing Editor of *The Chimurenga Chronic*, the Cape Town-based journal of politics and ideas.

Karen Bouwer is Professor of French in the Department of Modern and Classical Languages at the University of San Francisco. Her ongoing research interests include Francophone African literature, African cinema, gender and, more recently, literary and cinematic representations of urban spaces. Her abiding interest in the

Democratic Republic of the Congo culminated in the publication of her book *Gender and Decolonization in the Congo: The Legacy of Patrice Lumumba* (Palgrave Macmillan, 2010).

Jacques de Villiers is a doctoral student at the Centre for Film and Media Studies, University of Cape Town, South Africa, where he is busy writing a dissertation on temporality in African cinemas and teaches part-time. He is also an award-winning documentary and fiction film editor, whose work has played at major festivals around the world, including Sundance, Berlin, and Rotterdam.

Vlad Dima is Associate Professor at the University of Wisconsin, Madison. He has published numerous articles, mainly on French and Francophone cinemas, but also on Francophone literature, comics, American cinema, and television. He is the author of *Sonic Space in Djibril Diop Mambety's Films* (2017, Indiana University Press). He is currently working on a second project titled, *The Beautiful Skin: Clothing, Football and Fantasy in West African Cinema, 1964–2014.*

Lindiwe Dovey is Reader in Screen Arts and Industries and the Chair of the Centre for Media and Film Studies at SOAS University of London. She co-founded Film Africa and the Cambridge African Film Festival, festivals which she has also directed, and she works as a film curator and filmmaker. She has published widely on screen media, and her most recent book is *Curating Africa in the Age of Film Festivals* (2015), which Cameron Bailey (Artistic Director of the Toronto International Film Festival) has called "an essential read."

Rachel Gabara teaches Francophone African and European literature and film at the University of Georgia. She is the author of *From Split to Screened Selves: French and Francophone Autobiography in the Third Person* (Stanford, 2006), and her essays on African film in a global context appear in *Italian Neorealism and Global Cinema* (Wayne State, 2007), *Global Art Cinema* (Oxford, 2010), and *The Global Auteur: Politics and Philosophy in 21st Century Cinema* (Bloomsbury, 2016). She is currently at work on a book-length project on documentary film in West and Central Africa.

Carmela Garritano is Associate Professor of Africana Studies and Film Studies at Texas A&M University. She is author of *African Video Movies and Global Desires: A Ghanaian History* (Ohio University Press), a 2013 *Choice* Outstanding Academic Title and winner of the African Literature Association Best First Book award. Her research has been supported by Fulbright IIE and the West African Research Association, and her writing has appeared, or is forthcoming, in *African Studies Review*, *Black Camera*, *Cinema Journal*, *Critical Arts*, *The Cambridge Journal of Postcolonial Literary Inquiry*, and *Research in African Literatures*.

Suzanne Gauch is the author of *Maghrebs in Motion: North African Cinema in Nine Movements* (2016) and *Liberating Shahrazad: Feminism, Postcolonialism, and Islam* (2007), as well as numerous articles on African film and literature. She teaches gender, film, and postcolonial studies in the Department of English at Temple University.

Lindsey Green-Simms is Assistant Professor of Literature at American University, Washington, DC. Her book *Postcolonial Automobility: Car Culture in West Africa* is published by University of Minnesota Press (2017). She has also published articles in *Research in African Literature, Camera Obscura, Transition,* and the *Journal of African Cinemas.* She is currently drafting a manuscript on queer African cinema.

Kenneth W. Harrow is Distinguished Professor Emeritus of English at Michigan State University with specializations in African literature and cinema. He has taught in the Université de Yaounde and l'Université Cheikh Anta Diop in Dakar. He is the author of *Thresholds of Change in African Literature* (Heinemann, 1994), *Less Than One and Double: A Feminist Reading of African Women's Writing* (Heinemann, 2002; trans. as *Moins d'un et double,* L'Harmattan, 2007), *Postcolonial African Cinema: From Political Engagement to Postmodernism* (Indiana University Press, 2007), and *Trash! A Study of African Cinema Viewed from Below* (Indiana University Press, 2013). He has edited numerous collections on such topics as Islam and African literature, African cinema, and women in African cinema.

Jonathan Haynes is Professor of English at Long Island University in Brooklyn. A former Guggenheim Fellow and Fulbright Senior Scholar, he wrote *Cinema and Social Change in West Africa* (1995) with Onookome Okome and edited *Nigerian Video Films* (1997, 2000) and a special issue of *Journal of African Cinemas* (2012). His new book is *Nollywood: The Creation of Nigerian Film Genres* from University of Chicago Press (2016).

MaryEllen Higgins is Associate Professor of English at the Pennsylvania State University, Greater Allegheny. Her books include *The Western in the Global South* (Routledge, 2015, co-edited with Rita Kerestezi and Dayna Oscherwitz) and *Hollywood's Africa After 1994* (Ohio University Press, 2012). She has published articles in *Research in African Literatures, African Studies Review, African Literature Today,* and *Tulsa Studies in Women's Literature,* among other scholarly venues. She is the associate producer of two films: Jean-Pierre Bekolo's *Naked Reality* (2016) and Bekolo's *Les Choses et les mots de Mudimbe* (2015).

Justin Izzo is Assistant Professor of French Studies at Brown University. His research deals with literature, film, anthropology, and philosophy from Francophone Africa and the Caribbean. He is the author of *Experiments with Empire: Anthropology and Fiction in the French Atlantic,* forthcoming with Duke University Press. Current and forthcoming publications include articles in *Research in African Literatures*, *Small Axe*, *African Studies Review*, and *Contemporary French and Francophone Studies*.

Alessandro Jedlowski is a Belgian Scientific Research Fund (F.R.S.-FNRS) post-doctoral fellow in anthropology at the University of Liège (Belgium) and a lecturer in African Studies at the University of Turin (Italy). His main research interests include African cinema and media, urban cultures, media and migration, and South-South media exchanges. He is the author of numerous publications, including essays in academic journals such as *Television and New Media*, *African Affairs*, *Journal of African Cultural Studies*, and *Journal of African Cinemas*, and the co-editor of the books *Cine-Ethiopia: The History and Politics of Film in the Horn of Africa* (Michigan State University Press, 2018) and *Mobility between Africa, Asia and Latin America: Economic Networks and Cultural Interactions* (Zed Books, 2017).

Valérie K. Orlando is Professor of French and Francophone Literatures in the Department of French and Italian at the University of Maryland, College Park. She is the author of six books, the most recent of which are *The Algerian New Novel: The Poetics of a Modern Nation, 1950–1979* (University of Virginia Press, 2017) and *New African Cinema* (Rutgers University Press, 2017). She has written numerous articles and chapters in books on Francophone writing from the Caribbean, North and West Africa, the African diaspora, African Cinema, and French literature and culture.

Dayna Oscherwitz is Associate Professor of French and Francophone Studies and Chair of the Department of World Languages at Southern Methodist University in Dallas. She is author of *Past Forward: French Cinema and the Postcolonial Heritage* (SIU Press, 2010) and co-editor, with MaryEllen Higgins and Rita Keresztesi of *The Western in the Global South* (Routledge, 2015) and has published widely on French and francophone African cinema.

P. Julie Papaioannou is a Senior Lecturer in the Department of Modern Languages and Cultures at the University of Rochester, in Rochester, NY. Her teaching and research interests include French and Francophone literature and film, literary and postcolonial theory, feminist and film theories.

Sheila Petty is Professor of Media Studies at the University of Regina, Canada. She has written extensively on issues of cultural representation, identity, and nation in African and African diasporic screen media. She is author of *Contact Zones: Memory, Origin and Discourses in Black Diasporic Cinema* (2008). She is co-editor of the *Directory of World Cinema: Africa* (2015). Her current research focuses on transvergent African cinemas, new Maghrebi cinemas, and interpretive strategies for analyzing digital creative cultural practices.

Robin Steedman is an AHRC Creative Economy Engagement Fellow at the University of Sheffield where she studies data, diversity, and inequality in the creative industries. She recently completed her doctorate in African Languages and Cultures at SOAS University of London. Her doctoral research explores how and why Nairobi-based female filmmakers can be considered to constitute a film movement and is the first major work on these filmmakers and their unique female-led industry. She is also currently working on a project examining African documentary film production funds.

Melissa Thackway lectures in African Cinema at Sciences-Po and at the Institut des Langues et Civilisations Orientales (INALCO), in Paris. She is also a researcher, freelance documentary filmmaker, and translator. Author of *Africa Shoots Back: Alternative Representations in Sub-Saharan Francophone African Film* (James Currey/ Indiana University Press/David Philips, 2003), she has published numerous articles and speaks regularly on the subject in international conferences and seminars.

Noah Tsika is Assistant Professor of Media Studies at Queens College, City University of New York. His books include *Nollywood Stars: Media and Migration in West Africa and the Diaspora* and *Pink 2.0: Encoding Queer Cinema on the Internet*, and he is the editor of a special issue of *Black Camera* on the marginalization of African media studies.

Introduction

Critical Approaches to Africa's Cinema, From the Age of Liberation and Struggle to the Global, Popular, and Curatorial

Kenneth W. Harrow and Carmela Garritano

African Filmmaking and Criticism

What would an ideal approach to African cinema look like today? For us, the question lies less in approximating an answer, but in providing a focus on critical approaches that do more than reflect current trends, that impose a demand.

In the past, critical emphases fell on opposing approaches. One emphasized the sociological or sociopolitical, often using ethnology to critique, explain, or even to judge the contours of African cultural production, across the board. The underlying question was how faithful is this film, or novel, to the cultural and social reality. Linked to this way of reading, the writings of many of the first theorists and critics of African film elucidated or amplified the anti-colonial or cultural nationalist intent of the African filmmaker. The critic sometimes operated as a cultural translator or historian, providing the information that an "outsider" audience might require to understand or accept the film's truth. Politically, the 1960s and 1970s insured that the focus was grounded in Marxist revolutionary analysis. The names of filmmakers who drove this platform consistently marked the era: they included Sembène Ousmane, Med Hondo, Haile Gerima, and Sarah Maldoror. Their inspiring work and deep engagement were measures of revolutionary, Fanonian consciousness. Unfortunately, this approach, which was dominant for perhaps two decades after independence, ultimately led to dead-ends as what we now call postcolonialism could only be post-revolutionary. In other words, Third Cinema, like the term Third World, had its moment when it first

A Companion to African Cinema, First Edition. Edited by Kenneth W. Harrow and Carmela Garritano.
© 2019 John Wiley & Sons, Inc. Published 2019 by John Wiley & Sons, Inc.

stirred its audience to action, a moment that started to pass in the 1980s, to be supplanted by the postcolonial.

In contrast, ideological analysis developed in harmony with the growing importance of cultural studies. In cultural studies work, analyses examined the construction of the class-bound and racial subject, eventually, with the work of Stuart Hall and Paul Gilroy, giving us the postcolonial subject and postcolonial subjectivity, which lie at the heart of African cultural studies and especially film studies. Cultural studies enabled us to take into account manifestations of the political changes brought by neocolonialism and the waning of the Cold War, with the conclusions of the struggle for national independence: the Portuguese colonies completed the historical task of revolution, and the Rhodesian and South African struggles finally terminated roughly by the end of the decade.[1]

Several critics of African film, aligning themselves with film theorists associated with the journal *Screen*, such as Stephen Health and Laura Mulvey, drew on psychoanalysis to theorize subjectivity and desire.[2] Psychoanalysis offered a theoretical vocabulary to explore the truly new shift that was taking place in the films. It came not in the raising of consciousness, with femininst conscientization, or with ideological analysis that explained how neocolonialism affected the people, the masses, the underclass, the workers, etc., but with the issues surrounding desire. The cinematic harbingers there include Henri Duparc, whose *Bal Poussière* (1989) and Désiré Ecaré's *Visages des femmes* (1985) never received their due because they appeared to make an embarrassed acknowledgment that sexuality and desire might be acceptable topics of African cinema (Tcheuyap, 2011). These films seemed not to be attending Med Hondo's continual pressure for a cinema of liberation, following the critical impulse established by Teshome Gabriel (1982) and Ferid Boughedir (1983), and later Frank Ukadike (1994), and thus we can see a dialectical contrast between Duparc's light *Bal Poussière* and Hondo's serious *Sarraounia* (1986), between Sembène's *Xala* ([1994] 1975) and Moussa Touré's *TGV* (1998); between Gerima's brilliant LA Rebellion work, notably *Bush Mama* (1979) and Mweze's delighting the audience with charm, romance, and music in *La vie est belle* (1987).

Simultaneously, there was a shift of the critical target of many novels and films from the European metropoles, or white racism, to the corruption or abuse of power of the independent African state (notably in such works of fiction as Ayi Kwei Armah's *The Beautyful Ones Are Not Yet Born* (1968) or Ahmadou Kourouma's *Les soleils des indépendences* ([1968] 1970). This was replicated in a cinema and theatre of struggle against the Big Men in Power, with theatre meeting cinema in Wole Soyinka's *Kongi's Harvest* (1970), a film generally regarded as a cinematic failure, but still a harbinger for a host of works, from Gerima's *Harvert 3000* (1976) to Souleymane Cisse's *Finyé* (1982) and *Yeelen* (1987), Idrissa Ouedraogo's *Tilai* (1990) and *Yaaba* (1989), to finally the corpus of Sembène's films. The figure of the domineering patriarch appears early in his *Tauw* (1970), but systematically in his works since then. The shift of target in Sembène's *Faat Kine* (2001) is most instructive. We still have the Big Man, patriarchal, sexist, and dominant, but only dominant in the flashbacks, in the past when Kine was young. In his earlier period the dream of women's emergence could take the form of an ideal princess, as in *Ceddo* (1977), or a woman leading the revolution of the future, as in Rama, El Hadj's daughter in *Xala* (1975).

The ideal of a rise in women's cinema depended on an infrastructure of training, financing, and eventually of information, which Beti Ellerson with her Women Make Movies project developed. Safi Faye and Sarah Maldoror inspired the new generation. Their training and importance in the list of African filmmakers came despite the obstacles they faced as women, and their successes in overcoming them. Safi Faye was trained with Jean Rouch, as an assistant. Sarah Maldoror worked with French TV, but married an Angolan revolutionary, Mario Pinto de Andrade, who became a major figure in the MPLA when fighting the Portuguese. Maldoror was of Guadeloupian origins, and created the first black theatre troop in Paris, "Les Griots." She learned filmmaking at VGIK in Moscow and by 1969 had directed a short film, *Monagambé* that won an award at the Carthage film festival. She produced dozens of documentaries, in addition to *Sambizanga* (1972), now considered a classic of African revolutionary cinema.

Safi Faye first met Rouch in 1966 and played a role in his *Petit à petit* (1969). She moved on to Paris where she studied ethnology. In 1975, she produced a major documentary, *Kaddu Beykat* (Peasant Letter), now considered a classic. She has directed eight films since then, inspiring other women filmmakers like Rose Bekale, Aminata Ouédraogo, and Yangba Léonie.

Following in the path of Maldoror, whose work she has honoured, Anne-Laure Folly studied law and decided to go into filmmaking after returning to France after a visit to Togo on the occasion of her grandmother's funeral. Her film *Femmes aux yeux ouverts*, made in 1994, marked the direction of the second wave of women directors. She served on the board of FEPACI from 1997–2006, and has made some 20 documentaries, including *Sarah Maldoror ou la nostalgie de l'utopie* in 1998. Faye and Maldoror followed paths that were compatible with the approaches and scholarship of the 1970s and 1980s (see *Ngambika*, 1986). Folly and Fanta Nacro marked the new direction of third wave feminism.

The 1990s initiated massive, structural and technological changes world-wide. Under globalization, media and movies, like capital, flow across open borders, though in grossly uneven patterns, and the result has been a major shift in the films and media viewers have access to, in how viewers watch content, in who makes movies, and even in what counts as film. In Africa, the liberalization of national economies and the imposition of structural adjustment policies; the opening-up of media environments; and the widespread availability of video technologies, radically altered film production, viewing, and distribution, and initiated what has come to be an unprecedented diversification of the African cinematic landscape. The most obvious product of these new global processes was the emergence of informal and independent commercial movie industries in Ghana and Nigeria. (Later, the English-language formation of West African commercial video production came to be known as Nollywood.) The wide availability of video equipment coupled with a flourishing market in imported content pirated to video created the conditions for the local production of feature-length narrative films on video. These early movies were screened exclusively in neighborhood video parlors and, in Ghana, in cinema theatres, but in only a few years, the straight-to-video model of distribution flourished and remained dominant in African cites such as Accra, Kumasi, Lagos, and Kano for almost 20 years, through the transition from analog to digital video modes of production and circulation and the rise of television as a viewing platform.

These popular movies were disarticulated from the cultural nationalist and postcolonial paradigms that thus far had shaped the discourse of African cinema – the films, the manifestos, and the scholarship. Though some popular videomakers were loosely linked to state institutions, the National Television Authority in Nigeria, and in Ghana, the Ghana Film Industry Corporation (GFIC), most entered movie production as untrained lovers of cinema and storytelling. Their notions about narrative and cinema, for the most part, derived from the films and media they had been exposed to as viewers – colonial documentaries, martial arts films, Bollywood, and Hollywood B movies – as well as from deep stores of oral culture and, more immediately, the rumors and stories that shaped African urban, popular imaginaries.

For African film critics to come to terms with commercial videos such as William Akuffo's *Zinabu* (1987) or Kenneth Nnebue's *Living in Bondage* (1992), they needed research methodologies that borrowed from ethnography and history so as to situate these popular forms in their local contexts and make sense of the pleasures they offered African audiences. More importantly, they had to learn to approach the film in terms of popular culture, not high culture, nor as direct expressions of political ideologies. Although Karen Barber (1987) had already carved out a path for such approaches to popular literature, and even theatre, it had not yet been done for cinema. Onookome Okome's and Jonathan Haynes' (1995, 2000) early writing on Nigerian film mapped out these new directions, making it impossible to merely dismiss Nollywood as a manifestation of cultural imperialism, or crude entertainment. More critically, commercial video raised urgent questions about globalization, questions made visible in the groundbreaking essay "Millennial Capitalism: First Thoughts on a Second Coming" (Comaroff and Comaroff 2000). What that essay provided was the possibility of seeing African cinema as participating in a cultural frame that had developed in response to the new economic order brought about by globalization. When the wealthy Nigerians in *Living in Bondage* (1992) celebrate their newfound access to astounding wealth, to control over the nefarious and satanic forces of capital that would provide them with all the cars, homes, women, whiskey, etc., that their hearts desired, they were willing to strike the Faustian bargain for their souls. This was represented in the magical contents that the cargo cults always believed were to be found in the ships' holds, and that, today, come in the form of containers. The millennial capitalism the Comaroffs signaled could only be understood with the old beliefs about magic deployed by Big Men, and that could now be represented in the Old and the New, the Old being the foundation for Nollywood that began with *Living in Bondage* (1992). The New appeared with the same themes and tropes, the same new styles of the commercial, with liberal capitalism marked by the commodity, and the genres of the melodramatic and the occult.

1992, the year *Living in Bondage* appeared also saw the appearance of the New spirit in Jean-Pierre Bekolo's *Quartier Mozart* and Jean-Marie Teno's *Afrique je te plumerai*. During this period, a new generation of African auteurs, perhaps best represented in Bekolo's *Aristotle's Plot* (1999), demanded that the "fathers of African cinema" make room. By then, Bekolo had already introduced the new generation of cinema with *Quartier Mozart* (1992) and its youthful characters. The saucy, hot, hilarious comedic qualities, earlier denied in Duparc now emerge full blown with Chef du Quartier, Chien Méchant, Mon Type, and in the figure of the comedian Essindi Minja who played the tailor in *Quartier* and concluded the film with a hilarious routine that put down the Big Man of the past. *Quartier Mozart* embodied the hip dance music associated with video culture, and is marked especially by quick cross cutting and chic stylishness in the falling-in-love scene between Mon Type and Samedi. Similarly, Teno's *Afrique je te plumerai* rewrote how the African voice could speak back with the saucy figure of Marie who parodied De Gaulle, mocking how the new Big Men carried on France's charge in Africa. Mostly Teno introduced us to his own sarcastic voiceover, rewriting how this new, personal ironic tone supplanted the severe Master's voice of political engagement in the past. His figure, that of a *"bonimenteur,"*[3] was like the narrative voiceover employed in Bekolo's *Saignantes* along with the figures of the two impudent prostitutes (Majolie and Chouchou). They embodied the "clitoral power" of Mevoungou, rewriting notions of sterner feminist discourses, moving away from the earlier miserabilism in recounting the "women's condition" to the current New African Woman so desired by Sembène in *Faat Kine*. It paved the way for Fanta Nacro's short films like *Puk Nini* (1996) where the men's imaginary of a dominant patriarchy was taken down several notches through humor. Now, the impact of globalization would come to replace the older imperative for close readings, for ideological analysis, for demands that the critic join the filmmaker in advancing the struggles for liberation and progressive change.

This change in the political and economic landscape would lead to Arjun Appadurai's five scapes (1996), to the distance readings of Franco Moretti (2013), to developments in Asian cinema readings as seein in the work of Rey Chow (1993) and Sumita Chakravarty (2003), that re-created how feminist and political analysis could be developed.

What would have to become an "ideal" approach to African cinema would have to come from the "ideal" approach to world cinema itself, addressing the problems of funding, acquiring adequate production technologies and apparatuses, developing adequately trained actors, and most of all breaking the logjams of distribution and exhibition. For if globalization meant untold wealth and goods to be made available to the rich, the question for African cinema would have to be where its films could be made and seen. Ironically, as the 1990s saw the breakthrough in the expansion of video film, it also saw the drastic decline in theatrical venues, resulting in the death-throes of most theatres across much of the continent in the course of the new millennium. That death of theatrical venues occurred across the world for the same reasons: celluloid was too expensive, not only to make, but also to show as the equipment required expensive maintenance. Across Africa, the theatres and urban downtowns became uninviting venues. On the other hand, anyone with enough money could buy a video player, and could make a video film for the family. Ramon Lobato (2012) has shown how the video revolution radically shifted the work of the film industry, so that grade-b genre films made as STV (straight to video) were produced for increasingly large home audiences. These video films stretched the limits of the respectable by privileging the spaces of private viewings where pornography could be seen, and pushed the limits of entertainment where religious videos could be seen. All this meant increases in the corner video shop and home video viewing, and the reduction of downtown or quartier theatre spaces to local bars (cf. Teno's *Lieux saints* (2009 *Sacred Places*) or to neighborhood people's homes where a few chairs could be rented out and where cooked chicken and beer might be sold, All this meant exhibition no longer entailed a trip to the downtown Rex, Regal, Royal, Palace, or Rialto, among many in Nigeria, the Normandy in N'djamena, Le Paris in Dakar, or the Abbia or Rex in Yaounde.

The "ideal" approach to African cinema would have to take into account the kinds of films that have become so prevalent today. On the one hand we have *Timbuktu* (2014), with its immediacy in addressing the hottest topic on the continent, the issue of Al Qaeda in the Maghreb, and the threat of the fundamentalists to take over the state, in this case Mali. From Abderrahmane Sissako's earlier, auteurist creations like *La Vie sur terre* (1998) and *Heremakono* (2002), to the more recent polemics against the World Bank and IMF in *Bamako* (2006), we now see how the context has shifted away from the nation-state, from national liberation and neocolonialism, and even from the Big Men who replaced the colonialists, to the threat posed by the militias and the jihadists, the local movements whose indigeneity combines with the world-scape of religious extremist movements seeking to establish a New Order. Not only does *Timbuktu* evoke the puritanical, repressiveness of that religious order, it thematizes it in the scene in which the jihadists make personal films about the primacy of adopting a new religious code of living. Everything in the film calls out for a new kind of contextualizing and an approach that poses the question, how can the African filmmaker make a successful, popular, and yet ultimately serious film about the dangers of jihadism? How can a poetic, essayist filmmaker make a film about a serious political issue, a contentious issue that risks aligning the film with conservative Western European warnings about Muslims as terrorists.

Simultaneously, as Africans responded to globalizing by seeking to leave the continent in droves, seeking to cross the dangerous waters to the Global North, films like *Frontières* (2001), *Bamako,* and especially *La pirogue* (2012) called upon the conventional modes of representations of Africans daring the elements and especially defying the authorities in order to find new lives. The dangers of the journey include all the middlemen, especially *passeurs*, those selling the passage and often endangering or even killing their passengers: The ugliest of faces of globalization. Whatever contextualizing *Timbuktu* required, whatever the questions about the filmmaker's political alignments might arise (like Sissako becoming a cultural advisor to the Mauritanian government), along with moral questions involved with the ugly, deadly face of global migration, there had to be a simultaneous global equivalent in the filmmaking itself where consumerism and its attendant guilts form the core of the melodrama, or where the issue of representation verges on the exploitative (such as the scene of the Ghanaian woman who dies in the desert, seeking to migrate, in *Bamako*). In short, the shift from the generation of "serious" African filmmaking to commercial Nollywood, poses questions for the act of filmmaking under globalization more broadly, and specially for the world of what we had once called "African cinema."

In Manthia Diawara's recent study of African cinema, *African Film: New Forms of Aesthetics and Politics* (2010), he sets about the task of presenting the "new" in a manner that is totally different from his first, programmatic study, *African Cinema: Politics and Culture* (1992). What is new are two things. First, the kinds of films that are now emerging: Nollywood of course, and especially its amorphous, latest iteration dubbed New Nollywood; but also other "art" categories that Diawara finds in films that have appeared in the conventional African cinema venues during the past quarter century, that is, in the period following "oppositional cinema." The line between the older, so-called "FESPACO" celluloid films encased within an established understanding of African cinematic language, and the newer forms like "New Nollywood" have become increasingly difficult to sustain. If "video films" had typically been associated with greater commercial cinematic values, they now have begun to include "transnational films," typically associated with greater post-production values, "experimental" or "innovative" New Nollywood styles and genres, as might be seen in Andy Amadi Okoroafor's dark neo-noir *Relentless* (2010), Djo Munga's dystopic *Viva Riva* (2011), or Kenneth Gyang's *Confusion Na Wa* (2013). The conventional framing of African cinema is increasingly shifting, as now seen with Biyi Bandele's epic adaptation of Adichie's *Half a Yellow Sun* (2014), or Wanuri Kahiu's sci-fi feminist short "Pumzi" (2013). In other areas, too, like the most conventionalized of genres such as genocide films, a totally new approach has been taken as seen in Kivu Ruhorahoza's psychologically troubled drama *Matière gris* (*Grey Matter*) (2011). No longer is it just FESPACO that is defining what is to be admitted to the competitive ranks of "African film"; festivals in Zanzibar, South Africa, and Nigeria now compete for the status of premier award-givers, supplanting the often dated FESPACO.

New critical approaches have emerged with a new generation of critical writings sparked by Jonathan Haynes (1995) when he called for new work on popular genres and sociopolitical studies.[4] The emphasis on material readings and new global configurations has necessitated revisions of theoretical frames, as seen in Akin Adesokan's *Postcolonial Artists and Global Aesthetics* (2011), Carmela Garritano's *African Video Movies and Global Desires: A Ghanaian History* (2013), and Moradewun Adejunmobi's groundbreaking essay "Nigerian Video Film as Minor Transnational Practice" (2007). The questions of materiality and of the cinematic apparatus now redefine the limits of critiques of commodity culture and neoliberalism. In Adesokan's work, institutional structures, aesthetic values, and genre formation have come to lend new complexity to notions of "context," redefining what constitutes committed critique in an age of globalization.

Diawara's approach forges the bridge between the panegyrics for Blackness in the past and the tensions engendered by the rhetoric of post-racialism in the present conjuncture. His new formulations have nothing to do with the pigeon-holing approaches that delimited the value of past criticism, and yet he aspires to a systemization and separates the aesthetics of Nollywood, a cinema he sees as dominated by the tropes of movement and change, from the new waves of cinema that enable us to retain a sense of connectedness to past trends.

The three new waves of cinema that Diawara identifies are "Arte," "La Guilde des Cinéastes," and the "New Popular African Cinema." Unlike his earlier categories, Social Realist or Colonial Confrontation, which are defined in well-recognized genre or thematic terms, these three are very nebulous, allowing for any kind of genre or theme. What marks them, rather, are the conditions of production, reception, and exhibition.

If the first wave is the most auteurist, and the second most marked by diaspora sensibilities, the third wave, vaguely termed "New Popular African Cinema," is at once the most diffuse and at the same time "African" – a notion, in this context, as charged as the term "authenticity." After praising Senghor's call for an African specificity associated with qualities like rhythm – qualities that return in a more productive frame in cinematic terms than in the lexicon of affect (which degrades Negritude into a cheap essentialism) – Diawara looks to films like *Finyé* (1982) or *Le retour d'un aventurier* (1966) or *Love Brewed in an African Pot* (1981) for the use of "African ingredients" to combat the "recognized genres of the West." While they employ familiar genres like romance or melodrama, they take new popular forms, deploying "African ingredients and spices within old genres" (pp. 142–143). He claims that these directions, so commonly associated with Nollywood, also mark the important work of Mansour Wade, Moussa Sene Absa, Zola Maseko, Zézé Gamboa and others who employ techniques of melodrama, and deploy narratives and mises-en-scène associated with musicals, action films, and Westerns. "Popular" is the term Diawara uses to distinguish this body of work from the first two waves that he associates more loosely with "art" cinema (p. 144). He finds in the popular, "narrative structures, the motifs and emotional expectations [that] they borrow from African popular culture." He continues, "The films rely on popular religious beliefs and superstitions, folklore and the common sense of everyday life, unlike the consciousness-raising narratives of Sembène or the metafilmic and intellectualized films of Bekolo and Bakupa-Kanyinda" (p. 144). Here Diawara might be describing Nollywood were it not that the distance these filmmakers take is not from the commercial norms of Hollywood, but from "Africa cinema" itself in the forms of the above two waves and in its Sembenian influenced past. Popular is measured in the relationship of this cinema to its audience, in which he says the films have served to "constitute the first beginning of African cinema for Africans" (p. 145). How these films, still not readily exhibited in Africa, and certainly not in theatres that are almost nonexistent, might constitute a first beginning of an African cinema for Africans, rather than video films from Ghana and Nollywood, is a mystery. But the aspiration, if not the fulfillment of this claim, does much in defining its essential traits. The "real culture," the "real people," to whom this cinema relates is, strangely enough in an age of globalization, defined broadly in national terms. Thus, Diawara finds the film language informed by the national elements of dance, language, oral traditions, etc., like Mouridism and the Sabar, Senegalese religious and dance forms. For the cosmopolitan and global scholar, these might be termed local cultural formulations, not national, and the circulation of these filmmakers' work – like Joseph Gaï Ramaka's *Karmen Geï* (2001) or Mansour Sora Wade's *Le prix du pardon* (2002) – cannot be separated from the international festival circuit and transnational commercial venues, such as are found on the websites dedicated to African films. The division of African cinema along these lines of popular and art still leaves the latter burdened with the question of distribution, as has been the case from the start.

Distribution and Exhibition

The question of how to rethink critical approaches to African cinema cannot be easily separated from the films' spaces of exhibition. After all, a "curatorial" approach already implies an approach shaped by festivals, not by theatrical distributors. The history of the failure to provide African audiences with ready access to African films in Africa has been well documented, including in Diawara's first study *African Cinema: Politics and Culture* (1992) and in innumerable accounts of FEPACI and the desperate struggle to establish national film boards that would accommodate the distribution of African films (Diawara (1992), Thackway (2003); Barlet (2000)). In Senegal the Société National du Cinéma, headed up by Sembène himself, lasted only a short while, and the establishment of a film archive and center in Ouagadougou ultimately failed to produce the spur to national distribution across the continent. Sporadic semi-success in Ouagadougou was not matched, although well-known attempts in post-revolutionary societies, like Algeria and

Mozambique, succeeded briefly. In the end, the model of a commercial distribution system as the only meaningful measure of success continued as the cinema palaces across most of the continent crumbled or became disreputable quartier theatres, often enough limited to grade-b film showings, and especially Bollywood showings.

In Europe, there was very little outside of the occasional Arts et Essais theatre showings of African films, little outside of Odeon-type art theatres in Anglophone venues, little, really, outside the growing festival circuit. What provided the impetus for festivals might originally have had the panache of Cannes or Toronto, but eventually smaller festivals burgeoned, and as with other independent productions, became the favored sites for distribution [Dovey, 2015: pp. 13–14]. In the United States, as black studies prospered in the 1970s and even 1980s, the radical Third World movement generated Third World cinema distribution models, including most importantly the California Newsreel project aimed at distributing educational and feature films that supported the goals of leftist progress and revolutionary change. California Newsreel was founded in San Francisco in 1968 as part of Third World Newsreel, itself created in 1967 at the height of the counter-cultural movement. Its themes included race, social justice, revolutionary politics, and most importantly, the Library of African Cinema, whose mission is described on the California Newreel site thus: "Films from Africa made by Africans offer restorative images and oftentimes a new film language. The unique films in this collection not only showcase the works of master filmmakers but also innovative new talents who are embracing video technology. To see Africa through African eyes will break stereotypes and enlighten viewers about life in Africa as well as about the issues facing the continent" (http://newsreel.org/African-Cinema). This sums up the ideological impress that was intended to sustain the first generation of African and black filmmakers like those of the L.A. Rebellion, but especially those on the continent desperately seeking venues for distribution.

The California Newsreel model was based to a large extent on distributing their video tapes at US$200 for a single film, and US$500 for five, to university campuses where a few began to create significant collections. The curator for the Library, Cornelius Moore, became an important figure in his choice of films that emphasized the value of political lucidity and Afrocentric perspectives that would serve to provide the audience with a clear, counter-colonial understanding of African society and history. His films suited courses in African humanities that were inevitably intended to counter Western stereotypes and prejudices against African cultures and peoples. With the rise of major studies units in Northwestern University, the University of Wisconsin, along with similar departments in UCLA and eventually NYU, inevitably the fostering of black studies led to the creation of black film studies as well. It has been the case since the 1980s that festivals and American university library collections have remained the dominant venues for African films. At least that has been true as long as "African films" did not include video films that came to be produced in

Ghana and Nigeria for local distribution. The latter led to vast changes in models for distribution and exhibition which the "serious" or "FESPACO" filmmakers inevitably had to take into account, as the circuits of festivals and libraries barely enabled the filmmakers to sustain their production. The shift to digital platforms can be seen in the change in California Newsreel itself. A glance at its site showing its recent films includes only a handful of African American, not African films, and they are now streaming the films, selling rights to access to the streaming for three years, alongside US$50 DVDs. Almost all its films were made between 1990 and 2006, with the rare exception being a 2007 film *This is Nollywood*! The only African film in the collection since then was 2009 *The Manuscripts of Timbuktu*, after which no more African films appear. By 2009 more than a thousand Nollywood films a year were being churned out, and the model of digital filmmaking across the continent had become dominant. The changes in genres that bespoke the new technological breakthrough with video in the late 1980s and 1990s attested to the radical break with a past commitment to "see Africa through African eyes [so as to] ... break stereotypes and enlighten viewers about life in Africa as well as about the issues facing the continent" (http://newsreel.org/African-Cinema).

New Critical Approaches

What might be thought of as the key question for African cinema criticism, "what is the ideal approach to African cinema," becomes increasingly a question that depends on the larger issues now marking the field, namely, what is an African film. Across the world, digital and Internet technologies and flow of media and capital across national borders have enabled an enormous proliferation of film and media forms, platforms and distribution venues, film festivals, and screen sizes and types Likewise, the authors included here are at the forefront of an enormous expansion of African film studies. Focusing on new objects of study and drawing on a multiplicity of approaches, contributors place African visual forms at the center of major conversations in film and media studies and engage theoretical work on time, sound, genre, queering, and biopolitics. The methods deployed here move away from, and in some cases challenge, approaches that have been dominant in the field since its earliest years. Contributors share a concern with making sense of what Achille Mbembe identifies as the "third moment" in the history of "the vertiginous assemblage that is Blackness" (2017, p. 2). This is a time, he writes, "marked by the globalization of markets, the privatization of the world under the aegis of neoliberalism, and the increasing imbrication of financial markets, the postimperial military complex, and electronic and digital technologies" (2017, p. 3). It is a moment that compels new poetics and new theoretical engagements.

The chapters included in the first section of our volume attend to the temporal dimensions of African films, challenging the unremarked conception of time as linear and teleological that remains dominant in African cinema discourse. These chapters follow the work of Africanists Charles Piot, Jane Guyer, James Ferguson and others, who have shown that in the twenty-first century, time is being recalibrated. Time, Guyer writes, "is punctuated rather than enduring; of fateful moments and turning points, the date as event rather than as position in a sequence or cycle" (2017, p. 104). In a similar vein, Justin Izzo's reading of films by Abderrahman Sissako and Mahamat-Saleh Haroun elaborates on the intensity of the now, which Izzo describes as the hypercontemporary, as it is thematized and expressed formally in the award-winning films of these African auteurs. We might say that Izzo participates in the what Jacques de Villiers calls the "uncertain turn" in African Studies, which proposes "a complete conceptual reversal of the teleological paradigm." Crisis, contingency and uncertainty "cease to be temporal aberrations and instead become the *a priori* basis for understanding human experience." De Villiers tracks "the temporal dynamics" at play in Nigerian and Ghanaian commercial movies and argues that the movies' enactment of time "project an aesthetic mirror back at a world frantically connecting through all the objects of consumer modernity, while simultaneously mired in widespread scarcity and forms of disconnection." Finally, Karen Bouwer's chapter on *Viva Riva!* (2010) and *Nairobi Half Life* (2012) draws attention to the temporalities of suspension, moments between stasis and motion, experienced by the films' protagonists as a feature of the African city. The states of suspension portrayed in these films challenge the opposition that defines the African city as a stagnant dystopia or a site of flow and invention.

This volume seeks to disrupt not only African film studies, but the larger field of conventional film studies with its grounding in major Western critics and theorists, from Krakauer to Bazin to Bordwell; those who followed dominant film studies trends barely noticed that African film existed outside Western colonial films, and at most gestured toward *La noire de ...* (1966). It has become necessary to extend their original theoretical work, to reread them as Lindsey Green-Simms has done with queer criticism oriented around African subjectivities, used, in her case, to analyze the work of Jo Ramaka. Similarly, the question of the poetic and the political is reread by Adesokan in his exploration of Ramaka's *So Be It* (1997), an adaptation of Soyinka's *Strong Breed*. Akin Adesokan explores a set of difficult questions about the constraints placed on the African artistic imagination under processes of neoliberal globalization and the place of the postcolonial artist in a context where the social is "the ground of the collusion of authoritarianism and neoliberal globalization." These studies rework Foucault's biopolitics along unfamiliar lines that have revised the primacy of other, earlier identitarian approaches, requiring reorientations, like the curatorial or queer turn.

In our current moment, the field of human rights, too, has had to be expanded to produce readings of the poetic film-essays, as with the newly charged, committed films of Sissako, no longer driven by ideological grand narratives, or Haroun's *A Screaming Man* (2010) that turns us to questions of globalization (Oscherwitz). Not incidentally, it was at the most celebrated of film festivals, Cannes, that Haroun's film won the prestigious Jury prize in 2010, just as Sissako's *Timbuktu*, turned down in FESPACO 2015, won the major award for Best Film at the Césars in 2015. MaryEllen Higgins' contribution on Haroun's *Grisgris* (2013) investigates the intersection of trauma theory and the notion of precarity, re-reading these concepts through Haroun's film. Trauma and precarity, terms made so familiar from the work of Butler and Athanasiou (2013), remind us that African cinema, with its own history, its own horizons of possibility, its own pressures to find new ways to use the camera as one's own, to find one's own "African" vision, has been always grounded in oppositionality in its need to forge images and stories that are one's own. What is new is that that oppositionality itself has had to be revised, rewritten, rethought, both for today's globalicity as for yesterday's colonial world. In that regard, notions of trauma, violence, structural inequality, as well as aesthetic value, cannot be abstracted, much less simply repeated.

Returning to old questions with new provocations, Abdalla Uba Adamu's chapter pushes against the boundaries of what constitutes "African film." So is a film African when an African language is substituted for a non-African language? Is the French spoken in Cameroon, sung in *Afrique je te plumerai*, taken from the French song, "Alouette, alouette, je te plumerai," reterritorialized adequately when used ironically? When a Bollywood film is re-fashioned in adaptation, is it adequately African? When the original Indian version of an African adaptation is dubbed over in Hausa, or when the commentator adds his "bonimenteur" comments, summarizing the action; when a Tanzanian bonimenteur explains the action for a Swahiliphone audience watching Nollywood film, where is the "African" sauce, the lifeblood, the racial, ethnic, geographic definer that makes it adequately African to merit scholarly definition of the work as African? In Adamu's fascinating study of the transformations of Bollywood, Hindi language, or Tamil language films into Hausa fare for the Northern Nigerian audiences, the question must be posed, is this sufficient to define such films as "African" when dubbed in Hausa? Does the visual or aural prevail, or at least destabilize the conventions? Vlad Dima's chapter further reorients the "harmonious narrative relationship between image and sound." Focusing on the films of Abderrahmane Sissako, Dima draws on the work of Michel Chion and Jacques Lacan to attend to the function of sound, which he claims, supersedes image, leading "to the creation of an imagined space." Similarly, the film score of *Karmen Geï* (2001) is central to Green-Simms queer reading. Its musical sounds coordinate with its form so that *Karmen Geï* "opens itself up to queerness."

When distribution platforms and environments have changed radically, leaving the TV screen, computer screen, or cell phone as the primary technology for viewing, when the experience has changed to such an extent that viewing a movie on a bus, at home is in-between trips to the kitchen, at restaurants or in hotels, when images are viewed through glimpses, when familiar characters and story-lines are paraded partly as decoration, as creations of ambience, like football games in sports bars – when the films and their new stars are stylishly promoted in the new festivals, with new African Movie Awards – the scholarship has become so completely, radically altered as to require that ALL questions about African cinema be posed in new ways.

For scholars of Nollywood, transformations in content distribution and delivery and in audiences' experiences of movies have raised important questions about the materiality of the film form. As Nollywood boomed, the distinction between films shown in theatres and those sold directly as VCDs led to the question of what could continue to be considered serious enough, artistic enough, professional enough, to aspire to the label "cinema," to be included in IMDB listings, rather remaining mere "video," "amateur," "local," "unprofessional," "home" movies unworthy of the label "cinema." It was video, first analog and later digital, that created the technological conditions of possibility for the development of commercial movie industries in Nigeria and Ghana. The term *video film*, first used by Jonathan Haynes and Onookome Okome, represented an attempt to capture the materiality of the new form: A feature film made and distributed on video. Later, Lindiwe Dovey (2010) made an argument for adopting *screen media*, an expansive term that encompasses film and video formats as well as a variety of screen types, while Carmela Garritano (2013) has suggested that *video movie* is most appropriate to Ghanaian features shot on video. In her chapter included here, Adejunmobi builds on her previous work on the televisual to define African "cinema" as those features shown in theatres, in distinction to African "films," "movies" shown on streaming platforms. Noah Tsika, finally, considers the degradation and disappearance of the material stuff of Nollywood. He asks crucial questions about Nollywood's "missing archive," going so far as to claim that Nollywood be characterized by "the lack of preservation of its audiovisual heritage."

Today, a multiplicity of forms and creative practices, in various African languages, are stretching the boundaries of African film. Centering African film in francophone West Africa is now as dated as FESPACO, once the premiere African film festival, which now has been displaced by Durban, Zanzibar, and the African Movie Awards. The entry into the global is being read by Jonathan Haynes as a result of the industrial shift that began in the informal sector, and that is now becoming, rapidly, formalized. The changes, not unlike those signaled by Moradewun Adejunmobi as characteristic of "slow" and "fast" film signal precisely how conditions of distribution change the product, and eventually the temporalities that play into the horizons that delimit notions of "African cinema." Temporalities linked to the straight-to-DVD model of distribution and to Internet streaming differ radically from those associated with film festivals and theatrical releases. Strategies of combining the two, as Kunle Afolayan and Tunde Kelani have long had to calculate, change almost every year as new possibilities for distribution displace older ones. The same could be said of critical approaches. As Haynes playfully observes, "There is no cinema without electricity," but the electricity that a generator might produce, so that the router could work, the connection might function, operates at a ground level that enables informal as well as formal mechanisms to function.

Alessandro Jedlowski's comparative analysis of the distinct constellations of video production in Nigeria, Ethiopia and Côte d'Ivoire advances the work of pioneers like Haynes, Larkin, Meyer, and Okome. Jedlowski describes "the complex patterns of continuities and discontinuities" that characterize each of these singular cultural formations, and while Jedlowski insists on the significance of the nation-state in directing the development of video technologies toward film or television production, Robin Steedman finds that in Nairobi, the influence of state institutions and national imaginaries has diminished under globalization. Based on extensive interviews with female filmmakers in Nairobi, Steedman's chapter situates the success of emergent Kenyan women filmmakers within the transnational networks of Nairobi, a global city, the significance of which has superseded the nation-state. Like their counterparts in Ghana and other parts of Africa, these women move easily among media and platforms and do various forms of creative work for their own production companies, as well as for corporations and NGOs, and not surprisingly, their artistic sensibilities are more entrepreneurial and extroverted than cultural nationalist or oppositional.

"What's new" can be answered by the term "genre," or, simultaneously, mise-en-scène – compelling those notions to expand broadly outside their conventional usage: When the "scène" has been "real Africa," or "real African," the question of venue had typically been posed in the form of oppositionality to mainstream American or European conventions of representation, dating back to the colonial period. Analysis of work produced during that period allows us to review how the original genres created today are refashioning the ongoing postcolonial project of rewriting the critical work of the field. Another outstanding effort to re-view African filmmaking as a refashioning of older forms in newer guises, now centered in African locations and perspectives, can been seen in Suzanne Gauch's analysis of Moroccan film noir. It is no longer simply a question of the importation of an established genre, but of deterritorializing and reterritorializing it. Moroccan noir is not approached by her as derivative of Western genres, but as the contemporary site for new noir global formulations – in this case Moroccan, although Egyptian and Maghrebian filmmakers are now engaged in similar work. Rachel Gabara's chapter on documentaries takes us back to the earliest European documentaries about the continent, and carries forward to more recent essay-films, or self-reflexive, creative documentaries, by African filmmakers. Her reading of Haroun's *Bye, Bye Africa* (1998) represents a crucial intervention into the film studies scholarship on documentary, which has failed "to recognize reflexivity with African cinema, preferring to read African film as informative ethnographic documents rather than works of art." Gabara places Haroun's poetic documentary in conversation with "the great family of cinema," a phrase quoted from the manifesto of the African Guild of Directors and Producers, a group of young, daring African filmmakers that included Haroun and Sissako whose work insisted on African cinema's place in the artistic field of world cinema (cited above as one of Diawara's three categories of contemporary African cinema).

For Julie Pappaioannou, it is in Global South thinking that new theoretical formulations are being created. She focuses on Jean-Pierre Bekolo's notion of "mantis," a "new contemporary African film aesthetics" that also resonates with Adesokan's reading of Ramaka's work. Pappaioannou describes mantism thus: "Bekolo's discursive tropism to 'mantisme' is a foretelling that implies the desire for an imagined future that is projected in multiple mises en abîme, and a constant negotiation with the self and the world in the understanding of present." This follows from Bekolo's notion that mantism is a way of apprehending the world based on his own experiences: "a way of apprehending the world based on my experience, my education, my culture and my environment," with which his reading of the future, as in *Les Saignantes* (2005) becomes possible. Notably his recent *Naked Reality* (2016), like *Les Saignantes*, signal the increasing attention paid to Afrofuturism, a tendency seen increasingly in Kenyan films (Steedman).

Thackway's work on borders and Sheila Petty's on journeys both take us to the consideration of aesthetics and space, categories that run through a number of our chapters. For Thackway "frontiers, borders, map lines – be they geographic, imaginary, mental, visible or invisible – traverse the history of African and diaspora auteur film with the striking constancy and recurrence of the leitmotif." She explores that leitmotif by returning, like Gabara and Dovey, to early African cinema and its "pioneers": Paulin S. Vieyra (*Afrique-sur-Seine*, 1955) and Ousmane Sembène (*Borom Sarret*, 1962), who take into account the compartmentalization of the colonial, and later the postcolonial city, with their creation of distinct spaces of belonging or exclusion. She cites Mbembe who analyses neoliberalism's pressures to open borders to capitalist exchanges, the movements of goods and people, leading to the "race towards separation and *unbonding*" (Mbembe 2016). Similarly, for Petty, journeys are the outcome of modes of diaspora, exile, and migration that are to be understood best in relational terms that account for identity formation, as seen in Alain Gomis's (*L'Afrance*, Senegal/France, 2001) and Rachid Djaïdani's (*Rengaine*, France, 2012) work. Exploring terms such as diaspora, exile, migritude, Afropolitanism, Afropeanness, pensée-autre and Maghreb pluriel, her work examines how these filmmakers search for a new cinema aesthetic to reflect journeys, relational movement and identity construction within fluid spaces of Africa and Europe.

In the volume's closing chapter, Lindiwe Dovey revisits the archive of African film studies. She engages the writing of Paulin Soumanou Vieyra to propose a more nuanced narrative of the early years of African filmmaking and to suggest new practices of writing about, teaching, and curating African films that take seriously the acts of care and feelings of astonishment the films inspire. Dovey insists that we must also consider that the attachment to the film aside from ideological or scholarly analyses now include curatorial judgments that engage new modes as viewing. What impact on scholarship must follow as the festival and the library function as principal venues for viewing and collecting the less-commercial productions? Can we claim the relationship between films and venues is changing the films themselves? The "curatorial turn" celebrated by Dovey might be increasingly oriented around the celebration of what becomes standardized or normalized genres adapting to mass circulation technologies; what had once been dismissed as mere TV might be celebrated precisely because it has managed to enter onto the mainstream stages and extended to commercial option, or, conversely, because of being now judged "artistic," the very directions New Nollywood aspires to follow, indicating that there is a new history to be created for these films (Haynes; Tsika). If the terms "African" and "cinema" are emptied of meaning when used so as to conflate all the variegated forms to be found on the continent, they are refilled with specificity, depth, and new meanings when read through the lens of the chapters that constitute this volume. If, as Dovey claims, we as scholars are to find joy and cinephilia, and celebrate African film for its accomplishments and beauty, so, too, are we bound to follow the vision of African film scholars themselves with the same notion of generosity and comprehension as an apparatus that generates positive knowledge about African film itself.

Notes

1   Angola achieved independence in 1975, Guinea-Bissau in 1974, and Mozambique in 1975. Rhodesia was established as a white majority independent state in 1965, and became a democratic, black majority independent state in 1979. Lastly, in South Africa, Nelson Mandela was released in 1990, apartheid laws ended in 1991, and a democratic state was created in 1992. We could use these dates as markers for the end of armed struggle for independence – the end of the revolution in Africa. Notably Cabral was assassinated in 1973, and with the ascension to power of the ANC and the concessions it made, the last real revolutionary movement also capitulated to postcolonial exigencies.
2   See, for example, Kenneth Harrow's *Less Than One and Double: A Feminist Reading of African Women's Writing* and *Postcolonial African Cinema: From Political Engagement to Postmodernism*.
3   A humorous term, in its original meaning of a bullshitter. But it also means a commentator, and especially the person who provides a live voice-over that explains the action and dialogue. Initially prevalent in the silent era, it became important with the showing of foreign films in popular venues. It has become widespread in certain areas, such as in the showing of Nollywood films in East Africa. The commentator has become a personality of enormous entertainment value in himself or herself.
4   This was seen initially in *Cinema and Social Change in West Africa* (1995, co-edited with Onookome Okome), in which Haynes published his important essay "Nigerian

Cinema: Structural Adjustments." His groundbreaking work on Nollywood, "Evolving Popular Media: Nigerian Video Films" (co-authored with Okome, 1997), appeared in his edited volume *Nigerian Video Films* (1997).

References

Adejunmobi, Moradewun. 2007. "Nigerian Video Film as Minor Transnational Practice." *Postcolonial Text* 3.2. Web.

Adesokan, Akin. 2011. *Postcolonial Artists and Global Aesthetics*. Bloomington: Indiana University Press.

Adichie, Chimamanda Ngozi. 2006. *Half of a Yellow Sun*. New York: Alfred A. Knopf.

Appadurai, Arjun. 1996. *Modernity at Large: Cultural Dimensions of Globalization*. Minneapolis: University of Minnesota Press.

Armah, Ayi Kwei. 1968. *The Beautyful Ones Are Not Yet Born*. Boston, MA: Houghton Mifflin.

Barber, Karin. 1987. "Popular Arts in Africa." *African Studies Review* 30.3: 1–78.

Barlet, Olivier. 2000. *African Cinemas: Decolonizing the Gaze*. Chicago, IL: Zed Books.

Boughedir, Ferid. 1983. "Les Grandes Tendances du Cinema en Afrique Noire." *CinémAction* 26: 48–57.

Boyce Davies, Carole and Anne Adams Graves. 1986. *Ngambika: Studies of Women in African Literature*. Trenton, NJ: Africa World Press.

Butler, Judith, and Athena Athanasiou. 2013. *Dispossession: The Performative in the Political*. Cambridge, UK and Malden, MA: Polity Press.

Chakravarty, Sumita S. 2003. "The Erotics of History: Gender and Transgression in the New Asian Cinemas." In *Rethinking Third Cinema*, eds. Anthony Guneratne and Wimal Dissanayake. London: Routledge.

Chow, Rey. 1993. *Writing Diaspora: Tactics of Intervention in Contemporary Cultural Studies*. Bloomington, IN: Indiana University Press.

Comaroff, Jean and John L. Comaroff. 2000. "Millennial Capitalism: First Thoughts on a Second Coming." *Public Culture*, 12.2: 291–343.

Diawara, Manthia. 1992. *African Cinema: Politics and Culture*. Bloomington: Indiana University Press.

Diawara, Manthia. 2010. *African Film: New Forms of Aesthetics and Politics*. Munich, London, New York: Prestel.

Dovey, Lindiwe. 2010. "Editorial: African Film and Video: Pleasure, Politics, Performace." *Journal of African Cultural Studies*, 22.1: 1–6.

Dovey, Lindiwe. 2015. *Curating Africa in the Age of Film Festivals*. New York: Palgrave Macmillan.

Ferguson, James. 2006. *Global Shadows: Africa in the Neoliberal World Order*. Durham, NC: Duke University Press.

Gabriel, Teshome. 1982. *Third Cinema in the Third World: The Aesthetics of Liberation*. Ann Arbor: University of Michigan Research Press.

Garritano, Carmela. 2013. *African Video Movies and Global Desires: A Ghanaian History*. Athens: Ohio University Press.

Guyer, Jane. 2016. *Legacies, Logics, Logistics: Essays in the Anthropology of the Platform Economy*. Chicago, IL: University of Chicago Press.

Haynes, Jonathan, ed. 2000. *Nigerian Video Films*. Athens: Ohio University Press.

Kourouma, Ahmadou.1970. *Les soleils des independances*. Paris: Éditions du Seuil.

Lobato, Roman. 2012. *Shadow Economies of Cinema: Mapping Informal Film Distribution*. London: BFI-Palgrave Macmillan.

Mbembe, Achille. 2016. *Politiques de l'inimitié*. Paris: La Découverte.

Mbembe, Achille. 2017. Trans. Laurent Dubois. *Critique of Black Reason*. Durham, NC: Duke University Press.

Moretti, Franco. 2013. *Distant Reading*. Brooklyn, NY: Verso.

Okome, Onookome and Jonathan Haynes. 1995. *Cinema and Social Change in West Africa*. Jos, Nigeria: Nigerian Film Corporation.

Piot, Charles. 2010. *Nostalgia for the Future: West Africa after the Cold War*. Chicago, IL: University of Chicago Press.

Tcheuyap, Alexie. 2011. *Postnationalist African Cinemas*. Manchester and New York: Manchester University Press.

Thackway, Melissa. 2003. *Africa Shoots Back: Alternative Perspectives in Sub-Saharan Francophone African Film*. Bloomington: Indiana University Press.

Ukadike, Frank. 1994. *Black African Cinema*. Berkeley: University of California Press.

Filmography

Akuffo, William. (1987). *Zinabu*. Ghana. World Wide Motion Pictures.

Alassane, Moustpha. (1966). *Le retour d'un aventurier*. Niger: Argos Films.

Ansah, Kwah. (1981). *Love Brewed in an African Pot*. Ghana: Film Africa.

Bandele, Biyi. (2013). *Half a Yellow Sun*. Nigeria: Slate Films.

Bekolo, Jean-Pierre. (1996). *Aristotle's Plot*. Zimbabwe: JBA Production.

Bekolo, Jean-Pierre. (1992). *Quartier Mozart*. Cameroon: Kola Case.

Bekolo, Jean-Pierre. (2005). *Les Saignantes*. Cameroon: Quartier Mozart Films.

Bekolo, Jean-Pierre. (2016). *Naked Reality*. South Africa: Jean Pierre Bekolo Sarl.

Cissé, Souleymane. (1982). *Finye*. Mali: Les films Cissé.

Cissé, Souleymane. (1987). *Yeelen*. Mali: Centre National de la Cinématographie (CNC).

Djadjam, Mostéfa. (2002). *Frontières*. 2002. Algeria: Vertigo Productions.

Djaïdani, Rachid. (2012). *Rengaine*. France: Or Productions.

Du Parc, Henri. (1988) *Bal Poussière*. Côte d'Ivoire: Focale 13.

Ecaré, Désiré. (1985). *Visages de femmes*. Côte d'Ivoire: Films de la Lagune.

Gerima, Haile. (1979). *Bush Mama*. USA: Mypheduh Films

Gerima, Haile. (1975). *Harvest 3000 Years*. Ethiopia: Haile Gerima Production.

Gomis, Alain. (2001) *L'Afrance*. Senegal: Centre National de la Cinématographie (CNC).

Gyang, Kenneth. (2013). *Confusion Na Wa*. Nigeria: Cinema Kpatakpata.

Haroun, Mahamat-Saleh. (2010). *A Screaming Man*. Chad: Pili Films.

Haroun, Mahamat-Saleh. (1999). *Bye, Bye Africa*. Chad: Images Plus.

Haroun, Mahamat-Saleh. (2013). *Grisgris*. Chad: Pili Films.

Hondo, Med. (1986). *Sarraounia*. Mauretania: Direction de la Cinematographie Nationale.

Kahiu, Wanuri. (2013). *Pumzi*. Kenya: Changamoto.

Maseko, Zola. (2009). *The Manuscripts of Timbuktu*. South Africa: Black Roots Pictures.

Munga, Djo Tunda Wa. (2011). *Viva Riva! Democratic Republic of the Congo: uFilms.*

Ngangura, Mweze and Lamy, Benoît. (1987). *La vie est belle*. Zaire: Lamy Films.

Nacro, Fanta. (1995). *Puk Nini*. Burkina Faso: Les Films du Defi.

Nnebue, Kenneth (producer). (1992). *Living in Bondage*. Nigeria: NEK Video Links.

Okoroafor, Andy Amadi. (2010). *Relentless*. Nigeria: Clam Production.

Ouedraogo, Idrissa. (1990). *Tilai*. Burkina Faso: Les Films de l'Avenir.

Ouedraogo, Idrissa. (1989). *Yaaba*. Burkina Faso. Les Films de l'Avenir.

Ramaka, Joseph Gaï. (2001). *Karmen Geï*. Senegal: Les Ateliers de l'Arche.

Ramaka, Joseph Gaï. (1997). *So Be It*. Senegal.

Rapu, Chris Obi. (1992). *Living in Bondage*. Nigeria: NEK Video Links.

Rouch, Jean. (1970) *Petit à Petit*. France and Niger: Les Films de la Pléiade.

Ruhorahoza, Kivu. (2011). *Matière grise*. Rwanda: Moon Road Films.

Sacchi, Franco. (2007). *This is Nollywood!* USA: Eureka Film Productions.

Sembène Ousmane. (1963). "Borom Sarret." Senegal.

Sembène Ousmane. (1976). *Ceddo*. Senegal: Films Doomireew.

Sembène Ousmane. (2000). *Faat Kine*. Senegal: Films Doomireew.

Sembène Ousmane. (1970). *Tauw*. Senegal: Films Doomireew.

Sembène Ousmane. (1974). *Xala*. Senegal: Filmi Doomireew.

Sissako, Abderrahmane. (2006). *Bamako*. Mali: Chinguitty Films.

Sissako, Abderrahmane. (2002). *Heremakono*. Mauretania: Duo Films.

Sissako, Abderrahmane. (2014). *Timbuktu*. Mauretania: Les films du Worso.

Sissako, Abderrahmane. (1998). *La vie sur terre*. Mali: Centre National de la Cinematographie.

Soyinka, Wole. (1970). *Kongi's Harvest*. Nigeria: Calpenny Nigeria.

Teno, Jean-Marie. (1993). *Afrique, je te plumerai*. Cameroon: Les Films du Raphia.

Teno, Jean-Marie. (2009). *Lieux saints*. Cameroon: Les Films du Raphia.

Touré, Moussa. *La pirogue*. (2012). France: Les Chauves souris.

Touré, Moussa. (1998). *TGV*. Senegal: Les Films du Crocodile.

Paulin S. Vieyra (1955). *Afrique-sur-Seine*. France: Groupe Africaine.

Wade, Mansour Sora. (2001) *Le prix du pardon*. Senegal: Banfilm, Les Films du Safran.

Wade, Mansour Sora. (2001). *Ndeysaan*. Senegal: Films du Safran / Kaany Productions.

Part I
Time / Crisis / Uncertainty

1

Cinematic Economies
of the Hypercontemporary
in Haroun and Sissako

Justin Izzo

Two pre-millennial films, released just one year apart, set the scene for this chapter on narrative and economic understandings of post-millennial contemporaneity in Francophone Africa. I focus in this chapter on recent cinematic work by Abderrahmane Sissako (Mauritania) and Mahamat-Saleh Haroun (Chad), but two of their films from before the turn of the century signal the set of anxieties and narrative problems I want to examine here. The first of these films is Sissako's *La vie sur terre* (*Life on Earth*, 1998): This is a fictionalized documentary dealing with the return of a middle-aged man (played by Sissako himself) from France to his father's village in rural Mali. The man, Dramane, arrives in the run-up to the new millennium, and as he cycles through the dusty streets we see the village's residents going about their everyday lives while news bulletins from Radio France Internationale (RFI) relay the excitement of new year's celebrations taking place in other parts of the world. The lack of obvious mise-en-scène in Sissako's shots communicates to viewers a sense of documentary immediacy, drawing us into the everyday as a cinematic narrative category. At the same time, ambiguous voice-over quotations from Aimé Césaire's *Cahier d'un retour au pays natal* (1939) about colonial marginalization suggest a transitional cultural-political context that is no longer "postcolonial" in the conventional sense, but that is not yet fully millennial, either.

La vie sur terre communicates Mali's uneven integration into the global cultural and economic landscape by playing with the uncertainty of its ill-defined historical moment; the film's sense of immediacy nonetheless gives us to understand that we are on the cusp of a new understanding of the present that has yet to take shape. Mahamat-Saleh Haroun's *Bye Bye Africa* (1999), my second filmic example, offers a similar narrative of homecoming: Haroun plays himself as a fictional character who returns after a long absence to his native Chad following the death of his mother. *Bye Bye Africa*, like *La vie sur terre*, weaves fiction into a documentary aesthetic, and we watch Haroun's character film street scenes, record interviews with producers and aspiring actors, and gather footage for a new film that, as it turns out, may or may not be the one we are actually watching. *Bye Bye Africa* evokes a sense of anxiety akin to the one we witness in Sissako's film: Haroun's return to Chad also signals a transitional moment, one whose attendant uncertainty causes the director to inquire ceaselessly about the economic future of big-screen African cinema, its viability in Chad's fragile post-conflict society, and its desirability when faced with competition from low-rent video clubs.[1] *Bye Bye Africa* asks, how can cinema mark this transition and communicate its urgency as well as its most pressing filmic stakes? Like *La vie sur terre*, this film links African cultural production with cinematic attempts to define and characterize the immediacy of a cultural moment that overlaps with the turn of the new millennium.

These films situate global economics and the future of film in Africa within localized and intensely felt experiences of the now; they bespeak a desire to record, imagine, and narrativize the actuality of millennial transitions. At the same time, they indicate a desire to periodize and to outline changing experiences of historical time in the face of the "promise" offered by the new century, as Alain Badiou has put it (2007, p. 17). Building on the themes explored and questions raised by these early-millennial films, in this chapter I turn to Haroun's and Sissako's post-millennial cinematic archive in order to investigate the development of their cinematic approaches to an aesthetic economy of immediacy. How do their post-millennial films – specifically those about economics and war – communicate "now-ness" to spectators? In what ways do Haroun and Sissako endow everyday life with a current of urgency? How do they visualize and narrativize the everyday as a cinematic category that has an aesthetics as well as a political economy? Relatedly, but more generally, how do filmic narratives designate historical periods and cultural moments, and how does film attribute narrative value to contemporaneity as a post-millennial aesthetic category? These are the interrelated questions I take up in this chapter, and the responses Haroun and Sissako propose to them comprise what I call cinematic economies of the hypercontemporary. This formulation references how a thematics of urgent contemporaneity intersects with visualizations of warscapes, post-millennial capitalism, and with new narrative strategies designed to express in film emerging relations to immediacy. The economic here refers to the ways in which cinematic narratives thematize and visualize political economy; more metaphorically, it also refers to modes of attributing value to key elements of filmic narrative.

The hypercontemporary refers not just to narrative experiences of "now-ness," but more importantly, as the prefix "hyper-" suggests, to the fact that these experiences can possess a surfeit of intensity that speaks to a broader historical moment. As Paul Rabinow (2008) reminds us in his work on "the anthropology of the contemporary," the now is not necessarily synonymous or coterminous with "the new," and for him the contemporary is the shifting terrain upon which "older and newer elements" interact and are negotiated (2008, pp. 2–3). My reading of the hypercontemporary here focuses on forms of cinematic periodization, but Rabinow's reminder helpfully points toward the co-presence of contrasting experiences of temporality within an emerging historical moment. This co-presence helps explain why the now appears in multiple forms in the films I study here. On the one hand, cinema expresses the now thematically: For example, in this chapter's first section I examine how economic urgency is woven into filmic narratives of everyday life, and Sissako's *La vie sur terre* takes as its central theme the very moments marking the changeover from one millennium to the next. On the other hand, the idea of the now goes beyond the realm of the thematic and also enters into questions of cinematic form. Thus, certain films slow time down or even seem to pause it completely (as in Sissako's 2014 film, *Timbuktu*), drawing out the now into an expanded temporal moment, whereas others condense the now into an increasingly saturated immediacy, heightening the tension and intensity of "real time." What these disparate renderings of the now have in common is that each one also articulates and accounts for a new historical moment; these related but distinct expressions of temporal intensity and periodization are what make up the hypercontemporary.

We can consider several brief examples from Haroun and Sissako that illustrate more concretely what the hypercontemporary looks like in the context of cinematic narratives of everyday life. In *La vie sur terre*, for instance, Sissako's camera lingers in six different shots on a group of men lounging in chairs and listening to the radio (presumably RFI) in the little shade offered by a building. These shots punctuate his hour-long film, and the men do little more than inch their chairs closer to the building as their strip of shade grows smaller. They communicate intense feelings of boredom that contrast sharply with the foreign news bulletins excitedly describing how the world plans to celebrate the arrival of the year 2000. This set of shots pulls viewers at once into the excruciating actuality of the men's boredom and into a globalized millennial moment that seems to have left this rural Malian village behind. Filming boredom, that most unproductive of conditions, is actually a productive mode of communicating now-ness since the viewer comes to feel the weight of useless instants all the more acutely as they connect to the broader articulation of a new post-millennial historical period. Numerous shots of everyday labor in Sissako's *Bamako* (2006) have a similar function: As African civil society faces off against global financial institutions in a mock trial, daily life proceeds unimpeded in the neighborhood where the film is set and shots of a local open-air dyeworks bring the trial's political-economic rhetoric into highly localized focus. Labor both compresses and stretches transitional time in Haroun's *Daratt* (2006): The young Atim begins a baker's apprenticeship with Nassara, the man who killed his father during Chad's civil war. Sequences of the two preparing bread, sweating from their painstaking efforts, extend wordlessly as the political time of post-conflict reconciliation seeps into the elongated moments of Haroun's shots. These examples convey to viewers intense cinematic experiences of the now while, at the same time, pointing to and defining much broader cultural moments that coalesce into a post-millennial period whose contemporaneity, as I show in what follows, becomes an especially pressing problem for cinematic narrative.

Manthia Diawara has grouped Haroun and Sissako together with other African directors (Serge Coelo, Gahité Fofana) in what he calls the Arte Wave of new African filmmaking (2010, p. 100). Arte is the French and German television network that has produced and funded many of Haroun's and Sissako's films, allowing them free rein to experiment with *essayiste* (aestheticized, almost literary) approaches to cinema with little regard for the immediacy of popular acclaim.[2] The films by Haroun and Sissako I examine here bring a sense of popular urgency to everyday life even if they are not distributed or produced in the same way as, say, Nollywood video films. Other scholars have highlighted Sissako's engagements with globalization and economics, pointing to the contested "rationality" of structural adjustment in *Bamako* (Olaniyan, 2008) and to this film's difficulties in communicating an economic didacticism from an African perspective (Limbu 2013, p. 48).[3] Critics engaging with Haroun's work have tended to emphasize corporeal aestheticism, that is, the way bodies create new forms of cinematic language (Barlet 2011) or new intersections of masculinity and postcolonial nationalism (Williams, 2014). My emphasis here diverges from this work because it situates political economy, warscapes, and corporeality as thematics that gain cinematic salience through the intensity of temporal compression and through a periodizing impulse that urgently traces the outlines of the post-millennial now. As such, the perspective I articulate in this chapter considers how cinematic experiences of new temporalities generate economic visions of contemporaneity.

Anthropologists Jean and John Comaroff (2001) periodize millennial economic ideologies by turning to the eschatological (but not apocalyptic) metaphor of capitalism's "Second Coming" to describe how capitalism in the early twenty-first century is both resolutely contemporary and "salvific, even magical" (p. 2). They refer to "the odd coupling … of the legalistic with the libertarian; constitutionality with deregulation; hyperrationalization with the exuberant spread of innovative occult practices and money magic, pyramid schemes and prosperity gospels…" and point toward "a capitalism that, if rightly harnessed, is invested with the capacity wholly to transform the universe of the marginalized and disempowered" (p. 2). The periodizing impulses of Haroun and Sissako I examine here chronologically overlap with those of the Comaroffs. But, in the films I examine here, they drain millennial capitalism of its "salvific" potential (notwithstanding *Bamako*'s sequence set in a charismatic Christian church) and position it as a temporal problem whose weighty immediacy can be produced and communicated cinematically. For Haroun and Sissako, millennial capitalism's paradoxical characteristics yield temporal uncertainty rather than salvation, and it is the task of cinema to visualize and narrativize negotiations in everyday life of this emergent contemporaneity.

In the following section of this chapter, I turn to a set of films that thematize the temporal dimensions of post-millennial economic precarity. In these films, Haroun and Sissako combine cinematic storytelling with political economy, bringing ideological debates about new social relations into the realm of everyday life and the opportunities for narrative immediacy it provides. These debates may flare up explicitly, as in *Bamako*, or they may drive a given narrative from below the surface, as in Haroun's *Grigris* (2013), but, in all the examples I draw on, economics plays an outsized role in (over)determining visualizations of contemporary uncertainty. The next section deals with cinematic warscapes: Here I consider how conflict introduces new understandings of the now into daily life and how the warscape spurs cinematic periodizing impulses. The films I approach in this section deal less obviously with a thematics of political economy, but they attribute value to narrative immediacy in ways that complement the forms of periodization at work in the previous, "economic" set of films.

Economic Precarity and Everyday Urgency

I would like to begin by proceeding along three axes that nonetheless speak to each other: In an important set of films, debt, development, and the pervasive unease of economic precarity function as thematic lynchpins holding together more abstract economic debates and stories about everyday life. The films comprising this series of texts are Sissako's *Le rêve de Tiya* (*Tiya's Dream*, 2008), *La vie sur terre* (1998), and *Bamako* (2006); as well as Haroun's *Grigris* (2013). Taken alongside one another, these films help us understand how debt and development can be translated as economic concepts into the temporality of the hypercontemporary. The cinematic expression of these ideas and their attendant ideologies takes on special salience through stories of economic precarity that double as visual narratives of urgency.

Sissako's *Le rêve de Tiya* offers a particularly striking example of how these processes of translation and expression play out on screen. This short, roughly ten-minute film is part of a longer anthology called *8*, in which directors (including such figures as Wim Wenders and Gus Van Sant) made short films corresponding to the eight United Nations Millennium Development Goals (2016) to which all member states signed up in the year 2000.[4] These goals were wide-ranging (touching on such domains as gender equality, universal primary education, and HIV/ AIDS prevention), and member states set themselves the deadline of 2015 to meet them.[5] Sissako's film corresponds to and visualizes the first development goal, "to eradicate extreme poverty and hunger."

Tiya is set in Ethiopia and follows a young girl, the film's eponymous heroine, as she arrives late for school. The film opens as Tiya, sitting on the front stoop preparing her school satchel, is called back by her ailing father who reminds her to finish sewing a shirt before she leaves. This establishing sequence contains didactic overtones: We are given to understand that the economic expedient of child labor unfortunately trumps the prerogative of primary education. Tiya finally arrives at school during a lesson on the UN Millennium Development Goals (MDGs) but is quickly distracted by a chaotic game of pickup rugby taking place in the courtyard. Sissako's camera cuts back and forth between the game and the classroom, and we see Tiya drop one of the two pieces of fruit she has brought with her out the window for a shoeshine boy. During this sequence the other students dutifully recite their interpretations of the MDGs and the teacher shakes our protagonist from her reverie by asking her to name the first goal, that is, the very one Sissako's film is meant to illustrate. Tiya answers correctly but in too soft a tone for the teacher's liking; she explains herself by revealing that she does not believe in this goal, since "To reduce poverty, we must share wealth more evenly. But people don't like sharing." The film ends with a shot of Tiya staring dreamily out the window again, this time at an older boy who has come to serenade her with promises of affection and support when she loses her father.

The uncertainty communicated by *Tiya* stems, first, from the fact that we as viewers remain unsure of the film's decisive moment: Does it occur when Tiya initially drops her fruit for the shoeshine boy, or does it come later when she declares her skepticism of the MDG and philosophically validates her earlier action, challenging viewers to prove her wrong? I would suggest, however, that the more evocative moment in the film is the series of shots of Tiya staring out the window at either the rugby players or at her older suitor. In all these shots, Tiya appears somewhat dazed, and it is unclear whether she is truly absorbed in the activity taking place outside her classroom or whether she is unable to focus on the day's lesson because she is simply hungry. The uncertainty in this sequence intersects with the MDG Sissako is tasked with communicating in the film: He must visualize extreme poverty and hunger as well as their potential eradication, and before the credits roll statistics appear on screen to remind viewers of the numbers of people who either go to bed or die hungry each day. Upon seeing these statistics, we might be tempted to attribute to *Tiya* a certain uncritical moralizing; the film manages to skirt such charges, though, by highlighting its own uncertainty and immediacy. Tiya's remark challenges Western viewers but also casts doubt on the viability or accountability of the MDGs. At the same time that we process this thematic uncertainty, we watch Tiya watching the other children and experience her hunger and distraction at their most urgent through a cinematic mise-en-abîme. The combination of these two processes (and the fact that we are forced to take them in simultaneously) allows Sissako to translate critically "development" as an abstract UN mandate/goal into the visceral immediacy of hunger in daily life.

Sissako's earlier *La vie sur terre* engages in similar processes of conceptual translation, but the perspective he adopts in this docu-fiction is much more obviously poeticized, not least because citations from Césaire's *Cahier d'un retour au pays natal* punctuate the film's millennial narrative. Sissako's character, Dramane, assimilates himself to Césaire's poetic *je* in imagining his return to his father's village of Sokolo. He initially couches his desire to film the village as it transitions into the new millennium in Césaire's lines about arrival, which he reads in a voice-over: "I would arrive sleek and young in this land of mine and I would say to this land whose loam is part of my flesh: 'I have wandered for a long time and I am coming back to the deserted hideousness of your sores'" (Césaire 2001, p. 13). Despite the colonial context of Césaire's masterpiece, its presence in the film is part of a much more ambiguous reading of millennial temporality, since Sissako is primarily interested in how millennial ideals of development and global connectivity reach everyday life in rural Mali, a place that appears in the film as in but not of the millennial global ecumene.

We have seen how Sissako shows local villagers consuming global connectivity in his collection of shots of intense boredom, that is, the shots of men listening to RFI excitedly announce the world's plans for new year's celebrations. But in *La vie sur terre* local experiences of connectivity belie the triumphalist rhetoric of these ideals. These experiences come across most clearly in the tongue-in-cheek scenes set in the local post office, where villagers come to place local and overseas phone calls. We have the impression of laughing along with Sissako as some of the callers, Dramane included, do not succeed in reaching the people with whom they want to connect: Shoddy lines, absent interlocutors, and wrong numbers all prevent communication from taking place. In several shots from these scenes, the slogan for SoTelMa (Société des télécommunications au Mali) is visible on an advertisement: "The telephone for all! This is our priority." The irony here, of course, is that although the telephone is indeed available to Sokolo's residents they do not manage to use it to good effect.

In a sharp contrast with the irony and levity of these telephone scenes, Sissako's critique of the ideal of connectivity as lived experience takes on a more pathetic and urgently economic tone at the end of the film, when one of the village's residents dictates a letter in which he implores his brother living abroad to send money back to Mali. This man is coping with a poor harvest and medical problems, and he filters connectivity through the immediacy of kinship ethics: "If we don't help each other, the family cannot prosper," he pleads in the letter. On the one hand, kinship connections bestow certain obligations upon the man's unknown addressee; on the other hand, though, arriving as it does at the end of the film we never find out what becomes of this request, and the circumstances of its enunciation leave us less than optimistic about its viability. Connectivity, from this perspective, is both urgently real and idealized, almost fictive, at the same time: It is supposed to index development and herald new forms of global belonging, but it also enables expressions of economic precarity to take on transnational dimensions even if the fact of connectivity as such does not guarantee a certain outcome.

The tenor of Haroun's *Grigris* matches the plaintive immediacy of this final expression of precarity from *La vie sur terre*. But *Grigris* thematizes political economy more implicitly than Sissako's millennial "economic" films. Haroun's eponymous protagonist is a disabled part-time dancer in the Chadian capital, N'Djamena, where he moved from Burkina Faso with his mother. The film turns on the questions of economic urgency and precarity, as Grigris must turn to his friend Moussa for work in order to help his adoptive and ailing father pay off his hospital bills. Moussa works in the shadow economy, and Grigris ends up becoming a getaway driver in his friend's gasoline-trafficking scheme. Pressed for cash, Grigris steals a shipment of gas and sells it himself; in the rest of the film he evades Moussa's henchman by fleeing to the countryside with his love interest, a local sex worker.

The most striking scenes in *Grigris* show Haroun's protagonist dancing in a local bar. These scenes capture our attention both because and in spite of Grigris's disability, what Moussa calls his "dead leg": his brilliant dancing relies on exceptional bodily strength and on the use of his leg as a corporeal prop, such as when he holds and "fires" it like a machine gun. But in the context of my argument here, these scenes' aesthetic success lies in the fact that Haroun never quite lets viewers forget that these captivating displays of eroticized masculinity are, first and foremost, forms of labor: shots of a hat being passed through the crowd for donations remind us that Grigris's dancing is not so dissimilar from the work of his love interest, Mimi, an aspiring model who seduces clients in the bar where she meets our protagonist. Alongside the aestheticized and eroticized bodily labor visualized in the film, though, what drives Haroun's narrative here is debt. Grigris's adoptive father incurs a crippling debt due to his illness, which prompts Grigris to incur a life-threatening debt to Moussa when he steals the gasoline. The film presents these debts as following logically from economic urgency, since this is a world where the state is absent (save for the police apparatus), and where social protection, welfare, or what James Ferguson (2015) has called a "new [African] politics of distribution" are unthinkable. In this cinematic landscape the shadow economy morphs into the real economy, and a thematics of debt introduces immediacy as the only narrative temporality possible.

Debt is accompanied by urgent immediacy as its attendant form of temporality, for although debt is a promise projected into the future its uncertain resolution comes to weigh on every instant of the present. At first glance, the end of *Grigris* would seem to abolish both this thematics and its sense of time: Our hero and his girlfriend escape to a hamlet in the countryside, and when Moussa's hired muscle tracks them down, the women of the village come to their rescue and kill the henchman, vowing never to speak of the incident again. The film ends with this incident, suggesting at first glance a satisfactory resolution of the narrative. From the point of view of debt, however, this final sequence remains entirely uncertain: Grigris has not made good on his debt to Moussa and with the killing of his employee has in fact incurred another one. The film's supposed crescendo, its apparent moment of resolution, is a doubling-down on the cycle of debt that trapped Grigris in the first place. Although the film ends, then, the temporal dimensions of debt the narrative reveals remain steadfastly open-ended and Grigris becomes something of a tragic hero, a figure with whom we identify but who comes to embody debt as the emblematic relation of subjection in contemporary life (Lazzarato, 2015). And it is this seemingly irresolvable relation of subjection that signals Haroun's periodizing impulse in the film. The uncertainty of the film's ending is of a piece with its sense of temporal immediacy, as Grigris's debts continue to hang over his head as ever-present threats. But these elements of urgency and precarity also intersect with debt's open-endedness, what Maurizio Lazzarato (2015, p. 73), summoning Nietzsche, refers to as its "infinity."[6] Haroun's idea of the now in *Grigris* encompasses all of these qualities and he communicates them in a narrative whose ambiguity only grows as the film comes to a close.

The thematization of debt in the hypercontemporary is more implicit in *Grigris*, driving the (unresolved) narrative from below the surface. In Sissako's *Bamako*, however, sovereign debt, alongside structural adjustment programs and globalization, takes center stage as African civil society brings the World Bank to trial in a Malian courtyard. What makes this film so striking is Sissako's embedding of the highly formalized trial, whose political-economic issues are real but whose stakes are purely hypothetical, in the banality and boredom of everyday life going on around the trial. Although the trial, with its expert testimonies and cross-examinations, is *Bamako*'s narrative focal point, it would be wrong to consider these elements of daily life as somehow peripheral to the debate the film stages on neoliberal ideologies of development in post-millennial Africa. My reading of this film is situated instead at the interface of the judicial proceedings and the happenings of everyday life that impinge upon them. These are seemingly extraneous moments of disruption or cinematic framing, like when a toddler waddles across the judges' line of sight or when Sissako stages a shot of the trial from across the courtyard, taking in people and activities that are uninvolved in the proceedings. It is at the juncture of the juridical and the everyday that Sissako locates the film's temporal thrust; *Bamako* communicates to viewers its sense of the now by connecting debates about political economy, debt, and development to the immediacy and ordinariness of everyday life with its lack of obvious mise-en-scène. *Bamako* is indeed "anti-imperialist art" (Benjamin, 2012), but it is also hypercontemporary free play, a narrative where images of urgency confront the "textuality" (see Harrow 2013, p. 180) of the trial's argumentative logic.

The trial's procedural rigor constitutes the film's structural backbone, but the ill-defined (in the sense that it lacks the hyperorganized rationality of the court case) bustle of everyday life going on around the proceedings grabs our attention in a no less forceful manner. Thus, for instance, very early on in the film as the lawyers and spectators sit silently, waiting for the day's events to begin, an elderly man approaches the witness stand out of turn. In Sissako's shot, we look out at an angle, presumably from near the judges' bench, as the old man stands just to the left of the frame's center. At the center itself sit the lawyers, but our eyes are not drawn to them: For several seconds, as these individuals in the foreground stand and sit silently, the only movement we catch in the frame is that of a woman in the background washing clothes in a bucket. Although the woman appears smaller because of her distance from the camera, she demands our attention because she too is near the center of the frame and because her movement drags our eyes away from the individuals in the foreground, all of whom are "inside" the trial. And we can read the comings and goings of Melé, the lounge singer, in a similar manner. The trial takes place in the courtyard of the residence she shares with her husband, Chaka, and other families, and *Bamako* traces their growing estrangement as a secondary cinematic focal point. Throughout the film, Melé walks through shots of the trial, often looking stony-faced and uncomfortable, as she prepares to leave for work at the bar. Her movements and appearances disrupt the linearity of the court's proceedings, to be sure, but in terms of my argument here they also point to the forms of ordinary labor taking place in this Bamako neighborhood as the (mis)deeds of the World Bank are being hashed out and contested in the trial. The immediacy of everyday labor contrasts with the abstract political-economic arguments of the trial, bringing both of these narrative categories into sharp relief even as Sissako's camera holds them together in a single shot or sequence.

At times, our attention plunges directly into the trial's visual paratext: The most telling example of this is the interpolated short Western film, *Death in Timbuktu*, that Sissako inserts into his narrative. This film, starring Danny Glover (among others), is a very loosely structured tale of a shootout in the historic Malian city; we are only afforded a several-minute glimpse of the film, and thus are not aware of its stakes or its narrative resolution. Sissako shows off his virtuosity here, cheekily reminding viewers that cinema's generic categories can be provided with unexpected geographic genealogies – a Western set in Africa is hardly what the first-time viewer of *Bamako* expects to see in the middle of this film. But the function of this cinematic interpolation, I think, is to periodize and to reassert the film's sense of time, that is, to remind viewers of the immediacy it wants to communicate alongside the abstract political-economic debates of the trial. *Death in Timbuktu* is presented as a film the neighborhood children are watching at night on an outdoor television set, and at times Sissako's takes us outside the interpolation, back to the "real time" of the film, to one of the children laughing at the antics of one of the cowboys on screen. As viewers, we become aware that we are watching what the children are watching, at the same time, and this is how *Bamako* visualizes an intense now-effect that comes to characterize the entirety of the film.[7]

It is in terms of this "now-ness" that we experience Sissako's visualization of labor in the film. Thus, for instance, one witness, a Malian intellectual trained in France, gives testimony to the court about the one-way flow of information from the West to Africa, such that the "foundations" of local societies erode in the face of Western ideals and cultural models: "they take our minds, too," he concludes. This commentary seems to stray from the realm of the strictly political-economic and rests on certain shaky assumptions about supposed African "authenticity" (about which he is duly questioned during cross-examination), but the key moment of this sequence comes when Sissako cuts away from the trial to the interior of a house, where a young girl is sorting and spinning cotton by hand with an old woman, perhaps her grandmother. The relationship here between image (the production of a material to be used as a commodity, as value) and text (the description of alienation provoked by Western-led globalization) is a visual reversal of commodity fetishism, wherein the social relations that inhere in local forms of production become concrete while a disembodied voice comments on contemporary forces of social estrangement.

Production enters into the framing of Sissako's shots, as well. His camera returns time and again to images of a dyeworks operating in the compound. We see local women creating lovely, brightly colored lengths of cloth, although it is unclear to whom they are destined. One morning, as the day's proceedings are about to begin, Sissako cuts to an establishing shot of the bench framed by clothes and a length of the cloth drying on a clothesline – the framing is akin to a theater stage whose curtain has just opened. This shot brings the production of goods together with the production of domesticity, commercial labor with affective labor (Hardt and Negri 2000, p. 217). It also underscores the fact that debt, development, and production (or anti-production, as the plaintiffs might put it) taken as abstract political-economic categories have everyday visual referents that interface with broader critical debates in a medium that signals its own immediacy.

Bamako ends with a quotation from Césaire's poem "Les pur-sang" ("The Thoroughbreds"): "My ear to the ground, I heard tomorrow pass by" [L'oreille collée au sol, j'entendis passer demain]. In this context these words have a futuristic bent, and they signal utopian longing for a new kind of economic time, one divorced from neoliberal ideologies of structural adjustment, and for an alternate reality where civil society's request for justice (namely that the World Bank perform community service in perpetuity) is actually enforceable. This same citation also figures in Sissako's *La Vie sur terre*, where it performs different temporal work. In this earlier film it indexes stasis, the emphasis now falling on a millennial tomorrow that "passes by," occurring elsewhere but hardly registering in the village of Sokolo. But Césaire's words intersect with the periodizing drive expressed throughout the set of "economic" films I examine, for the idea of tomorrow is conceived and expressed here through a diagnostic of the now that endows political economy with a cinematic phenomenology of urgency and immediacy.

Warscapes and the Hypercontemporary

In turning our attention to Haroun's and Sissako's warscapes we do not rid ourselves so easily of Césaire's poetic influence: Haroun's *A Screaming Man* [*Un homme qui crie*] borrows its title from the *Cahier*: "For a screaming man is not a dancing bear," reads the full line. This is anti-spectacular logic ("For life is not a spectacle, for a sea of pain is not a stage" are the two preceding clauses in the poem (Césaire 1956, p. 42)), and it suggests that suffering or traumatic upheaval might be rendered narratively in their barest banality and facticity, shorn of "theatrical" (following Césaire's imagery) adornment.[8] We can read Haroun's *Daratt* and *A Screaming Man* and Sissako's *Timbuktu* as cinematic translations of Césaire's assertion. We can also read them as explorations of how the warscape as felt cinematic contemporaneity tells a story about time: How do Haroun and Sissako film conflict so as to create cinematic value from intense narratives of the now? This set of films is not "economic" in the strong, thematic sense that characterizes the films I took up in this chapter's previous section; but we are dealing nonetheless with narrative economies of the hypercontemporary that valorize the communication of temporal immediacy by periodizing cinematic warscapes.

Haroun's war films are slow-moving texts that communicate now-ness through silences, awkward pauses, ambient sounds, and the painstaking arrangement of bodies in frames. Many of his shots are reminiscent of tableaux vivants, in which the careful distribution of bodies signals an elongated and expanded sense of immediacy: Haroun forces us to take in shots that go on far longer than we feel they should, and in so doing he narrativizes war and its aftermath by burrowing into his characters' interiority rather than by pulling back and contextualizing the stakes of civil conflict. These shots elongate now-ness by slowing down and stretching out the immediacy of private moments, rendering them all the more intense for their reduced speed. In *Timbuktu*, by contrast, Sissako conceives of cinematic immediacy by filming armed occupation (by Islamist militants Ansar Dine) as a time outside of time, as a temporal subtraction from the normal working order of everyday life. If African war fiction creates historical narratives (see Coundouriotis, 2014), it also uses warscapes to visualize new experiences of the contemporary that are shot through with and overdetermined by the urgency of conflict.

Haroun's *A Screaming Man* was released in 2010, four years after his *Daratt*, but this later film offers a provocative starting point because it visualizes the warscape in real time whereas the earlier film periodizes post-conflict reconciliation. *A Screaming Man* is set during the Chadian civil war that began in 2005 and deals with the deeply wounded pride of a father, Adam, once a Central African swimming champion, who loses his job at an upmarket hotel pool to his son, Abdel. The hotel has recently gone under Chinese management and the new proprietress is eager to cut costs, but Adam takes his replacement to heart and this dismissal opens up the film's broadly Oedipal conflict. At the same time, Adam is relentlessly pressured by a neighborhood government functionary to make a financial contribution to the state's "war effort," an informal tax he cannot afford. Stinging from his career's abrupt end, Adam decides to give Abdel to the army in lieu of a monetary donation, a choice that eventually leads to the latter's death in combat. In keeping with the themes of this chapter, then, the crux of this film is transactional and the principle of (coerced) exchange is seen as part and parcel of the cinematic warscape. But the transaction upon which Haroun's narrative turns is embedded in a much broader visualization of war as a form of felt urgency, even or especially when the war in question remains unseen or only tangentially experienced. The obliqueness of the warscape in *A Screaming Man* seeps into Haroun's shots and also comes to condition his sense of the contemporary.

Early in the film, for instance, a sequence set indoors shows Adam and his wife, Miriam, feeding each other watermelon. The sequence begins in a medium close-up that moves in even closer as Adam and Miriam kiss, the juices from the fruit dripping onto their lips and chins. Haroun's close-ups compound the extreme tenderness expressed here: They make us uncomfortable, and we have the impression that we are intruding on a display of intimacy that we should not be seeing. Playing in the background during these intimate moments is a television newscast about the ongoing war, but we can only glimpse with difficulty the images on the screen as extreme close-ups fill the frame. The newscast's audio, however, comes through clearly, and, as the pro-government broadcast denounces the rebels, it becomes increasingly challenging to concentrate on the information conveyed in what under other circumstances would be a helpful moment of contextualization. Visuality and textuality overlap here without coinciding (akin to what we have seen in Sissako's *Bamako*), and Haroun pulls our attention in two contrasting directions as he refuses to let the war come fully into view, favoring instead the affective immediacy of Adam and Miriam's intimacy.

This sequence lacks dialogue (until a neighbor calls and interrupts our characters), and it highlights the way in which Haroun uses wordlessness to convey a sense of immediacy to viewers. Dialogue is sparse in his war films, and in *A Screaming Man* wordlessness allows the warscape to coexist with psychological interiority on screen. Wordlessness is not silence, however: Ambient noise around Haroun's characters brings the immediacy of everyday life to the fore while dialogic reticence paradoxically communicates the intense urgency of war even as the conflict hardly ever takes center stage in the film's shots.

The sequence in the film that most effectively illustrates this paradoxical communicative conduit occurs when Adam decides to "donate" his son to the government's war effort. While walking to work at the hotel where he is kept on as a gate attendant after Abdel is given sole custody of the pool, Adam is picked up by the neighborhood government functionary and informed once again of the urgent matter of his contribution. Adam insists that he cannot afford to pay the informal tax when the man proceeds to explain suggestively that he donated his own son to the army. After this conversation Haroun cuts away to a series of shots of Adam walking silently through the hotel, the sounds around him magnified by his introspection: Children splashing in the pool as Abdel gives swimming lessons, machines whirring and beeping in a back room, cars driving past in the distance. Haroun follows up this conjunction of silent bodily movement and ambient noise with a long-take shot of Adam sitting in his chair at the hotel's front gate, staring stonily into the camera. This shot lasts for over 50 seconds as the camera slowly zooms in on Adam's face, situating him just off center in the frame. This weighty sequence condenses war, alienation, and characterological interiority into the cinematic relationship between background noise and pensive silence, a relationship that intensifies the instantaneousness of Adam's thought processes. By visualizing this interaction between sound and wordlessness, Haroun brings the warscape into the immediacy of his character's consciousness without actually filming the conflict.

From this point of view, then, the title of *A Screaming Man* appears tragically misdirected: In the face of Adam's reflective silence, the only screams that stay with us viewers are those Abdel makes as he is hauled off to join the army while his father listens shamefacedly from his bedroom. However, within the anti-spectacular logic opened up by the title's Césairean roots, we come to recognize that wordlessness communicates the warscape not only as woven into everyday life but also as immediate to consciousness in ways that can be unexpectedly visualized in film.

If wordlessness signals the hypercontemporary in *A Screaming Man* by bringing the warscape and the logic of transaction into the immediacy of consciousness, this same quality functions differently in Haroun's *Daratt*. In this earlier film, the hypercontemporary is bound up with the periodization of post-conflict reconciliation and not with the experience of war in real time, as it were; the now, in this case, indexes the types of affective investment that emerge in the political time of the postwar moment. *Daratt* also tells the story of a troubled and troubling father figure, but here we are dealing with a case of paternal substitution: The film's protagonist, a teenage boy named Atim ("orphan," as he explains in a voice-over), travels from Abeche in the Chadian hinterland to N'Djamena in order to kill the man who murdered his father during the civil war. For Atim and his grandfather, revenge appears as ethically necessary since the state (or what we hear of it in the film via a radio broadcast) has granted amnesty to all war criminals. Once in the capital, Atim reluctantly befriends Nassara, his father's killer, and goes to work for him as an apprentice baker. Atim rebuffs Nassara's attempts to formally adopt him as his son, but he is nonetheless ultimately unable to kill Nassara when finally presented with an opportunity. Whereas in *A Screaming Man* the thematics of transaction involves coercion and renunciation, in *Daratt* transactional logic mobilizes an ethics of substitution: Atim allows Nassara to occupy the place of his father (even if he does not replace him outright) in a makeshift familial structure that sets in motion the time of national reconciliation.

Haroun's shots in *Daratt* are just as wordless as those in *A Screaming Man*. Dialogue is hard to come by in this film, and the tension expressed in Atim and Nassara's wordless sequences seems to stand in allegorically for the uncertainties involved in the establishment of a lasting sense of post-conflict political time. Relatedly, but even more fundamentally, our protagonists' lengthy periods of silence bespeak a relationship between labor and the production of affect that overlaps with the broadly allegorical elements of Haroun's story.

Much of the film is given over to the affection (grudging in Atim's case and desperate in Nassara's) and emotional dependence that grows between the two characters as Nassara teaches Atim the ropes of the bread-making trade. They rarely exchange words during these sequences – indeed, Nassara uses speech only sparingly since he must use an electrolarynx after an attacker slit his throat during the war – and the ambient noise of the ovens or other machines takes the place of the conversations we might expect them to be having. But the labor they undertake in concert compensates (the economic pun here is intended) for the shortfalls in their capabilities of verbal expression. Production in these sequences does double duty as both economic necessity and affective conduit, for it becomes a vehicle for the visualization of ways of feeling that cannot manifest in conventional forms of cinematic dialogue.

Haroun draws out the connections between this thematics of production and his film's periodizing impulse by returning occasionally to the national context, reminding us that his characterological intimacy has much broader referents. This is how we understand the brief sequence of Atim and Nassara silently eating outside and listening to a radio newscast describing protests against the government's decision to grant a blanket postwar amnesty to former combatants. As an interviewee angrily describes how "amnesty" here is synonymous with "impunity," Haroun's camera slowly zooms in on Atim looking accusingly at Nassara, whose face we cannot see. The interviewee refers to the need for "payback" as Nassara gets up from the ground and goes to turn off the radio, the upper half of his body leaving the frame entirely. Haroun then cuts to Nassara seated once again, angrily biting into his food and avoiding Atim's glare. The protester being interviewed voices sentiments that Atim seems unable to articulate, and the sequence's final cut showing Nassara tearing into his food while looking away from his young apprentice signals wordless acceptance of Atim's grievances. This moment reminds us of *Daratt*'s temporal stakes: The film makes its claim on the hypercontemporary by condensing redemptive possibilities and national narratives of postwar reconciliation into intense instants of wordless labor and silent communication.

In contrast to Haroun's hypercontemporary aesthetics of wordless instants developed in *A Screaming Man* and *Daratt*, Sissako's *Timbuktu* explores the temporality of the warscape using an effect of cinematic bracketing. Timbuktu is under occupation by the jihadists of Ansar Dine, and as ordinary residents push back against the dictates of Islamic law we are presented with a city that has come to a standstill – this is true even in a literal sense, as in the nighttime shots of soldiers patrolling the streets, ensuring that residents do not go about their lives as before. Sissako constructs the "now" of the warscape through a narrative of temporal subtraction and by portraying occupied Timbuktu as withdrawn from ordinary life, stuck in a time outside of time, as it were. The hypercontemporary here certainly expresses a state of exception, but it is one whose relationship to the law requires us to adjust Giorgio Agamben's understanding of exceptionality and *nomos*. Agamben (2005, p. 39) argues that "The state of exception is an anomic space in which what is at stake is a force of law without law," in which sovereign decrees take on an aura of legal authority even though the juridical order has been suspended. Sissako's *Timbuktu* accounts for a similar act of suspension, to be sure, but this film visualizes a state of exception in which ordinary juridical norms have been replaced not by the whims of a dictator but by the importation and (selective, it must be said) articulation of a different legal order entirely, namely sharia law. The immediacy of *Timbuktu*'s time outside of time is of a piece with an understanding of "exceptional" law as divine intervention, that is, as imposed from without but possessing the rigor of God-given systematicity in the here and now.

The film's atmosphere is one of stifling expectation, as occupying forces and locals standoff in a narrative of open-ended near-confrontation, the former issuing Islamic decrees through megaphones in the streets (women must wear socks at the marketplace, residents must not congregate outside after hours or listen to music) and the latter resisting by forcing everyday life back into the time of occupation (by playing music at home, for instance, or not wearing gloves at the market). In spite of these activities, though, what drives Sissako's narrative are images of people waiting, killing time until some resolution of the siege occurs. The Tuareg family, whose tent lies just outside of town, has not moved away because Kidane the patriarch wants to see what will happen; Abdelkerim, the leader of the occupying army, takes driving lessons in the desert from his translator; another soldier steals away to dance to music he cannot hear; and the city's imam tries to soften the application of sharia through counterreadings of the Qu'ran while realizing that he is powerless outside the space of his mosque. Sissako's sense of the now in this film involves immediacy without urgency, in the sense that *Timbuktu* narrativizes the real time of occupation without offering a horizon of resolution for the film's understanding of bracketed time. He does not let us glimpse any potential return to normative, non-occupied temporality and we are left with a succession of immediate instants comprising an occupied time that appears endless.

The film's most striking example of this time of waiting, of bracketed time, is a sequence that is paradoxically not about inactivity but about action as enforced make-believe. Following a scene in a makeshift courtroom in which young men are sentenced to 20 lashes for playing soccer, Sissako cuts to a sequence showing boys playing a soccer match without a ball. This sequence is silent but overlaid with music, and we observe the intricately coordinated movements of players who make tackles, passes, and saves as if the ball were at their feet, interrupting their imaginary match and pretending to stretch or do calisthenics when soldiers on patrol drive by the field. The looks on the boys' faces lead us to believe they are taking the match seriously, but at the same time we realize that there cannot be any result or rules-based endpoint to their play when the sport's crucial instrument has been outlawed. Coming as it does on the heels of the courtroom sentencing, we can of course read this sequence as illustrating a sly act of resistance to the strictures of Ansar Dine's interpretation of sharia. But it also offers a ludic analogue to the idea of the now that Sissako wants to convey: An unwinnable match with an imaginary ball maps onto the uncertainty and amorphousness of occupied time, and the players appear to make up their own rules in a moral economy that strictly circumscribes the distribution of bodies and activities in social space. This moral economy is a contested ideological site involving competing notions of justice and the good life and, in a stronger sense, the imposition of and resistance to a new moral order artificially grafted onto everyday life (Figure 1.1).

Another figure in the film embodies this idea of the now as hanging in suspension, as "time out of joint," to borrow the Shakespearean phrase. This is a woman who has the bearing of an eccentric Vudu priestess, a *mambo*; she walks through Timbuktu's streets in a long, brightly colored robe (that contrasts sharply with the ubiquitous light ochre of the city's streets and buildings) and is largely unchallenged by the Islamic police or other occupying soldiers – they observe her but pay her little mind, it seems at first. But they do not avoid her entirely, and her rooftop offers certain soldiers a respite from the rigors of occupation and sharia enforcement (this is where one soldier silently dances, for example).

In one sequence the woman, Zabou, offers a brief monologue explaining her presence in Timbuktu in a way that intersects with the theory of the hypercontemporary warscape as suspended time: Three soldiers stand in the foreground watching her tear up cloth at a bench or work station before she tosses one man a magical charm for protection. She proceeds to proclaim theatrically (speaking perhaps to her chicken named Gonaïves after the city in Haiti, perhaps to no one in particular) that she was instantly transported to Timbuktu from Haiti on 12 January 2010, at the exact moment that a devastating earthquake struck the country. "Time doesn't matter," she exclaims, "the earthquake is my body. I am the

Figure 1.1 A player lines up to take an imaginary penalty kick. Source: *Timbuktu* (2014), dir. Abderrahmane Sissako, Arte France Cinéma / Canal + / Ciné + / CNC / TV5 Monde.

cracks! Cracked from my head to my feet, from my feet to my head. My arms, my back, and my face cracked! What is time? I am cracked." In describing herself as "cracked" or "split" [*fissurée*], Zabou positions herself as torn between the time of the "real world" and the timeless now of the occupation, between time as chronological progression and time as indefinite suspension. For her, the concept of temporality is either uncertain or unimportant but, at the same time, extremely precise: It was at 16:53, "the same time as in Miami," that the earthquake struck Haiti and she found herself in Mali. The paradoxical experience of time that Zabou expresses in this sequence encapsulates Sissako's sense of the hypercontemporary in *Timbuktu*, for throughout the film we observe characters on both sides of the occupation recalling normative chronological time as they make do with the constraints of occupied time and the moral economy imposed through this temporal subtraction or suspension.

For Haroun and Sissako, warscapes signal new understandings of cultural and political time and, as *Timbuktu* shows, are capable of constituting periods in their own right. They do so by visualizing and narrativizing forms of temporality and immediacy that both respond to conflict and imagine social forms existing outside of it, as with Sissako's soccer players or Haroun's thematics of uncertain reconciliation in *Daratt*. The hypercontemporary warscape thus appears as perpendicular to everyday life in these films, intersecting with it and overdetermining it, but also, at the same time, leading it away from its normative forms of temporal organization. The richness of this perpendicularity is what makes the warscape such a fecund narrative site for new cinematic conceptions of the now.

*

We might conclude with a final nod to Agamben. In an essay titled "What Is the Contemporary?," he writes that "Contemporariness is, then, a singular relationship with one's own time, which adheres to it and, at the same time, keeps a distance from it. More precisely, it is *that relationship with time that adheres to it through a disjunction and an anachronism*" (2009, p. 41, emphasis in original). This idea of the contemporary involves temporal distance, the idea of being "out of phase" with one's cultural and historical moment, as well as studied curiosity, that is, the desire to account for one's own time even as it confounds our attempts to do so. But what, precisely, sustains this relationship and renews it in spite of the contemporary's constitutive elusiveness? Haroun and Sissako suggest that this relationship is primarily one of narrative, one that can be managed and (re)fashioned through stylized storytelling about everyday life. Further, their cinematic treatments of political economy and warscapes lend the contemporary a sense of urgent immediacy, transforming it from a narrative category into what we might call a narrative imperative, an idea of the cinematic now that demands exploration and theorization. The appearance in narrative texts (filmic ones, in our case) of these demands is what I have been calling the hypercontemporary. This is not just a thematic concern but one that enters into cinematic composition, as well. Haroun's and Sissako's films create temporal distance by expanding or compressing now-ness, effects that throw into relief the broader historical and cultural periods these films articulate. The gaps and distances generated by this setting into relief create the sort of "anachronisms" and "disjunctions" of which Agamben speaks. And the disparate temporal intensities at play in these operations of periodization are the markers of the hypercontemporary in cinematic form.

In a broader sense, though, the hypercontemporary provokes African directors to rethink their relationships to cinema as a medium. Beyond the translation of war, debt, or development into narrative markers of the now, the hypercontemporary as a form of narrative intensity urges filmmakers to devise new ways of communicating time through engagements with the immediacy of everyday life. To do so involves setting in motion new theories of periodization that redirect now-ness through the African continent by narrativizing abstract debates of global import (such as how to challenge radical Islam, or how to critique the operative assumptions of Western political economy). From this perspective, periodization becomes a powerful cinematic impulse, one that drives African cinema's changing interactions with pressing worldwide questions.

Notes

1   Cameroonian filmmaker Jean-Marie Teno examines a broadly similar series of questions in his 2009 documentary, *Sacred Places*. As I have written elsewhere, Teno filters these questions through an investigation of cinema's relationship with other African art forms. See Justin Izzo, "Jean-Marie Teno's Documentary Modernity" (2015).

2   From this point of view, it seems ironic that Haroun in *Bye Bye Africa* would articulate his concerns for the future of cinematic consumption in Africa using a rather esoteric pseudo-documentary form. But in this earlier film, Haroun does not hide his aestheticized approach, and I would argue that he implicitly wrestles with this irony when he asks, over and over, what the future of African film might be.

3   Tsitsi Jaji (2014, p. 156) reads the political overtones in Sissako's oeuvre as reminiscent of the Spaghetti Western genre, beginning from the Western film inserted into *Bamako*. I return to this sequence later in this chapter, although I am less interested in generic attributions in Sissako's work.

4   This film, as well as the others in the anthology, was released on YouTube in 2010: www.youtube.com/watch?v=3JGjljTLYgA.

5   See the United Nations website on the Millennium Development Goals and their relevance beyond 2015: www.un.org/millenniumgoals/.

6   In his book *Governing by Debt*, Lazzarato is primarily concerned with the public debt of nation-states, not the debts of private individuals, but his remark about infinity still holds for private individuals insofar as debt appears in his analyses as the pre-eminent relation of subjection of our times.

7   Sissako returns to this cinematic effect at the end of the film, as well: Chaka commits
     suicide and, as a local videographer films his funeral, Sissako shifts back and forth bet-
     ween shots of this man filming and shots from his camera. This is the same sort of
     mise-en-abîme that occurs during the *Death in Timbuktu* sequence.

8   Sissako also reads this quotation in a voice-over from *La Vie sur terre*, and in this early
     film Césaire's anti-spectacular language leads Dramane further into the as yet unex-
     plored banality of millennial life in Sokolo.

References

Agamben, Giorgio. 2005. *State of Exception*. Translated by Kevin Attell. Chicago, IL:
     University of Chicago Press.
Agamben, Giorgio. 2009. *"What Is an Apparatus?" and Other Essays*. Translated by David
     Kishik and Stefan Pedatella. Stanford, CA: Stanford University Press.
Badiou, Alain. 2007. *The Century*. Translated by Alberto Toscano. Malden, MA: Polity.
Barlet, Olivier. 2011. "African Film's Meaningful Body." *Black Camera*, 2 no. 2: 138–144.
     DOI: 10.1353/blc.2011.0007.
Benjamin, Bret. 2012. "Making the Case: *Bamako* and the Problem of Anti-Imperial Art."
     In *The Megarhetorics of Global Development*, edited by Rebecca Dingo and J. Blake Scott,
     199–232. Pittsburgh, PA: University of Pittsburgh Press.
Césaire, Aimé. 1956 [orig. 1939]. *Cahier d'un retour au pays natal*. Paris: Présence Africaine.
Césaire, Aimé. 2001. *Notebook of a Return to the Native Land*. Translated and edited by
     Clayton Eshleman and Annette Smith. Middletown, CT: Wesleyan University Press.
Comaroff, Jean, and John L. Comaroff. 2001. "Millennial Capitalism: First Thoughts on a
     Second Coming." In *Millennial Capitalism and the Culture of Neoliberalism*, edited by
     Jean Comaroff and John L. Comaroff, 1–56. Durham, NC: Duke University Press.
Coundouriotis, Eleni. 2014. *People's Right to the Novel: War Fiction in the Postcolony*. New
     York: Fordham University Press.
Diawara, Manthia. 2010. *African Film: New Forms of Aesthetics and Politics*. Munich and New
     York: Prestel Verlag.
Ferguson, James. 2015. *Give a Man a Fish: Reflections on The New Politics of Distribution*.
     Durham, NC: Duke University Press.
Hardt, Michael, and Antonio Negri. 2000. *Empire*. Cambridge, MA: Harvard University
     Press.
Harrow, Kenneth W. 2013. *Trash: African Cinema From Below*. Bloomington: Indiana
     University Press.
Izzo, Justin. 2015. "Jean-Marie Teno's Documentary Modernity: From Millennial Anxiety
     to Cinematic Kinship." *African Studies Review*, 58 no. 1: 39–53. DOI: 10.1353/
     arw.2015.0008.
Jaji, Tsitsi. 2014. "Cassava Westerns: Ways of Watching Abderrahmane Sissako." *Black
     Camera*, 6 no. 1: 154–177. DOI: 10.1353/blc.2014.0021.
Lazzarato, Maurizio. 2015. *Governing by Debt*. Translated by Joshua David Jordan. South
     Pasadena, CA: Semiotext(e).
Limbu, Bishupal. 2013. "Ab-Using Enlightenment: Structural Adjustment, Storytelling, and
     the Public Use of Reason." *Cultural Critique*, 84: 35–69.

Olaniyan, Tejumola. 2008. "Of Rations and Rationalities: The World Bank, African Hunger, and Abderrahmane Sissako's *Bamako*." *The Global South*, 2 no. 2: 130–138.

Rabinow, Paul. 2008. *Marking Time: On the Anthropology of the Contemporary*. Princeton, NJ: Princeton University Press.

Williams, James S. 2014. "Male Beauty and the Erotics of Intimacy: The Talismanic Cinema of Mahamat-Saleh Haroun." *Film Quarterly*, 67 no. 4: 33–43. DOI: 10.1525/fq.2014.67.4.33.

United Nations. 2016. "We Can End Poverty: Millennium Development Goals Beyond 2015." Accessed 25 May 2016. www.un.org/millenniumgoals/.

Filmography

Haroun, Mahamat-Saleh. (1999). *Bye Bye Africa*. Chad: Images Plus, La Lanterne, Télé Chad.

Haroun, Mahamat-Saleh. (2006). *Daratt*. Chad and France: Chinguitty Films, Goï-Goï Productions, Entre Chien et Loup, Illuminations Films.

Haroun, Mahamat-Saleh. (2013). *Grigris*. Chad and France: France 3, Goï-Goï Productions, Pili Films.

Haroun, Mahamat-Saleh. (2020). *Un homme qui crie*. Chad: Pili Films, Entre Chien et Loup.

Sissako, Abderrahmane. (2006). *Bamako*. France and Mali: Archipel 33, Chinguitty Films, Mali Images, Arte France Cinéma.

Sissako, Abderrahmane. (2014). *Timbuktu*. Mali: Les Films du Worso.

Sissako, Abderrahmane. (2008). *Le rêve de Tiya*. France: LDM Productions. Accessed 25 May 2016. www.youtube.com/watch?v=3JGjljTLYgA.

Sissako, Abderrahmane. (1998). *La Vie sur terre*. France and Mali: La Sept Arte and Haut et Court.

Teno, Jean-Marie. (2009). *Lieux saints*. Cameroon and France: Les films du Raphia, Raphia Films Production.

2

Approaching the Uncertain Turn in African Video-Movies

Subalternity, Superfluity, and (Non-)Cinematic Time

Jacques de Villiers

Without much doubt, the question of how one thinks about Africa ... demands answering difficult, irritating and sometimes almost teleological questions about the human. It also entails having to live with the indetermination of seeking to keep open what others struggle to keep closed.

(Jeremiah Arowosegbe 2014, p. 245)

When I was a boy they told me that everything happens for a reason. But they were wrong. Some things don't happen for a reason. Some things just happen.
Opening voiceover, Confusion Na Wa *(Kenneth Gyang, Nigeria, 2013)*

Persisting from the cradle of colonial orthodoxy through to the present, narratives of teleological predetermination have long beset the temporal imagining of that geopolitical invention we call "Africa" – an imagining that has all too often been goal-oriented, unilineal, and programmatic. The origins and critique of this kind of thinking are well known. Coercively inscribed by a colonial and Eurocentric arche-writing that relationally defined Africa as lack (Mbembe 2001, 2006b, p. 147), the continent was forced to partake in a game of catch-up, with Europe at the finish and Africa at the start. "The advance of Progress" becomes the teleological mantra in which colonialism was cloaked; a discourse "already given, definitely fixed," and rooted in the "forward-thinking" "conversion of African minds" (Mudimbe 1988, p. 47). Thus, presides what Mahmood Mamdani (1996, p. 12) calls a "history by analogy," in the sense that "African reality has meaning only insofar as it can be seen to reflect a particular stage in the development of an earlier [European] history" (cf. Chakrabarty 2000 and Fabian 1983). Nor, unfortunately, is

A Companion to African Cinema, First Edition. Edited by Kenneth W. Harrow and Carmela Garritano.
© 2019 John Wiley & Sons, Inc. Published 2019 by John Wiley & Sons, Inc.

this an outmoded way of thinking. It is a conception of Africa that is still very much with us: A tenacious teleology changing its appearance while retaining the same linear assumptions, each time cloaked in different ideological and programmatic banners (*"mission civilisatrice,"* "modernization," "development," "Third World liberation," "Marxist-nationalism," "return to the source").

This is a mutually invented teleological conception, as V.Y. Mudimbe (1988) so influentially demonstrated, wielded by (neo)colonizer and (neo)colonized alike. Indeed, African cinema scholarship has not been innocent of its teleological allure. While scholars militated against a legacy of colonialism and ongoing neocolonial hegemony, Kenneth Harrow (2007, p. 28) has persuasively argued that the dominant thrust of this discourse actually endorsed and *recapitulated* the sort of homogenizing teleological paradigms first introduced into Africa by colonialism under the banner of "progress" and "Enlightenment." Rather than remaining open to the contingent and diverse paths that African cinemas (understood as inherently plural) *could* take, too often African film scholars have been intent on prescribing the path that their homogenized object of study *should* take.[1] Apposite in this regard is Nwachukwu Frank Ukadike's criticisms of Idrissa Ouedraogo's *Yaaba* (Burkina Faso/Switzerland/France, 1989), from his seminal *Black African Cinema*. Ukadike (1994, p. 282) chastises the film for "not seem[ing] to have a clear vision of the African future" – as if a continent as diverse as Africa and as wracked by contingent developments does not deserve a more nuanced, necessarily ambiguous treatment of its temporal horizons. Similarly, one can point to the late Teshome Gabriel and his influential theories about Third Cinema; writings that helped set the proscriptive tone and teleological paradigms for much of the film theory that has followed (cf. Harrow 2007, pp. 24–26). Modeled after a rather reductive reading of Fanon, Gabriel (1989) advocated a three-phase hierarchy of cinematic "progress," which is proposed as a measuring stick for all African (and indeed "Third World") films. Moving from "unqualified assimilation" where the aim is to imitate Hollywood, through a reactionary "remembrance phase" bogged down by romanticized pre-colonial nostalgia, to finally find synthesis in a politically engaged "combative phase," Gabriel's teleological paradigm is not interested in evaluating the vast corpus of "Third World" (let alone African) films on their own terms. Instead, he imposes the homogenizing terms and singular direction in which all Third World filmmakers are *expected* to move and according to which their work must be judged.

Gabriel's paradigm offers a good example of Harrow's (2007, p. 12) contention that, too often, "history and time or temporality have been taken for granted" in African film scholarship. By sharp contrast, one of the defining trends in African Studies today is its insistent interrogation of temporality. Both the understanding and experience of temporality are being urgently reformulated on a continent where a proliferation of widespread factors – the dynamics of mass migration; intrastate conflict; the global neoliberal turn and its attendant structural adjustment; infrastructural absences derived from "the dramatic retreat of the state at the level of the everyday" (Sundaram 1999, p. 63); the very unstable existences of many states themselves (Nolutshungu, 1996) – have rendered all too common an experience of the everyday in the temporal indexes of "the contingent, the ephemeral, the fugitive, and the fortuitous – radical uncertainty and social volatility" (Mbembe in Shipley 2010, p. 658). In response to such factors, theorists from a wide range of disciplines – including anthropology (James Ferguson, Jane Guyer), urban studies (Abdoumaliq Simone), diasporic Afro-futurism (Kodwo Eshun), and the cross-disciplinary thought of Achille Mbembe – can be read as advancing a complete conceptual reversal of the teleological paradigm, a kind of Copernican revolution in our understanding of the relationship between structure and uncertainty, between predetermination and contingency. Contra the teleological conception, here contingency and uncertainty cease to be temporal aberrations and instead become the *a priori* basis for understanding human experience. To quote Jane Guyer (2002, p. x) on the subject, from her preface to a study of economic conditions in Nigeria during the years of structural adjustment and dictatorship: "condition[s] of turbulence" now enter "as an empirical topic, as a theoretical horizon, and as a methodological challenge. Chronic uncertainty is pervasive and compounds all problems." But more than just a challenge, uncertainty becomes a conceptual tool – "a resource, a mode of travel," as Abdoumaliq Simone (2014, p. 21) has recently put it.

Indeed, over roughly the last two decades, African Studies has witnessed a shift in thought that one might call the "uncertain turn,"[2] albeit one that has yet to permeate African *cinema* studies. The aim of this chapter is to suggest ways in which we might bridge this gap, demonstrating how the paradigm of uncertainty/contingency can foster new sensibilities of engagement with African cinemas, in turn generating new concepts that resonate and contribute to current debates in both African Studies and the broader field of cinema studies. To this end, going beyond a mere overview of the literature on uncertainty in Africa, I begin by drawing connections between the uncertain turn in African Studies and what one might call the "process-oriented" paradigm in continental philosophy – personified by a line of philosophers including Henri Bergson, Gilles Deleuze, Félix Guattari, Benedict de Spinoza, Alfred Whitehead, Brian Massumi, and others. I then demonstrate how recent African cinemas can help us both expand and historicize the uses to which process philosophy has been put in the broader, transnational field of cinema studies. Here I turn to the African video-movie phenomenon of the last two-plus decades, whose emergence coincided with the rise of neoliberalism and structural adjustment, but also with the uncertain turn in African Studies as well as the Deleuzian process-oriented turn in Euro-U.S. film-philosophy.[3] With a particular focus on that gargantuan, rhizomatic web of commercial "video-film" operations affectionately dubbed "Nollywood," I then read certain Nigerian video-movies (and one Ghanaian video-movie) from the 1990s and 2000s as indicative of how linear conceptions of time are out of touch with the temporal dynamics underpinning not just the making of movies, but the more general conditions of global political economy in the twenty-first century.

In this regard my analysis of video-movies owes a debt to the pioneering work of Brian Larkin (2008), Carmela Garritano (2013), Jonathan Haynes (2002), and others, who have demonstrated how video-movies frequently translate into cinematic terms the more general uncertainties that inform the social, economic, and political lives of many African nations and its peoples. But unlike these authors, I have sought to focus more directly on temporality itself, "carry[ing] out a temporalization of the image," to reassign Deleuze's (2005, p. 37) famous task from the filmmaker to the scholar. Combining the concepts of African philosophers like Emmanuel Eze and Mbembe with writings on cinema by the likes of Deleuze, Lúcia Nagib, and William Brown, I posit a connection between cinematic contingency and what I call "money-time"; the latter producing a temporal split in the cinematic image that undermines its claims to linearity and continuity, claims which are undone and instead replaced by bifurcation and *dis*continuity. While I posit that this monetary-temporal disruption has always haunted cinema as its "most internal presupposition" (Deleuze 2005, p. 76), it is most clearly manifested in our current neoliberal age, particularly the kinds of contexts that African video-movies reflect and in which they must operate. These are contexts of predatory capitalism that have forged imaginaries of "unrepentant commercialism" amidst a desert of human superfluity (Mbembe 2008, p. 38). To this end, I show that intrusions of money-time in African video-movies do not only signal a lack of money, but additionally a certain human superfluousness, which comes to haunt the frame as a presiding absence, taking the guise of what I call the "virtual subaltern."

What is most central to my reading of African video-movies, the crucial point I have sought to bring home in this chapter, is that ruptures in the continuity of the video-image point beyond cinema to the temporal entanglements undergirding the geopolitical interdependencies between consumer capitalism and the superfluous populations capitalism produces. Since the 1990s, numerous video-movies have emerged from countries like Nigeria and Ghana whose images and aesthetics enfold both sides of this globalized coin, articulating a temporal tension between the linear time of the video image and those other occluded times that accost the video image as both its margin and its aporetic center. In this sense, African video-movies perform a spatiotemporal enfolding, where the kinds of economic, infrastructural, and human inequalities we tend to read in *global* geopolitical terms – typically divided along the axis of Global North and South – here take on claustrophobically *local* forms and temporal configurations.[4] Such an enfolding is not particular to Lagos, the hub of Nollywood's video-movie production. Nor even to other cities of the so-called "Global South." It also undergirds much of European and the United States, which have long had to deal with (or violently ignore) their own transnational "excesses" in the form of "superfluous" migrant labor, waves of asylum seekers, and their simmering legacies of colonialism and slavery. The video-movies and images analyzed below project an aesthetic mirror back at this uncertain and entangled world, a world frantically connecting via the objects of consumer modernity while mired in widespread scarcity and forms of disconnection. In this way these video-movies exhibit a truth about globalization at the same time as this truth structures their forms, aesthetic possibilities, and temporalities.

Considering Contingency: A Processual Account

It is dangerous in life not to take a risk, because life itself is a risk.[5]

Spoken by a Nigerian refugee shortly after surviving a boat crossing to Italy, these words undo a central assumption that most of us cling to and construct as an everyday reality: The notion that life is inherent stable, that it doesn't change under our feet, and that if it changes then it does so in predictable ways, usually as a consequence of human intention. Whatever their differences and specificities, it is the undoing of this notion that connects process philosophy and Africanist theories of uncertainty. In both contexts, contingency and indeterminacy are no longer aberrations of structure – as they are in teleological accounts – with structure pre-given. Rather, contingency and indeterminacy now become the basis of human experience from which various structural forms might or might not arise. Duration, then, equals uncertainty, and contingency becomes the foremost principle of time (cf. Bergson, 1944; Meillassoux, 2008). Here it is *structure* that becomes provisional, contingent on an entangled knot of circumstances, and subject to change and flux. Brian Massumi aptly sums up this reversal. "The problem," Massumi (2002, pp. 7–8) posits, "is no longer to explain how there can be change given positioning" – "positioning" here synonymous with a spatially fixed or predetermined structure. Rather, "the problem is to explain the wonder that there can be stasis *given the primacy of process*" (my emphasis). This is not to say that structure vanishes. Rather, it is to stress the fact that structure is forged from, and is in constant interaction with, contingency and process. If time precedes any attempts to determine the course it has taken and will take in the future, then it follows that any attempts to forge a sense of continuity (by way of identity, historical construction, explanations of difference, or narrative construction) can only emerge as an attempt to retrospectively freeze time (and hence apprehend it) in the midst of its passing. It is only from the contingency of shifting circumstances that any sense of permanence can be constructed and (temporarily) held in place.

One finds this same processual principle at play in the last major work by the late philosopher Emmanuel Chukwudi Eze (2008), *On Reason*. Eze never makes reference to Massumi or explicitly cites process philosophy. Yet in a section where he explores the imposition of colonialism and the attendant violence that led to the fragmentation of indigenous knowledges, histories, and traditions, Eze offers an implicitly process-oriented understanding of the nature of these categories. For in violent and disruptive limit cases like colonialism, Eze argues, one is able to grasp a profound universal truth about the relationship between process and structure. "What happens when a culture's tradition breaks down," he asks? "Well, one could say, history reveals in a remarkable way *its own constitution as contingency, and it is then that the meaning of time is most obvious*" (p. 197, my emphasis). As in cases such as the Nigerian refugee quoted above, such extreme experiences of fragmentation draw attention to the artificiality informing *all* human constructions of social and historical continuity: The notion that process precedes structure, that continuity is a virtual construction that can only be forged from discontinuous fragments. And to Eze's citing of colonialism, one can add innumerable and more recent *neo*colonial forms, as I did near the start of this chapter. Indeed, whether or not one is inclined to read Eze's and Massumi's processual theses as transhistorical truisms, it seems clear that characteristics of the current globalizing age have made this process-oriented approach more applicable than ever. It is hardly coincidental that most of the aforementioned literature dealing with uncertainty in Africa emerges from and addresses contexts where the dominance of uncertainty is, at least partially, the consequence of the globalized advent of neoliberalism and the sorts of deregulation introduced by economic structural adjustment. As Jean and John Comaroff (2001, p. 8) have pointed out, one encounters an economic and psychological dissymmetry between the intensified "produc[tion] of [consumer capitalist] desire and expectation on a global scale," alongside a "decrease" in "the certainty of work or the security of persons." Policies of deregulation have the paradoxical effect of bringing a world of consumerism closer to many Africans, while moving many Africans further from that world (cf. Ferguson, 1999). Similarly, Simone (2004, p. 8) has emphasized the rather obvious but crucial point that structural adjustment not only introduced "policies that restructure the economy," but also restructured "the time and space of African lives." For this reason, he draws the provocative conclusion that "neoliberal, urban ways of thinking" are the intellectual "ground on which we have to operate" if we want to find a language and paradigm with enough accuracy to usefully critique the ways this same neoliberalism has shaped contemporary imaginations, desires, and the spatiotemporal dynamics of life itself (Simone, 2015).

It is for this reason that I now turn to African video-movies, with a particular focus on the Nigerian industry dubbed Nollywood. Nollywood is an apt site for considering the uncertainties of neoliberalism, since its emergence is inextricably bound to the widespread imposition of structural adjustment in Africa. In its production and distribution conditions, as well as the consumer capitalist imaginaries that fuel the content of its movies, Nollywood both reflects and navigates a cutthroat neoliberal mediascape marked by contingency and tangled rhizomatic trajectories. To briefly rehearse its history, the informal industry burst to life in the early 1990s amidst what Guyer, Denzer, and Agbaje (2002, p. xix) have called "some of the worst conditions of policy incoherence of any country in the world": The drastic and sustained depression of the value of oil in a country where oil was the only major export; the transition between two brutally ineffectual dictatorships; and the withering effects of structural adjustment (first implemented in Nigeria in 1986), which both exacerbated poverty and social instability through the privatization of public services and state withdrawal, and enabled a degree of deregulation whose upshot was the considerable enlargement of the informal economy. Nollywood emerged on the back of this deregulation: An industry whose largely untrained practitioners forged their aesthetics out of sheer necessity, filming at breakneck speed on miniscule budgets and cheap video technology after celluloid became an impossibly expensive format, and who possessed an undisguised commercial desire to seduce an untapped audience through informal channels of distribution (McCall 2012, p. 12). From these threadbare methods an industry has emerged that releases several dozen movies per week, generates annual revenue estimated in hundreds of millions of dollars[6], serves as a crucial source of job creation, and whose viewership is thoroughly global.[7]

While clearly a financial success story, it would be wrong to equate Nollywood's particular conditions of production, distribution, and reception to those of its U.S. namesake. The industry is composed of mutating multiplicities: Networks of creative and entrepreneurial actors, both local and transnational, long operating beyond the purview of government and skirting the lines between legality and illegality (Tade, 2016). This is not to overlook the signs of formalization and greater regulation that have emerged in recent years: A growing number of technically polished and higher budget movies categorized under the loose title "New Nollywood" (Haynes, 2014); the novelty in recent years of government funding (Ekenyerengozi, 2014); an upswing in theatre distribution (Odejimi, 2016), although the percentage of movies exhibited is still infinitesimal compared to the total number produced; the South African broadcaster M-NET, whose Africa Magic channels broadcast across Nigeria and the broader continent; and Internet streaming platforms, both legal and illegal – although given most Nigerians' limited broadband and connectivity, streaming is primarily targeted at an international diaspora (Jedlowski, 2013).

Contrary to the industry's mobile and contingent origins, one would be forgiven for not finding these conditions readily reflected within the diegeses of the video-movies themselves. Jonathan Haynes (2002, p. 214) has described video-movies as "commendably straightforward," emphasizing the ways they seem to project a sense of linearity, stability, and closure – more inclined to tame contingency than allow it free rein. Observing the prevalence of melodrama in numerous Nigerian video-movies, Brian Larkin (2008, chapter 6) has argued that they work to localize and render visible the vagaries and anxieties produced by global economics and Nigeria's oil-rentier state.[8] In this light they are a reflection of classical melodrama's tendency "to move toward a clear nomination of the moral universe" (Brooks 1976, p. 17). But at the same time as they reassure, they also function as nodes of consumerist fantasy, primarily to an audience that cannot afford to consume (Haynes 2002, p. 212). As many critics have observed, most video-movies furnish ordinary Nigerians with ostentatious "image-commodities": Images of fancy cars and wardrobes, large mansions, and storylines usually lodged in an urban, middle-class locale (Haynes, 2002; Ukadike, 2014). As such, they manifest what Mbembe (2008, p. 38) has called the "aesthetics of superfluity" endemic to global capitalism: "the inter-twined realities of bare life (mass poverty), the global logic of commodities, and the formation of a consumer public." In cinematic contrast to the francophone founding fathers of *cinema engagé* or the anti-capitalism of Third Cinema, here the image is unabashedly offered and consumed as a commodity, at the same time that commod-ities are presented as images (cf. Diawara 2010, p. 185). Yet these same video-movies typically bring a moral tone to bear on such ostentatious visuals, with narratives dra-matizing greed, deceit, infidelity, and murder in the tenor of good (and frequently God) versus evil – conflicts dependably resolved through the triumph of the former over the latter (cf. Adejunmobi 2003, p. 52; Alamu 2010, pp. 166–167; Diawara 2010, p. 171). As Peter Brooks (1976, p. 20) demonstrates, this is precisely the teleological task that melodrama performs. Melodramatic narratives start from and express "the anx-iety brought by a frightening new world in which the traditional patterns of moral order no longer provide the necessary social glue" (Brooks 1976, p. 20). In Nigerian and more broadly African contexts, this moral order is undermined by conditions of uncertainty and instability, arising with the advent of neoliberalism and structural adjustment (cf. Comaroff and Comaroff 2012, chapter 7; Ferguson, 1999; Garritano, 2013). The melodramatic structure of video-movies both envisions and overcomes this uncertainty by organizing narratives around a specific telos, which "plays out the force of that anxiety with the apparent triumph of villainy", before "dissipating it with the eventual victory of virtue" (Brooks 1976, p. 20).

In this manner Nollywood – like practically every mainstream cinema – often functions as one more mechanism "for provisioning … subjects with a sense of continuity in experience" (Eze 2008, p. 197). However, things are not so simple. In describing early Nigerian video-movie narratives, Brian Larkin (2008, pp. 184, 186) evokes the notion of an "aesthetics of outrage," a term that captures the manner in which video-movies are often structured around "continual shocks that transgress religious and social norms and are designed to provoke and affront the audience … often heightened by exaggeration and excess." Such affective transgressions, Larkin argues, work to the ends of communicating "the instability of modern Nigerian life." In processual terms, an aesthetics of out-rage counters the stabilizing transformation of discontinuity into continuity, of process into structure, troubling the telos of the happy ending, to the extent that scholars like Larkin (2008, p. 182) and Harrow (2013, p. 278) have suggested that these obligatory resolutions often feel tacked on and insufficient in the face of what precedes them. However, what I want to focus on in this chapter is not the ideologically subversive work performed by certain movies that upset the working of closure. Nor is it simply an analysis of narrative content on the level of the diegesis. I want to expand the analysis of uncertainty to encompass the aesthetic dimension of video-images and the extra-diegetic dynamics that funda-mentally inform most video-movies' processes of production. For it is here, in the oscillation between the time of the diegesis and that of the video-movie's production process, that we are able to fully grasp the fraught temporal relationship between process and structure.

Multiplicity, Discontinuity, and the Fissures of Non-cinema

As Mary Ann Doane (2002, p. 30), Harrow (2007, pp. 16–17), Deleuze (2005), and numerous others have reminded us, the constructed flow of onscreen time is always haunted by other times. A process-oriented approach helps us grasp this fact on the level of film production. In cinema, temporal continuity is never a given, but must be constructed out of the discontinuous fragments of different spacetimes. In this sense, the filmmaking process offers a medium-specific demonstration of the more general manner in which process always precedes structure. Consider things on the level of the shot. Every onscreen shot has been abstracted from its original spatiotemporal context – torn from the details that fall outside its frame, isolated and transplanted from its original temporal flow – and cut and tailored to the very different spacetime of the movie into which it has been inserted. By virtue of its appearing as one in a sequential flow of shots, it comes to form an integral part of the completed movie, dressed up to seem as if it always already belongs in this context. In this manner the fragmentary, the contingent, and the discontinuous are seamlessly sutured in order to construct and maintain the "virtual continuity of experience" of which Emmanuel Eze (2008, p. 197) speaks. Harrow (2007, p. 17) refers to this as the "work of naturalization," noting that "what would function to interrupt that work of naturalization is deprived of "presence," made invisible, pushed off-frame," and thereby giving the impression of a unified sense of space, time, and narrative.

This "work of naturalization" posits a kind of second or invisible cinema, which hides within the dominant one and threatens to undermine its hegemony. Here one can think of Jean-François Lyotard's (1978, p. 53) emphasis on "what is fortuitous, dirty, confused, unsteady, unclear, poorly framed, overexposed" in the filming of a movie, which dogs the margins separating cinema from what he terms "acinema." One is also reminded of the related and more recent formulation by Lúcia Nagib (2016, p. 132) of what she calls "non-cinema," "instances in which the medium disregards its own limits" by coming into contact with the fortuitous contingency of "life itself." Nagib demonstrates this principle with examples of movies that keep in what is unplanned, or emphasize the evidence of their own making. Although Nagib does not put it this way, it seems clear that such a gesture puts cinema back in touch with its non-cinematic origins; the place and time from whence it came, but which it always already has to disavow in order to be cinema.

Concurrent with Nagib, William Brown (2016, p. 109) has also recently evoked the concept of non-cinema. His definition places particular emphasis on "the low end of filmmaking: Micro- to zero-budget movies, shot on digital video, and/or on other devices such as phones or tablets." Such filmmaking lacks "the same aesthetic values of the [Western] mainstream", and his definition clearly encompasses most African video-movies, even though they are very much dominant and mainstream within their own national and regional contexts. Like Nagib, Brown argues that non-cinema is not a different kind of cinema, but rather "an intrinsic component, or quality, of cinema," which has "been in or with cinema since its inception" (p. 105). Nor are these qualities just with cinema. They *precede* cinema, just as process precedes structure. They are "the *a priori* from which cinema and the cinematic emerges" (p. 127), even though they can only be visibly grasped as a disruptive excess within cinema itself. I say "disruptive excess" because Brown, like Lyotard, defines non-cinema by its imperfections and seeming malfunctions. Underexposure, overexposure, intrusion of equipment or crew into the frame, "bad" editing, "bad" framing, "bad" acting, "unusable" sound, dead time – all of those "mistakes" and elements most filmmakers habitually try to expel surge to the fore in non-cinema and gain validity, becoming a central aesthetic tenet.

But what is brought back on screen in non-cinema is not just the cinematic excess that usually ends up on the proverbial cutting room floor. In Marxist fashion, Brown (2016, p. 123) argues that such imperfections are visible traces of the *time of labor* embedded in all filmmaking. By foregrounding imperfection, non-cinema de-fetishizes the image by revealing and reinstating the toil that birthed it, the labor that almost all movies (including Nollywood's) attempt to disavow. This foregrounding also troubles the linear experience of time that structures most films, by drawing attention to the temporally heterogeneous fragments a movie needs in order to build itself up. Brown's and Nagib's concepts of non-cinema thus offer a paradigm for reading contingency back into the image, exposing those *other* times that have been re-appropriated by the filmmaker in order for the cinematic illusion of continuity to persist – indeed, for such continuity to exist at all. In short, by tracing a fissure along the linear time of the diegesis, non-cinema reverses the process by which discontinuous multiplicity is translated into linear continuity.

Now we certainly cannot regard a mainstream industry like Nollywood as non-cinema per se – it lacks the intentional image-making politics of Brown's and Nagib's examples, which include the controversial documentary *The Act of Killing* (Joshua Oppenheimer et al., Denmark/Norway/United Kingdom, 2012), the work of politically defiant director Jafar Panahi, and the provocative "anti-cinema" aesthetics of no-budget filmmaker Khavn de la Cruz. Nonetheless, I want to suggest that many African video-movies furnish examples where the non-cinematic (all that is "confused, unsteady, unclear, poorly framed") manifests unintentionally and symptomatically. Of course one grows tired of the endless criticisms levelled at Nollywood for what are taken to be its practitioners' amateurish attempts at filmmaking (see for instance Irobi, 2014, 42fn; Isola, 2008; Soyinka, 2013). These criticisms are aimed not just at the industry's supposed generic imitation of industries and genres emerging elsewhere (the old Afrocentric dismissal), but also at the ways in which mistakes are often preserved onscreen: Boom mics appearing in shot, sound dropout and the drastic shifting of room tone from one shot to another, poor delivery of dialogue, unsteady framing and camera movement, editing that unnecessarily prolongs scenes, ill-conceived and inappropriate soundtracks "thrown down everywhere like cheap carpeting" (Haynes 2000, p. 3), etc. Others have posed the counterargument that such aesthetic practices are valid within their own particular context (Marston, Woodward, and Jones 2007, pp. 56–57). Nor have Nigerian filmmakers occupied a neutral position in this debate. One of the functions served by the banner of "New Nollywood" is to signify a teleological flight from such "mistakes." As Noah Tsika (2016, p. 109) observes, from his own experience interviewing filmmakers, industry veterans are often reticent to talk about their past endeavors, angling instead toward their role in a New (i.e. Better) Nollywood future that attempts to tar over the industry's past.

However, what all these positions miss is the ways in which such "mistakes" are equivalent to what Harrow (2013, p. 63) calls cinematic "trash." Less oppositional and more ambivalent than Brown's or Nagib's concepts of non-cinema, Harrow's emphatically non-pejorative notion of trash encompasses images that are out of place, "despite all efforts to amalgamate [them]." Like Mary Douglas' (2005) notion of dirt as "matter out of place," these non-cinematic images and moments are "included and excluded, in an indefinite state, an ambiguous state" (Harrow 2013, p. 76). Applied to Nigerian video-movies, they possess a spectral presence that has no bearing on the diegesis – sometimes even *counteracting* the diegesis, as we shall see. The undesirable miscarriages of the filmmakers, such "mistakes" are – like Lacan's notion of the Real circa his seminar on Poe's "Purloined Letter" – irrefutably and nonetheless *there*. These "mistakes" and their spatiotemporal indeterminacy project the more general struggle between structure and uncertainty; between Africans' attempts to forge a sense of continuity and the instabilities that both hamper and shape this enterprise. While this struggle has always haunted cinema everywhere, it is demonstrated in particularly acute ways in many African video-movies, whose considerable scarcity of time and resources leave these images particularly vulnerable to the intrusions of contingency and discontinuity.

Take the example of *Stupid: Mr Sharp Sharp* (Nigeria, 2002) – an early film by highly regarded director Teco Benson and starring Nkem "Osuofia" Owoh. In one scene, two characters try to blackmail a man with whom their employer is having an affair, catching him as he sneaks half-naked out of the house after her husband unexpectedly returns home. While the diegesis of this comedic scene is perfectly linear – "commendably straightforward," to repeat Haynes' description – such a sense of linearity is undermined by the drastic shift in lighting continuity from one shot to the next. Here the contingencies of a rushed production – in which the crew ran out of time and daylight – disrupt the impression of continuity the video-movie is trying to maintain. The temporal fragments with which the movie has carved out its form and flow come to trouble the veneer of linear time.[9] But the constructed illusion of diegetic continuity is not only threatened by contingencies of production. It also undergoes contingent mutations in the distribution and reception processes, which introduce their own discontinuities. Describing the process of distributing Nigerian video-movies on VHS during the 1990s and early 2000s, Larkin (2008, p. 237) notes how "[r]eproduction takes its toll, degrading the image by injecting dropouts and bursts of fuzzy noise, breaking down dialogue into muddy, often inaudible sound." Following Haynes (2007, pp. 137–138), one similarly notes how Nigeria's ongoing power cuts sabotage the unbroken and uninterrupted continuity of the video-movies. For those watching on television, the cuts not only disrupt the movie's linear progression but also plunge the illusion into a void. Similarly, reliance on old playback technology imposes a temporally unstable experience of media "where gaps in space and time are continually anni-hilated and reinforced" (Larkin 2008, p. 241). Other factors emerge in illegal online streaming, where unlicensed copies often fail to present the movies in their entirety. In short, to appropriate Simone's (2004, p. 15) analysis of the instability of life in various African cities, one can speak of African video-movies subjected to trajec-tories of distribution and patterns of reproduction that "twist them out of shape," so that "it is difficult to be confident that one is working with stable and consistent entities over time" (cf. Jedlowski, 2013).

Such temporal disruptions can also be of a sonic nature. Sound has often been a major concern amongst industry practitioners, particularly the clarity of dialogue and the manner in which it is often prone to distortion when characters raise their voices. Often dialogue is too soft or distorts to the point of illegibility, while even a movie like *Maami* (Nigeria, 2011), directed by the highly acclaimed Tunde Kelani, suffers from the occasional momentary sound dropout. To take a more sustained example, let us consider *Sacred Lies* (Ikechukwu Onyeka, Nigeria, 2011), a crime thriller-cum-romantic drama starring megastar Genevieve Nnaji. Through its use of music, cinematic continuity in *Sacred Lies* is fissured in a particularly distinctive manner. Take the obligatory scene designed to demonstrate Nnaji's character becoming enamored with her future husband. The two stroll, chat, eat ice-cream, embrace each other; a kind of romantic *gest* that drives home the idea: These char-acters are falling in love. The scene is comprised of languidly paced shots – hand-held, casually following after the couple in a manner reminiscent of both Bazin's (1971) advocated adherence to the actual duration of the event and Haynes' (2002, p. 214) contention that Nigerian video-movie narratives are generally "realistic." But the soundtrack that accompanies them – the only sound in the scene, since we watch them talk but do not hear them – completely undermines this sense of con-tinuity. Every two or three seconds the music changes suddenly and arhythmically. A romantic theme collides with a suspenseful stinger more suited to a thriller, which gives way just as quickly to the momentary aural intrusion of bombastic melodrama. At one point the music even cuts out mid beat, replaced by the library-sampled sound of a gunshot; elsewhere it simply collapses into several seconds of complete silence, in a manner not all that removed from the audiovisual estrangement practiced by the likes of Godard. This is in radical contrast to the traditional function of non-diegetic music, which subordinates and reorganises the temporal plurality of different images in line with its own sonic continuity. Rather than welding a sense of continuity from one shot to the next, the soundtrack makes each languid shot (continuous within itself) feel *dis*continuous, as virtual fragments of other scenes sunder the spatiotemporal coherence of the scene we are watching. It is as if the sum total of *Sacred Lies'* soundtrack, all of its various moods and genres, are haphazardly spliced and compressed together within the space and time of a single brief scene.[10] The sum effect is almost equivalent to Kodwo Eshun's (1998, -3) notion of sonic "Afro-futurism"; a musical descriptor for the kinds of electronic dissonances and discontinuities sampled and propagated by black diasporic musicians across multiple decades and genres, whose approach Eshun terms an "alien discontinuum" operating "not through continuities, retentions, genealogies or inheritances but rather through intervals, gaps, breaks." "Realistic" sounds are abandoned for "the power[s] of falsity" that audio technology's impossible juxtapositions make audible.

Money-time and Virtual Subalternity

Obviously, just as a movie like *Sacred Lies* does not constitute a straightforward instance of non-cinema, neither can it be considered an exemplar of Afro-futurism. Rather, what unites video-movies like *Sacred Lies* to Eshun's theory of Afro-futurism or the concept of non-cinema are the challenges that all three pose to the naturalization of temporal continuity and the fixities of structure. At the same time, what distinguishes many African video-movies is the manner in which the temporal split we witness in the image is, contra Brown's concept of non-cinema, less due to labor-time than it is an effect of what I am calling "money-time."

Fully testifying to neoliberal dynamics in Africa, money is what video-movies are often about, both in their narrative content and the *raison d'être* of their being made in the first place. But they are also paradoxically what many video-movies lack, an absence that in turn heightens the movies' vulnerability to the disruptive intrusions of contingency. If the volatility and absence of money have often generated great uncertainty in Africans' lives, both for rich and for poor (cf. Mbembe, 2006a), then this has always been a truism in filmmaking, where money = time – "the old curse which undermines the cinema" (Deleuze 2005, p. 75). If Deleuze argues that time "is the phantom which has always haunted the cinema" (p. 40), then time (understood as process, multiplicity, and contingency) is inextricably bound up with money, or its lack. Because money equals time, every movie must negotiate a tension between the constructed linearity of onscreen time and the constrained and contingent process by which this linearity is produced. And in the case of many video-movies, this process is rendered ever more contingent precisely by the lack of money, which translates into a lack of time – time for scripting, time for planning shots, time for rehearsal, time to redo a shot when the first take encounters unforeseen problems, and time to effectively disguise all of these problems in editing. In short, lack of money intensifies contingency, or at least diminishes the means by which contingency can be kept at bay.

But more than simply observing a truism about cinema, Deleuze suggests that this link between money and time is sometimes made present onscreen through an implicit reflexivity, which is present in all movies whose stories are concerned with money. "Money is the obverse of all the images that the cinema shows and sets in place, so that films about money are already, if implicitly, films within the film about the film" (p. 75). This assertion rings true for numerous Nigerian video-movies. From originary Nollywood classics like *Living in Bondage* (Vic Mordi, 1992), *Glamour Girls* (Chika Onukwufor, 1994), *Domitilla* (Zeb Ejiro, 1996), and onward into the present, one observes a mirroring of off-screen means and onscreen ends: Characters who desire money and pursue its elusive unattainability, rendered onscreen by filmmakers striving for commercial success against the same marginalizing neoliberal forces. Writing about the 1990s wave of Nigerian video-movies, Haynes (2002, p. 213) notes how, "[v]ery often, the films are all about a specific sum of money that needs to be raised but is simply beyond the [characters'] resources" – hardly a foreign concern in the world of movie financing. But in my own analysis I have demonstrated another way in which Deleuze's connection between time and money (what I am calling money-time) is made visible in the image, through the non-cinematic "mistakes" that pepper so many Nollywood movies. What we register in the image in these moments is an uncertainty about money and the contingencies it produces, which confounds (but inadvertently also shapes) Nigerian attempts to propel an industry forward. Here money (or rather its lack) makes itself felt as a virtual image of time, one that both mirrors and obstructs what filmmakers have planned and actualised on the screen.

Taking this analysis further still, I want to suggest that intrusions of money-time in African video-movies do not just signal a lack of money. They additionally signal a certain *human superfluousness*, which comes to haunt the frame as a structuring absence. Here we need to take a step back and observe the political and economic conditions from which African video-movies emerge. One of the central crises wrought by neoliberalism and structural adjustment in Africa has *not* been the all-encroaching multiplication of forms of labor exploitation – the globalization argument made by media theorists like Beller (2006) and Shaviro (2010) and reiterated in Brown's concept of non-cinema through his emphasis on labor-time. Rather it has been capitalist enterprises' relegation of Africans to the status of superfluous populations.

Nigeria is apposite in this regard. From 1970 to 2000 – a period overlapping with the country's oil boom and its conversion to an oil-rentier state servicing multinational corporations – the national population living on less than a dollar a day grew from 36% (19 million inhabitants) to a staggering 70% (90 million inhabitants) (Watts 2008, p. 62). As of 2005, two-thirds of Lagos state was designated a slum, its actual population size not even fully accounted for (Watts 2005, p. 189). Unemployable, such populations are not just outside the capitalist mode of production, but also of *consumption* as well, in the sense that many lack the basic means to be consumers. I am certainly not jumping to the conclusion that such superfluous populations are entirely passive tools of oppression or lacking in agency. My assertion is rather that they are subaltern *par excellence*. They fall outside the purview of the state, outside the "connected" spaces of globalization (cf. Ferguson 2006, chapter 1), and are not even fully accounted for by any census. They evade accurate or clear representation in most senses of the word. And as one might expect, given the way video-movies tend to fetishize an ostentatious consumerism "lived by a tiny fraction of the population" (Haynes 2002, p. 212), Nollywood is by and large not an industry in which they can easily or often speak.

This is an insight that has not always come readily to scholars writing about the industry. In a recent polemic, Nyasha Mboti (2014) takes swathes of this scholarship to task for serving little more than a cataloguing function: Merely explaining, enumerating, and defining what the industry has produced. What is lacking, he argues, is any kind of deconstructive impulse to interrogate what these movies seek to omit or conceal – a failure to move beyond the superficiality of what is already in plain sight. In particular, Mboti takes issue with a failure to properly analyze the manner in which Nigerian video-movies often erase the subaltern, who are only ever given presence in the majority of video-movies as a present absence. His chief example is the frequent (non)presence of the gate-man, a character who stands guard over the houses of the rich in numerous movies, and whose only function is to obediently open and close the gate in order to let more important (read "wealthier") characters gain entry and exit. As such, Mboti sees the gate-man as a subaltern figure that exists in the narrative and (occasionally) the frame without being properly acknowledged. "[T]he Nollywood script and its performance often pass through [the gate-man] but without noticing or acknowledging him and – even more importantly – without appearing to have passed through him at all" (p. 51). Entirely superfluous to the narrative, the gate-man is simultaneously inside and outside the movies' worldly concerns. He exemplifies the notion of superfluous populations referred to in the previous two paragraphs.

But this notion of the subaltern as a superfluous body can be extended to the video image itself, not just certain characters that inhabit (or do not inhabit) it. The video image can itself be regarded as an entity whose sights and sounds are orchestrated around a whole *aesthetics of superfluity* (Mbembe, 2008). Mbembe's concept of the aesthetics of superfluity offers a means of grasping the entanglements that bind together global capitalism, modernity, and the spatiotemporal elusiveness of superfluous populations; a means of enfolding the space and time of consumer capitalism's ostentatious surfaces with its superfluous (subaltern) "outside." Akin to Derrida's (2003) notion of the supplement, Mbembe posits the superfluous as something that is both necessary and extraneous, valuable without having any value, simultaneously originary and excessive. This concept, applied to an analysis of the cinematic image, is synonymous with the presence of what I am calling the virtual subaltern. What I mean here by the virtual subaltern is something very different from those movies that occasionally and unabashedly privilege subaltern concerns in their storylines.[11] Rather, the virtual subaltern is made manifest through the aesthetic operations of what I have defined as money-time and non-cinema, or Harrow's aforementioned notion of "trash cinema." Returning briefly to Brown's definition, non-cinema *is* a cinema of the subaltern. But this derives from its aesthetics, not its narrative content. To reorient Brown's concept in relation to Judith Butler's (1993) formulation of bodies that do not "matter," that do not register as human bodies, non-cinema is comprised of the images that do not matter as cinematic images, do not count as cinema. But if non-cinema constitutes a kind of virtual "outside" to cinema, this is also an "outside" that is simultaneously always already inside, since it also enables cinema's shape and definition. This is precisely the status of superfluous bodies in Mbembe's definition: The superfluous are those who are both necessary and erasable.

To be clear, in drawing this connection between subaltern images and subaltern lives I am not attempting to conflate human and cinematic subalternity and suggest that the one can be reduced to the other. Rather, my point is that one can detect analogous operations of disavowal in cinemas (like Nollywood's) that attempt to erase a) the money-time of their own non-cinematic origins and b) the poverty that these movies largely keep out of frame. Conversely, because many African video-movies operate according to an aforementioned aesthetic of superfluity, they are beholden to a particular spatiotemporal organization of the image; an organization that disavows the conditions of the subaltern while being fundamentally shaped by these conditions, and therefore inadvertently drawing attention to them through the subaltern's unwitting emergence as a virtual image of time. In the collision of neoliberal wealth and its attendant violence and poverty, the subaltern becomes imminently erasable within the structuring of onscreen time (just as they are erased within the spatiotemporal coordinates of global capitalism). But crucially, they are still virtually present within these spaces, even if only as a structuring absence and through the traces left by their erasures. Adapting Deleuze (2005, p. 37) to our purposes, we can say that the virtual subaltern "occup[ies] a place in time which is incommensurable with the… [onscreen] space", but which nevertheless haunts that space as its virtual, ghostly correlate.

To clarify what I mean by all this, let us turn from Nigeria to the Ghanaian video-movie industry and consider the high-profile example of *Beyoncé: The President's Daughter* (Frank Rajah Arase, Ghana, 2006). On first inspection, *Beyoncé* seems to have gotten around many of the financial constraints that plagued other 1990s and early-2000s video-movies – what Haynes (2000, p. xv) calls these movies' "ambient poverty", and what I am reading as a symptom of the virtual subaltern. A product of transnational collaboration between Ghanaian and

Nigerian industries – the movie was produced by the Ghanaian Abdul Salam Munumi and directed by the Nigerian Frank Rajah Arase – *Beyoncé* is regarded by Carmella Garritano (2013, p. 170) as "perhaps the most successful and influential" of a wave of Ghanaian "glamour" movies that emerged in the 2000s: "flashy, big-budget, English-language domestic dramas…showcas[ing] fantastically luxurious urban locations." As is evident from the movie's title, and apropos Mbembe (2008, pp. 38, 60), *Beyoncé* is "structurally shaped by…the global logic of commodities," the entire film an instance of a constructed "spacetime" that "exist[s] first and foremost as interfaces of other local and faraway places." The movie brazenly appropriates the looks, sounds, and signs of U.S. and European pop culture, its very title and character names signaling its global influences (Garritano 2013, p. 171). Moreover, the movie ties its "worldliness" to an "unrepentant commercialism" (Mbembe 2008, p. 38) and illustration of the "good life." Numerous scenes evoke opulent fantasy spaces, none more so that the titular character's presidential mansion, which is featured prominently over the opening credit sequence, dwarfing her as she moves from room to room (Figure 2.1). Elsewhere, characters rendezvous in shopping malls and similar architectural markers of consumer modernity.

With this ostentatious display in mind, Garritano (2013, p. 171) suggests that "the materiality of the postcolony … stays safely out of frame" for the duration of the movie. Yet this is not an entirely accurate description. Given Garritano's claim that "[n]othing of its scale had been seen before" in the Ghanaian industry (p. 170), it is curious that *Beyoncé*'s lavish expenditure is somewhat inconsistent. While no

Figure 2.1 In *Beyoncé: The President's Daughter*, numerous scenes conjure opulent spaces of consumerist fantasy, none more so than the titular character's presidential mansion.

costs are cut on the interiors, wardrobes, and possessions of the wealthy, these contrast starkly with the mise en scène of scenes in which characters are consigned to state institutions like hospitals or police stations. Here a doctor's room has little more than the barest furnishings: A table with a handful of books and a token poster of human anatomy plastered to the gaping white wall, whose ascetic surface is accentuated in size by the establishing wide-shot (Figure 2.2). Similarly, the "police station" in the film lacks all official insignia, and is reduced to a veranda upon which three plainly dressed men unconvincingly assume the part of police officers. Whether intentional or not, there is something depressingly appropriate in *Beyoncé*'s lack of attention to the visualization of these public institutions vis-à-vis the opulence of Beyoncé's abode. Given that the character is the president's daughter, one could hardly ask for a better aestheticized treatment of the neoliberal state's retreat from public life and its transformation into a private domain of self-enrichment (cf. Mbembe 2001, chapter 2).

But what is striking about these threadbare settings is not just their contrast with other scenes. More important is the way in which such settings signal a temporal excess and irreconcilability within the video-image. In these scenes from *Beyoncé*, the onscreen rich and the virtual subaltern confront one another within one and the same image, although not on a level that is accounted for either by the narrative content or the movie's edited structuration of onscreen time. Instead the cinematic image experiences a split in time, simultaneously coursing along the linear time of the diegesis and folding back into the white wall that carries the trace of the image's own superfluous, non-cinematic

Figure 2.2   In starkly furnished public institutions the powerful confront the powerless, and the visible characters confront the virtual subaltern.

origins. In moments such as these, *Beyoncé* reveals the non-cinematic reality of the world from which it emerges. The white wall signals the time of a virtual subalternity, which momentarily grazes the image, revealing the yawning and impoverished gap out of which Nollywood marshals its images and performances of ostentation, but which these same ostentatiously mediated surfaces work to conceal. The virtual subaltern signals a temporal excess and split in the image; an excess outside the bounds of narrative or perceived structuration, which signals a splitting of time and puts us in touch with the process from which such structures are formed. A spatiotemporal irreconcilability emerges, however briefly, belying the ways in which the frame, much like the African metropolis of Mbembe's (2008, p. 48) description, is "constantly marked by a dialectics of distance, proximity, and reciprocal dependencies" – dependencies between cinema and non-cinema, between the spacetime of the enframed diegesis and the fact that this diegesis is in turn enfolded and dependent upon the spacetimes of production and the world of the subaltern that the frame has sought to frame out. Betraying its function as a site of segregation and spatiotemporal organization then, the image instead becomes a space of "strange mappings and blank figures" – to which the bare white walls testify – "discontinuous fixtures and flows, and odd juxtapositions," which reveal the image's "discontinuities, its provisionality," its non-cinematic but all too human "superfluousness" (pp. 47, 64).

Conclusion

This chapter has avoided providing a(nother) totalizing theory of African cinemas, let alone a generalized evaluation of African video-movie production. In place of such a theory, I have sought to encourage a greater attentiveness to the *processes* that all movies are subjected to and which, as texts that draw their fundamental form from time and movement, they often exhibit in temporally entangled ways – more than ever in our global present. By way of example I demonstrated how a range of video-movies from Ghana and Nigeria offer us aesthetic forms and temporal configurations that articulate the fraught dynamics and contradictions informing experiences of neoliberalism and consumer capitalism in Africa. Such a case study makes clear that under conditions characterized by the provisional and contingent, the task is to inject time back into our analyses and find ways of laying hold of texts whose very cinematic being consists in change and temporal multiplicity. In this regard we would do well to mimic Simone's (2013, pp. 112) marginalized city dweller, who must establish a place of belonging amidst a sea of contingency: "[a] place…where the 'where' is not prescribed or always knowable, but where the uncertainty does not foreclose the capacity to act in new ways."

Acknowledgment

This chapter would not have been completed without the financial assistance of the National Research Foundation (NRF) of South Africa, whose support I gratefully acknowledge.

Notes

1   In recent years such teleological and proscriptive models have been the objects of detailed critique in African cinema studies (Harrow 2007; Niang 2014; Tcheuyap 2011; Zacks 1999). This space-clearing work already accomplished, I have kept my own critique brief.

2   Testament to the imminent rise of this uncertain turn is the fact that it is in the midst of being anthologized. See Cooper and Pratten (2015) and Goldstone and Obarrio (2016).

3   Perhaps not insignificantly, this process-oriented paradigm started gaining traction in Euro-American cinema studies around the same time the uncertain turn took hold in African Studies. Emerging in the late 1990s with a renewed interest in Deleuze's two *Cinema* books, the process-oriented paradigm has by now been applied, critiqued, and engaged far beyond its "Euro-centered" origins. For applications of Deleuze and broader process philosophy in Latin American, Asian, Middle Eastern, and diasporic contexts, see for instance Deamer (2014), Lim (2009), Marks (2000 and 2016), Martin-Jones (2011), Pisters (2010), and Tong (2008). Tellingly, such theory has been little utilized in African contexts, and what engagement there has been – i.e. Pisters (2003, pp. 72–74) and Rodowick (1997, pp. 162–167) – has not come from specialists in African cinemas.

4   For a related critique of the fallacy of North/South divisions and their enfolding in our age of global capitalism, see Comaroff and Comaroff (2012) and Simone (2014, chapter 1).

5   Quote taken from the recent documentary *Fire at Sea* (*Fuocoammare*, Gianfranco Rosi, Italy, 2016).

6   Although precise figures are periodically offered, the deregulated informality of distribution and the pervasiveness of piracy make total revenues "largely unverifiable" (Haynes 2007, p. 134).

7   On Nollywood's transnational reach, see Krings and Okome (2013).

8   For an in-depth analysis of the political practices and socio-economic consequences of the oil-rentier state, of which Nigeria is by far the largest African example, see Soares de Oliveira (2007), Watts (2008), and Yates (2012).

9   For a similar example of this kind of discontinuity in the context of early Ghanaian video-movies, see Garritano (2013, pp. 81–82).

10 It is hard to say whether this effect is intentional or not. Regardless, on iRokoTV, the streaming site where I watched the movie, all comments about the soundtrack were decidedly negative.

11 The likes of *Agony of the Rich* (Caz Chidiebere, 2014), *Domitilla, Lady Gagaa* (Ubong Bassey Nya, 2011), *Dry* (Stephanie Okereke Linus, 2014), *Newman Street: Life As it Is* (2014–2015) and *Taxi Driver* (Daniel Oriahi, 2015) come to mind.

References

Adejunmobi, Moradewun. 2003. "Video Film Technology and Serial Narratives in West Africa." In *African Video Film Today*. Edited by Foluke Ogunleye. Swaziland: Academic Publishers.

Alamu, Olagoke. 2010. "Narrative and Style in Nigerian (Nollywood) Films." *African Study Monographs*, 31(4): 163–171.

Arowosegbe, Jeremiah O. 2014. "Introduction: African Studies and the Universities in Postcolonial Africa." *Social Dynamics*, 40(2): 243–254.

Bazin, André. 1971. *What is Cinema? Volume II*. Translated by Hugh Gray. Berkeley, Los Angeles and London: University of California Press.

Beller, Jonathan. 2006. *The Cinematic Mode of Production: Attention Economy and the Society of the Spectacle*. Hanover, NH and London: University Press of New England.

Bergson, Henri. 1944. *Creative Evolution*. Translated by Arthur Mitchell. New York: Random House.

Brooks, Peter. 1976. *The Melodramatic Imagination: Balzac, Henry James, Melodrama, and the Mode of Excess*. New Haven, CT and London: Yale University Press.

Brown, William. 2016. "Non-Cinema: Digital, Ethics, Multitude." *Film-Philosophy*, 20: 104–130.

Butler, Judith. 1993. *Bodies that Matter: On the Discursive Limits of "Sex."* New York and London: Routledge.

Chakrabarty, Dipesh. 2000. *Provincializing Europe: Postcolonial Thought and Historical Difference*. Princeton, NJ and Oxford: Princeton University Press.

Comaroff, Jean and John L. Comaroff. 2001. "Millennial Capitalism: First Thoughts on a Second Coming." In *Millennial Capitalism and the Culture of Neoliberalism*. Edited by Jean Comaroff and John L. Comaroff, 1–56. Durham, NC and London: Duke University Press.

Comaroff, Jean and John L. Comaroff. 2012. *Theory From the South: or, How Euro-America is Evolving Toward Africa*. Boulder, CO and London: Paradigm Publishers.

Cooper, Elizabeth and David Pratten, eds. 2015. *Ethnographies of Uncertainty in Africa*. London: Palgrave Macmillan.

Deamer, David. 2014. *Deleuze, Japanese Cinema, and the Atom Bomb: The Specter of Impossibility*. New York and London: Bloomsbury.

Deleuze, Gilles. 2005. *Cinema 2: The Time-Image*. Translated by Hugh Tomlinson and Robert Galeta. London and New York: Continuum.

Derrida, Jacques. 2003. "Structure, Sign, and Play in the Discourse of the Human Sciences." In *Writing and Difference*. Translated by Alan Bass. London and New York: Routledge.

Diawara, Manthia. 2010. *African Film: New Forms of Aesthetics and Politics*. Munich, London and New York: Prestel.

Doane, Mary Ann. 2002. *The Emergence of Cinematic Time: Modernity, Contingency, the Archive*. Cambridge, MA and London: Harvard University Press.

Douglas, Mary. 2005. *Purity and Danger: An Analysis of the Concept of Pollution and Taboo*. London and New York: Routledge.

Ekenyerengozi, Michael Chima. 2014. "Nollywood is a Genre of Nigerian Film and Not the Entire Nigerian Film Industry." Accessed 20 April 2016. https://tns.ng/nollywood-is-a-genre-of-nigerian-film-not-the-entire-nigerian-film-industry/

Eshun, Kodwo. 1998. *More Brilliant Than the Sun: Adventures in Sonic Fiction*. London: Quartet Books.

Eze, Emmanuel Chukwudi. 2008. *On Reason: Rationality in a World of Cultural Conflict and Racism*. Durham, NC and London: Duke University Press.

Fabian, Johannes. 1983. *Time and the Other: How Anthropology Makes its Object*. New York: Columbia University Press.

Ferguson, James. 1999. *Expectations of Modernity: Myths and Meanings of Urban Life on the Zambian Copperbelt*. Berkeley: University of California Press.

Ferguson, James. 2006. *Global Shadows: Africa in the Neoliberal World Order*. Durham, NC and London: Duke University Press.

Gabriel, Teshome H. 1989. "Towards a Critical Theory of Third World Films." In *Questions of Third Cinema*. Edited by Jim Pines and Paul Willemen, 30–52. London: BFI Publishing.

Garritano, Carmela. 2013. *African Video Movies and Global Desire: A Ghanaian History*. Athens: Ohio University Press.

Goldstone, Brian and Juan Obarrio, eds. 2016. *African Futures: Essays on Crisis, Emergence, and Possibility*. Chicago, IL: University of Chicago Press.

Guyer, Jane I. 2002. "Preface." In *Money Struggles and City Life: Devaluation in Ibadan and Other Urban Centers in Southern Nigeria, 1986–1996*. Edited by Jane I. Guyer, LaRay Denzer, and Adigun Agbaje, ix–xvi. Portsmouth, NH: Heinemann.

Guyer, Jane I., LaRay Denzer, and Adigun Agjabe. 2002. "Introduction: The Nigerian Popular Economy – Strategies toward a Study." In *Money Struggles and City Life: Devaluation in Ibadan and Other Urban Centers in Southern Nigeria, 1986–1996*. Edited by Jane I. Guyer, LaRay Denzer, and Adigun Agbaje, xvii–xlv. Portsmouth, NH: Heinemann.

Harrow, Kenneth W. 2007. *Postcolonial African Cinema: From Political Engagement to Postmodernism*. Bloomington and Indianapolis: Indiana University Press.

Harrow, Kenneth W. 2013. *Trash: African Cinema from Below*. Bloomington and Indianapolis: Indiana University Press.

Haynes, Jonathan (ed.). 2000. *Nigerian Video Films: Revised and Expanded Edition*. Athens: Ohio University Centre for International Studies.

Haynes, Jonathan. 2002. "Devaluation and the Video Boom: Economics and Thematics." In *Money Struggles and City Life: Devaluation in Ibadan and Other Urban Centers in Southern Nigeria, 1986–1996*. Edited by Jane I. Guyer, LaRay Denzer, and Adigun Agbaje, 207–217. Portsmouth, NH: Heinemann.

Haynes, Jonathan. 2007. "Nollywood in Lagos, Lagos in Nollywood." *Africa Today*, 54(2): 131–150.

Haynes, Jonathan. 2014. "'New Nollywood': Kunle Afolayan." *Black Camera*, 5(2): 53–73.

Irobi, Esiaba. 2014. "Theorizing African cinema: Contemporary African Cinematic Discourse and its Discontents." In *Critical Approaches to African Cinema Discourse*. Edited by Nwachukwu Frank Ukadike, 23–45. Lanham, MD: Lexington Books.

Isola, Akinwumi. 2008. "In Whose Image?" In *Africa Through the Eye of the Video Camera*. Edited by Foluke Ogunleye, 7–15. Manzini: Academic Publishers.

Jedlowski, Alessandro. 2013. "From Nollywood to Nollyworld: Processes of Transnationalization in the Nigerian Video Film Industry." In *Global Nollywood: The Transnational Dimensions of an African Video Film Industry*. Edited by Matthias

Krings and Onookome Okome, 25–45. Bloomington and Indianapolis: Indiana University Press.

Krings, Matthias and Onookome Okome, eds. 2013. *Global Nollywood: The Transnational Dimensions of an African Video Film Industry*. Bloomington and Indianapolis: Indiana University Press.

Larkin, Brian. 2008. *Signal and Noise: Media, Infrastructure, and Urban Culture in Nigeria*. Durham, NC and London: Duke University Press.

Lim, Bliss Cua. 2009. *Translating Time: Cinema, the Fantastic, and Temporal Critique*. Durham, NC and London: Duke University Press.

Lyotard, Jean-François. 1978. "Acinema." *Wide Angle*, 2(3): 52–59.

Mamdani, Mahmood. 1996. *Citizen and Subject: Contemporary Africa and the Legacy of Late Colonialism*. Princeton, NJ: Princeton University Press.

Marks, Laura U. 2000. *The Skin of the Film: Intercultural Cinema, Embodiment and the Senses*. Durham, NC and London: Duke University Press.

Marks, Laura U. 2016. "Real Images Flow: Mullā Sadrā Meets Film-Philosophy." *Film-Philosophy*, 20: 104–130.

Marston, Sallie A., Keith Woodward, John Paul Jones. (2007). "Flattening Ontologies of Globalization: The Nollywood Case." *Globalizations*, 4(1): 45–63.

Martin-Jones, David. 2011. *Deleuze and World Cinemas*. London and New York: Continuum.

Massumi, Brian. 2002. *Parables for the Virtual: Movement, Affect, Sensation*. Durham, NC and London: Duke University Press.

Mbembe, Achille. 2001. *On the Postcolony*. Translated by A.M. Berrett, Murray Last, Janet Roitman and Steven Rendall. Berkeley, Los Angeles and London: University of California Press.

Mbembe, Achille. 2006a. "On Politics as a Form of Expenditure." In *Law and Disorder in the Postcolony*. Edited by Jean Comaroff and John L. Comaroff, 299–335. Chicago, IL and London: University of Chicago Press.

Mbembe, Achille. 2006b. "On the Postcolony: a Brief Response to Critics." Translated by Nima Bassiri and Peter Skafish. *African Identities*, 4(2): 143–178.

Mbembe, Achille. 2008. "Aesthetics of Superfluity." In *Johannesburg: the Elusive Metropolis*. Edited by Sarah Nuttall and Achille Mbembe, 37–67. Johannesburg: Wits University Press.

Mboti, Nyasha. 2014. "Nollywood's aporias part 1: Gatemen." *Journal of African Cinemas*. 6(1): 49–70.

McCall, John C. 2012. "The Capital Gap: Nollywood and the Limits of Informal Trade." *Journal of African Cinemas*, 4(1): 9–23.

Meillassoux, Quentin. 2008. *After Finitude: An Essay on the Necessity of Contingency*. London and New York: Bloomsbury.

Mudimbe, Valentin Y. 1988. *The Invention of Africa: Gnosis, Philosophy, and the Order of Knowledge*. Bloomington and Indianapolis: Indiana University Press.

Nagib, Lúcia. 2016. "Non-Cinema, or The Location of Politics in Film." *Film-Philosophy*, 20: 131–148.

Niang, Sada. 2014. *Nationalist African Cinema: Legacy and Transformations*. Lanham, MD, Boulder, CO, and New York: Lexington Books.

Nolutshungu, Sam C. 1996. *Limits of Anarchy: Intervention and State Formation in Chad*. Charlottesville: University Press of Virginia.

Odejimi, Segun. 2016. "TNS Exclusive Report on Nigerian Cinema in 2015." Accessed 20 April 2016. Available https://tns.ng/tns-exclusive-report-on-nigerian-cinema-in-2015

Pisters, Patricia. 2003. *The Matrix of Visual Culture: Working with Deleuze in Film Theory.* Stanford, CA: Stanford University Press.

Pisters, Patricia. 2010. "Violence and Laughter: Paradoxes of Nomadic Thought in Postcolonial Cinema." In *Deleuze and the Postcolonial.* Edinburgh: Edinburgh University Press.

Rodowick, D. N. 1997. *Gilles Deleuze's Time Machine.* Durham, NC: Duke University Press.

Shaviro, Steven. 2010. *Post-Cinematic Affect.* Washington and Winchester: O-Books.

Shipley, Jesse Weaver. 2010. "Africa in Theory: A Conversation Between Jean Comaroff and Achille Mbembe." *Anthropological Quarterly*, 83(3): 653–678.

Simone, AbdouMaliq. 2004. *For the City Yet to Come: Changing African Life in Four Cities.* Durham, NC and London: Duke University Press.

Simone, AbdouMaliq. 2013. "Majority Time: Operations in the Midst of Jakarta." *The Sociological Review*, 61(1): 109–123.

Simone, AbdouMaliq. 2014. *Jakarta: Drawing the City Near.* Minneapolis and London: University of Minnesota Press.

Simone, AbdouMaliq. 2015. *Entangled Cities* (digital recording). Berkeley: University of California Humanities Research Institute.

Soares de Oliveira, Ricardo. 2007. *Oil and Politics in the Gulf of Guinea.* New York: Columbia University Press.

Soyinka, Wole. 2013. "FESPACO 2013: A Name is More Than the Tyranny of Taste." *Black Camera*, 5(1): 237–250.

Sundaram, Ravi. 1999. "Recycling Modernity: Pirate Electronic Cultures in India." *Third Text*, 13(47): 59–65.

Tade, Oludayo. 2016. "The who and how of pirates threatening the Nollywood film industry." Accessed 20 April 2016. Available http://theconversation.com/the-who-and-how-of-pirates-threatening-the-nollywood-film-industry-56952?utm_medium=email&utm_campaign=Latest%20from%20The%20Conversation%20for%20April%2020%20 2016%20-%204703&utm_content=Latest%20from%20The%20Conversation%20 for%20April%2020%202016%20-%204703+CID_9582128ba4fd3d84e2a318d5e9a1a31e &utm_source=campaign_monitor_africa&utm_term=The%20who%20and%20 how%20of%20pirates%20threatening%20the%20Nollywood%20film%20industry

Tcheuyap, Alexie. 2011. *Postnationalist African Cinemas.* Manchester and New York: Manchester University Press.

Tong, Janice. 2008. *Chungking Express*: Time and its Displacements. In *Chinese Films in Focus*, 2nd ed. Edited by Chris Berry, 64–72. New York: Palgrave Macmillan.

Tsika, Noah. 2016. "Introduction: Teaching African Media in the Global Academy." *Black Camera*, 7(2): 94–124.

Ukadike, Nwachukwu Frank. 1994. *Black African Cinema.* Berkeley: University of California Press.

Ukadike, Nwachukwu Frank. 2014. "Video Book and the Manifestation of 'First' Cinema in Anglophone Africa." In *Critical Approaches to African Cinema Discourse.* Edited by Nwachukwu Frank Ukadike. Lanham, MD: Lexington Books.

Watts, Michael. 2005. "Baudelaire over Berea, Simmel over Sandton?" *Public Culture*, 17(1): 181–192.

Watts, Michael. 2008. "Anatomy of an Oil Insurgency: Violence and Militants in the Niger Delta, Nigeria." In *Extractive Economies and Conflicts in the Global South: Multi-Regional Perspectives on Rentier Politics*. Edited by Kenneth Omeje, 51–74. Burlington, VT and Farnham: Ashgate.

Yates, Douglas A. 2012. *The Scramble For African Oil: Oppression, Corruption and War for Control of Africa's Natural Resources*. London: Pluto Press.

Zacks, Stephen. 1999. The Theoretical Construction of African Cinema. In *African Cinema: Postcolonial and Feminist Readings*. Edited by Kenneth W. Harrow, 3–19. Trenton, NJ and Asmara: Africa World Press.

Filmography

Arase, Frank Rajah. (2006). *Beyoncé: The President's Daughter*. Ghana: Venus Films.

Benson, Teco. (2002). *Stupid: Mr Sharp Sharp*. Nigeria: Ossy Affason Video.

Ejiro, Zeb. (1996). *Domitilla: The Story of a Prostitute*. Nigeria: Zeb Ejiro Productions.

Gyang, Kenneth. (2013). *Confusion Na Wa*. Nigeria: Cinema KpataKpata.

Kelani, Tunde. (2011). *Maami*. Nigeria: Mainframe Film and Television Productions.

Mordi, Vic. (1992). *Living in Bondage 1*. Nigeria: NEK Video Links.

Onukwufor, Chika. (1994). *Glamour Girls*. Nigeria: NEK Video Links.

Onyeka, Ikechukwu. (2011). *Sacred Lies*. Nigeria: Divine Touch Productions.

Oppenheimer, Joshua, Christine Cynn, and Anonymous. (2012). *The Act of Killing*. Denmark: Final Cut for Real.

Ouedraogo, Idrissa. (1989). *Yaaba*. Burkina Faso: Arcadia Films.

Rosi, Gianfranco. (2016). *Fuocoammare*. Italy: Stemal Entertainment.

3

Life in Cinematic Urban Africa
Inertia, Suspension, Flow

Karen Bouwer

Mouvement perpétuel qui ne sait où il va mais qui y va à fond.

(Barlet, 2011)[1]

The city, in spite of all its movement, becomes an inert, monolithic embodiment of paralysis in which any action seems thwarted or limited.

(Launchbury, 2014)

In an era of unprecedented urbanization, African cities are commonly seen as dystopias characterized by extreme poverty, lack of urban planning, inadequate service delivery, and decaying infrastructure (Robinson, 2010).[2] Countering this familiar Afro-pessimistic narrative is the work of urbanists who celebrate what they see as exciting, new modes of urbanism.[3] At the center of this positive vision are the creativity, ingenuity and resilience of inhabitants who make the city work under trying circumstances. In their evocations of Kinshasa (the 2010 noir thriller *Viva Riva!*) and Nairobi (a gangster movie-inflected drama *Nairobi Half Life* released in 2012), Djo Tunda wa Munga and David Tosh Gitonga eschew the extremes of these binary positions. They bring to life, on the screen, cities they love and claim as their own while creating characters who confront the harsh and sometimes deadly realities for those living on the margins of large urban agglomerations in the Global South.[4] They show that while cities are places characterized by the circulation of bodies and goods,[5] this perpetual motion is not necessarily supportive of life and opportunity. For, although the protagonists of *Viva Riva!* and *Nairobi Half Life* are vital young men, they can be read as dead men walking. Riva is pursued not only by Azor, the big man of Kinshasa's underground, and his goons

A Companion to African Cinema, First Edition. Edited by Kenneth W. Harrow and Carmela Garritano.
© 2019 John Wiley & Sons, Inc. Published 2019 by John Wiley & Sons, Inc.

but also, more menacingly, by Cesar, his former boss and Angolan gangster. Having "stolen" Cesar's oil and Azor's woman Nora, Riva is as good as dead (Barlet calls him suicidal). Shortly after his arrival in Nairobi, Mwas tells a group of gangsters led by Dingo that he wants "a life." They laugh in his face, telling him, "There are no lives for sale here." This early scene and the title *Nairobi Half Life* prompt us to ask what makes a complete or full life.[6] Toward the end of the film Mwas and his gang will explicitly be identified as "walking dead." They can disappear without consequence and it becomes clear that they have been disposable from the outset.

While acknowledging the vulnerability to premature death of the inhabitants of their respective cities in Africa, the filmmakers create characters that demonstrate tremendous vitality and sublime moments of overcoming. Both protagonists are brimming with life and energy; Mwas's entrepreneurial ingenuity, his grit and wit are matched by Riva's seductive verve and insouciance. But Munga and Gitonga do not unambiguously celebrate resiliency, especially not if it leads to an acceptance of the status quo.[7] I therefore propose to read their films focusing on a continuum of mobility: from inertia (forces of stagnation and death) to flow (not simply motion but also moments of possibility and affirmation of life). Between these two poles, suspension represents intermediary states, moments of temporary stillness, or vulnerability to the forces of inertia, moments of ambiguity and uncertainty as to the possible re-insertion into some form of flow. Because in addition to the noun's evocation of "a temporary halting or deprivation," the verb "to suspend" can also mean to make uncertain, render doubtful, to stay, stop, interrupt (www.etymonline.com/).

Although I am analyzing films, this approach was inspired by photography, with its ability to draw our attention to moments of suspension between motion and stillness.[8] In "On Hold: Urban Photography as Interruption" (Donald and Lindner, 2014), Shirley Jordan studies Denis Darzacq's images of suspended bodies in *The Fall*. In this series the French photographer explores the entrapment of young people "somewhere between energy and disorientation" (2014, p. 23). In one photo, for example, a young man is floating horizontally about two feet above the ground in front of a door, an example of what Jordan calls "anonymous, transferable modern architecture" (p. 23). We know that it takes athleticism and strength for the body to hoist itself off the ground in this way. The camera captures this brief moment before gravity exerts its inexorable power. The author compares the suspended bodies in this series to those of 9/11 and concludes that the difference between the highly mediated and mourned bodies of the New York attacks and the anonymous urban individuals represented in the photos is that "nobody may notice when they hit the pavement" (p. 25). The photographer, as will the film directors, draws attention to the precariousness of certain lives in current "spatio-temporal and economic global configurations" (p. 26). The bodies that Darzacq photographs, captured in a moment of weightlessness and suspension, are "dancing and athletic" but *also* "falling, endangered, blasted and vulnerable" (p. 24). The bodies in the two films are not foregrounded, nor frozen in time, in the same way but they are also vital yet intensely vulnerable.

A similarly provocative take on suspension is offered by Congolese photographer Kiripi Katembo's *Un regard* series. His images, saturated in vibrant colors, often portray people on the move, going about their daily business. Reflected in puddles of stagnant water in the city of Kinshasa, his subjects appear suspended on the liquid surfaces. One of the most often circulated of these images (also appearing on the cover of Jean Bofane's 2014 novel *Congo Inc.*)[9] figures women walking close to the main market in Kinshasa. Titled "Moving Forward," it is Katembo's homage to women and their role in the society (*The Guardian*, 2015). The edges of the puddle ("floating" above the heads of the figures, because the photograph has been inverted so that the world reflected is upright again) are made up of dirt and bits of trash. Despite the beauty of the image and the clear mirror-like reflection, the trash along with the pooled water remind us of the realities of life in the city of Kinshasa: The lack of garbage collection and the lack of sidewalks that allow the pools of water to collect in the first place. Similarly, at one point in Munga's film we see the white-socked and sandaled feet of the Commander dressed as a nun, walking over the compacted trash and mud that have come to symbolize Kin-la-poubelle [Kinshasa the trashcan]. This image coincides with the Angolan gangster Cesar's use of the term "poubelle." (During the colonial and early post-independence era, Kinshasa had been considered a model city and had been affectionately called Kin-la-belle, Kinshasa the beautiful. The more recent, derogatory term of course includes homophonic play.) The interference caused by the inversion and the muddy frame also create a link to the biography of the photographer. We cannot but remember how Kiripi Katembo himself belonged to a group that is globally situated to be vulnerable to premature death; he died of malaria at the age of 36, succumbing because he did not receive adequate and timely medical care in Kinshasa, where he lived and worked.[10]

The cities the men and women have to navigate represent the forces of inertia in various ways. The foregrounding of the "dead men walking" trope invites us to investigate what creates these conditions of vulnerability. Agamben's notion of "bare life," life stripped of political significance and "exposed to death" (1998, p. 88) seems to describe the situation of these characters well. Although they are not explicitly thrust into a state of exception or emergency whereby legal protections are abrogated, they are either abandoned to their own devices (the collapse of the state in the Democratic Republic of the Congo (DRC)) or they are actively targeted for death by agents of the law (extrajudicial killings in Nairobi). But, Weheliye reminds us, Agamben has been criticized for founding "a biological sphere above and beyond reach of racial hierarches" (p. 53). While, in the films, the characters inhabit racially homogeneous spaces, these spaces have been shaped by colonial pasts and experience acutely the harmful effects of current neoliberal economic policies. Because they have been subjected to structures and institutions "that have served repeatedly to relegate subjects to the status of western modernity's nonhuman other" (p. 31), Africans are among the populations that continue to find themselves "marked for violent exclusion" (p. 86) in the global order, "suspended in a perpetual state of emergency" (p. 88),[11] vulnerable to premature death (p. 55).

Profoundly aware of how their societies are situated globally, the filmmakers will lead us through the cities exposing the daunting forces of inertia (poverty, inequality, lack of infrastructure, corruption, conflictual relationships) that have a significant impact on the lives of their inhabitants. Yet, the lively mobility of the characters and the camera will simultaneously emphasize the characters' occasional ability to burst out into flow (through resourcefulness, redefinition of gender/sex roles, violence, group membership). Focusing on the continuum from inertia to flow, marked by moments of suspension, will allow us to foreground how the films show life in the in-between spaces of African urban centers.[12]

Gitonga's film includes several explicit references to the Kenyan capital. Early in *Nairobi Half Life* Mwas's father says the city is "as socially rotten as Babylon," repeating an age-old suspicion of cities. In this instance, his fallen state (disillusioned alcoholism) seems to be at least in part due to his own past experiences in the city. In prison, Oti (the leader of the gang that Mwas will join) tells Mwas that "for survival in Nairobi you have to be smart." And Mose's gangster friends tell him to give up his dream of becoming a musician because "[t]his is Nairobi. You can't make it here without connections." In addition to these explicit verbal messages, class is strongly emphasized as Gitonga maps out the city for us, creating clear distinctions between various neighborhoods, many inherited from the colonial era (De Lame, 2010). We see the Hilton hotel, the fine Phoenix theatre where the actors practice, the upscale Westgate Mall, the gates and walls protecting the luxurious homes of the rich that Mwas and his gang target when they turn to carjacking. In contrast, we see the slum areas where Mwas and his friends live. In addition to extreme long shots of the Nairobi skyline, Gitonga privileges frames that capture areas where the two halves of the city meet, often a border between formal and informal structures.

Figure 3.1 *Nairobi Half Life* (33:41). Courtesy of One Fine Day Films.

The physical space itself represents the extremes of wealth and poverty and suggests prohibitions in terms of access, blockages to crossing the borders among neighborhoods, impediments to upward mobility. To further emphasize the divide, there is a small bridge that the characters cross as they move back and forth between the sprawling informal settlement and the rest of the city. The forces of inertia in this city are therefore presented as marked socio-economic inequality. Gitonga includes a theatrical mise-en-abîme in this film that reframes and comments on the criminal behavior of Mwas and his gang. The play that Mwas acts in foregrounds the struggle of the lower classes to have their plight be noticed and acknowledged by the well-off.

In contrast, although some class distinctions in Kinshasa can be gleaned in *Viva Riva!* (for example, the contrast between Azor's mansion filled with consumer goods versus the modest homes of JM or Riva's parents), the city we are shown in the film is surprisingly homogenous. For example, we never see the upscale Gombe district with its iconic Grand Hotel de Kinshasa (formerly the Intercontinental Hotel). Nor do we see extreme slum poverty. *Viva Riva!*'s opening sequence starts with a crane shot of a street filled with pedestrians and then offers a series of close-ups of money alternating with scenes of vehicles being pushed and signs at gas stations announcing that there is no gasoline available. The city has literally come to a standstill. A quick zoom sends us tumbling into the dark hole of a car's gas tank and to the opening credits. At no point does Munga give an aerial shot attempting to capture Kinshasa from above or offering a view of its skyline. The camera is almost always at ground level; the action takes place at street level, with only an occasional crane or balcony shot. The audience sees Munga's city close-up, as its inhabitants do. It is never seen from afar, not even when Riva returns after his long absence. But significantly, Riva brings with him barrels of oil, the stuff that can get (at least some) moving again. Frassinelli points out that the oil is "a resonant geopolitical signifier. [It points] to the extractive economy that through the exploitation of the continent's natural resources, especially minerals and oil, is repositioning Africa within the 'neoliberal world order' as (yet again) a global supplier of raw materials" (2015, pp. 297–298).

Inertia is also represented in the cities' state of disrepair. The marks of time on the surfaces of the buildings are more prevalent in Kinshasa where the majority of the buildings we see have succumbed to various degrees of dilapidation. In *Kinshasa: Tales of the Invisible City*, De Boeck emphasizes that colonial Europeans created "the primitivist idea of the Congo and its counter-image, the urban landscape" (p. 20). Like other colonial cities, Kinshasa was socially segregated from the outset (p. 30) but the breakdown of the colonial city model had already started during the colonial period. (In addition to whatever lack of maintenance there was, the colonial powers were not able to provide enough living units to keep up with demand, leading to the development of informal settlements.) Today, "modernity as exemplified by the city is contested or unfinished" (43). There is a particularly striking moment in the film that perhaps best captures the thwarting of the city's dreams of modernity. Riva has been injured and is trying to get to his parents' home. He waits on the curb while Anto tries to thumb down a ride for him. Riva is seated in front of a building that has large sections of steel piping sticking out and one is not sure whether the building was ever completed or not; whatever the case may be, the concrete seems to have simply fallen away and there is an open trench (men at work or collapse?) at Riva's feet. Both Riva and the country seem to be in a state of suspension: The wounded Riva between life and death and the country between an unfinished process of postcolonial (re) construction and decay.

The most notable reference to the failed dreams of independence comes when Cesar says the country is nothing but a "pile of shit" and that perhaps the Congo "should have stayed colonized."

It is these spaces, marked by the vagaries of time or (differential) neglect, that the characters navigate, guided by their diverse levels of experience and outlooks vis-à-vis the future. Through its depiction of Mwas's journey to Nairobi, *Nairobi Half Life* joins a long line of films centered on the trope of a country bumpkin coming to the city and suffering through all the accidents that come about due to his unfamiliarity with his surroundings and his naiveté regarding the predatory intentions of many of the people he meets.[13] Although Riva travels to the city from a village, it is as a consummate urbanite returning after a long absence. Mwas's disorientation and smallness (reinforced in the framing of the aerial shots) can be contrasted with Riva's easy navigation of a city despite his decade-long absence. In Kinshasa, Riva is in familiar territory. And despite the threats to life and limb, he continues to flow freely and easily through the city, even when he is scaling the wall of Azor's house, fleeing from the goons and the dogs after coming to see

Figure 3.2   *Viva Riva!* (1:17:17). Reproduced with permission from Suka Productions.

Nora. Only Cesar and his men will eventually manage to stop him. Or as Barlet insists, it is the city that finally gets the better of him: "Riva slips between walls, women, dangers, until the city catches up with him and seizes him."[14] In contrast to Riva's easy mobility, Mwas's movements are often curtailed. In an initial moment of suspension, he is literally shaken down upon his arrival in Nairobi (four men lift him off the ground and turn him upside down to make sure everything falls out of his pockets). Some of the obstacles Mwas faces seem temporary. During his first incarceration shortly after his arrival in Nairobi (he had been mistaken for a street vendor without a permit) he befriends Oti, the leader of a gang that operates in an area he calls "Gaza." Oti assures the neophyte that he will be released the next morning. And in response to Mwas's question about his own release he laconically states, "Ah, we always get out." Oti's relationship with the warden and casual attitude tell us that the prison door is a revolving door for him. But his statement to Mwas will of course turn out to be untrue when at the end the gang members get picked to be "dead men walking."

As the characters move through the streets of the city, they live by their wits, trying to resist the forces of inertia and attempting to create opportunities of flow. In Kin, "la débrouillardise" or resourcefulness has long been a mode of survival in a country where the state's ability to provide even basic services has been catastrophically eroded. Corruption and bribes therefore characterize the vast majority of interactions. For example, Cesar and his men, their status as grand miscreants notwithstanding, are arrested for no obvious reason and will eventually be released in exchange for the handsome sum of US$10,000. The Commander explains that they may as well pay because the price will just keep going up. When Riva is presumed dead, the Commander wants to sell the gas that Riva has brought to town to the priest. She asks for the going price plus a bit more "to help the family." In these interactions, the Kinois understand each other. After all, as the Commander points out: "among Congolese, we can work something out." Although there are some violent encounters among Congolese characters (and Munga's close-ups in the scene of domestic violence when JM beats his wife breaks the noir aesthetic and offers pointed social commentary), the only truly scary characters are the foreigners (i.e. Cesar and his men who constantly denigrate the Congolese as backward and do not hesitate to pour burning embers on the truck driver who can not or will not tell them where to find Riva).

Yet, the characters, who have few or no hopes of a better future and live with the daily awareness of the precarity of their existence, can be said to be suspended in a kind of "perpetual present" (Launchbury, p. 175). Oti explicitly says: "We live for the day." And as he orients Mwas to the neighborhood where the gang lives, he explains that Gaza is known for providing (stolen) spare parts. But "there's also cocaine, booze and pussy." Although this embrace of pleasure in the now can be seen as self-defeating behavior, seeking instant gratification is not an irrational choice in a situation where the future seems foreclosed. Barlet emphasizes the lack of hope and explains it in the following terms: "The colonized was already a body of exception, that could be subjugated at will. Decolonized, the bodies remain subjected to the uncertainty of a constant experience of danger."[15] These young people are neither immobile nor passive but their lives are nonetheless threatened by the forces of inertia: The inertia "of the dead, the poor, the wounded, [that] looks back at the city and asks for recognition" (Donald 2014, p. 160). Whether they are living for the day or, like Mwas and a few others, still hanging on to dreams, these characters show that subjection can never "annihilate the lines of flight, freedom dreams, practices of liberation, and possibilities of other worlds" (Weheliye 2014, p. 2).[16] But the day-to-day acts of "débrouillardise" take a huge toll.

A few of the characters in *Nairobi Half Life* have not yet been completely crushed by the harsh conditions of the city. The dreams of these characters are evoked with great pathos. In one scene, the gang is in the flophouse that they share with Amina, and Mose is trying to write a song. As his roommates mock his efforts, he puts his hands over his ears to block out their jeers. When Mwas asks Amina about her plans, she reveals her desire to become a beautician with her own salon. In Munga's Kinshasa, such dreams no longer exist. Barlet tells us that the characters try to draw on the strength of their imagination to dream and hope. But "[i]n Kinshasa it's a hopeless undertaking and Riva does not escape his destiny."[17]

Whether they are future-oriented or not, all the characters display a form of "desperate resilience" (Robinson 2010, p. 173), an excellent example of which occurs in an early scene in *Nairobi Half Life* that sorely tests Mwas. Soon after his arrival in Nairobi, he is mistaken for an illegal vendor and arrested. In jail, he is sent to clean up a filthy bathroom covered in excrement in which he slips and falls, and then vomits. Next we see the other detainees gathering at the entrance to the bathroom, lured by the sound of his singing. They see him energetically sweeping the floor as he whoops and belts out a tune. We had earlier witnessed Mwas's entrepreneurial spirit as a DVD salesman. He attracted potential clients by acting out famous movie scenes (ranging from *Kill Bill* to *300*) with great dramatic flair. Later in the film, Mwas will use not only his self-professed ability to read body language but also his acting skills to negotiate higher prices for stolen car parts. But these examples pale in comparison to the abjection he needs to overcome in the jail's bathroom. The scene encapsulates the resilience of many characters in these films who overcome the forces of inertia that threaten their emotional and physical survival.

Riva's resilience is of a different quality. Rather than having to live by his wits like Mwas, Riva flirts with disaster and death, defiantly affirming "life is good." He continues to laugh after withstanding serious beatings on several occasions, but the best illustration of his reckless abandon occurs in a short, rapid cross-cutting sequence between him dancing in the club (after tempting fate by openly flaunting his interest in Nora) and Cesar shooting police officers after his release from the holding pen. In the clever climax to this brief sequence, Riva moves as if he himself had been shot by Cesar: His body is loose, his arms are flung above his head, and he momentarily looks as if he is about to fall. This brief flash reminds us of

Darzacq's bodies suspended in space. Here, rather than an isolated image, the sequence puts two different spaces in dialogue with each other to expose the precariousness underlying the surface images of pleasure and vitality.

The films abound with examples of characters trying to overcome the forces of inertia or affirm their vitality in the face of death. These forces influence women in specific ways. Both films, for example, include women practicing survival sex. In *Nairobi Half Life* Oti's girlfriend (and Mwas's love interest) is the only notable female character. Although she works as a prostitute her body is never sexualized in the film and she is aligned with Mwas and Mose in that they continue to dream of other kinds of lives in the midst of a crushing dearth of opportunities. On the other hand, there are multiple female characters in *Viva Riva!* Congruent with the noir aesthetic, Nora's body is constantly sexualized and there are many moments in the film that portray Riva's voyeuristic pleasure and his obsession with the redheaded beauty. Unlike Amina in *Nairobi Half Life*, the prostitutes in *Viva Riva!* are treated as objects of male pleasure. For example, at Ma Edo's brothel, they wear face paint, raffia skirts, and even African masks. In a telling scene, the image of one of these fantasy women morphs into that of Nora as Riva gazes at her, almost oblivious to the woman sitting astride him. But Nora is not treated cinematically as a mere object of male desire, robbed of subjectivity. She fully embraces her sexuality and her right to pleasure (in a startling scene she offers herself to Riva through the bars of the bathroom in Azor's house for cunnilingus, what she calls "a real kiss"). In her affirmation of her right to pleasure (her aspiration to a kind of flow) she has to resist powerful forces of inertia. She constantly and even violently needs to defend herself from being called a whore, a perception that perhaps harkens back to earlier days when women first arrived in the male-dominated colonial cities and were considered "loose." Melanie Malone, the actress who plays Nora, expressed in an interview that she approved of the female roles in the film, saying that it showed women "en érection" (Rousseau-Dewanbrechies), women standing strong. But one can of course not miss the play on words which associates these women with a kind of virile sexuality. Other female characters include the Commander (who not only shows cunning but also physical strength when she and Jorge tackle one another toward the end of the film), Malou (who in addition to working as a prostitute is highly skilled in getting crucial and sensitive information), Ma Edo (the outspoken and shrewd brothel owner), and even JM's wife (who fights back physically when her husband beats her, leaving her battered and bleeding). Each tries, in her own way, to overcome the forces of inertia, whether in the shape of economic hardship, dysfunctional family relations, or social pressure. All except Nora and JM's wife die in the course of the film.

Children are not foregrounded in *Nairobi Half Life* since Mwas and his peers themselves represent the future generation. In *Viva Riva!* the protagonists are for the most part a little older than the Nairobi gang and it is Riva's young friend Anto who represents the uncertain future. Riva's as well as Nora's families show signs of serious dysfunction; Anto never mentions his family and seems to be fending entirely for himself. Munga eschews pathos when introducing him. Riva meets him peddling his wares at night and gives him some chicken saying, "You look hungry." But his street smarts are evident; he refuses to give Riva his contact for the cell phones he is selling since it would put him out of business. Anto, the shégue or street child, represents the most vulnerable of the inhabitants of the socio-economically divided cities but he too has already seemingly mastered the art of "la débrouillardise," preventing us from seeing him as a simple victim.

After his brutal introduction to Nairobi, Mwas will learn how to survive in the city and his progressive mastery of Sheng, a form of Nairobi slang, shows his acquisition of various forms of urban literacy.[18] He will continually move back and forth between his societally assigned place in the slums and the world he aspires to join, exemplified by the theatre. Because in Nairobi, echoing the stark contrasts among the different neighborhoods, the inhabitants are clearly divided between the haves and the have-nots, and the plainclothes policemen patrolling the Gaza neighborhood (who perhaps also represent the corruption of the entire state) inspire the greatest fear. They literally have the power of life and death over the young gangsters.[19] From the point of view of the gang, those with means are featured primarily as targets of crimes: First the petty theft of car parts; later the big-league hijacking of SUVs and other luxury vehicles. The only space in which Mwas can interact with those who are privileged is in the theatre where he "passes" (an accomplishment of flow for Mwas) since the other theatre members are oblivious to the rest of his life. A few key moments in particular showcase the socio-economic divide. When Mwas's gay actor friend takes him to an upscale club, Mwas replies to Cedric's complaints about his father (who is footing the bill) that he would welcome a father who showed that much interest in his life. During a reading and discussion of the play for which he successfully auditioned, Mwas is again an outsider. The play is about criminals who break into houses but do not steal: Instead they pile up all the objects of value (fridge, television, furniture, and other consumer goods) in the living room in order to shame the owners for their inordinate wealth, given that 10% of the country holds 90% of the wealth. Mwas jokes: "Why don't they just steal the goods?" His question highlights that the very existence of the play and its conceit depend on privilege. Mwas aspires to enter into this economic and discursive space, but he is still rooted in an entirely different reality. His art is that of survival: It is by play-acting, passing himself off as crazy, for example, that he manages to get away with a cart loaded with stolen goods when he is intercepted by the police. Faced with possible imprisonment, he draws on his wit and resourcefulness and is able to secure a moment of respite, of freedom and mobility. The viewer is momentarily left in suspense before joining in the characters' relief and celebration. Mwas's regular transgressions, crossings, can only take place thanks to his skills at pretense. He is play-acting his life, seemingly suspending his true identity as a thief when he comes to the theatre. Yet, in the play, he takes on the role of a thief who does not steal. Gitonga hereby creates a different frame for us to evaluate his criminal activities, once again emphasizing his aspirational universe (one in which one can make plays about "thieves" making a point about the inequalities of the society) and his actual life (in which he is obliged to revert to stealing in order to survive). One could say that he has to suspend his identity in order to cross these boundaries, but which identity is suspended?

Despite Mwas's regular transgressions, even spaces that initially seem to allow flow can turn out to be dead ends. At one point, Oti grabs a woman's cell phone. He and Mwas run, pursued by the woman. As they get to an alleyway, she stops dead, afraid to enter. Here the divided city benefits the gangsters who can escape the repercussions of the theft. But the gangsters' smug sense of security is short-lived. It is now Oti's turn to stop in his tracks. He sees plainclothes policemen in an adjacent alley. They are the men who will come and get their cut of the gangsters' earnings. And we will discover that they are as ruthless as Riva's pursuer, Cesar. As Barlet points out in his review of *Viva Riva!*, the merciless laws of the villains have become those of the society as a whole.[20]

An important moment of suspension in Mwas's trajectory takes place when he is forced to move from petty thieving (car parts) to carjacking in order to pay for the goods that were stolen from him upon his arrival in Nairobi. After the first hijacking, Mwas and another gang member are beaten by Dingo and his men who want to teach them a lesson about the big leagues. During their escapade they had been euphorically chanting, "We're living it up like pimps!" Now we see them regain consciousness in a deserted parking lot just as the city also slowly starts to come to life. This time they will be reanimated from this state of suspension; they will live to see another day (just like Riva does after he is believed dead). While the scene acts as a moment of foreshadowing for the viewer, it also reminds Mwas and the others of the extreme precarity of their lives.

While Riva is generally on the move, there is one scene of quiet introspection early in the film. As he puffs on a cigar, the smoke hangs in the air. A close-up captures Riva's pensive face. The electrical socket on the wall in front of him provokes a short flashback to two young boys running down an alley and arriving at the door of a modest abode. The sparking from an electrical connection in the flashback, along with photo of two young boys, tells the story of the traumatic loss in Riva's past. The stillness and suspension, rather than signaling the potential for decision-making that could influence the future, reconfirm Riva's reckless embrace of pleasure; we will learn later that his family blamed him for his brother's death, leading to his exile in Angola. This is the only moment of reflection in Riva's manic existence before he plunges back into the bustling, noisy life of the city. Riva's "suicidal" bent is evidenced from the outset. Riva is a hard-liner.[21] Barlet insists:

> Confronted with tragedy / the tragic, Riva has no other choice, in order to exist, than to forge ahead, head down, to take the blows without giving them much thought, to sacrifice his body on the altar of the big / great city.[22]

Riva's manic partying seems to be an end in itself whereas Mwas's lived reality is in constant contrast to his aspirational universe. We only see the mimetic desire of JM who looks longingly at the glamor of Riva's life. Thinking he can get his hands on the money when Riva is presumed dead, he abandons without conscience or afterthought the modest life (including a job and his wife and two young children) he had created for himself in the unforgiving capital of the DRC.

In Kinshasa, the city of no hope, even the church has lost its role as a safe space. Toward the end of the film, when Riva is believed dead, there is a gathering in the church where the Commander, Malou and JM have come to sell the gas to the priest. The priest's complicity in black market wrangling had already been exposed and he is clearly no different from his lay compatriots in other official capacities. The church fails to be a sanctuary when Cesar and his men arrive. The characters are all positioned in front of the altar when Cesar shoots Malou in cold blood for being of no use to him. Munga is clearly asserting that there are no sacred spaces left in Kinshasa.

Viva Riva! offers some explanation for the state of disrepair that has even infiltrated family life. Recent events explaining the dire situation in the Congo are referenced through the family histories of Riva and Nora. Riva's father rails about the cost of educating a child (who then turned to a life of crime) in a country that had seen lootings and war (situating us first in the early 1990s and then the period between 1996 and 2003). Nora's story evokes the predatory excesses of the Mobutu era during which it is said that the cars of rich politicians would line up outside the gates when school was out to pick up their high school "mistresses." But the film downplays this power relationship because Nora does not position herself as a victim and emphasizes the fact that she disgraced her father. In his review of the film, Barlet uses the word rape (2011) and it is in fact quite possible that this was a case of statutory rape. But the responses of the characters demonstrate how common these kinds of unequal and money-based relationships have become. Riva simply refers to Nora's assailant as her "Sugar Daddy."

Riva's relationship with his family is equally fraught, pointing to significant conflicts between the generations. Although Riva has returned to the city of his birth, he appears to have no home there. Rather he circulates from bars to clubs, from hotels to brothels, and it is only well into the film that we discover his parents are still in Kinshasa. Ironically he appears to be most at home at Ma Edo's brothel where she welcomes him with open arms, calling him her "baby." Ma Edo is fiercely protective of him whereas his parents not only give him an icy reception but end up accusing him of killing his brother (who died accidentally due to an electrical short circuit). When Riva responds to this unfair accusation by punching his father in a symbolic act of parricide, Ma Edo's status as a surrogate parent to him is reinforced. Munga's choice of the honorific nickname Ma (common usage in the Congo) also points to her *in loco parentis* relationship with Riva. Munga contrasts her maternal attitude toward him with his mother's cold-heartedness and her negligence of him and his brother when they were young. Through this reversal of roles, Munga offers commentary on the perversion of social relations strained by the difficult circumstances of life. Unlike Riva's mother, whom he resents for having been at church "praying, praying, praying" when his brother died, Ma Edo steps up to defend Riva in his time of need, confronting and fighting the bad guys in order to give him a chance to escape. In the end, she sacrifices her life, in essence leaving Riva orphaned. A small ray of hope is offered by Munga, however, that at least Nora may be able patch up her relationship to her estranged family. Riva and Nora share a last encounter at Ma Edo's brothel that is markedly different from their previous encounters in the hotel. The room is shown for the first time in a lighting that appears natural and we see a different, demure Nora who has shed her sexy outfits and make-up. There is no sex, only talk, and at the end of their sober and honest conversation she heads out to confront her future.

The painful dramas that play out in the domestic spaces point to severely compromised relationships in the urban spaces evoked. Nora and Azor are constantly insulting each other and at times Azor's bodyguards (who seem to be quite protective of Nora) have to physically separate them. The most heart-wrenching scene, though, is when JM beats his wife in front of their small children, telling her that she is ugly and talking about the great life he is going to have now that he will be rich. Munga focuses on their teary and traumatized faces, reinforcing the pathos of the moment. Waiting outside in the car, the Commander and her bisexual prostitute friend Malou ignore the woman's cries and turn their gazes away in indifference. Money, a resource that via its circulation should help alleviate poverty and create opportunities, certainly appears to poison everything, as Nora had proclaimed.

The endings of these films that evoke the precarity of life for those who are susceptible to premature death represent final moments of suspension. Both Munga and Gitonga take their characters to abandoned buildings in their closing sequences, a conventional trope for final showdowns. These out-of-the-way spaces remove the characters from their daily itineraries, the paths of their (relative) flow through the cities. Here they are isolated from any potential assistance. *Viva Riva!* presents us with the irony that Riva is going to die in a brick making factory; his destruction will occur in a place for making building materials, albeit the old-fashioned way as Cesar disparagingly points out. Perhaps this, along with his defiant cry "life is still good" while he is suspended over the flames, is yet another testimony to qualities that De Boeck (2004) describes in *Kinshasa: Tales of the Invisible City*: "In ways that often leave the observer perplexed, the city constantly activates and undergoes the effervescent push and pull of destruction and regeneration" (p. 19), thanks, no doubt, to the famed débrouillardise – or "desperate resilience" – of its inhabitants.

Nairobi Half Life offers viewers more breathing room by letting the story end in the theatre, the one place that has served as a kind of escape for Mwas. It is therefore in the penultimate sequence of *Nairobi Half Life* that Mwas and others are taken to the abandoned warehouse to be "dead men walking." It is important to note that they were about to be incarcerated after the brawl that ended in Dingo's accidental death. Instead the plainclothes policemen interrupt the regular process of arrest and take the gang aside. Manacled and lumped together in the back of the station wagon, their faces reflect the gravity of this extraordinary, extrajudicial situation. Oti explains to Mwas that the police will keep them in the warehouse until they need a body to "solve" a case, at which point they will be killed. Their energy has been depleted and they sit listlessly staring into space; they have given up. They are all but dead. Nobody will investigate their disappearance; their bodies will be used to represent those of criminals, and they will neither be recognized nor honored in death. The scenes are shot in a dark room traversed by the occasional sharp shaft of light. The lack of color and the strong contrasts create striking images that emphasize the dire situation in which they find themselves. Once again Mwas's resilience comes through. He encourages the others to fight back, but all his friends are killed and he alone escapes. As he runs across the city, we are reminded of Lola's running in Tykwer's film, and as Webber points out, she is "caught in a kind of suspended animation, recursive in her performances, running as it were on the spot" (p. 205). Mwas does make it to the theatre, his destination. But is it really the haven he had hoped it would be? Although he goes on stage, the mask he usually wears in the theatre starts to slip down, his beaten-up face is revealed for all to see. The play ends with him being shot and, even though it is a play, it is treated cinematically. The characters freeze and the lights go down, mimicking a filmic freeze-frame and fade to black. He is alive but not well. As the audience applauds, he looks out to Amina who is still blissfully unaware of the death of her boyfriend and the others. She is momentarily oblivious to the sudden increase in the precariousness of Mwas's life and by extension hers. In that moment of suspension, the uncertainty weighs heavily. Despite Mwas's resilience having been highlighted in the past, here, the film seems to suggest, the obstacles are such that even formidable entrepreneurial energy and vitality may not be enough to help an individual overcome them. The final shot is a close-up of Cedric holding Mwas's hand. The ending, while offering an example of solidarity, amplifies the appeal made by Mwas's character in the play, imploring the audience to stop averting their gaze from those reduced to "bare life." They have a choice: "To look or to look away." Gitonga's refusal of the status quo marked by inequality and flagrant injustice is more explicit than Munga's. And both filmmakers, while presenting us with characters whose verve we can admire, dramatize the toll these acts of resilience take on individuals and communities.

    Viva Riva!, although it ends with the protagonist's death, also leaves us in a space of suspension. After the truck with the fuel has literally gone up in flames, the young boy Anto finds a large bag of money in Cesar's vehicle. At first, he does not seem very interested in the cash. He flips through a wad of bills and then replaces it in the bag and closes it. He is more interested in playing like the kid he is, despite the heavy responsibilities he has already had to bear. He gets behind the wheel and, imitating car noises, he pretends to drive the SUV. A small Congolese flag perched next to the gearbox alerts us to the metaphorical importance of this scene that represents the future of the country as a whole. Munga offers us a long close-up shot of Anto facing the right side of the screen, the more hopeful orientation in film language. This perhaps adds a sliver of hope for our desire to will the young boy into a better future. But money has been seen to be like poison, and the vehicle is stationary. As the credits begin to roll, Franklin Boukaka's pan-African anthem calling for independence, "Le Bûcheron," plays. This emblematically Congolese song from 1970 gives way to the beats we had heard in the club. The dreams of independence were not realized. What future can the present possibly lead to? The driving beats bring us back into the nightclub, a space associated with the suspension of the "perpetual present" of Riva's generation. The nostalgia of the Boukaka song is no doubt an invitation to revisit, with a view to the future, the hopeful moment of decolonization.

I started this reading of the two films by asserting that Munga and Gitonga eschew the extremes of Afro-pessimism and unconditional celebration of the ingenuity and inventiveness of the inhabitants of African cities that make the cities work despite the insufficiencies of infrastructure and services. Even if the characters are marked as "dead men walking," their tremendous vitality in the face of tough odds confirms Weheliye's challenge to "the equation of domination and violence with the complete absence of subjectivity, life, enjoyment, hunger, and so on" (p. 52). Even these "dead men walking" are therefore not reduced to "bare life": "Agamben's theorization of bare life leaves no room for alternate forms of life that elude the law's violent embrace. What seems to have vanished from this description is the *life* in the *bare life* compound" (p. 131).

By drawing out moments of flow and overcoming, albeit often temporary, I have attempted to show how the filmmakers acknowledge the energy and vitality of characters living in African cities without downplaying either their vulnerability or the toll their required daily performances of "débrouillardise" take on them. Furthermore, the films reflect a great fondness for Kinshasa and Nairobi and their inhabitants on the part of the directors. Munga has been asked whether his film is a "love letter" to Kinshasa (Valley, 2011) and Kenyan viewers of *Nairobi Half Life* reported how happy they were to see their city on the big screen (Kinuthia Gathenji, n.d.). Shot on location in two vibrant cities whose shared and idiosyncratic qualities they bring to life, the films provide an opportunity to analyze representations of large urban agglomerations "from below" (Harrow, 2013). They capture the struggles of its inhabitants who counter the threat of death through vitality, resistance, and resilience. As spectators we are mostly left holding our breath, observing a suspension of life with no clear indication of whether the characters will fall back into inertia (always running on the spot without making discernable progress) or will be reinserted into some kind of life-giving flow. What we desperately yearn for as we view these films and the realities we associate with them is not linear, teleological progress, but *life*, or at least the horizons of possibility for life.

Notes

1   "Perpetual movement that does not know where it's going but goes at full tilt." All
    translations are my own.
2   Both Nairobi with its 3.5 million inhabitants and Kinshasa with its sprawling urban
    agglomeration of over 10 million are representative of the rapid urbanization of the
    continent. Kibera, for example, is not only the largest slum in Nairobi but also the larg-
    est urban slum in Africa.
3   Rem Koolhaas (2006) is one of the most prominent figures associated with this celebra-
    tory kind of reading, of Lagos in particular. See also *Mutations* (Boeri, Koolhaas et al.,
    2001), a joint project of Rem Koolhaas OMA and the Harvard Project on the City. For
    a range of productive approaches to African cities see *Rogue Urbanisms* (2013) edited by
    Edgar Pieterse and AbdouMaliq Simone. This work is the outcome of a research explo-
    ration by the African Center for Cities at the University of Cape Town.
4   African film, from its inception, has been linked to urban spaces. Paulin Vieyra, who
    later became a founding "father" of African film criticism (Ellerson, 2012), introduced
    us to Africans in the iconic city of Paris in his pioneering effort *Afrique sur Seine* (1955).
    Ousmane Sembène, considered the "father" of African cinema, chose a cart driver
    (Borom Sarret, 1963) as his first protagonist, a figure representative of those surviving
    in the informal economy on the margins of society. Sembène's debut film portrays
    Dakar as clearly divided between the upscale, former colonial downtown and the plains
    of the African quarter. Aerial shots alternate with traveling shots capturing the point of
    view of the cart driver as he moves through his familiar neighborhood and then, anx-
    iously, through the forbidden "ville." In "African Cities as Cinematic Texts" (*Focus on
    African Films* 2004), Françoise Pfaff postulates "an aesthetics of spatial dualism" in the
    works of Francophone African filmmakers who repeatedly contrast "representation of
    alienating archetypical urban contexts that highlight an unmistakable relationship bet-
    ween spatial and sociopolitical/economic spheres" (2004, p. 105). Much reflection on
    urban spaces in African film tends to be integrated into analyses focused on other
    thematic concerns, but examples of other studies that directly address the cinematic
    city include Wynchank on Dakar (2007), Haynes on Lagos (2007) and Ellapen (2007),
    Parker (2012), and Bickford-Smith (2013) on South African cities and townships.
    To a significant extent, African films have situated their stories in cities. Many films
    include the name of the city in their title, among them *Bamako* (Sissako, 2006), *Clouds
    over Conakry* (Camara, 2007), *Kinshasa Palace* (Laplaine, 2006) and *Ouaga-Saga* (Kouyate,
    2004). This is also the case with a few original and engaging documentaries, for
    example *Bamako Sigi Kan* (2003) and *Conakry Kas* (2004) by Manthia Diawara, *Rostov-
    Luanda* (1998) by Abderrahmane Sissako and the short film by Kiripi Katembo,
    Symphony Kinshasa (2009). In Nollywood films, Lagos of course has pride of place.
    Directors who foreground cites and who have contributed significantly to our
    perceptions of urban life include Djibril Diop Mambéty, Ousmane Sembène, and
    Sene Moussa Absa for Dakar, Jean-Pierre Bekolo for Yaounde, Jean-Marie Teno
    for Yaounde and Ouagadougou, Ivunga Imanga for Libreville, Gaston Kaboré for
    Ouagadougou, Mweze Ngangura for Kinshasa, Zeze Gamboa and Maria João
    Ganga for Luanda, and Oliver Schmitz, Suleman Ramadan, Gavin Hood, Neill
    Blomkamp, and Teddy Mattera for Johannesburg and Soweto. Other less often

represented cities have started joining the list, a recent example being Hermon Hailay's portrayal of Addis Ababa in *Price of Love* (2015). For the most part, in contrast to much of the mainstream literature dealing with African urban spaces, these films do not treat cities as inherently dystopic, with the exception of Bekolo's *Les Saignantes* (2005) with its urban noir setting.

5   "Infrastructures are the institutionalized networks that facilitate the flow of goods in a wider cultural as well as physical sense" (Larkin 5). In his book, Brian Larkin analyzes the role of media technologies in producing "what we call urban Africa" (p. 2).

6   The term "half life" also refers to decay, often in relation to radioactivity. In this context, it perhaps also evokes the persistence of the toxicity of the colonial legacy in Nairobi.

7   Although resilience, the ability to adapt in the face of adversity, is generally positively valued, it can create a sense of complacency that takes attention away from the need for real change.

8   It was only after returning to *Inert Cities* to check references that I realized to what extent I had adopted Donald and Lindner's vocabulary in my title. Their introduction is titled "Inertia, Suspension and Mobility in the Global City." I owe a deep debt to this collection of essays; it significantly shaped my readings of the films.

9   The English translation will be published by Indiana University Press in 2018.

10 Ruth Wilson Gilmore, quoted by Weheliye (2014), defines racism, "the state-sanctioned and/or extra-legal production and exploitation of group-differentiated vulnerabilities to premature death" (p. 55).

11 Mbembe notes that "the colony represents the site where sovereignty consists fundamentally in the exercise of power outside the law" (p. 23).

12 I would like to thank the faculty of the 2016 NEH Summer Institute held at Indiana University and titled "Arts of Survival: Recasting Lives in African Cities" for a stimulating and enriching experience: Eileen Julien and James Ogude (co-directors), Akin Adesokan, Grace A. Musila, and Oana Panaïté. Akin Adesokan specifically addressed the interstitial space between the urban apocalypse and celebrations of inventiveness.

13 A notable predecessor is Mweze Ngangura's rags-to-riches musical comedy set in Kinshasa, *La vie est belle*.

14 "Riva se glisse entre les meurs, entre les femmes, entre les dangers, jusqu'à ce que la ville le rattrape et le happe."

15 "Déjà le colonisé était un corps d'exception, que l'on soumettait à merci. Décolonisés, les corps restent déterminés par cette incertitude de faire en permanence l'expérience du danger."

16 At the same time Weheliye eschews the language of resistance and agency because "these concepts have a tendency to blind us […] to the manifold occurrences of freedom in zones of indistinction" (p. 2).

17 "À Kinshasa c'est un projet désespéré et Riva n'échappe pas à son destin."

18 I thank Grace Musila for pointing out the character's linguistic evolution.

19 This, according to Mbembe, is the ultimate expression of sovereignty (2003, p. 11).

20 "Des lois sans pitié des truands, qui sont devenues celles de la société."

21 Barlet speaks of his "jusqu'au-boutisme."

22 "Face au tragique, Riva n'a d'autre choix pour exister que de foncer tête baissée, de ramasser les coups sans y penser, de sacrifier son corps sur l'autel de la grande ville."

References

Agamben, Giorgio. 1998. *Homo Sacer: Sovereign Power and Bare Life*. Stanford, CA: Stanford University Press.

Barlet, Olivier. 2011. "*Viva Riva!* de Djo Tunda wa Munga." *Africultures*. Accessed April 2016. www.africultures.com/php/?nav=article&no=10467

Bickford-Smith, Vivan. 2013. "Cinematic Cities: A 'Film and History' Overview for South Africa's Major Metropolises from the 1890s to the 1950s." *Journal of Southern African Studies* 39.3: 681–699.

Boeck, Filip de, and Marie-Françoise Plissart. 2004. *Kinshasa: Tales of the Invisible City*. Ghent: Ludion.

Bofane, In Koli Jean. 2014. *Congo Inc.: Le testament de Bismarck*. Arles: Actes Sud.

Boeri, Stefano and Multiplicity, Rem Koolhaas and Harvard Design School Project on the City, Sanford Kwinter and Daniella Fabricius, Hans Ulrich Obrist, and Nadia Tazi. 2001. *Mutations*. Barcelona: Actar.

De Lame, Danielle. 2010. "Grey Nairobi: Sketches of Urban Socialities." *Nairobi Today: The Paradox of a Fragmented City*, edited by Rodriguez-Torres, Deyssi, 167–204.

Donald, Stephanie Hemelryk. 2014. "Inertia and Ethical Urban Relations: The Living, the Dying and the Dead." *Inert Cities: Globalization, Mobility and Suspension in Visual Culture*, edited by Stephanie Hemelryk Donald and Christoph Lindner, 152–169. London: Tauris.

Donald, Stephanie Hemelryk and Christoph Lindner, eds. 2014. *Inert Cities: Globalization, Mobility and Suspension in Visual Culture*. London: Tauris.

Ellapen, Jordache Abner. 2007. "The Cinematic Township: Cinematic representations of the 'township space' and who can claim the rights to representation in post-apartheid South African cinema." *Journal of African Cultural Studies* 19:133–137.

Ellerson, Beti. 2012. "Reflections on Cinema Criticism and African Women." Special issue, *African Feminist Engagements with Film. Feminist Africa* 16: 37–52.

Frassinelli, Pier Paolo. 2015. "Heading South: Theory, *Viva Riva!* and *District 9*." *Critical Arts: A SouthNorth Journal of Cultural & Media Studies* 29.3: 293–309.

Harrow, Kenneth W. 2013. *Trash: African Cinema from Below*. Bloomington, IN: Indiana University Press.

Haynes, Jonathan. 2007. "Nollywood in Lagos. Lagos in Nollywood Films." *Africa Today* 54.2: 131–150.

Jordan, Shirley. 2014. "On Hold: Urban Photography as Interruption." *Inert Cities: Globalization, Mobility and Suspension in Visual Culture*, edited by Stephanie Hemelryk Donald and Christoph Lindner, 16–38. London: Tauris.

Kinuthia Gathenji, Helen. n.d. "Nairobi Half Life, the Story behind the Magic." *East African Destination*. Accessed May 2016. www.eadestination.com/pop-culture/78-nairobi-half-life-the-story-behind-the-magic

Koolhaas, Rem, and Bregtje van der Haak. 2006. *Lagos Wide and Close: An Interactive Journey into an Exploding City*. The Netherlands: Submarine DVD.

Larkin, Brian. 2008. *Signal and Noise: Media, Infrastructure, and Urban Culture in Nigeria*. Durham, NC: Duke University Press.

Launchbury, Claire. 2014. "Urban Inertia and Dealing with the Disappeared in Postwar Beirut: *A Perfect Day* (2004) and *Here Comes the Rain* (2010)." *Inert Cities: Globalization, Mobility and Suspension in Visual Culture*, edited by Stephanie Hemeryk Donald and Christoph Lidnner, 173–186. London: Tauris.

Mbembe, Achille. 2003. "Necropolitics." *Public Culture* 15.1:11–40; doi:10.1215/08992363-15-1-11.

Parker, Alexandra. 2012. "Gangsters' Paradise: The Representation of Johannesburg in Film and Television." *International Journal of the Image* 2.3: 167–178.

Pfaff, Françoise. 2004. *Focus on African Films*. Bloomington: Indiana University Press.

Pieterse, Edgar, and AbdouMaliq Simone. 2013. *Rogue Urbanism: Emergent African Cities*. Johannesburg and Cape Town: Jacana; African Center for Cities.

Prakash, Gyan. 2010. *Noir Urbanisms: Dystopic Images of the Modern City*. Princeton, NJ: Princeton University Press.

Robinson, Jennifer. 2010. "Living in Dystopia: Past, Present, and Future in Contemporary African Cities." In *Noir Urbanisms: Dystopic Images of the Modern City*, edited by Gyan Prakash, 170–185. Princeton, NJ: Princeton University Press.

Rodriguez-Torres, Deyssi ed. 2010. *Nairobi Today: The Paradox of a Fragmented City*. African Books Collective.

Rousseau-Dewambrechies, Pascale. "Viva Riva de Djo Tunda wa Munga: du Congo où règne le chaos." *Acqui!* Accessed May 2016. www.aqui.fr/cultures/viva-riva-de-djo-tunda-wa-munga-du-congo-ou-regne-le-chaos,6433.html

Valley, Dylan. "Viva Kinshasa." *Africa is a Country*. Accessed May 2016. http://africasacountry.com/2011/10/viva-kinshasa/

Webber, Andrew J. "Slow Motion Pictures: Casting Inertia in Contemporary Berlin Film." *Inert Cities: Globalization, Mobility and Suspension in Visual Culture*, edited by Stephanie Hemelryk Donald and Christoph Lindner, 202–218. London: Tauris.

Weheliye, Alexander. 2014. *Habeas Viscus: Racializing Assemblages, Biopolitics, and Black Feminist Theories of the Human*. Durham, NC: Duke University Press.

Wynchank, Anny. 2007. "Promenade avec Djibril Diop Mambéty: Dakar pris sur le vif." *Enseigner le monde noir: Mélanges offerts à Jacques Chevrier*, ed. Beïda Chikhi, 365–380. Paris: Maisonneuve.

Filmography

Bekolo, Jean-Pierre. *Saignantes, Les*. (2005). Cameroon: Quartier Mozart Films.

Camara, Cheick Fantymadey. *Clouds over Conakry*. (2007). Guinea: Conakry-Ouagadougou-Paris Films.

Diawara, Manthia. *Bamako Sigi-Kan*. (2003). Mali: K'a Yéléma Productions.

Diawara, Manthia. *Conakry Kas*. (2004). Guinea: K'a Yéléma Productions.

Gitonga, David "Tosh." *Nairobi Half Life*. (2012). Kenya: One Fine Day Films.

Hailay, Hermon. *Price of Love*. (2015). Ethiopia. HM Film Production.

Hamadi, D., Katembo, K., and Lusala, D. *Congo in Four Acts*. (2010). DRCongo: Suka Productions.

Kouyaté, Dany. *Ouaga-Saga*. (2004). Burkina Faso: PM Audiovisuel, Sahélis Productions.

Laplaine, Zeka. *Kinshasa Palace*. (2006). DRCongo: Bakia Films, Les Histoires Weba.

Munga, Djo. *Viva Riva!* (2010). DRCongo: MG Productions, Suka Productions.

Sarr, M. and Vieyra, P. (1955). *Afrique sur Seine*. France: Groupe Africain.

Sembène, Ousmane. (1963). *Borom Sarret*. Senegal: Filmi Domireew.

Sissako, Abderrahmane. (2006). *Bamako*. Mali: Archipel 33, Chinguitty Films, Mali Images.

Tykwer, Tom. *Run Lola Run*. (1998). Germany: X-Filme Creative Pool, Westdeutscher Rundfunk (WDR), Arte.

Part II

Trauma / Violence / Precarity in an Age of Global Neoliberalism

4

At the Intersection of Trauma, Precarity, and African Cinema
A Reflection on Mahamat-Saleh Haroun's Grigris

MaryEllen Higgins

After its flourishing in the 1990s, Trauma Studies is under review. One recurrent critique is that the model of the singular, catastrophic event does not adequately consider trauma-inducing structural violence and persistent or cumulative trauma.[1] A linked critique points to the marginalization or omission of traumatic experiences beyond Europe and the United States, as well as the presumption that trauma as a conceptual apparatus can be universally applied.

Michael Rothberg (2014) argues that trauma encompasses not just a catastrophic, shocking event, but also "a system of violence that is neither sudden nor accidental: Exploitation in an age of globalized neo-liberal capitalism" (p. xiv). Stef Craps (2014) concurs: "Particularly contentious is the definition of what constitutes a traumatic stressor. This is typically thought of as a sudden, unexpected, catastrophic event – indeed, since the beginning of its discussion, trauma has been associated with an image of a single devastating blow or an acute stab that breaks the protective shield of the psyche" (p. 49). When trauma-producing events are relegated to the past, Craps argues, individual psychological therapy and recovery become "privileged over the transformation of a wounding political, social, or economic system," function as "a political palliative to the socially disempowered," and thus "negates the need for taking action towards systematic change" (2014, p. 50).

If systematic wounding beyond the usual locales is to be attended to, and if the definition of trauma in those locales cannot be taken for granted, then what do we mean when we say trauma? If there is to be a revision of the individualized, event-based model of trauma, a revision that takes into account traumas induced by pervasive, systematic forms of violence such as racism, sexism, neocolonialism and other ongoing forms of abuse – what Maria P. Root (1996) has called insidious trauma – how does the diagnostic criteria of trauma expand? Does the "post" in post-traumatic become like the "post" in postcolonial – a remembrance of the past with an acknowledgment of the continuation of that past into the present? If I explore a fictional film that features a man and woman in Chad who suffer from cycles of violent wounding, does the word trauma apply?

In some ways, trauma theory never really has been about a singular event. Instead, it examines the return of the event in the present, the repetition of the blows, the presence that haunts the psyche, the open wounds that resist closure. As Annie G. Rogers (2006) describes it, trauma is a "lasting terror" (p. xii). Trauma Studies conceptualize and analyze the relentless replay of wound-inflicting blows in the present, the perceived, or real inescapability of woundedness, being held in captivity, the crisis of being trapped in the time of trauma, trauma's freezing of time. Moreover, given that the well-studied catalysts for trauma – war, rape, and genocide – are calculated events wrought with racism and sexism, instances of perpetual, systematic wounding were already there at the outset, even if what Hamish Dalley (2015) aptly calls "trauma-inducing structures" were not the primary foci of trauma studies (p. 388).

Thus insidious traumas compel a revision to Cathy Caruth's interpretation (which owes much to Freud) of the sudden traumatic event, an event "not assimilated or experienced fully at the time, but only belatedly, in its repeated possession of the one who experiences it" (1995, p. 4). In the revised formulations of insidious trauma, events may not be singular. They may even become tragically predictable, yet there are still rich interpretive possibilities in Caruth's analyses. We might ask, for example, about "repeated possession": How do initial wounds impact further wounds? And for the sake of a chapter that contemplates film, how might the cinema's maneuvering of time – or its simulation of time – project repeated possessions? How might trauma's manipulations of perceived time be illuminated by the cinema's artistic devices: Flashbacks, ellipses, superimpositions, the tampering of the image track, dropped scenes, extended cuts? Might we read trauma embedded in some films as subtext, a subtext such as that conceived by Garrett Stewart (2007), following Michael Riffaterre, a series of "undue returns," or undisclosed seeds of origin (pp. 62–63)?

One element that changes in the analysis of insidious trauma is the role of memory. When blows to the body and the psyche are pervasive, trauma is less a matter of memory that inserts itself in a manner that is out of place or out of time.[2] It is less a matter of a memory that interrupts and invades the present. When the violent blows recur, one only need remember yesterday and the day before, and to anticipate that today and tomorrow could very well bring more of the same. It is not, thus, reliving a prior, shattering event *as if* it is occurring in the present, but reliving a shattering event *because* it is ongoing. It is reliving an event because the event has returned, often in various guises, like an incessant motif, or an inescapable genre. Trauma, in this context, is not a broken narrative; it is woven into the narrative.

Well before the resurgence of trauma theory in the 1980s and 1990s,[3] Franz Fanon (1963), who is notably absent from Caruth, wrote at length about pervasive traumata in the colonies. Fanon's descriptions of colonized subjects who are "scarred by the whip," "penned in," "in a permanent state of tension," and "kept on edge like a running sore flinching from a caustic agent" (pp. 15–19) resonate with the diagnostic criteria of trauma, which include, as Fanon does, experiences with threats of death and threats to the integrity of the self.[4] Craps notes that in *Black Skin, White Masks*, Fanon describes the alienating and dislocating effects of race-based trauma using "surgical metaphors": Amputation, knife blades in the body, dissection (2014, p. 30). As Dalley (2015) observes, Fanon takes the concept of trauma as puncture and violation and applies it to the physical and psychological invasions of colonization. Pernicious trauma is perhaps most famously portrayed in Fanon's final chapter of *The Wretched of the Earth,* titled "Colonial War and Mental Disorders." In it, Fanon speaks of "the scope and depth of the wounds inflicted on the colonized during a single day under a colonial regime" (1963, pp. 181–182).

If, as Bessel Van der Kolk (2015) writes, the way out of trauma's entrapments is to "take bodily action to regain ownership of your life" (pp. xiii–Viv), and if I place Fanon in an imagined dialogue with the strand of trauma theory that highlights somatic agency and recovery via bodily action, then for Fanon, bodily action translates as violent resistance. Violent action and masculinist agency, for Fanon, function to break the colonist's "spiral of violence" (1963, p. 9). For Fanon, violent resistance paves an escape from the colony's traumatic loops, puts a halt to the pernicious invasions, and asserts one's humanity (especially one's manhood), providing a means of not just of "working through" the psychic wounds of colonization, but of changing the course of the trauma itself. Yet violent revolution and Fanon's versions of compensatory masculinist action were not followed by new versions of the human, as Fanon had hoped, and the traumatic still replays in the postcolony.

In order to test the some of the limits and possibilities of trauma theory's applicability to African cinema, and also to examine traumatic looping, precarity, and imagined pathways out of the loop,[5] I contemplate multiple instances of wounding in a film by Mahamat-Saleh Haroun. Haroun's films are particularly inviting in this endeavor because they accentuate trauma's repetitive wounds. His films, like trauma theory, narrate the aftereffects of violent events; in Haroun's own words, his film *Daratt* "does not deal with civil war, but with its aftermath. I observe the landscape after the storm, the life that goes on after the debris, ruins and ashes. How to live with each other after so much violence and hatred?" (qtd. in Diawara 2010, p. 283). Wounded and damaged bodies punctuate Haroun's films *Abouna* (2002), *Daratt (Dry Season,* 2006), *Un homme qui crie (A Screaming Man,* 2010) *Grigris* (2013), and *Hissein Habré: une tragédie tchadienne (Hissein Habré: A Chadian Tragedy,* 2016). Elsewhere, I have analyzed Haroun's projection of cycles of war, damage, masculine violence, invasion, absence, memory, and agency in contexts of civil wars, and the reliance of those wars on youthful male bodies.[6] Here, I turn to Haroun's *Grigris* (2013), in part because the replay of wounding – trauma's root – is pronounced in the film, and in part because the film's dénouement stages women who inflict conclusive, fatal blows. For viewers familiar with Haroun's films, the violent pounding and bloodiness in *Grigris* is a shock, uncharacteristic of Haroun's other films, which tend to place direct representations of violence on the body in off-screen space. Dayna Oscherwitz remarks that *Daratt* "minimizes dialogue while elevating ambient or background noise to symbolic status" (2014, p. 238). In *Grigris*, the sounds of violent pounding are heightened, visceral, pronounced, as if one is hearing a boxing match up close, a crescendo of blows. Before death-inducing blows can be inflicted upon the eponymous character Grigris, women intervene to deliver their blows, clubbing the perpetrator. It is a move that revives Fanon's violent somatic agency but turns the counter-aggressors into women. If pronounced violent action performed by men has failed as a means of emancipatory agency that ushers in the new human, if it has failed to provide an escape route out of trauma's time loops, what happens when the violent agents are women?

But first, back to trauma: In *Unclaimed Experience* Caruth writes, "the language of trauma, and the silence of its mute repetition of suffering, profoundly and imperatively demand" from us "a new mode of reading and of listening" (1996, p. 9). If new readings are called for, and if, as Craps argues, traumas in postcolonial contexts must be recognized "on their own terms," (2014, p. 48) then what are the terms? References to wounds, their unspeakability, and their various traces appear in classics of African literature and scholarship – for example, in Ousmane Sembène's *Tribal Scars*, in Irène Assiba d'Almeida's *Francophone African Women Writers: Destroying the Emptiness of Silence* (1994), and in Tejumola Olaniyan's *Scars of Conquest/Masks of Resistance* (1995).[7] One example from African cinema, Cheick Oumar Sissoko's *La Genèse* (*Genesis,* 1999) traces the origins of fratricidal trauma to Genesis through its re-staging of chapters from the Bible. In it, somatic metaphors combine with images reminiscent of recent civil wars. In the wake of brotherly betrayal, in the aftermath of the loss of kinship, the biblical character Esau calls his brother Jacob "the scar." In fratricidal aftermaths, Sissako narrates the erasure of women's traumatic experiences; the very footsteps of Dinah leave no traces. Literature and cinema, like trauma theory, are ways of "attending to and addressing the representation of human suffering and "wounding," both literal and metaphorical, both personal and communal" (Eaglestone 2014, p. 12).

Haroun's *Grigris* plays with trauma's timeline of wounds: The first signs of bodily injury are internal, and summon intertextual recall external to the film. The protagonist, Souleymane Deme (played by Souleymane Deme), known by all as Grigris, learns that his father-in-law Ayoub (Marius Yelolo) is terribly ill. There appears to be a looping back to Haroun's previous film, *A Screaming Man*. The actor Marius Yelolo plays the part of David in that film; Yelolo as David, like Yelolo as Ayoub, also lies sick in the hospital. In *Grigris*, helplessness sets in when the hospital requires 700,000 francs to pay for Ayoub's treatment, an overwhelming sum that Grigris and his mother (Hadjé Fatimé N'Goua) cannot afford, despite their persistent labor – Grigris's dancing, his work in the photography studio, and his mother's physically demanding work as a laundress. Grigris implores an acquaintance, Moussa (Cyril Guei), to allow him to work in a profitable, but dangerous oil-smuggling ring. After his initial performance in Moussa's smuggling venture falters, Grigris pleads for a second chance, and is assigned to the position of driver. Desperate for money, and now in control of the wheel, Grigris transports and sells Moussa's jerry cans of oil surreptitiously to Alhadj (Youssouf Djaoro), a man to whom he is in debt. After Grigris scatters the bills gained from his loot on Ayoub's hospital bed, relief is only temporary. In his attempt to convince Moussa that the police roughed him up and confiscated the oil, Grigris bashes his head against a wall several times until it bleeds profusely. Thus, the initial bloody wound in *Grigris* is already an imitation of woundedness one might expect from the state's police who protect its oil revenues. Grigris's self-inflicted wounding, his first attempt out of the loop of blows, is a violent but protective measure in an environment where security means escape. However, self-wounding is just a delaying tactic for Grigris; Moussa demands payment for the missing jerry cans of oil, and as the payment deadline approaches, Grigris's wound-count increases. When Moussa eventually discovers that Grigris has been lying about the confiscated oil, violence and wounding escalate. Moussa's *homme de main* (Abakar M'Bairo) forces Grigris into the trunk of his car, beats him in a field at night, fires shots near his body, and threatens to fatally wound him if payment is not delivered in two days. In the aftermath of the initial, self-inflicted wounding, there are more blows and even greater wounds.

But first, there is the dance. Before the film credits commence, it is dark. As the credits appear, the first voices heard are cheering, then chanting "Grigris! Grigris!" Techno music plays and Grigris, wearing a suit and tie, strips off his jacket. As he dances in the club, the crowd claps and cheers – in that crowd his future girlfriend Mimi (Anaïs Monory), Moussa, and the future aggressor (the man who will try to murder him) are celebrating. For Stewart, a film's beginning is initially "all shaping and plotting with no clear story showing through" – there is nothing, at the beginning, to measure the first scene against. Such a scene "hover[s] on the verge of articulating the very structure it will then interact with as plot goes forward"; only later will there be a sort of "retroactive clarification" (p. 62). This reading of first scenes resembles Caruth's first wound, hovering, understood only belatedly and literarily in subsequent scenes of wounding. The first dance scene of *Grigris*, however, has no clear unraveling in subsequent scenes; instead, like the film's further dance sequences, it operates as a diegetic interlude – a somatic, poetic commentary on injury and resilience. If there is a hint of unraveling in the first dance, what it previews is a series of entanglements, a mix of disability and agility, injury and maneuverability, strenuous bodily labor and aesthetic pleasure.[8] And perhaps these interludes harness what Badiou (2013) describes as the cinema's potential to be an "affirmation of human presence" (pp. 5–6). Indeed, there is a link between the character Souleymane Deme (nicknamed Grigris) in the film, and the dynamic actor/dancer Souleymane Deme whom Haroun first saw dancing at FESPACO. Perhaps these interludes, as I will explore later, are the pathways out of trauma's repetitive loops.

In Grigris's case, it not a matter of understanding wounds belatedly. Rather, his actions will be governed by the imagined fast-forward, by the anticipation of future blows, by the predictable aftermath of wounds. The anticipatory awareness of woundability – something akin to Judith Butler's (2004) formulations of precarity and injurability – is there just after the inaugural scene of Grigris's dance performance in the club. Grigris is in the hallway, expecting his payment – "cash-cash-cash!" – from the man who passes the tip hat. It becomes clear that much of Grigris's earnings have been taken by this man. Moussa shows up as Grigris's protector – he says that Grigris, "C'est mon petit," and threatens the thief in a brief gesture of violence, pulling him behind the neck in a move that exhibits the potential for future damage. These gestures that preview future aggression occur repeatedly, as Moussa will direct the flows of future violence. Moussa's *homme de main* (right-hand man) will later point his finger at Grigris as if it were a gun; the same man fires shots close to his body. Moussa's gestures, and especially the movements of his *homme de main*, constitute what Craps calls "daily microaggressions," motions that operate alongside more explosive and deadly forms of violence and promise future violence if the addressee does not comply (2013, p. 26). When Moussa says to Grigris, "If you ever mess up…" the rest of the sentence is already understood. These gestural, unspoken messages contrast with the motions of Grigris's dancing, which at times mimic violent gestures only to absorb and transform them into movements that resemble flight. In *Grigris*, the most significant vulnerability is not in Deme's paralyzed leg, which can be lived with, "worked through," turned into poetic dance movements and controlled, but in his powerlessness to control impending loss, his inability to pay for its prevention. The threat of being fired, as in *A Screaming Man*, is yet another form of micro-aggression in a world where security and health are bought for an overwhelming price. Impending loss resides in a present system where care for the body is not a given and threats to the body reign; it is not a loss understood backward, but now and into the future.

Given the persistence of threats and blows in *Grigris*, perhaps the characters' predicaments would be more adequately described using Lauren Berlant's (2011) appellation, "crisis ordinariness" (p. 10). In *Grigris*, violence and disempowerment become predictable, quotidian. Carmela Garritano's analysis of Haroun's film corpus as a cinema of precarity in the African postcolony draws on Berlant's insights. While Garritano does not explicitly address what Nouri Gana calls "trauma ties" (2014, p. 77), her work on intimate, affective debt relations in Haroun's films attends to "the subjective damage inflicted by globalization processes under the current regime of neoliberal capitalism (the liberalization of economies, the extraction of raw materials oriented toward external markets, the reconfiguration of the functions of the state, as well as the expansion of zones of insecurity and crisis that lead to forced migration and displacement)." Ultimately, Garritano writes, the business of exporting oil has "has engendered corruption, political repression, and a deepening of poverty and insecurity." We might then merge what Dalley (2015) calls a *critical politics of trauma-inducing structures* (p. 388, original italics) with Garritano's "critical methods that attend to the experience of *feeling* postcolonial precarity" (original emphasis). Indeed, wounds in *Grigris* are bound to intimate debt relations; the business of debt seeps into the community's moral structures as oil spreads into the waterways. Moussa's team prays together just before smuggling oil; Grigris is forced to swear on the Qu'ran to support his story about the confiscated jerry cans; the threat of eternal damnation awaits those who attempt to escape paying up. Moussa explains his aggression against his "petit" in these words: "This is a business. A business." As in Haroun's earlier films, paternal figures who claim to provide security – and by extension, the patriarchal state – not only fail to protect vulnerable citizens; they are the very participants in the business that ails everyone, including themselves.

In *Grigris*, as in Haroun's *Abouna*, *Daratt*, *A Screaming Man*, and *Hissein Habré: A Chadian Tragedy*, wounding does not break the time of narrative but is woven into the narrative. Images of illness and somatic damage abound: Asthma (in *Abouna*); blindness, amputation, and speech emitted through wounded throats (in *Daratt*); bandaged bodies of wounded soldiers (in *A Screaming Man*); tortured bodies (in *Hissein Habré: A Chadian Tragedy*). The wound is not a rupture of expectations of a just world, but reinforcement of an already unjust world in which precarity is taken for granted and even perpetrators with resources, such as Moussa's criminal gang, scramble for a way out of state insecurity. The word *systemic* denotes both "affecting the entire body" and "relating to an entire system." Conducting business is in itself traumatic for Grigris's girlfriend Mimi, a prostitute, whose business is in the body. Mimi displays some of the more classic, dissociative symptoms of trauma: She wears a wig to create a separate persona, and when referring to her prostitution, she speaks of herself in the third person – "She has to eat, Mimi. Do you think she does it for pleasure?" Moussa treats her as an expendable person, a "*vaut-rien*" (good-for-nothing) and "*le bas-fond*" (the pits). The characterization of trauma as displaced experience – as triggered memory and affect out of place and out of time – transforms when the wounded are led to believe that they (and not the memory) are the ones out of place, *le bas-fond,* trapped, to adapt Butler, in an "uninhabitable identification" (2004, p. xix).

Desires for changes for the better – Mimi's hope to become a model and Grigris's aspirations in dance – devolve into what Berlant (2011) calls cruel optimism. Grigris first meets Mimi when she asks him to take pictures of her for a modeling competition. The backdrop behind the curtain in Ayoub's studio is a fantasy, an image of clichéd paradise: The beach, the palm trees. To this image, Grigris adds a pretty flame-colored scarf, which Mimi drapes around her slim, bikini-clad figure. A romance is sparked. Yet Mimi will not win: She is considered out of her element in the modeling world; she is told she is "too fat"; her slender frame has not been adequately starved. In the city, she is told that she does not belong because she belongs too much; she is "everyone's girlfriend," too trashy (to borrow from Ken Harrow, 2013) to sit at the dinner table with Moussa and his Asian host. The gentle Ayoub offers his studio to Grigris, but Grigris responds that photography is done for; his studio is out of place in new economy in which everyone is a photographer. The very name Grigris is supposed to yield optimism about the possibilities for good fortune, yet even after a successful performance that opens the film, a performance that starts when Grigris removes his business jacket, the jacket is placed back on his shoulders before he discovers that he has been cheated out of his tip money. Grigris's dancing is exceptional, outside of the usual, *"le tonnerre"* (thunder) as Moussa celebrates it, but also part of the quotidian, part of a financial transaction that culminates in disappointment. It would seem, then, that Haroun's pessimism has settled in, hopes for a pathway out of repetitive patterns of overwhelming insecurity are mere illusions, at least until we reach the protective space of a village governed temporarily by women.

Before then, an analysis of wounding need not decide between precarity and trauma. In an chapter about trauma in African cinema, there are films that might fall more clearly into a trauma genre – Yamina Bachir Chouikh's *Rachida* (2002), Fanta Régina Nacro's *La nuit de la verité* (*The Night of Truth*, 2004), Ramadan Suleman's *Zulu Love Letter* (2004), Kivu Ruhorahoza's *Matière grise* (*Grey Matter*, 2011), Judy Kibinge's *Something Necessary* (2013), or Sékou Traoré's *L'oeil du cyclone* (*Eye of the Storm*, 2014), to name a few. Yet the intricate patterns of wounding and quotidian precarity intertwine, and in *Grigris*, they interact as if in a blended genre. In Judith Butler's *Precarious Life* (2004), she asks "what form political reflection and deliberation ought to take if we take injurability and aggression as two points of departure for political life" (p. xii). In the language of trauma, the blow, or puncture, is the aggression. The initial injury takes the form of a wound, which in the traumatic situation lives on to haunt the injured, and in some formulations, the spectators, and quite possibly the perpetrator of the aggression. Before, and perhaps in between the blow and the wound is an already-existing injurability, precarity. Traumatic events often lead to the discovery of one's place among a community of the damaged, to an awareness of vulnerability that was always there, to a profound understanding that the horizon is an insecure line. As Butler acknowledges, a breaking of a protective shield, and especially the protective shield of a nation like the United States whose inhabitants are assured by their leaders that they will be protected, often leads to greater militancy and resolve to defeat perpetrator-others at all costs. In Butler, an acute awareness of human injurability should lead to the conclusion that "no final control can be secured, and that final control is not, cannot be, an ultimate value" (2004, p. xiii). "To be injured," Butler writes, "means that one has the chance to reflect upon injury, to find out the mechanisms of its distribution, to find out who else suffers from permeable borders, unexpected violence, dispossession, and fear, and in what ways" (2004, p. xii). For Susan J. Brison

(2002), individual trauma brings one to terms with an inescapable vulnerability, and resilience is less about the recovery of security and more about learning to live without protective illusions, and simultaneously discovering activist communities that work collectively toward healing, awareness building, justice, and methods of prevention.

In their counterargument to the acceptance of vulnerability as a condition of existence, as a premise, Brad Evans and Julian Reid (2014) resist "the language of insecurity as the natural order of things," a language that, in their estimation, requires the accumulation of "complex skills of adaptation and bouncebackability" (p. xii). An unsettling acceptance of vulnerability, paired with the consequent reliance on resilience in the wake of that vulnerability, prompts questions about subjects who live in a danger that is perceived as the usual, and who remain anxious about the prospect of "future trauma" (p. 98). "What does it mean," Evans and Reid ask, "to suffer or mourn what is yet to materialize? How does it feel to inhabit the ruins of the future?" (p. 98). In their contemplation of a movement "beyond the resilient subject," Evans and Reid adapt Nietzsche's conception of life as a work of art to propose an artful subject, a self that is "actively produced as a non-stable subject that does not seek to emulate some normative standard, but instead forcefully challenges the vulnerable ground which it is said to occupy" (p. 174). Grigris is somewhere in between the vulnerable, yet resilient subject whose body cannot outrun the forces that wound him, and the challenger of that vulnerability who does not accept impending loss or ruin as a given ground. He is not, however, Evans and Reid's subject who is "openly committed to the affirmative potential of the autonomous subject" (2014, p. 13). It is in his dance and in his interdependent connection with others, in his relation to Ayoub, his mother, Mimi, and the women and youth of the village, that he imagines a ground beyond states of insecurity.

Chronic wounding can be striking in its very "ordinariness," in the pervasive return of wounds that serve as mechanisms of oppression and reminders of injurability. Images of suffering viewed from a distance that is presumed safe, however, evoke various manifestations of awareness. Susan Sontag (2003), for one, writes of a "bemused," almost flat awareness that "terrible things happen" at a place beyond, over there (p. 13). As Dalley (2015) observes, there is an ambivalence about the capacity of representations of trauma to evoke solidarity among distant strangers in postcolonial narratives. An awareness of the gaze of distant others is embedded within Haroun's films, as Oscherwitz (2012) has demonstrated, and in a gesture to Aimé Césaire (1939), Haroun's title *A Screaming Man* suggests that we should not see suffering in the form of a distant spectacle of a dancing bear. It is interesting then that the cinematic successor to *A Screaming Man* focuses so intently on Deme's dancing.

A mixture of injury and agility, of labor and art, of resilience and resistance, unravel in Grigris's bodily performances. The film opens with cheering – the sounds of a spectatorship that encourages – and then exuberant faces of those spectators who make room for the performer. Grigris's leg has been damaged – paralyzed – but his dancing is not. Grigris is in possession of his leg – somatic damage may impede certain movements, but it is not, in his dance, disabling. It is, to use the classical terminology of trauma, damage that he can work through. In his dances, there are a series of repeated, mechanical movements, but also the generation of unpredictable new rhythms, variations and illusions. Outside of the space of the club, Grigris's rehearsals – his *répétitions* – demonstrate the physical toil required to balance a damaged body, to gymnastically maneuver the injury, to resist the pressure of gravity. His rehearsals are quiet; he cradles his damaged leg, leaps, choreographs a fall to the floor, then a laborious rise into a handstand. The entanglement of injurability, agility, and aggression are visible in Grigris's dance performance just after his initiation into Moussa's smuggling ring, after he nearly drowns. As sounds of techno music mimic machine gunfire, Grigris lifts his paralyzed leg like a machine gun and pretends to fire, as people cheer (see Figure 4.1). It is a reenactment of violence, a performance of the gestures of firing an automatic weapon that departs from the usual generic scenes of gunfire, a dance that turns repetitive, familiar postures of violence into creative motion. It is a dance that plays with the spectacle of violence, one that sees violence as choreography. After the machine gun poses, Grigris plays with fire on his skin to the sounds of drums (see Figure 4.2). He does not project the fire outward toward the crowd, but caresses the skin of his arms with it, then ingests it orally, bringing fire into a magical illusion of consumption. It is wholly unlike the bodily movements of Moussa's hired man, who points his fingers outward at Grigris as if they were barrel and trigger, a bodily move that repeats the gestures of so many gangster films

Figure 4.1   The entanglement of injurability, agility, and aggression.

(see Figure 4.3). The hired man's actions follow the rituals of violent intimidation: The forcing of Grigris's body into the trunk of the car, the trek to the desolate field, the shots designed to instill terror, the repetitive kicking of the suffering body in the grass. The movements of the gangster film are generic movements in a theatre in which violence is business, lacking in empathy, a theatre that Césaire's poem critiques, a

Figure 4.2   Grigris plays with fire.

Figure 4.3   Moussa's hired man.

sterile spectatorship that responds to a human scream as if it were an entertaining, dancing bear ("Un homme qui crie n'est pas un ours qui danse"). From the very beginning, spectators of the film *Grigris* hear the spectator-characters who watch Grigris dancing. The question of spectatorship lingers, and adds to the film's murky entanglements: Why does the crowd cheer on the body as machine gun, and what is the appeal of the dance – is it the testimony to resilience, the maneu-vering of injury, the eccentricity, the space that celebrates the accomplishments of creative human labor, even when that labor is not, outside the club, viewed as sufficient enough to earn a means to secure its health?

In his discussion of trauma, loss and trash, Harrow (2013), citing Butler, Nicolas Abraham and Maria Torok, summarizes the distinction between loss that is resolv-able through speech, through spoken acts of mourning, and the melancholic man-ifestation of traumatic loss which lingers somatically – loss "incorporated" into an empty space within the body. In a nod to Jacques Rancière, Harrow asserts that speech substitutes for the loss, spoken words become a metaphorical signification, a repeatable act of naming and substitution. In the construction of national memory, decisions about whom and what is to be spoken of (or memorialized), and whom or what is to be forgotten and dismissed, what Harrow calls "the trash of the past," becomes the site, following Derrida, of archive violence (pp. 141–143). Quotidian threats of trauma to the body are incorporated metaphorically in Grigris's physical dance with fire; his dance is also a poetic expression of vulnera-bility, malleability, and internalized danger, a reenactment of mechanical gun violence, rendered in the dance, through illusion, into performance. Simultaneously, the dance is a stripping, a pleasurable seduction of Mimi, the person who is referred to as everybody's girlfriend, trash, the pits, unwelcome at the dinner table, the *vaut-rien*. She is Grigris's focus of attention among the cheering crowd. This brief, somatic performance in the public dance club is a temporary metaphoric substitution, an interlude; as Francesca Castaldi writes, dance is "a form of expres-sion that vanishes at the moment in which it is performed" (2006, p. 3). Yet dance is also choreographed, rehearsed, repeated in multiple performances or rituals, sub-ject to variation, subject to dreaming, subject to various forms of spectatorship, to archiving within a film and elsewhere, to what Lindwe Dovey calls "repetition-with-difference" (2009, p. 11). Building on Alexie Tcheuyap's (2011) insight into a trans-formative poetics of adaptation that rewrites as it repeats, Dovey detects possibilities for imaginative change within projections of repetition, "repetition as a result of human agency rather than the simulacra of technological and industrial machinery" (2009, p. 11). Grigris's dance intertwines the active, choreographed movement of material body and fantasy, machine and illusion, labor and spectacle, somatic "disability" and agility.

Like Haroun's own cinematic projections, Grigris's dancing is an imaginative recreation of repetitive cycles, motions that evoke trauma's looping of old experi-ence, and simultaneously variations on a somatic rhythm that venture beyond repetitive ordinariness. Dancing becomes, as Tcheuyap writes, an integral part of the narrative, "postcolonial dramaturgy" (2011, p. 75). Before the last dancing sequence, Grigris detects the car of Moussa's *homme de main,* who is searching for him after Grigris and Mimi have fled to a village presided over by women while the men have left for the harvest. At night, Mimi and Grigris are close; he caresses her face and her hair. Then the music just happens as he caresses her. We hear the sound of Wasis Diop's singing, no playing machine is visible. Cut to Grigris dancing on a rooftop at night. In the dream space, what seems at first like a vigilant watch on the roof for the adversary who hunts him becomes an agile performance of flight, a bare performance of the body in shorts in a space unlike anything we have seen in the village (see Figure 4.4). His motions evoke the looping wingtips of birds and an athletic defiance of gravity. This vision of Grigris's self-propelled rooftop choreography combines agency and fantasy. The agents of disappointment, the crushers of optimism, are external to the dance. If dance, as Tcheuyap writes, brings the quotidian to cinema, and if cinema rediscovers the ordinary, then Grigris's cinematic dancing exhibits his quotidian surmounting of injury – the agile maneuvering of a paralyzed leg – alongside his injurability beyond the dance.

After the dance scene on the rooftop, the next scene features Mimi searching for Grigris in the morning. She finds him under a tree just beyond the perimeter of the village. It is here that Moussa's *homme de main* finds Grigris, who cannot escape him. Before the arrival of Moussa's right-hand man, Grigris and Mimi's experiences in the village might be characterized by what Virginia Held (2006) calls an ethics of care, an ethics that operates in contrast to a society preoccupied with the dictates of marketplaces and business, and in contrast to moral codes that value

Figure 4.4   The rooftop dance.

the autonomous, self-interested individual. Indeed for Held, the figure of the autonomous individual is an illusion; like Butler's notion of precarity, an ethics of care recognizes enduring human interdependence, from the dependence of every human on others during infancy, to the dependence of the wounded on those who care for them, to the dependence of the frail and elderly on supportive others. As Held writes, "Instead of a society dominated by conflict restrained by law and preoccupied with economic gain, we might have a society that saw as its most important task the flourishing of children and the development of caring relations, not only in personal contexts but among citizens and using governmental institutions" (2006, p. 18). The ability or inability to provide care is at the center of *Grigris*: The desire to care for the surrogate father propels Grigris's actions. An ethics of care exists in his mother's presence at Ayoub's side in the hospital, in Ayoub's adoption of Grigris as his son, and in Mimi's dressing of Grigris's wounds. An ethics of care initially guides the village: Mimi casts aside her wig; she is cared for when she has morning sickness; she is welcome, called darling, shown affection. She is no longer a "good-for-nothing." The women tell her that she is their sister, the baby she carries is a shared joy. Grigris is valued as a teacher of fitness to children, a repairer of radios. It is as if he has entered the protective women's space imagined in Sembène's *Moolaadé* (2004) and now attends to the women's formerly confiscated radios.[9] Grigris and Mimi flirt playfully by the river; Grigris accepts Mimi's forthcoming child as his own; the community lives harmoniously. Ogaga Ifowodo (2013) sees the "return to the past" motif in much of postcolonial literature as a response to the traumatic dismemberment of the past of the colonized. But this is not the village of the return to the source film, not an imaginative recuperation of a lost, authentic past before the blows of imperialism.[10] Grigris and Mimi seem to inhabit a relative utopia created by women in which their vulnerabilities make them subject to affection. The treatment they receive in the village contrasts with the practices of care in the city: Moussa ultimately tries to destroy the man he calls "mon petit"; Alhadj tells Grigris that Ayoub is not his father and therefore not his problem; the grotesque pile of money on the coughing Ayoub's bed demonstrates the overwhelming price of care in institutional spaces.

Initially, the contrasting, protective space of the village of women and children seems to provide passage out of the violent loops, a path out of a world punctuated by the movements of a familiar action/gangster genre in which men's hands and fingers mimic the movement of gunfire before they speed away in their cars. Yet the next scenes knock us out of our reverie, out of the dream-flight of the rooftop dance. When Grigris is caught, Mimi calls to her friend Fatimé (Rémadji Adèle Ngaradoumbaye) for help, and Fatimé shouts, "Women, attack!" The women emerge with sticks and clubs. They demand that Grigris be released. The aggressor refuses, and responds, "Go back to your business." The ensuing violence enacted by the women appears to be rehearsed, performed ritualistically, as if the timing of their movements has been practiced, as if no directions are needed beyond "women, attack." Suddenly the aggressor is hit from behind. They women pound him, one by one, wordlessly. They know what to do without speaking; their clubs and sticks rain down one by one in a rhythm of unsettling, thudding sounds. After the clubbing, they encircle the body, presumably dead, and stare at it. It is a performance that echoes Fanon's call to end trauma with violent action, but with a difference. The women make a pact to keep the murder a secret. They place their hands on top of one another, a gesture that solidifies the pact, a series of movements that also seems to be a practiced ritual. The violence is not followed by articulations of triumph, but by the somber lighting of a match, and the burning of the assailant's car. As they watch it burn, there is the sound of hissing flames. We see their faces watching the flames, then see them again at the burning car, their backs to us. The women turn from the flames, one by one. There are sounds of small explosive bursts from the car. Images of smoke billow up to the left side of the screen. At the end of *Grigris*, like the end of *Daratt*, figures walk away into the distance, their backs to us. In *Daratt*, the figures with their backs to us are a grandfather and grandson, holding hands. In this film, Grigris, Mimi, and Fatimé become barely visible bodies walking onto paths that have changed the narrative, but in ways that elude us.

After a series of films in which men with power – particularly Chadian patriarchs, soldiers and policemen – inflict numerous wounds, it seems significant that Haroun positions women as the dealers of final blows. Grigris has moved from the home of his mother, who shrugs when men do not behave, to a community of women who impose their rules with striking force when the menfolk are not around. Yet there is no systematic change in the clubbing, no enduring peace in this somber ending. It is a disappointing conclusion, a rupture from the previous scenes of peaceful cooperation in the village, an anticlimax, like the hiss of the smoldering car. In a discussion about negligent patriarchs, Haroun once said, "We are like orphans in Chad, and in much of Africa too. It's like a relay race; when you don't have somebody to hand you the baton, you are lost and can't progress" (qtd. in Stuart Jeffries, 2002). If cinema, as Lizelle Bisschoff and Stefanie Van de Peer (2013) suggest, can participate in healing, can point to pathways out from the repetition of blows, the women who carry the batons of violence in the film do not provide a route out of the insidious loop.

Butler asks, rhetorically, whether "experiences of vulnerability and loss have to lead straightaway to military violence and retribution." She follows with "There are other passages" (2004, p. xii). Instead of discovering the alternate passage, the women follow the path taken by the typical action genre in which escape and retribution are achieved through violent bodily action. The women perform their actions ceremoniously, as if following the motions of a genre – the rescue, the beating of the bad guy, the exploding car. In Fanon, violent, masculinist agency compensates for insidious wounding. *Grigris* gives way to a world in which women act as violent protective shields; however, in Haroun this role is a ritual, part of the machinery that produces a continuous cycle of wounding. We have been maneuvered in the film's timeline, returned to a scene of blows. It is a repeated possession, to go back to Caruth, of an agency entangled in violence and wounding, a reversion to the time of multiple blows. The film itself seems to seek a passage out of the loop even as it re-enacts some of the gangster genre's raw materials. After all, within the film's narrative timeline, the figure whose presence inhabits the majority of the film's frame is Grigris, who is not a masculinist hero who calls for the violent defeat of a wound-inducing perpetrator, not a conveyor of masculine agency calling for final control. He is an awkward lover, a quiet presence, a fabulous dancer who creates poetic motion out of paralysis. Grigris' most rigorous action is his dancing.

In its projection of cumulative wounding, how might *Grigris* engage with, adjust or challenge trauma theories? If *Grigris* does participate in a trauma genre – what Berlant sees as one genre among others that manages overwhelming events – just one route (with its generic variations) that narrates catastrophic wounding, then the question posed by Lindsey Moore and Ahmad Qabaha (2015) could be applied to Haroun's film: "What sort of 'working through' is possible when trauma is mundane, material, quotidian, repeated, and eminently repeatable?" (2015, p. 19). Cinema, as Jean-Pierre Bekolo puts it, is not just the story but how it is told.[11] Trauma is not just the wounding event but how it is experienced, comprehended, remembered, articulated, lived with. In its most vivid and brutal visualization on the flat wall, damage in the film is not a spectacle of vivid horror, not a spectacular circus. When Grigris pounds his head against a wall, what is seen during the pounding is the increasingly bloodied curtain on the wall – a sanguine aftermath that will linger on the flat space as a sign of the blow. For Jacqueline Maingard, the task of representing trauma looks to the future; ideally, artistic representations of trauma argue for a "sustainable peace" without "reducing the magnitude of events to the flat screen" (2013, p. xx). Beyond the flat wall of the first wound, beyond the unsettling "undue return" to blows in the finale, beyond the constraints of a genre of violence, is the language of the dance.

When Haroun (2013) says, in his interview with Alexandra Topping, "I feel a responsibility not to leave this country invisible," when he speaks of filmmaking as struggle against invisibility by "raising awareness" about Chad – a country, at the time of the interview, with merely two lone filmmakers, of what kind of aware-ness does he speak? The title of the interview, "Mahamat Saleh Haroun Brings Chad to the World, and Vice-Versa, through Film" (25 February 2013), reads as if Chad *is* invisible, not in the world until it is filmed and screened to others. Haroun's words about invisibility echo Edward Said, for whom "Palestinian cinema dis-covers a world that has been frequently hidden, and makes it visible" (2006, p. 5). Said was writing about the creation of a national narrative, a narrative that finally reveals suppressed, dismissed testimonies of Palestinian trauma. *Grigris* steers away from the route of the nationalist narrative, and moves toward a vision of inhabiting the body differently, of inhabiting the corpus of cinema genres differ-ently. There are at least two projections of "the invisible" in *Grigris*. First, there is the visibility of what Harrow calls "trash," the people whose fates are dismissed in the arena of global neoliberal capitalism, the people whose everyday lives become entrenched in debt relations, as Garritano aptly puts it. Second, what is also rendered visible are the assumptive worlds that structure cinema's action genres. Previously, I have written about Haroun's trashing of the classic Western genre in *Daratt*. The classic Western glorified the wounding of colonial subjects in its screen violence, then circulated and recycled spectacles of masculine valor and retributive wounding. In *Grigris*, the repetition of the raw materials of usual gangster and action films (micro-aggressions, gesticulant death-threats, violent wounding, retribution) might be read as a reflexive choreography that takes on the conceptual tools of a genre that render violence spectacular. In *Africa Shoots Back*, Melissa Thackway cites an African proverb: "A full calabash holds no water" (2003, p. 29). In order to change the contents of a calabash full of violent action cinema, something has to be poured out in order to make room for fresh water, for the innovation. Pervasive assumptions about trauma inhabit action genres: That trauma is outside the range of everyday human experience, that the world is usually secure, that swift-moving, muscular action heroes will safeguard security and save the good and the vulnerable. Trauma, like a genre, has its own constraints: The experience of wounding repeats, the time of the wound seems to loop as the film reel loops.

It is Deme / Grigris's dancing that provides a respite from the storyline – the pace changes to celebrate poetic labor. Coping with traumatic wounding, Ronnie Janoff-Bulman asserts, entails "reconstructing an assumptive world, a task that requires a delicate balance between confronting and avoiding trauma-related thoughts, feelings, and images" (1992, p. 169).[12] Recovery does not mean "a return one's previous condition"; rather, it is a return to the "ability to give energy to everyday life" (1992, pp. 169–170). Looping is encoded in Grigris's dance, but it is transformed into the motion of flight, enacted with incredible balance that seems to defy the codes of gravity. Ultimately, in *Grigris,* the imagined road out of the loop is not in the finale in which women enact scenes of murderous punishment, but in the interludes, in the dancing.

Notes

1   A special issue of *Studies in the Novel* (2008, volume 40, issue 1/2) on postcolonial trauma novels provides a collective challenge to the singular event-based model of trauma. In addition, Stef Craps' *Postcolonial Witnessing: Trauma Out of Bounds* (2013) and Abigail Ward's edited collection, *Postcolonial Traumas: Memory, Narrative, Resistance* (2015), provide helpful overviews of interdisciplinary trauma theories that employ various terms to mark everyday forms of trauma, including continuous traumatic stress syndrome (Gill Straker, 1987), insidious trauma (Maria P. Root, 1992, 1996), shattering of fundamental assumptions (Ronnie Janoff-Bulman, 1992), and race-based trauma (Lisa B. Spanierman and V. Paul Poteat, 2005).
2   In Pierre Janet's analysis in his 1889 *L'automatisme psychologique: Essai de psychologie expérimentale sur les formes inférieures de l'activité humaine*, trauma is characterized by

reactions based on memories of prior threatening events that are, in the aftermath, out of place. See Van der Kolk's (2015) discussion of Janet in his introduction to Peter Levine, *Trauma and Memory: Brain and Body in a Search of the Living Past* (Berkeley, CA: North Atlantic Books, pp. xi–xviii).

3   For a more detailed study of the various phases of trauma studies, see E. Ann Kaplan, 2005, *Trauma Culture: The Politics of Terror and Loss in Media and Literature* (New Brunswick, NJ: Rutgers University Press), pp. 24–41.

4   See Andrew P. Levin, Stuart B. Kleinman, and John S. Adler. 2014. "DSM-5 and post-traumatic stress disorder." *The Journal of the American Academy of Psychiatry and the Law* 42 (2): 146–158.

5   In a conversation with Jean-Pierre Bekolo in Germany in 2015, we discussed trauma. At one point in the conversation, Bekolo compared healing to finding a route out of a circular road. This conversation has sparked my analyses of the search for a passage out of trauma's cyclical loops.

6   MaryEllen Higgins, (2015). "Trashing the Western's Revenge Narrative in Mahamat-Saleh Haroun's *Daratt*." In *The Western in the Global South*. Edited by MaryEllen Higgins, Rita Keresztesi, and Dayna Oscherwitz (New York: Routledge), pp. 96–109.

7   See also Tim Woods, 2007, *African Pasts: Memory and History in African Literatures* (Manchester: Manchester University Press).

8   Many thanks to the editors, Carmela and Ken, for inspiring me to think carefully about the various entanglements performed in Demme's dance movements.

9   I am assuming here that readers are familiar with Sembène's film. In the film, the invocation of the Moolaadé by rebellious women provides shielding for vulnerable girls about to undergo circumcision. In an effort to counter the women's rebellion, patriarchal men in the film order that women's radios be confiscated and burned.

10 Diawara (1992) introduced the "return to the source" film in *African Cinema: Politics and Culture* (Bloomington: Indiana University Press), pp. 159–166.

11 From Bekolo's April 2015 interview with Phyllis Taoua at the University of Arizona in Tuscon: www.youtube.com/watch?v=YAwdgyWEoxM&feature=share

12 Janoff-Bulman takes the term "assumptive worlds" from Hadley Cantril and C.M. Parkes. See Janoff-Bulman, *Shattered Assumptions* (1992), p. 177, note 2.

References

Badiou, Alain. 2013. *Cinema*. Translated by Susan Spitzer. Cambridge: Polity.

Berlant, Lauren. 2011. *Cruel Optimism*. Durham, NC: Duke University Press.

Bisschoff, Lizelle, and Stefanie Van de Peer. 2013. "Representing the Unrepresentable." In *Art and Trauma in Africa: Representations of Reconciliation in Music, Visual Arts, Literature and Film*, edited by Lizelle Bisschoff and Stefanie Van de Peer. 3–25. London: I.B. Tauris.

Brison, Susan J. 2002. *Aftermath: Violence and the Remaking of a Self*. Princeton, NJ: Princeton University Press.

Butler, Judith. 2004. *Precarious Life: The Powers of Mourning and Violence*. London: Verso.

Caruth, Cathy, ed. 1995. *Trauma: Explorations in Memory*. Baltimore, MD: Johns Hopkins University Press.

Caruth, Cathy. 1996. *Unclaimed Experience*. Baltimore, MD: Johns Hopkins University Press.

Castaldi, Francesca. 2006. *Choreographies of African Identities*. Chicago: University of Illinois Press.

Césaire, Aimé. 2013. *The Original 1939* Notebook on a Return to my Native Land. Translated and edited by A. James Arnold and Clayton Eshleman. Middletown, CT: Wesleyan University Press.

Craps, Stef. 2013. *Postcolonial Witnessing: Trauma Out of Bounds*. New York: Palgrave Macmillan.

Craps, Stef. 2014. "Beyond Eurocentrism: Trauma Theory in the Global Age." In *The Future of Trauma Theory: Contemporary Literary and Cultural Criticism*, edited by Gert Beulens, Sam Durrant, and Robert Eaglestone. London: Routledge.

Dalley, Hamish. 2015. "The Question of 'Solidarity' in Postcolonial Trauma Fiction: Beyond the Recognition Principle." *Humanities* 4: 369–392. DOI: 10.3390/h4030369

D'Almeida, Irène Assiba. 1994. *Francophone African Women Writers: Destroying the Emptiness of Silence*. Gainesville: University Press of Florida.

Diawara, Manthia. 1992. *African Cinema: Politics and Culture*. Bloomington: Indiana University Press.

Diawara, Manthia. 2010. *African Film: New Forms of Aesthetics and Politics*. Munich: Prestel.

Dovey, Lindiwe. 2009. *African Film and Literature: Adapting Violence to the Screen*. New York: Columbia University Press.

Eaglestone, Robert. 2014. "Knowledge, 'Afterwardsness,' and the Future of Trauma Theory." In *The Future of Trauma Theory: Contemporary Literary and Cultural Criticism*, edited by Gert Beulens, Sam Durrant, and Robert Eaglestone. London: Routledge.

Evans, Brad, and Julian Reid. 2014. *Resilient Life: The Art of Living Dangerously*. Cambridge, UK: Polity.

Fanon, Franz. 1963. *The Wretched of the Earth*. Trans. Richard Philcox. New York: Grove Press.

Gana, Nouri. 2014. "Trauma Ties: Chiasmus and Community in Lebanese Civil War Literature." In *The Future of Trauma Theory: Contemporary Literary and Cultural Criticism*, edited by Gert Beulens, Sam Durrant, and Robert Eaglestone. London: Routledge.

Garritano, Carmela. 2018. "Living Precariously in the African Postcolony: Debt and Labor Relations in the Films of Mahamat-Saleh Haroun." 58 (2) *Cinema Journal*.

Harrow, Kenneth W. 2013. *Trash: African Cinema From Below*. Bloomington: Indiana University Press.

Held, Virginia. 2006. *The Ethics of Care: Personal, Political, and Global*. Oxford: Oxford University Press.

Higgins, MaryEllen. 2015. "Trashing the Western's Revenge Narrative in Mahamat-Saleh Haroun's *Daratt*." In *The Western in the Global South*. Edited by MaryEllen Higgins, Rita Keresztesi, and Dayna Oscherwitz, 96–109. New York: Routledge.

Ifowodo, Ogaga. 2013. *History, Trauma, and Healing in Postcolonial Narratives: Reconstructing Identities*. New York: Palgrave Macmillan.

Janoff-Bulman, Ronnie. 1992. *Shattered Assumptions: Towards a New Psychology of Trauma*. New York: Free Press.

Jeffries, Stuart. 14 Nov. 2002. "Out of Africa." [Interview with Mahamat-Saleh Haroun]. *The Guardian*. Web.

Kaplan, E. Ann. 2005. *Trauma Culture: The Politics of Terror and Loss in Media and Literature*. New Brunswick: Rutgers University Press.

Levin, Andrew P., Stuart B. Kleinman, and John S. Adler. 2014. "DSM-5 and Posttraumatic Stress Disorder." *The Journal of the American Academy of Psychiatry and the Law*, 42 (2): 146–158.

Maingard, Jacqueline. 2013. Foreword. *Art and Trauma in Africa: Representations of Reconciliation in Music, Visual Arts, Literature and Film*. Edited by Lizelle Bisschoff and Stefanie Van de Peer. London: I.B. Tauris.

Moore, Lindsey, and Ahmad Qabaha. 2015. "Chronic Trauma, (Post)Colonial Chronotopes and Palestinian Lives: Omar Robert Hamilton's Though I Know the River is Dry/Ma'a Anni A'rif Anna al-Nahr Qad Jaf." In *Postcolonial Traumas: Memory, Narrative, Resistance*. Edited by Abigail Ward, 14–29. London: Palgrave Macmillan.

Olaniyan, Tejumola. 1995. *Scars of Conquest/Masks of Resistance: The Invention of Cultural Identities in African, African-American, and Caribbean Drama*. Oxford: Oxford University Press.

Oscherwitz, Dayna. 2012. "Bye Bye Hollywood: African Cinema and Its Double in Mahamat-Saleh Haroun's *Bye Bye Africa*." In *Hollywood's Africa After 1994*. Edited by MaryEllen Higgins, Athens: Ohio University Press.

Oscherwitz, Dayna. 2014. "*Dry Season* Directed by Mahamat-Saleh Haroun (Review)." *African Studies Review*, 57 (2): 237–239.

Rogers, Annie G. 2006. *The Unsayable: The Hidden Language of Trauma*. New York: Ballantine Books.

Root, Maria P. 1992. "Reconstructing the Impact of Trauma on Personality." *Personality and Psychopathology: Feminist Reappraisals*. Edited by Laura S. Brown and Mary Ballou, 229–265. New York: Guilford Press.

Root, Maria P. 1996. "Women of Color and Traumatic Stress in 'Domestic Captivity': Gender and Race as Disempowering Statuses." In *Ethnocultural Aspects of Posttraumatic Stress Disorder: Issues, Research, and Clinical Applications*. Edited by Anthony J. Marsella, Matthew J. Friedman, Ellen T. Gerrity, and Raymond M. Scurfield, 363–387. Washington, DC: American Psychological Association.

Rothberg, Michael. 2014. "Preface: Beyond Tancred and Clorinda – Trauma Studies for Implicated Subjects." In *The Future of Trauma Theory: Contemporary Literary and Cultural Criticism*. Edited by Gert Beulens, Sam Durrant, and Robert Eaglestone. London: Routledge.

Said, Edward W. 2006. "Preface." *Dreams of a Nation: On Palestinian Cinema*. Edited by Hamid Dabashi, 1–5. London: Verso.

Sembène, Ousmane. 1974 [1962] *Tribal Scars*. Translated by Len Ortzen. London: Heinemann.

Sontag, Susan. 2003. *Regarding the Pain of Others*. New York: Picador.

Spanierman, Lisa B., and V. Paul Poteat. 2005. "Moving Beyond Complacency to Commitment: Multicultural Research in Counseling Psychology." *Counseling Psychologist*, 33 (4): 513–23. DOI: 10.1177/0011000005276469

Straker, Gill. 1987. "The Continuous Traumatic Stress Syndrome: The Single Therapeutic Interview." *Psychology in Society*, 8: 48–79.

Stewart, Garrett. 2007. *Framed Time: Toward a Postfilmic Cinema*. Chicago, IL: Chicago University Press.

Taoua, Phyllis, and Jean-Pierre Bekolo. 4 April 2006. "Phyllis Taoua's Conversation with Jean-Pierre Bekolo." University of Arizona. Accessed 26 March 2018. www.youtube.com/watch?v=YAwdgyWEoxM&feature=share

Tcheuyap, Alexie. 2011. *Postnationalist African Cinemas*. Manchester: Manchester University Press.

Thackway, Melissa. 2003. *Africa Shoots Back: Alternative Perspectives in Sub-Saharan Francophone African Film*. Bloomington, Indiana University Press.

Topping, Alexandra, and Mahamat Saleh Haroun. 25 Feb. 2013. "Mahamat-Saleh Haroun Brings Chad to the World, and Vice-Versa, through Film" (Interview). *The Guardian*. Accessed 26 March 2018. www.theguardian.com/world/2013/feb/25/mahamat-saleh-haroun-chad-film

Van der Kolk, Bessel. 2015. "Foreword." *Trauma and Memory: Brain and Body in a Search for The Living Past*, by Peter A. Levine. xi–xviii. Berkeley, CA: North Atlantic Books.

Ward, Abigail, ed. 2015. *Postcolonial Traumas: Memory, Narrative, Resistance*. London: Palgrave Macmillan.

Woods, Tim. 2007. *African Pasts: Memory and History in African Literatures*. Manchester: Manchester University Press.

Filmography

Haroun, Mahamat-Saleh. 2002. *Abouna*. Chad. Duo Films, Goï-Goï Productions.

Haroun, Mahamat-Saleh. 2006. *Daratt*. 2006. Chad. Chinguitty Films, Entre Chiens et Loups, Goï-Goï Productions.

Haroun, Mahamat-Saleh. 2010. *Un homme qui crie (A Screaming Man)*. Chad/France. Pili Films, Goï-Goï Productions.

Haroun, Mahamat-Saleh. 2013. *Grigris*. Chad. Pili Films, Goï-Goï Productions.

Haroun, Mahamat-Saleh. 2016. *Hissein Habré: une tragédie tchadienne (Hissein Habré: A Chadian Tragedy)*. Chad/France. Pili Films, Goï-Goï Productions.

Kibinge, Judy. 2013. *Something Necessary*. Kenya. One Fine Day Films, Ginger Ink Films.

Nacro, Fanta Régina. 2004. *La nuit de la verité (The Night of Truth)*. Burkina Faso. Acrobates Film, Les Films du Defi.

Ruhorahoza, Kivu. 2011. *Matière grise (Grey Matter)*. Rwanda. Storymakers TV, Camera Club, POV Productions, Scarab Studio.

Sembène, Ousmane. 2004. *Moolaadé*. Senegal/Burkina Faso. Ciné-Sud Promotion, Centre Cinematographie Morocain, Cinétéléfilms, Films Doomireew, Les Films Terre Africaine.

Sissoko, Cheick Oumar. 1999. *La Genèse (Genesis)*. Mali. Kora Films, Balanzan, CNPC.

Suleman, Ramadan. 2004. *Zulu Love Letter* (2004). South Africa. Jacques Bidou, Bhekizizwe Peterson, Marianne Dumoulin.

Traoré, Sékou. 2014. *L'oeil du cyclone (Eye of the Storm)*. Burkina Faso. Avalon Films.

5

Reframing Human Rights
Hotel Rwanda *(2004)*, A Screaming Man *(2010)*, *Global Conflict, and International Intervention*

Dayna Oscherwitz

Mahamat-Saleh Haroun has become one of the most critically acclaimed African directors of the past two decades. His films, from *Bye Bye Africa* (1999) to *GriGris* (2014), have, like the works of his compatriots Issa Serge Coelo and Abakar Chene Massar, done much to bring the African nation of Chad to the screen, foregrounding the complexities of civil conflicts that have been ongoing during much of Chad's post-independence existence, but also looking beyond the conflict to the experience of ordinary people leading or trying to lead ordinary lives. The complex, often understated, and multilayered nature of Haroun's films permits engagement with the full range of human experience, exploring an array of conditions and concerns and their impact on the lives of people from various walks of life.

One of the leitmotifs of Haroun's filmmaking has been an exploration, both at the narrative and the aesthetic level, of the ways in which individuals perceive and interact with those around them in conditions of hardship and strife. Specifically, Haroun's films explore the conditions under which individual characters choose or choose not to consider other people's needs, desires, rights, or lives as equal to or greater their own. The exploration of individual agency and equality and the degree to which these are recognized in contexts of uncertainty – such as war or economic hardship – points to the broader issue of human rights, the principal subject of Haroun's filmmaking. This focus on human rights appears in various guises in his films, ranging from the treatment of those who are HIV positive or believed to be in *Bye Bye Africa* (1999) to the question of war crimes and reconciliation in *Daratt* (2006). It is, however, Haroun's 2010 film, *A Screaming Man*, which offers the most sustained exploration of human rights, its role and failures in contemporary Africa and its relationship to the parallel discourses of

A Companion to African Cinema, First Edition. Edited by Kenneth W. Harrow and Carmela Garritano.
© 2019 John Wiley & Sons, Inc. Published 2019 by John Wiley & Sons, Inc.

globalization and development The film, which won the Jury Prize at Cannes in 2010, raises questions of foreign interventions, of the status of refugees from war-torn nations, and the actions – or lack of action – of the UN and other NGOs in conflict zones as well as the civilians who find themselves caught in them. However, its principal investigation concerns the relationship between human rights and development, and the ways in which neoliberal globalization has adopted and intertwined itself with the rhetoric of human rights, promoting privatization and unrestricted markets as essential guarantors of individual liberty.

This investigation is embedded in a parallel exploration of the relationship bet-ween observation and action, both in the context of human rights and in film spectatorship. Observation and intervention form not only two of the central poles of international human rights, but also the two poles of engaged art, in which spectatorship is intended to lead the spectator to action. The double focus of Haroun's film leads to a meditation on the relationship of individual observa-tion and action for both human rights and neoliberal development, but also for the role of art, and the image specifically, in reflecting, promoting, or sustaining dominant discourses and practices. Ultimately, the film suggests that both privat-ization and the ensuing focus on the individual erodes communal relations and encourages individuals to promote individual status at the expense of the community or collective identities. Similarly, the film finds that the individual gaze or the witnessing, either directly or through mediation, of individual suffering does not necessarily produce empathy, as the rhetoric of human rights has for centuries presumed, much less humanitarian intervention. Therefore, in both cases – development and observation – the film finds a privileging of the individual – either as actor or spectator – that is incompatible with the universalist ideals and egalitarian ambitions of human rights.

Individualism, Bearing Witness, Development, and Human Rights

Both human rights and cinema are organized around two fundamental and inter-twined concepts – that of the individual and that of witnessing or watching. In the context of human rights, the principal unit of measurement – the metric against which the presence or absence of rights is measured – is the individual, and it is the degree to which the rights and agency of the individual are respected that deter-mines the degree to which human rights are seen to be in force.

Human rights, as defined by the United nations office of the High commissioner are "universal and inalienable" rights "such as the right to life, equality before the law and freedom of expression; economic, social and cultural rights, such as the right to work, social security and education, or collective rights, such as the rights to development and self-determination..." (2016). The paradigm of human rights has risen to prominence in public discourse in the past several decades. However, it has a much longer evolutionary arc. Historians of human rights note that, while elements of such rights-based thinking date to antiquity – elements may be found in for example in the Babylonian Code of the Hammurabi or in the Persian policy of religious tolerance under Cyrus the great from the sixth century BC – the evolution of what we now understand as human rights evolved from thinking about the relationship of the individual to the state in the European Enlightenment (Anderson, 2006; Freeman, 2011; Hunt, 2007). The concept of natural rights evolved in the Enlightenment as a fusion of new principles of equality and universalism with pre-existing theories of natural rights, such as the Roman concept of *jus naturis* (Millgate 2006, pp. 56–60). In the early nineteenth century, this conception of rights fused with nationalism to produce a nation-based conception of rights in a national context (Hunt 2007, pp. 20–21, 177). The result is a politicized concept of rights conceived of in national terms (the relationship of individual to society or the state), that holds that all individuals are equal, possessed with the same rights and privileges and entitled to the same opportunities. This is the vision that is articulated in the Universal Declaration of Human Rights of 1948, and the one that governs conceptions of human rights to the present day.[1]

In this model of human rights, the guarantees of equality and opportunity are presumed to be everywhere applicable, desirable and possible; all nations in the world are held to equivalent standards both in terms of the relationship of citizen to state and in terms of individual opportunities within and outside of the nation state. This is the conception that governs the UN Convention on Human Rights, for example, which has been signed by all nations. Those places in the world where the relationship of individual to state does not correspond to the human rights-based model are seen to be either evolving toward that or in need of being brought to that point. Thus, human rights-based interpretations of social and political relations are both national, focusing more on the behaviors of states than individual, and developmental, regarding all nations as somewhere along a fixed trajectory toward a common point (Donnelly, 2013; Howard-Hassmann, 2010; Uvin, 2002).

While they are independent and in many ways antithetical discourses, development discourse has, particularly since the fall of the Soviet Union, progressively fused itself with the rhetoric of human rights (Ake, 2001; Ishay, 2004; Uvin 2002). As Micheline Ishay has noted, those "who hold this position are generally confident that economic liberalization, once it takes root… will promote… affluent societies and stable democratic institutions" (2008, p. x). This is, at least in part, due to points of overlap already present in the two discourses. In this model, the global circulation of goods and services and the unrestricted markets associated with globalization lead, at least theoretically, to economic growth, which leads to greater individual economic prosperity, which in turn leads to greater personal freedom and individual rights (Howard-Hassmann 2010, p. 18). It is this fusion of the discourses of development and human rights, and the ensuing emphasis on individual prosperity and individualism more broadly as the guarantor of collective liberty and equality – that which Jean and John Comaroff have termed "millennial capitalism" – that *A Screaming Man* challenges.

Benedict Anderson has argued that the framework and apparatus that permitted and disseminated the type of thinking that led to human rights, the nation state, and the discourse of economic liberalization or development was born in the rise of "print capitalism" which created a media for disseminating information in such a way that it would easily circulate across geographic borders (2006). Lynn Hunt, following from this, points to the rise of new media and narrative forms, such as the novel, and suggests that these newly evolved forms, and the novel, specifically, contributed to the universalist, rights-based thinking that emerged in the eighteenth century (2007, pp. 70–76). The novel, in Hunt's view, was critical to the evolution of rights-based thinking because novels made *visible* other realities, created a window onto them, permitted the reader to see and observe other people and modes of being, creating empathy and encouraging action or intervention from the reader on behalf of those in need (Hunt, 2007). Thus, the novel, in Hunt's analysis, creates a kind of seeing that leads to doing, a mechanism to translate observation into action. Subsequently, other narrative forms, such as cinema, emerged and became the dominant media through which people are persuaded to act to guarantee the rights of others. Regardless of the specific narrative or representational form, therefore, from relatively early, the paradigm of human rights has relied upon the principle of translating observation into action and the principle that seeing or witnessing something, even in mediated form, produces a sense of empathy that motivates the spectator into action.

During approximately the same period in which human rights and development discourse became fused, there emerged a number of "engaged" narrative films whose purpose seems to be to draw attention or make visible human rights abuses or related causes or issues to audiences in the Global North. Recent examples of such narrative human rights films include *Blood Diamond* (Zwick, 2006), which draws attention to role of conflict minerals, *Tears of the Sun* (Fuqua, 2003), which depicts the human costs of civil conflict, or *The Constant Gardener* (Meirelles, 2005), which foregrounds abuses of the pharmaceutical industry in Africa, and, perhaps the best-known example, *Hotel Rwanda* (George, 2004), which explores international non-intervention in the Rwandan genocide. What these films have in common is their tendency to use popular narrative cinema to publicize contexts of conflict and oppression, potentially in order to motivate spectators to care about the distant people and places and to act – directly or through monetary contributions or political action – to correct a past or present injustice (Gibney and Betsalel, 2011).

Such films would seem to constitute the twenty-first-century equivalent of the novel in Hunt's analysis – mediated representations that reflect on human suffering and rights abuses in places remote from the implied audience, representations that could or should motivate the spectator to act to correct the injustices depicted. In these films, however, the act of seeing and witnessing seems to function in a way that is antithetical to producing such outcomes. First, these films employ the aesthetics of classical film narration, which, Adorno and Horkheimer have suggested, "denies its audience any dimension in which they might roam freely in imagination – contained by the film's framework but unsupervised by its precise actualities" (2002, p. 100). They function, therefore, to train the spectator "to identify the film directly with reality" (Adorno and Horkheimer 2002, p. 100). Moreover, Adorno and Horkheimer argue that such films also enact a substitution of a fictive resolution for an actual one, thus each is a representation that "endlessly cheats its consumers out of what it endlessly promises" (2002, p. 111) or that demand a type of real-world action that is foreclosed by the narrative resolution of the fictional film.

Jacques Rancière has similarly meditated upon the relationship between art and reality and the capacity for "engaged" art to motivate a spectator to act in the real world. He notes that engaged artists, like the directors of the film in question, seek "to produce a form of consciousness, an intensity of feeling, an energy for action" (2009, p. 14). However, he similarly finds that "mediation… can be nothing but a fatal illusion of autonomy, trapped in the logic of dispossession and its concealment" (2009, p. 15). Moreover, he finds the image to be particularly fraught in this regard, arguing that films, like those under consideration, participate in a representational "system that drowns us in a flood of images, and images of horror in particular, thereby rendering us insensitive to the banalized reality of these horrors" (2011, p. 96). Thus, for Rancière, it is not only the case that individual films, such as the human rights films noted, undermine any impetus for action they seem to create, but it is also the case that such films participate in a broader system of representation that functions, progressively, to erode the empathy and sense of urgency necessary to such action.

As Rancière's analysis suggests, human rights films such as *Hotel Rwanda* are not the first films, nor even the first collections of images to exploit the process of seeing or observing in order to promote and simultaneously defer or foreclose spectator engagement on the subject of human rights. Images have been a central component in constructing narratives about Africa, in particular, that have circulated globally since the colonial era (Landau and Kaspin 2002 pp. 4–40), and they have likewise been integral in constituting the continent as a site for both development-based globalized action and human rights-based interventions. Whereas, in earlier centuries the images used to promote Africa as a site of intervention took the form of paintings, etchings, postcards and photographs, in the contemporary era, it is the moving images of television and cinema and more recently the Internet that have reframed old rhetoric through the double filter of economic and democratic development. Such images of Africa may be heterogeneous, but, over time they have formed a related system of images that operates in ways consistent with the mechanism of banalization that Rancière identifies. Moreover, because this particular set of images has origins located within a particular set of power relations, it is, as Giorgio Agamben has asserted, a restrictive apparatus that functions to "capture, orient, determine, intercept, model, control, or secure the gestures, behaviors, opinions or discourses of living beings" (2009, pp. 2–14).

The apparatus function to which Agamben refers is particular to the filmic image, which plays another game of substitution and deferment in that cinema is a highly ideological but erases or conceals this ideological function. As Jean-Louis Baudry asserted, this ideological sleight of hand is a result of the cinematic process – the formal properties of visual construction, from camerawork to editing – which function to "conceal" the cinematic work, producing "ideological surplus" rather than a "knowledge effect" (Baudry 1986, pp. 40–41). This combination of effects means that in narrative films, in particular, the cinematic image imposes the ideological, social, and economic weight of its cultural context upon the spectator precisely by convincing the spectator that it is doing no such thing (Heath 1976, p. 226). Thus, conventionally narrative human rights films, like *Blood Diamond* or *Hotel Rwanda* persuade the observer or spectator through his or her mediated witnessing of the narrative resolution to a particular problem or issue that he or she has addressed that issue, all the while deferring any such action.

The cinematic image took on this function from its origins, at the height of the colonial era. As early as 1896, a mere one year after the successful projection of the inaugural films of Auguste and Louis Lumière, the brothers sent Alexandre Promio, one of their cameramen, to North Africa, Egypt, and Palestine. A few years later, Pathé, one of the first major French film studios, likewise sent Albert Machin into Sub-Saharan Africa, resulting in a number of African documentaries for that studio. Machin and Promio's films and other early documentaries' cinematic texts were invested with the ideological baggage of colonialism. They allowed spectators in the Global North to see Africa, and in seeing to perceive the need for active intervention. These early films were informed, as Peter Bloom has argued, with assumptions of a dichotomy between "civilized" and "uncivilized" populations and "developed' and "undeveloped" economies (2008, p. 135), reflecting and projecting the ideology of European superiority and colonial privilege in both the colonies and the metropole. As Frank Ukadike notes, these films were also consumed by African audiences and functioned to "instill into the minds of the viewers the 'dominating image' of the white man over the African" (1991, p. 74).

Later narrative films, including those grouped under the rubric of "colonial cinema," similarly "reflected and reinforced the machinery of cultural hegemony…[and] legitimated the racial privileges of European workers, diverted attention away from their own exploitation, and disabled impulses toward solidarity with women and colonial peoples" (Slavin 2001, p. 3). These films did so not only through the images and narratives that composed them, but also through their visual composition, character-driven linear plot lines, rising action, and narrative trajectories of progress. Such films, according to Slavin, also relegate colonial peoples to the background of the action, using Africa, primarily, and other colonial locales, as exotic backdrop to narratives of European progress, both encouraging and justifying European interventions on the continent.

While the contemporary human rights narrative films are not identical to colonial-era cinema, they nonetheless inherit its ideologically invested cinematic practices which they fuse with the observation to action paradigm of the discourse of human rights. Terry George's *Hotel Rwanda*, one of the best-known examples of this type of film, deploys the observation / action paradigm to both alarm and reassure the spectator on the subject of human rights, tacitly affirming discourses of development in the process. On the surface, *Hotel Rwanda* differs from many of the other rights-based narrative films from the Global North dealing with Africa. The film's protagonist, Paul Rusesabagina, although played by American actor Don Cheadle, is an African character, not an American or European. This is atypical of such films, which usually feature an American or European character as the protagonist. Moreover, the film provides some historical specificity to the events it depicts, rather than exploring human rights issues in vague, fictionalized contexts, as several of the other films of this type do. In fact, because the film explores a well-known and historical failure of human rights and international bodies such as the UN, it seems to question to validity of the human rights paradigm, altogether, as well as the observation to action model it represents.

However, upon closer inspection, *Hotel Rwanda* engages very efficiently in the ideological game of foregrounding an injustice only to reassure the spectator that such injustice has been resolved. Moreover, this resolution is presented in the film as a consequence of economic neoliberalism, making *Hotel Rwanda* a vehicle for the fusion of development discourse and human rights. The film starts, for example, just prior to the violent massacres that occurred as part of the genocide, and its narrative arc results in the conflict coming to an end. Therefore, despite the brutality and violence, there is a positive, developmental trajectory to the film's narrative arc. Moreover, because the film deals with past historic events widely regarded as finished or closed, the sense of closure offered by the film is not merely cinematic. *Hotel Rwanda* is also paradoxical in the sense that it reinforces ideologies it ostensibly serves to question. As Heike Härting has observed, for example, the film's prominent display of the bodies of the victims of the genocide participates in "the cultural politics of affect" reinforcing the interventionist rhetoric of human rights even as it displays its obvious failure (2008, p. 61) and normalizing the brutality of political violence in the ways Rancière has suggested.

The film's linear, progressive, rising narrative and its use of suspense force close identification with the protagonist, Paul, who is distinct, in the beginning of the film, for his appreciation and adept mastery of globalized capitalism, and for his close association with the European-owned hotel in which he works. Paul "evolves" over the course of the film, from indifferent individualist to engaged activist, and works to correct or at least mitigate the violence and abuse that surrounds him. His entire evolution, however, is grounded in his association with the hotel – which he ultimately turns into a safe-haven. The evolution from indifferent observer to humanitarian, therefore, is on one-level an evolution away from individualism and toward communalism – a worldview in which the well-being of others takes priority over self-advancement, but it occurs and is dependent upon the presence and resources of a global multination corporation – the very symbol of global economic neoliberalization. Thus, the film seems to support the assertion of the proponents of development that economic liberalization leads to stability and democratization. The spectator, through the vicarious witnessing of the violence in Rwanda and the end to that violence is made to feel enlightened and aligned with the egalitarian rhetoric of human rights, but is also, unwittingly, reassured of the value of globalized capitalism.

There is another aspect to *Hotel Rwanda* that draws attention to the contradictory and paradoxical function of narrative human rights films. *Hotel Rwanda* restages probably the best-known example of mass killing from the contemporary era, and it was so precisely because it was a widely mediatized and therefore widely *seen* and *observed* event. This observation, however, yields, in real terms, no compensatory or corrective action, at least at the historical moment of the violence, and in many ways, yielded little in the way of empathy, at least from elites in the Global North. In restaging and visually correcting this failure to act, therefore, *Hotel Rwanda* inherently questions the observation to action paradigm that it appropriates and embodies. It "corrects" the failures of human rights in Rwanda by depicting a narrative resolution and end to the violence, a resolution that the film attributes indirectly, to the economic liberalization of Rwanda.

Like *Hotel Rwanda*, *A Screaming Man* recounts the violence associated with civil conflict in an African nation through the experience of a married, family man. The film is set in a hotel in Ndjamena, Chad's capital city, in a period of détente in the civil conflicts that have marked that nation since shortly after independence. The film's protagonist, Adam (Youssef Djaoro) is a former national swimming champion, still called "Champion" by those who know him, and he has worked as a pool attendant in a hotel for many years. Adam's grown son, Abdel (Diouc Koma) also works as a pool attendant, and is beginning to outshine his father in terms of his popularity with the guests. The hotel in which they work, which is frequented by foreign tourists, has been taken over by Chinese owners, and the new manager, Madame Wang (Heling Li) begins process of restructuring that costs several people, including Adam's best friend, a cook and Congolese immigrant named David (Marius Yelolo), their jobs. Adam is also ultimately displaced from his position as a pool attendant in favor of his son, although he is assigned to take the position of gatekeeper, instead, displacing his friend Étienne (John Mbaikoubou) from that job.

The family and interpersonal drama (or melodrama) that would one would normally expect from a story centered on the displacement of the father by the son is both complicated and disrupted, in the logic of the narrative, by the resumption of hostilities among the warring parties. Adam is ordered by the local military commander, Ahmat (Émile Abossolo M'bo), to either send his son, Abdel, to fight

Figure 5.1   Adam and Abdel in competition in the hotel swimming pool.

in the war to pay a large tax to exempt him from combat. Adam, without telling either his son or his wife, Mariam (Hadje Fatime N'Goua), neglects to pay the tax, a decision motivated both by his recent demotion from his job and the economic and personal insecurity this demotion provokes. Adbel, who unbeknownst to his father, is expecting his own child with his girlfriend Djénéba (Djénéba Koné), is ultimately forcibly conscripted into the army and is subsequently gravely injured during battle. As conflict engulfs the city, many of the residents, including a disguised Ahmet, flee to neighboring Cameroon. Adam journeys to recover Abdel and bring him back to the family and potentially to correct his earlier actions, but Abdel dies during the return journey, near the banks of the Chari river. Adam releases Adbel's body into the river, and the final scene is of Abdel's body floating downstream, with Adam looking on.

Observation is both thematically and narratively central to *A Screaming Man*. The film is structured through an interplay of gazes – Adam's, Abdel's, Madame Wang's, Mariam's Djénéba's, the army's – all of which drive the events in the narrative and suggest the relative power or powerlessness of the characters within it. Moreover, observation is tied directly to the themes of both neoliberal privatization – through the surveilling gaze of Madame Wang, the hotel manager, and to human rights, through the gazes of UN troops who appear both at the hotel, and later on the roads as Adam journeys to find Abdel. In addition to the personalized observation and looking enacted by the characters within the film, there is also a camera – Abdel's camera – and its unseen images, both of which figure centrally in the narrative. This camera, of which Adam disapproves, connects the personal act of looking with the official observations of the international community and the multinational corporate boss because Abdel asserts that he uses the camera

Figure 5.2   Abdel takes a selfie.

precisely to document what is going on around him, but it also stands in for the filmic gaze, or the documentation of the external film. Thus, *A Screaming Man* negotiates multiple gazes, all of which observe and are, to some degree, impli- cated in the military and civil conflict that unfolds. Finally, the film draws attention at various points to the act of looking engaged in by the filmic spectator, who is often positioned – quite overtly – as a spectator watching the action and interper- sonal relations as they unfold, which in turn inscribes the spectator in the relational network of gazes and the actions they observe. This raises the question of whether looking leads to empathy, not only on the character-to-character level – where the film suggests it does not – but also at the level of spectatorship of the film itself.

In addition to positioning observation and spectatorship as central to concerns about empathy, action, development, and human rights, *A Screaming Man*'s self- conscious staging of the act of spectatorship draws attention to the fact that the various conflicts in Chad have been largely unseen in international media, despite the protracted nature of the violence and its connections to other, more widely mediatized conflicts, such as the conflict between the government of neighboring Nigeria and the forces of Boko Haram (Skinner, 2016). This raises questions about the role of seeing and acting at the multinational level, and questions the motives and actions of governments and allied actors, all of whom tend to privilege certain groups and regions over others, for reasons that have less to do with the nature and severity of rights infringement than with national and economic interests (Simms and Trim, 2011). In this way, the film collapses the presumed relationship between intervention and observation in human rights narratives – the two poles in international rhetoric surrounding both conflict and human rights – and it challenges the assumption of both discourses that observation leads to empathy which then leads to benevolent intervention. Similarly, the film undermines the asserted link between economic liberalization and respect for human rights, presenting a nuanced exploration of the potential roles of individual, corporate, state, and international actors in times of strife and conflict.

If looking and acting form the thematic framework for *A Screaming Man*, the film's narrative framework derives from a set of embedded conflicts, the one national and the other both personal and economic. The personal/global conflict is that of Adam's attempt to keep his job at the hotel where he has worked for many years. The hotel, which is specifically presented as a previously nationalized and newly globalized hotel, becomes the site of meditation on the impact of privatization – which is a key component of economic liberalism and development, as defined by the World Bank and the International Monetary Fund, and which is argued to increase both prosperity and liberty by these institutions and proponents of development (Nellis and Kikeri, 1989). The hotel in the film was, to some degree, was a globalized space even prior to the privatization that precedes the narrative action, in that it serves foreign tourists and business people who travel to Chad. However, in the film's pre-history, the hotel's nationalization embodied a collective and national sense of community or ownership, and a specifically Chadian presence in the global economic network. In the narrative present, however, the hotel has been taken over by a (presumably) Chinese corporation, and it is in the context of that takeover, and a subsequent focus on profitability over job-creation, that the downsizing that triggers the personal conflict in the film occurs.

The solidarity that seems to have previously existed among the workers is progressively supplanted by a self-interested survivalism that not only pits friends against one another for the same job (Adam versus Étienne), but also pits father against son. Thus, the change in the ownership structure of the hotel from collective/socialized or state ownership, to private, corporate ownership, produces a parallel breakdown in social relations and a shift in emphasis, at the personal level, from collective appurtenance and solidarity, to rugged individualism, and this shift works not to promote democracy and equality, but rather to undermine them.

If discourses of development are to be believed, the privatization of the hotel should lead to increasing prosperity and democracy, and liberty for all characters in the film. After all, the privatization of the hotel follows the prescription for development set out by such multinational agencies as the IMF and the World Bank, who often link neoliberalism to an expansion of democratic practice (Ake, 1996). What occurs, however, is a decline in prosperity for all actors, and a related decline in both personal liberty and security as well as a growing disregard for the liberty and security of others, which could be equated to a deterioration of human rights. The personal/economic conflict embodied by Adam's fear for his job, for example, is embedded in a widening national and regional conflict marked by family, the resumption of hostilities among the warring parties in Chad, one that is driven, as the films suggests, by the self-interested actions of local military commanders, like Adam's friend Ahmat (Émile Abossolo M'bo), who order him to either send his son, Abdel, to fight in the war to pay a large tax to exempt him from combat.

The film never makes clear, nor can the spectator of the film easily discern, through watching, what Adam's real intentions are. He does not pay the tax, but there is insufficient information to indicate whether this is because he is unable to pay, because he is paralyzed by indecision, or because this is a deliberate decision. This inability to resolve, through spectator observation, one of the central questions of the film, calls the connection between observation and empathy into question. The spectator, as noted, observes all of Adam's actions, but despite this, can't understand what he is thinking or feeling, or why he does what he does. Adam's failure or decision to pay the military tax parallels Abdel's decision to accept the position at the hotel once held by his father, a decision about which he also remains silent. Similarly, the film does not make it clear how much Abdel knew about that decision prior to its enactment, or whether there might have been something he could have done to mitigate the impact on his father. These two decisions, along with the decision of Adam to accept the job of his friend Étienne are all cases of acquiescence or inaction that guarantee individual security at the expense of other members of a community. The intertwined structure of these decisions in the film links the downsizing of staff at the hotel to the resumption of hostilities, suggesting that the conflict is also the result of globalized actors intervening in the local context, a suggestion reinforced by the presence of UN troops both at the hotel and on the road to the front. Thus, in the logic of the film, economic liberalism has not only altered economic structures in Chad, but has been a significant factor in conflict in the region. This points to the external

Figure 5.3   Madame Wang determines Adam's fate.

political reality in which foreign entities, particularly those located in the Global North, actively vie for control of Chad's oil resources, and in so doing, influence socio-political realities in the region (Carmody, 2009). The military conflict, in life as in the film, is an escalation of the divisions and deteriorations produced by neo-liberal economic practices, such as the corporate restructuring that occurs at the hotel, and both events serve to produce parallel disruptions and deteriorations in both the local economy and in human rights.

Human Rights, *Hotel Rwanda*, and *A Screaming Man*

There are a number of similarities between *A Screaming Man* and *Hotel Rwanda*. Both films, as noted, are set in multinational hotels in capital cities of African nations experiencing civil conflict. In both films, the protagonist is an employee of the hotel, and the hotel plays a central role in the film. The conflict, in both cases, is introduced early in the film and has the effect of modifying or destroying familial and communal relations. The protagonist, in both cases, is challenged by the circumstances of the conflict and undergoes a personal transformation as a result of that. At the end of both films, the conflict makes it impossible for many of the inhabitants of the country to stay in their native country. In both films, the action moves from the space of the hotel, to various spaces in the city, including the protagonist's home. And in both films, the television and the radio play central roles in commenting on the conflict and in informing the characters about its evolution. Finally, both films use the conflict and its effect on the protagonist to explore questions of human rights in the contemporary era.

There are also a number of divergences between the two films. Where *Hotel Rwanda* restages a well-known and widely viewed civil conflict, *A Screaming Man* makes visible a civil conflict that has often, from a global perspective, been largely ignored. Whereas *Hotel Rwanda* uses the space of the multinational hotel as a sanctuary site that offers refuge to victims of the conflict, *A Screaming Man* points presents the hotel as part of a global complex of interventions that leads to violence and conflict. *Hotel Rwanda*, on many levels, affirms a certain type of masculine individualism, that is a combination of masculine self-reliance and a willingness to challenge the existing order, as integral to human rights. Paul's ability to act in ways that diverge from the dominant course in his country is a function of this individualism. In *A Screaming Man*, a similar type of masculine individualism fragments the relationship between Adam and Abdel, as both men compete for the same economic opportunity in an effort to remain self-supporting rather than looking to the welfare of the extended family, as a collective unit, as the measure of stability and continuity. Similarly, both men are willing to challenge the dominant order, and this willingness leads Adbel to accept his father's job and Adam to the inaction that costs him his son. Finally, *Hotel Rwanda* depicts the violence of the

Rwandan genocide as central and in many ways inexplicable, whereas the violence *A Screaming Man* is one of many forms of conflict caused by an individualism and an economic liberalization that shreds the fabric of the nation, the community, and the family.

The similarities and divergences between the two films suggest that they deal with similar issues but reach different conclusions. *Hotel Rwanda,* despite its recognition of the failures of international human rights discourses, for example, ultimately works to reaffirm their validity and particularly reinforces the equation that binds observation to action in the human rights context. *A Screaming Man,* on the other hand, challenges such discourses, and it does so by challenging both the implied relationship between development discourse and human rights that has emerged in international discourse and by challenging the presumption that individual prosperity is the appropriate metric through which to measure human rights in a local or international context. However, and equally importantly, the film questions the equation established by human rights narratives and rhetoric between observation and intervention, and it challenges the basic premise that understanding or witnessing another person's reality necessarily produces empathy or motivates benevolent intervention. The film therefore defies the basic paradigm of development and improvement that is common to human rights narratives, and it does so in spite of its depiction and suggestion of various forms of intervention, both national and transnational, designed to produce such development.

In many ways, the divergences between *Hotel Rwanda* and *A Screaming Man* illustrate the ways that *A Screaming Man* diverges from the typical paradigm of human rights narratives. The civil conflict in *A Screaming Man,* for example, is not the central structuring device of the narrative, as it would be in many human rights films; rather, it is an element that interrupts or encroaches upon the life of the protagonist, and it is one of a number of pressures and encroachments he is forced to navigate. The evolution undergone by the protagonist, Adam, cannot be seen as a journey toward universal ideals of human rights or an epiphany concerning the justness and appropriateness of such ideas, and so the film cannot be seen as attempting to produce such an epiphany in the spectator. Moreover, the action in the film does not produce a narrative arc of ascendance and development; indeed, the film does not ever provide narrative closure, nor does it convey the sense that watching or bearing vicarious witness to the conflict produces closure. Indeed, *A Screaming Man's* suggests that individuals like Adam and Abdel are increasingly caught between transnational (as embodied by Madame Wang) and local and national elites (as embodied by Ahmat and the army) and that all entities function to erode both individual rights and communal and familial bonds, and that this process is expanding, not ending.

What is more, the function of watching and observing in *A Screaming Man* undermines the implicit relationship between observation and action that underpins much of the rhetoric of human rights films. Many characters in the film watch or observe other characters, and they often see them in moments of crisis. Madame Wang watches Adam and Abdel as they tend the pool. Adam watches Abdel as he interacts with hotel guests. Mariam watches Adam and Abdel as they fight. Ahmat watches Adam as he struggles to decide what to do about the demand that he either pay Ahmat or send his son to serve in the army. At almost no point, however, does this observation lead to a positive intervention, one that would measurably improve either the quality of life or the personal liberty of the person observed. On the contrary, watching in the film often serves as a form of intelligence gathering, both in the case of Ahmat and Madame Wang, a kind of surveillance that is ultimately used against the person being watched.

The role of observation in the film's interior also raises questions about the way the film engages the spectator in the act of observing. The filmic strategies employed by *A Screaming Man* in many ways disrupt the typical mechanisms of cinematic identification, which depends upon both the projection of an image and the careful concealing of that act of projection and of the real distance that separates the spectator from the image. In classically realist filmmaking, close character identification – the aligning of the spectator's gaze with that of a character, and the revelation of that character's thoughts and motives – produces a constructed point of view that seduces the spectator into ignoring or forgetting the fictive distance of the film, ultimately imposing the view or vision embodied by the image, adopting the film's projected vision as his or her own interior view (Dayan, 1974; Oudart, 1977). This permits the cinema, as Kaja Silverman has argued, to function as an extension of existing power structures and as a central mechanism of ideological transmission, creating a particular subject position for a given spectator and then "suturing" or stitching the spectator into that position (Silverman 1983,

Figure 5.4   Adam observes the civil conflict on television.

pp. 221–223). This stitching is a function of the close alignment – through realist processes – with the point of view of the film and with the sense of resolution or closure this alignment conveys.

In *A Screaming Man*, these processes are disrupted, both by the periodic disruption of the process of character identification – the camera is often centered and static, offering an apparently neutral gaze that is distanced from any of the characters. This, coupled with the difficulty in understanding the motives or feelings of Adam, Abdel, or even Madame Wang prevents close identification with any of the characters and blocks the sense of empathy needed to assume their point of view. Moreover, the spectator is positioned as both observer and potential actor, placed at the same time within the frame and outside of it. This occurs quite clearly in the opening scene in swimming pool, in which the spectator is positioned between Adam and Abdel, and at other points in the narrative, such as in the dinner scenes in Adam and Abdel's home.

The film opens with a transition from a silent black background against which the acting credits appear in white, to Adam and Abdel in the pool. During the transition, while the acting credits are still visible, the sound of chirping birds becomes audible in the background, and at 52 seconds into the film the screen goes completely black and then cuts to a shot of the two men standing in the swimming pool, centered in the frame, with the pool ladder visible behind them. The scene is shot with a static camera, in a brightly lit long take, with the sun visibly reflecting on the water. Adam is facing Abel (looking to the right of the frame), and stands slightly higher than Abdel (Adam is visible from the shoulders up, but Abdel is only visible from the neck up). Abdel is turned away from his father, his eyes turned down and toward the right, facing the camera. The two men discuss a competition they are having regarding who can hold his breath the longest underwater. The contest between the two of them results in a tie, and Adam challenges Adam, who turns to face his father, to a final round to determine a winner. Abdel agrees, and the two men submerge, at which point the final credits – the director's name and the title of the film – appear, superimposed over the image of the submerged men. Finally, Adam re-emerges from the pool, followed by Abdel, who taunts his father, telling him he had let him win the last competition, saying that he, not his father is the champion. Abdel and Adam playfully wrestle, positions reversed, with Abdel higher in the frame, and his father, in his grip, firmly below him. As the scene ends, Adam and Abdel, their backs to the camera, continue to wrestle, both again at equal height in the frame.

Although there is no hint of war in this opening scene, the interaction between father and son suggests alternate forms of civil conflict and unseen realities. The emerging rivalry between father and son, which at first seems playful, transforms, by the end of the scene into a real conflict whose playful surface masks deeper tensions and divisions. The contest between father and son is clearly a play for dominance between an aging former hero and his younger and stronger son, whom he perceives, on some level, as a threat or rival. The mentioned, but not depicted, previous rounds in the father-son contest point to ongoing processes that shape the action that is to come, processes that are not fully visible to the spectator. This introduces a theme in the film, in which the action will, indeed, be shaped by events and actions that are not always revealed in the narrative, that are not seen, but whose effects are clearly felt. Finally, the scene – which features the father watching the son and the son watching the father as the spectator watches them both – questions the relationship among observation, empathy, and action. First and foremost, it is clear that the type of watching that occurs between father and son is competitive in nature, and therefore yields action, but not empathy.

The film's title, *A Screaming Man*, which interrupts this opening scene, seems self-referential, inviting a reflection on the role of films, such as this one, that depict human suffering, and those who watch them. The static camera and the long take used to shoot this opening scene heighten that suggestion, as the spectator of the film is positioned as if in the pool with Adam and Abdel, a spectator, watching what unfolds, poised between action and observation. As the film progresses, it becomes clear that the title raises broader questions concerning the relationship of action and observation. The implied quote of the title also points to the role played by those who consume images of conflict throughout the world, but also to the role played by transnational agencies such as the UN – whose forces will be briefly visible in the film – and who observe and do not intervene. This raises broader questions about the role, nature, and motives governing individual, national, and transnational interventions on the personal, national, and global scale. This tension between action and observation is raised elsewhere in the opening sequence, in Abdel's initial hesitation to accept his father's final challenge, and is a motif that structures the action of the film as a whole.

The opening scene is followed by a series of short scenes that reinforce the motif of action versus observation and that expand the scope of the film's inquiry to the double contexts of globalization and conflict. The second scene in the film opens with a long shot on Adam, who is centered in the frame with the hotel grounds in the background. He is facing toward the left and walks in that direction as the camera tracks left along with him as he passes the pool and lounging guests. At 2 minutes 10 seconds into the film, the camera stops moving, but Adam keeps walking and at 2 minutes 11 seconds, he disappears off-screen behind a woven straw screen. At that moment, Abdel emerges from the background, dressed in black and white and walks toward the camera. We hear Adam's voice from off-screen call to Abdel, and he re-emerges. At this point, Adam is in the left side of the frame, Abdel in the right. The two come together and walk along. The camera tracks right and follows them as they walk. At two minutes 31 seconds, the camera and Adam and Abdel stop. The two are centered in the frame. Adam reproaches Adbel for not being dressed entirely in white. Abdel responds that he had to wear a black shirt because the washing machine was broken. Abdel tries to take a photograph of Adam, who refuses and asks Abdel why he is always taking photographs, and Abdel replies that it is to document his life. At that moment, Adam signals the presence of the hotel manager, and the camera cuts to Madame Wang, in extreme long shot, as she walks around the hotel pool with the manager, Souad, as the two survey the pool and grounds.

This brief scene introduces Madame Wang as an external observer or onlooker to the unfolding story between Adam and Abdel. As subsequent events in the film show, she witnesses the contest between father and son, and uses it to her own ends as she decides which positions to eliminate in restructuring the hotel staff. Her observation, although apparently passive and neutral, serves as a pretext to self-interested intervention. Adam's reaction to her observation signals the potential peril in her gaze and indicates both his awareness of his vulnerability and his inability to meaningfully deflect either her gaze or her action. Madame Wang stands in, in many respects, for the forces of transnational intervention, ranging from multinational corporations, to the World Bank, to the UN, to foreign military forces sent to observe or advise in the conflict in Chad. Madame Wang's role is a suggestion that in all such cases, observation and action are deeply intertwined and that there are, in the transnational context, only self-interested observers who lack empathy for those they observe and who frequently transform into self-interested actors.

There is another context in which observation is evoked in this swimming pool scene, and that is the failed photograph Abdel attempts to take of Adam. Abdel's camera is, in his own words, his attempt to document his life, a form of self-observation or representation in which Abdel is both actor and observer. We never see the photographs Abdel takes, but the film, in many ways, stands in for them. Even in their absence, the evocation of the photographs creates a tension between the type of observation in which Madame Wang engages – a self-interested

Figure 5.5   Adam passes UN troops on the road.

observation used to justify or further specific ends – and the documentary gaze of Abdel's photographs. This contrast is highlighted elsewhere in the film, between the television images of the widening conflict seen in Adam's home, for example, and the tape recordings of the experience of the war Abdel sends home from the front. The first type of observations are motivated, external observations of life in Chad, and the second set are self-representations meant to communicate or document personal realities. These various forms of looking, when combined with the passive and powerless nature of Adam's gaze throughout the film foreground multiple types of looking, some of which do and some of which do not produce action or empathy. They function, therefore, to problematize the question of the relationship of looking to action and to suggest that what looking means, in any given context, and what type of action – if any – it leads to are a function of the type of person who looks, their motivations for looking, their capacity for action, and the consequences of any action they might undertake. Following this brief scene, the film cuts to a scene of Adam tending the pool as the camera tracks very slowly in toward him, and then stops, conveying the idea of observation and surveillance, as if someone, perhaps Madame Wang, were walking around the pool and observing him. The scene then cuts to Adam and his friend David, walking through a white-tiled hallway leading out of the hotel kitchen and out to the back of the hotel. The camera is located behind them as they walk, and tracks with them as they walk past boxes of produce. The spectator is again, in this scene, positioned as an observer who listens to their conversation and surveys their actions. As they walk, David expresses fear and concern. Adam asks if David if he is worried about the war, and David responds that he is worried, instead, about the privatization of the hotel. As the men exit into the hotel yard, the sound of a helicopter flying overhead can be heard. The men then sit in the yard, which is filled with crates of Coca-Cola, and attempt to reassure one another about the future, as David feeds a local stray dog he has taken under his care.

The film's title, *A Screaming Man*, provides clues to the film's interrogation of the relationship between observation and action, and the relationship between the filmed image and human rights. In the opening scene, the title cuts across the image of Adam and Abdel submerged in the swimming pool. The apparent intrusion of the title into the action of the film invites reflection on both observation and intervention and the relationship between those two options. The title is, as Rachel Gabara rightly notes in her review of the film, a reference to Aimé Césaire's *Cahier d'un retour au pays natal/ Return to My Native Land*. It is, in fact, part of a quote from the text, which reads "beware of assuming the sterile attitude of a spectator, for life is not a spectacle, a sea of miseries is not a proscenium, a screaming man is not a dancing bear" (Gabara 2015). The quote asserts that there is no necessary relationship between observation and action, but rather that any spectator has a choice of how to respond to the injustice and inequalities of the world. The film's title, therefore, reminds the spectator from the beginning that watching a film about inequality and injustice is not equivalent to acting to correct that injustice, and it raises broad questions of action, human suffering, and spectatorship and the relationship among them. It calls out for active involvement, as opposed to "sterile" or passive observation, invoking a dichotomy between watching and acting that has structured both human rights discourses (which similarly compel action and intervention as opposed to watching) and theoretical discussions of film spectatorship. The reference also suggests the act of film spectatorship, as it evokes Abderrahmane Sissako's 1999 film *La vie sur terre/Life on Earth* which also addresses the relationship between film spectatorship and human suffering, and which also features the Césaire quote prominently.

Through the double reference to Césaire and Sissako, *A Screaming Man* interrogates the idea of "sterile" observation, suggesting observation in interpersonal interaction is never neutral or "sterile." The dynamic of observation and intervention invoked in the title is at play in the film in both personal and global terms, and involves both the actions (or inaction) of characters within the film and the broader political and economic contexts in which those actions occur. This intertwined personal/global dynamic is evident in the sequences that start the film, and it becomes more and more apparent and disruptive as the film progresses. The rivalry between Adam and Abdel, for example, which is foregrounded from the opening scene, is both a personal and economic and political rivalry, structured by competitive dynamics that are purely familial, but also by an economic insecurity that occurs in the face of globalization and that becomes more acute in the political insecurity brought on by the escalation of the war. This rivalry is characterized by a dynamic of observation and intervention that is also on display from the opening sequence in which Abdel must make the choice to act or not act in his competition with his father, and in which both Adam and Abdel are watched by Madame Wang, the focus of whose observation is the degree of action and each man demonstrates in the pool.

In both cases – the competition between father and son and the management decisions made by Madame Wang – neutral observation is rejected, or serves only as a precursor to action or intervention. Abdel, after a pause, decides to end his father's competitive game by beating him decisively, and Madame Wang uses the information gathered from her observation to remove Adam from his job, on the grounds he is not active enough (he describes his job to her as one of oversight, of observation, a role she clearly rejects).

Nor does Adam do anything to attempt to help his friend David, who is the first character in the film to lose his job, or even anything to help the stray dog David cared for when the new cook throws stones at him. Perhaps most importantly, Adam, faced with the choice of paying to keep his son out of the war or doing nothing, does nothing, becoming an inactive observer both to the war – which he witnesses only through images on the television – and to his son's forcible conscription. Adam's reversal and intervention, which comes too late to save his son, occurs only after he realizes that the nation he has believed he was serving is a nation that controls through observation, a nation composed of old men who start and then observe wars in which they have no intention of fighting, wars in which

they will sacrifice their sons and the sons of others to safeguard their own positions. The film makes it clear that these forms of observation and inaction are
costly, as Adam regains his job when Abdel is sent off to war, but finds himself
tending a pool in an empty hotel, and Ahmat, who conspired to protect his own
position of power, ends up fleeing a country on the verge of collapse.

Conclusion

At the narrative level, *A Screaming Man* questions the central premise of human
rights narratives, which is that observation of the reality of another leads to com-
passion and egalitarian intervention on the part of the spectator. There is much
watching, on both a personal and national level in the film, but at no point does the
observation or witnessing of the reality of someone else produce compassionate
action. Instead, the characters in the film, at least those who, like Madame Wang
and Ahmat, are empowered to act, use their observations to better calculate their
interventions, or lack of intervention, so as to better advance their own interests,
with little regard for the consequences of their actions or inaction on others. Other
characters, such as Adam's wife, Mariam, or Abdel's girlfriend, Djénéba, observe
but are rendered unable to act by their positions in society, or the circumstances in
which they find themselves. The film, also, indirectly, questions the motives and
intentions of its own filmmaker, or of any filmmaker of a film that depicts human
suffering, and it recognizes that such an endeavor to capture, to make palpable the
experiences of those suffering in Chad and elsewhere, without turning their experiences into a spectacle, from which the spectator of the film is aesthetically,
politically, and actively distant, may well be impossible.

This points to one of the central ironies of the film, and that is that the title, *A
Screaming Man*, seems to refer to Adam, the protagonist, who at no point in the
film, either screams or cries. On the other hand, Adam is surrounded by people
who suffer and cry out, people like his wife and son, the anonymous soldiers on
the television, or his fellow employees at the hotel. For this reason, Adam is not, in
all likelihood, the screaming man evoked by the title. Rather, he is the sterile spectator, who watches, transfixed, as those around him suffer as the world around
him collapses. The film, through the periodic shift in the gaze – during which
periods the spectator become unaligned with Adam's point of view – provides
another perspective and therefore fails to fully stitch the spectator into Adam's
point of view. Thus, *A Screaming Man* functions as what Jacques Rancière has called
"a pensive image" a double construction in between which lies a zone of
indeterminacy" (2009, p. 107). This zone of indeterminacy, in Rancière's assessment
"liberates" the spectator from presumed alignment with the aesthetic or ideological point of view of the image, releasing him or her from the author or filmmaker's imposed compulsion to act in a particular way. It thus creates a deliberate gap

between observation and action, and, like the title of the film, asks the spectator to reflect and make a conscious choice about how to feel about what he or she has seen, and whether and how to act in response.

A Screaming Man, moreover, does not generalize or universalize Adam's choices or actions, at least beyond the context in which they occur. Rather, they are presented as the product of a particular character with a specific history operating in a specific context. As a result, the film deals with issues of conflict and change in Chad without reference to the discourses of globalization and human rights that are almost inevitably bound to them, and this is heightened by the film's lack of a linear narrative structure and its fragmenting of classical audience identification. If the film follows Adam's point of view, it also distances the spectator from it, presenting it as limited and problematic, and suggesting that all such perspectives, which lock the spectator or viewer into a particular point of view, are similarly limiting and problematic. *A Screaming Man* therefore reveals several strategies for exploring human rights and violence and conflict in Africa without reinforcing problematic discourses and without recycling old stereotypes. Moreover, it demonstrates that it is possible to investigate African issues and even conflicts separate from the intervention, non-intervention, and development paradigms of the Global North, all of which it explicitly questions.

For both narrative and aesthetic reasons, any film that deals with the relationship of human rights and the Global South risks becoming simply another text that reinforces the codes of meaning already in place. Mahamat Saleh-Haroun has been keenly aware of the double-bind of the African filmmaker who undertakes to film the continent, and particularly one who wishes to engage questions of rights, development, and equality in countries deemed to be "under-developed." Haroun's first feature-length film, *Bye Bye Africa,* is a long, cinematic meditation on the nature of filmmaking in Africa. The film, a fictional documentary in which a filmmaker named Haroun, played by Mahamat-Saleh Haroun returns to his native Chad to make a movie called *Bye Bye Africa* – a movie he never makes – questions the orientation of the filmic gaze the ideological consequences of filmmaking in general, and filmmaking in Africa in particular. *A Screaming Man* repeats and expands upon the gesture made by *Bye Bye Africa.* Like the first film, *A Screaming Man* opens up a space of negotiation that lies between existing discourses. In that regard, the film both critiques existing narratives of human rights, which in this model, are too unidimensional, too rigid, to produce sufficient understanding or empathy, much less ethical action. However, the film also, perhaps, paradoxically, affirms the centrality of observation, and of images of observation, to the production of such empathy and action. It is through watching the act of watching, through observing the observer and our own observations that we are able to see, the film suggests, beyond our own point of view. Moreover, because no character in *A Screaming Man* is able to achieve this emancipated perspective – it is a perspective only available to the external observer – the film also affirms the necessity of outside or transnational cooperation, even if it rejects the terms of such cooperation as it is currently configured.

Note

1   For more on the history and evolution of human rights, see Hunt (2007) and Ishay
    (2004).

References

Adorno, Theodor and Max Horkheimer. 1947 (2002). *The Culture Industry.*
Ake, Claude. 2001. *Democracy and Development in Africa.* Washington, DC: Brookings
    Institution Press.
Agamben, Giorgio. 2009. *What is an Apparatus and Other Essays.* Translated by David
    Kishnik and Stefan Pedatella. Stanford, CA: Stanford University Press.
Anderson. Benedict. 2006. *Imagined Communities: Reflections on the Origin and Spread of
    Nationalism.* London: Verso.
Baudry, Jean-Louis. 1986 (1970). "The Apparatus: Metaphysical Approaches to the
    Impression of Reality in Cinema." In *Narrative, Apparatus, and Ideology,* Philip Rosen,
    ed. New York: Columbia University Press, 299–318.
Bloom, Peter. 2008. *French Colonial Documentary: Mythologies of Humanism.* Minneapolis:
    University of Minnesota Press.
Carmody, P. (2009)
Césaire, Aimé. 1939 (2014). *Return to My Native Land.* Brooklyn, NY: Achipelago Books.
Dayan, Daniel. 1974. "The Tutor-Code of Classical Cinema." *Film Quarterly* 28.1: 22–31.
    doi: 10.2307/1211439
Donnelly, Jack. 2013. *Universal Human Rights in Theory and Practice.* Ithaca NY; Cornell
    University Press.
Freeman, Michael. 2011. *Human Rights.* Malden, MA: Polity Press.
Fukuyama, Francis. 1989. "The End of History." *National Interest* (Summer): 3–18.
Gabara, Rachel. 2015. "War by Documentary." *Romance Notes* 55.3: 409–23.
Gibney, Mark and Ken Betsalel. 2011. "Human Rights Begin with Seeing: A Review of
    Human Rights Films." *Human Rights Quarterly* 33.4: 1186–94.
Härting, Heike. 2008. "Global Humanitarianism, Race, and the Spectacle of the African
    Corpse in Current Western Representations of the Rwandan Genocide." *Comparative
    Studies of South Asia, Africa, and the Middle East* 28.1: 61–77.
Heath, Stephen. 1976. "Narrative Space." *Screen* 17.6: 68–112. doi: 10.1093/screen/17.3.68
Howard-Hassman, Rhoda. 2010. *Can Globalization Promote Human Rights?* University Park
    PA: Pennsylvania State University Press.
Hunt, Lynn. 2007. *Inventing Human Rights: A History.* New York: W.W. Norton.
Ishay, Micheline. 2004. *The History of Human Rights: From Ancient Times to the Globalization
    Era.* Berkeley and New York: University of California Press.
Landau, Paul S. and Deborah D. Kaspin. 2002. *Images and Empires: Visuality in Colonial and
    Postcolonial Africa.* Berkeley and Los Angeles: University of California Press.
Millgate, Michael. 2006. "Human Rights and Natural Law: From Bracton to Blackstone."
    Legal History 10.1–2: 53–70.
Oudart, Jean-Pierre. 1977. "Cinema and Suture." *Screen* 18.4: 35–47. doi: 10.1093/
    screen/18.4.35

Rancière, Jacques. 2004. *The Politics of Aesthetics: The Distribution of the Sensible.* Translated by Gabriel Rockhill. London and New York: Continuum.

Rancière, Jacques. 2009. *The Emancipated Spectator.* Translated by Gregory Elliot. London: Verso.

Silverman, Kaja. 1983. *The Subject of Semiotics.* New York: Oxford University Press.

Simms, Brendan and D.J.B. Trim. 2011. *Humanitarian Intervention: A History.* Cambridge and New York: Cambridge University Press.

Slavin, Henry David. 2001. *Colonial Cinema and Imperial France: White Blind Spots, Male Fantasies, Settler Myths.* Baltimore, MD: Johns Hopkins University Press.

Ukadike, Frank. 1991. "Anglophone African Media." *Jump Cut* 36: 74–80.

United Nations Office of the High Commissioner. 2016. Accessed 278 March 2018. www.ohchr.org/EN/Issues/Pages/WhatareHumanRights.aspx

Uvin, Peter. 2002. "On High Moral Ground: The Incorporation of Human Rights by the Development Enterprise." *Praxis: The Fletcher Journal of Development Enterprise* XVII: 1–11.

Filmography

Fuqua, Antoine. (2003). *Tears of the Sun.* Los Angeles: Sony Pictures.

George, Terry. (2004). *Hotel Rwanda.* Los Angeles: United Artists.

Haroun, Mahamat-Saleh. (2013). *Grigris.* Pilifilms.

Haroun, Mahamat-Saleh. (2010). *A Screaming Man.* Paris: Pilifilms.

Haroun, Mahamat-Saleh. (1999). *Bye Bye Africa.* Paris: Imagesplus.

Meirelles, Fernando. (2005). *The Constant Gardener.* Nairobi: Blue Sky Films

Zwick, Edward. (2006). *Blood Diamond.* Los Angeles: Warner Brothers.

6

"The Invisible Government
of the Powerful"
Joseph Gaï Ramaka's Cinema of Power

Akin Adesokan

Introduction

A preoccupation with power, that is, power as the structural capability to exercise control and dispense violence across the social realm, is a major feature of the work of Senegalese filmmaker, poet, and playwright, Joseph Gaï Ramaka. Even though his output has not manifested itself with a prolificacy comparable to that of Abderrahmane Sissako, with whom he entered the arena of African filmmaking in the late 1990s, and is thus likely to elude concentrated critical attention, Ramaka has worked with an artistic principle confident enough, holistic enough, to convince an educated viewer that he knows what he is doing. With seven films of varying lengths and in different genres, and a strong record of achievements in the area of production and curating, he is worthy of being considered a compelling force in institutional terms. In this chapter, I focus on the preoccupation with power, an important aspect of Ramaka's work which puts the record of his achievements on the rope of paradox: The social, through which the artistic process can only be manifested in production, poses severe challenges to a poetic imagination, and in institutional terms, those challenges are intimately connected to the idea of censorship. By censorship I mean both the disciplinary response of the sovereign to art and the effect of a process for which no one can be held accountable, in the "natural" character of the market, for example. My primary focus is on Ramaka's *So Be It* (1997) and through this film I analyze complex forms of socio-political and economic control in West Africa and the world at large. The chapter's larger aim, however, is to explore the output of this remarkable artist in

A Companion to African Cinema, First Edition. Edited by Kenneth W. Harrow and Carmela Garritano.
© 2019 John Wiley & Sons, Inc. Published 2019 by John Wiley & Sons, Inc.

relation to a thorny issue in contemporary African and postcolonial art: The structural connection between the poetic imagination and the creation of cultural prestige, through the figure of the artist. What is the economic status of "difficult" or obscure subject-matters to the institutions which confer value on art? How does an artist with a style that could be called "surrealist," which is another way of saying "poetic" or "non-narrative," pursue a career in a context where having "an audience" and producing work with commercial viability count as measures of professional excellence? The social challenges the poetic imagination because it is the ground of the collusion of authoritarianism and neoliberal globalization, and censorship is their mutual, reactionary instrument in relation to art. But it is also the ground on which production takes place. Without the social, those institutional forms which artists, scholars, and audiences alike have come to take for granted, even the most "difficult," "inaccessible" works of art might be grateful to escape the fate of works which have never been made, "produced" – because no one knows about them.

I focus primarily on *So Be It* because my interests are specifically conceptual. The aspect of Ramaka's work which allows me to discuss the challenges that the social poses to a poetic imagination is difficult to grasp but there is, indeed, a much narrower aspect of this problem. This is the idea of censorship, both as the disciplinary response of the sovereign to art and as the effect of a process for which no one can be held accountable. Although based on *The Strong Breed*, an early dramatic work by Wole Soyinka, the Nigerian playwright and Nobel laureate, Ramaka's version ("re-imagining," as he prefers to call it) strikes me as the statement of a very profound artistic principle. It is not his best-known work (that honor goes to *Karmen Geï*), but it is the most decisive from my understanding of his career, the film that made it possible for him to produce the universally acclaimed one. Institutionally, the short film serves as a launching-pad for the feature film. Aesthetically, the artistic liberties which Ramaka takes with *So Be It* become indispensable to his re-imagining of Prosper Mérimée's *Carmen*. In this 30-minute film, most of the distinguishing features of Ramaka's work are present: A philosophical concern with the social rendered in poetic terms; the relationship between sexuality and power; a preference for the spectacular and the anti-illusionistic; the relationship between otherness and violence, both psychic and physical.

In an interview with film historian Michael Martin, Ramaka characterizes the mental disposition from which he works as a "'surrealist' understanding of the world." (Martin 2008, p. 25). But what does it mean to have a "surrealist understanding of the world" when, again, as Ramaka claims in the interview, this sense predates the canonized idea of surrealism as a modern European literary movement? Eileen Julien once described this filmmaker as a poet with a camera and I think that the quality which Julien attempts to capture through this description is not rare in African filmmaking.[1] Indeed, Ramaka as writer and director is comparable in certain aspects of his poetics to his compatriot, Djibril Diop Mambéty, who once described himself as the history of a dream.[2] African cinema is still a relatively young field, though quickly expanding into subfields, so I think we make useful contributions to knowledge when we distinguish directors like Ramaka and Mambéty from Ousmane Sembène and Gaston Kaboré on the basis of the general philosophical orientations of their art. In the first set of directors, there is a well-established preference for conceiving of experience as primarily a function of individual consciousness, whereas in the second set there is a comparatively higher investment in the dramatization of such an experience as a part of broader socio-political phenomena. Second, there is a higher degree of mimetic representation in Kaboré's work than in Ramaka. For example, the figure of the mute child in *Wend Kuuni* (1982) serves explicitly narrative purposes whereas this figure is primarily symbolic in *So Be It*.

This kind of distinction is useful, but it also conceals one important fact. The social, that is, the embodied relations of power, of exchange, and the like in the different dimensions of lived experience, is not a discrete, preconstituted domain, as Ato Quayson has argued in *Calibrations* (2003), nor is it exhaustive of experience as such. There are dimensions of experience that are irreducible to socio-historical processes, so when Ramaka defines his aesthetic philosophy in terms of surrealism, and qualifies this definition by distinguishing its history from a European provenance, it seems to me that a productive way of coming to terms with such self-conception is to take the logic of a dream as its point of departure. Thus, a preliminary inventory of this logic in African art might include the quality of light and visuality in the fictions of Amos Tutuola and Emmanuel Dongala, the principle of synthesis in the poetry of Wole Soyinka, the concept of formula in *oriki* and *yere don*, and the amorality of discursive practices such as taboo and the proverb. What is called "poetic" in the filmmaker's work, I think, is not a refuge in the irrational from an overdose of reality, but a self-conscious labor on behalf of complex pleasures which, as Bertolt Brecht famously says, are "more intricate, richer in communication, more contradictory and more productive of results" (1992, p. 181).

But this presents another question, a most important one in terms of my purposes in this chapter: How is it that an artist with such a profoundly aesthetic apprehension of experience is also one for whom socio-political engagement is a moral imperative? More persistently than Mambéty, Ramaka proceeds from the point of view of a citizen, an individual artist with a sense of responsibility toward the *civis*. And it is not enough of a solution to think of Ramaka the filmmaker as separate from Ramaka the citizen: In the first place, the idea of citizenship is inconceivable outside of a locality, so Citizen Ramaka is not the same person in every particular in Dakar and New Orleans, although this would be a little complicated if he were to naturalize as an American; second, this individual citizen would not be of much analytical interest were he not also, and primarily, a filmmaker. There is really no solution here, and this is the kind of problem I am interested in regarding Ramaka's work, the problem which defies solution but draws attention to art as the basis for thinking through it.

The idea of censorship I deploy in this chapter is two-fold: The more common notion of the state using its power as the monopolist of violence to legislate what is permissible utterance or action in a social setting, and the less common but no less consequential one of what the prevailing relations of production prohibit. The culprit behind this second form of censorship is sometimes identified as "the invisible hand of the market." In *Firing Back*, one of his last works, the French sociologist Pierre Bourdieu (2003) implicitly suggests a synthesis of the two culprits as "the invisible government of the powerful" (p. 14), pointing to Benito Mussolini's characterization of fascism as corporatism, as an earlier instance of the collusion between the sovereign and the market. For Bourdieu, who was not interested in artistic censorship as such, the problem with determining what is permissible action has to be located in "the novel forms that domination assumes" (p. 20). Where there is a mobilization and concentration of cultural capital, Bourdieu argues, there is less corresponding need for the spectacular demonstration of power. Bourdieu's term, "invisible government of the powerful," is useful for many conceptual reasons, primary among which is its character as a synthesis. However, for my purposes here, I would slightly amend the term by substituting "governance" for "government" because the impersonal, administrative ring of the former word accords more with the "naturalness" of neoliberal idea of free market. The prevalence of poststructralist concept-metaphors like "stakeholders" and "good governance" in contemporary, everyday usage points to the unfelt effect of a corporatist worldview. Besides, more than "government," "governance" rings true of notions such as "governmentality" and "biopolitics," which, as I show later by turning to the example of Michel Foucault, makes the structural link between power and domination/control serviceable in the discussion of Ramaka's work.

In addressing Ramaka's work, however, I find that it is important not to lose sight or steer clear of the vulgar displays of power in the authority of the sovereign who, in an African context is indeed an autocrat, an Abdoulaye Wade or a Paul Biya, but who is constrained by the political demands of global corporatism to pretend to be a democrat. There is a terrifically funny moment in *And What If Latif Were Right?*, Ramaka's documentary film about the authoritarian ways of former President Wade (of Senegal) when the president, sitting on an imposing throne, says to a political adversary: "But for the fact that I am a democrat, I would send you to jail for saying that!" Such a display of power in relation to a work of art does not have to manifest itself as or translate into a ban on a film or a book; it is significant enough that there is a structural connection between a given political atmosphere and the production of a particular work, for example the Nigerian civil war and its immediate repressive aftermath and Soyinka's production of *Madmen and Specialists* during a period of self-imposed exile, or the Israeli military attacks on Lebanon in 1982 and the poetry that Mahmoud Darwish, who was resident in Beirut at the time, wrote, as we can glimpse from Jean-Luc Godard's *Notre Musique/Our Music*. This is where to locate the problem I am trying to address: The social as the ground of the collusion of authoritarianism and neoliberal globalization, and censorship as their mutual, reactionary instrument in relation to art. When I say that Ramaka has displayed greater civic-mindedness in his work than, say, Mambéty, what I mean is that we have more evidence from him of works that respond to baldly political emergencies, such as *And What If Latif Was Right?* and *Plan Jaxaay!* But I also want to resist the temptation to distinguish these works from others like *So Be It, Karmen Gei,* and *It's My Man* (2009) solely on generic grounds, in part because of what I say below about *So Be It.* Also, in the play *A Thousand and One-Voiced Fragments,* which has not been widely performed and may yet emerge as a film script, Ramaka has brought these aspects of his work together in a very compelling manner, dramatizing illusions of power without losing sight of the compositional principles at work in anti-illusionistic theater. The censorious collusion between authoritarianism and neoliberalism works in indiscriminate ways, and Ramaka's films also provide us with some evidence of this.

How the form of power that is characterized by censorship operates in Ramaka's work deserves a careful attention. A major controversy surrounded the reception of *Karmen Gei* in Senegal. The outrage expressed by the clerical authorities in the country over the use of Mourid sacred music during the funeral for the prison warden Angélique, a lesbian who committed suicide following a heartbreaking separation from Karmen, is a ruse for the unexpressed reactionary view of spectacular lesbianism (or bisexuality), and it is clear from Ramaka's prior film, *So Be It,* that a concern with sexual tensions represents a resolve to confront authority on the sources of its legitimacy. It is in this sense that it is productive to speak about censorship in the filmmaker's work, the idea of taking on subjects so critical of authority and authoritarianism, perhaps in politically direct ways as in *And What If Latif Was Right?,* perhaps in poetically concentrated ways as in *So Be It,* as to attract suspicious attention from the cultural or the political dominant.

What remains little-explored but incredibly important is the role of sexuality and ritual as the forms in which political domination is calibrated. This is slightly different from the amoral "aesthetics of vulgarity" that we have come to understand from the works of Jean-Pierre Bekolo (*Les Saignantes*), Sony Labou Tansi (*La Vie et demie*), or even in early Achille Mbembe. I think that the focus on the body and bodily functions through grotesque and excessively parodic imageries in these works tends to undermine the deeper aspects of the relationship between sexuality, ritual, and power. If this literature is to speak meaningfully to the problem, it will also need to see the relationship in the sense of James Baldwin's "unspeakably, dark, guilty, erotic past" (1998, p. 267) because the taboos that are attached to sex and ritual have practical political implications and purposes. Besides, it seems to me that the interest in the comical aspects of the nexus of power and sexuality is overdramatized and even its more critical aspects hardly ever go beyond the cathartic effects of the critique, thus leaving the tyrannical resources generated in the nexus intact. It would be more productive, I think, to deepen this interest by paying attention to the relationship between human sacrifice and the maintenance of order in precapitalist societies as a sign of homoerotic power, along with the standard practice of using women, the young, and foreigners as victims. A detailed look at *So Be It* will clarify what I am aiming at.

Invisible Governance: The Return of the Stranger

So Be It is Ramaka's cinematic re-imagining of *The Strong Breed*, Soyinka's play about the practice of carrier and the demands of personal sacrifice. Michael, a medical doctor has come to live in the small village in which the story takes place, out of a commitment to serving the needy and love for Sunma, his girl-friend, who is a native of the village. The action revolves around the event of selecting a victim to carry away the "sins" of the village in the style of ritual scapegoating, and Michael's futile efforts, against Sunma's warnings, to save the helpless victim, Ifada, a mute but lovable boy whom he has befriended. In *The Strong Breed*, the plot is stretched over two periods – between the present time of Eman attempting to stop the cult-elders from using Ifada as the scape-goat, and the past, rendered in flashback, of Eman as a young boy, who fails to complete his tutelage because he disagrees with his tutor's amorous advances toward his (Eman's) young friend, Omae. In the film, the made-for-cinema flashback sections disappear completely, although there is a brief sequence near the beginning where a young man departs hurriedly and a woman follow-ing him also pauses to cast a gestured spell of irrevocable departure. In place of these, the film presents emotional tensions between the couple consisting of Michael, the village doctor, and Sunma, his girlfriend and native daughter, and those triangulated between them and the two little children loitering around the house. These tensions are expressed through interrupted sexual acts. In scenes remarkably poised between the cinematic and the theatrical, Ramaka frames the drama of incommunicable anxieties manifested in Michael's silent moments of reading and Sunma's own of literal hairsplitting through indoor, low-light sequences.

While Sunma is frustrated by Michael's refusal to heed her warnings and leave, she also suggestively thrusts her pelvis at him in a series of taunting moves that are not meant as invitation, or libidinal "call to action." The sexual acts are, practically, attempts by Michael to physically dissuade her from these taunts. The attention given to sexual acts in the film is one of the major innovations Ramaka brings to the plot of Soyinka's play, where such acts are suggested largely through Eman's suspicion of his tutor's actions toward the young Omae. Indeed, the break with tradition that Eman's departure from his town and its ritual expectations signifies is an ethical reinforcement of the principled defense of his girlfriend's honor, which is also a rejection of the tutor's irresponsible conduct. The same principle earlier has Eman retorting to the elders in his new station that "A village which cannot produce its own carriers contains no men" (Soyinka 1973, p. 129). The prominence given to the sexual acts in *So Be It* is thus significant for a variety of reasons.

First, the emotional intensity is a symptom of other things – the taboo of the scapegoat which the opening ritual by the elders and the closing ritual of seizing Ifada seek to enact, and the otherness of Michael as foreigner and physician professionally trained to oppose the logic of secretive rituals. Second, as the highly charged love-making between the lovers is repeatedly begun and interrupted, Sunma barks in frustration: "Get your crazy little pal to rub up against us," thus giving voice to the homoerotic fantasy attached to the mute Ifada as one who competes with her for Michael's attention. And, in fact, Ifada is sustained emotionally by attentions from Michael. At one point, the boy manifests the pleased contentment of a pet while being stroked by the doctor. Third, the most sustained of the attempts at intercourse is witnessed by the sick girl and thus interrupted, deepening Sunma's dread of ill-omen either in relation to Ifada's presence or the advancing horde from the village. The love-making is not for only physical gratification, but also serves to create intimacy between them and thereby provide a refuge from the hostile environment. Finally, the revulsion Sunma feels toward Ifada also comes from a primordial fear that potential mothers might have for blemished or disabled children. It is a well-known taboo in some West African societies that pregnant women are prohibited or discouraged from walking in the noonday sun, the time of the day when evil spirits are believed to be abroad, looking for a vulnerable body to inhabit. In Soyinka's play, Sunma explicitly connects her revulsion toward Ifada to the fact that she is a woman, and "these things matter. I don't want a mis-shape near me" (p. 117).

I argued earlier that the fact of the film being based on *The Strong Breed* only serves to give wings to Ramaka's imaginative flight, showing his assured command of the ethical grounds of the dramatic conflict. The originality of *So Be It* manifests itself in the idea of using cinematic techniques to turn the merely suggestive or poeticized in *The Strong Breed* to an ineffable spectacle. The charged emotional states occupied by Michael and Sunma are foreshadowed in the hermetic ritual in the opening scene, witnessed by only Ifada, who flees the scene, literally followed by the diegetic sound of a pig grunting, most likely a sacrificial animal. This grunting denotes a lack of articulation, a condition that thus attaches itself to the scene through association with the mute Ifada. The lack of articulation and the impossibility of full communication are, for Sunma and Michael, displaced onto the repetitive and desperate attempts at love-making. It is logical thus that the mute boy is seen as the potential victim, even if he runs or is driven away from the scene, and that his fate is connected to that of the couple – Michael the foreign doctor, and Sunma the native daughter who is revolted by the amorality of her people. Indeed, Ifada's muteness makes it possible for him to be present (he is tolerated because of the assumption that he is not in a position to tell of what he has seen) but also seals his fate at the end. Taken with the image of the sick girl looking silently on copulating adults, this incident, Ifada's witnessing of the brief, bloody ritual, dramatizes Ramaka's imaginative response to the earlier work, in which none of these moments is present.

The opening ritual is accompanied by a chant in Wolof which goes:

> This friend of mine cures whatever illness he comes across
> What I do not know,
> Is the one he does not know about or does not come across.
> But I know he cures whatever illness he falls on.[3]

The same chant returns in the final sequence, when the crowd arrives to seize the sacrificial animal, Ifada, and the very image of a crowd arriving in the night with torch lights vividly recalls the scene of the expulsion of the stranger Mercenary in Sembène's *Moolaadé* and in a couple of scenes in Mambety's *Hyenas*. Michael, who so identifies with Ifada as to become his protector, tries but fails to prevent his capture, and the final image in the film, the horrific face of an infantile Michael staring at the girl and reciting a nursery chant, appears to make this identification concrete. He is unable to save Ifada, but he now takes the child's place through the recitation of the formulaic chant, this voicing itself making up for Ifada's irreparable blemish.

An important achievement of this film is therefore its careful linking of this traumatic experience of unpremeditated sacrifice to the fact of Michael's alienation from the village. In one of the short, fragmentary sequences at the beginning of the film, right after the opening ritual witnessed by Ifada discussed earlier, we see a figure hauling a bag on his shoulder and walking angrily away – toward the camera – against the background of the diegetic sound of a pig's grunting. He is followed by a woman, Sally, whom he entreats to walk faster, and who pauses, makes an ominous "swearing" gesture of breaking with the place she is leaving behind by running her hand over her head. This sequence is not really integrated with the plot, and the couple does not make a subsequent appearance. This is part of the film's residual connection to *The Strong Breed* where stage directions detail the presence of a couple passing by Eman's house, going to catch the lorry leaving the village. The sequence about the departing figures symbolizes Eman's psychic break with his own community, which is dramatized in the play in a flashback. In *So Be It*, it is supplemented through another sequence of a scattered crowd moving through the open grassland, in a move indicating angry leave-taking. While these sequences contribute more to the poetic, fragmented look of the film than to its narrative depth, they validate the main tension between Sunma and Eman. The opening dialogue between the three elders actually prepares the grounds for these developments:

> "Will he get out alive?" says the old man.
> "And her," one of the women adds. "I warned her. What does he know about us?"

Details of why Eman and Sunma "return" to this village are thus as fragmentary as the challenges of departing are urgent. The strong bond between them, the basis for the film's thematic investment in romantic love, is tested by this challenge, the recognition by Sunma that Eman's commitment – to his profession, to the village, to Ifada – is straining their relationship. They are the kinds of details to analyze, and one opportunity for this interpretive task can be seen in the quite opaque exchange between Eman and the little girl. The girl, who is sick, persistently voices the belief that a doll, the item she plans to display at the impending rites, will carry her sickness away, and this in the presence of a medical doctor. It says a lot about the villagers' needs and expectations, and brings greater clarity to the opening dialogue as well as to Sunma's trenchant statement, that Eman is viewed as an interloper. To her, the relationship is sustainable only if they leave. To him, full self-accounting is inseparable from the deep care for the unlucky and vulnerable Ifada. The problem is that both sentiments are incompatible, and this is where to look for the film's gestures to a fatal condition.

The custodians of the ritual in Soyinka's play are the Ogboni, the judicial body connected to Earth worship in traditional Yoruba society and the nature of whose power has often intrigued scholars. As Peter Morton-Williams (1960) writes in "The Yoruba Ogboni Cult in Oyo," his illuminating essay on the Ogboni, even the religious duties of this body are ultimately connected to the exercise of control, the maintenance of order, in the social realm.

> The senior grade of Ogboni will collectively know all that pertains to the orisa cults. They will also have been active participants in them and many will have gone deeply into their esoterica. The ritual of the orisa ceases to captivate the most thoughtful of them and to be reduced to a technique for gaining magical power from the orisa; through their experience, age, and closeness to death they have transcended the ordinary orisa "truth" – the conceptions expressed through the cults – leaving only Earth as the absolute certainty in their future. (p. 373)

Ramaka's framing of sexuality in this ritual discourse is uncanny because, although membership in the Ogboni is gendered, the importance of the elderly female as mother is also the reason for making a woman indispensable to the group. This woman, a mother of the palace according to Morton-Williams, is a representative of the king, and this inclusion is in recognition of the power of women as mothers and as wives, possessors of the XX chromosomes and thus, in this cultural context, of the erotically charged powers of life and death.[4] In *So Be It*, two women take part in the ritual, and when the torch-bearing crowd arrives to seize Ifada at Eman's door, there is a woman at its head, chanting to the boy's face as the crowd finally seizes him. The filmmaker's larger poetic investment, certainly in this film, is to be sought in the non-mimetic ways it confronts the dramatic conflict, which is between the administration of a sovereign but closed system and an intellectual alienation from the idea of hermetic ritual.

It is because of this connection between sovereign or authoritarian control and the ideological openness simultaneously enjoined and withheld by neoliberalism that I find Michel Foucault's reflections in *The Birth of Biopolitics* (2003) to be relevant. I an mindful of the now-standard critique of the intellectual pitfalls of deploying terms generated through the analysis of specific external problems, in this case a European-derived concept as external to African needs. In addition, Foucault repeatedly postpones his discussion of biopolitics in this book; yet I think that the conception of power in relation to ritual, to violence both psychic and physical, and to sexuality, suggests the immanence of the mode of control at play in this film as informed by the originating discourse around the Ogboni. Foucault's central aim in using the concept, to explore "what concrete content could be given to the analysis of power – it being understood … that power can in no way be considered either as a principle in itself, or as having explanatory value which functions from the outset" (p. 186) actually dates back to the first volume of *The History of Sexuality* and receives far more detailed treatment in *Society Must Be Defended!* But it is in *The Birth of Biopolitics* that he connects the concept more directly to neoliberal economics, especially through his reading of his economic writings of Jeremy Bentham, an eighteenth-century English social historian of *laissez-faire* capitalism. In particular, Bentham's formulation of *sponte acta* derives from a view of economic activities spontaneously developed by members of a community without governmental intervention, as distinct from agenda and non-agenda, economic activities of a government according to whether they maximize pleasure or minimize pain. Reading Bentham, Foucault argues that the even more provisional term, governmentality, "the way in which one conducts the conduct of men, is no more than a proposed analytical grid for these relations of power" (p. 186), and that the most meaningful term, "biopolitics," represents "the attempt, starting from the eighteenth century, to rationalize the problems posed to governmental practice by phenomena characteristic of a set of living beings forming a population: Health, hygiene, birthrate, life expectancy, race…" (p. 317).

Far from suggesting that the neoliberal system unfavorably views a work of incredible erotic charge such as *So Be It*, or that the political and clerical authorities in Senegal are in cahoots with the agents of the World Bank to sanitize the country's cinema industry, I am making a different but specific argument. This is that Ramaka's artistic preference for complex subject-matter and his poetic, highly aestheticized approach to filmmaking both complicate the desire for producing work with the kind of commercial viability in which neoliberalism is ultimately invested. The World Bank may not be in cahoots with the political establishment in Senegal to clean up the filmmaking industry, but Kodak will promptly set up shop in Dakar if there is money to be had. I argue further that the neglect of culturally esoteric topics – like the connection in *So Be It* and Ogboni society between erotic powers and political rituals – under the prevalent economic conditions is systematic. It pertains to other artforms (contemporary literary fiction, for example), and it amounts to a form of censorship for which it is not easy to hold anyone accountable. This explains why I opted for "governance," rather than "government" in Bourdieu's term, "invisible government of the powerful." The objective, impersonal attitude toward any and all kinds of activity through which to safely and profitably do business runs into a conflict when an ungovernable artistic temperament makes its appearance, and censorship is the administrative way of removing or controlling such a conflict. It seems to me that the elaborate, diffracted process of executing this form of control is what Foucault calls "biopolitics," and that it acquires a potent force in contexts where it involves bodily control in erotic terms. The critique of authoritarian power in *So Be It*, though still suggestive, has an added significance in the context of neoliberal globalization because, even at that early stage in his career, Ramaka was working within a production context in which the contingencies of funding and commissioning were consequential enough to shape, if not absolutely determine, what a film was or is – what films get made.

Producing Romantic Love

So Be It was one of four short films on the theme of love produced for Arte, the French television programming company, and collectively titled *Africa Dreaming* (1997). The remaining three are Abderrahmane Sissako's *Sabriya* (Mauritania/ Tunisia), Pedro Pimenta's *The Gaze of the Stars* (Mozambique), and Richard Pakleppa's *Sophie's Homecoming* (Namibia). According to promotional information about the project, Jeremy Nathan, an executive producer for Arte conceived of television programming designed "to give Africans a rare opportunity to speak directly to each other in their own words and images." There was already a series in place, and this particular project was aimed at generating collaboration between broadcasters, television producers, writers, and film directors across the continent. So Nathan "asked for script proposals for 26-minute dramatic shorts on the broad theme of 'love in Africa'... [and the channel chose] four of the six films which were selected and produced." Ramaka has also disclosed that he was hired to work as a production consultant on the project (Personal communication/Interview, 23 September 2016).

Clearly, this was a film commissioned for television, a form of cinematic production which is oriented toward the institutional protocols of film scripts as "grant writing," competitive submission, and jury selection. Prior to the emergence of Nollywood and apart from the Egyptian and South African industries (and excepting the corpus of directors like Ousmane Sembène and Souleymane Cissé as well), this was how much of what has come to be known as African cinema had been produced. Commentaries on this complex, "exogenous" production context for a cultural form aimed at self-representation are just as complex and diverse, but one of the most insightful so far happens to come from an insider – Rod Stoneman's reflections as Commissioning Editor for the United Kingdom's Channel Four. First published in 1993, incidentally on the occasion of the thirtieth anniversary of the release of Sembène's *Borom Sarret*, Stoneman's reflections articulated the issues surrounding the politics of funding for film and television in African cinema at a time when the large part of funding and technical resources originated from outside the film's primary economic and aesthetic concerns. Characterizing as "ultra-auteurism" the position of many African filmmakers, "directors who are also, at one and the same time, the producers of their own films," Stoneman makes a case for a "body of professional, entrepreneurial, cultural producers ... to articulate potential funding sources and, it can be argued, to strengthen individual production processes" (1996, p. 176). To underscore this dire situation, Stoneman incidentally quotes Ramaka (though without providing context) who sees the writer/director/producer complex as unacceptably obstructive of professional sanity: "They have always gone on the long, solitary and labored quest for international aid, accepting all its criteria and demands, making one film every ten to four years" (p. 176). From this picture, a tension between "the directorial id" and "productorial superego" arises, and the result is best imagined in the questions that Stoneman subsequently poses:

> Is there an unconscious predilection for certain types of products, a selective prioritization of certain types of films? What kind of African films are more difficult, or even impossible for European television? Do specific interventions change particular films? No commutation test exists when asking how these relations may affect the organic development of African cinema – it is not possible to know those films which have never been made! (p. 177).

It is true that current developments in digital technology, bold imaginaries of global blackness, and new channels of distribution may have complicated or even changed some of the premise from which this argument is launched. The Nigerian breakthrough film, *Living in Bondage*, was conceivably in "pre-production" (note the euphemism) as this was being written in the early 1990s, and the case of a director/producer like Kunle Afolayan has shown that it is possible to be both and still make a film every two to three years – even three films in a year, as his 2017 output demonstrated.[5] An explosion of small but well-publicized film festivals has occurred with the last decade across the continent, as well as at non-African venues, promoting the work of African directors in very unique ways, coming out of sensibilities and cultural innovations that Stoneman's admirably sympathetic point of view did not anticipate. These festivals, such as African International Film Festival (London), Lights, Camera, Africa! (Lagos), African Diaspora Film Festival (New York), and Nollywood in London, are closely linked to new processes of imagining audiences and communities, which are easier to do through social media-based marketing and crowdfunding, and which also enable modes of distribution that could not have been contemplated at a time when the concept of the Internet was non-existent. Within Nigeria and in much of West Africa, different kinds of Nollywood films are broadcast round the clock on the Africa Magic channel of MNET, the South African satellite broadcasting company which contracted

Afolayan's three films of 2017, while the Chinese-owned company Starfilms and the online streaming portals of iROKOtv have taken to producing original Nollywood content.

Nonetheless, I think that some of Stoneman's points bear returning to because of a paradoxical situation. Recent developments in the production and distribution of varieties of African cinema have also increasingly resulted in the marginalization of the kind of filmmaking which ought to serve as aesthetic alternative, or complement, to either Nollywood, "extraverted productions" or other, strong "national" industries – in Egypt or South Africa.[6] These developments have not eliminated the dire circumstances under which African or "non-industrialized" directors operate, and which continue to put their works in a special category, especially when compared to those of their contemporaries in the United States, the United Kingdom, France, or Germany. To be sure, certain operational modes of neoliberalism, in the ubiquitous form of globalization, play a role in determining the fortunes of a film as a final product, if it succeeds in making the transition from a script. Even international film festivals such as the Sundance and the Independent Film Channel (IFC) which were designed to rescue filmmaking from the so-called "Hollywood model" cannot totally escape this logic, and when an African director appears at any of these festivals, he or she is rarely scheduled in a major event, far from the prestigious "A-list," as the industrial pecking order reasserts itself anew. As the scholar Bérénice Reynaud puts it in her famous report on the 2005 Sundance Festival, "film professionals, when they come to Sundance, want to be a part of the "discovery" of the "new Tarantino" – not marvel at the bold cinematic language of an *auteur* from Burkina Faso, whose commercial prospects are close to nil" (Reynaud, "Shades"). In this regard, the particular production and aesthetic situations from which Ramaka made *So Be It* ought to be discussed in more specific ways.

That any director would be selective in his choice of material for a 30-minute film goes without saying. As a matter of fact, Ramaka has also disclosed, during the interview I mentioned earlier, that his screenplay based on *The Strong Breed* was much longer than the filmed script. While getting into the head of the creator of an artwork is not always a sufficient guarantor of informed reflection on the said work, it is sometimes useful to have an idea of what may not be reflected on the surface of a film – if that film manages to get made at all. Besides the production exigencies which ensured that only four out of six successful scripts made it to film in a project which seeks to explore the theme of love, there is also the question of the specific directorial choices through which the film is calibrated. This is relevant because *So Be It* is one of two films in the project which are based on published works – Pimenta's *The Gaze of the Stars* is also inspired by a story by the Mozambican writer Mia Couto. Both the appeal and the discomfort of Soyinka's dramatic assumptions become grist for the mill of Ramaka's directorial options, but the thematic pressures of making the film address issues of love would result in a work that shifts the focus of action and diegesis from the primary issues of sacrifice and self-accountability.

There is nothing intrinsically wrong with this – the field of signification is a field of infinite possibilities. In the same interview, Ramaka disclosed that he did not agree with some of Soyinka's choices in creating a self-sacrificing character like Eman, nor did he intend to suggest a homoerotic bond between Eman and Ifada – but he was fully aware of the erotic power of the female role in secretive rituals, and even as a mode of public censure.[7] The fact is worth stressing, however, that between reducing Ramaka's script to a 30-minute drama and downplaying the originating ideas in *The Strong Breed*, important analytical questions arise which further underscore the tensions between the social and the poetic imagination. On a certain level, it is conceivable that the treatment of the romantic impulse which is truncated in *So Be It* makes a return in *It's My Man*, a film which is admittedly of a different generic order and comes out of a more independent production process than in the earlier film.[8] I think that it is more helpful to view Ramaka's oeuvre in this incremental or supplementary manner; that which does not have the opportunity for full manifestation within the parameters of a sponsored or commissioned work makes a return in another where the production strictures are lax. The point I am making is that the dramatic intensity of Soyinka's play is differently calibrated (not to say "degraded") in film, a medium which prioritizes meaning-making through the narrative demands of a theme-based curating or selection. It may sound unseemly, but Arte's ostensibly bold idea of television programming designed "to give Africans a rare opportunity to speak directly to each other in their own words and images" is hard to conceive outside the pressures of neoliberalism. This was a reality that Soyinka, working as a research fellow courtesy of a Rockefeller grant and with the benefit of young, enthusiastic actors, did not have to confront. Ramaka is afforded the privilege of limited enunciation because the challenges which the social poses to the poetic imagination manifest themselves through the invisible governance of the powerful, in this case through the deleterious effects of the free market. They are the challenges that a director of Ramaka's artistic orientation faces in dealing with the contending forces of authoritarianism and neoliberal globalization.

The point is that in purely aesthetic terms, Ramaka's work ranks very high among scholars and critics, and with audiences on the evidence of *Karmen Gei*, and his poetic approach does not necessarily eventuate in obscure or inaccessible work. On the strength of *Karmen Gei*, Ramaka has attained something close to canonical status in the annals of African filmmaking. To the best of my knowledge, the film is one of the few works in African cinema about which an entire monograph has been written.[9] While this fact in itself represents a potentiality, the implications of such status for Ramaka's earlier and later works are considerable. His more recent films, especially the short films *Plan Jaxaay!*, *Madame Plastig*, and *L'arbre qui crie!*, have been privately produced and not formally distributed. All three of them are about specific social problems – urban flooding, the ubiquity of plastic as an issue of environmental concern, and deforestation – across West Africa, not just in Senegal. If the problem of censorship as I have conceptualized it in this chapter is consequential in Ramaka's career, the challenge is to probe further into the role that the forces of authoritarianism and neoliberalism have played in this situation, and how the director's aesthetic options, if properly harnessed, could constitute a real alternative in African filmmaking. This is the issue to which I now turn.

Conclusion: The Stories We Choose to Tell

Of these two forces, the devil and the deep blue sea of postcolonial art, neoliberalism is the more implacable, a fact with implications for consequential artistic confrontation with authoritarianism. Given his predilections so far discussed, Ramaka is the kind of director to make a film for which the System (read imperialism, neoliberalism) has no use, as the proponents of Third Cinema once wrote to characterize revolutionary filmmaking. The incorporative and absorptive nature of the commodity form has certainly shown how much this characterization underestimated capitalist culture: There are hardly any films which the System may find useless to the point of being surprised by their potential for subversive politics, and as I noted earlier, neoliberalism is sustained by the constant, restless search for spaces in which to do business safely and profitably. The singular example of Gilo Pontecorvo's classic, *The Battle of Algiers*, is a case in point. This was a film dramatizing the history of the Algerian War of the 1950s but which, 50 years later, became a useful weapon for the U.S. Department of Defense, a sort of how-to film in the war against terror. To understand the process leading to this transformation of a revolutionary classic in cinema history into a tool of high-wire warfare, I think it is useful to pay attention to how and why Pontecorvo made this film. According to Carlo Celli in *Gillo Pontecorvo: From Resistance to Terrorism*, the director was already well-established within the international context of cinema as an industry, ranging from Italian neorealism to contractual Hollywood. The treatment for a film which Pontecorvo wrote before *The Battle of Algiers* actually imagined either Paul Newman or Warren Beatty as the lead (2005, p. 50). Celli writes further that the "Pontecorvo-Solinas treatment is apparently imbedded with an admiration for the cool, macho professionalism of the French paratroopers ... but the film was never made, in part because producers at the time were wary of the Organization de l'Armée Secrète (OAS), a terrorist group active in maintaining French rule in Algeria through intimidation and terrorism" (p. 50). Although the film was never made, the contacts which Pontecorvo made while traveling in Algeria played a role in the well-known film. The relevant point in this example is that the director was a player in a production context in which the sense of film as a commodity was decisive.

The subject-matter of Ramaka's three short films – *Plan Jaxaay! Madame Plastig*, and *Un arbre qui crie!* – is localized and "difficult," and may seem too middling to merit the kind of attention usually given major works, on the basis of critical opinion which confers canonical status on such works. But if we consider these films alongside *And What If Latif Was Right?*, a different interpretation suggests itself, one which approaches the films as a series of much-needed activist interventions in the social sphere, a significant body of work about socio-political issues in Senegal, with reverberations across the West African region, and thus reinforcing Ramaka's self-characterization as a "citoyen engagé." The main issue in *Plan Jaxaay!* is less the flooding than the neglect of the Jaxaay neighborhood, and it might even be possible that this is a calculated neglect aimed at preparing the grounds for prime property by office-holders and their business allies.[10] The environmental risks constituted by the pervasive presence of plastic may come across as "elitist" from the perspective of the long line of laboring women seen in the opening scene of Sembène's *Faat Kine* carrying water on their heads, the haunting voice of the singer Yande Codou Sène hovering above their burdened heads. Yet it is precisely the kind of morality informing the film's critique that is missing in so many cinematic attempts at acknowledging the ingenuity of ordinary people – in a world where the ordinary people unsustainably, unreflectingly (and perhaps inescapably?) reproduce the conditions for their own continued exploitation.

Further down the scale, it is also the case that these examples of activist subject-matter are not entirely resistant to corporate or large-scale funding. The challenge is to determine the scale of their importance as ideas or social issues that can find company in the imaginaries of others – which is always a complex blend of many things, including cultural and material conditions. The historical basis for the opportunistic canonization of *The Battle of Algiers* which I mentioned earlier ought to be discussed in a broader context. The position of Theodor Adorno and Max Horkheimer about the culture industry as reinforcing conservative ideology is well known. Less known is the view of Andrei Tarkovsky on the relationship between a filmmaker's poetic imagination and so-called popular audience. In *The Genius, the Man, the Legend*, a film which follows Tarkovsky around as he works on films, the Russian director makes the compelling argument about the poetic imagination in cinema and its relationship to the popular commercial success. According to Tarkovsky, poet-filmmakers such as Satyajit Ray, Ingmar Bergman, Luis Buñuel, and Akira Kurosawa "have difficulty getting their works out, not because they want to be obscure, but because they want to listen secretly, to give expression to what is deep inside those we call the audience" (Tarkovsky, 1988). It seems to me that the challenges that the social poses for the poetic imagination in the work of Ramaka are to be met at the intersection of these three approaches. It is a problem that defies a simple solution, because for Ramaka, there are two additional institutional issues: The contexts of filmmaking in contemporary West Africa, and diasporicity as a social fact.

Some years ago, the Cameroonian filmmaker Jean-Marie Teno wondered wryly if the success of Nollywood might intimidate scholars to abandon Africa cinema, which he believed to have more to offer on African experiences than the ostensibly commercialized Nigerian form.[11] Recent scholarship on African cinema shows an interest in subthemes and subfields, and we have the paradoxical situation of a cinematic practice that, having attained a level of institutional viability on the evidence of the scholarship, is also at the risk of stasis in terms of production and dissemination. A film such as Sissako's *Timbuktu* attracts an Academy Award nomination, as Nigerian director Afolayan releases one well-distributed film after another, whereas Souleymane Cissé's entire oeuvre remains unknown except to specialists of African cinema. These are important issues in the development of African cinema and, for a filmmaker like Ramaka, they are material. A poet-filmmaker is audible or visible in the world *as a filmmaker* to the extent that she is able to reproduce herself, and the social is the ground for this possibility.

Notes

1   Eileen Julien made this statement during the oral presentation of her paper at the joint conference coordinated by Frieda Ekotto and Ken Harrow at Michigan State University (MSU) and the University of Michigan in October 2010. The remarks did not appear in the version of the essay published in *Rethinking African Cultural Production* (2015).

2   See "Interview with Djibril Diop Mambéty," http://itutu.com/djibril/Interview.html. Last accessed 20 August 2009.

3   I am grateful to Moustapha Ndour and Moussa Thiao for helping with the translation of this Wolof chant.

4   Morton-Williams (1960, p. 368) also notes that the membership of an Ogboni society included six women.

5   By August 2017, Afolayan had released three films – *Omugwo*, *Roti*, and *The Tribunal* – all commissioned by MNET. The director discussed these commissions in a YouTube video produced shortly before the release of the third film.

6   I characterize as "extraverted production" the different tendencies which Oliver Barlet (2010) ascribes to contemporary African filmmaking in response to "Western audiences' demands for both exoticism and reality." See his "The New Paradoxes of Black Africa's Cinemas," especially p. 223.

7   During the interview, Ramaka also provided an anecdotal example of a French colonial officer in Casamance who died shortly after an encounter with rioting women who confronted him with bared breasts.

8   *It's My Man* (2009), is a film based on the relationship between the scholar Eileen Julien and the Senegalese artist Kalidou Sy, narrated from Julien's point of view. At screenings, Ramaka often stated that the film was a love story, and not about Sy.

9   The film *The Figurine* (2010) by the Nigerian director Kunle Afolayan is the subject of an edited volume, *Auteuring Nollywood*, published in 2014.

10 One might note a similar impulse in the latest film by the director Femi Odugbemi which is about the floating school at Makoko in Lagos, and note in addition that Ramaka and Odugbemi also collaborate on institutional projects.

11 Although Teno made this observation in private conversation, it is consistent with his publicly expressed view of Nollywood. For an example of this criticism, see Martin and Moorman (2015, pp. 9–10).

References

Baldwin, James. 1998. "Alas, Poor Richard." In *Collected Essays*, 247–268, New York: The Library of America.

Barlet, Oliver. 2010. "The New Paradoxes of Black Africa's Cinemas," In *World Cinemas, Transnational Perspectives*, edited by Natasa Durovicova and Kathleen Newman, 217–224. London: Routledge.

Bourdieu, Pierre. 2003. *Firing Back: Against the Tyranny of the Market 2*, New York: The New Press.

Brecht, Bertolt. 1992. "A Short Organum for the Theater." In *Brecht on Theater: The Development of an Aesthetic*, 179–205, translated by John Willett, New York: Hill and Wang.

Celli, Carlo. 2005. *Gilo Pontecorvo: From Resistance to Terrorism*, Scarecrow Press.

Foucault, Michel. 2003. *The Birth of Biopolitics*, New York: Picador.

"Interview with Djibril Diop Mambéty," http://itutu.com/djibril/Interview.html. Accessed 27 October 2017.

Interview with Joseph Gai Ramaka (Akin Adesokan), 23 September 2016.

Julien, Eileen. 2015. "The Critical Present: Where is 'African Literature'?" In *Rethinking African Cultural Production*, edited by Frieda Ekotto and Kenneth W. Harrow, 17–28. Bloomington and Indianapolis: Indiana University Press.

Martin, Michael T. 2008. "I'm Not A Filmmaker Engagé. I'm A Citizen Engagé." *Black Camera* 22/23: 1, 24–34.

Martin, Michael T. and Marissa Moorman. 2015. "The Civilising Mission of Globalisation." *Third Text*, 29: 1–2, 1–14.

Morton-Williams, Peter. 1960. "The Yoruba Ogboni Cult in Oyo." *Africa*, 30: 4, 362–374.

Quayson, Ato. 2003. *Calibrations: Reading for the Social*, Minneapolis: University of Minnesota Press.

Reynaud, Bérénice. 2005. "Shades of Globalization: The 24th Sundance Film Festival." *Sense of Cinema*, 5. http://sensesofcinema.com/2005/festival-reports/sundance2005. Accessed 17 October 2016.

Stoneman, Rod. 1996. "South/South Axis: For a Cinema Built by, with and for Africans." In *African Experiences of Cinema*, edited by Imruh Bakari and Mbye Cham. London: British Film Institute, 175–180.

Tarkovsky, Andrei Arsenevich, 1988. *The Genius, The Man, The Legend Andrei Tarkovsky*, edited by Michal Leszczylowski. Stockholm: Swedish Film Institute.

Filmography

Godard, Jean-Luc. (2005). *Notre Musique*. New York: Wellspring Media.

Mambéty, Djibril Diop. (2003). *Hyènes/Hyenas*. New York: Kino on Video.

Pontecorvo, Gilo. (2004). *The Battle of Algiers*, Irvington, NY: Criterion.

Ramaka, Joseph Gai. (2009). *It's My Man*, New Orleans, LA: Colored People's Production.

Ramaka, Joseph Gai. (2005). *And What if Latif Were Right?/Et si Latif avait raison?* Senegal: L'Observatoire Audiovisuel sur les Libertés.

Ramaka, Joseph Gai. (2001). *Karmen Gei*. Senegal and France. California Newsreel, Arté France Cinéma, and Euripide Productions.

Ramaka, Joseph Gai.(1997). *So Be It*. San Francisco: California Newsreel.

Ribeiro, João. (1997). *The Gaze of the Stars*. San Francisco: California Newsreel.

Sembène, Ousmane. (2004). *Moolaade*. Senegal: Filmi Doomirev.

Part III
Sound/Form/Dub

7

Transcultural Language Intimacies
The Linguistic Domestication of Indian Films in the Hausa Language

Abdalla Uba Adamu

Indian cinema has had a powerful influence on African audiences with whom Indian films are extremely popular (Desai, 2004; Kaur and Sinha, 2005; Kasbekar, 2006; Dönmez-Colin, 2007; Hawley, 2008). The popularity of Hindi cinema in Africa came about because of the perceived cultural similarities between Indian and African social structures, particularly with regards to traditional culture and gender treatment, which generated interest in, and feelings of affinity for, Hindi film cultures among African communities (Larkin, 1997; Steene, 2008; Fair, 2009). Among the Muslim Hausa of northern Nigeria, the influence of Hindi film goes beyond audience consumption and has led to the appearance of local video-film productions, in Hausa, based loosely on Indian film creative templates (Adamu, 2007). Consequently, from 1990 when the Hausa video-film industry was created until the present, hundreds of Indian films have been "remade" as Hausa-language equivalents (Adamu, 2010). From 2014, however, Hausa filmmakers adopted a new remake strategy: The direct dubbing of Hausa-language dialogue on selected predominantly action Telugu films from India. These films are referred to as Indiya-Hausa in the local commerce. This act of dubbing Indian, Telegu-language films in Hausa can best be referred to as *interorality*. Popularized as a literary concept by Hanétha Vété-Congolo (2016), the term refers to the systematic transposition of previously composed storytales into new and distinct tales. Although Vété-Congolo used the term in reference to her analysis of Caribbean literature, the fundamental concept of transposition of two different and in this case, unrelated, languages to create a narrative of understanding to an audience of one of the languages, is perfectly captured in the dubbing of Hausa-language translated dialogue onto Telugu films in northern Nigeria.

The Trajectories of Hausa Film Development

The popularity of Indian films in northern Nigeria followed three trajectories. The first, starting in Kano, northern Nigeria, from the early 1960s up to about 1982 reflected itself in the way songs from predominantly Hindi-language films were domesticated by local secular and religious singers into Hausa equivalents. Local popular and secular performers often used the meters of Indian film songs and substituted the lyrics with Hausa onomatopoeic equivalents (Adamu, 2010). From 1983, religious performers, often singing the praises of Prophet Muhammad, formed themselves into singing groups (using the bandiri frame drum) called Ushaqu Indiya (Lovers of India) and also adapted the meters of Indian films songs into songs praising the Prophet (Larkin, 2002). These cross-cultural popular culture adaptations served to entrench Indian films into the hearts of local audiences of Indian films. The second trajectory started in 1982 when local drama clubs hired videographers to experiment with VHS cameras and record their dramatic performances. These dramas were based loosely on famous Indian films popular in that period and featured mimed songs, called Sidiya, which were inserted into the narrative and danced by a local female artist. These taped dramas were shown in video parlors in local communities and attracted great interest. By 1999, a commercial, Hausa industry had formed and was tagged Kanywood. During this period, the Hausa film industry adopted a variety of production strategies with the industry approximating and, in many cases directly appropriating, Hindi-language films from India in terms of storyline, cinematography, and narrative focus. From 1990 to 2015, more than 150 Indian films were directly appropriated and remade as Hausa film equivalents.

In his discussion of the remake, Thomas Leitch identifies "four possible stances a remake can adopt, each with its own characteristic means of resolving its contradictory intertextual claims" (1990, p. 142). These are the "readaptation," the "update," the "homage," and the "true remake." These stances refer to intertextual relationship between the remake and the source text – rather than the general approach (model) that motivates the need for the remake. Thus Leitch's "stances" gives us another perspective on the specific strategies adopted when a decision to remake is taken.

Here, I am arguing that Hausa remakes be understood not merely as adaptations of Indian films, but as appropriations of those films. In trying to distinguish between adaptation and appropriation, Sanders (2006) argues that "adaptation signals a relationship with an informing source text," while "appropriation frequently affects a more decisive journey away from the informing source into a wholly new cultural product and domain" (Sanders 2006, p. 26). This distinction does apply significantly to the political economy of video-film production in northern Nigeria because films appropriated into Hausa from Indian source texts, and occasionally from Hollywood, clearly share a creative relationship with their orig-inals; None-the-less, the Hausa video filmmakers go out of their way to combine a series of Indian films together in one film in order to re-create them as a new film. A typical example of this was *Gwaska* (dir. Adam A. Zango, 2015), a Hausa-langauge film that drew from at least four films: *Krrish* (dir. Rakesh Roshan, 2006); *Kick* (dir. Sajid Nadiadwala, 2014); and the Telugu films, *Billa* (dir. Meher Ramesh, 2009) and *Shadow* (dir. Meher Ramesh, 2013). In "translating" the four Indian films into one, Zango not only enacted the action sequences of the originals, but also donned the Zorro trademark mask of each of the main characters in the two Indian films in the original source films. This act of cultural remediation draws attention to the transnational origins of "Gwaska," a Hausa word meaning a Robin Hood-kind of folk hero, who robs the rich and feeds the poor with the pro-ceeds. Such acts of cross-cultural appropriation through Hindi films that are then translated into a form of Hausa popular culture was what sustained the creative impulse of Hausa video films.

Thus in analyzing transnational media flows in popular culture, it becomes inevitable to discuss the issues of adaptation and appropriation. While adaptation is clearly intermedial – shifting from source text to another (for instance, adapting a book to its film version), appropriation is "a more decisive journey away from the informing source into a wholly new cultural product and domain" (Sanders 2006, p. 26). Thus, appropriation is often intramedial – circulating within the same media (for instance, from a film version to another one).

Hausa cinema in northern Nigeria draws its main inspiration from Hindi cinema, such that over 130 Hindi films were appropriated in one form or the other as Hausa video films (see Adamu, 2009). This is further illustrated by the fact that when the Nigerian government provided grants for training Nigerian filmmakers in 2014, Hausa filmmakers chose to be trained in India to be as close to their cine-matic models as possible (Ciroma, 2014). A sample of 12 is shown in Table 7.1.

Table 7.1 is based on the entire range of appropriation styles adopted between Indian films and the corresponding Hausa video films; some were shot-by-shot remakes; others used the Hindi songs and thematically re-arranged them using Hausa lyrics or borrowed scenes here and there. Yet, others used artwork (poster and editing techniques) from Hindi films. Finally, some use similar special effects to create similar scenes from Indian films. An analysis of the main list of 124 shows that 77 of the Hausa video films were directly based on the storylines of a corresponding Hindi film, while 30 adapted the songs, 17 used various scenes and one simply used the title of the equivalent Hindi film.

Finally, the third historical trajectory of cross pollination between Indian and Hausa saw the substitution of Indian film dialogue in Indian films with Hausa nar-ratives, a process which started from 2001. As this is the main subject of this chapter, I will first provide a broader picture of the process of the appropriation of Indian films by Hausa filmmakers before contextualizing the interorality of the new productions.

Table 7.1   Hausa video-film and Hindi film inspirations/appropriations

Original Hindi film	Hausa remake	Element remade
Agni Shakshi	Izaya	Storyline
Azaad	Jirwaye	Scenes
Bhoot	Almuru	Storyline
Chandni	Ayaah	Storyline
Chori Chupke	Furuci	Storyline
Jurm	Jumurda	Storyline
Judwa	Abin Sirrine	Storyline
Major Saab	Kasaita	Song
Dillagi	Mujadala	Scenes
Hum Aapke Hain Kaun	Kudiri	Scenes
Sanam Bewafa	Akasi	Scenes
Yaraana	Hakuri	Scenes

Interorality and Audiovisual Translation

Interorality and audiovisual translations share a common ground in that they both involve transposition and substation of dialogue from one language to a different one. While interorality is mainly in a folktale domain, audiovisual translation achieves its effects through digital technologies.

While in northern Nigeria this translation came in the form of direct cinematic appropriation, in East Africa it took the form of narrative oral translation. Lagarriga (2007) reported that in Uganda the process was initiated by a VJ called Lingo in 1988. While more a commentator than a translator, Lingo proved catalytic to the professionalization of the film translation in Uganda. As Lagarriga's informant noted, "in 1998 we started dubbing films, with two video decks, one plays, one is dubbing, so we translate it and it was recorded. We did copies and we put them in the video library, so people could come and rent them." In Tanzania, Englert noted in 2010 that "the translation of films from languages such as English, Hindi/Urdu or Chinese into Swahili is a phenomenon that has quickly grown into a successful business in … the last couple of years" (Englert 2010, p. 138). The stars in this translation were video DJs or VJays. Englert further argues that the task of translating foreign films into Kiswahili in Tanzania was not framed by notions of "resistance" to Western cultural hegemony, but employed as devices to enable a faster and more domesticated understanding of international films for local audiences. These locally translated versions, or filamu zimezotafsiriwa, as they were referred to, proved to be extremely popular, especially among the youth in Tanzania. The mechanism of the translation provides an insight into the process. As Englert further reported, "the oral translations provided by the film translators are neither proper dubbings nor voice-overs but rather what could be termed as "delayed dubbing," i.e. the voice of the translator is inserted after the original voice which remains to a large extent audible" (Englert 2010, p. 148).

This would seem to indicate that at least two voices can be heard in the same film – the original voice and the translator's voice. It goes beyond this, however, as the translators also provide running commentaries on the film and the actors, thus providing a third script to the translated film – two scripts from the source and the target, plus a third exposition from the narrator which is not part of the original source dialogue. English-language source films were much easier to translate more accurately, while non-English films, such as Hindi or Chinese, were translated based on their English subtitles. Even then, the lack of subtitles in non-English films was not a barrier to the translation; for, as Englert's interview with one of the translators indicated, he was able "to understand any filmed story – even if he does not know the languages" (Englert 2010, p. 150).

Similar interoral devices were also adopted in Congo in which foreign films, particularly those from Nigerian "Nollywood," were translated into kiKinois, "a mixture of Lingala, French, and Hindubill (youth slang that originated during the early postcolonial period)" (Pype 2013, p. 220). In Uganda, Dominica Dipio (2014) reports that Nigerian Nollywood films, recorded in English, were remixed in Luganda language by local VJs and proved to be immensely popular.

These various modalities of interoral translation – which transpose the target narrative over the source – often extend beyond the film narrative.Miller (2016, p. 85) reports that "narrators can localize this foreign content, connecting, for instance, a destructive fire in a Nollywood movie to one that recently destroyed a local market, affecting the lives of many in the market video hall audience." This practice became an established VJ tradition in Uganda because at times during the film, the translator bestowed the actors with local nicknames (Dipio, 2014).

In the first instance, as indicated earlier, Hausa filmmakers directly appropriate mainly Hindi-language films as Hausa equivalents, with a parallel storyline structure, which more or less domesticates the original Indian film as a Hausa version. In the second stage of the transnational appropriation, Hausa marketers experimented with the idea of language dubbing – a practice long-established in East Africa. In northern Nigeria, this process started with the first direct voice dubbing of a Tamil-language film, *Namma Ooru Poovatha* (dir. M. Manivasagam, 1990) in late 1990s. It was marketed by Ace J. Ventures and Video Palace of unknown location but most likely in Jos, northern Nigeria, where Indian films were more popular than anywhere else in the north of the country. Figure 7.1 shows the VHS cassette cover of the film.

The Hausa translators named it "B. Manic" after one of the characters in the film. Appearing as it did at the time, the film created a flurry of interest in that it provided Hausa viewers of Indian films with a direct access to the dialogue. The film is quite rare. The only copy I was able to locate on a VHS cassette has deteriorated considerably and was barely audible – but it was definitely in Hausa and marketed as "the first Indian film in Hausa" on the cover artwork of

Figure 7.1 *Namma Ooru Poovatha* as Hausa "B. Manic."

the film's cassette packaging. *B Manic* was moderately successful. Since there were no details on how the dub-over translations were done, one might assume that the dubbing into Hausa was most likely based on a deductive understanding of the dialogue, rather than a linguistic understanding of Tamil. This deduction device was used by Tanzanian translators of particularly Hindi films who based their linguistic expertise on their understanding of the dialogue in the source films and creating vocal narrative equivalents. This method works well only in dubbed-over translations, rather than live rendering of the source film dialogue, since some members of the audience could have a superior understanding of the source film's dialogue than the narrator. This mode of audiovisual translation differs remarkably from the strategies of video narration adopted by East African VJs. For whereas the VJ translation phenomena in East Africa started with live rendering of the dialogues of the foreign films into Kiswahili, the Nigerian translators, perhaps operating in a stronger economy, bypassed the live narration and launched directly into the voice-over dubbing. translations. After B. Manic, one or two other films were translated into Hausa, but the practice was discontinued. My field work indicated that this was caused by the high cost of doing the dub-over translations, coupled with a technology (VHS recorders) that was cumbersome to use.

The dub-over translations were revived some years later in Kano by Algaita Music Studios, which was established in Kano in 2003 as a general-purpose music recording. These dubbed films were targeted at capturing a share of the burgeoning soundtrack music for Hausa video films before eventually branching into Hip Hop music. The founder of the studio, Sadiq Salihu Abubakar (who goes by the stage name of Buzo Danfillo), had established himself as an accomplished session musician (and a Rapper). By 2012, he had started the business of Hausa dub-over translations, which the youth language in Kano refers to as "suburbuɗa" – a coined Hausa word that simply suggests a transformation. Buzo Danfillo started with Hausa dubbing of an Iranian TV series, *Yousuf-e-Payambar* (dir. Farajollah Salahshoor, 2008) or "Joseph, the Prophet." Some of the episodes in the series had English voice-over dubs. It was these that Algaita retranslated into Hausa by first translating the English subtitles. Using an Audio Dialogue Replacement technical process, Algaita then substituted the original Farsi dialogue of the film with Hausa translations. To achieve this substitution, Algaita used Sonar X1 music software to separate the sound tracks and remove the English voice track. He then transcribed the dialogue on that track into Hausa, recorded it in Hausa and dubbed it back onto the video. This process created a Hausa version of the original, the first in a series to follow and established a sub-industry of transnational translation. The poster artwork for both the original and the translated is shown in Figure 7.2.

 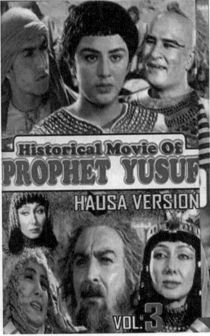

Figure 7.2 *Joseph the Prophet* DVDs in Kano markets – original and dubbed both pirated.

Released as "Historical Movie of Prophet Yusuf – Hausa Version" on eight DVDs for the entire 45 episodes, the translations proved massively successful for a number of reasons. First, there was the inherent popularity of the story of Joseph (Yusuf), which, as narrated in the Qur'an (Chapter 12), taught many lessons, especially perseverance, hope, patience, forgiveness, etc. Second, the Hausa translations, rather than subtitles (which would require a level of literacy) domesticated the narrative and delivered it in a form easily digestible by the Hausa. By "speaking" to the audience, the Hausa narration engages the audience in a personal encounter, as if talking directly to the viewer. This personalization created avenues for debate and discussions on the film in many conversational groups – thus immersing the audience in a way the original Farsi and English versions would have done.

The success of the Prophet Joseph translation DVD in Kano and other northern cities created a new business model for translation of transnational films into Hausa and attracted the attention of a resident Indian merchant, K. Pawan, whose company, Speedy Ventures Nigeria Limited, imported films from India. Seeking to experiment with translated dub-overs, Pawan sought out Nazeer Magoga, a Hausa performer resident in Kano who had a high standard of Hindi. He had published Hausa to Hindi phrase books in 1996. In 2005, he was given a one-hour slot on Radio Kano FM during which he presented *Mu Kewaya Indiya* [Let us visit India], a program in which he translated Hindi film songs into Hausa. His fluency in Hindi was such that in 2007 the BBC World Service in London showed interest, which resulted in a live-on-air interview with him about his life with an Indian journalist, Indu Shekhar Sinha, in Hindi. This attracted so much attention in India that the BBC Delhi office sent a crew to interview Magoga in Kano in July 2008. The crew was led by Rupa Jha, who recorded the entire interview in Hindi at the Tahir Guest Palace Hotel in Kano and was broadcast in India. It was this latter broadcast that came to the attention of the Indian merchant resident in Kano, K. Pawan, who immediately thought about getting a Hausa person to translate films from India with Hausa voices. The desirability of such a venture was supported by the success of the Joseph films in Kano.

Interestingly, southern Indian films, which started the India-Hausa voice translations, were themselves dubbed in Hindi to appeal to wider Indian audiences – which seems to indicate a divergence in southern Indian languages and Hindi films. One would have thought that their proximity would have made such interorality superfluous. Yet, despite being in the same country, they were of course, radically different. As Subramonyam (2000, pp. 37–38) noted,

> ...some of the biggest hits in the "Hindi Belt" in the 1990s are South Indian films remade or dubbed in Hindi. While this kind of crossover is not new, and while over the years Hindi hits have been remade in various South Indian languages as well, dubbing of films across the nation, including Indian versions of everything from Jurassic Park to Jumanji, has never been as popular as it is today.

However, such a practice of language dubbing seems to have slightly waned, perhaps triggered by the bigger international market share of mainstream Hindi films that eclipsed regional films.

The four regional cinemas have characteristics that are particular to their respective regions, yet thanks to the practice of dubbing films into other south Indian languages initiated early by the studios in Chennai, each of the southern regions is also familiar with films from their neighboring states. South Indian films dubbed into Hindi have never been very popular in northern markets, however. It was these southern Indian films, dubbed into Hindi, that Pawan brought to Kano. He contracted Magoga, who transcribed the Hindi dialogue into Hausa, creating a new script. Magoga was able to transcribe the Hindi voices into Hausa due to his understanding of Hindi, which he acquired exclusively from watching Hindi films since early childhood. In the early stages, there were licenses obtained from the film studios in India which granted Pawan the right to translate the films into Hausa and distribute them locally. For the next stage, Pawan sought voice-over artists in Kano. His search led him to Buzo Danfillo, then a guest session musician at Hikima Studios in Kano and contracted him to translate Bhojpuri- and Telugu-language films (already dubbed in Hindi) into Hausa. The recordings were done at Algaita, rather than Hikima, since Danfillo was the owner of Algaita Media Entertainment Group, of which Algaita Dub Studio, dedicated to voice-over translations and dubbing, was a subsidiary. The first film translated was the Bhojpuri film, *Hukumat Ki Jung* (dir. S.S. Rajamouli, 2008). It was translated as "Yaƙi da Rashin Adalci" (Fighting Injustice). Others that followed included *Dabangg* (dir. Abhinav Kashyap, 2010), *Racha* (dir. Sampath Nandi, 2012) and *Nayak: The Real Hero* (dir. S. Shankar, 2001). In an interactive session in June 2016, Buzo Danfillo told me that the Algaita Studio had translated 93 films by 2016. During the period of the partnership with Pawan, the translators were paid NGN80,000, or about US$501, according to Central Bank of Nigeria (CBN, 2013), when the U.S. dollar was worth 157 Nigerian Naira.

The first few films produced by the Algaita Studio in 2012 were considered novelties, providing relief from watching complete remakes of Hindi films by Hausa filmmakers, or even from watching the originals themselves. What made them more attractive, however, was the translation of the titles of the films in a single powerfully expressed word, or couple of words, that seemed to take a life of their own and communicate adventure, danger, or defiance. For instance, *Nayak: The Real Hero* (dir. S. Shankar, 2001) was translated as "Namijin Duniya" (lit. Brave); *Indirajeet* (dir. K.V. Raju, 1991) as "Fargaba" (Fear), and *Velayudham* (dir. Mohan Raja, 2011) as "Mai Adda" (Machete). Referred to as "India-Hausa" (Hausa versions of Indian films), they quickly became the new form of transcultural expression in the Hausa entertainment industry. In giving the Hausa versions their titles, the translators often move away from the direct literal translation from the original film; instead, they often affix a title that seems to capture the main plot of the story; for example, *The Shadow* (dir. Meher Ramesh, 2013) was translated as

"Inuwa" (Shadow), although the Hausa version of the word was intended to convey a more sinister implication). This device was useful because it created a subtext and, therefore, a hidden commentary on the film even before one watches it. This served as another basis for domestication and offered an alternative to the cinematic appropriation of Hindi films by Hausa filmmakers. Figure 7.3 shows the selective use of stills from the films to convey the same meaning to different audiences.

It is instructive that the Hausa translators of *Dabangg* used a different shot from the picture used on the official Telugu film DVD cover. The original, from a low angle, raised the profile of the character and, by bringing the pistol closer to the viewer, emphasizes the strong character of the hero, whose face is covered by dark glasses. The Hausa version shows a grim-faced character without any adornment on his face, but with a fixed gaze – something the Hausa would certainly appreciate as approximating a fearless person.

The Hausa translations, at least in the beginning, were backed by licenses which Algaita insisted on seeing before embarking on the Hausa translations. This is the first time that copyright was respected in the transnational appropriation of

Figure 7.3   *Dabangg* ("Fearless"), original and Hausa version covers. Photo: Abdalla Uba Adamu.

popular world cultures by Hausa performers. Certainly, all the cinematic remakes and appropriations that characterize the mainstream Hausa film industry were done without any licensing agreement with the original – a stance Hindi film-makers themselves appropriating Hollywood films take. However, the success of the first few films in 2014 opened up the doors. Whereas Algaita and Pawan were marketing the films they exclusively translated, soon enough other marketers entered into the process and started getting dub-over translators to translate the same southern Indian films illegally downloaded from YouTube and other Internet streaming sites. To bypass the process of getting a Hindi translator, the marketers simply downloaded those films with English subtitles. The subtitles were then copied out and translated into Hausa. Since there were many music studios in Kano, it was relatively easy to find voice-over artists to dub the Hausa dialogue onto the films. This considerably broke the monopoly Algaita had over the southern Indian film translations in northern Nigeria. Eventually, the studio also entered the business of unlicensed translations—especially as Pawan seemed to have faded from the scene—foraying into both mainstream Hindi, southern Indian and occasional Hollywood films, the latter of which included *Shrek*, translated as "Botorami" (monster), *Apocalyto* as "Gudun Tsira" (Deliverance) and *The Expendables*. Since they could not translate this title into Hausa, they just marketed the dubbed version with the same title. This is critical in the sense that it shows the political economy of the process and also shows how transnational markets operate in the domestication of overseas films for African audiences.

It is significant that the translations were mainly for non-Hindi language films in the beginning. There were several reasons for this. First, obtaining a license to translate the dialogue of mainstream Hindi films in other languages and marketing the resultant product as a new repackaged film was difficult. This is because these films have a high visibility internationally, featuring megastars. Second, the Hausa foreign film market was already saturated with Hindi films which are, familiar to the Hausa. Translating them into Hausa, when they were already understood by the fact of their being part of the staple visual entertainment of the Hausa, would not seem profitable. Third, non-Hindi language films are hardly known in northern Nigeria and Pawan wanted to change all this. Finally, the subject matter of the films translated were more social – dealing with injustice, insecurity, corrupt offi-cials, poverty – subjects Nigerians would have readily identifed with. Translating these "message" films would seem to provide an alternative to the saccharine romance of mainstream Hindi films.

Unlike East African VJ translators, the India-Hausa translators did not pass through an evolutionary oral stage of live translation before dubbing the transla-tions on the foreign films. This might reflect the different nature of the approaches to community folk theatre between the Hausa and the East African audiences. For the Hausa, spectatorship is often a personal, and silent, statement. Films were often viewed in the personal and private medium of home entertainment, instead of a collective public space and, therefore, not amenable to running commentaries.

This was more so with the death of the cinema in the 1990s which came on the heels of a new Shari'a (Islamic Law) reinforcement during which many Muslim scholars discouraged cinema attendance. This forced people to watch films on TV at home.

Further, in contrast to the India-Hausa dubbers, East African VJs apparently insert themselves in their live translation of foreign films, substituting items for local versions as well as providing a commentary on a particular scene. As Hoad (2012, par. 3) noted, "VJs do more than simply describe the action – they frame the action in a context familiar to east Africans and add their own brand of humour." India-Hausa dubbers conspicuously remove themselves from the originals and maintain a high fidelity in their translations. What emerged was a new sub-industry that provided alternatives to the endless appropriation of Hindi films by Hausa film producers. The India-Hausa translations differ in the sense of being officially licensed and a much easier mode of immersion in transnational popular culture, than English subtitling which will not appeal to the vast majority of Hausa audiences in the same way the interoral dubs do. There was no pretext that a new film was made – the antecedent origin of the translated film was indeed its main selling point; for the translated dialogue brings the film much closer to the Hausa audiences than the appropriated remakes by Hausa filmmakers. They offer authenticity of being from India, with the credibility of being understood because they are in Hausa. Further, the subject matter of fighting injustice and corruption touches a raw nerve in a country rated as 136 out of 187 in the list of countries with a high corruption perception (Transparency International, 2016).

The India-Hausa translations have been massively successful and have attracted audiences not attuned to Indian films in the first place. This can be deduced from the numerous comments on the Facebook pages of the Algaita Dub Studio (www. facebook.com/algaitadub/). Their success created a public debate mainly online in social networks about their cultural impact. In the first instance, there does not seem to be any attempt by the translators to censor some of the bawdier dialogues of the originals – translating the dialogue directly into Hausa. Kanywood filmmakers latch on to this as an indication of cultural impropriety of the translated films. Additionally, the often romantic scenes revealing inter-gender sexuality were not edited out by the translators, since their focus is not the visuals, but the voices. This, again, was pointed out by Hausa filmmakers as a direct attack on Hausa cultural sensibilities. Kanywood filmmakers do accept that they appropriate Hindi films; but they argue that they culturally adapt the stories to reflect Muslim Hausa sensibilities.

Audiences, however, do not accept these arguments against the translated Indian films. This was evidenced in a debate a Kano local FM radio station opened on its Facebook pages to discuss the merits or otherwise of India-Hausa translations on 13 October 2014. A total of 2,027 comments were posted reflecting various views about the translations. Out of these, about 1,326 were considered valid posts and were content analyzed and categorized into five. The results are shown in Table 7.2.

Table 7.2   Radio Freedom Facebook responses to India-Hausa translations

S/N	Comments	Number	%
1.	Translated Indian films corrupts Hausa audiences	179	13.5
2.	Translated Indian films do not corrupt Hausa audiences	509	38.4
3.	Kanywood films corrupt Hausa audiences	451	34
4.	Kanywood films do not corrupt Hausa audiences	31	2.3
5.	Indifferent/neutral	156	11.8
	Total comments	1326	100.0

Data *source*: www.facebook.com/freedomradionig/posts/10152810476008035, retrieved 3 December 2015.

The comments focus on what is more corrupting on youth: Kanywood or the India-Hausa translations. It should perhaps be pointed that "corruption" (gur6ata tarbiya in Hausa) is a general expression for any inter-gender relation in which men and women touch each other, as well as for obscenities, thuggish behavior, and other socially undesirable traits. The corruption variable came into play because of the constant accusations by the more puritanical Hausa critical views that suggests inter-gender mixing, particularly in Hausa video films, has the potential of corrupting the morality of vulnerable youth.

From Table 7.2, it is clear that a significant number of people do not accept that the translations have any corrupting influence on Hausa audiences. This view goes beyond any media effects theory since the responses were referring basically to sexuality and offensive language in the translated films. Those defending the Hausa films point to the fact that there had been a long public debate about the desirability of Hausa films appropriating Indian films and the skimpy attire the female actresses wear, especially during the song and dance sequences. These public criticisms actually led to the establishment of a Kano State Censorship Board in 2011 to regulate the films sold in Kano markets.

From the general postings, it was also clear that a considerable number of those who hold favorable opinions about translated Indian films believed that the issues raised in the film portray a lot of Nigerian social and political realities, particularly the leadership/followership crisis and social injustice between the haves and have-nots. These motifs were rarely explored in mainstream Hausa films due to fears by the filmmakers that the political establishment will take umbrage at any portrayal of the social realities – poverty, unemployment, crime, insurgency, corruption – that bedeviled Nigerian society. Those with unfavorable views about the translations believed that the translations would kill the Hausa film industry, since there was a decline in sales of the films after the intense appearance of the films since 2014. Consequently, the commercial, if not artistic, success of the India-Hausa films generated a backlash among the mainstream Hausa filmmakers, who saw the translations as a threat to their own business. As reported by Ciroma (2014),

Hausa filmmakers have raised the alarm that the infiltration of Indian movies translated into the Hausa language into the industry is silently killing the Hausa movie industry. In unison, stakeholders believe that the act is being hamstrung by piracy and dishonest traders. Kanywood Trends understands that marketers of the said products engage the services of Hausa linguists who understand Hindi to translate and lip-synch dialogues in the movies such that both the audio and video are perfectly synchronized with the actions that produce them. They also ensure that the movements of a speaker's lips match the sound of his speech.

The Hausa filmmakers that Ciroma talked to were upset by the trend. A famous Hausa actress, Hauwa Maina, voiced the feelings of most of the producers and directors when she lamented:

> I am totally against it. If the pirates want to produce Hindi movies, why don't they go to India and shoot, or go on joint productions rather than [engage in] this nonsense? Our marketers have succeeded in killing Kanywood. People should know that Hausa movies were originally inspired by the Indian films. Back then, teeming Hausa communities see Kanywood movies as a recipe for what they need. But now, it is as if the marketers are taking them back to where they were coming from, making our Hausa movies irrelevant. (in Ciroma, 2014)

The reaction of the Hausa filmmakers to translations of foreign, especially Indian films, echoes similar reactions from Bengali filmmakers, where the film industry in Bangladesh also faced the challenges of the popularity of Hindi films dubbed with Bengali voice-overs. A survey of selected Bengali filmmakers' views about Hindi films dubbed into Bengali came up with the following

> Let Hindi films run parallel to films made in Bengali by people here. We urge everybody concerned not to screen any dubbed film in theatres and serials on television any more … we are not issuing any threat to anybody. But the local industry has its stake. This is our united stand and we mean it … this is no threat, but is a request for allowing the survival of local industry. (Press Trust of India. 2014)

The Hindi film that caused the furor was *Gunday* (dir. Ali Abbas Zafar, 2014). Dubbed into Bengali, it caused insecurity and fear among the industry practitioners. Even the songs were in Bengali and *Gunday* belonged to one of the most powerful Mumbai studios, Yash Raj Films. However, as Chatterji (2014) reported,

> the issue is not West Bengal's alone. [In February 2014], the Karnataka film industry formed a solid wall of unity in protest against dubbed versions of Kannada films released in the state. Umashree, actress and Kannada Culture Minister of Karnataka who is against dubbing of content in Kannada, said, "We oppose dubbing of other language films in Kannada and will not accept it. We have to give prominence to the people who are working in the Kannada industry."

Mainstream Hindi filmmakers also often made the occasional foray into "foreign" language dubbing. This was noted by Grimaud (2006), who recorded the experiences of Hindi filmmaker, Yash Chopra, who in 1998 dubbed one of his most popular films, *Dil to Pagal Hai*, into French. The target audience was putatively the French diaspora, but the actual market was Mauritius. The filmmaker rejected the idea of using native French-speakers in Paris to dub the film into French, insisting on Indian voice artists who will read the French translations with Indian accents because "he was convinced that a film in an exportable Indianized French was the best way to attract not only the diaspora but other viewers, since the dialogue itself would convey a kind of exoticism" (Grimaud 2006, p. 168). This search for authenticity in interoral insertion introduces another dimension the dubbing process – for neither the East African or Hausa dub artists attempted accentual authenticity of the original voices they translated.

Conclusion

What film translation shows us, therefore, is the eddy of messages that kept swirling around cultural spaces throughout the world in attempting to enter the hearts and minds of cinematic audiences by any means necessary. Thus, through VJeeing, dubbing, translations and running commentaries, media circulates from its point of origin to another, perhaps not intended, audiences. The fact this circulation follows all directions – from the West to developing countries and within developing countries themselves – indicates the breaking down of barriers to the consumption of these media messages.

The transnational travel of foreign films in Africa has been domesticated in various ways. However, the most ingenious would seem to be cases of domestication of some of these films through what I can call "narrative territoriality" in which new forms of engagement with the media, or what can be called remediation and not a sentence – are created by young media entrepreneurs to create new narratives domesticated to local understanding. By following Sander's "adaptation," Hausa translators took a more domesticated path by dubbing voice-over translations of Hindi film (and occasional Hollywood film) dialogue into Hausa. This proved to be a tremendous success; indeed, so much that the sales for the appropriated Hindi films remade as Hausa films declined significantly. Comments on newspaper websites and Facebook groups clearly indicate a more direct cultural relationship between the source text and the resultant "Hausa version."

Hausa voice-over translators of foreign films in northern Nigeria do not seek to maintain continuity with the original source films. In the process of translating the dialogues into Hausa, they indeed go out of their way to domesticate the original scenes to reflect Hausa communities in speech and lexicon. The accuracy of the Hausa versions is often confirmed by the fact that some of the source films had English subtitles. Merely following the spoken Hausa translations as against the English subtitles attests to the accuracy of the Hausa translations. For these reasons, Sander's adaptation theory could not neatly fit into the audiovisual practices of Hausa translators. I would advocate interorality as a closer label in the sense that it describes the oral juxtaposition and dependencies of two radically different, but contextually related oral narratives describing the same set of events.

References

Adamu, Abdalla Uba. 2007. "Currying favour: Eastern media influences and the Hausa video Film." *Film International* 28(4): 77–91.

Adamu, Abdalla Uba. 2009. "Media parenting and construction of media edentities in northern Nigerian Muslim Hausa video films." In *The media and the construction of African identities*, edited by John Middleton and Kimani Njogu, 171–186. London: International African Institute/Twanzega Communications.

Adamu, Abdalla Uba. 2010. "Transnational flows and local identities in Muslim northern Nigerian films: from Dead Poets Society through Mohabbatein to So…" In *Popular media, democracy and development in Africa*, edited by Herman Wasserman, 223–234. London: Routledge.

Central Bank of Nigeria (CBN). 2013. "Monthly average exchange rates of the Naira (Naira per unit of foreign currency) – 2013." Accessed 12 July 2015. www.cbn.gov.ng/rates/exrate.asp?year=2013.

Chatterji, S. 2014. "From one language to another: What's at stake?".Accessed 6 May 2017, http://www.indiatogether.org/controversy-over-dubbing-films-media

Ciroma, Amin. 2014, "Indo-Hausa flicks killing Kanywood." Leadership newspaper (Nigeria), 29 August,2014.Accessed September 2014.http://leadership.ng/entertainment/382373/indo-hausa-flicks-killing-Kanywood.

Desai, Jigna. 2004. *Beyond Bollywood: the cultural politics of South Asian diasporic film.* New York: Routledge.

Dipio, Dominica. 2014. "Audience pleasure and Nollywood popularity in Uganda: an assessment." *Journal of African Cinemas* 6(1), 85–108.

Dönmez-Colin, Gönül. 2007. *The cinema of North Africa and the Middle East.* London: Wallflower Press.

Englert, Birgit. 2010. "In need of connection: reflections on youth and the translation of film in Tanzania." *Stichproben (Vienna Journal of African Studies)* 18: 137–159.

Fair, L. (2009). "Making love in the Indian Ocean: Hindi films, Zanzibari audiences, and the construction of romance in the 1950s and 1960s." In *Love in Africa*, edited by J. Cole, J., and L.M. Thomas, 58–82. Chicago: University of Chicago Press.

Grimaud, Emmanuel. 2006. "Maps of audiences: Bombay films, the French Ttrritory and the making of an 'oblique' market." In *Globalizing India: perspectives from below*, edited by C.J. Fuller and Jackie Assayag, 165–184. Anthem South Asian Studies. London: Anthem Press,

Hoad, Phil. 2012. "Tanzania's VJs bring Hollywood to Africa." *The Guardian (UK)* 10. Accessed July 11 2012. www.theguardian.com/film/2012/jul/10/tanzania-vjs-hollywood-africa/print.

Kasbekar, Asha. 2006. *Pop culture India!: media, arts, and lifestyle*. Santa Barbara, CA: ABC-CLIO.

Kaur, Raminder and Ajay J. Sinha. 2005. *Bollyworld: popular Indian cinema through a transnational lens*. New Delhi: Sage.

Lagarriga, Dídac P. 2007. "Vee-jay translators in Uganda." Accessed 3 May 2015. www.oozebap.org/text/uganda-vj-eng.htm.

Larkin, Brian.1997. "Indian films and Nigerian lovers: media and the creation of parallel modernities." *Africa* 67: 406–440

Larkin, Brian. 2002. "Bandiri music, globalization and urban experience in Nigeria." *Cahiers d'études africaines* 168 (XLII-4): 39–762.

Leitch, T.M. (1990) "Twice-told tales: the rhetoric of the remake." *Literature/Film. Quarterly* 18(3): 138–149.

Miller, Jade L. 2016. *Nollywood central*. London: Palgrave.

Press Trust of India. 2014. "Tollywood against dubbing Hindi films in Bengali." Accessed 28 March 2018. www.business-standard.com/article/pti-stories/tollywood-against-dubbing-hindi-films-in-bengali-114021800424_1.html.

Pype, Katrien. 2013. "Religion, migration, and media aesthetics: notes on the circulation and reception of Nigerian films in Kinshasa." In *Global Nollywood: the translational dimensions of an African video film industry*, edited by Matthias Krings and Onookome Okome, 199–222. Bloomington: Indian University Press.

Sanders, Julie. 2006. *Adaptation and appropriation*. London: Routledge.

Steene, G.V. (2008). "Hindu dance groups and Indophiles in Senegal: The imagination of the exotic other." In *India in Africa, Africa in India: Indian Ocean cosmopolitanismso*, edited by J.C. Hawley, 117–148). Bloomington: Indiana University Press.

Subramonyam, Radha. 2000. "India." In *The international movie industry*, edited by Gorhan Kindem, 36–59. Carbondale, IL: Southern Illinois University Press.

Transparency International. 2016. *Corruptions perception index 2015*. Berlin: TI. Accessed 28 March 2018. www.transparency.org/cpi2015/.

Vété-Congolo, Hanétha. 2016. "Caribbean interorality: a brief introduction." In *The Caribbean oral tradition: literature, performance, and practice*, edited by Hanétha Vété-Congolo, 1–54. New York: Springer International Publishing.

Filmography

Hausa Films

Bello, Hafizu. 2001. *Jumurda*. Kano, Nigeria: HB Productions.

Bello, Hafizu. 2004. *Almuru*. Kano, Nigeria: HB Productions.

Ibrahim, Rabi'u. 2001. *Furuci*. Kano, Nigeria: HRB Productions.

Ibrahim, Tijjani. 1999. *Abin Sirrine*. Kano, Nigeria: HRB Productions.

Ibrahim, Tijjani. 1999. *Hakuri*. Kano, Nigeria: Iyan-Tama Multi Media.

Ibrahim, Tijjani. 2001. *Mujadala*. Kano, Nigeria: FKD Productions
Ishaq, Sidi Ishaq. 2000. *Akasi*. Kano, Nigeria: Ibrahimawa Film Production.
Ishaq, Sidi Ishaq. 2001. *Izaya*. Kano, Nigeria: Kajol Productions.
Mohammed, Yakubu. 2000. *Ayaah*. Kano, Nigeria: 2Effects Empire.
Sabo, Aminu Muhammad. 2002. *Jirwaye*. Kano, Nigeria: Sarauniya Films.
Umar, Yusha'u Idris. 2001. *Kasaita*. Kano, Nigeria: Bright Star Pictures.
Yakasai, Aminu Hassan. 2001. *Kudiri*. Kano, Nigeria: FKD Productions.
Zango, Adamu Abdullahi. 2015. *Gwaska*. Kaduna, Nigeria: Prince Zango Productions Nig. Ltd.

Hollywood Films

Adamson, Andrew and Jenson, Vicky. 2001. *Shrek*. United States: PDI/Dreamworks
Stallone, Sylvester. 2010. *The Expendables*. Los Angeles, CA, United States: Millennium Films/Nu Image.

Iranian TV Series

Salahshoor, Farajollah. 2008. *Yousuf-e-Payambar* [Prophet Joseph]. Tehran: Islamic Republic of Iran Broadcasting.

Films in Indian Langauges

Anand, Tinnu. 1998. *Major Saab*. Mumbai, India: Amitabh Bachchan Film Corporation Limited/A B Corp.
Barjatya, Sooraj R. 1982. *Hum Aapke Hain Koun*. Madhya Pradesh, India: Rajshri Productions Pvt. Ltd.
Bhatt, Mahesh. 1990. *Jurm*. Mumbai, India: Vishesh Films.
Chakravorthy, Pramod. 1978. *Azaad*. Mumbai, India: Pramod Films.
Chopra, Yash. 1989. *Chandni*. Mumbai, India: Yash Raj Films
Deol, Sunny. 1999. *Dillagi*. Mumbai, India: Vijayta Films Pvt. Ltd.
Dhawan, David. 1997. *Judwaa*. Mumbai, India: Nadiadwala Grandsons Entertainment Pvt. Ltd.
Ghosh, Partho. 1996. *Agni Sakshi*. Uttar Pradesh, India: Neha Films
Kashyap, Abhinav. 2010. *Dabangg*. Mumbai, India: Arbaaz Khan Productions Pvt. Ltd.
Kumar, Rakesh. 1981. *Yaarana*. Mumbai, India: A.K. Movies.
Manivasagam, M. 1990. *Namma Ooru Poovatha*. Chennai, India: Raaja Pushpa Pictures.
Mustan, Abbas. 2001. *Chori Chori Chupke Chupke*. Mumbai, India: Eros Multimedia Pvt. Ltd.
Nadiadwala, Sajid. 2014. *Kick*. Mumbai, India: Nadiadwala Grandson Entertainment.
Nandi, Sampath. 2012. *Racha*. Hyderabad, India: Megaa Super Good Films Pvt. Ltd.
Raja, Mohan. 2011. *Velayudham*. London, UK: Ayngaran International.
Rajamouli, S.S. 2008. *Hukumat Ki Jung*. Mumbai, India: Sai Entertainment Pvt. Ltd.
Raju, K.V. 1991. *Indrajeet*. Mumbai, India: Rose Audio Visuals Pvt. Ltd.

Ramesh, Meher. 2009. *Billa*. Hyderabad, India: Gopikrishna Movies Pvt. Ltd

Ramesh, Meher. 2013. *Shadow*. Hyderabad, India: United Movies.

Roshan, Rakesh. 2006. *Krrish*. Mumbai, India: Filmkraft Productions Pvt. Ltd.

Shankar, S. 2001. *Nayak: The Real Hero*. Chennai, India: Sri Surya Movies

Tak, Saawan Kumar. 1991. *Sanam Bewafa*. Mumbai, India: Saawan Kumar Productions Films Pvt. Ltd.

Varma, Ram Gopal. 2003. *Bhoot*. Gujarat, India: Dream Merchant Company.

8

The (Aural) Life of Neo-colonial Space

Vlad Dima

Abderrahmane Sissako's four most important films[1] – *La vie sur terre* (Life on Earth, 1998), *Heremakono* (Waiting for Happiness, 2002), *Bamako* (2006), and *Timbuktu* (2014) – generally deal with issues of identity that stem from various forms of exile. The word "exile" comes up, in fact, in all the interviews and special features that the director includes in the DVD version of the films (and in the promotional interviews for his latest). In spite of their dealings with exile, limits, and forbidden spaces, Sissako's films are also a space of inclusion for the director who occasionally inserts himself into the material fabric of the stories, as an actor or as a (literal) voice. The latter narrative practice – using his own voice – allows him to tower over the diegetic and non-diegetic spaces of the films, which is a fairly common practice among auteurs.[2] As a result, the narrative focus tends to shift toward the aural. As the director's voice gives a material quality to the aural, one begins to pay more attention to the sound, voices, and music, which in turn leads to the creation of aural spaces – entire rural and urban aural spaces that materialize through sound rather than through the image. It is thus sound that breathes life into the neo-colonial[3] town and city, spaces that are traditionally rife with colonial visual markers such as buildings, clothes, signs, and posters written in the colonizers' language. A different kind of space is thus born, out of sound, out of noise and song, and it is a space that pairs itself with the visual neo-colonial town and city, not in order to complete it (as one would imagine given the traditional relationship between image and sound in cinema – a symbiotic enterprise, as it were), but rather in order to supplant it. Ultimately the aural spaces that emerge in African cinema, and specifically in Sissako's films, are no longer defined by attributes such as, "colonial," "postcolonial," or "neo-colonial." Instead, they become freeing spaces

A Companion to African Cinema, First Edition. Edited by Kenneth W. Harrow and Carmela Garritano.
© 2019 John Wiley & Sons, Inc. Published 2019 by John Wiley & Sons, Inc.

of fantasy, mental images, and maps of an imagined space that transcends politics, global divisions, and subaltern relationships. Therefore, this chapter argues that whatever "life" one may speak of concerning the neo-colonial town and city is much more animated and vociferous at the aural level rather than when we take into consideration only the visual (which, of course, never completely disappears).

Sound (as noise, song, or voice) plays a fundamental narrative role in the pioneering, and by now canonical, work of African directors such as Ousmane Sembène, Djibril Diop Mambéty,[4] Safi Faye, Souleymane Cissé, and Idrissa Ouedraogo. Sound continues to be employed effectively by a younger generation of African directors, gifted filmmakers such as Jean-Pierre Bekolo (Cameroon), Moussa Touré (Senegal), Yamina Benguigui (France/Algeria), and of course Sissako. While Sissako's use of sound is not as subversive or revolutionary as Mambéty's, for example, his voice(s) and sound(s) do effectuate multiple narrative trips and provide us with interesting venues of inquiry: They travel within and around the space of the town; they provide an expansion of sorts to the visually limiting space of the city, and they also traverse and extra-diegetically connect the four films mentioned above into a somewhat cohesive narrative. Moreover, I would like to propose that the layered use of sound in Sissako's films operates according to a rhythm closely resembling the narrative device of the Russian doll effect: With each uncovered layer, one is closer to finding the hidden meaning, the smallest kernel of truth in the very last incarnation of the Russian doll. Yet, this narrative device is about misdirection – there is no ultimate truth. In Sissako's films, too, meaning is more likely to be found on the fringes, in the outer layers of the story, which are produced by the aural layers surrounding the films. It is within these layers that one finds the most significant meaning(s).

The idea of sound as an outer narrative layer brings to mind the physical effect that sound has on the spectators; in other words, sound's most outer layer is likely completely removed from the narrative of the film and it lives on its own in the space of the theatre, in between the screen, the speakers, and the ears of the spectators. Therefore, as it penetrates the space of a theatre, sound offers a sensation of corporeality that the image (unless in 3D) does not. This materiality of sound is what allows for the construction of the aural rural and urban spaces. To take but one example at this point, the camera rarely ventures outside of closed spaces in *Bamako*, which is a technique that ends up limiting the spectators' access to the visual city of Bamako. We hardly see anything beyond the yard in which the trial that guides the visual narrative of the film unfolds, and the club where one of the main characters, Melé, sings. Instead, the city comes to life aurally. Sound envelops the visual action of the film like a protective layer of sorts, similar to a replication of the Russian doll. Significantly, and to reiterate the observation from above, it is the layer itself that is important, and not what it holds within, which is in actuality nothing. What matters is what surrounds and conceals the "nothing," which in this case study is the visual city; what matters is the sound.

It must be said, though, that in spite of the obvious connection with orality and the tradition of African stories and storytellers (griots), the use of cinematic sound for narrative purposes and artifice is not unique to African directors. Experimentation with sound defines in some measure the European avant-garde cinema, Russian formalism, the French New Wave, and even parts of mainstream, classical Hollywood. Furthermore, the link between orality and aural cinema may prove to be perhaps too reductive. In the particular case of Sissako, sound certainly seems to be more than a simple remnant of an oral tradition. It functions as a narrative device and certainly as narration, but also as a remedy, as a way to deal with an artistic form of exile: The director finds himself situated within the context of a quintessentially European art form (cinema was born in France after all) that has generally favored the visual, and through sound, he and his characters find a personal, familiar (aural) space of inclusion that may hold the key toward a tangible form of freedom.

Sound on Earth

The construction of an aural space of inclusion begins with *Life on Earth*, a film that lacks what one might call a traditional plot and presents itself as quasi-documentary. The main character and narrator, played by Sissako, returns to his native town, but in the first scene of the film he is alone in a French supermarket. Amid several sounds – the supermarket loudspeaker, voices of customers, and the main character's steps – one stands out. It is the repetitive beeping sound of an unseen cash register that we first begin to hear during the long tracking shot of the cheese aisle. The beeping sound (likely that of the machine reading the barcodes of purchased items) is occasionally accompanied by the sound of receipts being printed out, which reinforces the aural reference to the cash register. The only other clearly noticeable sound (the sounds mentioned above function as ambient noises in the supermarket) is that of a siren coming from the outside, but it disappears rather quickly. To my mind, then, the rhythmic sound of the cash register is the aural element that anchors the entire scene and not the visual presence of the character. Crucially, the importance of the cash register is underlined by the lack of a visual confirmation that it is indeed a cash register making that sound. At the end of the sequence, when the main character steps on the escalator, to his left (and the right of the screen), we notice the word "caisse" (checkout) plastered on the wall and an arrow pointing upward. Therefore, the sound that seems to dominate this initial scene technically comes from a floor above. It is a logical sound, of course, but its original source is rather ambiguous – in effect, the beep comes from off-screen throughout the scene.

As Mary Ann Doane notes about sound (as voice) coming from off-screen, "there is always something uncanny about a voice which emanates from a source outside the frame" (1985, p. 164). In addition to the attached uncanniness, Michel Chion's notion of the *acousmêtre* – necessarily a voice whose origin is not obvious – assigns the unseen voice various degrees of omniscient, panoptical, and magical powers (1999, pp. 21–24). These powers are "usually malevolent, occasionally tutelary" (1999, p. 23), and Chion finishes his commentary on the acousmêtre by giving two examples: "The greatest Acousmêtre is God – and even farther back, for every one of us, the Mother" (1999, p. 27). Chion's and Doane's observations about voice can be extrapolated to other off-screen noises like the constant aural intrusion of the acousmatic beep. Because it remains unseen and because it likely comes from the floor *above* (which is suggestive of a hierarchy of sorts or of God), the beep acquires the magical powers mentioned by Chion, as well as the degree of uncanniness suggested by Doane. But, the beep and the receipt printing also quite clearly symbolize Western money, which will eventually become the focus of *Bamako* (so the extra-diegetic dialogue between Sissako's films does not limit itself only to common sounds, as certain themes repeat themselves, too). Given the connections of the acousmêtre to omniscient forces such as God, or to the tutelary value of Mother, the aural symbol of the beep then takes on a larger meaning – the Mother-like (*la France*, feminine gender) or God-like (*L'empire*, masculine gender) uncanny figure of the colony.

As a hovering sound, the beep establishes a magical presence, whereas its physical value (hear "beep," think "money") offers a material dimension meant to emphasize its significance. Moreover, the constant, metronomic beep may suggest the passage of time and lead one to recall the old Western adage, "time is money." When the film moves to Africa, time will slow down, stretch, and become less relevant. In the supermarket, there is one particular visual detail that accompanies the beep and that presages this temporal change of pace. As Sissako-the actor moves about the space of the supermarket, the film offers a very brief, slow-motion shot of twirling cases of jewelry through which the audience gets a glimpse of him shopping. The slow-motion effect is used again when Sissako-the actor walks onto the escalator carrying his purchases (one in particular stands out as incongruous – the large toy polar bear). In the space of the supermarket he is out of place, and the slow pace of the visual renders his displacement more obvious. It is then worth reiterating that the visual cannot be completely erased, even symbolically, by the aural; however, the visual may be presented as lacking its normal capacity to dominate the narrative space of the film. I believe this is what happens in this first sequence: The visual slows down (and, consequently, so does the passage of time), almost as if it were having difficulty moving forward, while the aural remains a constant focus and even thrives narratively.

In addition to the aural marker of the beep, two more aural elements arise at the beginning of the film, fully emerging as the film transitions to the outside, to the open space of Mali. First, the director reads a letter addressed to his father in voice-over and cites Aimé Césaire; second, the music of renowned Malian musician Salif Keita takes over the soundtrack. In *Cahier d'un retour au pays natal* (1939) Césaire dreams of returning to his native Martinique. Akin to Césaire, the voice-over that reads the letter mentions the desire to leave (it even uses the same verb "partir"). Crucially, the voice itself becomes lost because it is detached from the physical body of the actor/director. Since the body of the director is visible in the previous scene, the audience knows where the voice comes from – it is a logical sound – and yet the physical separation persists. A voice that remains conscribed to the soundtrack, without it ever being "assigned" to a body, is a purely non-diegetic sound. Once the diegetic body appears, the voice/sound transforms into intra-diegetic; this is also called a process of deacousmatization. The narrative construction of this first scene, though, features an interesting symmetry: Visible body (in the supermarket), off-screen voice, back to visible body (in the dusty Malian roads). In other words, the voice is only temporarily detached from the body but that suffices to consider it "lost."

As Mladen Dolar claims, such a departed voice never fully returns to the body, once the latter becomes visible. In other words, *"there is no such thing as disacousma-tization"*[5] (2006, p. 70, original emphasis). In the process of establishing voice as an object fetish, Dolar also declares the following: "The acousmatic voice is simply a voice whose source one cannot see … but even when it finds its body, it turns out that this doesn't quite work, the voice doesn't stick to the body, it is an excrescence which doesn't match the body" (2006, pp. 60–61). In essence, the body is never *complete* again once the voice either leaves or returns to it. Both Sissako and his voice want to return, and both will find that such a return is impossible, maintain-ing Sissako's voice in Doane's category of the uncanny rather than rendering it entirely logical. So, in the end, Sissako's voice is arguably the most memorable element of the film, as it floats freely away from the body and becomes the narra-tive cog that seemingly connects France (supermarket) and Mali (town), past (Césaire) and present (Father), soundtrack and visual. Moreover, the overlapping of three authorial voices – Sissako, Césaire, Keita – provides the audience with a perfect example of layered, aural narrative planes, between which the narrator travels on his return voyage. What he finds at the heart of his journey back home is less relevant – it remains uncertain whether he has truly found himself, whether he will stay or leave again – than the journey itself and the multi-layered aural spaces through which he travels. Once again, in the middle of it all, in the physical proof of the visual, there is much less than meets the eye, as it were.

The return home and the futile search to recapture the lost blissfulness brings to life the question of fantasy and *the objet petit a*. Sissako, as Dramane, the name of the character he plays, finds himself in the middle of his native town, a part of this town, yet it often feels that he remains removed from it. His situation parallels the relationship between sound and image in which the former may narratively sepa-rate itself from the latter. In cinema, the spectators naturally desire to know the source of the various sounds and voices at all times. It is unsettling not to know, and such occurrences may lead to distanciation. In classical cinema, the manifesta-tions of extra-diegetic sounds are rare because one strives for the impression of reality – sound logically matches the visual and completes it. But when counter cinema practices deny the audience knowledge of the sound's source, we are basically denied *jouissance* in the Lacanian sense. We, as spectators, continue to want to see those images, images that are "lost" to us. It is fantasy, fantasy that acts like a protective veil, that allows us to negotiate the pain which comes from desiring what we cannot have (Dramane is on a similarly superfluous quest), and thus desire and *jouissance* can never coexist in a relationship of contingency. The way we deal with this pain is, of course, through the *objet petit a*, and the *objet petit a* only becomes apparent when looked at "from aside," with a distorted look of desire:

> This is precisely the Lacanian *objet petit a*, the object-clause of desire, an object which is, in a way, posited by the desire itself. The paradox of desire is that it posits retroactively its own cause, i.e., an object that can be perceived only by the look "distorted" by desire, an object that does not exist for an "objective" look. In other words, the *objet petit a* is always, by definition, perceived in a distorted way, because, outside this distortion, "in itself" it does not exist, i.e., because it is nothing but the embodiment, the materialization of this distortion...Objet petit a is "objectively" nothing, it is nothing at all, nothing of the desire itself which, viewed from a certain perspective, assumes the shape of "something." (Žižek 1989, p. 34)

This "certain perspective" may very well be that of an audio point of view, because the audio comes from an outer perspective and contributes to altering the meaning of the visual (or "distorting" to use Žižek's word). Moreover, voice is an embodiment of the *objet petit a* in the Lacanian world, because voice carries the signifier outward, while in essence being "nothing" (i.e. it is the signified, the meaning of what the voice carries, that is relevant). Therefore, the overlapping of three voices mentioned above – Sissako, Césaire, Keita – provides the audience with a hyperbolized *objet petit a*, a choral *objet*, as they all refer to (impossible) returns.

The protective feeling, though, may be naïve. Fantasy protects us from the Real, but it can also reveal the exact object of our horror (Žižek 2008, p. 6). Žižek complicates this issue even further: "If what we experience as 'reality' is structured by fantasy, and if fantasy serves as the screen that protects us from being directly overwhelmed by the raw Real, *then reality itself can function as an escape from encountering the Real*" (2008, p. 57, original emphasis). The reality we hear throughout Sissako's film is radically different from the visual reality. It prevents us from actually seeing the reality, and therefore, "we never pass from the spectral Real to reality" (Žižek 2008, p, 201). The spectral Real is akin to the aural space I have been referring to, since they are both figments of the imagination. As a result, it becomes imperative to consider sound a quintessential and necessary ingredient in the creation of both the neo-colonial fantasy and its space.

The ambiguous nature of fantasy is analogous to how we perceive the film's narrative with or without the contribution of sound. Žižek also refers to a similar deadlock: "Fantasy is the primordial form of narrative, which serves to occult some original deadlock" (2008, p. 11). He refers here to the myth of primordial accumulation, but we can generalize and look at the visual and sound as being in a deadlock. To reiterate, classic Hollywood cinema uses sound in order to enhance the image, or to complete what the image is telling us, and sound should not be "noticed." This is the original setup – our deadlock – and this also happens to be the original Law. Later, in the traditions of avant-garde and experimental cinemas, sound became a transgression: Film and its sound went against an established Law and from that point of conflict sound emerged solitary and independent. Lacan (1998) finds a similar point of conflict in Seminar XX, but at a more personal level. This point explains how fantasy works with the following famous declaration: There is no sexual relationship. We can never have an ideal partner; instead we make them (in our heads) into one. This practice works really well in the context of understanding image and sound as a "couple." Nowadays, disjoining sound from image is not as transgressive or uncommon an act anymore, but I believe that the continuation rules of the classic Hollywood narrative are still the dominating norm. However, West African film continues to challenge more systematically the preferred harmonious narrative relationship between image and sound. So in essence it challenges the Big Other, which in the case of cinema is still represented by the rules according to which image and sound should function congruously.

Among his many contributions to cinema theory, Rick Altman gives us a capital volume, *Silent Film Sound* (2004), on the history of sound and sound rules from the very beginning of cinema. While his historical approach and focus on American cinema are not necessarily complementary to current sound theories, this is a tremendously ambitious project that marks important moments in the timeline of the relationship between sound and image. It begins with establishing sound as initially discontinuous in its relationship with the image (2004, pp. 92–93). It then moves slowly toward uniting the two, bypassing the "oppressive" period of vaudeville (during which film was secondary to the theatrical act, 2004, pp. 104–115), and the early nickelodeon years, to arrive at the conclusion that sound and image together could "create realistic pseudo-events" (2004, p. 155), which was one of Edison's points of insistence, too (2004, p. 175). The general impetus toward marrying image and sound, or toward the standardization of sound, slowly eliminated attempts, such as placing voices behind the screen or adding live music, that might have competed for the attention of the audience to what happened on screen (2004, p. 318). The process ends in a simplification: "Limit the soundscape to a single sound source, standardize sound practices, gentrify sound choices. In this classical approach film exhibition found its first stability, and cinema thereby its initial identity" (Altman 2004, p. 390).

Michel Chion is the one theorist who has most consistently challenged this initial identity of cinema. In the first part of his book *Film, a Sound Art* (2009, pp. 2-18), he follows a similar historical path as Altman, beginning with an understanding of sound as it was suggested through images. Chion had also originally discussed the "dream" of voices in *The Voice in Cinema* (1999); to him, cinema was never silent, it was deaf, and every time we saw the actors' mouths move we must have dreamed (for my purposes here, "imagined") what they were saying (1999, pp. 7–9). This segregation of our senses, of our understanding of what happens on screen was what threatened the state of cinema at the time. Following Chion's ideas, one can easily consider that sound in general must have been imagined (i.e. seeing a vase drop, then imagining the sound it makes when hitting the ground). I think that a reversal is taking place in West African cinema in general, and in the films of Sissako in particular. There is sound, but the image is lacking its usual narrative strength and therefore it must be imagined (or, at least, mentally completed), which in turn leads to the creation of an imagined space. To invoke another theorist who has dealt with the issue of imagined, cinematic space – André Bazin – film comes to "life" in the minds of the spectators in the following way: "We need to believe in the reality of what is happening while knowing it to be tricked … so the screen reflects the ebb and flow of our imagination which feeds on a reality for which it plans to substitute" (1967, p. 48). Cinema has been a medium that encourages an active imagination, but it is sound that has installed that imagination as the most necessary tool of the viewing process.

Let us now return to the third voice that makes itself heard during the film's transition to the Malian town, Salif Keita's voice. This is a purely non-diegetic voice – it remains in the nebulous space of the soundtrack – and therefore constitutes the most outer layer of the aural Russian doll. Keita's voice seems to spring out of Sissako's spoken words and plays its part to remind the audience of the back and forth movements between France and Mali, or past and present. The song itself, *Folon* ("The Past"), speaks indirectly to the first movement through the use of the regional Malinke dialect and directly through a shift in the actual lyrics from *folon* / past to *sissan* / today. Before the song begins in earnest, though, the mechanical sounds of capitalism (the beep, the loudspeaker in the supermarket, etc.) are replaced by a soft, instrumental prelude to the song that incorporates the sounds of nature. The non-diegetic sound of the song harmoniously meshes with the diegetic natural sound. The movement away from the Western world is alluded to later in the film when an aural contrast opposes Keita's music with classical music by Schubert. The film also loops back to Césaire's words which appear on screen, "L'oreille collée au sol, j'entendis passer Demain" (Ear to the ground, I heard Tomorrow pass), as the camera films the ground. Visually, the camera follows the indications in Césaire's quote, and a key transference takes place: The camera is the ear mentioned by the poet. It is as if the camera itself functions like an ear or is reduced to a microphone, which further underlines the critical importance of sound. Just as in the example of the slow-motion shot in the French supermarket, the camera being pointed needlessly toward the ground reignites the sentiment that the visual is somehow lacking scope, lacking its usual narrative control.

In this film, sound also materializes and travels through an ever-present material embodiment – the radio.[6] In Dramane's town, an interesting dynamic arises between the broadcast of the diegetic radio station, Radio Colon (carrying the subtitle, "la voix du riz"/the voice of rice), which is done in the local dialect, and the French news broadcast. The former is not followed by shots of actual radios and people listening in, while the latter is: We see a group of men sitting in the shade by a wall listening together, then a solitary man puts a small radio to his ear, then another group of men sitting under a tree listens to the same French broadcast. It would appear that the broadcast in the colonizers' language draws more interest and has a wider reach, which would sustain the invisible reach of colonialism. The town is filled with several other physical embodiments of the radio: A man walks by carrying a large boom box, another one bikes with a radio wrapped around his neck,[7] Dramane's father has one in his room, and a minor character named Danté keeps a radio by his side when he showers. In spite of this overwhelming presence, connecting people actually remains a challenge on the cusp of the new millennium. For example, a postal worker ominously declares, "It's hard to reach people. It's a question of luck," when he tries to find someone over the phone. It would not be a stretch to extrapolate this comment to the difficulties of the local, cultural reach of Sissako's film, especially given the lack of cinemas in Mali that the director often criticizes in his interviews. However, one possible positive result yielded by the presence of the radio is that the many visual encounters with it throughout the film continue to show that sound travels around the town. In doing so, it acquires a flanerial quality and it remaps the neo-colonial rural space.

Sound, Space, and City Limits

The traveling quality of sound poses a problem to the visual representations of both rural and urban spaces in that it appears to stretch their perceived limits. The visual can also push these limits when it "hovers" in an establishing shot, but these types of shots usually follow conventions of continuity (i.e. they place the spectator in the proper spatial context or they act as transitions from one scene to another). The point is that the visual can push the (seen) spatial limits to a perceived infinity, but for the most part the visual is restricted to tighter frames, long shots to close-ups. In stark opposition with this limitation, sound can truly hover over a space and in doing so, it redraws the perceived limits. Off-screen sound, especially, widens the spectators' perspective of the frame – it elongates the image – which reaches out into the space off screen. Therefore, in short, sound expands space.

   If we take the familiar example mentioned above (Sissako at the beginning of *Life on Earth*), a siren is also heard when the director/actor is in the supermarket. The sound, coming from outside, expands the visual field by adding an aural coda, which reminds the audience that the outside space is necessarily urban. According to Michel Chion: "No other noise is as symbolically and dramatically effective in marking territory as a vehicle horn or siren" (2009, pp. 242–243). He then elaborates that "The sound of a horn or siren in a movie doesn't just evoke its source – police car, fire engine, taxi – but instantly allows our ear to get the feel of the urban landscape" (2009, p. 242). It is important, though, that Sissako's film does not feature any outdoor shots during the short episode in France. This conspicuous lack helps set up a more poignant contrast with the outdoor shots in the Malian town and the surrounding countryside. In essence, Sissako is "stuck" inside this supermarket and the aural expansion of space via the siren only hints at the possibility of conquering the outdoors. Furthermore, the sound of this first scene is seemingly reduced just to natural sound, to the ambient sound that logically accompanies the visual. Sound proves that it can travel further than the visual but it, too, might be limited to the space of the city. Michel Chion observes that acoustically the city can be a "container," in which sounds bounce between different urban surfaces (2009, p. 242). In this particular case, sound mostly bounces of the walls of the supermarket. A few seconds later, though, the sound is freed to roam alongside the outdoor shots. Not only that but sound now boasts three kinds of output: Natural sound (birds chirping), voice off, and non-diegetic music. The overlap of and dialogue between the three aural narrative layers emphasize that a sudden narrative shift has taken place, even though the visual briefly remains restrictive (the transition shot to Africa zooms in on a single, large baobab tree).

It seems natural that such a shift should occur in the African context, which has long been mediated by colonial visual markers. For example, visual reminders about colonialism abound in West African film, particularly in the cinema of Senegal, which often focuses on Dakar, a city with "more colonial structures than other major African urban centers" (Pfaff 2004, p. 92). While Françoise Pfaff's declaration may prove to be too reductive, as it ignores other (more) sizeable traces of colonialism in Ivory Coast or Nigeria, for example, colonialism and neo-colonialism certainly do linger visibly in Senegal. Historian James Genova also remarks to this point: "It's been more than fifty years since Senegal … achieved independence … but the scenes of contemporary Dakar, marked by coterminous signs of renewal and decline, belie the heritage of that half century" (2013, p. 1). It must not be forgotten, though, that similar traces persist audibly as well. Brian Larkin's groundbreaking book, *Signal and Noise* (2008), draws attention to the radio as a colonial technology and infrastructure, and subsequently documents how the media (especially the radio) creates "unique aural and perceptual environments, everyday urban arenas" (pp. 2–3) in postcolonial Nigeria. These environments lead to the construction of a "colonial sublime," which is "about Europeans' tactile and symbolic effort to make technology mean" (Larkin 2008, p. 42). Of course, technology was first introduced through the operations of colonialism and then, partially "protected" by the operations of neo-colonialism. It continued to produce an audible materiality meant to function like an echo of colonialism. The control exercised over the colonized was perpetuated thanks to the visual form of the infrastructure (including the physical radio), but more insidiously, through the

dissemination of English broadcast radio: "Radio diffusion … continued the process of mediating urban space … creating new types of aural experience" (Larkin
2008, p. 49).[8] Larkin's findings can be extrapolated to Senegal, where French-language broadcasts flourished during the Senghor years (it is less so the case nowadays, as the broadcasts are equally in African languages), and also to Sissako's Mali
and Mauritania. While the visual markers of colonialism and the presence of radio
diffusion in the colonizers' language(s) have contributed to perpetuating an echo
of colonialism, they do not necessarily dominate the visual and aural landscapes of
the neo-colonial city. But Sissako's films do create "types of aural experiences" by
focusing first on the aural, and then looking for new meanings in the visual. Gilles
Deleuze (1986) rightfully claimed that the advent of the talkies changed the way
one looks at the cinematic image, that the image itself became something else
thanks to the sound attached to it. It stands to reason, then, that culturally specific
noises, voices, sounds, and music would do the same. Following *Life on Earth*,
Sissako's next three films would continue to buttress the narrative trend of this
aural specificity and the creation of aural spaces.

Waiting for Sound

In *Waiting for Happiness*, the wind, the sand, and the radio (a malfunctioning radio
appears in the first few sequences) seem to emerge as the main characters. The
director moves the setting of the story from Mali to Nouadhibou, a transit city in
Mauritania according to Sissako in the notes to the DVD version. The geographical
shift does not affect the overall direction of Sissako's narrative arc, as the film
returns to the themes of exclusion and exile. Any resemblance to a traditional plot
hinges on the story of young Abdallah who is spending some time at home with
his mother but does not speak the local language. His inability poses some communication problems and makes him an outsider, but one with whom music resonates. For example, when he overhears the neighbors' party, where several women
take turns singing, Abdallah goes out of his room, and dances by himself on the
rooftop. He does not respond well to the language, or to the customs of the place,
yet somehow the music speaks to him (and, through him, to us). In the impromptu
dance, Abdallah connects himself to the city. The sound and the music hover over
the space of the city, pushing quasi-foreigners to become part of the city.

It is not just Abdallah who is touched by the music filling up the city. For
example, a Chinese man who sells watches sings karaoke in Chinese to a local
woman, random characters sing in the street, and, most importantly, a little girl
learns the craft of singing from an older woman. All these instances of singing
cross over and unify urban space(s); music acts as the great common denominator
that brings people together. The director returns several times to the interaction
between the young girl and her teacher, and the camera patiently waits for their

song to end. Music traditionally features on the soundtrack, but in Sissako's films the soundtrack descends into the diegesis. The action (which lags anyway) comes to a full stop in order for the camera to focus on these two women and their singing. The result is that the scope of the visual is momentarily reduced in order to emphasize the expansive powers of the aural.

The power of the sound is established in the beginning of the film through a playful shift between non-diegetic and intra-diegetic music: The music the audience initially associates with the soundtrack (non-diegetic) is revealed to be coming from the radio of a car (intra-diegetic), which Abdallah turns off. Whatever control the characters have over the narrative manifests itself aurally rather than visually; by the same token, the wonderful scene when Abdallah dances showcases the opposite effect – the control of the sound over the people. A repeated scene in Abdallah's home, where the young man is mostly bored, emphasizes the lack of visual range or control over the surroundings. Abdallah, lying down, often looks through a rectangular hole, a window of sorts placed right on ground-level. His view is rather limited by the very low angle of the hybrid window. In a moment that pushes the metaphor beyond the obvious, a donkey with a cart carrying a television goes by slowly, but the sand obscures most of our view. Through transference (what he sees is what the audience sees), the window fulfills its diegetic purpose: It is indeed a metaphor for cinema; it is in fact a view from below.[9] Kenneth Harrow's wonderful 2013 study of cinema from below offers this exact perspective. In this instance, though, it is not simply a cinema from below, but a cinema with sand in its eyes, or lens, as it were. Moreover, Sissako's camera occasionally does not want penetrate beyond drapes and hanging cloths, as it is the case when Nana, a prostitute with whom Abdallah seems fascinated, receives male company. Instead of showing us the interaction between Nana and the two men, the camera stops in front of the hanging cloth and essentially records the dialogue of the three. This choice technically renders the camera into a microphone, which is a technique similar to transforming the camera into an ear in *Life on Earth*. Therefore, the sound yet again emerges as a viable, more encompassing alternative to telling a story. From his viewpoint Abdallah does not get a full image of the city; how could he? And neither do the spectators, as Sissako limits their access, too. The visual life of the city is stunted, but the aural life moves over the buildings and reaches Abdallah (and the audience) even in his retreat, where he does respond to the sound of the city, to its music.

The Sounds of *Bamako*

Bamako is another cinematic effort that circumvents a traditional plot. In short, the locals of the Malian capital put the World Bank on trial, which takes place in a courtyard, and the film follows the events of the trial, along with a few underdeveloped side stories. The trial is broadcast through loudspeakers into the sandy streets of Bamako, so one of the most interesting aspects of the film is, once again, the way in which the director employs sound, which materializes more clearly (i.e. "visibly") than in the previous two films. If the radio was the stand-in fetish-object that replaced the idea of sound in the first two films, *Bamako* offers several shots of the loudspeakers but also of the microphones in the courtyard in order to substantiate the metaphorical uses of sound. Because of the insistence of such shots containing either a loudspeaker or a microphone, sound itself seems to take on a material quality. A series of three shots featuring microphones occurs during one of the breaks from the trial and reinforces the physical presence of sound: First, a man prays, while next to him the boom microphone rests against the wall. Second, a woman speaks on a cell phone, while two mics appear in the foreground in an out of focus medium close-up. Third, the camera moves further away and changes angle too, but the mics remain in the foreground and out of focus. It is interesting that the microphones should be mostly out of focus (another visual fail of sorts), as if the director decided to cover up their presence: They are both *there* and *not quite there* at the same time, much like how sound functions in cinema, too (i.e. it is always present in some form, even as silence, but not always clearly visible). There are several other examples of microphones, instances which amount to the film occasionally being reduced to the singular power of sound.

The voices of the people partaking in the trial travel to the outside of the courtyard through the aforementioned loudspeakers. The people outside of the courtyard go about their daily lives, but what is being said, and consequently what is being broadcast into the city is rather relevant. For example, the voice of one of the lawyers warns that though Africa will accept the rules of globaliza-tion, it does want an even playing field economically. Other people at the trial speak against President George W. Bush, against Western policies, against ter-rorism and immigration, and against the war in Iraq; other voices suggest that the West could provide Africa with potable water and medicine for AIDS. The loudspeaker reappears when the guardian at the door is shown either letting people in or not allowing them to enter, but again it is visible on either side of the frame, almost out of sight, like an afterthought, which happens on multiple occasions. Finally, tired of the arguments, the people listening from outside turn it off, but it is only temporary, as the trial still makes its way onto the street. They turn it off again, but the problem is that the sound of justice and the voices of the people cannot be turned off.

In one of the most moving scenes of the film, an old man finally gets his chance to "speak" after waiting since the beginning of the film, and at last he just sings, untranslated. As Sissako explains in an interview for the DVD, the old man is a peasant from the South and almost no one understands his dialect. Sissako claims he wanted something universal for this scene – everyone understands the emotion transmitted via the song. The old man also provides the audience with a cinematic transition to the singer, Melé, who ends the film on a high note, as it were. While in the bar, framed in a medium close-up, on a mostly empty background, Melé's voice travels to several places because the scene starts by focusing on her wedding photo, then goes to her daughter (Ina) sleeping, then to her husband Chaka sitting outside. While visually the film is built following an atemporal style of editing, the voice covers up and smooths out the narrative space, linking it to the old man's tune, reaching further back (for the audience familiar with Sissako) to Salif Keita's song: Melé, like Keita in *Life on Earth*, talks about going back, as she wants to return to Dakar. The ending of the film captures her beautiful singing, now in a close-up, as she begins to cry. It is a very long song contrasting with the usual bits of music offered by a film that does not belong to the genre of the musical. Just as it did when the old man sang in the courtyard, or even further back, to the girl and teacher from *Waiting for Happiness*, the film essentially stops; the camera stops moving and contents itself with filming this beautiful, aural moment.

Killing the Music

In another extra-diegetic connection, Sissako's latest effort, *Timbuktu*, is announced by the short film within the film in *Bamako*, in which the director casts himself as a villain. The title of the film is "Death in Timbuktu," and it is an aimless comedic Western that features random shootings, Danny Glover, Western music, and generally speaking, plot confusion. It is perhaps the reason why the words "Directed by," shown on screen, are never followed by a name, as if Sissako did not want to take credit for such an intervention. In interviews, Sissako has said he wanted to put himself in a film, to be like a spectator, and to play with a genre that is important to him (the Western), because he grew up with it. *Timbuktu*, the actual feature film, centers around death and the tragedy of guitar-playing cattle herder, Kidane. When a fisherman kills one of Kidane's cows (ironically named GPS, the animal had become entangled in his fishing net), the latter looks for justice and accidentally shoots the former. What follows is perhaps one of the most beautiful scenes directed by Sissako. The conflict is initially framed in a long shot. The camera tracks Kidane going toward the fisherman, then during the struggle it stops moving. The sounds of nature are rather subdued throughout the struggle between the two men, as if to defer to this important, visual moment. We only hear the water splashing under their tangling feet and later the bubbling noise of water from under the fallen bodies. The moment the gun goes off, though, birds and insects begin chirping and the sounds of nature come to life, which is odd: Normally one would think that nature would briefly go quiet because of the violent aural intrusion of the gun. But the bullet that essentially settles Kidane's fate also jumpstarts the surrounding aural soundscape. In the moments after this terrible death, Sissako moves the camera way back on an adjacent hill and follows Kidane's stumbling in an extreme long shot, while the sounds of nature continue on the soundtrack. Kidane is both visually and aurally reduced: First he becomes a moving dot in the immensity of the open landscape, and second, his feet sloshing in the water are covered up by nature noises and then by the emergence of soundtrack music. The camera waits for the character to cross the shallow waters from right to left, without moving in closer, maintaining this exaggerated distance. The visual distance suggests the director's removal from the emotion of the scene, which might have been shot in close-ups in conventional cinema, but it also establishes the power of nature, in which the man is impotent, a moving dot. This shot is the closest equivalent to the way in which sound is able to hover over all of Sissako's films. All of non-diegetic sound is really sound from a distance, from an extreme long shot (or farther even) perspective.

While the film is certainly more vigorous and topical in its attack on extreme manifestations and interpretations of Islam, sound and music remain focal points through opposition and absence: In the city of Timbuktu, Muslim fundamentalists (the ISIL flag is shown on several vehicles) do not allow music playing or singing.[10] The opening sequence includes a hunted, running antelope as well as target practice on African statues. The source of the bullets remains invisible, and, because of the destructive force of the bullets, the acousmêtre seemingly takes on a larger degree of omnipotence. These bullets coming from nowhere mutilate the wooden statues placed directly in the sand. It is an interesting commentary that reminds one of Franz Fanon's (2008) critique of President Senghor's admiration for the African rhythm observed in the wooden sculptures: "And this race staggered under the weight of one basic element. *Rhythm!* Listen to Senghor, our bard … Have I read it correctly? I give it an even closer reading. On the other side of the white world there lies a magical black culture. Negro sculpture!" (2008, p. 102; original emphasis). According to Senghor, rhythm is indeed at the heart of African aesthetics, and by extension then at the heart of Negritude. Unlike the European order and reason, rhythm is emotion, the vital force that explains the imbalances or misperceived asymmetry of African sculpture. In her study of Negritude, Ima Ebong looks at four values – intuition, emotion, rhythm, and vital force, or rather the "abstract characterization of the values it [Negritude] imagined as ancestral African art forms" – in order to explain why "Negritude was limited as an aesthetic" (1999, p. 132). Souleymane Diagne offers us a more direct link with Negritude and Senghor when he looks at the notion of rhythm in the context of African poetry which, he claims, emphasizes parataxis – juxtaposition and coordination (2011, p. 93).[11]

Parataxis is an element that the cinema of Sissako clearly exposes in its treatment of sound and image, especially during this opening scene. Ultimately it is the sound of the whizzing bullets, which remain unseen, of course, that carves into the statues. These statues, disfigured, now boast rough edges, and the true, lighter color of the wood beneath is revealed. The message is clear: African heritage is under attack by these extreme ideologies, but it almost feels as if the true enemy here is sound. At the very least, sound appears to hold some kind of magical power that can shred wood, so sound materializes under our very eyes. The source of the

violent sound is invisible, yet the weapons are likely Kalashnikovs, also known as
AK-47s, the famed Russian assault weapons, a fact confirmed visually moments
later. It is perhaps ironic that Sissako spent seven years in Russia learning filmmaking,[12] a tool for construction, while the characters of *Timbuktu* destroy the world
with different Russian tools.

Conclusion

Sissako's films challenge the spatial limits and limitations of the town and of the
city through constant movement and engagement with their surroundings. As the
films unfold visually, it becomes increasingly clear that the stories generated by
sound, the stories on the margins, the outer layers of this cinematic version of the
Russian doll effect, represent the "place" where meaning is birthed. Space is
certainly reconstructed through and by the eye of the camera, but also, more
meaningfully and eloquently, through an aural remapping of Malian and
Mauritanian neighborhoods. In the process, the life of the neo-colonial town and
city takes clearer shape at the aural level.

It is worth repeating that, inevitably, the camera generates and controls space to
an extent. However, the narrative tendency to shift from the visual to the aural
cannot be ignored, because sound transgresses the visual, physical space. Moreover,
the inherent mobility of sound helps the audience mentally map out cities and
neighborhoods. The noises and voices thus have the capacity to generate new
spaces, diegetically and extra-diegetically, as the neo-colonial space and its characters keep changing. The cinematic sound of these films, and of West African
cinema in general, embodies this constant change, a change that has been at the
heart of the neo-colonial transition for several decades now. In the tumultuous
political context of West Africa during the second part of the twentieth century,
and moving into the new century as well, it is the cinematic sound that emerges
not only as an ingenious artistic tool and as an aesthetic artifice, but also as an
expression of absolute (narrative) freedom.

Notes

1   Sissako has also made a number of short films.
2   Orson Welles and Jean-Luc Godard are but two famous examples. This chapter intends
    to sidestep the outdated issues of authenticity, auteurship, and originality in African
    cinema. In other words, and in spite of a few necessary referential examples, I do not
    intend to speak of African film and of Sissako through oppositions, comparisons, or
    categories: African cinema is just cinema. Consider Kenneth Harrow's take on the
    matter: "The very notion of tradition is a concoction of modernism; the attempt to

validate African authenticity, or traditional identity, is a reaction to western domination and is betrayed by its dependence on western epistemological tools, western
categories of knowledge" (2007, p. 27).

3   As opposed to the term "postcolonial," which may be wrongly applied to contexts
from which colonialism has never really disappeared, the term "neo-colonial" offers
more ambiguity and is therefore more appropriate for the current argument. Here I
am following Ella Shohat's perspective: "The 'neo-colonial,' like the 'postcolonial,'
also suggests continuities and discontinuities, but its emphasis is on the new modes
and forms of the old colonialist practices, not on a 'beyond'" (2006, p. 241).

4   In *Sonic Space in the Films of Djibril Diop Mambéty* (2017, Indiana University Press), I investigate the work of the mercurial Senegalese director in order to argue that sound first
effectuates a deterritorialization of the image, of its narrative primacy, and second, that
culturally-specific uses of sound reterritorialize the African cinematic narrative space.
This chapter revisits theories exposed in this book and expands on earlier findings.

5   There seems to be some discrepancy between Chion's and Dolar's terminology
(disacousmatization and de-acousmatization). I have kept the original choices of the
authors, as they mean the same thing.

6   The radio is a crucial prop, a fetish-object really, in several West African films: Mambety's
Le franc and *La petite vendeuse de soleil*, Sembène's *Moolaadé*, are but three examples.

7   This example brings to mind the expression "albatross around one's neck": One may
be weighed down by the radio and the constant news stream. Since this is an idiom, it
does not translate well into French. However, the French equivalent, "boulet au pied"
(heavy ball attached to the feet) conjures images of slavery: One is a slave to the news.

8   For a more detailed perspective, see the chapter titled, "Unstable Objects: The Making
of Radio in Nigeria" (Larkin 2008, pp. 48–72).

9   Sissako's intentions here are further explained in the notes to the DVD: Sissako
remarks that there is an unequal relationship between North and South and that the
TV brings in "an outside culture to the detriment of an existing culture." There is a
TV show on but the reverse shot reveals that no one watches it. In the same room,
Abdallah sits and his clothes are made of the same cloth that adorns the entire room.

10 There are other interdictions that occur, as well. They also confiscate a soccer ball,
which leads to a beautiful scene in which children play without the ball.

11 Souleymane Bachir Diagne's book, *African Art as Philosophy: Senghor, Bergson, and the
Idea of Negritude* (2011), defends Senghor's legacy, and deals at length with his engagement with Bergson's philosophy. Diagne claims that Senghor's distinction between
reason and emotion, reductively Hellenistic art and African art, does not mean that
the two are conclusively opposed.

12 Eisenstein's Russian formalism often subtly emerges in his approach to filmmaking,
which represents another incarnation of parataxis.

References

Altman, Rick. 2004. *Silent Film Sound*. New York: Columbia University Press.
Bazin, André. 1967. *What is Cinema?* Berkeley: University of California.
Césaire, Aimé. 1939. *Cahier d'un retour au pays natal*. Paris: Volontés.

Chion, Michel. 1999. *The Voice in Cinema*. New York: Columbia University Press.
Chion, Michel. 2009. *Film, A Sound Art*. New York: Columbia University Press.
Deleuze, Gilles. 1986. *Cinema 2*. Minneapolis: University of Minnesota Press.
Diagne, Souleymane Bachir. 2011. *African Art as Philosophy: Senghor, Bergson, and the Idea of Negritude*. Trans. Chike Jeffers. London: Seagull Books.
Doane, Mary Ann. 1985. "The Voice in the Cinema: The Articulation of Body and Space." In *Film Sound*, edited by Elisabeth Weis and John Belton, 162–176. New York: Columbia University Press.
Dolar, Mladen. 2006. *A Voice and Nothing More*. Cambridge, MA: MIT Press.
Ebong, Ima. 1999. "Negritude: Between Mask and Flag – Senegalese Cultural Ideology and the *École de Dakar*." In *Reading the Contemporary: African Art from Theory to the Marketplace*, edited by Olu Oguibe and Okwui Enwezor, 128–143. Cambridge, MA: MIT Press.
Fanon, Frantz. 2008. *Black Skin, White Masks*. New York: Grove Press.
Genova, James. 2013. *Cinema and Development in West Africa*. Bloomington: Indiana University Press.
Harrow, Kenneth. 2007. *Postcolonial African Cinema. From Political Engagement to Postmodernism*. Bloomington: Indiana University Press.
Harrow, Kenneth. 2013. *Trash: African Cinema from Below*. Bloomington: Indiana University Press.
Lacan, Jacques. 1998. *The Seminar of Jacques Lacan, Book XX: On Feminine Sexuality, the Limits of Love and Knowledge*, translated by Bruce Fink. New York: Norton.
Larkin, Brian. 2008. *Signal and Noise: Media, Infrastructure, and Urban Culture in Nigeria*. Durham, NC: Duke University Press.
Pfaff, Françoise. 2004. "African Cities as Cinematic Texts." In *Focus on African Films*, edited by Françoise Pfaff, 89–106. Bloomington: Indiana University Press.
Shohat, Ella. 2006. *Taboo Memories, Diasporic Voices*. Durham, NC: Duke University Press.
Žižek, Slavoj. 1989. "Looking Awry." *October*, 50, 30–55.
Žižek, Slavoj. 2008. *The Plague of Fantasies*. London: Verso.

Filmography

Diop, Mambéty Djibril. (1994). *Le franc*. Senegal: Waka Films.
Diop, Mambéty Djibril. (1998). *Le petite vendeuse de soleil*. Senegal: Waka Films.
Sembène, Ousmane. (2004). *Mooladé*. Senegal/Burkina Faso: Doomireew Films.
Sissako, Abderrahmane. (1998). *La vie sur terre*. Mali/France: Haut et court.
Sissako, Abderrahmane. (2002). *Heremakono*. France/Mauritania: Arte France Cinéma, Duo Films.
Sissako, Abderrahmane. (2006). *Bamako*. Mali: Archipel 33, Arte France Cinéma, Mali Images.
Sissako, Abderrahmane. (2014). *Timbuktu*. Mali: Les Films du Worso, Dune Vision, Arte France Cinéma.

9

"Outcast Orders" and the Imagining of a Queer African Cinema
A Fugitive, Afro-Jazz Reading of Karmen Geï

Lindsey Green-Simms

By many accounts, African Queer Studies or a Queer African Studies now constitutes a recognizable and emerging field of scholarship (Nyanzi, 2015; Currier and Thérèse Migraine-George, 2016; Osinubi, 2016). Though there is still debate about the applicability of the term "queer" to same-sex practices and desires in Africa, it has been the case that for at least the past decade "queer" has become a mode of thinking through and about diverse, non-conforming African sexualities and challenging normative assumptions. Used both by North American Africanists as well as those on and from the African continent, "queer" refers to modes of inquiry that, as Stella Nyanzi writes, take on a "two-pronged approach, namely queering African Studies on the one hand, and Africanising Queer Studies on the other hand" (2015, p. 127). Those using the term contend that queer provides a shifting and flexible epistemological positionality that can account for rather than erase the complexity of regional identities and local categories. In a much-needed intervention outlining the often fraught relationship between Queer Studies and African Area Studies, Ashley Currier and Thérèse Migraine-George write that "Queer African studies can therefore be seen as the space in which the contours of cultural and sexual identities become questioned and blurred – a space that may allow for the forging of new forms of alliance, sociality, and kinship but also transcends limited assumptions about location, belonging, and identity" (2016, p. 291). Writing about the combined effect of queer-labeled African literary collections and "the increasing deployment of *queer*...by African scholars in African universities," Taiwo Adetunji Osinubi states in his introduction to the first queer-focused special issue of *Research in African Literature (RAL)* that "the relevant question in 2016 is less about the applicability of queer and more about the already-existing

A Companion to African Cinema, First Edition. Edited by Kenneth W. Harrow and Carmela Garritano.
© 2019 John Wiley & Sons, Inc. Published 2019 by John Wiley & Sons, Inc.

applications of queer in Africanist research" (2016, p. xiv). Though not without its faults and limitations, which are arguably being addressed by contemporary scholars, artists, and activists, Queer African Studies and queer African literary production gather together multi-directional writing that gives shape to the complexity, resistance, and precarity of queer African lives.

Within this emerging and increasingly prolific discourse, discussions of African film tend to be grouped together with discussions of literature, as in the above-mentioned *RAL* special issue titled "Queer Valences in African Literatures and Film." Thinking about what aesthetic forms have to offer, scholars often make note that both film and literature's "focus on narrative processes of meaning mak-ing rather than on the empirical and archival fieldwork" (Osinubi 2016, p. xv) calls for and allows for different methodologies and models of analysis than those used in the social sciences. Osinubi notes that queer African film and literature should be seen in terms of a "restorative project," one with "a *proleptic designation* that also questions asserted norms" (2016, p. viii). Currier and Migraine-George argue that queer aesthetic representations of Africans often "offer a productive alternative" to less imaginative modes of disciplinary inquiry and can focus on what Keguro Macharia, paraphrasing Neo Musangi, calls "conditions of livability" (2016, p. 295). Though I agree with these assessments, what I want to focus on in this chapter are the specificities and potentialities of a queer African cinema.

While the African literary scene has seen several queer-identified authors, like Binyavanga Wainaina, Jude Dibia, Unoma Azuah, and Frieda Ekotto, making public statements or publishing work that explicitly challenges homophobia and many more allies doing the same, the same cannot be said of the African film scene. Currently, the majority of representations of LGBT Africans are occurring in Nigerian and Ghanain video films.[1] In nearly all of these films, gay characters are associated with witchcraft, prostitution, or criminality and these characters are, accordingly, punished for their sins – they wind up in jail, dead, or are saved through the acceptance of Jesus into their lives. Following formulaic plots and arbi-trary rules set up by national Censors Boards, these films, then, are not about forg-ing new forms of alliance and sociality, but about repeating stereotypes and tropes of criminalization. Elsewhere (Green-Simms, 2012a; Green-Simms, 2012b; Green-Simms and Azuah, 2012), I have engaged with these films in detail, discussing their relation to genre, melodrama, and rumor and examining the role they play in pro-ducing discourse around the figure of the homosexual. Here, however, I would like to think about an African cinema that opens itself up to queerness, a cinema that practices modes of belonging, unbelonging, and solidarity that are particular to African and African Diasporic queers. Though there are more than a handful of films that I might turn to, I want to look at Joseph Gaï Ramaka's *Karmen Geï* (2001), an exemplary film in part because of the richness of its form and in part because it gestures to a trans-Atlantic imaginary that forces one to think beyond the geographical area of Africa and, therefore, beyond an essentialized notion of Africa. As Eve Kosofsky Sedgwick writes, one thing that "queer" might refer to is "the open mesh of possibilities, gaps, overlaps, dissonances and resonances, lapses and excesses of meaning when the constituent elements of anyone's gender, of anyone's sexuality are made (or *can't be* made) to signify monolithically" (1993, p. 8). What this chapter explores, then, are the "open mesh of possibilities" and "excesses of meaning" present within *Karmen Geï* and made audible in its echoes.

Perhaps one of the most widely written about African films, *Karmen Geï*, which was banned in Senegal, is a Senegalese adaptation of Prosper Mérimée's 1845 novella *Carmen* that was famously turned into an opera by Georges Bizet in 1875. In both of these versions, Carmen, a Gypsy and outlaw in southern Spain, seduces the officer Don José who destroys his career for Carmen and joins her fellow bandits. But when Carmen turns her affections to a bullfighter (Escamilo in the opera, Lucas in the novella), Don José murders Carmen. *Karmen Geï*, the first African adaptation of the story, follows this basic plot with one major change: In the original *Carmen*, and in most of the 80-some filmic adaptations, Carmen is caught in a love triangle between two men; in Ramaka's version Karmen loves both men and women. Because of laws against homosexuality in Senegal, Karmen's list of illicit activities therefore includes her choice of lovers. And while most *Carmen* adaptations do diverge from Bizet's operatic score, Ramaka's soundtrack is also unique: He combines jazz music with *sabar* drumming, Wolof songs, call and response rhythms, and Mouride religious music, creating a hybrid Afro-jazz score. Thus far, scholars have written about *Karmen Geï's* musical form (Petty, 2009; Powrie, 2004; Dovey 2009) as well as its focus on queer, or what Babacar M'Baye calls "variant," sexualities (Coly, 2015; M'Baye, 2011; Ekotto, 2007; Nelson, 2011; Stobie, 2016; Powrie, 2004). What I want to do is to think about the film's form and music in relation to its queerness, to place the Afro-jazz score at the center of a queer reading so as to underscore the modes of solidarity, sociality, and kinship that the film calls forth. Part of my contention, then, is that thinking about what a queer African cinema might be or might offer means paying attention to the cinematic form itself, to thinking through the power and possibilities of the image and its soundscape. I therefore offer a heuristic reading of *Karmen Geï* as a queer Afro-jazz musical that imagines, or improvises, structures that lead to other possible modes of being and doing.

Ramaka's *Karmen* has the same discourse on love, resistance, and freedom that has become the hallmark of all global Carmen stories. Throughout these different iterations, Carmen is consistently an outsider, an Other, and an outlaw who refuses to be owned; she is "willfully transgressive" (Harrow 2013, p. 108). But what the Senegalese Karmen does, perhaps more explicitly than other Carmens, is to multiply the concept of Other. Karmen is not just a postcolonial subject; she's a prisoner, a queer, a woman. And throughout the film she performs her opposition to patriarchy, the national bourgeoisie, compulsory heterosexuality, and what Ken Harrow calls "the economy of the market" (2013, p. 112). Ramaka links these struggles together and connects Karmen to histories of colonial oppression and slavery and to a long line of historical and divine resisters. And he does so, I argue, not only through the plot and dialogue, but through the film's improvisational structure and its trans-Atlantic black fugitive imagination, an imagination predicated on shedding constraints and fleeing toward the open mesh of possibilities.

An Afro-Jazz Musical

In the opening sequence of *Karmen Geï*, the audience sees Karmen, a prisoner at Kumba Kastel women's prison, dancing with and seducing Angelique, the prison warden. After sleeping with Angelique, Karmen is granted her freedom. In the following scene, Karmen gatecrashes the wedding of the soldier Lamine Diop (the Don José equivalent) and accuses him, and the state in general, of swallowing up the country. Lamine nevertheless falls madly in love with Karmen and neglects his duties. After Lamine is put in jail, Karmen and her friends break him free. She allows him to join her gang of smugglers as they plot illicit operations off of Dakar's coast. But Karmen does not return Lamine's love, a love her friend Samba calls a "bad love." After aiding in an operation, Karmen hands Lamine his share of the earnings – refusing to take any of the money herself – and encourages him to go back to his fiancée. Other love interests appear for Karmen, like the singer Massigi (the Escamilo/Lucas equivalent) played by the famous Senegalese singer and guitarist El Hadj N'diaye, but after a lonely Angelique commits suicide by drowning, Karmen admits it is Angelique, the one who gave her her freedom whom she loves the most. At the end of the film, as at the end of all Carmen stories, the scorned Lamine kills Karmen, an event predicted in Karmen's visions of death and painted-face ghosts.

In order to make the Carmen story more specifically Senegalese, Ramaka spells Karmen with a K in line with Wolof names and spelling (Dovey 2009, p. 248). Moreover, Ramaka gives his Karmen the last name of Geï. As a few critics have noted, Karmen's last name, pronounced the same as the word "gay," could be a pun, but Ramaka (who also bears the name) stated a different reason. He says, "I thought of the rhythm of the *sabar* [drums] called 'Ndèye Guèye'. The person who gave her name to this particular rhythm was a beautiful and exceptional dancer. She was a Carmen. So the title of my film is *Karmen Geï*" (qtd. in Powrie 2004, p. 286). And throughout the film, one can hear echoes of the story of Ndèye Guèye' (Guèye'and Geï are different spellings of the same name), a beautiful Senegalese woman who made all the men of Dakar fall in love with her but never consented to marry any of them (Maasilta 2005, p. 171), along with *sabar* drumming led by Doudou N'Diaye Rose, head of Dakar's National Ballet. But just as important as the drumming is the jazz score composed by David Murray, an American tenor saxophonist who has a history of collaborating with several Senegalese musicians including Rose. Also prominent throughout the film is Yandé Coudu Sène, the griot who sings the story of both Ndèye Guèye and, at the end of the film, Karmen Geï. And the film also features songs by Massigi, including a controversial holy song sung during Angelique's funeral procession, and by Karmen herself who sings with a strained and sometimes shaky voice.

Despite the presence of song and dance, critics have disagreed as to whether the film should be called a musical, a "quasi-musical," a "musical drama," a "musical comedy," or even a "dance review" (Dovey 2009, p. 221). Indeed, the film contains many of the familiar elements of a musical, most notably the breaking into song and dance, but it also feels more muted and less committed to fulfilling the expectations of the musical genre than American musical films, Bollywood movies, or Broadway shows. Ramaka himself rejects any categorization and says, "I do not make a difference between that which is said, that which is movement, and that which is sung…Everything is a question of tempo: The emotion that we express determines the need either to sing or speak it" (qtd. in Powrie 2004, p. 285). That *Karmen Geï* is named after Ndèye Guèye, both the name of a woman and the name of a rhythm, underscores the centrality of rhythm and music to the film and emphasizes the imbrication of plot and musical score.

I am calling the film a queer Afro-jazz musical, a category that brings to attention the fact that Karmen does not neatly fit into established genres, that the film, like its soundtrack, blends and mixes forms. The category of queer therefore refers to Karmen's non-conforming and non-heteronormative sexuality as well as to the film's resistance to generic categorization. The fact that in French, as Jacques Derrida points out, the word for gender and genre are the same (*genre*) adds multiple meaning to the blurring of *genre* that the film performs. What I want to think about is the way that the music in the film circulates sound and meaning, the way that it supplements the visual and the dialogue to create new ways of understanding and queering the film and new ways of reading its complex layering of intersecting marginalities or what Nathaniel Mackey calls "outcast orders."

In his book *Africa Speaks, America Answers: Modern Jazz in Revolutionary Times,* Robin D.G. Kelley turns to the era of decolonization and explores the conversations and collaborations between African and African American musicians. He describes "how modern Africa figured in reshaping [American] jazz during the 1950s and 1960s" and how that same music, in turn, "figured in the formation of a modern African identity" (2012, p. 5). Both African musicians and their African American counterparts saw jazz as "a path to the future" and a way to articulate a "deeply spiritual, antimaterialist" vision of modernity (2012, p. 6). Discussing artists from both sides of the Atlantic, artists like Max Roach, Randy Weston, John Coltrane, Guy Warren, and Sathima Bea Benjamin, Kelley writes, "They were modernists in search of radically different elements in harmony (the use of modal music), rhythm, and timbre. African music (not just West African but North, South, and East African music) offered rich possibilities for 'freeing' the music from the prevailing harmonic and rhythmic constrictions of swing and bebop" (2012, p. 7). And in addition to finding new forms of music and expressions, these African and African American artists often saw their music as speaking to "linked struggles" during a particularly charged historical moment (2012, p. 10). In her dazzling book *Africa in Stereo: Modernism, Music, and Pan-African Solidarity*, Tsitsi Jaji echoes and expands this sentiment by claiming that "music has quite literally *rehearsed* transnational black solidarity" (2014, p. 7). Analyzing a range of cultural production from music to film to print magazines, Jaji explores the way in which a black trans-Atlantic "stereomodernism" shaped expressive forms that articulated both pan-African struggles and aspirations for a resistant modernity. *Karmen Geï*, I suggest, participates in this (stereo)modern performance by recalling the "freeing" possibilities of jazz, the forms of solidarity it improvises, and the (queer) futures it imagines.

Black Fugitivity and The Cut

As the opening credits of *Karmen Geï* role, the audience can hear the jazzy saxophone of David Murray playing over a chorus of *sabar* drumming. The music continues as the first image of the film appears: Karmen Geï is seated and smiling between two of the drummers, her legs spread apart and her black *boubou* draped to reveal her thighs that open and close to the rhythm (see Figure 9.1). A reverse shot reveals that Karmen is smiling at Angelique, a lighter-skinned woman dressed in a khaki uniform who sits off to the side and watches Karmen lustfully. Murray's saxophone recedes into the background as the drumming picks up and the camera pans out to show the full ensemble of drummers and a circle of cheering, clapping

Figure 9.1   Karmen in the prison courtyard just before her dance for the warden. *Karmen Geï* (2001), California Newsreel.

women, some of whom have joined the drummers by keeping the rhythm on overturned plastic buckets. Karmen stands up and moves to the center of the circle where she dances for the crowd and then moves towards Angelique. Placing Angelique's closed legs in between her open, gyrating ones, Karmen reveals her silver waist beads and red-orange *sous-pagne,* a provocative undergarment. Placing one finger under Angelique's chin, Karmen guides Angelique to a standing position and the two dance an intimate *sabar* duet as the circle around them tightens.[2] A high angle shot shows Karmen and Angelique in the midst of the dancing crowd and then, as the sound of the saxophone returns, the camera pans out to reveal prison guards positioned in a circle above the crowd. Suddenly, the audience becomes aware that the dancing women, including Karmen, are prisoners and that Angelique is their warden. A whistle blows and the women are herded back to their cells. As the camera pans out further, the audience can see that the courtyard where the women were dancing is both a fictional prison, with guards positioned in panopticon style, and the real House of Slaves on Gorée Island where slaves, from the fifteenth to the mid-eighteenth century, were housed before being taken across the Atlantic.

Once back in the cell, Karmen leads the other women in call and response singing as they celebrate Karmen's successful seduction of the warden. When night falls, Karmen is led to Angelique's quarters, and images of intertwining limbs, contrasting skin tones (Karmen is jet black, Angelique much lighter), and sensual gyration fill the screen in the first ever depiction of same-sex intimacy between women in African cinema. As the women make love and a soft piano plays on the soundtrack, the camera cuts back to the other prisoners who are tapping out a slow rhythm with spoons against the prison bars. The next morning Angelique, who knows better than to keep Karmen locked up, sets Karmen free. As the jazz score and saxophone pick up again, Karmen flees the prison and Gorée, running down the dark passageway of the prison, kissing one of the guards goodbye, and leaving the House of Slaves for the open air and sunshine. Though historians now refute claims that Gorée was a major site in the trans-Atlantic slave trade – plaques on the wall at Gorée claim that millions of slaves passed through Gorée while historians estimate it was around 33,000 – the House of Slaves still stands as a powerful visual symbol of the horrors of captivity (Fisher, 2013). But Karmen's departure is the reversal of the slaves' departure: She heads towards freedom rather than away from it. And though the setting of Kumba Kastel prison in the House of Slaves links Karmen to the history of trans-Atlantic slavery, throughout the film Karmen continually sheds constraints and refuses to be bound by anyone else's desires or rules. She works against sexual norms. She criticizes the state. She rejects any form of love that objectifies her, and she engages in piracy and smuggling though seemingly rejects the financial gains they bring her.

Here, then, I want to suggest that Karmen's departure from the House of Slaves and her flight throughout the film are part of a black fugitive imagination. Francesca Royster describes the fugitive as "the artistic impulse to escape the constraints of the objectification and social death of slavery – but also to never fully escape its embodied lessons" (p. 12). James Edward Ford III writes that "one can define fugitivity as a critical category for examining *the artful escape of objectification*" (2015, p. 110) and he emphasizes that fugitivity and the artful "act of fleeing" fosters "alternative spaces, ethics, and structures of feeling in the name of being otherwise" (p. 2014). Ford further defines fugitivity as that which "entails a critique of violence, engaging the forces sustaining, resisting, or overturning the status quo, and imagining what [Saidiya] Hartman calls a 'free state, not as the time before captivity' but as an 'anticipated future' still to be enacted" (2014). Karmen's jog down the dark prison corridor and subsequent emergence into the sunshine is therefore a paradigmatic fugitive moment, a moment when her artful fleeing and resistance of the status quo allows her to leave captivity and to imagine an otherwise that remains open to possibility. For Fred Moten, whose work is central to my understanding of *Karmen Geï* and its queer performance, the fugitive describes an aesthetic impulse that is linked to the "profound discourse of the cut" and to the embodied memories of dispossession and resistance (2007, p. 44). Here, then, one might also read Karmen's escape as a break or a cut.

The cut is both a musical term and a cinematic term. In music the cut refers to "an abrupt, seemingly motivated break" from a series (Snead 1992, p. 220). For James Snead, the "cut" is a key feature of black musical forms and one way to distinguish African and African American forms of music, with their rhythms and patterns of repetition, from the goal-oriented "accumulation and growth" of European music (1992, p. 220). In film, the cut refers to the splicing together of two different scenes and the transition between two different times and places. In the opening scene that I just described, the musical cuts and the cinematic cuts work together to create a fugitive structure of feeling. As Snead writes, "In jazz improvisation, the 'cut'… is the unexpectedness with which the soloist will depart from the 'head' or theme and from its normal harmonic sequence or the drummer from the tune's accepted and familiar primary beat" (Snead 1992, p. 222). And listening closely to the score, the audience can hear Murray's saxophone or a lead drummer depart from the theme and then return back to it. But Karmen herself also enacts a cut. When she dances for Angelique or leads the call and response or escapes from prison, she is the soloist who departs from the group, who breaks from the ensemble that surrounds her.

And once Karmen escapes from Gorée, there is another cut, one that cuts through the established orders and logical sequences. As Karmen flees the island, her silhouette running towards the ocean, the sound of the *sabar* drums heard in the opening dance re-joins the soundtrack. The next image is a cut to a medium shot of a *sabar* drummer leading a rhythm for a happy couple – Corporal Lamine Diop and Majiguene – who then enter their wedding celebration. Angelique, not in uniform, trails the couple and sits behind them. A *griot* begins to praise the couple, but suddenly, the lights turn off and a spotlight shines on Karmen who dances for the crowd (see Figure 9.2). Karmen pauses her dance, silences the drummers, and

Figure 9.2   Karmen performs at the wedding of Lamine and Majiguene. *Karmen Geï* (2001), California Newsreel.

begins a chant-like speech addressed to the wedding couple and the state officials seated behind them. "Let Kumba Kastel's spirit appear," she says, evoking the name of the water goddess who watches over Gorée Island (and for whom the prison is named). She continues: "Your rifles cannot bring me down. The eagles soar through the sky. Ramatou the little bird flies under his wings. You are evil. I say you are evil. You've swallowed up the country. We'll eat your guts." When the drumming picks up, she begins to dance, strips off a piece of cloth from under her *boubou* and tosses it to Lamine who lustfully sniffs the fabric much to his bride's dismay. Majiguene gets up to challenge Karmen in a dance duel but Karmen, who has the crowd's support, tosses Majiguene to the ground. Lamine, who has now been seduced by Karmen, is reprimanded and ordered to arrest Karmen. As Karmen is being arrested she repeats, "You've swallowed up the country, but it will stick in your throat." Lamine leads Karmen away in ropes but Karmen sings him a love song and easily escapes from him, again artfully fleeing towards her freedom.

   Though both the opening sequence of the film and the wedding sequence begin with dancing and drumming and end with Karmen's escape, the cinematic cut from the first sequence to the second privileges interruption over continuity: The order that is disrupted or cut is both the official order of the state and the order, or logic, of the film. It is not quite clear what Karmen is doing at the wedding, why this seems to be her first stop after she leaves prison, whether she knows the couple, or what, if anything at all, Angelique has to do with Karmen's presence at the wedding. Karmen simply appears and none of these questions are ever answered. The film, in fact, cares very little for conventional plot, often favoring the cut or the break over linearity. But, according to Ayo Coly, who reads *Karmen*

Geï as a way to underscore the inherent queerness of the postcolony, "the elliptical structure of the film, although critiqued by some reviewers, obeys the logistics of a queer assemblage…The film constructs Karmen as an irruption, an unplanned event whose occurrence interrupts, diverts, redirects, and confounds" (2015, p. 9). Another way to put this is that Karmen, the soloist, cuts the status quo, that her critiques of state power, her literal disruption of a heterosexual marriage, her disregard for conventions, and her fugitive spirit are enacted in the film's cinematic syntax, just as much as in its Afro-jazz score.

But it is also important to underscore that while the film is structured on breaks, and moments of individual becoming, Karmen, like the music itself, is also always tied into the collective ensemble. As Snead writes, "In black culture, the thing (the ritual, the dance, the beat) is 'there for you to pick up when you come back to get it.' If there is a goal (*Zweck*) in such culture, it is always deferred; it continually cuts back to the start" (1992, p. 220). Or, as Alexander Weheliye puts it, "While the cut or break deviates from the main theme or primary beat, it does so only in dialogue with these forces" (2005, p. 63). My argument is that Karmen, the free-spirited dancer, soloist, smuggler, and seducer of both men and women, exhibits a type of freedom and individuality that plays against and into the collective, that depends on community and modes of solidarity as much as it breaks with them. This is part of its queer organizing principle and part of its work as an Afro-jazz musical.

Circles and Borders

In order to elucidate the particular structure of *Karmen Geï*, I want to detour briefly to the fugitive law of movement that Fred Moten finds in Charles Mingus's concept of "rotary perception," a concept that seems to describe well what is at stake in Ramaka's queer Afro-jazz musical. Moten reads rotary perception as "a theory and practice of rhythmic flexibility" (2007, p. 33), a formulation of the improvisational structure of jazz itself. Moten quotes from Mingus' autobiography *Beneath the Underdog*:

> There was once a word used – swing. Swing went in one direction, it was linear, and everything had to be played with an obvious pulse and that's very restrictive. But I use the term "rotary perception." If you get a mental picture of the beat existing within a circle you're more free to improvise. People used to think the notes had to fall on the centre of the beats in the bar at intervals like a metronome, with three or four men in the rhythm section accenting the same pulse. That's like parade music or dance music. But imagine a circle surrounding each beat – each guy can play his notes anywhere in that circle and it gives him a feeling he has more space. The notes fall anywhere inside the circle but the original feeling for the beat isn't changed. If one in the group loses confidence, somebody hits the beat again. The pulse is inside you. (qtd. in Moten 2007, p. 38)

For Moten, what Mingus describes here are the "rigorously enacted and interarticulate temporal differences" (2007, p. 39) or the "free, rhythmic, de-centering preservation of structure" (2007, p. 39). For me, this is the queer structure that characterizes both the elliptical plot and the score of *Karmen Geï* and that emphasizes a responsibility to the others "in the circle."

Mingus uses the circle as a metaphor to contrast jazz to the rhythmic constrictions of more linear forms of music and asks his reader to think of jazz as circularity, to "imagine a circle surrounding each beat." But also implicit here is an actual circle of musicians, an ensemble grooving and improvising together where no one individual is self-sufficient. Mingus goes on to say, "When you're playing with musicians who think this way you can do anything. Anybody can stop and let the others go on" (qtd in Moten 2007, p. 38). With this in mind, I see a type of rotary perception being played out in the opening scene of *Karmen Geï*. Karmen sits, then stands, in the center of a circle surrounded by *sabar* drummers, drumming prisoners, and guards. She performs a solo, and then brings in Angelique for a duet. She dances in the center of a courtyard, itself a circle, guarded by canons and more guards who watch from above. When the guards blow the whistle, the circle collapses: Discipline and linearity cut the seductive improvisation and the prisoners are herded down a tight, dark hallway into their cells, back to captivity. But as Mingus says, "Each guy can play his notes anywhere in that circle and it gives him a feeling of more space." In *Karmen Geï* the circles formed in the opening sequence create space and new structures both for the soloist and for those who have kept the beat with her. They allow for fleeing and fugitivity and open up towards a being otherwise.

Moreover, once the inmates are back within their cell another "practice of rhythmic flexibility" emerges: The call and response that celebrates Karmen's seduction of Angelique as a collective triumph. Karmen chants, "Where does it go?" and the women respond, "Wherever you like." Karmen then sings, "It goes here," and the women repeat, "Wherever you like." Though it is clear that the women are praising Karmen, the English subtitled translation does not make much sense. However, in Wolof the women are chanting the words *"asaaloo* and *asabombe,"* words that have important meaning in Wolof folklore. Babacar M'Baye writes, "Pamela Munro and Dieynaba Gaye say that the word *asaaloo* means 'to throw (something desirable) up in the air or away so that someone in a group can get it,' while the term *asabombe* is the response that the audience offers to the person who gives away things" (2011, p. 120). Moreover, M'Baye explains, "This song is part of the large repertoire of under-explored African oral poetry that is known as *taasu…Taasu* poetry is often expressed through a language that connotes desire and pleasure while having a covert subtext of opposition and belligerence against the established power or men" (2011, p. 120). Though it is Karmen who has seduced the warden, Karmen who leads the call and response, and Karmen who will gain her freedom, Karmen has also thrown something up in the air for the group to get.

What that something is remains unclear, but it is something, it would seem, that is cause for celebration and hope, something that can resist, mock, and parody the existing social order. This is why the women tap on the bars during Karmen's lovemaking scene: They are part of the circle, keeping the beat. As Moten says, the circle is one of shared responsibility to irresponsibility. While the individual player is freed, his or her escape is still bound to the law of the rhythmic circle (2007, p. 41).

In the call and response that Karmen leads, the "swinging back and forth from solo to chorus" (qtd. in Snead 1992, p. 221) places Karmen within a rhythm and structure that she both cuts and circles back to or performs alongside. Later in the film, another chorus indicates that Karmen is keeping the beat for a long line of ancestral spirits. After Lamine is imprisoned for failing to bring in Karmen, Karmen and her band of smugglers break Lamine out of jail. On the run from the law, Karmen visits her mother's restaurant with Lamine. When the police arrive and demand to search Ma Penda's establishment, they are chased out by Massigi and the chorus of patrons who circle around them and accuse the police of "scheming and dealing" and disrespecting their mothers. After the police leave, Ma Penda orders the party to continue and Murray begins to play his saxophone while the patrons celebrate the return of Karmen Geï, singing, "You've suffered so long but you've always had hope. Tell me you're here so I can hope again." But in order to understand the type of hope that Karmen represents, one must note that the song Massigi and the patrons sing to the police links Karmen to other Senegalese hero-ines like the women of Nder who burned themselves rather than being taken by Islamic invaders in 1820, Aline Sitoé Diatta, queen of the Casamance region in Southern Senegal from 1940–1942, who was arrested and deported when she tried to prevent children being taken by the French to fight in World War II (Dovey 2009, p. 248), and the water goddesses Mame Njare and Kumba Kastel. While Karmen flees and breaks free from the law, she is linked, through music, through call and response singing, to the rebellious women who broke from established structure but who are bound together by a radical fugitive impulse. Like the African structure of call and response and the rotary perception of African American jazz, Karmen is dependent on the dynamic relationship between the individual and the group, a dynamic that is made necessary, in part, by shared his-tories of oppression.

I'd like, therefore, to think about the relationship of *Karmen Geï's* musical score to the concept of *duende*. While Moten finds the law of fugitive movement most prominent in Mingus's rotary perception, in an essay titled "Cante Moro," poet and critic Nathaniel Mackey characterizes the fugitive spirit as *duende*. *Duende*, which means "spirit, a kind of gremlin, a gremlinlike, troubling spirit" (Mackey 1994, p. 73), is a term Mackey borrows from Federico García Lorca to describe painful and "dark sounds" or the *cante jondo*, deep song, of struggle. Explaining the title of his essay, Mackey says that *cante moro* goes back to a 1960s recording by the Gypsy flamenco musician Manitas de Plata. Mackey writes,

> At one point...a member of the group says, "Eso ese cante moro," which means "That's Moorish singing." Calling deep song *cante moro* summons the past rule and continuing cultural presences of the Moors in Spain; it acknowledges the hybrid heterogeneous roots not only of *cante jondo* but of Spanish culture generally, of, in fact, culture, collective poesis, generally. A Gypsy doing so, as in this instance, allies outcast orders, acknowledging hybridity and heterogeneity to entwine the heterodox as well – heterodox Gypsy, heterodox Moor. *Cante moro* bespeaks the presence and persistence of the otherwise excluded, otherwise expelled. (1994, p. 71).

Mackey's emphasis on the "Gypsy" (or Rom) is of particular interest for a few reasons. First, Lorca himself, in his essay on *duende*, links the concept to the "Gypsy singer" Manuel Torre who had said, "All that has dark sounds has *duende*" (1994, p. 72). Mackey notes that "a large part of [Lorca's] importance to Spanish poetry is the respect he accorded the vernacular culture of southern Spain. He sought instruction in the mixed cultural inheritance of Andalusia, in the music of outcast Gypsies, in reminders of the expelled Moors. The book which made him famous is *Gypsy Ballads*, published in 1928" (1994, p. 72). That Lorca's *Gypsy Ballads* was translated into English by none other than Langston Hughes shows that there's a correspondence between the Spanish vernacular cultures Lorca was invoking and the prominence of the vernacular in the Harlem Renaissance (Mackey 1994, p. 72).

Mackey argues that in his writing on *duende,* Lorca was in fact invoking a particular black aesthetic, noting that a more recent translation has Manuel Torre saying, "All that has <u>black</u> sounds has *duende*" and notes that Torre had urged Lorca to go back to the "Gypsies' fabled origins in Egypt" (1994, p. 72). Mackey pushes this connection further by linking Gypsies to African American fugitivity and turning to the poetry of Amiri Baraka where Gypsies "embody a mobile, mercurial non-investment in the status quo" (1994, p. 78) that resonates with enslavements and persecution of the African body. *Cante moro*, as Mackey says, "allies outcast orders," it acknowledges a "collective poesis" that is shared not just among a certain group or collective but across history and geography. And I think that that is precisely what Ramaka is doing by turning Mérimée or Bizet's Carmen into Karmen Geï, a queer Senegalese critic of postcolonial greed. And, of course, one must recall that the original Carmen was a Gypsy in southern Spain, very much a part of the vernacular culture so important to Lorca. I read this not simply as a coincidence, but rather as a way to think about the layers of meaning and music in the film. Ramaka is taking that Moorish singing, that deep sound of pain and struggle, and giving it a new, alternative voice, a voice that is, as Mackey says of *duende*, "manifold, many-meaning, polysemous" (Mackey 1994, p. 78). *Duende* is a way of thinking not only of longing and the troubled voice, but also trans-historical solidarity among outcast orders.

And just as *duende* emerges through the Andalusian and African/African American encounter, Mingus's rotary perception, it is important to note, is also a concept that relies on meetings and convergences. Moten explains,

Jazz biographer Brian Priestly argues that Mingus's practice and theory of "rotary perception" begins to emerge in an experience of the frontier, in the vexed circuits of politico-economic, aesthetic and sexual desire that mark the U.S./Mexico border, its cycles of conquest and conquest denial, its Afro-diasporic traces and erasures. Mingus' *Tijuana Moods,* an album recorded in late July and early August of 1957, just a few weeks before the National Guard had to be deployed in order to escort nine black kids into Little Rock Central, replicates that circularity. (2007, p. 36).

Tijuana becomes the location of Mingus's "own self-described hybridities" and the site where he develops a "new approach to negotiating the circle and its borders" (Moten 2007, p. 37). In other words, the actual border, a space of ambiguity, hybridity, and both licit and illicit crossings, helps Mingus think through jazz as a musical structure that, like the border, both contains and cannot contain.

What I am putting forth is a reading of *Karmen Geï* as a structure that, similarly, both contains and cannot contain, an eccentric structure that puts pressure on what is both in and outside the circle. For Moten, Mingus's border experience helps him to achieve a "kind of grounded eccentricity" (2007, p. 37), a structured way of experimenting with and liberating structures. Moten calls Mingus, and jazz music more broadly, "eccentric" because the improvisation that they utilize entails "opening a critique of traditions" and a time of "looking ahead" (Moten 2003, p. 64). *Karmen Geï's* eccentricity, or fugitive queerness, can be seen at its limits and borders, the very spaces where "excesses of meaning" and norms become the most audible.

Eccentricity and the Law of Genre

Thinking about *Karmen Geï* as eccentric means examining the way Karmen herself transforms the rhythms that she is grounded in, about the way she re-invents earlier Carmens, and the way she keeps the beat of Dakar's polysemous urban life while moving against its more constraining tempos. In her forward to *Recovering the Black Female Body: Self-Representations by African American Women,* Carla Peterson argues that the term eccentric connotes "a double meaning: The first evokes a circle not concentric with another, an axis not centrally placed (according to the dominant system), whereas the second extends the notion of off-centeredness to suggest freedom of movement stemming from the lack of central control and hence new possibilities of difference conceived as empowering oddness" (2001, p. xii). Building on Peterson's formulation of the eccentric as a way for black women to insist upon a "freedom of movement," Daphne Brooks discusses how black women in nineteenth and early-twentieth century America "employ their own bodies as canvases of dissent…restoring movement and history to individuals in the cultural margins" (Brooks 2006, p. 2). In *Karmen Geï,* Karmen's "empowering oddness" and her bodily performance of dissent act in the way these scholars suggest: Karmen's movement – her dancing, her lovemaking, her smuggling, and her agile mobility in Dakar's markets, bars, and underground spaces – shed light on the forms of control present in the postcolony and push back against them. In other words, Karmen might be seen as an eccentric who productively disturbs or decenters a closed circle.

Exploring a range of black post-soul performances, Francesca Royster expands on Brooks and Peterson to "consider multiple black sexualities, multiple black bodies" (Royster 2012, p. 15) and links eccentricity more explicitly with the category of queer. In an important essay on *Karmen*, Phil Powrie also links eccentricity to non-normative sexuality. He argues, that the homosexual narrative in *Karmen Geï* is

> an *eccentric* move, in two senses of the word. In a first sense, there is a triple decentering: lesbianism decenters normative sexuality; it decenters the myth of Carmen as excessively heterosexual (by which we mean Carmen as *femme fatale* with her dangerous heterosexuality); and in so doing it decenters the Western Carmen narrative. There is a second sense in which lesbianism is eccentric. The decentering is an excess (in the sense of spilling out of its container), because Karmen's sexuality is excessive. (2004, p. 287)

While I find much of what Powrie says here to be compatible with my own reading of the film, especially as he considers the importance of the jazz soundtrack alongside Karmen's embodied dissidence, I also want to push his reading a bit further and to consider the relationship between eccentricity and the queerness of the film in general. To begin with, "lesbian" does not seem to be the best rubric here. The category fits neither Karmen, who sleeps with men, nor Angelique who, as Cheryl Stobie (2016) points out, wears a wedding ring that indicates that she is likely married to a man. But my intervention is not primarily about terminology. By reading Karmen as lesbian, Powrie suggests that what is excessive is primarily her sexuality, which does not fit into Senegalese social norms and does not fit into heterosexual Carmen stories. And though he talks about the film's soundtrack as well as the circumstances surrounding its censorship, for Powrie, neither of these seem to enact the same form of eccentric decentering as Karmen's sexuality. But I want to pay attention to the multiple forms of excess and "spilling out" that the film enables.

To explore the intersecting forms of eccentricity at play in the film, let me turn briefly to the controversy surrounding the film when it screened in Dakar. After the film had been showing for about six weeks in Dakar, a *fatwa* was issued against the film by Serigne Moustapha Diakhaté, a high-ranking cleric in the Mouride Muslim brotherhood and host of a religious radio show (Nelson 2011, p. 76). Though Diakhaté had not seen the film, he was incensed upon hearing that the funeral procession for Angelique, a "lesbian" and Catholic who drowned herself in the sea, was combined with a holy song or, *Khassaïd*, of the Mouride founder Cheikh Amadou Bamba and sung by Massigi. The day after the *fatwa* was issued about 200–300 Mourides and Baye Fall, members of a Mouride sub-group, stormed the theater where *Karmen Geï* was playing, and, wielding machetes, swords, and clubs, threatened to burn it down. As Abdoulaye Babou of the Alliance of Forces of Progress stated, "The use of a poem of Cheikh Amadou Bamba...to accompany the burial of a lesbian in a Catholic cemetery is blasphemous" (qtd. in Nelson 2011, p. 76). Ramaka and his wife, the actress who plays Karmen, were out of the country at the time, but when they returned they received threatening phone calls (Nelson 2011, p. 76). In response, the government banned the film and impounded copies, and, despite Ramaka's efforts, Karmen was not shown again in Senegal.

Though there was a confluence of factors contributing to the *fatwa* and subsequent censoring of the film, it seems that the argument that finally won out, according to journalist Mari Maasilta, was that of verisimilitude. As Nelson puts it, "[The Mourides] argued that the meeting of Islam and Christianity, of a *Khassaïd* and a lesbian who had committed suicide, of homosexuality at all were somehow inauthentic representations, somehow not accurate social or religious depictions, in short, somehow not real" (Nelson 2011, p. 79).[3] While the Mourides could have criticized the explicit dancing at the beginning of the film, the lovemaking between Karmen and Angelique, or the scene of Angelique masturbating, these were not, in fact, their focus. They also did not seem to object to depictions of drug smuggling or the slams against state power at a time when that power was held by fellow Mouride Abdoulaye Wade. In a letter to the newspaper *Mouers*, Diakhaté demanded, not the removal of any of these possibly objectionable scenes, but simply of the *Khassaïd* itself, which he said is not to be used for entertainment purposes and was a threat to public security (Maasilta 2005, p. 265). In other words, what Diakhaté seemed to have found the most egregious was the contamination of the genre of *Khassaïd*, a genre that is supposed to be, in one word, pure. Though the articulated argument might have been about verisimilitude, the real issue it seems, had to do with various forms of pollution set off by an "improper" use of the *Khassaïd*. Misuse of the *Khassaïd* was a violation of a form (the holy song) that was queered in multiple ways: Literally associated with a queer body and also made to signify beyond its primary, intended meaning. Another way of putting this is that the *Khassaïd*, in the hands of Ramaka, becomes eccentric. Out of its holy context, it "implies purposeful oddness, and a simultaneous hijacking of our gaze and eardrums, jamming the system" (Royster 2013, p. 15), a system the Mouride brotherhood did not want jammed.

Interestingly, in a letter published in two local papers, Professor Madièye Mbodji argues that the film depicts religious tolerance, a tolerance that is, in fact, part of the very fabric of Senegalese society. Mbodji says that Ramaka had been influenced by an event ten years before he made the film in which a group of Baye Fall sang *Khassaïds* at the funeral of a Catholic person (Maasilta 2005, p. 266). Mbodji counters the claim of inauthenticity by claiming that an event like the one in the film did indeed happen. For both Mbodji and Diakhaté, the *Khassaïd* at a Catholic funeral contaminates, but for different ends: For one contamination is a utopian vision of Senegalese cosmopolitanism and tolerance, for the other it equals a dangerous unraveling.

To me, the controversy that the film provoked amplifies the eccentric queerness of *Karmen Geï*. What seemed to anger so many people was that the film violated categories of genre and, therefore, categories of respectability. But, as I have been arguing throughout, this is precisely the film's point: This is why the soundtrack, including the *Khassaïd*, is so central to the film's politics and aesthetics, to the way it destabilizes conventions and rules of law and creates a space of fugitivity. As Moten says, "music is understood as content that irrupts into generic form, enacting a radical disorganization of that form" (2003, p. 192). And if we are to follow Jacques Derrida, genre is something that always already evokes this type of instability. Derrida writes of the "the law of genre" that "it is precisely a principle of contamination, a law of impurity, a parasitical economy. In the code of set theories…I would speak of a sort of participation without belonging – a taking part in without being a part of, without having membership in a set" (Derrida and Ronell, 1980, p. 206). This, then, is what characterizes *Karmen Geï's* queerness or eccentricity, a "participation without belonging," a rotary perception in which Karmen, the individual player or soloist, is freed, but her escape is still bound to the rhythmic circle, or to the "set." In other words, the film is not queer simply because Karmen sleeps with Angelique. It is queer because it opens up spaces and rhythms that have been closed off. And "like Derrida's 'law of genre,' the one that extends and deepens the totality it ensures by way of violation" (Moten 2003, p. 158), it disorganizes the forms, conventions, and rules of law on which it depends.

Moreover, what the controversy around the film shows is that *Karmen Geï* disorganizes not only generic constraints and expectations of the Carmen narrative, but also the state itself. Though the state provided partial funding for the film and did not seem to object to its content at first, the Mouride brotherhood essentially forced the state's hand. In other words, as Nelson argues, the film was censored not because the state was too active in public affairs, but because its withdrawal from public culture left a void that religious groups could fill (2011, p. 77). In this way, the fate of *Karmen Geï* in Senegal is almost predicted in the film itself, which not only disorganizes laws of genre and form but also disrupts the law itself by pointing out the inefficiency and weakness of the postcolonial state. Throughout the film, the state seems powerless to keep Karmen, Lamine, or Samba in jail; it cannot get past Massigi and Ma Penda to search her restaurant; it cannot stop or arrest any of the members of Karmen's gang despite beating Samba to near death; and not one, but two representatives of the state (Angelique and Lamine) are undone by their attraction to Karmen. As Karmen says to the figures of state at Lamine's wedding, "You've swallowed the country, but it will get stuck in your throat." And *Karmen Geï*, I would argue, gets stuck in their throat. It spills out of its container and disorganizes. It exposes weaknesses and bodies, eccentric bodies that "cannot be successfully incorporated into the national body politic" (Peterson 2001, p. xvi), and it jams the system that funded it, then censored it, that was supposed to, as the postcolonial promise originally went, protect all of its citizens, and then gave way to corruption, greed, and homophobia.

"Tomorrow is Another Day"

Though my reading of *Karmen Geï* has been one that focuses on Karmen's resistance, several critics have pointed out that the film's liberationist politics are far from perfect. Carmela Garritano, for instance, writes that Karmen "becomes pure spectacle" who "never frees herself from the male gaze of the camera" (2003, p. 159). Frieda Ekotto reminds readers that Ramaka "could have changed the musical's narrative by keeping Karmen alive to continue her mission of liberating herself and other women" and notes that both Karmen and Angelique, the two characters who threaten the order and normativity of Senegalese society, wind up "erased" (2007, pp. 75–76). I take these claims seriously and offer them here as an attempt to temper a euphoric reading of the film and to further emphasize the particular queerness that the film offers. As Royster reminds, eccentricity offers "freedom of movement in an otherwise constraining situation" (2012, p. 15). And as Ekotto and Garritano make clear, this "constraining situation" remains despite the film's disruptive politics and form. *Karmen Geï* was after all, literally, constrained by the state in Senegal.

But *Karmen Geï* does indeed make waves, as Karmen says of herself. In a scene towards the middle of the film Karmen and Massigi are on the beach across from Gorée when Karmen picks up a flag from a fishing boat and starts waving at the ocean. Massigi asks her who she is waving to and Karmen responds, "My women, Massigi. And my jailer. They're there. Just there. In that lousy prison." Massigi smiles and says, "You're really quite a woman," to which Karmen replies, "No more than the others, Massigi. Only they don't show it. So as not to make waves." That Karmen should choose to frame her eccentricity and resistance in terms of waves is important on at least three different levels. First, it is a reminder that throughout the film Karmen is linked to the water goddess Kumba Kastel of whom she is said to be a descendent. Kumba Kastel is a local incarnation of the trans-Atlantic Mami Wata spirit (Mami Wata is pidgin English for "Mother Water") who is known as a seductress of both men and women and who can bring both wealth, as Karmen brings to her fellow smugglers, as well as madness and death, as Karmen brings to Lamine and Angelique. Moreover, as M'Baye notes, Kumba Kastel "is an important force in Karmen's revolutionary struggle since she provides her with ambiguous identities and a dual capacity to do good and evil at once" (2011, p. 118).[4] Second, the metaphor of the wave also perfectly captures the very form of Karmen's disruption. A wave might constitute a disturbance, an unsettling, a breaking point even, but it is still part of the ocean, part of what is contained within it. Though Karmen flees and enacts a cut, "the cut attempts to confront accident and rupture not by covering them over but by making room for them inside the system itself" (Snead 1992, p. 220). Or to put it differently, part of what makes a cut a cut is that the musicians who break from the series always return to it just as the wave that breaks always remains part of the ocean. Finally, in this scene with Massigi on the beach, Karmen makes waves but her gaze is towards a horizon, towards her lover and friends in the distance, and to what is not yet visible. In this sense, I would like to suggest Karmen/*Karmen Geï's* queerness is, as José Esteban Muñoz suggests of queerness in general, "always in the horizon" (2009, p. 11).

I therefore read Karmen's death as both a failure by Ramaka to imagine another possibility for this queer Carmen, as Ekotto suggests, and, at the same time, as a gesture towards a "forward-dawning futurity" (Muñoz 2009, p. 1) that might be otherwise. Here, then, the ending of the film, like the beginning, opens up fugitive space. In the final sequence of the film, Karmen and Lamine approach each other in the catwalks above the stage where Sène is singing over the *sabar* drummers. As the sound of Sène and the drummers fade out, Karmen sings to Lamine, "Love is a rebellious bird and no one can tame it… Love isn't a business deal. If you want to kill me do it quickly and do it well. Tomorrow is another day." Lamine stabs Karmen as Sène's voice re-emerges below and Karmen falls to the ground. The visuals then fade to wobbly images of colorful painted faces lining a street, the same vision of death that Karmen had seen earlier in the film when reading her cards with Samba and when being chased through the market by Lamine.

Here, Karmen's final words seem to underscore her stance throughout the film. The line "love is a rebellious bird and no one can tame it" is from the famous habanera in Bizet's opera. But, in the queer *Karmen*, it takes on further significance given that the film features same-sex love that is not sanctioned by the state. Moreover, Karmen's claim that "love isn't a business deal" highlights her antimaterialist position and the audience may recall that Karmen, when she refused the money from the smuggling operation, seemed to have little interest in financial gain. But it is the somewhat enigmatic line "tomorrow is another day," Karmen's final "sentence," that points to the utopic impulse of the scene and recalls both the hope that is sung about in Ma Penda's restaurant and the hopeful exuberance of Massigi in the marketplace singing about the possibilities of the year 2000. As Muñoz argues, "Queerness… allows us to see and feel beyond the quagmire of the present. The here and now is a prison house" (2009, p. 1). If the present is a prison house, then death, perhaps, is Karmen's final act of escape; it is that which "propels [her] onward" (Muñoz 2009, p. 1). Karmen joins the ghosts and the painted-face dead, and in the final image and final act of friendship, Samba carries Karmen's corpse, wrapped simply in fabric, to the cemetery on the island of Joal. As Samba carries Karmen, Sène can be heard on the soundtrack singing about Karmen and rejoined again by the *sabar* drummers. The music exceeds the image and the final cut skips the rhythm "back to another beginning which we have already heard" (Snead 1992, p. 221). Karmen is both contained – no longer a threat to order – and that which cannot be contained as the music of Sène carries her story onward, haunting the film like the images of the painted dead, but also implying that "tomorrow is another day," perhaps one that is open to new, queer horizons.

In *In The Break*, Moten invokes Sedgwick's queer performative (2003, p. 69) in order to explore the overlapping movements between music/improvisation, totality, and the "space of the black avant-garde," a space that is intimately connected to the "sexual underground" (2003, p. 163). Moten, then, finds a connection between the "temporal-affective disorder, displacement and disjunction" of black performance and syncopation and the sexual difference and dissonance that converges with radical blackness (2003, p. 153). A similar moment occurs in "Cante Moro" when Mackey writes about gay poets who saw the connection between Lorca's concept of *duende* and Lorca's troubled, conflicted homosexuality. For Moten, queer performance has a utopian, improvisational quality that, like jazz music, strives to be "beyond category" (2003, p. 25). For Mackey, the relationship between queerness and black music seems to be more about allying outcast orders. But Karmen's queerness is about both formal qualities, the "gaps, overlaps, dissonances and resonances" that Sedgwick describes, and about shared histories of oppression – queers, slaves, women, "Gypsies," the postcolonial disenfranchised – and their embodied resistance. In other words, the film opens itself up to a particular performative experiment that disturbs the status quo. It spills out over any categories, boundaries, or borders that might have been set up. It flees and escapes and becomes fugitive.

Notes

1   As Claudia Böhme (2015) demonstrates, depictions of homosexuality, specifically in two films about male homosexuality, are now also occurring in Tanzanian video-film and drawing attention from the Tanzanian censors.
2   According to Dovey, "The opening sequence of *Karmen Geï* is fashioned as a *sabar*, in which it is conventional to have six male *sabar* drummers (known as *géwëls*) pounding out rhythms that initiate the *sabar* dancing, the most popular and pervasive kind of dancing in Dakar. The dancing is characterized by its circular formation, with women moving in a provocative, energetic way very close to one another" (2009, p. 245). Women often dance in duets and because the more skilled dancers tend to be more risqué and explicit, the Senegalese audience will know that Karmen has "earned the social right to behave as she does in public" (Dovey 2009, p. 245).
3   Though, as Nelson points out, film critics and filmmakers (including Ramaka) argued that film is often not supposed to be realistic and that art does not often coincide with realities.
4   For a discussion of the role of Mami Wata spirits in Ghanaian video films about lesbianism, see Green-Simms (2012b).

References

Böhme, Claudia. 2015. "Showing the Unshowable: The Negotiation of Homosexuality through Video Films in Tanzania." *Africa Today* 61 (4): 62–82.

Brooks, Daphne. 2006. *Bodies in Dissent: Spectacular Performances of Race and Freedom, 1850–1910*. Durham, NC: Duke University Press.

Currier, Ashley, and Thérèse Migraine-George. 2016. "Queer Studies/African Studies: An (Im) possible Transaction?" *GLQ: A Journal of Lesbian and Gay Studies* 22 (2): 281–305.

Coly, Ayo A. 2015. "Carmen Goes Postcolonial, Carmen Goes Queer: Thinking the Postcolonial as Queer." *Culture, Theory and Critique* 1–17. DOI: 10.1080/14735784.2015.1056540

Derrida, Jacques, and Avital Ronell. 1980. "The Law of Genre." *Critical Inquiry* 7 (1): 55–81.

Dovey, Lindiwe. 2009. *African Film and Literature: Adapting Violence to the Screen*. New York: Columbia University Press.

Ekotto, Frieda. 2007. "The Erotic Tale of Karmen Geï: The Taboo of Female Homosexuality in Senegal." Ed. G. Vander and Keith Mitchell. *Xavier Review* 27(1): 74–80.

Fisher, Max. 2013. "What Obama Really Saw at the 'Door of No Return,' A Disputed Memorial to the Slave Trade." *The Washington Post* 28 June. Accessed 22 August, 2016. www.washingtonpost.com/news/worldviews/wp/2013/06/28/what-obama-really-saw-at-the-door-of-no-return-a-debunked-memorial-to-the-slave-trade/

Ford, James Edward III. 2014. "Call for Papers: Fugitivity and the Filmic Imagination." https://call-for-papers.sas.upenn.edu/node/54723

Ford, James Edward III. 2015. "Close-Up: Fugitivity and the Filmic Imagination: Introduction." *Black Camera, An International Film Journal* 7(1): 110–114.

Garritano, Carmela. 2003. "Troubled Men and the Women Who Create Havoc: Four Recent Films by West African Filmmakers." *Research in African Literatures* 34(3): 159–165.

Green-Simms, Lindsey. 2012a. "Hustlers, Home-Wreckers and Homoeroticism: Nollywood's Beautiful Faces." *Journal of African Cinemas* 4 (1): 59–79.

Green-Simms, Lindsey. 2012b. "Occult Melodramas: Spectral Affect and West African Video-Film." *Camera Obscura: Feminism, Culture, and Media Studies* 27.2 (80): 25–59.

Green-Simms, Lindsey, and Unoma Azuah. 2012. "The Video Closet: Nollywood's Gay-Themed Movies." *Transition* 107 (1): 32–49.

Harrow, Kenneth W. 2013. *Trash: African Cinema From Below*. Bloomington: Indiana University Press.

Jaji, Tsitsi Ella. 2014. *Africa in Stereo: Modernism, Music, and Pan-African Solidarity*. Oxford: Oxford University Press.

Kelley, Robin D.G. 2012. *Africa Speaks, America Answers: Modern Jazz in Revolutionary Times*. Cambridge, MA: Harvard University Press.

Mackey, Nathaniel. 1994. "Cante Moro." *Disembodied Poetics: Annals of the Jack Kerouac School*. Eds. Anne Waldman and Andrew Schelling. Albuquerque: University of New Mexico Press: 71–93.

Maasilta, Mari. 2005. "Transnational Senegalese Cinema between Nationalism and Globalism: The Case of Karmen." *Glocal Times*. Accessed 28 March 2018. www.gl0caltimes.k3.mah.se/viewarticle.aspx?articleID=79&issueID=0

M'Baye, Babacar. 2011. "Variant Sexualities and African Modernity in Joseph Gaye Ramaka's Karmen Geï." *Black Camera* 2(2): 114–129.

Moten, Fred. 2003. *In the Break: The Aesthetics of the Black Radical Tradition*. Minneapolis: University of Minnesota Press.

Moten, Fred. 2007. "The New International of Rhythmic Feeling(s)." In *Sonic Interventions*. No. 18. Eds. Sylvia Mieszkowski, Joy Smith, and Marijke De Valck. Amsterdam: Rodop Press: 31–56.

Muñoz, José Esteban. 2009. *Cruising Utopia: The Then and There of Queer Futurity*. New York: New York University Press.

Nelson, Steven. 2011. "Karmen Geï: Sex, the State, and Censorship in Dakar." *African Arts* 44 (1): 74–81.

Nyanzi, Stella. 2015. "Knowledge is Requisite Power: Making a Case for Queer African Scholarship." *Boldly Queer: African Perspectives on Same-Sex Sexuality and Gender Diversity*. Eds. Theo Sandfort, Fabeinne Simenel, Kevin Mwachiro, Vasu Reddy. The Hague: HIVOS: 125–135.

Osinubi, Taiwo Adetunji. 2016. "Queer Prolepsis and the Sexual Commons: An Introduction." *Research in African Literatures* 47 (2): vii–xxiii.

Peterson, Carla L. 2001. "Foreword: Eccentric Bodies." *Recovering the Black Female Body: Self-representations by African American Women*. Eds. Michael Bennett and Vanessa D. Dickerson. New Brunswick, NJ: Rutgers University Press: ix–xvi.

Petty, Sheila. 2009. "The Rise of the African Musical: Postcolonial Disjunction in *Karmen Geï* and *Madame Brouette*." *Journal of African Cinemas* 1 (1): 95–112.

Powrie, Phil. 2004. "Politics and Embodiment in Karmen Geï." *Quarterly Review of Film and Video* 21 (4): 283–291, DOI: 10.1080/10509200490446169

Royster, Francesca T. 2012. *Sounding Like a No-No: Queer Sounds and Eccentric Acts in the Post-Soul Era*. Ann Arbor: University of Michigan Press.

Sedgwick, Eve Kosofsky. 1993. *Tendencies*. Durham, NC: Duke University Press.

Snead, James A. 1992. "Repetition as a Figure of Black Culture." *Out There: Marginalization and Contemporary Culture*. Eds. Russell Ferguson, Martha Gever, Trinh T. Min-ha, and Cornell West. Cambridge, MA: MIT Press. 213–232.

Stobie, Cheryl. 2016. "'She Who Creates Havoc Is Here': A Queer Bisexual Reading of Sexuality, Dance, and Social Critique in *Karmen Geï*." *Research in African Literatures* 47 (2): 84–103.

Weheliye, Alexander G. 2005. *Phonographies: Grooves in Sonic Afro-Modernity*. Durham, NC: Duke University Press.

Filmography

Ramaka, Joseph Gaï. (2001). *Karmen Geï*. California Newsreel.

Part IV

Platforms / Informality / Archives

10

Streaming Quality, Streaming Cinema

Moradewun Adejunmobi

This chapter examines the changing status of cinema in the twenty first century in relation to the cultural and commercial value of feature films produced by Africans, as these films circulate within and beyond the African continent. The questions to be considered are the following: How does cinema matter for companies that specialize in streaming African feature films and television series? What kinds of "African cinema" matter on these streaming platforms? In exploring responses to these questions, the chapter contributes to a growing debate about the status of cinema given technological advances that are re-orienting the social practice of going to the movies and film spectatorship generally. Much of this discussion about the status of cinema in the twenty-first century has unfolded with respect to Hollywood movies in North America and Europe. I address some of the concerns animating this discussion from the perspective of African commercial cinema, and in particular Nollywood. In this regard, the chapter is less focused on contributing to the debate about what constitutes an authentic African cinema.[1] Instead, the discussion will consider the extent to which African film is also African cinema, as well as the relationship between both terms.

Trends in movie going in other regions of the world represent a useful starting point for framing the subsequent discussion regarding the status of cinema in the African context. One such trend is especially relevant: Although industry practices ensure that Hollywood films are making more money than ever before, cinema attendance itself is in decline in the United States and Western Europe (Acland 2008, p. 88). Digital delivery, in general, and streaming on mobile devices are becoming ever more popular. The explosive growth in Netflix subscriptions following the introduction of streaming options in late 2010 is pushing scholars to rethink media spectatorship broadly speaking, and especially cinema attendance. In their respective books published in 2013, Chuck Tryon and Wheeler Winston Dixon each weigh the implications of this sea change in viewing practices for the future of cinema. For Gabriele Pedulla, streaming and small screens in general represent cinema's unavoidable destiny in the early twenty-first century. She writes: "The purism of the big screen's champions and their almost religious cult of the movie theatre seem to have been vanquished by the common sense of the man on the street, who has never wondered whether [Frederico Fellini] La Dolce Vita [1960] on TV might be truly, deeply different from La Dolce Vita at the movies" (2012, p. 3).

At first glance, a discussion about streaming Video on Demand (SVOD) would appear to have minimal relevance for an understanding of African cinema today. After all, and in the early twenty-first century, the African continent had the lowest Internet penetration of any region in the world. Given bandwidth limitations, streaming remains a mostly inefficient and extremely costly medium for viewing both feature films and television shows for all but a sliver of the population across the African continent. And yet, as I intimated in a 2015 article, most locally produced films in Africa, currently are not viewed in cinema theatres, but on television screens.[2] Detheatricalization of film viewing is the current order of the day, and in general, African commercial "cinema" owes its circulation more so to Pay television (Pay TV) and to streaming than it does to theatrical exhibition. For viewers outside Africa, and with the exception of Western Europe where some Pay TV stations offer channels dedicated to popular African film, streaming is gradually becoming the default mode for viewing African films. Streaming is also gradually displacing the purchase of illegally reproduced VCDs for middle-class members of the African diaspora. Even as streaming and television viewing have become more widespread for fans of African film outside Africa, film festivals within and beyond the continent continue to provide an alternative, but highly circumscribed circuit for theatrical exhibition of African films. Still, the experience of viewers of African film outside Africa does not generally mirror that of viewers on the continent, but also cannot be simply dismissed out of hand. One might even say as a provocation, that African cinema refers to those independent feature films that have been more frequently viewed outside Africa than within the continent. To the extent that a canon of "African cinema" has been emerging from the mid-twentieth century onwards, it comprises feature films that are largely unavailable for viewing outside select venues and times in or outside Africa. By contrast, the African films available on streaming platforms dedicated to African content have often been viewed as much and probably more in Africa than outside the continent.

Recent developments in countries like Nigeria and Ghana might lead attentive observers to call into question claims about detheatricalization of film viewing in Africa. In particular, cinema culture appears to be experiencing a gradual and slow rebirth in Nigeria, with potential ramifications for Pay TV and streaming platforms on the African continent and beyond. In addition to the luxury cinema theatres located in malls in cities like Lagos and Abuja, Film House, a relatively new company on the local media scene has committed to establishing new cinema theatres across Nigeria.[3] Already, new cinema theatres have gone into operation across diverse suburbs in Lagos, as well as in cities like Ibadan, Akure, Kano, and Port Harcourt among others. Similarly, many of the new malls springing up across Accra, Ghana include a cinema theatre with one or more screens as an additional site for leisure in the mall. Still, some caveats are in order. First, the total number of available big screens is still low, perhaps no more than 35 in all of Nigeria.[4] Second, it seems likely that a majority of Nigerians and Ghanaians will continue watching local films on pay television or purchasing VCDs for the very same reasons that film viewers in Europe and North America have taken to streaming: Namely, for convenience and relative cost. Third, and while a growing number of locally produced films are now debuting in cinema theatres and avoiding the straight to video format, the majority of films shown in these new cinema theatres are still Hollywood blockbusters.[5] Furthermore, the majority of Nigerian features produced continue to adopt the straight to video, and or increasingly, the straight to television, and straight to streaming format.

At the same time, theatrical exhibition undoubtedly presents clear benefits for film producers and the management of local cinema theatres in African countries like South Africa, Nigeria, and Ghana to name a few. The fact that in Nigeria, some locally produced features in the past two years have not only turned a profit in local cinema theatres, but have also apparently done better than Hollywood block-busters in the same time frame suggests that many more films for exhibition in cinema theatres will begin to be produced.[6] It comes as no surprise then that the Nigerian cinema company, Film House, has begun to provide funding for film production through its distribution affiliate Film One. Film One was listed as joint producers for two highly successful Nigerian films from 2015: *Gbomo Gbomo Express*, and *Taxi Driver Oko Ashewo*. Two of the eight films selected for a spotlight on Nollywood at the 2016 Toronto International Film Festival 2016 were Film One co-productions. At the very least, the increase in opportunities for theatrical exhibition for Nigerian-produced commercial films makes reflexive default to African art and independent cinema for understanding African cinema less and less tenable. When the continuous output of commercial cinema in African countries like South Africa with a more developed cinema infrastructure is further taken into consideration, the growing range and variety of a commercial African cinema become even more evident. Against this background, one might wonder: What do these increases in the rate of theatrical exhibition of commercial films mean for streaming platforms and Pay TV platforms? The question is especially pertinent since these remain the primary points of access for Nollywood films and popular media content for fans outside the African continent, but also for many viewers in Nigeria who find a trip to the movie theatre inconvenient for a variety of reasons. In responding, there is room for both speculation and informed judgment. If, in particular, ready access to the highest number of cinema theatres per capita in the world has not prevented an upsurge in streaming in the United States and Western Europe, there is little reason to think that the construction of additional theatres in a few African countries will reverse the general trend towards growing consumption of African movies on small screens in a part of the world with much lower levels of disposable income for leisure activities. Instead then of a zero-sum game where one form of film spectatorship completely displaces other forms, spectatorship on small screens at home and on larger screens outside the home will very likely continue to shape the relative status of both types of screens and feature films watched on either screen.

Cinema and Streaming

In speaking of cinema in this chapter, I refer specifically to theatrical exhibition of film.[7] Given the intertwined histories of film and theatrical exhibition, cinema is also a widely understood shorthand for film. It is, however, worth reviewing what this shorthand might mean and the implications of those changing meanings for our subject of study when most African films are no longer viewed in cinema but on Pay TV and or on streaming platforms. Somewhat similar concerns with respect to television lead Amanda Lotz (2014) to question whether television studies will soon be supplanted by neologisms like "monitor studies" or simply "screen studies." For several reasons and despite the new points of access, Lotz maintains that television studies retains its relevance. Cinema too retains its relevance in this reconfigured media landscape. But, what cinema is, will be subject to redefinition in relation to specific media and in specific contexts.

Unlike recent discussions of the implications of streaming for cinema that focus on the varied dimensions of instant access and an on-demand culture (Wheeler Dixon, 2013 and Chuck Tryon, 2013 respectively), my interest here pertains to the value of cinema for the management of streaming platforms and for the spectators who make use of streaming platforms for their access to African feature films. Although streaming platforms offer quicker access to African films for viewers located outside Africa, the value of feature films that have been through theatrical exhibition depends on more than the speed of access. As such, the emphasis here will not be on instant access to films. Instead, the principal argument of this chapter is that cinema currently matters for streaming platforms dedicated to African content as one of several possible means for designating content with premium value on the platform and thus generating additional subscriptions. In other words, African feature films that have benefited from theatrical exhibition are valuable for streaming platforms in a way that is different for films that have not benefited from theatrical exhibition. I also argue in this chapter that streaming and pay television are contributing to a growing divergence between a slow and a fast cinema culture with respect to African cinema.

Some of the best-known streaming platforms dedicated to African content in 2016 include iROKOtv (mostly Nigerian and some Ghanaian content), ibakatv (Nollywood), ShowMax (South African and American content), Sparrowstation (films and television series by Shirley Frimpong Manso) and Bunitv (mixed content with a focus on East Africa). There are other less well-known platforms, such as for example tundekelanitv, dedicated to the films and other productions of the Nigerian filmmaker, Tunde Kelani, kwelitv, and Afrostream featuring content for French-speaking African audiences and many works in French, some Nollywood content and African American television dubbed into French. The satellite television giant in Africa, M-Net DStv, operated Africamagicgo, a globally accessible streaming platform for roughly one year before shuttering the streaming platform. M-Net DStv does have a streaming platform available in Africa, and which also delivers feature films to a subscriber's television called Box Office. Like ShowMax, DStv's Box Office's constantly updated catalogue shows a high number of American features and television relative to African content. By contrast, the balance between African and non-African content weighs heavily towards African content on platforms like iROKOtv and ibakatv.

Apart from these SVOD platforms, selected African feature films are also available on other platforms that are not specifically dedicated to African content or oriented at audiences in Africa including Google Play, iTunes, Netflix, Amazon, Distrify, Kanopy, and Vimeo among others. However, and if the question of interest here is how cinema might matter for African film in a world of streaming, Google Play, Netflix, and Kanopy will provide fewer answers to that question than streaming platforms dedicated exclusively to African content. The specific function of African cinema for streaming platforms can be more clearly ascertained on sites like iROKOtv and ibakatv that host a variety of types of African-produced content such as straight to video films, web television series, broadcast television series, and films that premiered in cinema and benefited from theatrical exhibition. It is principally on those sites dedicated to African content alone that African straight to video films are positioned side by side with African films that have a history of theatrical exhibition. By contrast, platforms like Kanopy and Mubi stream independent and art cinema from around the world, including, but not limited to, African cinema. It is thus on the Africa-focused sites that one can more clearly determine whether and how cinema still matters for the circulation of African film. Accordingly, and for the rest of this chapter, I will focus on iROKOtv as a pioneer in streaming African content, and as one of the most important, if not the most important streaming platform dedicated to Nigerian content. It should be pointed out, though, that this chapter does not set out to provide a comprehensive history of iROKOtv.[8] Rather, this discussion of iROKOtv aims to illustrate the ways in which the status of African cinema is changing for different types of viewers by referring to developments occurring within the field of operation of a major player in the field of streaming African content.

Launched in late 2011, iROKOtv currently describes itself on its site as "the world's largest online catalogue of Nollywood movies, with over 10,000 hours of incredible movie and tv content…" At its inception, iROKOtv offered two types of access to Nollywood movies: A free service supported by advertising, and a premium subscription service that was ad-free. With very few exceptions, the iROKOtv catalogue at that time consisted almost entirely of straight to video films. The New Nollywood wave which, from 2010 onwards, saw a small number of Nigerian filmmakers begin to invest in films with higher production values for theatrical exhibition was just starting, and the majority of the early New Nollywood films like *The Figurine, Mirror Boy,* and *Tango with Me* were not initially available on iROKOtv. However, and gradually, iROKOtv did begin to include a few theatrical features for streaming on the site. Understanding iROKOtv's early dependence on straight to video films is crucial for assessing the evolution and later positioning of feature films from local cinemas on the platform.

In April 2014, iROKOtv discontinued the free service and adopted a subscription-only format. Jason Njoku, the founder and CEO of iROKOtv described this bold move as "killing iROKOtvfree."[9] As he explained in his personal blog, the 15 cents per person that the ad-supported service was providing could not match up with the US$6 per person viewer subscribed to the premium service. With the benefit of hindsight, Njoku appears to have made the right decision. In six months following the introduction of the payment only service, the platform apparently acquired half a million subscribers. At the same time, the company began attracting international investment worth millions of dollars. Although the number of subscribers to iROKOtv outside Nigeria has declined substantially since then, the market for streaming African films and especially Nollywood continues to grow.[10] In fact, iROKOtv currently seems to be locked in a fierce battle with rival streaming platforms to expand its subscriber base outside Africa, and to compete more effectively with Pay TV on the African continent. Increasing recourse to cinema features is one of the many planks of a strategy to reclaim subscribers on both ends. The battle for subscriptions is being waged on at least two fronts: The cost of subscription, and types of content.

Cinema on Iroko

In its early days, iROKOtv was frequently accused of shortchanging local film producers, and paying bottom bargain prices for licensing the rights to show Nigerian-produced films on its site. If these claims are true, it would undoubtedly discourage producers of the more expensive films shown in local cinema theatres from licensing their work for streaming on iROKOtv. At the time of writing in 2016, straight to video films still accounted for some features available for streaming on iROKOtv. But iROKOtv has also since moved into production of original content and is now producing a high percentage of its own material (both feature films and television serials) for streaming. Many more films from cinema houses, or what I henceforth call cinema features are also available on the site now. To understand iROKOtv's "new" orientation, one must attend to the wider context for streaming Nigerian movies from 2010 onwards.

The profile of content on the iROKOtv site has been changing since the founding of the site in 2011.[11] In speaking about changing profiles, I do not simply mean that new content is being added as might be expected. I am also referring to the types of content being added. When iROKOtv was first launched, much of the content available on its precursor site, a YouTube channel called NollywoodLove migrated to the new site. These consisted primarily of straight to video films for which Njoku had purchased streaming rights. Within a year or so, other types of content began to be added to the iROKOtv site. A handful of films by New Nollywood filmmakers were added to the site starting in 2013. These included films like Obi Emelonye's *Last Flight to Abuja*, and Mahmood Ali-Balogun's *Tango With Me*. Having expressed repeated dissatisfaction with the business culture and practices of Nollywood producers who were making their films available for free on YouTube, Njoku decided to go into film production himself, and he established an affiliated production company with iROKOtv called ROK Studios in 2013. ROK Studios has been producing many of the features and series now available on the iROKOtv site since that move. In 2015, Njoku stated publicly in interviews and blogs that the iROKOtv management now rarely buys streaming rights from Nollywood producers making straight to video films.[12]

Following the launch of ROK Studios, the production division of iROKOtv also began partnering with independent producers to produce films which showed in local cinemas, and then migrated to the iROKOtv site after their theatrical run. In addition to feature films, whether produced in-house or licensed, iROKOtv also began adding television series to its site. Some of these television series were independently produced as was the case with season one of *An African City*, while others like *Festac Town*, and *Husbands of Lagos* were produced by Rok Studios. Finally, and at some point in 2014, iROKOtv began adding locally produced cinema features to the site in an accelerated and systematic way. Popular Ghanaian cinema features, and especially the films of Shirley Frimpong Manso and Leila Djansi were also increasingly available for streaming on the iROKOtv site.

Given an increasingly competitive environment, it is understandable that straight to video films for which iROKOtv could not secure exclusive streaming rights would become less and less attractive to the company, especially at a time when its own affiliated production company was ramping up its productions. Thus, and in August of 2016 for example, Nigerian cinema features like the following were available for streaming on iROKOtv: *Flower Girl, Confusion na Wa, Lunchtime Heroes, When Love Happens, Gbomo Gbomo Express, Taxi Driver Oko Ashewo*, and the film *Dry* about child marriage. The Ghanaian cinema features, *Potomanto*, and *Somewhere in Africa* were also available. By 2016, iROKOtv had come full circle. Not only was it acquiring many more locally produced cinema features from Ghana and Nigeria, it was now licensing its own television series for circulation on Pay TV,[13] and occasionally even producing a film for theatrical exhibition instead. For example, the cinema feature, *Thy Will be Done*, ROK Studio's co-production with another production company, The Nollywood Factory, premiered at an IMAX cinema in London.

Like Netflix, the global streaming platform, iROKOtv is a data-driven company. In his blogposts, Jason Njoku, has revealed that he is a man of numbers, and prefers to discuss developments in the Nigerian film industry based on verifiable statistics.[14] He has also boasted in interviews about the data on viewing habits and viewer preferences that iROKOtv is collecting from its subscribers. This data, he says, guides the management in deciding about investments in co-productions, and what kind of in-house productions to launch independently. For understandable reasons, this data is not available to the public. However, there are at least two additional sources of information about viewer preferences on the iROKOtv site that are visible to all subscribers. The first is the percentage of viewers that "like" any given feature or television series on the site. Subscribers are able to click on a like or dislike icon while watching any of the content on the site. Anytime subscribers log in, they can see what percentage of previous viewers have liked a film. The second source of information about viewer preferences lies in the copious comments left on the page for each film or television serial. The comments are often brief, and the sites indicate how long ago the comments were made (for example: 5 days ago, 6 months ago etc.). Some features attract hundreds of comments, while others attract less than 100 comments. As is to be expected, there is rarely a consensus judgment about any film on the site: Some of those who have left comments like the film in question while others detest it. In general though, films with a rating of more than 85% of likes attract more comments with the most recent comments tending to explain why the film deserves high credit despite complaints about the film by some of the earlier viewers. Perhaps more importantly for the subject of this chapter, the comments section after each feature and or television series has become the primary means through which subscribers communicate with iROKOtv staff about complaints, but also about which films they would like to see on the site in the near future.

The preferred practice on iROKOtv is to add new content to the site on a weekly basis. Rather frequently, the types of additions made to the iROKOtv library attract copious commentary from subscribers. It is clear from comments left on the site that many iROKOtv subscribers follow cinema and celebrity news in Nigeria and are aware of the feature films that have premiered in local cinemas and are being discussed on celebrity news sites. Questions such as: "When will you upload....?" "Please Irokotv, I really want to see...." are recurrent on the site. By and large, the films that are most frequently requested in the comments section are cinema features, or are associated with increasingly visible film directors. For example, one subscriber asked for films directed by Omoni Oboli like *Being Mrs. Elliott*, and *Wives on Strike* to be added to the iROKOtv catalogue. Another subscriber asked for Kunle Afolayan's *October 1* to be added to the site. Irokotv staff almost always respond to these requests for particular cinema features to be uploaded. In many instances they reply that the request has been noted, while in other instances, they apologize for not having the requested film, and invite the subscriber to try out other films on the site. Many of the films requested were being added to the catalogue from month to month in 2016, though several others were still not available on the iROKOtv site. Although the overwhelming majority of films specifically requested by subscribers are cinema features, there are some exceptions. For example, subscribers repeatedly asked for the film *Darima's Dilemma* to be uploaded. This was a straight to video film from 2014, but which apparently remained popular among Nollywood fans. It was eventually uploaded to the site in August 2016.

Between 2015 and 2016, the site was evidently adding cinema features at a more accelerated pace than when it was first launched. While we cannot categorically infer iROKOtv's strategy for adding new content simply from the comments section, the comments section would certainly appear to be one of many possible factors informing the pace at which cinema features are now showing up on the iROKOtv site. One subscriber, for example, thanked iROKOtv for finally adding *Gbomo Gbomo Express* to its catalogue. The subscriber wrote: "This movie was making the rounds out there before iROKOtv got a hold of it, the trailer was out for a while, I was thirsting for it." In asking for the films, *Dry, First Lady*, and *Rebecca*, a different subscriber admitted: "I know they're still in cinema but plz Irokotv inquire the right to have them. Thx," Of the three films requested by the last subscriber quoted, two, *Dry*, and *Rebecca*, were available on the iROKOtv site by August of 2016. In the each of these instances, subscribers apparently became aware of the requested feature through its theatrical run.

Premium Services, Quality Content

In late 2011 and for much of 2012, very few cinema features were accessible on the site, and the relationship between Jason Njoku and many Nigerian film directors appeared rather strained.[15] What, apart from Njoku's own professed love for cinema, had changed in the meantime to prompt iROKOtv management to take greater interest in cinema features?[16] For one thing, the number of YouTube sites offering free Nollywood films had multiplied several times over. Njoku, who himself started out offering free access on YouTube, was quick to complain about the practice of placing cheap Nollywood productions on YouTube for free. In a blog-post from February 2015, he wrote that the Nollywood "marketers" at Alaba market[17] in Lagos had "chosen to destroy all the value online with their YouTube strategy of taking their entire libraries and making it available for free."[18] In the same blogpost, he described the business strategy of Old Nollywood distributors as "Alaba-fueled madness." The abundance of Nollywood straight to video films available for free on YouTube no doubt accounts in part for the steep decline in subscriptions that iROKOtv experienced following an initial surge in subscriptions after the subscription-only platform debuted. With the sheer number of films available for free on YouTube, platforms like iROKOtv, requiring subscription and payment had to find some other way to distinguish themselves from the sites offering free films. Simply being a one-stop site for Nollywood films no longer sufficed, and for as long as Nollywood continued to churn out new films week by week that could be accessed for no fees. Furthermore, additional subscription and payment platforms offering Nollywood films also began to emerge following the creation of iROKOtv, so that iROKOtv was receiving competition from two ends: The free YouTube channels, as well as newer subscription based streaming platforms. Over time, purchasing exclusive rights to stream cinema features became a viable option for managing competition from both ends.

The most important of the subscription based sites offering competition to iROKOtv's dominance in streaming Nigerian film is a site called ibakatv. On its site, ibakatv describes itself as "world's largest online catalogue of Nollywood movies, with over 15,000 hours of incredible movie and TV content streamed on-demand."[19] Both ibakatv and iROKOtv use cinema features first to keep current subscribers from dropping their subscriptions, and second to reel in would-be subscribers, though each site currently pursues distinctive strategies as relates to cinema features and other types of content. In the first place, and while a handful of cinema features can be found on both sites, as a rule, most straight to video films and cinema features available on iROKOtv are not available on ibakatv and vice versa. In August 2016, the only cinema features that were present on both sites were: *Potomanto, Devil in the Detail, A Soldier's Story,* and *Love or Something Like That.* These are, by the way, all Ghanaian films. In other words and generally, neither streaming site simply duplicates the other. Nollywood fans who wanted to watch cinema features like *Diary of a Lagos Girl, Househusband,* or *Being Mrs. Elliott,* would have had to subscribe to ibakatv in addition to, or in place of iROKOtv. Likewise, Nollywood fans who wanted to see cinema features like *Lunchtime Heroes* or *Rebecca* would have had to subscribe to iROKOtv instead of, or in addition to ibakatv. None of the cinema features and even straight to video films that are available for streaming on either ibakatv or iROKOtv can be viewed on free YouTube channels. The exclusivity of the content in each site's library provides a clear rationale for subscription. In the second place, and as will be discussed subsequently, each site organizes its references to feature films differently.

At least some subscribers to each streaming service are aware of the rival site, and often make reference to the other site in addressing complaints to the company staff. A subscriber on iROKOtv who expressed frustration at having to read the subtitles on the film *Taxi Driver Oko Ashewo,* said s/he would simply go to ibakatv and watch a new film on the ibakatv site that did not require reading subtitles. On the ibakatv site, a subscriber complained about a film that had just been added to the ibakatv site but was also available on iROKOtv[20]: "This movie is on iROKOtv and it going up to four or five months, please u guys need to put new movie." Requests for new movies, and for specified cinema features is actually recurrent on both sites, with some subscribers toggling between both sites in order to find a desired cinema feature. It would seem, then, that on these streaming sites offering Nollywood films, cinema features can be considered what Amanda Lotz describes as "prized content." Lotz defines "prized content" as "programming that people seek out and specifically desire... prized content is deliberately pursued" (2014, p. 12). Although Lotz was referring to television programming in her definition of "prized content," her definition would seem equally applicable to streaming sites specializing in showing feature films, since these streaming sites either compete with, or also offer content that is free. Ibakatv, for example, sometimes offers fairly lengthy "trailers" comprising the first 20 minutes of a cinema feature film for free. When viewers then ask to see the rest of the film, they are advised to consider taking out a subscription. Here, it is also worth recalling iROKOtv's own history and prehistory here, starting out as a YouTube site offering free movies before becoming a standalone streaming site offering free movies, and then becoming a subscription-only site offering movies for paid subscription. Unlike straight to video films or even the free Nollywood films available on YouTube, which viewers outside Africa watch mainly because they happen to encounter the film on a streaming site, cinema features on iROKOtv and other streaming sites are often specifically requested for, by their titles, and thus become prized content.

In a context where so many films are available free of charge with or without interruption from commercials, subscription and payment make sense only if they open the door to services and content that are not available elsewhere. For these streaming platforms, cinema features represent premium or prized content, or, content that Nollywood fans are actually willing to pay for, unlike the free films that are widely available on the Internet. Cinema features can serve as desired and premium content, not only because the films often exhibit higher production values, but also because of the high levels of publicity that they have already generated in relation to their theatrical run, involving the use of trailers, a premiere, with photos in celebrity magazines, formal and informal reviews disseminated using mobile phone apps, and simple word of mouth. Theatrical exhibition itself bestows special recognition on the feature. What is true for Hollywood also appears applicable to Nollywood in this specific respect. As Acland (2008, p. 94) states, "Commercial theaters remain a space of high visibility for a text that may be encountered later in its multimedia life-cycle as a video, pay-per-view, DVD, VCD, cable, or broadcast commodity."

On virtually all the sites that legally stream Nollywood features, there is an awareness that cinema features drive traffic to the site. Both for free and subscription sites, cinema features are premium content. Even a YouTube and standalone site like tvNolly that hosts many forgettable straight to video films, including some that appear to be soft porn, was able to secure the rights to stream features by two eminent Nigerian filmmakers: Tunde Kelani's *Maami*, and Lancelot Imasuen's *Invasion 1897*. In turn, and as a subscription based site ibakatv draws would-be subscribers to the site using trailers of cinema features, described as "premium movies" on its YouTube site, and its own standalone site, although ibakatv generally appeared in August 2016 to have fewer cinema features to offer than iROKOtv, and many more straight to video films. In addition, the full-length films whose trailers continue to be featured on the ibakatv site, are not necessarily available on the site, or if they are, they are present for relatively short periods of time. In August 2016, for example, the ibakatv site had posted trailers for *The Meeting*, *October 1*, *Iquo's Journal*, and *Diary of a Lagos Girl*. *Diary of a Lagos Girl* was still available for streaming on the site, but none of the other films whose trailers were being shown was available on the site at that time. Obtaining the rights to keep trailers for films on the site when the films themselves are not available for viewing represents an unusual marketing strategy. The decision to retain trailers of films that were no longer available for streaming or had never been available for streaming would seem to be motivated by a desire to encourage subscription by individuals specifically seeking access to the better known cinema features.

In 2016, iROKOtv appeared to be engaged in competition to ramp up subscriptions and overtake ibakatv as well as even the streaming sites with free straight to video and feature films, by offering more prized Nigerian and Ghanaian content than virtually all the other streaming sites put together. In addition to offering more prized content, iROKOtv dropped its subscription price to US$14.75 for an entire year from US$6 a month in the United States, its initial price when it was first launched.[21] This makes iROKOtv cheaper than ibakatv which was still charging US$7.00 per month with fewer cinema features, and certainly cheaper for residents in Europe and North America than Netflix, which had relatively few of the best-known Nollywood cinema features. Although iROKOtv does not use trailers on their standalone site to draw in views like ibakatv does, once an individual completes the subscription process, and logs in, the site was organized at that point in such a way as to foreground its cinema features as a type of prized content. When iROKOtv first started operations in December 2011, feature films did not appear to be organized in any order, though one could filter a search for films by using names of famous actors, or broad generic classifications like drama and comedy. Between January and August 2016, the content on iROKOtv was being organized very differently. The categories showing on the iROKOtv opening page pointed to a new orientation, one in which a certain number of cinematic features were being added every month. Now films were grouped according to when they were added by month: June 2016 releases, January 2016 releases etc., so as to confirm that new films in general, and cinema features in particular were being added on a regular basis. One satisfied subscriber commented: "Irokotv still better ibakatv that loads two films for two weeks. And it's the same monthly charge fees. Pls let's appreciate."

New classifications have also been added to the iROKOtv site that speak to the aesthetic value of films: "Classics" for example, and "award-winning," as well as "blockbuster." These headings are ways of suggesting the quality of a film apart from its newness. In response, a number of subscribers to the site are also beginning to make aesthetic judgments about the quality of the films available for streaming. Writing about a particular film, for example, one subscriber wrote "the cinematography and aesthetics make you know they put a lot of effort into this movie." Another subscriber wrote in the comments section that s/he was happy to note that *Taxi Driver Oko Ashewo* was one of the selections for a spotlight on Nollywood films in the Toronto International Film Festival for 2016. iROKOtv and other subscription sites are now clearly positioning themselves as purveyors of "quality" content, as opposed to merely free content. In this respect, theatrical exhibition is critical as an indication of both the commercial and cultural value of the film.

The question of what constitutes "quality" mediated content by and for Africans is itself a subject of debate, that is likely to intensify at a time when film production by Africans is experiencing a notable increase, fueled, in large part, by film industries like Nollywood. If, from the 1970s to the late twentieth century, it was possible to position African cinema as a non-commercial, preferably "third" cinema in contrast to the first cinema of Hollywood, those protocols of differentiation no longer seem as compelling for African art and experimental filmmaking against the backdrop of a vibrant, homegrown and resolutely commercial filmmaking practice in the early twenty-first century. Now more, and more, art and independent cinema are described as representing quality cinema, presumably, unlike the more trashy films associated with film industries where video production predominates. The notion of quality and art has always been important as a way of distinguishing films curated in film festivals from more mainstream productions. Given the high visibility of Nollywood and other video film industries around Africa, references to quality and aesthetics are becoming an increasingly important basis for distinguishing African art and independent filmmaking from commercial filmmaking in film festivals. As Lindiwe Dovey (2015, pp.104–105) points out, for most curators working on African film festivals in Africa and beyond, African art and independent filmmaking represents cinema and aesthetic quality while video films do not. Some curators of African cinema for film festivals in Africa are willing to include local video films in their selection, but mainly as a way to encourage video film producers to pursue the kind of quality exhibited in art cinema (Dovey 2015, p. 148).

Discussions about "Quality TV" are perhaps even more relevant to the experience of streaming platforms focusing on African content than the references to "quality" filmmaking. Among scholars of American and European media, "Quality TV," often used to describe the kind of premium content that began to appear on HBO and other cable channels in the 1990s, is also a contested term.[22] Notwithstanding disagreements over definitions of the term, and the usefulness of the concept itself, it is hardly surprising that the notion of Quality TV first emerged in relation to programming on Pay TV, where both the subscribers to the cable channels and the Pay TV companies themselves had an interest in rationalizing payment for content. On its YouTube channel, ibakatv uses an analogue for Quality TV when it advertises some films as "Premium movies." As noted earlier, iROKOtv achieved a similar effect by designating some films as "award-winning" and "classic." The adjective "classic" serves the desired goal particularly well, in suggesting that films are not just old, but also have some special value by virtue of being old. In short, prized content on streaming platforms specializing in African content functions in much the same way as Quality TV did on American Pay TV. As was the case with Quality TV, prized content involves mobilizing aesthetic evaluation for specifically commercial purposes. To a large extent, the encouragement given to viewers to like or unlike a feature film, and the comments section where some subscribers school other subscribers on the value of a given film, perform this work of aesthetic judgment on iROKOtv. It should be mentioned here that ibakatv too has a comment section, though it is not nearly as heavily patronized as the comments section on iROKOtv. Subscribers on ibakatv also do not appear to use the available star rating system quite as frequently as subscribers use the like and unlike icon on iROKOtv. On ibakatv, the results of the star rating system reveal a clustering of a majority of films with similar rates of approval, and far fewer comments to justify the rates given.

Slow Cinema

All types of African cinema do not necessarily represent "prized content" or cultural and commercial value for the streaming platforms that specialize in streaming African content. Nor do the commercial cinema features have the same kinds of value on the streaming platforms or in the cultural life of communities more broadly. To understand how particular cinema features acquire value on streaming platforms, it is useful to consider other dimensions of their circulation. In this respect, tracking the feature films that have *never* been added to the catalogue of iROKOtv is just as critical as documenting those feature films that are currently in the catalogue or have been on the site at some point in time. A review of the "missing" features raises interesting questions about motivations on the part of the streaming platform, and on the part of the filmmaker. Curiously, and until late 2016, none of Kunle Afolayan's films were available on the iROKOtv site.[23] None of the films by Omoni Oboli had ever been on the site: *Being Mrs. Elliott, The First Lady, Wives on Strike* and others. None of the films of Tunde Kelani had ever been on iROKOtv. At some point in 2015, *The Figurine* was available for free on YouTube, and as stated earlier, Kelani's film, *Maami* is available for free on Nollytv, but both films were not available on the streaming platform with the largest number of cinema features. Other celebrated cinema features from the past few years like *The*

Meeting and *Journey to Self* have never been on iROKOtv. *The Meeting* was available on Distrify for several months in 2014, and is now available for sale as a DVD in Nigeria. From late 2015, *October 1* was available on Netflix, as was the immensely successful movie, *Fifty*.

Given the fact that iROKOtv subscribers in their comments have specifically requested for many of the films mentioned above and others that have had a fairly successful theatrical run, and given the fact that iROKOtv was, in 2016, staking its reputation as a subscription service on its ability to secure many notable cinema features for streaming, the absence of these films listed on iROKOtv is striking. It is not clear whether iROKOtv management declined to offer what the film producers considered an adequate fee for licensing rights for each of these films, or whether the filmmakers declined to make the film available to iROKOtv in particular for unspecified reasons. In some instances, the decision to bypass iROKOtv appears deliberate. For example, Kunle Afolayan recorded a brief commercial for ibakatv in 2014, and allowed the trailer for *Phone Swap* to be shown for several months, before the film itself was made available on ibakatv for a brief period of time. In 2015, that Kunle Afolayan initially decided to give *October 1* to Netflix instead of iROKOtv is also noteworthy, as is the decision of Ebonylife production to license the cinema feature *Fifty* to Netflix, but not iROKOtv.

For other features, another set of considerations would seem to be at work. In this instance, it does not appear to be a simple case of preferring other streaming services to iROKOtv, or simply wanting to thumb one's nose at iROKOtv. For example, only one of Omoni Oboli's films, *Being Mrs. Elliott* has been made available on any streaming platform, though her films have been fairly successful in Nigerian theatres and she herself is a popular and highly regarded actress. *Being Mrs. Elliott* was made available to ibakatv in 2016. Her other films are not available on any streaming platforms, nor have they been released as DVD. The Yoruba language film, *Aramotu*, which was nominated for many awards at the African Academy of Movies event in 2011 has never been released on DVD, or made available for streaming. Tunde Kelani's *Dazzling Mirage* is not available for streaming on any platform, or in DVD format. Recent films by Mildred Okwo and Rita Dominic are not available for streaming as well. These include *The Meeting* which was available for a year or so, on Distrify, and more recently, *Suru'Lere* which has not yet been made available for streaming. There is a pattern here which seems to be gathering steam with each year.

To account for the increasingly divergent circulation trajectories of most Nollywood films in comparison to African art and independent cinema, I would like to turn to the distinction that Charles Acland (2008, p. 102) makes between fast and slow cinema cultures. With respect to duration of the exhibition run in a cinema theatre, Acland (2008, p. 102) has observed: "With film, the short run of the blockbuster marks rapid economic gleaning and looks to lucrative prospects on DVD, where the smaller 'art' or 'indie' film has a slower release pace and may spend more time in its few theaters..." Acland further builds his

argument by referring to the work of Pierre Bourdieu who distinguishes between avant-garde and middlebrow theatre and their cultural temporalities.
Extrapolating from Bourdieu, Acland (2008, p. 102) concludes, "what we might
describe as 'slow' and 'fast' cultures become correlates of cultural and economic
capital." Works associated with fast cultures yield immediate commercial profit
but do not acquire much cultural and economic capital over time. For works
associated with slow cultures, it is the inverse. They may not have much
commercial value in the short term, but they grow in symbolic capital and eventually economic capital over time.

For my purposes here, however, I will define the difference between the slow
and the fast cinema cultures somewhat differently from Acland, while accepting
the principle of differing cultural temporalities. In this instance, I am concerned
with the temporality of release of the film in additional formats, and not simply
the duration of the film in a commercial cinema theatre. With some Nigerian
cinema features, we see "wide" release in local cinema theatres for several weeks
followed by total withdrawal of the film from circulation either on DVD or on
streaming platforms. These features belong to the Nigerian version of a "slow"
cinema culture. For African cinema then, I define the slow cinema culture as one
involving slow and restricted release of a film for viewing on additional formats
over time irrespective of the duration of a theatrical run.

Other Nigerian features whose distribution belong to a "fast" cinema culture
legally migrate to streaming platforms and or other distribution formats on Pay
TV or on DVD fairly quickly and once the theatrical run has ended. With some
films, we see a hybrid process: They migrate to streaming platforms quickly, but
then are withdrawn after several months and may not resurface on either streaming platforms or on DVD for a few years. This represents another version of the
slow cinema culture. While it may not have been a deliberately implemented
strategy, independent and art cinema by Africans helped initiate and consolidate a
slow cinema culture for African films. These films typically debuted at a cinema
festival either in Africa or elsewhere, and then moved from one film festival to
another over several years. In between film festivals, the films were shown on university campuses mainly in Europe and North America, or at conferences, and
frequently with the filmmaker in attendance. The cultural capital accruing to these
films over time derived, in part, from the specific attributes of the individual film
as recognized by critics, but also, in part, from their relative scarcity as cultural
goods. There are independent African filmmakers like Abderahmane Sissako
whose films transition to other distribution formats fairly quickly after a theatrical
run, and still retain a great deal of cultural capital. However, and interestingly, and
at a time when film formats are proliferating everywhere including in Africa, it is
actually becoming harder and more expensive to gain access to films by those
African filmmakers committed to independent and art cinema. In these instances,
the scarcity of the film would seem to be part of a deliberate strategy to increase
the film's value by ensuring that it can be viewed only at film festivals, or by direct

invitation to the filmmaker at special events or educational institutions around the world where academic and professional critics are likely to be present.

The fear of seemingly unstoppable piracy is undoubtedly a major consideration in the unwillingness of some Nigerian commercial film producers and directors to release their films even for streaming. Given Nollywood's well documented history of piracy, it comes as no surprise that virtually all of the highest grossing Nigerian cinema features have been pirated in the past few years. *Half of a Yellow Sun, Phone Swap, 30 Days in Atlanta*, and *Invasion 1897*, among others have all been massively pirated. Acland's description of piracy as "an unsanctioned acceleration of a film's life-cycle" (2008, p. 95) is especially apt here. On the same theme, Acland further adds, "Piracy is a form of cultural speeding" (Acland 2008, p. 95). If the film can acquire cultural and symbolic capital by being released slowly and intermittently, then the decision to minimize opportunities for piracy and "cultural speeding" can only be beneficial for the film and the filmmakers. Allowing a film which has had a successful theatrical run to acquire more cultural and symbolic capital over time also works to the advantage of the filmmaker in any future negotiations with streaming platforms that might want to license the film. Indeed, and if iROKOtv's experience is anything to go by, the longer the film is out of circulation on DVD or on other free and subscription platforms, the more subscribers are likely to clamor for it to be added to the site. Since access to successful cinema features has become one of the most important rationales for taking out a subscription, the management of these streaming platforms specializing in Nollywood films will frequently find that it is their best interest to pay to license often-requested films, even when the cost is high. From the filmmaker's perspective, unwillingness to make a film available for streaming now seems increasingly like a deliberate embrace of a slow cinema culture, and not only a response to the prevalence of piracy. Nigerian filmmakers adopting the slow cinema culture model also find it useful to license at least one of their popular films to a streaming platform, to generate a certain level of visibility for their status as filmmaker, while withholding their other films from circulation through streaming and DVD. This would appear to be Omoni Oboli's strategy. She has licensed *Being Mrs. Elliott* to ibakatv, but has kept her other films from circulating beyond their initial theatrical run. Obi Emelonye's *Mirror Boy* is still available for free on the OHBox site for free probably for a similar reason. In this case, the accessible and singular feature becomes a trailer for the entire body of work by the filmmaker. In allowing *October 1* to stream on Netflix, but keeping his other popular films locked away and unavailable for streaming on sites specializing in African content until fairly recently, Kunle Afolayan appears to be betting on a bigger and global stage, while also hoping to increase the value of his films for streaming platforms that specialize in African content. With Afolayan and Oboli as well as with other participants in the slow cinema culture approach, we see a willingness to privilege a certain kind of cultural prestige and exclusivity linked to material scarcity above opportunities for immediate financial remuneration.

In both instances of slow and fast cinema cultures in Africa, cinema matters as a way of generating initial publicity for a film that will then inform its standing beyond theatrical exhibition. Even given widespread piracy, and the relatively weak development of legal distribution pathways for films and other cultural goods, films benefiting from theatrical exhibition are like trailers (Acland 2003, p. 65), advancing subsequent distribution of the film on other platforms. Although the more expensive New Nollywood films have not yet become what Acland (2003, p. 65) and Thomas Schatz (2008, p. 37) calls "loss leaders," films that run at a loss during theatrical exhibition, but then make a profit in ancillary markets, the possibility that expensive Nigerian cinema features will increasingly depend on streaming and Pay TV to recoup production costs and or make a profit should not be ruled out. Cinema features are already an important way of constructing value for customers on streaming platforms specializing in Nigerian content. Nigerian and other African filmmakers pursuing higher production values, which entails increased production costs, may find themselves working in greater collaboration with streaming platforms like iROKOtv, and or with Pay TV as a way of recouping the cost of production.[24] But in order to leverage the value of the film with streaming platforms, the film will have to cycle through theatrical exhibition. African filmmakers engaged in a fast cinema culture may end up needing streaming platforms almost as much as the management of most streaming platforms needs cinema features to drive traffic to their site and encourage subscriptions. In other words, cinema will still matter in a world of streaming African media as an indicator of quality and prized content.

Conclusion

It is important to point out, however, that all cinema does not necessarily equate prized content on streaming platforms dedicated to African content, simply by virtue of being cinema. Art and independent cinema are almost completely missing from the iROKOtv and ibakatv libraries, as well as many other streaming platforms specializing in African content. Somewhat more controversial Nigerian or Nigeria-related films like *B for Boy*, or even *Mother of George*, are available for streaming on sites like Amazon and Google Play, but not on platforms specializing in African and Nigerian-related content. Some African art cinema was available on the Bunitv library for several months, but many of these features appear to have been removed from the site in 2016 or perhaps even earlier. In short, and while curators at film festivals are pushing the quality label for African art and independent cinema, this attribution of quality to independent and art cinema does not appear salient for streaming platforms focusing on mainstream commercial fare.

Furthermore, cinema features do not constitute the only kind of prized or premium content available on streaming platforms like iROKOtv and ShowMax.

Among the streaming platforms focusing on Nigerian content, iROKOtv has gone further than others in also adding televisual series that are popular with select audiences. These include *Jenifa's Diary, An African City* (season 1), *Festac Town, The V Republic, Lekki Wives* and *Husbands of Lagos* among others. That the star of a popular television series, *Jenifa's Diary*, featured from 2015 to 2016, on the log-in page of iROKOtv would suggest that television series and serials, too, can become prized content encouraging viewers to subscribe to the platform. Indeed, and on its YouTube channel, iROKOtv uses free access to single episodes of its prized tele-visual series to lure future subscribers, in much the same way as ibakatv uses cinema feature trailers for the same purpose. The prominence of television serials as prized content represents another point of contrast with ibakatv, which did not, in 2016, have any of the better known television serials on its site. Whether iRO-KOtv will continue to make use of cinema features as premium content or will increasingly rely on in-house television series and serials remains to be seen. There is no doubt that on iROKOtv and other streaming platforms specializing in African content, many different strategies are being pursued for increasing viewership numbers and attracting fee-paying as well as "free" subscribers.

In January 2016, Netflix announced that it was extending service to additional territories around the world, including all countries in Africa. Reacting to the news, Jason Njoku declared somewhat tongue in cheek on his blog that Netflix had come to Africa to "take food away from the bowls of his children."[25] On a more serious note, we might legitimately inquire to what extent and in which way might Netflix change iROKOtv's current understanding of quality content for African viewers. In response, both Njoku and the CEO of ShowMax have dismissed the possibility that Netflix might pose significant competition to their services.[26] While these declarations might simply represent corporate posturing for the sake of nervous share-holders worried about the entry of a global powerhouse into the market for streaming to African audiences, there might be some truth to these claims. As Njoku himself has admitted, most of the subscribers to iROKOtv currently reside outside Africa, and in places where Netflix has long been available to interested viewers. Since iROKOtv has been harvesting subscriptions in what Njoku describes in the same blogpost as Netflix's "backyard" for a while, it seems unlikely that the extension of Neflix services to the African continent will affect that subscriber base.

Second, and if iROKOtv and ibakatv have staked their success on fostering a cinema culture of fast release and expanding access using mainly African gener-ated content, streaming platforms from the global North may find themselves at a disadvantage in this particular fight. In 2016, Netflix had very little Nollywood content, and only three or four of the most desirable cinema features. Furthermore, and in its initial expansion to the African continent, Netflix has been associated with what Tryon (2013, p. 41) calls restricted access rather than expanding access. In particular, and after initial excitement at the arrival of Netflix, Netflix sub-scribers on the African continent quickly began to complain that many of the prized content American shows like *House of Cards* that were of specific interest were geo-blocked on Netflix in Africa due to licensing issues. At the same time, other streaming platforms like ShowMax already had the right to stream some of the American television series that Netflix could have offered those Africa-based subscribers less interested in Nollywood type content. Industry observers have discussed other potential challenges for Netflix in Africa relating to bandwidth and infrastructure. In my opinion, and where Netflix might yet make a big difference to the African media market is in the competition for prized African content, whether these are cinema features or television serials. Nigerian filmmakers who are currently pursuing a slow cinema culture strategy may find it advantageous to license their feature films to Netflix for much higher fees as a way of pressuring companies like iROKOtv that specialize in Nigerian content.[27]

It is possible to argue that the impact of streaming services for Nigerian and African cinema may be more circumscribed than I seem to anticipate in this chapter, in light of the fact that streaming options are still limited, even if the competition between streaming platforms serving customers on the African continent and in the African diaspora seems to be heating up. The more important point to note is that for the short and medium term, small screens will continue to play a major role in the African media landscape, and the competition between suppliers of small screen entertainment will have an impact on how African cinema is viewed and assessed.[28] Already, and in recognition of the competitive media landscape, iROKOtv took two bold initiatives for its Africa-based customers. First, it canceled its desktop service for subscribers in Africa in 2015, and introduced a mobile app that would allow subscribers to download content to their mobile devices without using up too much data. That is to say the company sidestepped streaming for its Africa-based customers. Second, however, it followed this up by signing contracts to make ROK Studio productions available on regional and international pay television stations. Then it signed a deal with the Chinese owned Pay TV provider in Africa, Star Times, to introduce two new linear television channels, iROKO Play, and iROKO Plus populated with iROKOtv exclusive content.[29] In 2016, Rok Studios consolidated this toehold on television delivery by signing contracts to license its in-house productions to Sky TV in the United Kingdom, and to M-Net DStv for broadcast across Africa and parts of the Middle East.[30] In other words, iROKOtv intends to compete on all fronts: Streaming for mainly African-Diasporic subscribers, mobile and Pay TV for Africa-based and African-Diasporic subscribers. To advance this multi-pronged approach, iROKOtv even adopted a new logo showing three sizes of screens all connected to each other, thus highlighting its commitment to providing content on different kinds of screens. Populating all these screens with payable or quality content will depend, at least in part, on cinema. At some point, the scramble for African generated premium and prized content may become intense enough to precipitate faster construction of cinema theatres in Nigeria and elsewhere in Africa. In the meantime, and no matter what happens, cinema will matter, even for those in Africa and the African diaspora who only watch African cinema on small screens.

Notes

1   For more on questions of authenticity, see for example, David Murphy (2000).
2   See Adejunmobi (2015, p. 124).
3   Film House was established by Kene Mkparu working with a few partners. They launched their first cinema theatre in Nigeria in December 2012. For more on Mkparu's plans for cinema theatre construction in Nigeria, please see Kene Mkparu, "Interview Filmhouse."
4   This was the estimate suggested by Kene Mkparu, CEO of Filmhouse cinemas in a 2016 interview on CNN. See "CNN's Zain Asher Meets Kene Mkparu – CEO of Filmhouse Cinemas."
5   One need only visit the websites for the best known cinemas in Nigeria to see what they are showing to get a sense of Hollywood's commanding position in Nigerian cinemas. For Ozone, see: http://ozonecinemas.com/now_showing.htm. For Silverbird, see http://silverbirdcinemas.com/.For Genesis Deluxe, see, www. genesiscinemas.com/.For Film House, see www.filmhouseng.com/.
6   See Shaibu Husseini (2016), *The Vanguard* (2014), and *The Guardian* (2016).
7   While scholars like Wheeler Dixon and Chuck Tryon are also concerned about digital projection, which is a related subject, my interests here pertain mainly to the functions of films that have enjoyed a successful box office at cinemas for streaming platforms.
8   For a more in-depth history of iROKOtv, see Adejunmobi (2014) and Miller (2016).
9   See Jason Njoku (2014b) for more on this.
10 In January 2016, *The Financial Times* was reporting as few as 65,000 subscribers for iROKOtv, but the same article also noted that iROKOtv had attracted US$19 million worth of international investments. See Maggie Fick (2016).
11 What I describe in the pages that follow represents the content profile for iROKOtv from 2015 to 2016. As will become evident in the subsequent discussion, the content profile on iROKOtv and other platforms specializing in African content undergoes frequent change.
12 For more on this, see Jason Njoku (2014c) "Interview, Jason Njoku" and Jason Njoku (2016b) "Death of an industry."
13 Both *Poisoned Bait* and *Losing Control* are ROK Studio television serial productions that were showing on DStv-M-Net's Africa Magic channel even before additional contracts, discussed in the latter section of this chapter, were signed with M-Net DStv in 2016.
14 Jason Njoju (2015a), "Iroko: Bad for the Industry? Part 1."
15 Although much of the information about iROKOtv's strained relationship with Nigerian filmmakers is admittedly anecdotal, Njoku felt sufficiently concerned about this to address the issue in two blogposts, titled "Iroko. Bad for the industry, Part I" (Jason Njoku 2015a) and "Iroko. Bad for the industry, II" (Jason Njoku 2015b). It was worth noting that Nollywood filmmakers were equally critical of DStv, when it initially began licensing Nollywood films to show.
16 See Jason Njoku (2014a) for his comments about cinema.
17 Alaba market in Lagos is a major hub for the wholesale purchase of straight to video films and streaming rights.

18   See Jason Njoku (2015c) for more on this.

19   Despite this claim on the ibakatv site, iROKOtv is clearly the dominant streaming platform in the streaming market. My own experience on both sites, albeit limited, makes me rather skeptical about the size of ibakatv's library in comparison to that of iROKOtv.

20   As indicated earlier, it is rare for both sites to have the same feature films. The feature film referenced by this displeased ibakatv subscriber is one of the three mentioned earlier in this chapter.

21   In the United Kingdom, the new subscription rate in 2016 was £10.00 a year.

22   For more on the debate about Quality TV, see Christine Geraghty (2003), Sundeep Dasgupta (2012), and Janet McCabe and Kim Akass (2007).

23   The films, *October 1* and *Phone Swap* began to stream on iROKOtv in November 2016, almost two years after *October 1* was made available on Netflix.

24   As evidence of this trend, one need only note that DStv's Africa Magic channel was listed as one of the producers of Kunle Afolayan's 2016 film, *The CEO*.

25   For Njoku's comments about the arrival of Netflix in Africa, see Jason Njoku (2016a).

26   For reactions from ShowMax to Netflix's arrival in Africa, see Loni Prinsloo (2016).

27   As indicated earlier, two of the most popular Nollywood cinema features of 2015 are already available on Netflix. Netflix also appears to be signing licensing deals with filmmakers from other African countries, as for example, in the case of the South African thriller, *Hard to Get*, which it acquired for its library in 2016. See Tambay Obenson (2016).

28   And by small screens, here, I do not only mean television, but increasingly also cell phones. Despite the high cost of data, expanding access to free wifi in some public areas in West Africa, such as upscale shops, cafés, and restaurants, means that a slowly increasing number of people can now watch films on their cell phones.

29   See Jason Nwokpoku (2015) and Gbenga Onalaja "StarTimes (2016).

30   See Mobisola Atolagbe (2016) and Tola Agunbiade (2016).

References

Acland, Charles R. 2003 *Screen Traffic: Movies, Multiplexes, and Global Culture*. Durham, NC: Duke University Press.

Acland, Charles R. 2008. "Theatrical Exhibition: Accelerated Cinema." In *The Contemporary Hollywood Film Industry*, edited by Paul McDonald and Janet Wasko, 83–105. Malden, MA: Blackwell.

Adejunmobi, Moradewun. 2014. "Evolving Nollywood Templates for Minor Transnational Film." *Black Camera*, 5.2, 74–94.

Adejunmobi, Moradewun. 2015. "African Film's Televisual Turn." *Cinema Journal*, 54.2, 120–125.

Agunbiade, Tola. 2016. "Rok Studios Is Launching a Channel on UK's Sky TV This Month." http://techcabal.com/2016/09/15/rok-on-sky/. Accessed 30 December 2016.

Atolagbe, Mobisola. 2016. "Rok Studios Is Launching a Channel on DStv in November." http://techcabal.com/2016/10/18/rok-studios-is-launching-a-channel-on-dstv-in-november/, Accessed 30 December 2016.

CNN. 2016. "CNN's Zain Asher Meets Kene Mkparu – CEO of Filmhouse Cinemas, Nigeria's Largest Chain of Theaters at His Recently Opened IMAX Theater." www. cnn.com/videos/world/2016/11/28/marketplace-africa-nollywood-b.cnn. Accessed 30 December 2016.

Dasgupta, Sundeep. 2012. "Policing the People: Television Studies and the Problem of Quality." *European Journal of Media Studies*, 1.1, 35–53.

Dixon, Wheeler Winston. 2013. *Streaming: Movies, Media, and Instant Access*. Lexington: University Press of Kentucky.

Dovey, Lindiwe. 2015. *Curating Africa in the Age of Film Festivals*. New York: Palgrave Macmillan.

Fick, Maggie. *Financial Times*. 2016. "iROKOtv Investors Back "Netflix of Africa" with $19 Million Funding." www.ft.com/cms/s/0/b02cab5e-c378-11e5-b3b1-7b2481276e45. html. Accessed 26 August 2016.

Geraghty, Christine. 2003. "Aesthetics and Quality in Popular Television Drama." *International Journal of Cultural Studies*, 6, 25–45.

Husseini, Shaibu. *The Guardian*. 2016. "30 Days in Atlanta Grosses over N100 Million in Box Office Sales." http://guardian.ng/art/30-days-in-atlanta-grosses-over-n100-million-in-box-office-sales/. Accessed 30 March 2018.

Lotz, Amanda. 2014. *The Television Will Be Revolutionized*, 2nd ed. New York: New York University Press.

McCabe, Janet and Kim Akass. 2007. *Quality TV: Contemporary American Television and Beyond*. London: I.B. Tauris & Co. Ltd.

Miller, Jade. 2016. *Nollywood Central*. London: British Film Institute.

Mkparu, Kene. 2016. "Interview: Filmhouse on Building 25 Cinemas in Nigeria by 2019." www.youtube.com/watch?v=k9614oePm5Y. Accessed 20 August 2016.

Murphy, David. 2000. "Africans Filming Africa. Questioning Theories of An Authentic African Cinema." *Journal of African Cultural Studies*, 13.2, 239–249.

Njoku, Jason. 2014a. "Nigerian Cinema, Hype and the Way Ahead." https://jason.com.ng/nigerian-cinema-hype-and-the-way-ahead-26ee3f625275. Accessed August 20 2016.

Njoku, Jason. 2014b. "Killing iROKOtv." https://jason.com.ng/killing-irokotv-7ce0bc1a6d6. Accessed August 20 2016.

Njoku, Jason. 2014c. "Interview. Jason Njoku on launching its production arm Rok Studios to test film and TV series." https://www.youtube.com/watch?v=h_JYhyK_8-8.

Njoku, Jason. 2015a. "Iroko: Bad for the Industry? Part 1." https://jason.com.ng/iroko-bad-for-the-industry-part-1-fbe922ec8bbf. Accessed August 20 2016.

Njoku, Jason. 2015b. "Iroko: Bad for the Industry? Part II." https://jason.com.ng/iroko-bad-for-the-industry-ii-a5515ffd9cbd. Accessed August 20 2016.

Njoku, Jason. 2016a. "Netflix in Africa." https://jason.com.ng/netflix-in-africa-b01fea9706da. Accessed August 20 2016.

Nwokpoku, Jason. *Vanguard*. 2015. "IROKOtv, StarTimes Sign Exclusive Channel Deal." www.vanguardngr.com/2015/04/irokotv-startimes-sign-exclusive-channel-deal/. Accessed 30 March 2018.

Obenson, Tambay. 2016. "South African Action Romance 'Hard to Get' Secures USA Netflix Deal." *Shadow and Act*, http://shadowandact.com/2016/06/14/south-african-action-romance-hard-to-get-secures-usa-netflix-deal-trailer/. Accessed 30 March 2018.

Onalaja, Gbenga. "StarTimes Could Steal Some of Africa Magic's Magic." *Techcabal*. 2015. http://techcabal.com/2015/04/12/irokotv-has-launched-two-channels-on-startimes-that-could-steal-some-of-africa-magics-er-magic/. Accessed 30 March 2018.

Pedulla, Gabriele. 2012. *In Broad Daylight. Movies and Spectators after Cinema*. Translated by Patricia Gaborik. London and New York: Verso.

Prinsloo, Loni. 2016. "ShowMax expands to 36 African countries to challenge Netflix." www.bloomberg.com/news/articles/2016-05-13/showmax-expands-to-36-african-countries-in-challenge-to-netflix. Accessed 30 March 2018.

Schatz, Thomas. 2008. "The Studio System and Conglomerate Hollywood." In *The Contemporary Hollywood Film Industry*, edited by. Paul McDonald and Janet Wasko, 13–42. Malden, MA: Blackwell.

The Guardian. 2016. "Fifty… Setting New Box Office Record." http://guardian.ng/art/fifty-setting-new-record-for-box-office/. Accessed 28 August 2016.

The Vanguard. 2014. "Half of a Yellow Sun Sets New Box Office Record." www.vanguardngr.com/2014/08/half-yellow-sun-sets-new-box-office-record/. Accessed 25 August 2016.

Tryon, Chuck. 2013. *On-Demand Culture: Digital Delivery and the Future of Movies*. New Brunswick, NJ: Rutgers University Press.

Filmography

Afolayan, Kunle (2007). *Ìràpàdà*. Nigeria: Golden Effects Pictures.

Afolayan, Kunle. (2009) *The Figurine*. Nigeria: Golden Effects Pictures.

Afolayan, Kunle. (2012) *Phone Swap*. Nigeria: Golden Effects Pictures.

Afolayan, Kunle. (2014). *October 1*. Nigeria: Golden Effects Pictures.

Akanni, Niji. (2010) *Aramotu*. Nigeria: Treasure Chest Entertainment Ltd.

Ali-Balogun, Mahmood. (2010). *Tango with Me*. Nigeria: Brickwall Communications LTD, Jungle FilmWorks.

Anadu, Chika. (2013). *B for Boy*. Nigeria: No Blondes Production.

Arase, Frank Rajah. (2011). *Somewhere in Africa*. Nigeria: Heroes Films Productions, Raj Films.

Attoh, Ken and Shirley Frimpong Manso. (2016) *Rebecca*. Ghana: Sparrow Productions.

Babatope, Seyi. (2014). *When Love Happens*. Nigeria: Future Gates Pictures, PHB Films.

Babatope, Seyi. (2015). *Lunchtime Heroes*. Nigeria: PHB Films, FilmOne Production.

Bandele, Biyi. (2013). *Half of a Yellow Sun*. Nigeria: Shareman Media, Slate Films.

Bandele, Biyi. (2015). *Fifty*. Nigeria: EbonyLife Films.

Bello, Michelle. (2013). *Flower Girl*. Nigeria: Blu Star Entertainment.

Dosunmu, Andrew. (2013). *Mother of George*. USA: Parts & Labor, Cunningham & Maybach Films, Fried Alligator Films, SimonSays Entertainment.

Egbe, Blessing Effiom. (2015). *Iquo's Journal*. Nigeria: B'concept Network Productions.

Emelonye, Obi. (2010). *Mirror Boy*. UK: The Nollywood Factory.

Emelonye, Obi. (2012). *Last Flight to Abuja*. UK: The Nollywood Factory.

Emelonye, Obi. (2015). *Thy Will be Done*. UK: The Nollywood Factory.

Frimpong Manso, Shirley. (2013). *Devil in the Detail*. Ghana: Sparrow Productions.

Frimpong Manso Shirley. (2013). *Potomanto*. Ghana: Sparrow Productions.

Frimpong Manso, Shirley. (2016). *Love or Something Like That*. Ghana: Sparrow Productions.

Gomis, Alain. (2012). *Tey*. Senegal: Belle Moon Productions.

Gyang, Kenneth. (2013). *Confusion na wa*. Nigeria: Cinema KpataKpata.

Imasuen, Lancelot (2014). *Darima's Dilemma*. Nigeria: Director is, Royal Arts Academy.

Imasuen, Lancelot. (2014). *Invasion 1897, Deposition of the Last African King*. Nigeria: Iceslide Films Production.

Kelani, Tunde. (2011). *Maami*. Nigeria: Mainframe Film and Television Productions.

Kelani, Tunde. (2014). *Dazzling Mirage*. Nigeria: Mainframe Film and Television Productions.

Kibinge, Judy. (2013). *Something Necessary*. Kenya: One Fine Day Films.

Oboli, Omoni. (2014). *Being Mrs. Elliott*. Nigeria: Dioni Visions.

Oboli, Omoni. (2015). *The First Lady*. Nigeria: Dioni Visions.

Oboli, Omoni. (2016). *Wives on Strike*. Nigeria: Dioni Visions.

Ogar, Frankie. (2015). *A Soldier's Story*. Nigeria: Frankie Ogar Films.

Oguamanam, Uduak Isong. (2015). *House Husband*. Nigeria: Closer Pictures.

Okereke Linus, Stephanie. (2014). *Dry*. Nigeria: Next Page Productions.

Okwo, Mildred and Rita Dominic. (2012). *The Meeting*. Nigeria: Mord Pictures Production.

Olatunde, Jumoke. (2014). *Diary of a Lagos Girl*. Nigeria: Parables Entertainment.

Omotoso, Akin. (2011). *Man on Ground*. South Africa. Tom Pictures.

Oriahi, Daniel. (2015). *Taxi Driver, Oko Ashewo*, Nigeria: FilmOne Production, House 5 Production, Obit Imagery.

Peters, Robert. (2014). *30 Days in Atlanta*. Nigeria: Ayo Makun.

Qubeka, Jahmil X. T. (2013). *Of Good Report*. South Africa: Spier Films.

Waltbanger Taylour, Walt. (2015). *Gbomo Gbomo Express*. Nigeria: Waltbanger 101 Productions.

Serials

Akindele, Funke. (2015–) *Jenifa's Diary*. Nigeria: Scene One Productions.

Amarteifio, Nicole. (2014–). *An African City*. Ghana: An African City.

Djansi, Leila. (2014–) *Poisoned Bait*. Ghana: Turning Point Media/Rok Studios.

Egbe, Blessing Effiom. (2012–). *Lekki Wives*. Nigeria: B' Concept Network.

Njoku, Mary Remmy. (2014–). *Festac Town*. Nigeria: Rok Studios.

Njoku, Mary Remmy. (2015–). *Husbands of Lagos*. Nigeria: Rok Studios.

Onyeka, Ikechukwu. (2015–). *Losing Control*. Nigeria: Rok Studios/Royal Arts Academy.

11

Between the Informal Sector and Transnational Capitalism

Transformations of Nollywood

Jonathan Haynes

The Nigerian video film industry was created and grew to enormous size in the informal economic sector – that vast untaxed zone of activity where little gets written down and law and government are mostly absent.[1] But as transnational corporations have recently inserted themselves into the industry, formal and informal structures are colliding in a dramatic struggle over the future of the industry.

Countability and Visibility

There is no cinema without electricity, and

> Sub-Saharan Africa is desperately short of electricity. The region's grid has a power generation capacity of just 90 gigawatts (GW) and half of it is located in one country, South Africa. Electricity consumption in Spain exceeds that of the whole of Sub-Saharan Africa…. Two in every three people – around 621 million in total – have no access to electricity. In Nigeria, an oil-exporting superpower, 93 million people lack electricity. (Johnston 2015, p. 16)

The eminent committee (chaired by Kofi Annan) responsible for this report eloquently describes the range of consequences of these dire facts. But what does it mean to "lack" or "have access to" electricity? Presumably (the report does not explain the basis of its figures) the statistics are based on the number people living

A Companion to African Cinema, First Edition. Edited by Kenneth W. Harrow and Carmela Garritano.
© 2019 John Wiley & Sons, Inc. Published 2019 by John Wiley & Sons, Inc.

in households that are hooked up to the grid – probably, households that are officially hooked up and are being billed. In Nigeria, those who have official connections to the grid complain that very often they still do not "have access to" electricity
because none is coming through the wires. One reason for this failure (not the
main one) is that whole streets and neighborhoods are connected to the grid
through haphazard illegal hookups, which endanger the physical infrastructure
and profitability of the supplier. So people use generators, if they can afford them.
And how many generators are there in Nigeria? They are hard to count, too: I
haveve seen estimates ranging from nine million (Moss and Gleave, 2014) to 60
million (Anonymous, 2009). Then there is electricity stored in batteries: The little
Chinese batteries sold in the remotest villages to power flashlights and radios, the
car batteries used to charge cell phones for a small fee. And there is the social
dimension of access to be considered: Those with connections to the grid and/or
generators may share their electricity with poorer relatives or social dependents.
Video parlors provide cheap entertainment in dark neighborhoods, and people
gather in the street to watch (for free) monitors set up by vendors of Nollywood
films (Okome, 2007).

My point is not that Nigerians are getting along fine through informality:
Generators are the most polluting and least efficient method of producing
electricity, and in 2009 the estimated amount spent on fuel for these generators
was almost exactly the same as the national capital development budget (Yusuf,
2014). My point is that the official statistics suggest that 93 million Nigerians spend
half their lives in darkness, perhaps (one might imagine) reading their Bibles by
hurricane lamp or doing something folkloric by torchlight, when in fact many of
them are managing, in one way or another, to watch Nigerian movies. Overlooking
this fact means ignoring their cultural reality.

Ramon Lobato makes the general point about "informal" film distribution: It
goes on everywhere in the world and is "a global norm rather than an exception or
deviation. The international pirate economy exceeds the legal film industry in
size, scale, and reach" (Lobato 2012, p. 4). If film distribution shapes public culture
by determining who sees what films and where and when they see them, then
informal film distribution has massive consequences. But film studies does not recognize its "epistemological authority" or give it attention commensurate with its
importance (Lobato 2012, pp. 1–6).

Informal distribution seizes on the products of more or less all film industries;
but alone among major film industries, Nigerian films are mostly produced in the
informal sector as well as distributed in it. This doubly informal character means
Nigerian films are regularly categorized out of existence in formal contexts – this
even though the African video boom, of which Nollywood is the most powerful
element, has utterly transformed audiovisual culture across Africa. In the new
edition of the standard textbook *Africa*, for example, there is a whole chapter
devoted to "African Cinema" but less than one paragraph about Nollywood and
the video phenomenon, and those few sentences are almost entirely devoted to

246

Jonathan Haynes

how the video films do not meet the standards and aspirations set by Sembène and Abderrahmane Sissako (Adesokan 2014, pp. 239–240). This would seem to be a case of an old-fashioned conception of "cinema" trumping social, economic, and cultural significance. (In many cases – not this one – a problem is that most African film scholars are not equipped to do work on both sides of the celluloid/video divide. See Haynes 2000, 2010b, 2011.)

The distinction between celluloid and video has been rapidly eroding if not disappearing everywhere, including in Hollywood. In the context of African cinema, when the distinction between the formats is enforced, it is usually a cover for other things. FESPACO's long resistance to admitting Nollywood films on equal terms clearly has had political dimensions. European film festivals have defended a notion of "quality" that found Nollywood films, cheaply made and springing from African popular culture, deficient and disorienting.

In the wider world of international commercial cinema, Nollywood has finally begun to make cameo appearances – in 2014, an official Nigerian committee was formed to nominate films for the Oscars (Anonymous, 2014); in 2015, a first small batch of Nollywood films appeared on Netflix. But for the most part, the brutal realities of money and power assert themselves with raw clarity. All of African cinema is nearly beneath notice. In a 2014 survey of world film industries, the section on Africa is all about North Africa; south of the Sahara, only South Africa is accorded treatment in the standard format of the study. But then, reflecting a dim awareness that something new and strange – and unignorably large, in its way – is coming out of Africa, there is a sidebar paragraph on Nigeria, full of reluctance to stretch the category of "film" to accommodate Nollywood:

> According to government figures, the country has overtaken South Africa as the continent's largest economy. The West African country is the second largest film producer in the world by number of productions; that is, understanding film in the broadest sense of the term, as most titles are no-budget guerrilla productions with few commercial perspectives, let alone a theatrical release. Nonetheless, Nollywood has found a new source of revenues in video and on-demand services thanks to the Nigerian diasporas, mainly in UK and the USA. (Kanzler and Milla 2014, pp. 60–62)

Part of the problem here is in how films are counted up in the international cinema business. There are two standard measures: Box office receipts and the number of films with budgets over US$500,000. (The Motion Picture Association of America recently increased the budget threshold for films to be counted to US$1,000,000.) Only a small handful of Nollywood films have had budgets over US$500,000. These are so-called "New Nollywood" films, and they also have brief runs in the new multiplex cinemas that have been built in Nigeria in the last decade, producing modest box office receipts. But Nollywood was created at a moment when there were virtually no functioning cinemas in Nigeria, and so box office receipts and a "normal" distribution system serving movie theatres have not been part of the Nollywood economy. Nigeria's National Bureau of Statistics released data in 2014 estimating that the Nigerian film industry was worth US$3 billion, but less than 1% was tracked from official ticket sales and royalties (Bright, 2015). The authors of the world film industry survey don't have a vocabulary for talking about what Nollywood is, until, in their last sentence, they arrive at the corporate exploitation of Internet streaming.

The claim that Nigeria "is the second largest film producer in the world by number of productions" is the result of another problem with counting Nigerian films. The claim seems to rest entirely on a single 2009 UNESCO report, whose information was compiled by asking film classification boards around the world to supply statistics (UNESCO Institute of Statistics, 2009). These boards followed normal practice by counting only films that had theatrical releases, except for the Nigerian Film and Video Censors Board (NFVCB), which counted all the video films it had processed. On this basis, Nigeria outstripped the United States (India was in first place), which it would not have done if every low-budget, straight-to-video American film had been counted. This problem has been pointed out (Bud, 2014b; Haynes, 2010a), but the claim was immediately picked up and constantly repeated until it has become unassailably ensconced in conventional wisdom and Nollywood's sense of itself. Tejaswini Ganti has written about how "fuzzy numbers" about the Indian film industry have been generative, not debilitating, leading to new investments, contacts, and discourses (Ganti 2015, p. 453; I owe this reference to Jedlowski 2016a, where the point is applied to Nollywood).

Alexander Bud points out that something similar had happened in 2006 when the NFVCB published a wildly inflated claim that Nollywood employed a million people and was therefore the second largest employer in the country. A story in *The Economist* legitimized the claim, which was then cited by the World Bank in justifying a US$25 million investment (Bud, 2014a).

And it happened again in 2014 when the Nigerian economy was "rebased" – that is, its gross domestic product recalculated for the first time in two decades, establishing the Nigerian economy as larger than South Africa's and therefore the largest in Sub-Saharan Africa. The new figures from the National Bureau of Statistics also included the claim that the film and music industries were making an enormous contribution to the national economy. Peace Anyiam-Osigwe (a leading Nollywood figure) and Dayo Ogunyemi point out how unrealistic the figures were, and therefore how inadequate as a basis for the film industry policies of the Goodluck Jonathan (GED) administration; and they indict a whole culture of fake expertise that attaches the names of prestigious organizations to bad numbers, thereby ensuring that journalists and everyone else will continue to cite them.

The Ministry of Finance led by NOI [Ngozi Okonjo-Iweala] had neither the sector expertise nor the data upon which to set sensible policy. As the old aphorism goes, you can't manage what you can't measure.

That administration's failure to gather, aggregate and understand firm level data and challenges is evident from the laughable dimensions of the macro level claims carelessly made about Nollywood – "it accounts for millions of jobs, second only to agriculture."

The rebasing exercise including the particularly vexatious claim that the film and music sectors contribute 1.4% of GDP – 23 times the aviation sector, 3.2 times the cement sector, three times the oil refining sector, 1.3 times the electricity supply sector, 1.3 times the road transport sector and 52% of the financial institutions sector (banks and insurance companies combined)! If anyone believe these numbers or, more importantly, believes that the GEJ administration believed these numbers, simply contrast the scale of its Nollywood initiatives to the interventions it made in financial services, agriculture, aviation, and the power sector. If that doesn't lift the wool from your eyes, nothing will.

Over this period, there was undue deference in strategy and policy development given to international players – the World Bank, the IFC, the Indian EXIM Bank – and a strange motley of "consultants." Let us state boldly – the World Bank Group has close to zero competence regarding the film industry....

The baseline would be to commission a comprehensive study of the Nigerian movie industry.... This study needs to be done by consulting (not importing from India, Europe or the US) the few people who understand the industry – people who aren't afraid to roll up their sleeves and go into [the grungy film marketing centers] Alaba, Idumota, Upper Eweka Rd, Oshogbo, Asaba among others. The industry's future cannot be divined from a desk in Asokoro or Victoria Island [exclusive neighborhoods in Abuja and Lagos]. (Anyiam-Osigwe and Ogunyemi 2015)

Odia Ofeimun (in Glasspiegel, 2012) and Eddie Iroh (2009), among others, have observed that Nollywood strongly expresses the self-aggrandizement and premature self-congratulation that they say are salient features of the Nigerian character. Nollywood itself and its sympathizers are glad to think of it as very, very big – including journalists wanting a compelling hook for their story and academics (such as myself) who want to believe, and to have others believe, that the object of study they are invested in is enormous and therefore important – and no one has the numbers to refute the claims.

There is a minor scandal of academic and journalistic rectitude here: Boastfulness, laziness, and ignorance are part of the story, as is the bad history of stereotypes about Africa that makes any kind of exorbitance creditable, and a framing belief that Nigeria is a wild and dangerous place where one would not want to stay long enough to verify facts. But it is unfair to heap too much blame on those who repeat bad numbers when good ones are unavailable.

Good numbers are unavailable because neither the film industry nor the Nigerian government provide them, and no one else is being paid to do the work of creating them. The film industry does not provide good numbers because the marketers who have controlled it operate in the manner of the informal sector, one of whose leading characteristics is that things are not written down. The marketers are regularly accused of being "stark illiterates," but many of them are quite literate and highly intelligent. They like informality and secrecy because these strategies work for them – to obscure the numbers of films sold, for example, which in turn lets marketers avoid full payment to producers or inflate the reputation of a movie. Moreover, the Nigerian film industry is really three separate ones, producing films in English, Yoruba, and Hausa, each with its own marketing system and set of professional organizations, with only limited communication between them. (This chapter is about the English-language branch, "Nollywood," though most of it applies to the other branches as well.)

Informality does not mean lack of organization. In Lagos, every two weeks the marketers' organizations determine which films will be released, and lists of the approved titles are circulated to video shops. (In recent years, an increasing number of films are being released outside this system.) If these lists were collected and published, we would know much more than we do now. But the lists are not published.

The government, in the form of the National Film and Video Censors Board, published three volumes of an index of all the films submitted to it for classification, including titles, producers, language, and other valuable information (Abua 2002, 2004; Gana and Edekor 2006). Under the leadership of director general Emeka Mba, in 2010 a website was created to make easily available all kinds of information, but budget cuts eliminated the money that was to pay the company that was given the contract to develop the website, so it never went live. For a while a couple of years later, the website (www.nfvcb.gov.ng/) began to post a wealth of data, only to subside again into a barebones operation devoted to guiding producers through the procedures of the agency's core function of classifying films submitted to it. I have been told repeatedly that one reason the NFVCB no longer publishes statistics and the titles of films is that it is embarrassed by how few films – perhaps half of the total produced – are submitted to it for classification. The percentage was much higher until the NFVCB tried to formalize the industry in 2007, which led to a major falling out with the marketers (see p. 252). The other parastatal charged with matters relating to the film industry, the Nigerian Film Corporation, has also long been accused of ineffectiveness and distance from the Nollywood film industry. While it has various training programs, a film festival, and other accomplishments to its credit, like the NFVCB it is for the most part a stagnant bureaucracy primarily devoted to meeting its payroll.

Nollywood's Informality

Nollywood was created in 1992 when informality from below met informality from above: The systems of West African markets could now sponsor and distribute movies, thanks to new video technologies; and the deregulation of the national economy and of the media enforced by Nigeria's creditors created a chaotic vacuum rather than the envisioned neoliberal economic boom.[2] The full-blown economic and social crisis created by the structural adjustment program from 1986 on devastated formal sector manufacturing, left the educational system in ruins, made civil servants' salaries nearly worthless, starved government television of resources, and so on. In this dire context, people turned to the informal sector to get by, and they turned to Nollywood for entertainment and for a creative interpretation of what was happening to their society.

The informal sector proved capable, in some instances at least, of turning into something much more than a survival strategy. Igbo informal business groups distinguished themselves by making the transition from trading to making things like car parts (Deborah Brautigam, cited in Meager 2010, p. 5). Kate Meagher has studied the informal shoe and garment manufacturing clusters in Aba; these industrial clusters began to flourish in the 1980s and by 2000 had an annual turnover of nearly US$200 million and employed 50,000 workers (Meagher 2010, p. 1). The Nollywood "marketers" (i.e. distributors, who are also the main source of film financing), who were originally importers of electronics, are organized in strikingly similar fashion: They too cluster together (Idumota Market in Lagos was the first center, followed by Iweka Road in Onitsha, Pound Road in Aba, and Alaba Market in Lagos,). Workers are brought in through an apprenticeship system that trains them and then, at the end of the apprenticeship period, sets them up with capital to launch their own businesses. This apprenticeship system helps give the film industry its shape: Many small enterprises sharing the market, competing but also cooperating with one another, with a dense network of social linkages. Filmmakers and outside observers of the industry have always complained about this system as a closed cabal and an ethnic (Igbo) mafia.

New video technologies allowed films to be made and distributed on this basis, on the model of the African popular arts, which are based in the informal economy as largely unregulated enterprises with low bars to entry in terms of capital, training, and equipment (Barber, 1987). The Yoruba traveling theatre tradition, which had already transitioned to television and celluloid filmmaking, quickly moved into producing video films.

The Nollywood branch of the new video film industry, which began in Igbo but quickly switched to producing in English, was accused from the beginning of being an "all-comers affair," because of the aforesaid low bar to entry. But the hegemonic element in the production side of Nollywood was a cadre of professionals who had been trained in television – in most cases, by the Nigerian Television Authority (NTA), which was at this time another formal sector institution in crisis – and who brought an aesthetics and culture with them, even as they also embraced the desire to make feature films. Bond Emeruwa estimates that at the end of the 1990s he was one of about 60 video film directors in Lagos who had experience working in television (personal communication). These people clustered in the Lagos mainland neighborhood of Surulere. Many of them were Igbo, and many of them were not. Like their leading actors, most of them had been to university.

The cultural hybridity of this grafting of the Surulere independent filmmakers onto the Idumota marketers contributed to the strength of Nollywood, but it was never an easy relationship and it has not gotten better with time. The filmmakers resented their dependence on the uneducated marketers, who they felt did not understand film or the potential of the film industry if it were organized on a more formal basis, as in the rest of the world. But the power and self-confidence of the marketers grew as improving video technology and experience being around filmmaking led them to launch into making their own films without the expertise of the Lagos professionals. The power struggle between the two groups came to a head in 2003 when the independent filmmakers attempted to set up their own parallel distribution system. The marketers crushed this initiative by isolating the startup system, which had few outlets and a small number of films to offer the public. By 2010–2012, the long-standing opposition had crystallized in two very different kinds of movie produced by two distinct formations: The so-called "New Nollywood" and "Asaba" films (see pp. 246, 255, 261).

The immediate basis of the new industry was what Brian Larkin calls the "infrastructure of piracy" (Larkin, 2004) – the system set up to provide cassettes for the VCRs that had become common middle-class possessions during the oil boom years. The electronics dealers who would become the Nollywood marketers imported blank cassette tapes, dubbed foreign films onto them without authorization, and distributed them through a national network of video shops and rental clubs. It was a short step to reproduce and distribute original Nigerian films.

Video technology is inherently vulnerable to unauthorized reproduction, and piracy has always been a basic structuring condition of Nollywood, determining the business model of rapidly cranking out cheap productions, since pirates will certainly exploit any film with a large budget.

Piracy is characteristic of informal markets, which often exist in a gray zone between legal and illegal. Piracy has strong and variable social, cultural, and political dimensions. Lobato lists six different conceptions of piracy: As theft, free enterprise, free speech authorship, resistance, and access (Lobato 2012, chapter 5); see also Lobato and Thomas, 2015). In Nigeria as in other places, pirates and legitimate marketers are often not different people. The marketers started out as pirates of foreign films, after all. The general public has been disinclined to take the problem seriously, in spite of various campaigns by filmmakers and the government. Alessandro Jedlowski describes how intellectual property laws introduced under British colonialism were meant to protect British, not Nigerian interests, and though local cultural producers have been agitating since the 1970s for the protections they need, they still have to struggle against a general sense that intellectual property laws continue to be foreign impositions. If intellectual property laws aren't seen as legitimate, they are very hard to enforce. And people have reasons to be grateful to the pirates – their prices are low, and they give almost instant access to films, including new Hollywood and Bollywood films, that would otherwise be unavailable (Jedlowski, 2016b). People argue, in defense of pirates, that they open up new markets: The whole enormous audience for Nigerian movies across the African continent and in the Caribbean was almost entirely created by pirates.

These arguments are cold comfort to filmmakers who have taken out a loan against their house to make a film that they then cannot sell because the market is already flooded with pirated copies. The government makes noises about protecting intellectual property rights but has never done so in a sustained, effective manner. The piracy problem is worse now than it has ever been; one aspect of the problem is that the piratical marketers have more money than anyone else in the industry and give some of it to politicians at election time, guaranteeing government inaction (Tunde Kelani, personal communication).

Government Interventions

As people in the industry have always pointed out, the Nigerian government did approximately nothing to help establish and build the video film industry. But eventually the government could not ignore the economic importance of the film industry, and – with trepidation – its primacy in shaping Nigeria's image.

In 2007, the NFVCB made a major effort to restructure the film industry by decreeing a new distribution framework (Bud, 2014a; Miller, 2016; National Film and Video Censors Board, 2007; Obiaya, 2012). This was basically an attempt to formalize the industry, thereby attracting formal sector investments and generally creating the conditions for expansion. Marketers were required to demonstrate all the trappings of formality: Written records, bank accounts, a certain level of capitalization, legal representation, and so on. The marketers of Idumota, Alaba, and Onitsha believed these measures were designed to put them out of business and fought back bitterly. There was a widespread sense that the people who had created the industry were being treated badly, though there was also a widespread frustration with the blocked potential resulting from the marketers' conception of the film business. The timing of the initiative was unfortunate, coinciding with the 2007 global financial crisis, which discouraged capitalist investors – in any event, very few of them appeared. The marketers fought the initiative to a standstill, but in the process the market was seriously disorganized, resulting in a sharp if temporary drop in the level of production and a dramatic and lasting increase in piracy, which had been running at a manageable 10% but jumped to 80 or 90%.

The federal government made dramatic new investments in the industry under President Goodluck Jonathan, who as governor of Bayelsa State had inherited the patronage of the African Movie Academy Awards, the most important such annual event, and remained interested in Nollywood. In 2010 he announced a US$200 million fund to support the entertainment industry, followed by another fund (of US$20 million) in 2013 and a third in 2015. The money was to make loans to filmmakers to make high-quality films, support training programs, and help create better distribution systems.

The dramatic first result of these funds was to demonstrate the chasm between the informal film industry and the formal procedures – gruelingly elaborate bureaucratic procedures – for getting access to the money. For years, no director based in Nigeria managed to negotiate the paperwork and to supply evidence of the collateral required for the loans. The first filmmaking loans were made to Nigerian filmmakers based in the United Kingdom and the United States who were used to negotiating formal sector film funding systems, and the resulting films were not commercially successful (Anyiam-Osigwe and Ogunyemi, 2015). What worked better was providing capital to companies constructing (or upgrading) multiplex cinemas, to the distribution companies set up to service those cinemas, and to some film studio facilities (Eniola, 2015). (The multiplexes had begun to appear in 2004; by 2015, thanks in part to the government money, there were 25 of them, with many more planned.) In other words, what worked was giving money to those who did not need it because they were already able to raise money in capital markets (Ihidero, 2015). Nollywood proper benefited little, but it (or certain elements within it) was sent into something of a frenzy by the tantalizing prospect of the big pile of money on the table. The training programs were the part of the funds that they could get their hands on, and these programs were widely seen as a "come and chop" opportunity (Anyiam-Osigwe and Ogunyemi, 2015). Chris Ihidero, in an open letter to the in-coming President Buhari entitled "Please, Don't Give Nollywood Money," complained that "A rent-seeking mentality has descended on the industry like evil spirit and it's eating away its soul." Commercial filmmakers should take risks, he argued; what the industry needs the government to do is ensure a working market by moving against pirates, and to help to build 1,000 community cinemas (Ihidero 2015).

These community cinemas would serve the mass of the population (as opposed to the elite audience at the multiplexes) and provide a strong, reliable revenue stream parallel to – and potentially larger than – the piracy-prone market for discs. Such small theatres have been much talked about, though so far (in July 2016) few such theatres are operating. Government participation in creating them – perhaps donating land, which can be very expensive in urban areas, facilitating permitting, and so on – is highly desirable if not necessary.

Government regulation of the market for discs (around 2000, the standard format for Nollywood films shifted from video cassettes to video compact discs – a cheaper alternative to DVDs) is fundamental, as filmmakers have been arguing since the beginning of Nollywood. When bankers or other potential formal sector investors look at the existing pirate-ridden market for Nollywood films, they cannot see how an expensive film could possibly make its money back. Only the government can clean up the market.

So government still has not acted as the partner the film industry needs. But they are thinking about one another and have begun to mix socially. In August

2014, Omoni Oboli premiered her film *Being Mrs. Elliot* at Aso Rock, the presidential palace, with Goodluck Jonathan, his vice president, and a roomful of chieftains of the ruling People's Democratic Party dining with her and watching the film. During the 2015 election campaign, film celebrities played high-profile roles in support of Jonathan and against him (Husseini, 2015). The actor/director Desmond Elliot was elected to Lagos State House of Assembly that year. Other famous actors have taken political appointments, including Kanayo O. Kanayo, Richard Mofe-Damijo, BobManuel Udokwu, and Sam Dede. In early 2016, it was announced that the Nigeria Police – the national force – was sponsoring a television series, designed to influence the public's image of the police, directed by the leading Nollywood figure Lancelot Imasuen (Njoku 2016). "Reciprocal convergence of elites" is the political scientist Jean-François Bayart's phrase for a fundamental African form of organizing and distributing power, as politicians, military men, businessmen, and traditional rulers jointly form a ruling class (Bayart, 1993). Nollywood celebrities have begun to figure in such configurations – in minor roles, but still, they are in the picture.

Corporate Interventions

Jade Miller, in her recent book-length study of Nollywood's informality, defines its "basic intersecting constituents" as follows:

> 1) *not documenting sales* or most other distribution figures in any publicly accessible or externally scrutinisable fashion, 2) *not utilizing prosecutable legal contracts* for employment or other business relationships, 3) *not using agents* or other formal inputs such as accredited schools for talent recruitment, 4) *not pursuing copyright violations* via legal frameworks and 5) *privileging undocumented financing and distribution networks* and spurning alternatives (collectively not pursuing in good faith any of the four aforementioned areas of potential formalization when opportunity presents). (Miller 2016, pp. 31–32)

According to Meagher, the formality/informality binary has come to be mostly defined in terms of state regulation or its absence (Meagher 2010, p. 14). But another way is through the contrast between the unwritten opacity of informal economic organization and the liquid clarity of corporate capitalism. It is on this basis that John C. McCall argues that the commercial business of Nollywood is not capitalist. He follows Hernando de Soto in arguing that the Third World suffers from the inability to turn wealth into capital because of lack of written documentation – a house owned for generations cannot be used as collateral for a loan for lack of a piece of paper demonstrating legal title, for example (McCall, 2012). Miller repeatedly stresses how the marketers have deliberately kept the whole distribution system opaque so that potential formal sector capitalist investors cannot get the numbers – for estimated sales and so on – that they need to conduct business, thereby ensuring the marketers' continued control of a domain only they can fully understand (and avoiding taxation).

And the business culture of the marketers discourages accumulation of capital. When marketers have made money from films they have not reinvested it in their business; rather than building studios or acquiring equipment, they invest in real estate or hotels. The more important marketers seem not to try to dominate the market. The enormous growth of Nollywood since 1992 has produced many small producers and marketers but no really big ones.

This has left them vulnerable to the intervention of corporate capitalism, which recently has decisively altered the Nigerian film industry and may come to control it.

The chains of multiplex cinemas that have already been mentioned are being built by Nigerian-owned companies. National capital, with government support, dominates this new sector, but, as Connor Ryan shows, these cinemas and the upscale malls in which they are found are nodes in a transnational neoliberal consumer economy and culture (Ryan, 2015). The multiplexes are socially exclusive, charging a forbidding US$8 per ticket – nearly a week's earnings for much of the population – and at first they showed Hollywood films exclusively. Lately cheaper midweek tickets have been introduced, broadening the audience, and Nollywood films are now regularly programmed.

The multiplexes are a crucial element in the business model for "New Nollywood" films – films by independent producer/directors, made with higher budgets, better equipment, and more care, so that they can plausibly fill big screens (Adejunmobi, 2014; Haynes, 2014). Foreign distribution, mostly to the African diaspora, is also crucial. New Nollywood is part of a new segmentation of the Nollywood audience and industry, which in turn is part of a new segmentation of Nigerian society into increasingly consolidated classes. Ryan argues New Nollywood films are made to be integral to the neoliberal consumer context of the malls (Ryan, 2015). The economic basis of New Nollywood is extremely precarious. Nigerian filmmakers complain they are given only short runs in the multiplexes, often at less desirable times, and they see only a fraction of the box office take. Few Nollywood films actually make much money in the theatres, though red-carpet premieres are crucial to publicity campaigns.

Larger transnational corporations have intervened in other sectors. They have always sponsored a corner of the Nigeria media through ad agencies that own their own studios; once concentrated in Surulere, these studios are now mostly in Ikeja, another Lagos neighborhood, near the companies they serve. Footage shot in Lagos is sent to South Africa or London for editing. There is very limited overlap between the professionals who produce slick ads for television or the impressively sophisticated and expensively-produced Nigerian music videos, on the one hand, and on the other, Nollywood people, who, brilliant as they may be at improvised location shooting, very seldom can afford to pay for studio time and seldom know how to use it efficiently (Pat Nebo, personal communication 2015). But these advertising and music video professionals and their equipment provide a reservoir of talent which corporations can draw on as they expand their range of activities.

Nollywood arose during a period when global capitalism largely lost interest in Africa, which seemed too poor, crisis-ridden, and corrupt to be worth troubling with, apart from the extraction of natural resources. But as the era of "Afropessimism" (very roughly, from the mid-1980s to about 2006) gave way to the "Africa rising" narrative, Nigeria enjoyed a sustained period of high growth rates and a sudden influx of foreign direct investment. Capitalism must keep colonizing new territories (or intensifying its exploitation) in order to keep up its rate of profit, and the enormous potential profits of Nollywood attracted its attention. But the marketers of Idumota and Alaba were determined to keep control of the industry and to do things in their own informal way, as the 2007 NFVCB new distribution framework debacle demonstrated.

Thwarted from entering directly into film production and distribution, transnational corporations came in around the edges. They exploited Nollywood's celebrity culture, using stars to advertise their products and then, from 2007, hired them as "brand ambassadors" who are kept on a stipend and expected to make frequent public appearances to support their corporate sponsors. The big stars (such as Funke Akindele, Genevieve Nnaji, and Jim Iyke) now make at least as much from such sponsorships as they do from acting (Osae-Brown, 2013). Telecommunications companies and breweries took the lead; they also dominated live entertainment through heavily branded tours by music and standup comedy acts. *Big Brother Africa*, a South African-coproduced version of the television reality game show, was an enormous hit across the continent from 2003, ushering in an epoch of corporately-sponsored reality television programs, often local franchises or imitations of successful transnational models. Reality television is extremely popular and cheap to make, and it generated its own crop of celebrities.

But it was dominating the international distribution of Nollywood films that gave transnational corporations real power in the film industry. Nollywood films always found their way across the African continent and the diaspora, but the informal character of the industry meant that it never controlled this dimension. Sometimes traders bought films in bulk in Idumota or Alaba and took them abroad, but mostly the export market was in the hands of pirates. Nollywood made virtually no profit from international distribution until around 2003, when the American market was organized to the extent that producers could sell a film's North American rights to a distributor in New York for a few thousand dollars, and the Odeon cinema chain in London began cultivating an audience that would turn out for red-carpet premieres and support a short run in four or five theatres.

In late 2003, a South African broadcasting conglomerate began broadcasting Africa Magic, a satellite television channel devoted to Nollywood films, on its DStv platform. It quickly attracted a wide audience across most of the countries in Sub-Saharan Africa, including Nigeria, which is the biggest market for Africa Magic's parent company MultiChoice. More channels were subsequently added, carrying Hausa and Yoruba films, and then Swahili ones for the East African market. "Africa Magic" now has seven themed channels, most of them heavily dependent on Nigerian content.

There may be 20 million Nigerians living overseas; in large part the product of brain drain, as a group this diaspora is very well educated and affluent, and it remains closely connected with Nigeria. As an audience, it is supplemented by other African emigrants who watch Nigerian films. This far-flung, dispersed community seized on the Internet as an important mode of communication with home and with itself. Businesses sprang up selling or renting Nollywood films on disc over the Internet or streaming them. Mostly these businesses did not bother to locate the films' producers and send them money. Fans put up their favorite films on YouTube, in ten-minute segments, producing a vast wiki-generated cultural commons of thousands of films.

Into this anarchic, scarcely monetized situation came iROKO Partners, founded by Jason Njoku, a London-born child of the Nigerian diaspora, whose YouTube channel NollywoodLove went live in 2011. Six months later, it had 500,000 registered users; a few months after that, it had a catalogue of 5,000 films, viewers in 178 countries, and US$8 million in startup capital from an American hedge fund (Anonymous, 2012). In 2015, iROKOtv announced it had hit a billion views on YouTube (Anonymous, 2015), though the center of its business had long since shifted from ad revenues from the YouTube channel to a Netflix-style paid subscription model. Nearly all this business is outside Nigeria, where broadband is still not fast enough to permit streaming of full-length films. (Constantly pressing against this limit, in 2015 iROKO introduced an Android-based service in Nigeria through which subscribers download films to their phones, however long that takes, and then watch the downloaded film without buffering problems.) iROKO dominates the business of streaming Nollywood films, though it has many competitors.

Nollywood experienced these encounters with corporate capitalism primarily as pain. The constant, ubiquitous television broadcasting of its films in Nigeria on many satellite and terrestrial stations has sharply reduced the profits for sales of films on disc, on top of the chronic problems of piracy and overproduction. The market for selling physical copies of films to consumers, always the heart of the Nollywood economy, has declined precipitously in Nigeria and also abroad, where easy access to films over the Internet has had the same effect as television broadcasting – why buy two films on disc for US$5 when the same amount buys a month's access to iROKOtv's enormous catalogue?

The payments that the corporations offer producers does not begin to compensate for the lost revenue from disc sales. When iROKOtv's office in Lagos first opened, Njoku was paying producers as little as US$100 for the rights to stream a film for three years; now he pays from US$4,000 to US$15,000 (Smartmonkeytv, 2014). Africa Magic has tried to shield its payments from publicity, but early on, rumor had it they paid only US$700 for three years' broadcasting rights, rising later to a few thousand dollars. Nollywood independent producers often expressed anger at these levels of payment, but marketers would sell rights they controlled more cheerfully – it was extra money after the films had had their run in the disc market, and if the payments were small, so were the budgets of the films. (The average budget was something like US$80,000.) The corporations justified their low payments in relation to international norms, where broadcast and streaming rights are a minor source of income after theatrical release and DVD sales. But for Nollywood, there normally was no theatrical release, and now that the profits had gone out of the disc market, they saw the corporations making money and expanding their reach by leaps and bounds while Nollywood went hungry. This led to bitterness.[3]

Njoku is stung by the accusation that iROKO is "bad for Nollywood"; this is one of the motivations of his blog, "Just Me. Jason Njoku," at jason.com.ng. He claims that, at the beginning, producers were ready to sell him permanent streaming rights for US$1,000 per film, but he passed because he thought it would be taking undue advantage. He complains that the Nollywood marketers declined to join forces with him as he struggled to reduce Internet piracy, which had been more or less total in the days when he was establishing the YouTube channel NollywoodLove. Google has software that instantly detects unauthorized video content, and iROKO's team pursued cases against pirates in Accra and several American cities. (Once he switched to the subscription model, he abandoned this fight.) The marketers also declined to heed his advice that they should look to the future because the disc-based market would inevitably die – he was aware of this happening in the West from 2010. The marketers have been content to throw their films up on the Internet by the thousands in return for tiny ad revenues. Njoku argues, bitterly, that the marketers have thereby destroyed the commercial value of the whole catalogue of Nollywood films and severely compromised the future by training consumers in the United States and the United Kingdom – the largest and most affluent markets for streamed Nollywood films – to expect free content. You cannot expect new good films to be made out of free, he says (Njoku, 2015b, 2016a).

These things happened in 2013: Al Jazeera headlined, "Africa on the verge of Internet boom: McKinsey study says continent could gain US$300 billion by 2025 if it embraces Internet as it did mobile phones" (Pizzi, 2013). Facebook and a number of corporate partners announced Internet.org, whose purpose, Mark Zuckerberg said, "is to make Internet access available to the two-thirds of the world who are not yet connected." Google announced Project Link, to build a model high speed fiber network in Kampala, later adding Ghana. And Shaibu Husseini of the Lagos *Guardian* wrote a dispiriting year-end survey of Nollywood, reporting that the Nollywood guilds were still busy squabbling and the government's large-scale investment in film production was still going nowhere because Nollywood filmmakers could not meet its bureaucratic requirements (Husseini,

2015). It was hard not to conclude that the transnationals were going to have their way with this situation and that they would own the future.

For Nollywood, the most portentous developments of the year were that iROKO Partners launched Rok Studios in Lagos, a new division to produce its own original films and television serials and to finance others with partners; and Africa Magic also began commissioning large amounts of original content. (Since 2008 it had been broadcasting *Tinsel*, an expensively-produced and popular serial about the entertainment industry made in Lagos under close supervision by South African executives.) In 2015 EbonyLife TV, a new affiliate of the conglomerate that owns Africa Magic, began commissioning the same sort of film as Africa Magic. They are short (an hour long), produced on budgets that are tiny even in the Nollywood context (about US$8,000), and are made to strict, corporately-mandated standards: The actors must be young and beautiful and speak clear, grammatical English, and the locations must be swanky. The opening graphics can be impressively sophisticated, but the scripts are negligible and the actors tend to come from reality television if they have any acting experience at all. Mo Abudu, the CEO of EbonyLife TV, reportedly tells her staff that *Real Housewives of Atlanta* should be their model (Tsika, 2015). The whole budget is spent creating a certain look.

These might be the emptiest productions ever offered to the Nigerian public and are a pure example of corporately-produced mass culture, designed to model consumption in a capitalist economy. Karin Barber's influential description of the African popular arts defines them (in terms derived from the Birmingham School of Marxist cultural and media studies) as being the opposite of this kind of mass culture: The popular arts are a grassroots phenomenon expressing the consciousness of a heterogeneous, non-elite public, and are produced by people who are not very different from the people they are made for (Barber, 1987). The popular arts are certainly commercial and express the masses' desire for wealth and what it can bring, but they are capable of scathing criticism of how wealth and power are generated and used. Nollywood was created as such a popular art and it has, from its first films about "money rituals" and other "get-rich-quick" schemes, mounted such critiques (Haynes, 2016b).

Africa Magic, iROKO Partners, and EbonyLife TV all plan to make hundreds or even thousands of hours of original content per year, and they are by no means the only companies moving into production. They are all creating television serials as well as feature films: Serials are cheaper to make per hour, a crucial consideration for corporations mass-producing content, and the corporate platforms have the stability for serials, as the market for discs does not (see Adejunmobi, 2003, who describes Nollywood's characteristic multi-part films as "short serials"). Television is in Nollywood's DNA; another influence may be the world-wide golden age in long-form television, pioneered in the US by HBO. Some of the new Nigerian serials are quite good (personal favorites include iROKOtv's *Jenifa's Diary* and *Festac Town*, see Haynes, 2016a).

The corporations invest in prestige projects as well as mass-producing filler. New Nollywood began with no support from media corporations, though several productions were rescued by subventions from telecommunication companies. iROKOtv began by ignoring any film it could not buy at rock-bottom prices, which excluded New Nollywood, but Njoku now boasts that he has put money into nearly all New Nollywood films. EbonyLife produced *Fifty* (2015), a glossy film directed by Biyi Bandele, the British-based director of the major international coproduction *Half of a Yellow Sun* (2013). For his current project *CEO*, Kunle Afolayan, the leading New Nollywood director, accessed funds from the government's loan scheme and got sponsorship from Africa Magic as well as Air France and others. It seems a sign of the time that the film is about the selection of a new corporate CEO through a process reminiscent of reality television shows like *Big Brother*; the story, casting, and locations all show a strong commitment to reaching an African continental audience, not just a Nigerian one.

New Nollywood has begun to overlap with the corporately-produced films, then, but it remains a distinct formation. New Nollywood is an auteurist director's cinema, and while this is of some interest to the corporations, they think differently. The New Nollywood directors are a diverse lot, but the corporate types are a new and different type, or array of types, from Mo Abudu, the force behind EbonyLife, "the African Oprah," who morphed from a human resources consultant for the international accounting firm Arthur Andersen to talk show host, television producer, and media personality; to Jason Njoku of iROKO Partners, a self-described geek whose graph-studded blog chronicles his life as a Silicon Valley-style tech entrepreneur, a heroic executive riding the turbulent waves of late capitalism; or iROKO's polished vice president of monetization, Oluchi Enuha, who went from Harvard to Merrill Lynch and then home to Nigeria as a business development analyst, getting a Gates Foundation grant for a project to bring mobile banking to rural areas before joining iROKO Partners.

In 2015 iROKO Global was created as a new division of the company, reflecting the explosive growth of a new dimension of its business: Packaging Nollywood content for corporate clients, including airlines and giant media companies like the French Canal + and the Chinese StarTimes. iROKO has acquired linear television channels on three carriers (Ochelle, 2015: Njoku 2015c). These deals are far more lucrative than consumer subscriptions, but Njoku declares that he is still laser-focused on serving African consumer audiences (Njoku, 2015a, 2015c).

iROKO is swimming with the big fish, who habitually swallow smaller ones. From the beginning, iROKO was called "the Neflix of Africa," but now Netflix wants to be the Netflix of Africa and everywhere else – it announced in January 2016 that it was expanding into 130 more countries, including African ones. This has refocused Njoku's attention on where he can hope to stay competitive or even dominant: Supplying Nollywood's audience with enormous amounts of Nollywood content (Njoku 2016b, 2016c). But, contradictorily, even as he embraces Nollywood as the heart and soul of his business, he has also become definitively fed up with the actually existing Nollywood, declaring that he is through with the Nollywood marketers and the kind of films they produce. Their market for discs has crashed and he thinks 90% of them will disappear in the very near future. He is trying to reduce his dependence on their films to zero as he sharply ramps up production of original content (Anonymous, 2015; Njoku, 2015b, 2016b). In January 2016, iROKO raised US$19 million from a second round of venture capital, most of it from the French media company Vivendi, which has declared an interest in eventually acquiring iROKO entirely. Most of this money will be spent on content creation (Fick, 2016; Njoku, 2016c).

The current Nollywood scene is more diversified – and unstable – than ever. By 2013, something like half of Nollywood films were being shot in and around Asaba, a pleasant, low-key city across the Niger River from Onitsha, which is a stronghold of the marketers. Asaba is cheap and offers a variety of kinds of location. All sorts of films are shot there, but the term "Asaba films" has come to be used to describe the low end of the Nollywood market. Old-school marketers have reacted to the crisis of profitability in the disc market by doing what they best know how to do: Grinding out very low-budget films (budgets are US$25,000 or so, less than a third of the Nollywood average) very quickly, designed for a short run in the VCD market. The broad middle range of Nollywood films, between Asaba films and New Nollywood productions, still exists.

But increasingly, employment in the film industry means working for the corporations. This is often very badly paid, and filmmakers resent being told what to do. The extremely profitable deals iROKO Global is making with its corporate clients happen far over the heads of the filmmakers whose movies are being resold. They get nothing. In part this is the result of their own business culture, the kind of contracts they entered into. Nollywood is almost entirely based on flat fee payments for outright sales, rather than percentages and residuals: The informal, unwritten character of all transactions means there is no practical way to operate more complex arrangements, even if one were not worried about the endemic piracy and cheating. Flat fee payments are safe and sensible in the context of informality, but are a disaster in the emerging corporate media economy. A new organization, the Audio-Visual Rights Society of Nigeria, was formed in 2014 to oversee payment of royalties (Akande, 2016), but changing the business culture is apt to take time. Tunde Babalola, who wrote for television in the United Kingdom for 15 years before returning to Nigeria to become a sought-after screenwriter for New Nollywood films, told me that he has residuals written into his contracts, but he does not know of anyone else who does this, and he expects to make money from the residuals only when the film is sold abroad, since there is no mechanism for accounting in Nigeria (personal communication, 2015).

So power, profits, and control of Nollywood have been shifting rapidly away from those who created it – who built the systems of production and distribution, assembled a huge transnational audience, and created a whole film culture of genres, themes, stars, stories, and styles. It is hard not to feel this as injustice and exploitation – as strip mining of cultural resources, another example of Africa's heritage being appropriated by those with different notions of property rights. But the capitalists are acting legally and, like Njoku, feel themselves to be acting virtuously – even saving Nollywood from itself. The Surulere independent filmmakers and many others in and around the industry have always thought breaking the power of the marketers was necessary for Nollywood to reach its potential. It is too early to say what the consequences of corporate power will be for the social and cultural character of Nigerian film and television production. I have already suggested that some corporate productions are very bad, but others are good.

One reason for guarded optimism is that both satellite television and the Internet can carry huge amounts of programming – the companies doing business on these platforms are operating big pipes for dispersed, various audiences, so unless they are invested in branding themselves in a particular way, as EbonyLife has done, it is in their interest to carry a broad range of content. Africa Magic has multiplied its channels broadcasting in African languages, and these channels seem to be popular beyond the native speakers of those languages (Ekwuazi 2014), as if the tendency towards cultural homogenization were not inevitable or at least has limits. There is something utopian about the staggering amount and variety of African culture now available at the click of a mouse or a television remote. Events like the Africa Magic Viewers' Choice Awards, with their various categories and continental participation (voting is through the WeChat app), create an awareness of a whole beyond the single channels. John C. McCall called Nollywood "the Pan-Africanism we have" (2007); the corporate media platforms, which would be inconceivable without Nollywood's massive supply of content, are helping to realize this project, though not in the form imagined by W.E.B. Du Bois or Kwame Nkrumah.

The intervention of corporate capitalism into Nollywood has been so dramatic in its speed and in the stark contrast between the corporate actors and the Nollywood marketers that it is hard not to see it in terms of a grand narrative, the classic grand narrative of capitalism overpowering and absorbing prior economic and social forms. In *The Informal Media Economy*, Ramon Lobato and Julian Thomas point out that Hollywood consolidated itself through a similar process of uncompensated appropriation and exploitation of all kinds of resources.

But I want to emphasize how unsettled the current situation is. It is dangerous if not foolish to predict how it will turn out. In her very recent book, Miller shares my sense of an acute conflict: Njoku feels himself to be at war with the Alaba marketers; he and Emeka Mba, architect of the NFVCB's attempt at formalization, are straightforward about their desire to replace the marketers with an oligopoly of fully capitalist firms; and the marketers are fully aware of this and mean to maintain their position of control (Miller 2016, p. 152). She thinks the marketers will win:

> Discourse on Nollywood, the industry, be it popular journalism or academic enquiry, frequently features the question: is this person or that initiative on the horizon going to formalise the industry? Are they going to change it forever to a

form that encourages or enables formal investment and the growth in budgets that comes with it? The answer has been and, at this point, still is always no. Any analysis must be clear about that. No, they probably will not. Despite numerous initiatives, regulations and investments, the industry remains in the hands of the marketers and the physical VCD market....A day will probably come when entertainment content is primarily delivered through virtual networks in Lagos. That day, however, seems to be a long way away. (Miller 2016, p. 155)

Several factors I take as crucial appear only minimally or not at all in her analysis: The new cinemas, mobile phones as an important platform, and the advent of corporately-produced content. So I believe things are moving quickly. But she has strong arguments: Nigeria's infrastructural problems are stubborn obstacles; to be profitable, films still need distribution in physical form in the Nigerian market; and that market remains firmly under the control of the marketers, who are not to be underestimated. And I agree with her conclusion that if and when a corporately-controlled system fully establishes itself, the old informal Nollywood will survive "wherever the gaps between connection to the Network Society then lie" (Miller 2016, p. 158).

Lobato and Thomas similarly tell a story – give us an analytic vocabulary and conceptual framework – that is much less linear, much more fragmented than the grand narrative of corporatization. They teach us to see that media economies normally include formal and informal elements whose relationships are nuanced and shifting, running through cycles of consolidation and fragmentation, sometimes parasitic, sometimes symbiotic, sometimes resistant (Lobato and Thomas, 2015).

In any case, the future will not be entirely up to the transnational corporations. Africa has a long history of thwarting, bending, or negotiating the purposes of foreigners. It is possible the government will decide to enforce the piracy laws, thereby reviving the market for discs. It is certain that many more cinemas will be built – more multiplexes, but also community theatres to serve a popular audience. The community theatres could become the most important revenue stream for Nollywood producers, and the result – one can reasonably hope – would be a continuation, in improved form, of the main lines of the Nollywood tradition and its independent, popular perspective. The corporations are certainly already established as an important element in the situation, but the extent and character of their cultural influence is still unclear.

Notes

1   The concept of the "informal" has proved to be slippery and difficult – as the name suggests, it has been easier to define it by what it is not than by what it is. Keith Hart introduced the concept of the informal economy into African studies (Hart, 1973). Kate Meagher provides a fascinating account of the recent history of the concept. She

collects statements of leading theorists from 2001 to 2007 suggesting that the African informal economy defies rational description and analysis (Meagher 2010, pp. 6–7); later, empirical studies began to catch up with the expanding and therefore more visible informal sector; and then, as neoliberal deregulation – "informality from above" – became the global norm, informality became so pervasive as to throw the concept into crisis. Responses to this global development also created tension between a global/comparativist framework and an Africanist idea that informality was the mark of peculiarly African institutions, histories, and cultures (Meagher 2010, chapter 2). In the story this chapter tells, Nollywood's informality and the formality of government and the corporations contrast so bluntly that the conceptual difficulties do not need urgent attention.

2   This history is described in some detail in Haynes (2016b, chapters 1 and 2).

3   Cf. Miller's useful description of iROKO, where she presents producers vying to sell to iROKO and Africa Magic as the most lucrative and prestigious options, and Njoku as the architect of a policy of paying more than he had to for film rights because he thought the films were worth more and because paying higher prices would discourage competing streaming companies (Miller 2016, pp. 134–142). This account does not actually contradict mine: Producers make the best of a situation they do not like.

References

Abua, Ferdinand O., ed. 2002, 2004. *Film and Video Directory in Nigeria*. Vols. 1 and 2. Abuja, Nigeria: National Film and Video Censors Board.

Adejunmobi, Moradewun. 2003. "Video Film Technology and Serial Narratives in West Africa." In *African Video Film Today*, edited by Foluke Ogunleye, 51–68. Manzini, Swaziland: Academic Publishers.

Adejunmobi, Moradewun. 2014. "Evolving Nollywood Templates for Minor Transnational Film." *Black Camera* 5.2: 74–94.

Adesokan, Akin. 2014. "African Film." In *Africa*, edited by Maria Grosz-Ngaté, John H. Hanson, and Patrick O'Meara, 233–249. Bloomington: Indiana University Press.

Akandeon, Victor. 2016. "Bond Emeruwa Wins as Audio-Visual Rights Chairman." *The Nation*. 30 March. Accessed 1 April 2016. http://thenationonlineng.net/bond-emeruwa-wins-as-audio-visual-rights-chairman/

Anonymous. 2009. "60m Nigerians Now Own Power Generators – MAN." *Vanguard*, 26 January. Accessed 4 December 2010. http://allafrica.com/stories/200901260005.html

Anonymous. 2012. "IROKOtv, the 'Netflix of Africa', Reaches 500,000 Subscribers in less than Six Months." *Balancing Act* 132, 21 June. Accessed 24 June 2012. www.balancingact-africa.com/news/broadcast/issue-no132/distribution/irokotv-the-netflix/bc

Anonymous. 2014. "OSCARS Approves Nigerian Committee for NOLLYWOOD Films." *Premium Times*, 1 Ma. Accessed 17 June 2014. www.premiumtimesng.com/arts-entertainment/159912-oscars-approves-nigerian-committee-nollywood-films.html

Anonymous. 2015. "iROKOtv Crosses One Billion YouTube Mark." *Technology Times Reports*, 19 February. Accessed 1 April 2015. http://technologytimes.ng/irokotv-crosses-one-billion-youtube-mark-sounds-death-knell-alaba-pirates/

Anyiam-Osigwe, Peace, and Dayo Ogunyemi. 2015. "Nollywood And the Creative Industries: A Tale of Two Possibilities." *TNS*, 7 June. Accessed 1 July, 2015. http://tns.ng/nollywood-and-the-creative-industries-a-tale-of-two-possibilities/

Barber, Karin. 1987. "Popular Arts in Africa." *African Studies Review* 30.3:1–78.

Bayart, Jean-François. 1993. *The State in Africa: The Politics of the Belly.* New York: Longman.

Bright, Jack. 2015. "Meet 'Nollywood': The Second Largest Movie Industry in the World." *Fortune*, 24 June. Accessed 22 March 2016. http://fortune.com/2015/06/24/nollywood-movie-industry/

Bud, Alexander. 2014a. "The End of Nollywood's Guilded Age? Marketers, the State and the Struggle for Distribution." *Critical African Studies* 6.1: 91–121.

Bud, Alexander. 2014b. "Hooray for Nollywood? Nigeria Isn't the World's Second-Biggest Film Industry After All." *The Conversation*, 11 April. Accessed 1 May 2014. http://theconversation.com/hooray-for-nollywood-nigeria-isnt-the-worlds-second-biggest-film-industry-after-all-25527

Ekwuazi, Hyginus. 2014. "The Perception/Reception of DSTV/Multichoice's Africa Magic Channels by Selected Nigerian Audiences." *Journal of African Cinemas* 6.1:21–48.

Eniola, Temilade. 2015. "NollyFund: BoI Meets Nollywood Filmmakers at AFFRIF 2015." *Express*, 5 November. Accessed 6 November 2015. http://expressng.com/2015/11/nollyfund-boi-meets-nollywood-filmmakers-at-afriff-2015/

Fick, Maggie. 2016. "iROKOtv Investors Back 'Netflix of Africa' with $19 m Funding." *Financial Times*, 25 January. Accessed 26 January 2016. www.ft.com/intl/cms/s/0/b02cab5e-c378-11e5-b3b1-7b2481276e45.html#axzz43HtbgRie

Gana, D.R. and Clement D. Edekor, eds. 2006. *Film and Video Directory in Nigeria.* Vol. 3. Abuja, Nigeria: National Film and Video Censors Board.

Ganti, Tejaswini. 2015. "Fuzzy Numbers: The Productive Nature of Ambiguity in the Hindi Film Industry." *Comparative Studies of South Asia, Africa and the Middle East* 35.3: 451–465.

Glasspiegel, Wills. 2012. "What Nollywood Tells Us about Nigeria." *TheGuardian.com*, 1 October 2012. Accessed 8 September 2014. www.theguardian.com/world/africa-blog/2012/oct/01/nollywood-nigeria-odia-ofeimun

Hart, Keith. 1973. "Informal Income Opportunities and Urban Employment in Ghana." *The Journal of Modern African Studies*, 1.1: 61–89.

Haynes, Jonathan. 2000. "Introduction." In *Nigerian Video Films*, edited by Jonathan Haynes, 1–36. Athens: Ohio University Press.

Haynes, Jonathan. 2010a. "History, Cyberspace, Borders, and Collective Action: Projects around Nigeria's film culture." Paper delivered at Nollywood: A National Cinema? An International Workshop, Kwara State University, Ilorin, Nigeria, July.

Haynes, Jonathan. 2010b. "What Is to Be Done? Film Studies and Nigerian and Ghanaian Videos." In *Viewing African Cinema in the Twenty-First Century: Art Films and the Nollywood Video Revolution*, edited by Mahir Saul and Ralph A. Austen. 11–25. Athens: Ohio University Press.

Haynes, Jonathan. 2011. "African Cinema and Nollywood: Contradictions." *Situations* 4.1: 67–90.

Haynes, Jonathan. 2014. "'New Nollywood': Kunle Afolayan." *Black Camera* 5.2:53–73.

Haynes, Jonathan. 2016a. "Neoliberalism, Nollywood, and Lagos." In *Global Cinematic Cities: New Landscapes of Film and Media*, edited by Johan Andersson and Lawrence Webb. 59–75. New York: Wallflower/Columbia University Press.

Haynes, Jonathan. 2016b. *Nollywood: The Creation of Nigerian Film Genres*. Chicago: University of Chicago Press.

Husseini, Shaibu. 2015. "How Political Campaigns Split Nollywood." *The Guardian*, 12 April. Accessed 13 April 2015. www.ngrguardiannews.com/2015/04/how-political-campaigns-split-nollywood/

Ihidero, Chris. 2015. "Open letter to President Buhari: Please, Don't Give Nollywood Money." *The Net*, 23 April. Accessed 6 June 2015. http://thenet.ng/2015/04/open-letter-to-president-buhari-please-dont-give-nollywood-money/

Iroh, Eddie. 2009. "Nigeria: Nollywood, Nolly What?" *ThisDay*, 25 May. Accessed 2 April 2011. http://allafrica.com/stories/printable/200905250137.html

Jedlowski, Alessandro. 2016a. "Post-Imperial Affinities: The Nigerian and the Indian Film Industries." Paper presented at New Directions in Nollywood and Nigerian Cinema conference, Columbia University, New York. April.

Jedlowski, Alessandro. 2016b. "Regulating Mobility, Reshaping Accessibility: Nollywood and the Piracy Scapegoat." In *Copyright Africa: How Intellectual Property, Media and Markets Transform Immaterial Cultural Goods*, edited by Ute Röschenthaler and Mamadou Diawara, 292–310. Canon Pyon, UK: Sean Kingston.

Johnston, Andrew, ed. 2015. *Africa Progress Report 2015*. Africa Progress Panel. Accessed 28 February 2016. www.africaprogresspanel.org/publications/policy-papers/2015-africa-progress-report/

Kanzler, Martin and Julio Talavera Milla. 2014. *Focus 2014: World Film Market Trends*. Cannes: European Audiovisual Observatory. Accessed 15 January, 2015. http://issuu.com/marchedufilm/docs/focus_2014

Larkin, Brian. 2004. "Degraded Images, Distorted Sounds: Nigerian Video and the Infrastructure of Piracy." *Public Culture* 16.2:289–314.

Lobato, Ramon. 2012. *Shadow Economies of Cinema: Mapping Informal Film Distribution*. New York: Palgrave Macmillan.

Lobato, Ramon and Julian Thomas. 2015. *The Informal Media Economy*. Malden, MA: Polity.

McCall, John C. 2007. "The Pan-Africanism We Have: Nollywood's Invention of Africa." *Film International* 5.4.28: 92–97.

McCall, John C. 2012. "The Capital Gap: Nollywood and the Limits of Informal Trade." *Journal of African Cinemas* 4.1: 9–23.

Meagher, Kate. 2010. *Identity Economics: Social Networks and the Informal Economy in Nigeria*. Rochester, NY: James Currey.

Miller, Jade. 2016. *Nollywood Central*. London: BFI/Palgrave.

Moss, Todd, and Madeleine Gleave. 2014. "How Can Nigeria Cut CO_2 Emissions by 63%? Build More Power Plants." Center for Global Development blog, 10 January. Accessed 21 February 2016. www.cgdev.org/blog/how-can-nigeria-cut-co2-emissions-63-build-more-power-plants

National Film and Video Censors Board. 2007. *Comprehensive Document on the Distribution, Exhibition and Marketing of Films and Video Works in Nigeria*. Abuja: National Film and Video Censors Board.

Njoku, Benjamin. 2016. "Lancelot Lands Multi-Million Naira Deals with Nollytv, Nigeria Police." *Vanguard*, 17 March. Accessed 18 March 2016. www.vanguardngr.com/2016/03/lancelot-lands-multi-million-naira-deals/

Njoku, Jason. 2015a. "iROKO at 4." *Just Me. Jason Njoku*, 1 December. Accessed 1 December 2015. www.jason.com.ng/post/134326162730/irokotv-at-4 Accessed 1 April, 2018. https://jason.com.ng/irokotv-at-4-bcc5fa050b89

Njoku, Jason. 2015b. "iROKO. Bad for the Industry II." *Just Me. Jason Njoku*, 20 July. Accessed 23 July 2015. www.jason.com.ng/post/124569515020/iroko-bad-for-the-industry-ii Accessed 1 April 2018. https://jason.com.ng/iroko-bad-for-the-industry-ii-a5515ffd9cbd

Njoku, Jason. 2015c. "iROKO goes global." *Just Me. Jason Njoku,* 3 November. Accessed 5 November 2015. www.jason.com.ng/post/132502411380/iroko-goes-global Accessed 1 April, 2018. https://jason.com.ng/iroko-goes-global-d9415dde0e37

Njoku, Jason. 2016a "The Death of an Industry." *Just Me. Jason Njoku*, 4 January. Accessed 1 April, 2018. https://jason.com.ng/the-death-of-an-industry-80b5cf9639d3

Njoku, Jason. 2016b. "Netflix in Africa." *Just Me. Jason Njoku*, 7 January. Accessed 7 January 2016. www.jason.com.ng/post/136800839840/netflix-in-africa Accessed 1 April, 2018. https://jason.com.ng/netflix-in-africa-b01fea9706da

Njoku, Jason. 2016c "Not another raise!" *Just Me. Jason Njoku*, 25 January. Accessed 25 January 2016. www.jason.com.ng/ Not another raise! Accessed 1 April, 2018. https://jason.com.ng/not-another-raise-1bb3e233c48c

Obiaya, Ikechukwu. 2012. "Restructuring the Nigerian Video Film Industry." Ph.D. dissertation, Department of Communications, Universidad de Navarra.

Ochelle, Felicia Omari. 2015. "iROKOtv is now on TV." *Ventures Africa*, 15 April. Accessed 6 June 2015. http://venturesafrica.com/irokotv-is-now-on-tv/

Okome, Onookome. 2007. "Nollywood: Spectatorship, Audience and the Sites of Consumption." *Postcolonial Text* 3.2:1–21. Accessed 4 December 2010. http://journals.sfu.ca/pocol/index.php/pct/article/view/763/425

Osae-Brown, Funke. 2013. "Firms Invest N500m in Celebrities for Brand Reach." *Nigerian Entertainment Today*, 6 March. Accessed 7 March 2013. http://thenet.ng/2013/03/firms-invest-n500m-in-nigerian-celebrities-for-brand-reach/

Pizzi, Michael. 2013. "Africa on the Verge of Internet Boom." *Aljazeera America*, 22 November. Accessed 10 January 2014. http://america.aljazeera.com/articles/2013/11/22/africa-on-the-vergeofinternetboom.html

Ryan, Connor. 2015. "New Nollywood: A Sketch of Nollywood's Metropolitan New Style." *African Studies Review* 58.3: 55–76.

Smartmonkeytv. 2014. "Jason Njoku, iROKO on launching its production arm" (interview). 9 July. Accessed 1 March 2016. www.youtube.com/watch?v=h_JYhyK_8-8

Tsika, Noah. 2015. "From the Chibok Girls to the Ebola Outbreak: Nollywood's Responsiveness to Current Events." Paper presented at the Society for Cinema and Media Studies Annual Conference, Montreal, 28 March.

UNESCO Institute of Statistics. "Analysis of the UIS International Survey on Feature Film Statistics." 2009. Accessed 8 September 2014. www.uis.unesco.org/FactSheets/Documents/Infosheet_No1_cinema_EN.pdf

Yusuf, Ibrahim Apekhade. 2014. "Nigeria: Overrun by Electric Power Generators." *The Nation*, 9 November. Accessed 4 December 2014. http://thenationonlineng.net/nigeria-overrun-by-electric-power-generators/

Filmography

Afolayan, Kunle. (2016). *The CEO*. Nigeria: Golden Effects.

Bandele, Biyi. (2015). *Fifty*. Nigeria: EbonyLife Films.

Bandele, Biyi. (2013). *Half of a Yellow Sun*. United Kingdom: Slate.

Big Brother Africa. (2003–). Television serial. South Africa: MultiChoice.

Festac Town. (2014). Web serial. Nigeria: Rok.

Jenifa's Diary. (2010–). Web serial. Nigeria: Scene One.

Oboli, Omoni. (2014). *Being Mrs. Elliot*. Nigeria: Dioni Visions.

Tinsel. (2008–). Television serial. Nigeria: MultiChoice.

12

Nollywood Chronicles

Migrant Archives, Media Archeology, and the Itineraries of Taste

Noah Tsika

Whether understood as a wellspring of VHS cassettes, a source of VCDs and DVDs, a producer of celluloid films for multiplex exhibition, or a fount of streaming media, Nollywood is characterized first and foremost by the missing archive – by the absence of consistent, reliable systems of classification and preservation for its audiovisual output. At present, a certain paradox appears to structure the intelligibility of this heritage: Nollywood films vanish with startling frequency while simultaneously appearing in unprecedented numbers on various websites. What to some might seem an unwelcome overabundance might, to others, seem a tragic loss. The digital turn has done little to ensure the survival of the so-called "old Nollywood" (low-budget films produced in a style associated with the industry's infancy), and no large-scale effort is currently underway to preserve even the biggest VHS hits – the landmarks of yesteryear. iROKOtv, for example – a subscription service devoted to streaming Nigerian and Ghanaian films – is firmly committed to recent fare and has rarely reached into the pre-2010 period; its business model rests on ideals of selectivity and contemporaneity that are patently incompatible with comprehensive historical preservation. In many cases, scholars committed to Nollywood history must rely on their own material collections (often garnered from the markets of West Africa), or on the occasional, ephemeral, altogether imperfect uploading of old films to YouTube, Vimeo, DailyMotion, and other video-sharing sites. Nigerian blogs may routinely publish retrospective celebrations – lists of the ten best Nollywood films of the 1990s, for instance – but the authors of such accounts must, in many cases, write from memory, without the aid of surviving films. This chapter addresses Nollywood's missing or "migrant" archives and how they have shaped popular and scholarly accounts of the industry over the past several years. How do we watch, teach, and write about Nollywood in the context of its simultaneous disappearance and proliferation?

Exploring a range of methods for making certain Nollywood histories more intelligible and contextual despite the losses and suppressions that have plagued the industry, I argue that structured obsolescence applies as much to Nollywood's films as to its constitutive technologies, promoting the blurring of all distinctions between audiovisual narratives and their material manifestations, and sustaining Nollywood's alterity in the context of "world cinema" (a designation that, in Kenneth W. Harrow's reading, "has sought to keep African cinema in its place" (Harrow 2015, p. 26)). The tendency to bifurcate Nollywood into "old" and "new" mimics the logic of structured obsolescence, whereby extant texts are understood not as reusable or destined for libraries, museums, and other archives but as current and future waste – the refuse against which imminent evolutionary developments must be framed. To be sure, this is a partly subjective bifurcation that is by no means characteristic of scholarship on Nollywood, but it appears to be increasingly convenient, at least among some producers of Nollywood content, as a means of distinguishing their work from stereotypes associated with low-budget, generic antecedents. As Moradewun Adejunmobi points out, Old Nollywood involves "a particular mode of film financing, production, and distribution" that is not necessarily limited to the historical past – that persists as a marker of "low quality," particularly in the face of big-budget productions aimed at the multiplexes. But these multiplexes, like any number of other sites or "platforms" for Nollywood content, impose their own limitations on how Nollywood films become intelligible as such. Jonathan Gray's notion of "clusters of authorship," which refers to the multiple and often contradictory pressures placed on any given media text as it travels through various streams (or atop the "waves" that Adejunmobi (2015), Manthia Diawara (2010), and MaryEllen Higgins (2015) have described in relation to African cinema), is thus central to this chapter, as I consider Nollywood's changing platforms and their effects on Nollywood content, framing this investigation in terms of a concern for film preservation and historiography. As Nollywood becomes "new," it not only loses its implicitly (and, often, explicitly) denigrated pasts, including those films that have never been preserved and those practices that have never been properly understood, much less mentioned in popular or scholarly accounts; it is also reinserted into a global market logic that militates against reuse, as though Nollywood films were mere appliances (like laptops or smartphones), rather than discrete entertainment forms or works of art. Nollywood has long offered resistance to imposed itineraries, however, and interspersed throughout this chapter are unheralded examples of extraction, recycling, and remediation that complicate conventional accounts of Nollywood history and point to some of the industry's possible futures.

I begin by interrogating the practice of media archeology as a means of bringing to light those aspects of African film history – both material and discursive – that are routinely left out of popular as well as scholarly surveys. Committed to the Foucauldian uncovering of the mediated "invention" of certain aesthetic standards, cultural practices, and social "certainties," media archeology, in the words of Erkki Huhtamo and Jussi Parikka, "rummages textual, visual, and auditory archives as well as collections of artifacts, emphasizing both the discursive and the material manifestations of culture. Its explorations move fluidly between disciplines, although it does not have a permanent home within any of them" (2011, p. 3). Media archeology has thus far served as a tool primarily for the excavation of Western artifacts, however (as in canonical accounts of European computing and early American cinema), even as the working definition that Huhtamo and Parikka provide seems especially relevant to an African popular industry like Nollywood, the study of which is as rootless and itinerant – as discursively slippery and institutionally elusive – as the production practices and audiovisual narratives that it generates. This chapter applies some of the central methods of media archeology – including the analysis of previously unexamined representational clichés or "topoi" (Huhtamo's preferred term) – to contemporary African screen media in an effort to engage urgent questions about obscure global flows of culture and commerce and their as yet unacknowledged impact on various African industries, especially Nollywood. How, for instance, did the theme music of the American television series *Twin Peaks* (1990–1991) end up a crucial part of the soundtrack of the Nollywood classic *Domitilla: The Story of a Prostitute* (Zeb Ejiro, 1996)? What can newly uncovered archives and novel media-archeological practices tell us about when, how, why, and with what immediate and lasting effects a program like *Twin Peaks* infiltrated African markets? How, moreover, might media archeology, which builds upon the new historicism of the 1980s, enable us to write alternative histories of Nollywood based precisely on the material formats, social practices, and representational techniques that are typically ignored in scholarship on African cinema?

This chapter is attuned to the possibilities of a media-archeological approach to Nollywood, but it is also alert to the many, multiplying obstacles to Nollywood-specific historiography. Perhaps the most daunting of these obstacles is the absence of an industrial, scholarly, or popular consensus about Nollywood's historical, national, cultural, ethnic, linguistic, and material contours, which partly explains another, equally unsettling absence: hat of Nollywood films themselves, at least in the kinds of institutional repositories that could facilitate their survival and aid their study. Currently, there is no agreed-upon Nollywood canon and there are no formal Nollywood archives. While resistance to canonization has long been fashionable in academic accounts of Western cinemas – an often-chagrined response to an embarrassment of available riches – such resistance assumes somewhat different valences in Nollywood studies, as scholars attempt to recognize and honor the mechanisms of an industry that is not designed to produce durable material objects, let alone cinematic masterpieces. If New Nollywood generates the occasional film (like Kunle Afolayan's *October 1* (2014)) that critics tout as an outstanding work, so, of course, did Old Nollywood (think, for instance, of the industry's "foundational" film, Kenneth Nnebue and Chris Obi Rapu's *Living in Bondage* (1992)). If these "classics" of the New Nollywood are disciplined into scarcity by the severe limitations of certain distribution patterns (with no formal DVD release following a run at the multiplexes for the vast majority of them), so have the products of Old Nollywood been circumscribed by a logic of (relatively) conservative circulation, as well as by structured obsolescence and the general degenerative capacities of analog technologies. Both remain "victims" of piracy – a mechanism that may boost their visibility and increase their circulation, but under idiosyncratic terms, to say the least. However generative of immediate access and material abundance, piracy is hardly a reliable engine of historiography (unless, of course, one is writing the history of piracy, but even then one would need a basic understanding of the licensed media and the authorized, proprietary avenues of distribution against which piracy becomes legible and operational in the first place). Whether constrained by the new corporate rights holders or conditioned through the apparatus of piracy, Nollywood is perhaps best characterized by the concept of the missing archive – by, that is, the lack of preservation of its audiovisual heritage. If Nollywood's archives are missing, they are hardly non-existent, however. They span an array of public and private sites that are both material and digital, African and diasporic, demanding that we turn to Rodrigo Lazo's theory of migrant archives, which for Lazo "reside in obscurity and are always at the edge of annihilation" (2009, p. 7). The migrant archives that characterize Nollywood history offer unique and profound challenges to media archeology. This chapter traces those challenges as it attempts to concretize some of Nollywood's crucial yet understudied interactions with a diversity of global media productions, practices, and theories. Media archeology, as I understand it, can facilitate the pursuit of Nollywood's migrant archives, in the process illuminating the intertextuality of those audiovisual narratives that rarely receive close analysis, and that are often distorted, denied, or eliminated through new, Internet-enabled avenues of distribution and modes of reception. The practice of media archeology can also answer crucial questions about media production in African contexts increasingly governed by external infrastructural forces and corporate entities, from South Africa's DStv to China's StarTimes and beyond.

Contemplating Nollywood's Contours

Before considering some of the negative consequences of Nollywood's online availability, it is necessary to sketch the historiographic operations by which the industry is divided into two "eras." In academic and popular writing, "Old Nollywood" refers to the production on VHS and VCD of multipart genre films for distribution via Nigerian marketplaces (based, for instance, in Idumota and Onitsha) and consumption in the home or in public video parlors; its emergence is typically dated to 1992 (and the production of *Living in Bondage*), and while some accounts cite 2010 as the year of its demise (Chamley, 2012), it is perhaps most accurate to suggest that Old Nollywood describes an ongoing style of production, distribution, and consumption (Adejunmobi, 2015). It coexists with "New Nollywood," a capital-intensive movement to improve the aesthetic quality of the industry's products, replace local marketers with corporate advertising and distribution firms, and centralize theatrical exhibition in Lagos, London, and New York, among an increasing number of other cities (Haynes, 2014). The most convincing and nuanced accounts of Old and New Nollywood stress the considerable overlap between the industry's two major "phases." Some films slated for New Nollywood success in fact fail to make it to the multiplexes and must be ported through Old Nollywood's more modest, less lucrative distribution channels; other big-budget productions plainly retain a certain interest in witchcraft and money rituals that, to some, smacks of the worst and most embarrassing elements of the industry's diverse representational traditions. Furthermore, several Old Nollywood films received what is now understood to be the New Nollywood treatment: *Domitilla*, for instance, got a heavily publicized theatrical release in early 1997, along with a series of star-studded events celebrating its premiere (Adesanya 2000, p. 44). In Nollywood, it seems, everything old is new again, made strange and shiny only by the attention of various corporate entities and by those self-appointed cultural mediators who proclaim their distaste for "obsolete" technologies and "shameful" representational tactics.

Recognizing the continuities between past and present production and distribution practices, some critics prefer the term "neo-Nollywood" to "New Nollywood," with the argument that "neo" signifies rejuvenation rather than separation – an amplification or revivification of familiar practices, and not a radical rupture from the past. Certain qualitative distinctions inevitably characterize critical uses of "neo-Nollywood," however, suggesting the persistence of dichotomizing tendencies in Nollywood historiography. When Nollywood producer-director Charles Novia first employed the term "neo-Nollywood" in 2010, he described it in terms of a "tasteful" itinerary – a move away from low production values, "a positive direction for better quality and improved storylines" (in Afolayan 2014, p. 26). For his part, Adeshina Afolayan insists that neo-Nollywood signals resistance to what he calls "paradigmatic Nollywood," becoming intelligible more by "introducing new rules of engagement" than by "transgressing the old rules" (2014, p. 28). According to Afolayan, these "new rules of engagement" rest on a refusal of Nollywood's "mushrooming tendency," featuring an emphasis on quality over quantity. Yet this very emphasis, which Afolayan reads in terms of a Deleuzian creativity (understood in contradistinction to commercial imperatives), is as much the product of corporate influence as of individual authorial designs. A celebrated auteur like Kunle Afolayan might favor a relatively slow gestation period for his projects, nurturing his ideas, cultivating potential funding sources, and testing new filmmaking equipment, but the limited distribution streams through which his works circulate are, in many ways, conditioned by his corporate sponsors as well as by contractual arrangements with various exhibitors. Viewed through the lens of corporate control, then, Afolayan's prominent anti-piracy crusades serve merely to distract from the ongoing manufacturing of scarcity by such corporate forces as Globacom, BlackBerry, and Honeywell, which have set many of the boundaries for Afolayan's recent work (Ryan, 2015). It is not so much that piracy is siphoning profits away from Afolayan (though this may well be happening, as Afolayan would be the first to suggest) but that profitability is at least partly determined by licensees and the frequently severe constraints that they place on availability.

Exploring the affinities between Old and New Nollywood permits us to consider what was once new about now-outmoded recording and playback technologies like VHS and VCD; it also encourages contemplation of potential reuses of the industry's earliest films – extractive and derivative practices that might telegraph the connectedness of analog and digital productions. In her essay "Neoliberal Rationalities in Old and New Nollywood," Moradewun Adejunmobi (2015) resists reductive bifurcations of old and new that, in scholarship on cinema, so often suggest the absence of any aesthetic, technological, or ideological continuities between past and present. Like other scholars who address New Nollywood, Adejunmobi echoes the media theorists J. David Bolter and Richard Grusin, who coined the term "remediation" in the late 1990s, writing, "Media need each other in order to function as media at all" (1999, p. 55). But if New Nollywood needs Old Nollywood, it is surely only in a limited number of ways: As a discursive construction against which to situate its "sophisticated" practices and "upscale" productions; as a source of star talent (Genevieve Nnaji, Stephanie Okereke Linus, and Dakore Egbuson are among the many who have made the transition from direct-to-VHS melodramas to big-budget, high-grossing multiplex films); and as an occasional, partial source of narrative inspiration. While some understandings of remediation look for the immediately recognizable, material survival of the old in the new, any consideration of the imbrication of Old and New Nollywood must be attentive to the material obsolescence of the former. New Nollywood hardly needs Old Nollywood as an audiovisual archive, nor could it conceivably sample its predecessor in an era of accelerated obsolescence, when VHS – a format once prized for its archival capacities – is largely being consigned to the trash heaps (Harrow, 2013). It is impossible to know exactly how many Old Nollywood films are discarded before they are digitized – an epistemological conundrum occasioned by the absence of reliable databases and the persistence of informal mechanisms of circulation and consumption for this most informal of major media industries. Derided by many, Nollywood's penchant for appropriation and pastiche can be seen in many films of the 1990s, which reproduce incidents – and sometimes incorporate actual footage – from earlier works (Haynes, 2016). If the global circulation of *Twin Peaks* can literally be heard in the *Domitilla* that samples its score, so can *Domitilla* be seen in Fred Amata's Nollywood film *The Prostitute* (2001), which revives and remediates its predecessor in multiple ways, constituting

its own kind of Nollywood archive. Old Nollywood may have routinely remediated Hollywood films, lifting sounds and images from any number of imported
texts (often as a means of signaling its own sophistication and engagement with
the wider world), but New Nollywood does not operate in this extractive
fashion – at least not with respect to its Nigerian counterpart – and it is unlikely to
embrace what many see as an aesthetically impoverished and altogether ignomin-
ious practice.

It is precisely this appropriative tendency that renders Old Nollywood – or parts
of it – unfit for distribution via new platforms. Whether understood as politically
resistant or ideologically "empty," the illicit extraction and reuse of American
media makes not merely for qualitative distinctions between Old and New
Nollywood (wherein the former is seen as derivative and morally suspect while the
latter remains "original" and law-abiding), but also for a strict separation between
the two in relation to extant distribution streams. New Nollywood gets Netflix,
and thus availability on any number of Internet-enabled mobile devices; Old
Nollywood got VHS and VCD, and thus the rubbish bin, becoming "trash" in
more ways than one (as in Kenneth Harrow's (2013) memorably adaptable formulation). For if Old Nollywood is "not good enough" for Netflix, at least according
to its detractors, that is due to a number of factors: Its association with "low"
cultural production, with "trashy" melodramas (and crime dramas, village comedies, 419 thrillers, and so on); its "low" production values, which are inseparable
from the distortions and degradations of such "dingy," corruptible formats as VHS
and VCD; its extractive practices, which are synonymous, in corporate terms, with
actionable piracy; and its association with the masses – with those who plainly
cannot afford the ticket prices at the Silverbird galleria, and who would surely be
denied entry by private security guards tasked with policing distinctions between
rich and poor, "classy" and "classless" (Ryan 2015, p. 60). As a number of critics
have pointed out, the "newness" of New Nollywood is very much a function of its
relationship to wealthy Nigerians, rather than of certain technical affordances or
narrative strategies. In this sense, Adejunmobi, Jonathan Haynes (2014, 2016),
Connor Ryan (2015), and other scholars of New Nollywood evoke the work of
Raymond Williams (1977), who argues that major developments in cultural industries always index altered social relationships, and of Arjun Appadurai (1986),
whose understanding of "regimes of value" is applicable to recent shifts in the
commercial configuration of Nollywood.

Paradoxically, Nollywood has become "new" by embracing "old" formats and
technologies – not VHS and VCD but 16mm and 35mm film. If the prohibitively
high costs and multiple infrastructural requirements of celluloid precluded its
uptake by those who would effectively invent the Nollywood industry, these same
stumbling blocks are what ensure that New Nollywood will remain "new" long
past its initial appearance. The scarcity and vulnerability of celluloid – its sensi-
tivity to, say, airport X-rays and other detection equipment that can effectively
"wipe it clean" – make it an ideal agent of production of the novelty of New

Nollywood, despite its "old," analog status. The director Izu Ojukwu, who has long experimented with competing production and storage technologies, and who shot his historical epic *'76* (2016) on 16mm, recounted to me many of the difficulties that he faced not only in shooting on film but also in attempting to transport his footage to various postproduction facilities (including in Germany). The ongoing absence of such facilities in West Africa, which famously presented obstacles to the first generations of francophone filmmakers and militated against the use of celluloid in Nigeria in the late 1980s, 1990s, and well into the first decade of the twenty-first century, thus represents a crucial link between Old and New Nollywood, even as the latter boasts regular attempts to embrace celluloid against considerable odds. What made Nollywood possible, in other words, is precisely what makes New Nollywood "new" – namely, an experience of infrastructural inadequacy that, once surmounted through the use of cheap camcorders and the development of grassroots home-video distribution streams, now catalyzes the "quality" and prestige of films that must be finished (and, in some cases, screened) far beyond Nigeria's borders.

Disappearing Inscriptions: Nollywood on the Internet

Like the eminently debatable demarcation between Old and New, Nollywood's multilingualism offers immediate historiographic challenges, particularly as online versions of the industry's formative films become the only available iterations of those films, bearing false inscriptions that often reflect the use-value of English as the Internet's "common language." Consider, for instance, the case of Funke Akindele's beloved 2008 melodrama *Jénífà* (directed by Muhydeen S. Ayinde), in which the title character attempts to shed her persona's rural trappings and become, as she puts it, "a big hit in the big city." "Jénífà" (short for "Jennifer") is her adopted name – one imposed on her by the Americanized girls who surround her at the University of Lagos, and who think that her birth name, Suliat, smacks of the village. As a measure of her tentative resistance to their strictures, however, Jénífà gives her assumed name the diacritics found in Yorùbá orthography, and so, of course, does the film itself, producing a pleasurably hybridized title, one that is both Western and Nigerian, both American and Yorùbá. But as the *Jénífà* franchise has migrated across multiple platforms, mutating from home video (the original work) to theatrical release (2012's *The Return of Jénífà*, also directed by Ayinde) to television-cum-web series (the thriving *Jenifa's Diary*), it has shed these thematically relevant diacritics – a consequence of some of the main demands of the digital age, which, in the name of content's "accessibility" and "spreadability," enforce normative English even as the Internet is touted as a global, uniquely inclusive medium. The pressure to drop Yorùbá diacritics did not come from a single source but rather derived from the general conditions of intelligibility for digital content that must "fit" any number of online spaces, becoming mobile and searchable through linguistic conformity. Standard English is thus the essence of an Internet that increasingly embraces Nollywood through such sites and services as YouTube, iROKOtv, Dobox, and Netflix, the global availability of which hardly entails linguistic diversity (and hardly accommodates Yorùbá diacritics as components of hypertext). Via a range of digital networked technologies, standard English masquerades as "universal access" in ways that directly affect Nollywood, as when iROKOtv and Silverbird Television (STV), operating in the name of online intelligibility, removed Yorùbá diacritics from the title of *Jenifa's Diary*, despite both textual precedent and the entreaties of producers (including Funke Akindele). If *Jenifa's Diary* represents Akindele's efforts to keep the *Jénífá* franchise alive amid the obsolescence of its foundational melodrama, one would need, in true media-archeological fashion, to encounter that melodrama on its earliest platform – VHS – in order to catch a glimpse of how Yorùbá diacritics functioned thematically, via a remarkable title sequence that has not been duplicated in later versions (despite the fact that digital software makes the addition of diacritics far easier than in the days of in-camcorder editing and patchwork graphics). The Internet thus offers innumerable obstacles to Nollywood's archivization – none more consequential than the transformation (whether deliberate or unintended) of the industry's linguistically diverse texts.

Nollywood's transition to online platforms has been far from seamless, and it may serve to further constrain the serious study of the industry's history. However much we may delight in its appearance, the occasional YouTube upload of an Old Nollywood product is simply not, in the field of film and media studies, admissible as a primary source of Nigerian audiovisual material; at best, it may be welcomed as a secondary source – as, that is, evidence that may be marshaled in the service of an argument about Nollywood's online "afterlives," or about YouTube itself. This is, indeed, as it should be – not because online viewing is somehow a travesty of film spectatorship, a YouTube version necessarily less "respectable" than a licensed DVD, but because of the sometimes dramatic omissions evident in a Nollywood film's migration from material to immaterial storage forms. It is the very lack of availability – the very absence of preservationist discourses surrounding – Nollywood's VHS cassettes and VCDs that make these omissions difficult to prove, or even to recognize. Entire sequences are missing from many online versions of Nollywood films, and one must be familiar with the earliest editions of those films in order to recognize such gaps. iROKOtv, for instance, is hardly in the habit of identifying its own elisions; like Netflix, it prefers to present those films that it streams as "complete," despite certain conspicuous absences (Tsika, 2015a). These missing pieces are not insignificant, although the ongoing stereotyping of Nollywood as an engine of repetition and redundancy would appear to suggest otherwise. Losing key textual dimensions may, in fact, lead to misrecognition even of Nollywood's most salient thematic obsessions and production practices. The industry has, for instance, long relied on stars who labor, through their film performances as well as through their diverse public appearances, to transcend the boundaries of nation and, perhaps especially, ethnicity (Tsika, 2015b). Consider the vast number of Nollywood stars who have played pre- and post-conflict Liberians, from Oge Okoye in the groundbreaking Ghanaian-Liberian-Nigerian co-production *Hatred* (Courage Borbor, 2012) to, somewhat less successfully, Mercy Johnson in *Liberian Girl* (sometimes titled *Two Dollars*, directed by Mykel C. Ajaere, and released in 2011). Born in Okene, Kogi State, Nigeria, Johnson, as the title character in *Liberian Girl*, speaks a language (Liberian Kreyol, combined with a series of "tribal dialects") that the film's Nigerian characters cannot understand, but that the film attempts to "transcend" through the "universal" language of American pop music. Sampling (and sharing the title of) a pop single from Michael Jackson's 1987 album *Bad*, the film pays obeisance to Jackson (a hardly uncommon Nollywood tactic), and offers its own, self-exculpating rejection of the nationalist complaints that have been leveled against Jackson's own "Liberian Girl." First released as a single in Europe and Australia, Jackson's song infamously opens with South African singer Letta Mbulu impersonating its Liberian subject by speaking not a Liberian language but, instead, Swahili, suggesting that the song is peddling a sense of interchangeable Africanity (an exceedingly familiar Western approach to the continent and its inhabitants). Viewed against the controversial backdrop of one of Jackson's lesser-known singles, Nollywood's *Liberian Girl* suggests its own convincing defense of Mercy Johnson: Unlike Letta Mbulu, at least she speaks – or attempts to speak – a Liberian language, in keeping with Nollywood's growing commitment to a wide range of African dialects (including those traditionally spoken far beyond Nigeria's borders). That said, it is worth considering what, exactly, is so objectionable about Letta Mbulu's performance on Jackson's record, as it would seem a clear reflection of national essentialism to suggest that no Liberian would ever speak Swahili – that Mbulu was the "wrong" choice for Jackson's spoken-word intro. That this intro can, in fact, be heard in the original version of Nollywood's *Liberian Girl* suggests the film's direct engagement with some of these issues. Incorporated, via piracy, into the film's soundscape, "Liberian Girl" comments on – and provides a discursive launching pad for – *Liberian Girl*.

Such incorporations are, of course, characteristic of Old Nollywood – a productive consequence of the sheer difficulty of regulating informal video production and distribution, and an indication of Nollywood's longstanding goal of global engagement – but they are decisively effaced by new developments in distribution. When Nollywood migrates to new platforms, the regulatory mechanisms that it has long evaded suddenly become disciplinary forces to be reckoned with, the results of which can be seen in the alteration of *Liberian Girl* to suit distribution via YouTube and iROKOtv. Shortly after its emergence, in collaboration with Disney and Time Warner, YouTube developed content-identification software – dubbed Content ID – that streamlines the detection of precisely the types of pirated sounds and images that have given Nollywood a famously syncretic flair. Content ID thus radically transforms Nollywood's formative films for "authorized" consumption (which, for the most part, is the only form of consumption available via a YouTube ruled by such effective content-identification software). When a new, shorter version of *Liberian Girl* was prepared for online distribution in 2012, Jackson's pop song – a principal source of inspiration for the film – was cut, presumably on the (correct) assumption that its inclusion would have triggered Content ID, leading to the removal of the film from YouTube and associated sites. Excavating the film's earliest iteration as a series of VCDs would, in true media-archeological fashion, provide one way of exposing the distortions of online platforms, as well as of understanding the logic of extractive practices that are automatically policed by Content ID and other forms of copyright protection.

At present, in the absence of any authoritative Nollywood database, the Internet reinvigorates Old Nollywood (to the extent that it reinvigorates it at all) only when individual users upload their own collections to YouTube and other video-sharing sites, although the operations of Content ID force us to question the "completeness" of these uploads, which may be missing key scenes (or, at the very least, key sounds). The survival of the old is thus placed in the hands of amateurs – left to the idiosyncratic determinants of database culture – which means, of course, that there is no way of knowing if or when a YouTube upload of *Living in Bondage* will disappear, or if and when the woman who uploaded *Glamour Girls* to Vimeo will cancel her account (or face suspension for some unintended infraction). Other, seemingly more stable sources of Old Nollywood exist, but they often prove to be far less reliable than the individuals who curate their own YouTube accounts. For example, the YouTube channel NollywoodWonder, which boasts 50,000 subscribers and purports to offer "the latest Nollywood movies," routinely uploads Old Nollywood films in an attempt to pass them off as New Nollywood ones; the channel uses an image of Izu Ojukwu's *'76* to advertise a 1999 Chico Ejiro film, labeling that film a 2015 release (and changing its title, to boot – from *Without Your Love* to *I'm Nothing Without Your Love*). To be sure, there are some excellent online sources of Old Nollywood films, such as the YouTube channel YorubaMoviePlanet, which offers English-subtitled versions of Yorùbá-language classics (including Tade Ogidan's 1997 masterpiece *Owo Blow*), but the vast majority of Nollywood's online repositories are bastions of inaccuracy, marking the Internet as an ineffective (and even counterproductive) engine of recovery of the Nollywood past. The Internet's power to distort is well known among collectors of "old" media (particularly VHS cassettes). As Kate Egan points out, reflexive valorizations of the Internet's archival capabilities often ignore "the pleasures and intricacies of VHS-centered video collecting, and its relationship to issues of authenticity, exclusivity, and the material life histories of objects" (2007, p. 218). Considering Ghanaian contexts of video production and consumption, Carmela Garritano argues that "[t]he technology, or medium, of the text is not incidental to its symbolic life" (2013, p. 26), offering a vital reminder that the experience of VHS and VCD cannot be perfectly reproduced online.

Local forms of censorship have long conditioned the content of Nollywood films, but these forms are very much in flux, at least with respect to representations of gender and sexual minorities, and they often influence the uptake of Nollywood on the Internet. Consider, for instance, the Nollywood film *Pregnant Hawkers* (Patrick Hogan and Okechukwu Ifeanyi, 2013), which directly depicts gay men enjoying anal sex. The film was completed on the eve of passage of Nigeria's Same-Sex Marriage Prohibition Act, which criminalizes all manner of gay identifications, including those inferred through film spectatorship and various online inscriptions. Since January 2014, the Nigerian government has worked to ensure that a thoroughly heterosexualized version of *Pregnant Hawkers* (dubbed *Desperate Hawkers*) replaces its predecessor on all digital platforms conceivably accessible to Nigerians, thus rendering it difficult to access the gay-inclusive, even gay-positive *Pregnant Hawkers* online (Tsika, 2016). When such forms of federal censorship intervene well after the completion of a Nollywood film, established and emergent distribution channels tend to follow suit, as when Africa Magic (the African satellite channel), iROKOtv, and other platforms promptly jettisoned *Pregnant Hawkers*, replacing it with its state-sanctioned successor. For its part, Africa Magic often broadcasts the types of distortions (including title changes) described above, whether through inattention or because licensees provide the channel with those film versions that they have already altered for online distribution. As Jonathan Haynes suggested to me at a 2016 Columbia University conference on Nollywood, the historiographic value of Africa Magic and iROKOtv lies in the paper trails that they leave – the records of contracts made and renewed, which enable us to learn who, exactly, has owned the rights to Nollywood content at a given time, and under what terms. Such records constitute precisely the kind of "nonfilmic evidence" that scholars of film and media increasingly value, often at the explicit expense of close textual analyses of individual films. But building a history of Nollywood on the materials (filmic and nonfilmic alike) that Africa Magic and iROKOtv provide is plainly insufficient and may even produce wildly misleading accounts. Media archeology does not deny the significance of "nonfilmic evidence" – quite the opposite, in fact – but its central methodology, committed to the search for multiple material iterations of media texts, offers a vital reminder of the importance of looking beyond such evidence to the formats and practices that it does not describe. Simply put, what we find online or on Africa Magic, however complete or otherwise evidentiary it may seem, is rarely all there is of audiovisual narratives that have experienced multiple material and medium-specific lives, demonstrating the dynamism of Nollywood's enterprise.

Corporatized Reductions: Nollywood as "Content"

The rise of broadband digital infrastructure has occasioned major shifts in global media production and consumption, as various cultural industries convert to what Anna McCarthy has called "a casualized, high-yield system of piecework, one in which a mysterious substance called *content* is at once the basic unit of production and a new form of value" (2014). Such conversions are increasingly characteristic of African and diasporic cultural industries, and they are often celebrated by academic disciplines that have relinquished the close textual analysis of films in favor of the production of data about their circulation and consumption. The digital humanities are presently leading the charge in this regard, but the denigration of textual analysis, which has dire consequences for Nollywood historiography, is hardly a new phenomenon. As early as 1975, in the journal *Screen*, Edward Buscombe was discouraging the close textual analysis of films, laying some of the discursive groundwork for the new historicism of the 1980s, with its rejection of the notion that a "complete" text exists and can be explicated according to its authorized contours. A pronounced distaste for "typical textual and narrative analysis" similarly structures Eric Smoodin's introduction to his 2007 anthology *Looking Past the Screen*, which Smoodin co-edited with Jon Lewis, and which takes as one of its central premises the notion that Hollywood films have survived in excess of the type of "nonfilmic evidence" (production files, censorship reports, audience surveys) that would enable their "legitimate" exegesis (p. 12). If conditions of filmic abundance lead to the exhortation to "look past the screen" in the study of American cinema, opposite conditions may make that exhortation necessary in the study of Nollywood, given the lack of preservation (and even of accurate identification) of its audiovisual materials. In the academy, textual analysis is increasingly considered a bourgeois pastime (Toby Miller, for instance, dismisses it as "apolitical formalism" (2010, p. 137)), but this approach is clearly a Western privilege, a product of the luxuriant overabundance of Hollywood media; after all, for textual analysis to be denigrated – deemed insignificant – it first needed to prove its mettle, becoming the dominant methodology in the field of film studies in the 1960s and early 1970s. In many accounts of Hollywood and other Western media producers, textual analysis is thus resisted as redundant or extraneous. When scholars apply the same resistance to Nollywood, however, it becomes one of the discursive mechanisms through which the industry's films become mere technologies – undifferentiated "content," their obsolescence inevitable. This is true of those who consider Nollywood only "in the aggregate," as Jonathan Haynes puts it (2000, p. xv), but it is also characteristic of African and diasporic corporations that revive Old Nollywood's ethos of speed and productivity while claiming a New Nollywood panache.

Collapsing Nollywood films and the formats that materialize them is not simply a squeamish, condescending Western strategy – a means of avoiding Nigerian sounds, images, and stories – but also a product of specific consumerist aspirations. Take, for example, EbonyLife TV, an entertainment corporation that often funds film production (via its subsidiary EbonyLife Films), and that consistently touts its "thousands of hours of content" in terms not of individual audiovisual texts but of converging distribution streams and playback platforms (satellite channels, VOD services like Google Play and The App Store, the corporation's own website, and so on). Based in Calabar, Cross River State, EbonyLife TV promotes a certain image of Nigeria that reflects an ideological investment in American reality television programs – particularly the globally syndicated *Real Housewives* franchise (2008–). The founder of EbonyLife TV, the London-born Mo Abudu, has partnered with the Cross River State government, which provides a measure of funding for film and television productions, but the majority of funding comes from South Africa, and many of the corporation's mandates uphold Hollywood as a model for representing wealth and glamor. Filmmakers who sign contracts with EbonyLive TV invariably receive instructions to make their films "look American" – meaning polished and professional – but some claim that the corporation also insists that film characters be extremely wealthy, or at least middle-class, urban, physically beautiful, well-dressed, and far removed from tribe, tradition, and any of the negative stereotypes that continue to hound Africa and Africans. The case of EbonyLife TV is thus emblematic of the "upscale" trends that have led to New Nollywood – and, indeed, the corporation directly contributes to New Nollywood through EbonyLife Films, which produced and distributed Biyi Bandele's *Fifty* (2015), a slick drama about wealthy, glamorous Lagosian women. Like other corporations, EbonyLife TV manufactures a monolithic vision of Nigeria as a technologically advanced, culturally sophisticated, cosmopolitan society populated by the fabulously wealthy and the stunningly beautiful. In so doing, however – and in consistently touting technological sophistication, media convergence, and "instant access" at the expense of identifying and promoting discrete audiovisual texts – EbonyLife TV contributes to the ongoing reduction of Nollywood films to undifferentiated "content" accessible via a range of mobile devices.

A related engine of reduction and obsolescence is, perhaps paradoxically, multiplex exhibition, a characteristic of New Nollywood that applies its own disciplinary pressures to the industry, creating and sustaining conditions of scarcity for films that, however "polished," are not prized as lasting commodities. The new multiplex release pattern appears rooted in a desire to mimic the perceived consumption habits of the Western world, with its constant search for new content. As Connor Ryan argues in his account of New Nollywood, "the material organization of the multiplex cinema conscripts the body in the constitution of 'modern' subjectivity and foregrounds the illusion of free and infinite mobility in the experience of that modernity" (p. 61). Consumption, in this context, is about immediate gratification – instant (and conspicuously public) association with glitz and glamor – and not the hard work of preservation or the lasting pleasures of home viewing and careful archivization. In many cases, New Nollywood films are available briefly via the multiplexes – and then never again. (A key example is Niyi Akinmolayan's 2010 science-fiction film *Kajola*, which was exhibited at Silverbird but has not been available – in any format – since.) New Nollywood can be considered sparse only from a certain perspective, however. If we expand the category to include more than the occasional 16mm or 35mm "event," we can see how its vastness has become the crux of arguments for Nigeria as a dazzling "new" content provider: EbonyLife

TV is among the corporations that link their "newness" to high turnover rates for their productions, and even companies rooted in the diaspora, like iROKOtv, make similar claims, presenting audiovisual abundance as a measure of technological progress and a marker of Nigeria's digital "relevance." The obsolescence of Nollywood films – their sudden disappearance after multiplex releases, or their sudden removal from streaming services – is thus a form of value and not a source of distress. As Jonathan Sterne (2007) suggests, obsolescence is often understood as an index of progress – a sign of renewal, a symbol of modernity. If a high rate of turnover positions Old Nollywood as an excessively active, even indiscriminate enterprise in accounts of its aesthetic impoverishment and "mushrooming tendency," it signals something else entirely in the context of New Nollywood – namely, prestige, a constant flood of "content" that makes New Nollywood seem metonymic of the always content-rich Internet.

The discursive transformation of Nollywood into a digitally sophisticated content aggregator is abetted by the disciplinary mechanisms of African multiplex chains like Silverbird, Genesis, and Filmhouse. Such mechanisms are major factors in the fracturing of New Nollywood, leading to multiple versions of a single film, some of which may remain unavailable through authorized distribution channels. When Izu Ojukwu produced a final cut of '76 in the spring of 2016, it ran to 138 minutes – an appropriate enough running time for a historical epic, but far too long for a multiplex system that regularly prescribes 90-minute running times for New Nollywood films. Silverbird, which booked '76, thus required Ojukwu to eliminate nearly 50 minutes of his film. It is therefore well worth considering a number of factors that are rarely addressed in Nollywood studies: The authoring function of African multiplexes that set certain textual terms; the operations of Africa Magic and other satellite distribution channels that impose their own restrictions on content; and the work of websites that must comply with various copyright restrictions, in the process jettisoning those aspects of Old Nollywood that are hardly at home on the commercial Internet. Abandoning, in true media-archeological fashion, conventional notions of authorship (with their romantic, individualist underpinnings), Jonathan Gray favors the notion of "clusters of authorship – their composition in ever-changing flux – to focus attention on the multiplicity of authors that attend any given text, and to the clustering of their activity around specific moments and times in a text's life: The moments of its authoring." Gray's emphasis is on Western media, but his words apply well to Nollywood's chaotic contexts. The fragmentation of Nollywood (Old and New) is not a Nigerian anomaly but, as Gray would have it, characteristic of all forms of cultural production: "A text's identity is never set, since not all of the text is ever already there. How the rest of the text gets there, who puts it there, and the times and places when and where this process occurs are all questions that lead us to finding the always shifting authors" (2013, p. 108). As Gray reminds us, "any text is always open, never concluded or complete, and thus any notion of authorship based on the assumption that the text has already been created is a problematic one" (pp. 107–108).

Promoting Nollywood's Archivization

Whatever the "clusters of authorship" that gave it life, Old Nollywood, perhaps more so than any other major media-making practice, is at risk of disappearing into the ether, and we would do well to develop rigorous methods for studying Nigeria's non-extant films and archival ephemera. Allyson Nadia Field's *Uplift Cinema* (2016), which examines the production and circulation of films that no longer exist, provides a model for looking at the "losers" of film history – those works that were never preserved and that simply cannot be seen. Field's project – an examination of early African American filmmaking – thus resonates with ongoing scholarship on Oscar Micheaux (whose vast body of work is similarly underrepresented in extant archives), as well as with Alexander Horwath's work on Josef von Sternberg's lost films (2007). The familiar denigration of Nollywood as a source of substandard audiovisual works has surely contributed to the lack of adequate preservation of its films, but one should not have to lie about the quality of those films in order to ensure their archivization. This is perhaps especially so at a time when more and more institutions are embracing "low" cultural forms in the construction of "counterarchives" – collections that call into question the very notion of archivization, and that are marked by the inclusion of precisely those texts that are typically *excluded* by various factors, whether bourgeois taste claims, institutional precedents, or historiographic conventions. For Tim Dean, a counterarchive "refers less to a determinate place or archival content than to a strategic practice or a particular style of constituting the archive's legibility. Less an entity than a relation, the counterarchive works to unsettle those orders of knowledge established in and through official archives" (2014, p. 11). No less illustrious an institution than Yale University is currently committed to the preservation of thousands of "bad," straight-to-VHS movies from the 1970s, 1980s, and 1990s – including *Sorority Babes in the Slimeball Bowl-O-Rama* (David DeCoctau, 1988) and *Hollywood Chainsaw Hookers* (Fred Olen Ray, 1988). Yale's new VHS collection is, however, firmly committed to European and North American fare (and to horror movies, at that); the inclusion of Nollywood videos would ostensibly undermine its precise counterarchival approach, which is to highlight those straight-to-VHS movies that once constituted the abundant underside of mainstream Hollywood production. The problem with Yale's particular counterarchive, then, is not so much that it represents the ethnocentric corollary to a possible engagement with African audiovisual texts, but that it appears to concretize and reproduce a particular illogic – a sense of European and American "home videos" as belonging to a different order of time, and to different constitutive conditions, than their African counterparts. The truth, of course, is far more complicated, and it suggests the very continuities that make it difficult to define Nollywood in dichotomous terms – whether as strictly separate from Western media practices or neatly divisible into Old and New.

The notion that Nollywood films are at all collectible might seem eccentric – or, at the very least, based on a fatal misunderstanding of the industry and its popularity. That is because, as Barbara Klinger (2001) has pointed out, video collecting is most commonly understood in terms of cinephilia, particularly when the collected object (whether a LaserDisc, DVD, or Blu-ray) appears to reproduce the polished technical qualities and authorized dimensions of its celluloid predecessor. As Nollywood films have, for the most part, famously lacked such polish, their collection can scarcely be understood as a conventional form of cinephilia or technophilia. Nollywood collecting is perhaps closer to Kate Egan's account of the idiosyncratic preservation of so-called "video nasties" – marginal, often low-budget horror and exploitation films that circulated (via small-time distributors) as some of the first commercially available VHS cassettes in the British market. As Egan points out, the preservation of video nasties is about more than just stubbornly maintaining a collection of "bad" media, as the practice may illuminate misunderstood textual properties and lay the groundwork for novel historiographic approaches. In sustaining Nollywood's alterity by avoiding considerations of preservation and archivization, we risk losing more than just a rich history of Nigerian media production. Early Nollywood – far more than the industry's more recent, glitzy iterations – constitutes an archive of the complex, unheralded global circulation of major media products and representations. Old Nollywood films are, more often than not, vivid, telling repositories of appropriated technologies and practices, not abstract indices thereof, nor vague symbols of such broad concepts as globalization, cultural imperialism, and the global postmodern. ("I hate the term 'the global postmodern,'" writes Stuart Hall, "so empty and sliding a signifier that it can be taken to mean virtually anything you like" (1992, 22).) There are two dominant ways of understanding the appropriations that are characteristic of Old Nollywood: As the "mindless," voracious acquisition of anything and everything (but particularly products that smack of American cultural legitimacy); and as activist or simply cynical responses to Western cultural imperialism. The latter approach, while motivated by a noble commitment to redressing racist and ethnocentric conceptions of African cultural production, is blind to certain authorial justifications for sampling – to specific artistic strategies, as well as to Nollywood's status as a producer of "small media." As theorized by Annabelle Sreberny-Mohammadi and Ali Mohammadi (1994), "small media" are marked by idiosyncratic borrowings that address local consumers, affording them the opportunity to engage with a diversity of cultural practices, away from the copyright-driven constraints that characterize the circulation and consumption of "big media." If Old Nollywood films constitute small media, New Nollywood films suggest something much bigger and, of course, less flexible, less mobile – and far more vulnerable to censorship and myriad copyright restrictions. Small media may be ephemeral, but media archeology offers a vital reminder that such a recognition need not preclude the search for material forms. It is one thing to theorize ephemerality as the defining characteristic of small media; it is quite another to proceed as if videocassettes no longer exist as material objects despite their cultural obsolescence (and whether in private collections, public trash heaps, or inadequate state archives), and to act as if this existence does not matter.

I want to end with a reminder of the significance of Nollywood's own archival practices, particularly those that are marked by piracy and thus effectively "screened out" of
platforms like YouTube, iROKOtv, Africa Magic, EbonyLife TV, and many others. As I
mentioned earlier, Zeb Ejiro's Nigerian melodrama *Domitilla: The Story of a Prostitute*,
which was first released on VHS in 1996, leans heavily on the soundtrack of David
Lynch's American television series *Twin Peaks* (as well as on the soundtrack of Michael
Caton-Jones' 1995 film *Rob Roy*), but for reasons that may seem elusive, and that are
hardly explicable according to the familiar cultural imperialism thesis. *Twin Peaks* had
become globally syndicated by the time *Domitilla* went into production, and it had
already spawned an official, commercially available VHS version of its pilot episode, as
well as a prequel film – all of which informs Ejiro's sampling of the Angelo Badalamenti
score. But Ejiro used that score for a specific reason, and not simply because it was
widely available or otherwise "imperialist." He used it to contest what would become
the dominant stereotype of Nollywood: The suggestion that the industry is a factory
for low cultural production – for irredeemably artless soap operas. Thus if David Lynch
could confer artistry and even auteurism on so lowly a genre as the American network
television soap opera, as he so famously demonstrated with *Twin Peaks*, then Zeb Ejiro
could confer some of the same qualities on his film *Domitilla*, sampling Badalamenti's
score as a means of making this connection explicit. As I write this, Ejiro is taking
another page out of Lynch's ever-provocative book, preparing a Nigerian television
miniseries based on *Domitilla*, much as Lynch is currently preparing a *Twin Peaks* reboot
for Showtime. But while the original *Twin Peaks* remains abundantly available – whether
on DVD or via Netflix and other streaming services – the original *Domitilla*, produced
on videocassette, is dying. The film never made it to DVD in any official capacity, it is
not streaming on Netflix, and it certainly has not been preserved and stored in any
archive (or, for that matter, counterarchive). Ejiro is all too aware of the disappearance
of his most famous film, and he is choosing to fight back by producing a television
reboot, much as Funke Akindele is now attempting to keep the *Jénífà* franchise alive by
adapting it for TV and the Internet. The intersections between Nollywood and Western
media are not incidental, and we must take them seriously; but we must also recognize
where and why they diverge. We must accept that Nollywood's itineraries, like those
of other African media industries, are complex and multidirectional, generative of
archives still waiting to be uncovered.

References

Adejunmobi, Moradewun. 2015. "Neoliberal Rationalities in Old and New Nollywood."
    African Studies Review 58.3: 31–53.
Adesanya, Afolabi. 2000. "From Film to Video." In *Nigerian Video Films: Revised and Expanded
    Edition*, edited by Jonathan Haynes, 37–50. Athens: Ohio University Center for
    International Studies.

Afolayan, Adeshina. 2014. "Introduction: Philosophy, (Neo-)Nollywood and the African Predicament." In *Auteuring Nollywood: Critical Perspectives on* The Figurine, edited by Adeshina Afolayan, 1–52. Ibadan: University Press PLC.

Appadurai, Arjun. 1986. "Introduction: Commodities and the Politics of Value." In *The Social Life of Things: Commodities in Cultural Perspective*, edited by Arjun Appadurai, 3–63. Cambridge: Cambridge University Press.

Bolter, J. David and Richard Grusin. 1999. *Remediation: Understanding New Media.* Cambridge, MA: MIT Press.

Chamley, Santorri. 2012. "New Nollywood Cinema: From Home-Video Productions Back to the Big Screen." *Cineaste* 37.3: 21–23.

Dean, Tim. 2014. "Introduction: Pornography, Technology, Archive." In *Porn Archives*, edited by Tim Dean, Steven Ruszczycky, and David Squires, 1–28. Durham, NC: Duke University Press.

Diawara, Manthia. 2010. *African Film: New Forms of Aesthetics and Politics*. New York: Prestel.

Egan, Kate. 2007. "The Celebration of a 'Proper Product': Exploring the Residual Collectible through the 'Video Nasty.'" In *Residual Media*, edited by Charles R. Acland, 200–221. Minneapolis, MN: University of Minnesota Press.

Field, Allyson Nadia. 2016. *Uplift Cinema: The Emergence of African American Film and the Possibility of Black Modernity*. Durham, NC: Duke University Press.

Garritano, Carmela. 2013. *African Video Movies and Global Desires: A Ghanaian History*. Athens: Ohio University Press.

Gray, Jonathan. 2013. "When is the Author?" In *A Companion to Media Authorship*, edited by Jonathan Gray and Derek Johnson, 88–111. Oxford: Wiley-Blackwell.

Hall, Stuart. 1992. "What Is This 'Black' In Black Popular Culture." In Michele Wallace and Gina Dent (eds.), *Black Popular Culture*, 21–36. Seattle: Bay Press.

Harrow, Kenneth W. 2013. *Trash: African Cinema from Below*. Bloomington: Indiana University Press.

Harrow, Kenneth W. 2015. "Manthia Diawara's 'Waves' and the Problem of the 'Authentic.'" *African Studies Review* 58.3: 13–30.

Haynes, Jonathan. 2000. "Preface to the Nigerian Edition." In *Nigerian Video Films: Revised and Expanded Edition*, edited by Jonathan Haynes, xv–xviii. Athens: Ohio University Center for International Studies.

Haynes, Jonathan. 2014. "New Nollywood: Kunle Afolayan." *Black Camera* 5.2: 53–73.

Haynes, Jonathan. 2016. *Nollywood: The Creation of Nigerian Film Genres*. Chicago: University of Chicago Press.

Higgins, MaryEllen. 2015. "The Winds of African Cinema." *African Studies Review* 58.3: 77–92.

Horwath, Alexander. 2007. "Working with Spirits – Traces of Sternberg: A Lost Film about the 'City of My Dreams.'" Trans. Peter Waugh, in *Josef von Sternberg: The Case of Lena Smith*, edited by Alexander Horwath and Michael Omasta, 9–42. Vienna: Synema.

Huhtamo, Erkki and Jussi Parikka. 2011. "An Archaeology of Media Archaeology." In *Media Archaeology: Approaches, Applications, and Implications*, edited by Erkki Huhtamo and Jussi Parikka, 1–24. Berkeley: University of California Press.

Klinger, Barbara. 2001. "The Contemporary Cinephile: Film Collecting in the Post-Video Era." In *Hollywood Spectatorship: Changing Perceptions of Cinema Audiences*, edited by Melvyn Stokes and Richard Maltby, 132–151. London: BFI.

Lazo, Rodrigo. 2009. "Migrant Archives: New Routes In and Out of American Studies." In *States of Emergency: The Object of American Studies*, edited by Russ Castronovo and Susan Gillman, 36–54. Chapel Hill: University of North Carolina Press.

McCarthy, Anna. 2014. "From Work to Content: Formats, Properties, Texts." cmap2 conference "Ubiquitous Streams: Seeing Moving Images in the Age of Digital Media," Vanderbilt University, 4 April 2014.

Miller, Toby. 2010. "National Cinema Abroad: The New International Division of Cultural Labor, From Production to Viewing." In *World Cinemas, Transnational Perspectives*, edited by Nataša Ďurovičová and Kathleen Newman, 137–159. London: Routledge.

Ryan, Connor. 2015. "New Nollywood: A Sketch of Nollywood's Metropolitan New Style." *African Studies Review* 58.3: 55–76.

Şaul, Mahir and Ralph A. Austen. 2010. "Introduction." In *Viewing African Cinema in the Twenty-First Century: Art Films and the Nollywood Video Revolution*, edited Mahir Saul and Ralph A. Austen, 1–8. Athens: Ohio University Press, 2010.

Smoodin, Eric and Jon Lewis. 2007. *Looking Past the Screen*. Durham, NC: Duke University Press.

Sreberny-Mohammadi, Annabelle and Ali Mohammadi. 1994. *Small Media, Big Revolution: Communication, Culture, and the Iranian Revolution*. Minneapolis, MN: Univesity of Minnesota Press.

Sterne, Jonathan. 2007. "Out with the Trash: On the Future of New Media." In *Residual Media*, edited by Charles R. Acland, 16–31. Minneapolis, MN: University of Minnesota Press.

Tsika, Noah. 2015a. "Elevating the 'Amateur': Nollywood Critics and the Politics of Diasporic Film Criticism." In *Film Criticism in the Digital Age*, edited by Mattias Frey and Cecilia Sayad, 137–154. New Brunswick, NJ: Rutgers University Press.

Tsika, Noah. 2015b. *Nollywood Stars: Media and Migration in West Africa and the Diaspora*. Bloomington: Indiana University Press.

Tsika, Noah. 2016. *Pink 2.0: Encoding Queer Cinema on the Internet*. Bloomington: Indiana University Press.

Williams, Raymond. 1977. *Marxism and Literature*. Oxford: Oxford University Press.

Filmography

Ajaere, Mykel C. 2011. *Liberian Girl* (also known as *Two Dollars*). Bold Steps Pictures.
Akinmolayan, Niyi. 2010. *Kajola*. Adonis Productions.
Amata, Fred. 2001. *The Prostitute*. Kingsley Ogoro Productions.
Amata, Jeta. 2006. *The Amazing Grace*. Jeta Amata Concepts.
Ayinde, Muhydeen S. 2008. *Jénífà*. Olasco Films
Ayinde, Muhydeen S. 2012. *The Return of Jénífà*. Olasco Films/Scene One Productions.
Bandele, Biyi. 2015. *Fifty*. EbonyLife Films.

Borbor, Courage. 2012 *Hatred*. God Glorious Entertainment/GG Film.

Ejiro, Zeb. 1996. *Domitilla: The Story of a Prostitute*. Zeb Ejiro Productions/Daar Communications.

Hogan, Patrick and Okechukwu Ifeanyi. 2013. *Pregnant Hawkers* (Patrick, 2013).

Ogidan, Tade. 1997. *Owo Blow*. First Call.

Onukwafor, Chika ("Christian Onu"). 1994. *Glamour Girls*. NEK Video Links.

Ojukwu, Izu. 2016. *'76*. Adonis Productions/Princewill's Trust.

Rapu, Chris Obi ("Vic Mordi"). 1992. *Living in Bondage*. NEK Video Links.

Part V

National Industries / Media Cities / Transnational Flows

Part V

National Industries, Media Cities, Transnational Flows

African Videoscapes

Southern Nigeria, Ethiopia, and Côte d'Ivoire in Comparative Perspective

Alessandro Jedlowski

Introduction

The emergence of video film production in West Africa has triggered the development of a fast-growing body of scholarship on African video film industries. Most of this academic production focused on the southern Nigerian case, Nollywood, producing a problematic homogenization of the field – something we could label as the "Nollywoodization" of African Video Film Industries Studies (see also McCain, 2013). Other instances of video film production in sub-Saharan Africa have been the focus of in-depth researches which highlighted the specificity of each experience (cf. Böhme, 2015; Garritano, 2013; Jedlowski, 2015a; Larkin, 2000; Meyer, 2015; Overbergh, 2015a, 2015b; Rasmussen, 2010; Santanera, 2015; Thomas, 2015), but a common assumption remained widespread in both academic and journalistic circles: The emergence of video film industries around Africa is a consequence of Nollywood's success and of the subsequent vernacularization of the Nollywood model in other regions of the continent.

As Matthias Krings and Onookome Okome put it in the introduction to their influential volume on the transnationalization of Nollywood,

> in Tanzania, Kenya, Uganda, and South Africa, for example, Nollywood has served as a model of film production and inspired the growth of local film industries .... In these countries and elsewhere, Nigerian video films are appropriated and reworked into local forms of filmmaking and other cultural models of narrativization with local inflections that borrow and copy heavily from Nollywood. (2013, p. 1)

A Companion to African Cinema, First Edition. Edited by Kenneth W. Harrow and Carmela Garritano.

This statement is supported by the wide range of empirical evidences included in the book chapters, but it risks hiding the complexity of each country's specific experience. As Alexie Tcheuyap emphasized, "film production on the African continent has never been as univocal as critics and journalists have generally tended to assert" (2011, p. 11). A similar point can be made also in what concerns video film production. Carmela Garritano, for instance, suggests that "by subsuming all West African video under the example of Nigeria, the region's dominant national power, critics have erased the movement, complexity and contestation that mark the West African regional videoscape" (2013, p. 3). This points to the fact that, rather than as a model, in some regions of the continent Nollywood has been seen as a hegemonic power threatening the development of other forms of cultural entrepreneurship (cf. Lobato 2012, p. 66).

The application of the "diffusionist" model implicit in much scholarship about the pan-African circulation of Nollywood and about the adoption of the Nigerian model of film production and distribution tends to conflate three separate processes which took place in different historical periods and influenced the emergence of video film industries around Africa in different ways. First came the introduction of analog technologies in the late 1970s and early 1980s. This phenomenon did not produce a singular, homogenous response around sub-Saharan Africa, but instead caused a wide range of highly diverse consequences in terms of both the production and circulation of media. Second, with the progressive growth of the Nigerian industry, throughout the 1990s Nigerian video films began to have a pan-African circulation via (mainly pirated) transnational networks. In this phase, non-Nigerian audiences around Africa became aware of Nigerian video films and, in some cases, started consuming them compulsively. This process at times interacted with local video film production, and at times did not. Third, after the invention of the term "Nollywood" in 2002 and the subsequent publication of a number of international reports rating it as the second or third largest film industry in the world, the Nigerian video industry's "success story" began to circulate widely around Africa and around the world as a news item. At the same time, with the switch from analog to digital technologies, video film production became even more affordable than before and new film production ventures emerged throughout the continent. This phase is the one that, in my view, partly generated the optical effect of convergence toward the Nollywood model that we read in much scholarship about African video film industries: In fact, it is mostly around this time that media professionals around the continent started referring to Nollywood's success story to legitimize their attempts at producing and circulating films locally, even when the films they were making had nothing to do with Nollywood aesthetic and narrative contents, or even with the Nigerian industry's modes of operation.

As I will argue in this chapter, in order to fully "problematize the transportability of the Nollywood model" (Mistry and Ellapen 2013, p. 47) it is important to make an attempt at separating the three processes mentioned above and highlight the complex patterns of continuities and discontinuities existing between the different sub-Saharan African contexts. In this chapter, I will make an attempt in this sense by producing a comparative analysis of the history of video film production and circulation in three sub-Saharan African countries (Nigeria, Ethiopia, and Côte d'Ivoire) where I conducted research over the past few years (between 2009 and 2015), as part of my doctoral and post-doctoral research projects. I will concentrate particularly on the first of the three phases that I highlighted above, the introduction of analog technologies, and then briefly discuss the other two phases (the circulation of Nollywood in Ethiopia and Côte d'Ivoire, and the reception of the Nollywood success story in these countries) in the conclusive section of the chapter.

Adopting a term recently proposed by Jean-François Bayart, the introduction of analog technologies can be considered as a "moment of historicity" in the long itinerary that constitutes the history of media and cinema in Africa. As Bayart puts it,

> the *moment of historicity* is a nodal point which delineates the longer or shorter durations of history, in Braudel's sense. It articulates the heterogeneous but synchronic temporalities of the different landscapes of globalization ... It is the point of concatenation of disparate temporalities. (2016, p. 34, my translation and emphasis)

As a moment of historicity, the introduction of analog technologies is a nodal point in the history of African cinemas. It is a moment of transformation that makes visible the long-term historical processes that preceded it, such as the modernization of communication technologies, the gradual neoliberalization of African economies, the liberalization of media production and distribution processes, and the decline of pan-African nationalist ideologies. At the same time, this is a moment whose analysis can offer us the keys to understand the development in African film and media production that followed it.

As I will argue in this chapter, while analog technologies have been introduced in Nigeria, Ethiopia, and Côte d'Ivoire around the same period, the outcome of their introduction has been shaped by local political, economic, and infrastructural specificities. If the southern Nigerian video film industry (Nollywood) is well known for having developed a straight-to-video system of distribution, in Ethiopia, video film production boomed only when locally produced video films were accepted for screening into the few still-existing, state-owned theatre halls. This gave rise to two profoundly different video film industries, in terms of contents, structure, and economic modes of operation. While Nigeria opted for a straight-to-video system and Ethiopia for a video-to-cinema one, in Côte d'Ivoire, after making a few attempts with VHS distribution, producers oriented themselves mainly toward television. As a result, within a context characterized by a protracted political and economic crisis, the introduction of analog and, later, digital technologies brought about the emergence of a dynamic and successful TV series industry, which has made Abidjan one of the leading cities for the production of visual popular culture in Francophone sub-Saharan Africa.

What are the historical factors that determined these different itineraries? How did different legal frameworks, economic contingencies, infrastructural specificities, and individual decisions participate in shaping the way the introduction of analog and, later, digital technologies were received by local media entrepreneurs and adapted to specific media environments? And how did these different paths of development impact the way these industries related to their audiences and to the everyday reality of the countries within which they have emerged?

In the following pages I will make an attempt at answering to these questions and at suggesting a few possible research itineraries for further investigation. In the first section, I will discuss the role of comparative analysis in the history of African cinema scholarship and underline the specificities of the methodology applied in the context of this study. In the second section, I will provide some general information about the history of the introduction of video technologies and its consequences on media industries worldwide. Finally, in the third and fourth sections, I will develop the comparison between the Nigerian, Ivorian, and Ethiopian video film industries and connect it to the key topics discussed in the first two sections of the chapter.

Comparing Video Film Industries in Sub-Saharan Africa

When one of the first historians of African cinema, Paulin Soumanou Vieyra (1975), famously argued for the use of the singular term "African cinema" instead of the more open and plural "African cinemas,"[1] he (perhaps inadvertently) left two major contrasting legacies to the African cinema scholarship that came after his work. On the one hand, by adopting a continental focus, he implicitly proposed a comparative approach to the study of film aesthetics and narrative formations across the continent. On the other hand, however, by inscribing this comparative effort into a singular, common denominator, the united and homogenous Africa of the post-independence pan-Africanist discourse, it limited it to an impoverished form of comparativism, unable to take into account and properly valorize the profound historical, economic, social, cultural and political differences existing between different African countries, and their impact on the films that were being produced.

Such a homogenizing approach was somehow justified by the specific modes of film production of the early post-independence period. Back then, African cinema was heavily dependent on foreign (mainly French) cooperation funding, and was made by a small elite of highly interdependent and connected filmmakers who trained mostly abroad, and who could aptly be described as being part of a group sharing similar ideas about the role of cinema in Africa. However, as highlighted by Harrow (2007) and Tcheuyap (2011), among others, with the emergence of new generations of African filmmakers (and critics), and with the seismic transformations generated by the introduction of new technologies, this early paradigm became obsolete. Harrow made an attempt at moving forward by developing a theoretical framework "concerned with the ways in which desire and fantasy play decisive roles in the ideological constructions of subjectivity and agency" (2007, p. 20), and thus by proposing to move from a paradigm centered on an "aesthetic of depth" (connected to post-independence nationalism and monolithic ideals of political engagement), to one based on what he provocatively suggested to define as an "aesthetic of surface." Similarly, Tcheuyap (2011) argued for a new scholarship able to account for two key dimensions left aside by the previous, politically-normative approach: Entertainment and audience's pleasure. As Tcheuyap underlined, the emergence of video film industries such as Nollywood "clearly signals that African cinemas have moved in the crucial direction of popular cinema" (2011, p. 23) and scholars approaching the field of African "screen media" (Dovey, 2009) cannot ignore these transformations.

Harrow's and Tcheuyap's works, as well as other attempts which can be seen as part of the same trend (Diawara, 2010; Dovey, 2009; Thackway, 2003), helped pluralizing the academic discourse on African cinemas by proposing innovative theoretical approaches and wider thematic and generic focuses. But they did not manage to fully overcome the simplistic comparativism put forward by Vieyra. In most of these works, in fact, even if the plurality of African cinema experiences is recognized, the particularity of specific regional and national trajectories is not fully considered. It is rather within the field of African video film industries studies, emerging throughout the 2000s, that a more sustained interest for the specificities of precise national contexts began to see the light (cf. Haynes, 2000; Meyer, 1999; and, more recently, Garritano, 2013; Meyer, 2015; Haynes, 2016).

The issue of the existence of "national cinemas" in Africa is particularly complicated to address, especially if we consider, as Karin Barber (2007) suggests us to do, that the relation between media and processes of nation-building in Africa worked in ways profoundly different from those analyzed by Benedict Anderson (1983).[2] However, the relevance of specific local, regional and national dynamics should be taken into account in order to understand the existence of different responses to similar phenomena (such as, for instance, the different responses to the introduction of analog and digital technologies around Africa). Furthermore, as Hjort and MacKenzie underscored,

> Although there is much talk these days about the erosion of nation-states and the need to rethink the link that has been assumed for some time to exist between nations and cinematic cultures ... film scholars should be intent, not so much on avoiding concepts of nationhood and nationality, but on refining them and clearly identifying their continued, although changing pertinence for film studies. (2000, p. 2)

Indeed, despite the worldwide impact of processes of globalization and neoliberalization, a growing number of scholars have begun to suggest that analysts have been too quick in discarding the nation-state as a frame of reference for interpreting individual and collective initiatives, in Africa as elsewhere in the world (Moyo and Yeros, 2011). The analysis proposed in this chapter, then, takes local specificities seriously and make an attempt at understanding their influence in shaping diverging itineraries of media transformation. It does so by looking at video film production in relation to the nation-state, that is, by inscribing it in specific national political and economic histories. But it also does so by underlying the role of specific cities and regions in wider national contexts. The video film production analyzed in this chapter, in fact, is more the outcome of the three "media capitals" (Curtin, 2003), Lagos, Addis Ababa, and Abidjan, than the expression of three distinct national cinemas. Nevertheless, the legal, economic, political, and historical frameworks that have influenced the emergence and development of these video film industries are largely connected to the specific trajectories that Nigeria, Ethiopia, and Côte d'Ivoire took as independent, postcolonial nations, that is, to specific *national* legal frameworks, economic measures, and political conjunctures which affected the development of media production in the contexts of these three media capitals.

Based on these premises, this chapter adopts an open-ended comparative approach which counters the narrow comparativism based on a monolithic conception of Africa, as seen in Vieyra's work. By considering comparison as an "epistemological technique of rupture" (Schmidt 2010, p. 80) and by highlighting areas of meaningful incomparability, the research presented here aims at using comparative analysis as a tool to "denaturalize" (Hallin and Mancini 2004, p. 2) our understanding of African video film industries. The reasons for the selection of Nigeria, Ethiopia, and Côte d'Ivoire are multiple. If Nigeria is the inescapable reference country for a discussion of video film production in Africa, the selection of Ethiopia and Côte d'Ivoire requires a brief explanation. These are two of the most culturally and politically influential countries of the sub-Saharan African region and they can represent in general terms the cultural, social, and political environment of two profoundly different areas of the continent (the Horn and Western Francophone Africa). Because of their size, their political and cultural history, and their present economic and military power, these two nations have a wide influence in their respective geographical areas. Furthermore, compared to other sub-Saharan African countries that have witnessed the development of local video film industries in the recent past (such as Ghana, Kenya, Tanzania, Uganda, and Cameroon), these are probably the two cases that have been studied the least, and which, as non-Anglophone countries, were less exposed to the direct influence of Nollywood video films in the early years of the development of their respective video film industries.

The Difference Video Makes

In one of the first book-length studies of the video format, Roy Armes cautioned that "video's very versatility and flexibility as a medium repulse any simple attempt to grasp its 'essence' or 'specificity'" (1988, p. 1, qtd. in Herbert 2014, p. 4). Indeed, video is better understood as a fluid technology which participated in transforming media industries around the world in many different and unpredictable ways. The definition of the term "video" itself is relatively fluid and, for the sake of clarity, my use of this term in this chapter needs a brief clarification. As the Oxford dictionary definition highlights,[3] the term "video" encompass both analog and digital technologies, remaining open to different meanings and uses. Its most important function is that of differentiating these technologies from the celluloid film format in order to underline the disruptive force that their introduction had on cinema history and on its previously unchallenged relation with the film format. Following this definition, in this chapter I thus adopt video as a generic term, and instead use the words "analog" and "digital" when referring to specific technologies and their specific impacts on the transformation of media production and distribution in the three analyzed countries.

Video made its first appearance in the 1950s and was used by "television broadcasters to transmit and archive programming" (McDonald 2008, p. 1), but it became available to consumers only two decades later. Since then, and for the following 20 years, it had a major impact on media industries all over the world and participated in revolutionizing their economy of production and distribution, as well as their relationship with audiences (Herbert, 2014; Hilderbrand, 2009; McDonald, 2007). In Hilderbrand's (2009) opinion, the most remarkable attribute of the video is "access." Indeed, video made media production and circulation accessible to a range of people who were previously excluded from these processes because of the economic and technological barriers attached to them. The introduction of these technologies had indeed a fundamental role in opening up the consumption of global audiovisual materials to regions of the world that were previously excluded from it. As Brian Larkin emphasized in relation to Nigeria,

> piracy has made available to Nigerians a vast array of world media at a speed they could never imagine, hooking them up to the accelerated circuit of global media flows. Where cinema screens were once filled with outdated films from the United States or India, pirate media means that Nigerian audiences can watch films contemporaneously with audiences in New York or Bombay. Instead of being marginalized by official distribution networks, Nigerian consumers can now participate in the immediacy of an international consumer culture – but only through the mediating capacity of piracy. (2004, p. 297)

In this sense, the introduction of the video has been, through piracy, a major accelerator of globalization processes worldwide. However, while most of us today tend to connect the introduction of video to the global explosion of movie piracy (cf. Athique, 2008; Larkin, 2004; Lobato, 2012; O'Reagan, 1991), it is important to consider that video also had a very important stake in the transformation of movie industries' official economy. In fact, from the 1970s, film industries in major producing countries adopted straight-to-video systems to diversify their production output and to respond to the increase in audience demand for cheap and affordable entertainment. As Ramon Lobato points out, reliable data on the nontheatrical movie sector is hard to find, but according to a study by the Harvard economists Anita Elberse and Felix Oberholzer-Gee [based on figures collected during a five-year sample (2000–05)], 59 per cent of titles in the US video/DVD marketplace are released straight-to-video. There are vast straight-to-video industries in nations such as Japan (home to "V-cinema" straight-to-video DVD releases and "OVA", or original video animation, movies), Thailand (where straight-to-VCD release is popular with independent directors) and Mexico (known for its "videohome" narcotraficante movies) … Despite its unsavory reputation, *straight-to-video is a big – and global – business*. In terms of the number of films released each year, straight-to-video is the *empirical norm* of contemporary cinema. (2012, p. 22, my emphasis).

It is useful to keep these data in mind as we advance in this analysis, because they help us "de-dramatize" (Bayart 2010, p. 31) the African case studies to which this chapter is dedicated. If it is certain that the introduction of video technologies had a particular impact in sub-Saharan Africa due to the specificities of the African context, it is important to remember that the emergence of straight-to-video industries such as Nollywood is less unique than what is often believed, and the straight-to-video model of distribution, far from being a specificity of less developed media markets, has been central for the economy of major film industries up to the 2000s.

African Videoscapes

Through the late 1970s, following profoundly different itineraries, Nigeria, Ethiopia and Côte d'Ivoire had managed to develop moderately efficient celluloid film industries. In Nigeria, a local popular cinema production had emerged from the tradition of Yoruba Travelling Theatre and artists such as Hubert Ogunde, Moses Olaiya Adejum (known as Baba Sala), Adeyemi Afolayan (known as Ade Love), Ola Balogun and Eddie Ugbomah had participated in developing one of the most dynamic celluloid industries in the region (Balogun 1983). Something similar had happened also in Côte d'Ivoire where, partly thanks to funding coming from the old colonial metropole, people like Henri Duparc, Roger Gnoan M'bala, and Desiré Ecaré had been able to produce a number of celluloid films which had managed to have substantial commercial success with local audiences (Bachy, 1983). In Ethiopia, the Derg regime in the late 1970s had created the Ethiopian Film Center (later transformed into the Ethiopian Film Corporation), and funded the training in Russia of a generation of filmmakers and technicians (including Tafese Jara, Getachew Terreken, Desta Tadesse, Taferi Bezuayo, Berhanu Shiberu and Abeba Kasala) who had later contributed in producing a large number of documentary and fiction films for release in both state-owned cinemas and local television channels (Jedlowski, 2015a).

The pauperization of most African economies that followed the global economic crisis of the late 1970s and early 1980s profoundly affected this artistic movement: Celluloid became too expensive because of the devaluation of local currencies, and audiences stopped patronizing local theatre halls for lack of economic resources and because of the growth of insecurity in the public spaces. As a result, celluloid film production and cinema-going culture in the three countries literally collapsed in the space of a few years. By the early 1990s, film production had practically disappeared and the few remaining theatre halls were struggling to keep their doors open. This situation influenced the way in which new technologies were received in these contexts, as well as all over Africa and in other regions of the world.

The video made its appearance in sub-Saharan Africa more or less at the same time it did in the rest of the world. It became accessible to the public toward the end of the 1970s and it quickly became a widespread commodity among the rising urban middle classes of expanding metropolises such as Lagos and Abidjan. The situation was slightly different in Ethiopia. In fact, while in the late 1970s Nigeria and Côte d'Ivoire were experiencing the late years of their post-independence economic booms (connected respectively to the export of oil and cacao), Ethiopia was ruled by a Stalinist regime, which enforced a number of programs to develop agriculture and to counter ongoing processes of rural-urban migration (cf. James et al., 2002). As a result, while the introduction of the new technology was quickly embraced by urban middle-class households in Lagos and Abidjan, its penetration remained very limited in Ethiopia and in its capital Addis Ababa. This difference remained relevant for the following two decades, characterizing Ethiopia as one of the African countries with the highest percentage of rural population and the lowest levels of television sets per family. According to Population Concern, a UNDP website cited by Assefa (2005, p. 37), in 2004 there were only four television sets per thousand people in Ethiopia. In the context of the comparison proposed here, this becomes particularly striking if we consider that according to Mitchell Land, in the late 1980s, Côte d'Ivoire and Nigeria, together with South Africa, had already five television sets per 100 of population, "the largest number of televisions per capita in Africa" (1992, p. 12).

In the three countries, the consequence of the economic crisis of the 1980s made video first and foremost a "collective technology." Its strongest impact on audience consumption habits, in fact, was not to be felt, as in most Western countries, through the individualization of viewing practices and the customization of movie culture (cf. Benson-Allott, 2013; Herbert, 2014), but through the emergence of video houses and video-parlors, that is, informal screening venues where video-cassettes of international releases (mainly American B-movies, Honk Kong kung fu films, Indian melodramas, Westerns, and pornography) were screened for derisory entry tickets to urban dwellers too poor to own a VCR and a TV set, or to buy a ticket for a cinema show (cf. Assefa, 2005; Bahi, 2011; Larkin, 2004; Okome, 2007). Coupled with the global phenomenon of movie piracy that video technologies helped develop, the emergence of video houses was the main agent of transformation in film culture throughout the African continent.

If video revolutionized African audiences access to international contents, it quickly had an impact also on content production. This happened in profoundly different ways in each of the three countries this research focuses on. In Ethiopia and Nigeria, the first to pick up the video camera were people involved in local theatre production. In northern Nigeria, for instance,

> Novelist and filmmaker Ado Ahmad Gidan Dabino, who started out his career in a drama group, and co-writer Bashir Mudi Yakasai claim that between 1980 and 1984 amateur drama groups like Gyaranya, Black Eagle, Dynamic Fighters, and Tumbin Giwa made around nine video films. (McCain 2013, p. 38)

In southern Nigeria, "Yoruba traveling theater artists began making video films in 1988" (Haynes and Okome 1998, p. 109), before the commercially successful Igbo-language film *Living in Bondage* (Obi Rapu, 1992) was released, marking the explosion of Nigerian video film production. In Ethiopia, just after the end of the civil war and the fall of the Derg regime in the early 1990s, local entrepreneurs and theatre artists came together to record and distribute Amharic stage plays on VHS. One of the first to be released was, according to Tesfaye Mamo (personal communication, Addis Ababa, 23 January 2013), the play *And Misht,* written and directed by Tesfaye Abebe and produced by Ambasel Music and Video Shop. This film was followed by several straight to VHS releases (Jedlowski 2015, p. 174), which however, contrary to what was happening in Nigeria, did not manage to achieve any particular commercial success. The low level of penetration of television sets and VHS readers in Ethiopia, as well as the low level of urbanization of the country's population, were probably the factors which contributed to this situation, slowing down the development of the Ethiopian video film industry until the beginning of the 2000s.

In Côte d'Ivoire, things went quite differently. In a context marked by the success of the TV satirical comedy series *Comment ça va?*, directed and produced by Léonard Groguhet for the only national television channel Radiodiffusion Télévision Ivoirienne (RTI) between 1975 and 1994 (cf. Bahi 1992), the first attempts at adopting the video technology happened in the field of cabaret-like sketches and TV-like comedy shows, with the production of the landmark video series *Les guignoles d'Abidjan* (Adédé, 2003; Gbanou, 2002). This series began production around 1993 thanks to the initiative of the Ivorian-Capverdian music and event producer (based in Abidjan at the time) Daniel Cuxac, and was produced and distributed in video format for several years before moving to television.[4] The most interesting particularity of this series, which makes the Ivorian case significantly different from the other two analyzed here, is that it was explicitly produced with the diasporic audience in mind, and thus was the first audiovisual media product to be produced in Côte d'Ivoire beyond the control (in terms of both production and distribution) of the national broadcaster RTI. As underlined by one of the show's main actors, the Ivorian star Gohou Michel (personal communication, Abidjan, 14 July 2014), while the cast and crew were Ivorian and the show was filmed in Abidjan, the VHSs were duplicated in Paris for distribution among the Ivorian diaspora in France and other European and (later) African countries. Paradoxically, then, the show became successful in Côte d'Ivoire only after a few years, when the local broadcaster became aware of the show's international success as a VHS series and decided to buy it. In the following years, the example of the tremendous commercial and popular success of *Les guignoles d'Abidjan* stimulated the emergence of a large and dynamic television series production sector, which led to the production of extremely successful titles such as *Ma famille, Class A,* and *Nafi* (Sangaré, 2011). The series *Ma famille,* an independently produced TV series created in 2002 by Loukou Akissi Delphine, also known as Akissi Delta (by then a well-known star thanks to her role in Groguhet's *Comment ça va?* and in some of Henri Duparc's films) is particularly significant because it became one of the greatest success stories in the history of Ivorian television production, reaching most Francophone African countries. This series managed to obtain such tremendous success also by explicitly positioning itself along the legacy of earlier Ivorian TV and VHS series, including in its cast star actors who had become known through such programs (such as Akissi Delta herself, and Gohou Michel), and combining the typical, soap-opera-like melodramatic style of foreign series with the specific Ivorian taste for comedy and humor.

The particular trajectory of video production in Côte d'Ivoire brings to our attention the specificity of each country's experience with video technology, particularly in what concerns the use of VHS as a means of distribution for locally produced contents. The local political, economic and infrastructural specificities of each country played a very important role in shaping these trajectories. As mentioned above, the economic differences between the three countries had a role in determining the success of straight-to-video distribution strategies, with, for instance, Ethiopian early video films struggling to find a market because of the low penetration of VHS recorders and TV sets in the country. But beyond the economic conditions, also the state of infrastructures played a very important role. If Lagos is well known for its erratic provision of electricity, Abidjan on the contrary boasts one of the most stable power supplies in the region. As the Abidjan-based Nigerian filmmaker and producer Chris Orji suggested to me, this is a factor that should be considered in order to understand why, if both Nigerian and Ivorian producers adopted video technologies for local audiovisual production around the same time, Nigerian producers oriented themselves toward film-length format productions to be distributed straight-to-video, while Ivorian producers opted for the series format to be distributed on TV. As Orji told me,

> In Nigeria people didn't watch TV series. They preferred VHSs and VCDs. It is because series need a certain type of environment; you need to watch them regularly. And in Nigeria you can't do that. Nigerian audience prefer to watch a film and

then forget about it. Series are too long. And you have to be there to follow them. But then maybe the evening you don't have light, and you cannot turn your TV on. While, with the VCDs, you watch them when you can, when you have the money to buy the fuel and turn your generator on. (personal communication, Abidjan, 21 September 2015)

Thanks to the partial improvement of infrastructural conditions in Nigerian cities like Lagos and the ongoing transformation in the local video film industry economy, today the TV series format is emerging as a valuable option also for Nigerian producers, but throughout the 1990s and the early 2000s, such a format would have struggled to find its audience in a country like Nigeria. At the same time, from the late 1990s and throughout the early 2000s, while Nigeria was experiencing the return of democracy after two decades of military regimes, Côte d'Ivoire was plunged into a very violent and divisive civil war, which, in a context of high penetration of television sets and relative stability of power supply, favored the success of the series broadcast on TV, to be watched at home rather than in crowded and "dangerous" neighborhood video houses" (Diao, 2014).

In Ethiopia, the specificity of the local political context, marked by the tight control of media production and distribution (cf. Reta, 2013), prevented local video producers to turn toward the local broadcaster to overcome the commercial failure of straight-to-video distribution. They instead turned themselves toward the few still-existing, state-owned theatre halls, which at the time (in the late 1990s and early 2000s) were surviving by programming old copies of celluloid Indian films and American B-movies. In order to do that, however, they had to wait a few years in order to obtain the authorization to screen videos, which, as a technology, suffered from the bad reputation connected to the circulation of pornographic videotapes in the neighborhood video houses throughout the 1980s and 1990s. The first theatrical screenings took place in the early 2000s, but the film that marked the turning point in the history of the local video film industry was Theodros Teshome's *Kazkaza Welafen* (2003). This film's commercial success convinced other video entrepreneurs of the viability of the video-to-cinema model, and the industry quickly grew to become one of the most productive in sub-Saharan Africa. The explosion in video production resulted also from the switch from analog to digital technologies which made video production faster and cheaper. As Tesfaye Mamo (personal communication, Addis Ababa, 23 January 2013) put it, this technological transformation was a "shifting point" for the Ethiopian film industry, allowing for a general increase of the average production quality which made Ethiopian videos better fit for theatrical release. Today, the number of theatre halls in the country has multiplied and audiences can be seen queuing in front of them during the afternoon, even in the middle of the week.

Continuities, Discontinuities, and Convergences

Thanks to the size of the Nigerian internal market, the pronounced dynamism of Nigerian media entrepreneurs (the well-known "marketers") and the advantage of producing the majority of video films in the English language, Nollywood grew faster than other video film industries around Africa and, through mainly informal and pirated networks of circulation (Adejunmobi, 2007), Nigerian videos began circulating all over the continent (Krings and Okome, 2013). In countries such as Ghana, Tanzania, and the Democratic Republic of Congo, their circulation had a controversial impact on local popular culture industries, at times disrupting the relationship between audiences and local productions, but also propelling, through commercial competition, the consolidation of local production ventures (Krings, 2010; Meyer, 2010; Pype, 2013).

In Ethiopia and Côte d'Ivoire, the circulation of Nollywood films was initially less important and influential than in other countries. As I discussed at length elsewhere (Jedlowski 2017), the circulation of Nollywood videos in Côte d'Ivoire evolved through a few different phases. Nigerian video films began circulating among the Nigerian diaspora residents in the country and, when local audiences began watching them, they were imported by local video film distributors who traveled to Lomé or Lagos to buy their stocks. If Nollywood's popularity grew throughout the 2000s, Nigerian videos remained a second choice if compared to local TV series and comedies. But things changed at the beginning of the 2010s when the new French-owned channel Nollywood.tv began screening Nollywood videos dubbed in French 24 hours a day. Since then, Nollywood has become extremely popular, and Nollywood.tv has almost overcome the local broadcaster RTI as the most popular channel in the country, to the point of attracting the interest of the French satellite company Canal+. This company ended up buying Nollywood.tv in 2014 as part of its expansion plans in sub-Saharan Africa, which culminated in the creation of the satellite channel A+, a 24/7 channel for Francophone (or French-dubbed) African entertainment products (cf. also Jedlowski, 2016).

In Ethiopia, Nigerian films had almost no circulation until recently, when the exponential growth of Pentecostalism (cf. Fantini, 2015) allowed for the penetration of a few Nigerian churches in the country, which brought with them an entire archive of Nollywood video films. Nigerian videos, however, remained mostly confined to Pentecostal circles and, at least for what I could understand from interviews and informal conversations with Ethiopian cinema audiences during my research, if Nollywood is known as a phenomenon, most people have never seen a Nigerian video film in their life. This points to the fact that it is analytically important to recognize the difference between the pan-African circulation of Nollywood videos and the pan-African circulation of the discourse about Nollywood

(Jedlowski, 2013). Indeed, in Ethiopia the discourse about Nollywood is more popular than the videos themselves. Nollywood works as a success story, a positive example that local filmmakers and entrepreneurs use as an inspiration, a motivation to support their continued efforts against the economic odds they face in order to produce films in an African country today. The distance between Nollywood films and the discourse about Nollywood as a phenomenon is well demonstrated by the fact that, while I was in Ethiopia, local filmmakers were very interested by my previous research experiences on Nollywood, and asked me to organize a seminar about the economy of the Nigerian video film industry for the local association of young filmmakers (Allatinos), but when I proposed to screen a Nollywood film as part of the event, they refused, telling me that they were not interested in the narrative or aesthetic aspects of the Nollywood video films, but only in the economic model adopted by the Nigerian industry.

In Côte d'Ivoire, despite the fact that Nollywood video films are popular among the local audience, people know little about the industry's modes of operation and use the Nollywood success story in order to legitimate claims which are connected to the local context. For instance, during an informal conversation with a few local filmmakers, a young Ivorian director told me: "You see, we need our government to act like the Nigerian one, and do something for the film industry. Nollywood developed because the government supported the industry, gave them money and infrastructures!" However, as researches on the Nigerian video film industry clearly evidenced, Nollywood thrived precisely because the government did not intervene in any substantial way until recently. And Nigerian film entrepreneurs look at government interventions with suspicion. This example thus shows how "Nollywood" as a term has become the signifier for a very wide and diverse set of meanings, related to the specificity of local contexts of film production and the work that Nollywood-as-a-success-story is able to do in relation to them.

With the success of Nollywood.tv in Côte d'Ivoire, local entrepreneurs started looking at Nollywood as a model, but they did it in the context of a country that has a long history of political intervention in the field of cultural production – somehow a legacy of French colonialism and of the French model of cultural policies. In this context, local producers, left at the margins by the hegemony of the series format and the influence of the television industry on it, used the Nollywood example as a discursive tool to push the government to promote and finance film production. It must be said that, beyond the commercially successful TV series production, Côte d'Ivoire has also witnessed, from around 2004, the emergence of smaller straight-to-TV video film production phenomenon around the work of filmmakers such as Alex Quassy, Owell Brown, Jaques Trabi, Alain Guikou, Guy Kalou and Marie Luise Asseu.[5] With the end of the political crisis in 2011–2012, this group of filmmakers and producers has become more vocal, and has found in the new government a proactive interlocutor for the development of film production in Côte d'Ivoire. If the international success of the (partially state-funded) film *Run* (2014) by Philippe Lacôte is the most evident example of the political will to revive the local film industry, other initiatives have seen the light. The most interesting of them for the argument developed in this chapter is the much publicized creation of the brand "Babywood" by the Ivorian state-owned broadcaster RTI (still the only authorized broadcaster in the country, Nollywood. tv and A+ being accessible only via satellite), as a tool to promote local film productions locally and internationally (*ScreenAfrica*, 2015; see also Noukoué, 2015). In this case, the importance the brand "Nollywood" has played in the success of the Nigerian video film industry (Jedlowski, 2011) is fully acknowledged through the attempt of replicating a similar process, even before something like an actual video film industry has fully developed in the country.

If the Ivorian producers have used the Nollywood example as a tool in order to make an attempt at moving from TV series to video film production, in Nigeria and Ethiopia, television series are progressively taking over the video film format. In both countries, in fact, satellite television channels and (in what concerns Nigeria) the new channels that emerged from the transition to digital television signal (see Jedlowski, 2016), are attracting many of the film professionals (above all, star actors and film directors, but also members of film crews and technicians) who have begun their careers in the local video film industries. In Nigeria, TV series like *Tinsel* (which began in 2008), *Meet the Adebanjos*, and, more recently, *Taste of Love* have become extremely successful, attracting more and more Nollywood veterans, and making new stars emerge (Tsika, forthcoming). Similarly, over the past few years in Ethiopia a number of series, such as *Wazema*, *Mogachoch*, *Bekenat Mekakel*, and *Welafen* have made their appearance on the independent satellite channel Ethiopian Broadcasting Service (EBS – broadcast from the United States) obtaining a wide popular success in Ethiopia and throughout the diaspora (Tadesse, 2018). In both contexts, this process is a sign of the growing interest of larger media corporations in the local production phenomenon. The switch to the TV series format, in fact, is better suited to the interest of broadcasters who are keen in developing stable and loyal audiences, whose free attention-labor is easier to sell to advertisers than that of shorter, one-off programs such as the video films (see also Cubitt, 2005).

In relation to these more recent developments, it is important to note the substantial difference between the broadcasting markets in the three countries. Nigeria is the only one among them to have a fully liberalized broadcasting sector since the mid-1990s. In Ethiopia and Côte d'Ivoire, the national broadcasters (the Ethiopian Broadcasting Corporation (EBC – formerly ETV) and the RTI respectively still have the monopolistic control of the national broadcasting systems. This situation has been partially transformed by the growing impact of satellite channels, including those that, as the already mentioned EBS, Nollywood.tv and A+, broadcast also African, and at times local, content. Nevertheless, within this context, the Nigerian television market is undoubtedly the most dynamic among the three, and one of the most dynamic in the continent – a situation confirmed by the multiplication of channels that resulted from the recent switch to digital broadcasting.

However, the effect of these different broadcasting environments on the development of video film industries in the three countries is far from linear.

While Nigeria has the most dynamic broadcasting market, television played, until recently, a very marginal role in the development of Nollywood. Quite to the contrary, it is precisely the crisis of the national broadcaster and the slow take-off of the newly created independent channels throughout the 1990s that can be regarded as one of the key factors which favored of the explosion of the local video film industry (Jedlowski, 2012). Still today, rather than local broadcasters, the companies which are battling to play the major role in the economy of Nollywood are foreign media corporations such as the South African M-Net-Multichoice, the French Canal+, and the Nigerian/American iROKOtv. In Côte d'Ivoire, RTI has exploited its monopoly to influence locally produced contents and maintain, as much as possible, a role as gatekeeper. Even the successful series, such as *Les guignoles d'Abidjan* and *Ma famille*, which have been independently produced and, at least initially (as in the case of *Les guignoles*) independently distributed, have been later acquired by RTI. This makes the broadcaster an ambiguous player in the history of local video production: It has somehow inhibited independent developments, but it has also been the most receptive partner for whoever was actually producing something. Finally, in Ethiopia, the specific priorities dictated by the government's authoritarian developmentalist agenda forced the national broadcaster to marginalize entertainment products and prioritize educational programs. This, combined with the very low penetration of television sets and VHR recorders in the country highlighted earlier, forced local entrepreneurs toward theatre halls. In both Côte d'Ivoire and Ethiopia, the situation is changing quickly because of satellite broadcasters' interest in attracting African audiences through local contents. This process is ultimately having a strong impact on African screen media production, participating to its progressive "televisualization" (cf. Adejunmobi, 2015; Tcheuyap, 2015).

Conclusion

As Karin Barber underlined, when looking at specific cultural texts or media we need to ask ourselves "why, at a certain time and place, we find these textual forms and not others; and how specific textual forms participate in constituting specific historical forms of consciousness" (2007, p. 41). In this chapter, I made an attempt at responding, at least partially, to this call. By looking at how video technologies have been adopted in different contexts, I made an attempt and understanding how specific forms of video film production have appeared in different contexts at specific moments in history, and why, while being the result of the introduction of the same technology (the video), they have developed differently. As Brian Larkin has suggested,

Technologies are unstable things. We think we know what a radio is or what a cinema is used for, but these phenomena, which we take for granted, have often surprising histories. ... The meaning attached to technologies, their technical functions, and the social uses to which they are put are not an inevitable consequence but something worked out over time in the context of considerable cultural debate. And even then, these meanings and uses are often unstable, vulnerable to changing political orders and subject to the contingencies of objects' physical life. (2008, p. 3)

As this chapter showed, then, the adoption of video technology in the three contexts analyzed here led to the emergence of profoundly different phenomena as a result of specific economic and political histories, cultural debates, and trajectories of infrastructural development.

What is missing from the analysis presented here, however, is an attempt at responding to the second part of Barber's quote. What about the interactions between the processes discussed in this chapter and the contents of the video films produced in these three countries? And what about the audiences? How did these different trajectories of media transformation interact with processes of construction of collective identities, political constituencies, and "aesthetic formations" (Meyer, 2009)?

These are questions that, for lack of room, this chapter cannot approach without risking to fall into exaggerated simplifications, but which will need to be addressed in order to fully develop the comparative analysis this research aims to do. And further analytical insights could be gained by enlarging the comparative analysis also to non-African case studies, in order to make the African experience of video production be compared with other similar instances which appeared in countries as different as Mexico, the Philippines, and Turkey over the past three decades. The African video boom is part of the larger story of video film production experiences triggered by the introduction of analog technologies throughout the world in the late 1970s and early 1980s: This is a story whose amazing complexity and diversity is yet to be fully explored.

Notes

1 Vieyra suggests using the term "African cinema" because "the national cinemas of this continent are not yet so important ... that we are led to divide them up and study them separately as Algerian, Senegalese, Nigerian, Moroccan, Guinean, Ivorian, or Nigerien cinema" (qtd. in Tcheuyap 2011, p. 32).

2 As Barber emphasizes in relation to Nigeria, for instance, the emergence of new forms of literature, oral culture and media production during both the colonial and the post-colonial eras, generated transversal rather than national audiences:

These new imagined constituencies did not necessarily coincide with the nation. In the formative years of multi-ethnic, multi-lingual, externally defined nations of Africa, emergent classes of literati experimented with new genres of print capitalism in order to convene shifting audiences, whose boundaries seemed to shrink and expand from moment to moment, sometimes consolidating ethnic linguistic communities far smaller than the national entity, at other times bypassing the nation to convoke a pan-African, black, or pan-human audience (Barber 2007, p. 202).

3   The Oxford Dictionary defines video as "a recording of moving visual images made digitally or on videotape." See https://en.oxforddictionaries.com/definition/video.
4   The first season of this series, which ran throughout the 1990s, was filmed in Betacam format and then edited and distributed in VHS. The second season, produced in the 2000s, was filmed in DVcam and then edited and distributed digitally on TV and via DVDs. I am grateful to Julie Dénommée and Alex Quassy for these and the following information on production and distribution formats of Ivorian series.
5   I do not include in this list Philippe Lacôte, whose recent film *Run* (2014) was presented at the Cannes International Film Festival, because, despite his connection with the grassroots filmmaking movement in Abidjan through the activity of his production company Wassakara Productions, his work is of another level (in aesthetic, technical and economic terms) and cannot be compared with the ongoing video film production in the country.

References

Adédé, Schadé. 2003. "Côte d'Ivoire: Les Guignols d'Abidjan : l'humour corrosif d'une troupe exceptionnelle." *AllAfrica*, 10 May. Available online: http://fr.allafrica.com/stories/200305120311.html (accessed 30 March 2018).
Adejunmobi, Moradewun A. 2007. "Nigerian video film as minor transnational practice." *Postcolonial Text* 3.2. Available online: http://postcolonial.univ-paris13.fr/index.php/pct/article/viewArticle/548 (accessed 30 March 2018).
Adejunmobi, Moradewun A. 2015. "African film's televisual turn." *Cinema Journal* 54.2: 120–125.
Anderson, Benedict. 1983. *Imagined Communities: Reflections on the Origin and Spread of Nationalism*. London: Verso.
Armes, Roy. 1988. *On Video*. London: Routledge.
Assefa, Emrakeb. 2005. *An Investigation into the Popularity of American Action Movies Shown in Informal Video Houses in Addis Ababa, Ethiopia*. Unpublished MA Thesis, Rhodes University.
Athique, Adrian. 2008. "The global dynamics of Indian media piracy: Export markets, playback media and the informal economy." *Media, Culture, and Society* 30,5: 699–717.
Bachy, Victor. 1983. *Le cinéma en Côte d'Ivoire*. Paris: L'Harmattan.
Bahi, Aghi. 1992. *Narration, traditions et modernité dans le discours filmique de* Comment ça va?, *une émission de la télévision ivoirienne*. Unpublished PhD Thesis, Université Lumière Lyon II.

Bahi, Aghi. 2011. "Piratages audiovisuels en Côte d'Ivoire, entre rhétorique du blâme et logiques des commerçants." In *Piratages audiovisuels: Les voies souterraines de la mondialisation culturelle*, edited by Tristan Mattelart, 163–182. Brussels: Ina-De Boeck.

Balogun, Françoise. 1983. *Le cinéma au Nigéria*. Paris: L'Harmattan.

Barber, Karin. 2007. *The Anthropology of Texts, Persons and Publics*. Cambridge: Cambridge University Press.

Bayart, Jean-François. 2010. *The State in Africa: The Politics of the Belly* (Second edition). Cambridge: Polity.

Bayart, Jean-François. 2016. "'Dessine-moi un MENA !', ou l'impossible définition des 'aires culturelles'," *Societés Politiques Comparées* 38: 1–43.

Benson-Allott, Caetlin. 2013. *Killer Tapes and Shattered Screens: Video Spectatorship from VHS to File Sharing*. Berkeley: University of California Press.

Böhme, Claudia. 2015. "Film production as a 'mirror of society': The history of a video film art group in Dar es Salaam, Tanzania," *Journal of African Cinemas* 7.2: 117–135. DOI: https://doi.org/10.1386/jac.7.2.117_1

Cubitt, Sean. 2005. "Distribution and media flows." *Cultural Politics* 1.2: 193–213. DOI: 10.2752/174321905778054809

Curtin, Michael. 2003. "Media capital: towards the study of spatial flows." *International Journal of Cultural Studies* 6.2: 202–228. DOI: 10.1177/13678779030062004

Diao, Claire. 2014. "Séries TV#1 : Qu'est-ce qu'on regarde à Abidjan ? – entretien de Claire Diao avec Yacouba Sangaré." *Africultures*, 15 September. Available online: www.africultures.com/php/?nav=article&no=12420 (accessed 30 March 2018).

Diawara, Manthia. 2010. *African Film: New Forms of Aesthetics and Politics*. Munich: Prestel.

Dovey, Lindiwe. 2009. *African Film and Literature: Adapting Violence to the Screen*. New York: Columbia University Press.

Fantini, Emanuele. 2015. "Go Pente! The charismatic renewal of the evangelical movement in Ethiopia." In *Understanding Contemporary Ethiopia: Monarchy, Revolution and the Legacy of Meles Zenawi*, edited by Gérard Prunier and Eloi Ficquet, 123–146. Oxford: Oxford University Press.

Garritano, Carmela. 2013. *African Video Movies and Global Desires: A Ghanaian History*. Athens: Ohio University Press.

Gbanou, Sélom Komlan. 2002. "Le rôle du petit écran: l'exemple ivoirien." *Notre Librairie* 149: 114–117.

Hallin, Daniel C., and Paolo Mancini. 2004. *Comparing Media Systems: Three Models of Media and Politics*. Cambridge: Cambridge University Press.

Harrow, Kenneth W. 2007. *Postcolonial African Cinema: From Political Engagement to Postmodernism*. Bloomington: Indiana University Press.

Haynes, Jonathan, ed. 2000. *Nigerian Video Films*. Athens: Ohio University Press.

Haynes, Jonathan, 2016. *Nollywood: The Creation of Nigerian Film Genres*. Chicago: University of Chicago Press, 2016.

Haynes, Jonathan, and Onookome Okome. 1998. "Evolving popular media: Nigerian video films." *Research in African literatures* 29.3: 106–128.

Herbert, Daniel. 2014. *Videoland: Movie Culture at the American Video Store*. Berkeley: University of California Press.

Hilderbrand, Lucas. 2009. *Inherent Vice: Bootleg Histories of Videotape and Copyright*. Durham, NC: Duke University Press.

Hjort, Mette, and Scott MacKenzie, eds. 2000. *Cinema and Nation*. London: Routledge.

Krings, Matthias. 2010. "Nollywood goes East: The localization of Nigerian video films in Tanzania." In *Viewing African Cinema in the Twentieth Century: Art Films and the Nollywood Video Revolution*, edited by Mahir Saul and Ralph A. Austen, 74–95. Athens: Ohio University Press.

Krings, Matthias, and Onookome Okome, eds. 2013. *Global Nollywood: The Transnational Dimensions of an African Video Film Industry*. Bloomington: Indiana University Press.

James, Wendy, Eisei Kurimoto, Donald Donham, and Alessandro Triulzi, eds. 2002. *Remapping Ethiopia: Socialism and After*. Athens: Ohio University Press.

Jedlowski, Alessandro. 2011. "When the Nigerian video film industry became 'Nollywood': Naming, branding and the videos' transnational mobility." *Estudos Afro-Asiaticos* 33.1–2–3: 225–251.

Jedlowski, Alessandro. 2012. "Small screen cinema: Informality and remediation in Nollywood." *Television and New Media* 13.5: 431–446.

Jedlowski, Alessandro. 2013. "Nigerian videos in the global arena: The postcolonial exotic revisited." *The Global South* 7.1: 157–178.

Jedlowski, Alessandro. 2015a. "Screening Ethiopia: A preliminary study of the history and contemporary developments of film production in Ethiopia." *Journal of African Cinemas* 7.2: 169–185. DOI: 10.1386/jac.7.2.169_1

Jedlowski, Alessandro. 2015b. "Avenues of participation and strategies of control: Video film production and social mobility in Ethiopia and southern Nigeria." In *Production Studies, The Sequel! Cultural Studies of Global Media Industries*, edited by Miranda Banks, Vicky Mayer, and Bridget Conor, 175–186. New York: Routledge.

Jedlowski, Alessandro. 2016. "Studying media 'from' the South: African media studies and global perspectives." *Black Camera* 7.2: 174–193.

Jedlowski, Alessandro. 2017. "African media and the corporate takeover: Video film circulation in the age of neoliberal transformation." *African Affairs* 116.465: 671–691. https://doi.org/DOI: 10.1093/afraf/adx017

Land, Mitchell. 1992. "Ivorian television, willing vector of cultural imperialism." *Howard Journal of Communications* 4.1–2: 10–27.

Larkin, Brian. 2000. "Hausa dramas and the rise of video culture in Nigeria." In *Nigerian Video Films*, edited by Jonathan Haynes, 209–241. Athens: Ohio University Press.

Larkin, Brian. 2004. "Degraded images, distorted sounds: Nigerian video and the infrastructure of piracy." *Public Culture* 16.2: 289–314.

Larkin, Brian. 2008. *Signal and Noise: Media, Infrastructure, and Urban Culture in Nigeria*. Durham, NC: Duke University Press.

Lobato, Ramon. 2012. *Shadow Economies of Cinema: Mapping Informal Film Distribution*. New York: Palgrave Macmillan.

McCain, Carmen. 2013. "Nollywood and its others: Questioning English language hegemony in Nollywood studies." *The Global South* 7.1: 30–54.

McDonald, Paul. 2008. *Video and DVD Industries*. New York: Palgrave Macmillan.

Meyer, Birgit. 1999. "Popular Ghanaian Cinema and 'African Heritage'." *Africa Today* 46.2: 93–114.

Meyer, Birgit, ed. 2009. *Aesthetic Formations: Media, Religion, and the Senses*. London: Palgrave Macmillan.

Meyer, Birgit. 2010. "Ghanaian popular video movies between state film policies and Nollywood: Discourses and tensions." In *Viewing African Cinema in the Twenty-first*

Century: FESPACO Art Films and the Nollywood Video Revolution, edited by Ralph Austen and Mahir Saul, 42–62. Athens: Ohio University Press.

Meyer, Birgit. 2015. *Sensational Movies: Video, Vision, and Christianity in Ghana*. Berkeley: University of California Press.

Mistry, Jyoti, and Jordache A. Ellapen. 2013. "Nollywood's transportability: The politics and economics of video films as cultural products." In *Global Nollywood: The Transnational Dimensions of an African Video Film Industry*, edited by Matthias Krings and Onookome Okome, 46–72. Bloomington: Indiana University Press.

Moyo, Sam, and Paris Yeros, eds. 2011. *Reclaiming the Nation: The Return of the National Question in Africa, Asia and Latin America*. London: Pluto Press.

Noukoué, Serge. 2015. "Abidjan, plaque tournante de l'audiovisuel africain." *Le Monde*, 2 September.

Okome, Onookome. 2007. "Nollywood: Spectatorship, audience and the sites of consumption." *Postcolonial text* 3.2. Available online: http://postcolonial.univ-paris13.fr/index.php/pct/article/viewArticle/763 (accessed 30 March 2018).

O'Regan, Tom. 1991. "From piracy to sovereignty: International video cassette recorder trends." *Continuum: Journal of Media & Cultural Studies* 4.2: 112–135. DOI: 10.1080/10304319109388202

Overbergh, Ann. 2015a. "Kenya's Riverwood: Market structure, power relations, and future outlooks." *Journal of African Cinemas* 7.2: 97–115. DOI: https://dx.doi.org/10.1386/jac.7.2.97_1

Overbergh, Ann. 2015b. "Innovation and its obstacles in Tanzania's Bongowood." *Journal of African Cinemas* 7.2: 137–151. DOI: https://dx.doi.org/10.1386/jac.7.2.137_1

Pype, Katrien. 2013. "Religion, migration and media aesthetics: Notes on the circulation and reception of Nigerian films in Kinshasa." In *Global Nollywood: The Transnational Dimensions of an African Video Film Industry*, edited by Matthias Krings and Onookome Okome, 199–222. Bloomington: Indiana University Press.

Rasmussen, Kristin A. 2010. *Kinna-Uganda: A review of Uganda's National Cinema*. Unpublished MA Thesis, San José State University.

Reta, Meseret Chekol. 2013. *The Quest for Press Freedom: One Hundred Years of History of the Media in Ethiopia*. Plymouth: Rowman & Littlefield.

Sangaré, Yacouba. 2011. "Séries télé ivoirienne: Pourquoi ça cartonne." *CenterBlog*, 2 February. Available online: http://meschak.centerblog.net/4-series-teles-ivoiriennes-pourquoi-ca-cartonne (accessed 30 March 2018).

Santanera, Giovanna. 2015. *Douala si mette in scena: Nuove esperienze video in Cameroun*. Unpublished PhD Thesis, University of Milan La Bicocca.

Schmidt, Robert. 2010. "Re-describing social practices: Comparison as analytical and explorative tool." In *Thick Comparison: Reviving the Ethnographic Aspiration*, edited by Thomas Scheffer and Jörg Niewöhner, 79–102. Leiden: Brill.

ScreenAfrica. 2015. "Welcome to Babiwood." 13 February. Available online: www.screenafrica.com/page/news/africa/1651546-Welcome-to-Babiwood#.V45Ve7MkrmQ (accessed 30 March 2018).

Tadesse, Bitania. 2018. "The new frontiers of Ethiopian film industry: TV serials and sitcoms." In *Cine-Ethiopia: The History and Politics of Film in the Horn of Africa*, edited by Michel W. Thomas, Alessandro Jedlowski and Aboneh Ashagrie. 141–160. East Lansing, MI: Michigan State University Press.

Tcheuyap, Alexie. 2011. *Postnationalist African Cinemas*. Manchester: Manchester University Press.

Tcheuyap, Alexie. 2015. "De las grandes a las pequeñas pantallas. Nuevas narrativas africanas de entretenimiento." *Secuencias* 41.1: 57–77.

Thackway, Melissa. 2003. *Africa Shoots Back: Alternative Perspectives in Sub-Saharan Francophone African Film*. Bloomington: Indiana University Press.

Thomas, Michael W. 2015. "The local film sensation in Ethiopia: Aesthetic comparisons with African cinema and alternative experiences." *Black Camera* 7.1: 17–41.

Tsika, Noah. Forthcoming. "Miracles from Mexico: Christianity, corporate restructuring, and the Telenovela in Nigeria." *Journal of African Cultural Studies*.

Vieyra, Paulin S. 1975. *Le Cinéma africain de ses origines à 1973*. Paris : Présence Africain.

Filmography

Lacôte, Philippe. (2014). *Run*. France/Côte d'Ivoire: Banshee Films, Diam Production, Wassakara Productions.

Obi Rapu, Chris. (1992). *Living in Bondage*. Nigeria: Nek Videos Links.

Teshome, Theodros. (2003). *Kazkaza Welafen*. Ethiopia: Teddy's Studios.

14

Nairobi-based Female Filmmakers
Screen Media Production between the Local and the Transnational

Robin Steedman

In 2002, Judy Kibinge's debut feature film *Dangerous Affair* burst onto the Kenyan film scene and sparked a new era of filmmaking in Nairobi. The film tells the story of Kui, a beautiful woman returned home to Nairobi from New York City looking to get married who falls for, and then marries, the notorious playboy, Murags. When his ex-girlfriend, Rose, also moves back to Nairobi the titular dangerous affair ensues, and while Rose and Murags end up together in the end, they do so as social pariahs. *Dangerous Affair* was a local success and "managed to secure distribution through local cinemas, and even establish a presence within Nairobi's VCD piracy networks" (McNamara 2016, p. 24) alongside winning Best East African Production at the Zanzibar International Film Festival in 2003. Kibinge's career is one that has been marked by transmedia fluency, and she has been active as a director, producer, and writer in Nairobi for over 15 years. Her career has spanned feature fiction, documentaries, television, and commissioned corporate work, and, additionally, she is now Executive Director of the East African documentary film fund Docubox, which she also founded. Films were being made in Kenya before *Dangerous Affair*, including *Saikati* (Mungai, 1992) and *The Battle of the Sacred Tree* (Kinyanjui, 1995), but it was *Dangerous Affair* that marked the start of a film-making renewal in which women have taken the lead (McNamara, 2016; Dovey, 2012), a shift made all the more significant because of the historical marginalization of women in African film industries (cf. Dovey, 2012). In Nairobi, the most successful and critically acclaimed filmmakers – both directors and producers – are women, and yet this creative formation remains woefully understudied, receiving only passing notes in the literature for being "interesting" (Bisschoff, 2012, p. 64,

A Companion to African Cinema, First Edition. Edited by Kenneth W. Harrow and Carmela Garritano.

2015, p. 73; Dovey 2012, p. 22; Wenner 2015, p. 190). This chapter is the first detailed study of these unique women and their industry.

The concept of national cinema is a longstanding organizational principle in film studies, but one that has also been strongly contested, for, viewing "the world as a collection of nations (as in the United Nations) is to marginalise if not deny the possibilities of other ways of organising the world" (Dennison and Lim 2006, p. 6). The concept retains its usefulness in certain circumstances. Indeed, film scholar Andrew Higson argues for its continuing relevance "at the level of policy" because "governments continue to develop defensive strategies designed to protect and promote both the local cultural formation and the local economy" (2006, p. 20). In a supporting argument African film scholar Aboubakar Sanogo observes "any serious study of world cinema, in particular in its independent auteurist version, must come to terms with the indispensable role of the state as an enabler of that tradition" (2015, p. 144). Yet, within the Kenyan context, the state has not played this facilitating role, and instead the parastatal responsible for promoting the Kenyan film industry – the Kenya Film Commission (KFC) – has taken the approach of "selling Kenya as a [film] destination instead of really trying to build within the industry" (Matere, 2015).[1]

In a situation where the state provides almost no support (Kenya), it becomes ever more tenuous to hold the nation as the logical boundary of analysis, and instead, a transnational framework becomes more productive. Rather than a nationally bounded approach, this chapter will examine how connections are taking place across national borders, all the while situated in Nairobi. The vibrancy of Nairobi's screen media market is sustained by a confluence of artistic, commercial, and institutional networks – some local, some transnational – that intersect in the city. Of critical importance is the particular mode of working in this space where Nairobi-based female filmmakers fluidly shift formats between commercial and creative, short and feature, and television and documentary projects to seize any possible opportunity to create.[2] The women filmmakers discussed here are connected by their shared Kenyan nationality, but their more important connection is their choice to live and work in Nairobi.

Foundations: *Saikati*

The first noted film by a Nairobi-based female filmmaker is the feature-length fiction *Saikati* (1992). Directed by Anne Mungai,[3] the film – its narrative, as well as its production – conforms to the conventions and processes of so-called FESPACO, or "serious" African cinema. Mungai was part of the first generation of Nairobi-based female filmmakers, and alongside fellow graduates of the government-run Kenya Institute of Mass Communication (KIMC) Jane Murago Munene and Dommie Yambo-Odtte, and German trained Wanjiru Kinyanjui,[4] formed what

Ellerson terms "the vanguard of Kenya's female visionaries" (2010, p. 122). KIMC was government run at the time[5] and its graduates were "automatically absorbed" into the Film Production Department of the Ministry of Broadcasting and Information "where their job was to make documentaries along government lines" (Kinyanjui 2014, p. 69). Mungai was thus making *Saikati* within an institutional context deeply connected to the national development goals and agendas of the Kenyan state. The film tells the story of a young girl named Saikati from a Maasai village, who travels to Nairobi to work and escape an arranged marriage, only to realize that she belongs not in the city but in the Maasai Mara, and that she must return home to confront her problems and pursue her dream of getting an education. The dominant theme of the film is depicted visually from the outset. When Saikati first appears onscreen in the opening sequence, she is in a neat school uniform of pencil skirt, blouse, and tie. She is on her way to her village and once she arrives she immediately changes into a cloth wrapper and layers of ornate beaded necklaces and headpieces. This visual juxtaposition of urban/"modern" and "traditional"/rural life is the central tension that structures the entire film.

Mungai faced a great deal of difficulty making the film because of her gender. At the time she made the film, there were very few women working in the film industry, so she found herself in the position of giving instructions to a male crew that had difficulty respecting female authority (Mungai, 2015). Despite these challenges, Mungai produced, directed, wrote, and edited *Saikati*. She made the film while working at KIMC, which was funded by the German Friedrich Ebert Foundation[6] – and it was through their support of KIMC that Mungai was provided with the materials to make the film (Cham and Mungai 1994, p. 95). *Saikati* was shot on 16mm film and the processing of the film was done in Kenya, with the exception of the optical soundtrack which Mungai did at Bavaria Studios in Munich because the necessary equipment did not exist in Kenya (Cham and Mungai 1994, pp. 96–97).[7] The film's crew was entirely Kenyan (Cham and Mungai 1994, p. 96). Financing the project was difficult and she "managed to get the crew... and the actors to work for only token pay from the school" since she "could not afford professional fees." She also received in-kind contributions from Serena Hotels and Air Kenya (Cham and Mungai 1994, pp. 95–96) – leading to product-placement sequences in the film. These struggles in film financing have been part of the African cinematic landscape since its beginnings in the 1960s.

Within a context of state supported filmmaking supplemented by transnational resources and corporate donations, Mungai was able to tell a personal and creative story. The film itself closely parallels Mungai's own life, and it was important to her to make a film that reflected her own experiences. She states:

> As a woman film-maker, I want to be free to describe what affects a woman from a rural background. After all, I did grow up in a village! … When I make films, I put a lot of myself into them, a lot of my childhood. It is what I want to express because it is what I know and what I've lived. (Mungai 1996, p. 65)

The need to tell her own story and assert her experiences as well as political views on those experiences helps explain why Mungai would go to the trouble of actually making the film. Mungai's film and early career are thus intelligible according to African film scholar Lizelle Bisschoff's argument that African women filmmakers often "enter the industry through a desire to tell their own stories" and that "commonly their main goal is to offer alternative representations of African women as a counter to western and masculinist hegemony" (2012, p. 168). *Saikati* argues against male gerontocratic control and asserts women's rights to independence through a story based closely on Mungai's lived experiences. African film scholar Melissa Thackway argues "the emergence of women's filmmaking has enabled women directors everywhere to deconstruct stereotypical representations of female characters that are generally filmed from a male point-of-view" (2003, p. 147). While Thackway's argument may stray toward the utopian, it cannot be simply discarded or we risk neglecting the very real structural inequality women in cinema face. For instance, "many of the great women directors who emerged on the continent in the 1970s, 1980s, and 1990s – such as Sarah Maldoror, Safi Faye, and Anne Mungai – have made very few films. Those that they have made have not been widely screened, and sometimes do not exist in modern, digital formats" (Dovey 2012, p. 22). As such, while Mungai is part of a generation of African filmmakers, both male and female, working to assert "authentic" national perspectives and create socio-political transformation, keeping gender in focus is essential to understanding Mungai's working context.

Transformations in the New Millennium

Many features of 1990s-era film productions such as *Saikati* continue to be enduring fixtures of Nairobi-based filmmaking, including the difficulty in finding financing for feature fiction films and the necessity of transnational sponsorship for this endeavor. Yet, there are key differences. Rather than being educated by, and working at, state institutions, the new generation has often trained at film schools abroad and frequently run their own small production companies, relying on their entrepreneurial instincts rather than state support. This generation is also part of a movement of young filmmakers on and off the African continent "whose cultural and educational backgrounds do not encourage a simple equation between political identity (as Africans) and artistic orientation" (Adesokan 2014, p. 248). The urban space of Nairobi is central to the emergence of a lively and sustainable screen media production industry in the new millennium. Much as Lagos is to Nollywood, Nairobi "is an environment that shapes [Nairobi-based films] materially" (Haynes 2007a, p. 13). While there is some film production elsewhere in the country (e.g. Mombasa (Overbergh 2015, p. 99)), Nairobi is the unquestionable center. Nairobi's centrality in filmmaking is paralleled by its significance in all business: Indeed, "'everyone who counts' has his business there" (De Lame 2010, p. 153). A fast-growing ICT sector with the "presence of major global players" and local "technology incubators and labs" gives Nairobi the feel of an ICT hub, and state policy goals include setting up "Kenya as Africa's ICT hub by 2017" (Overbergh 2014, p. 208). Further, confidence and entrepreneurialism in creative industries "resonates a more general feeling of 'momentum' in Kenya" (Overbergh 2014, p. 209). Contemporary Nairobi is an area of technological and entrepreneurial growth that is emerging as a significant node in global networks, while at the same time maintaining its historical importance as the business center of Kenya.

The large presence of NGOs and international organizations in the city is also of crucial importance to filmmakers. The United Nations headquarters in Africa are in Nairobi (established in 1996), and additionally Nairobi is a "central hub for connections with an international civil society network" (McNamara 2016, p. 29 citing Taylor, 2004). NGOs are an essential client for local filmmakers: They are the "bread and butter of this industry" (Kamau, 2015). Nairobi is also a regional center for producing commercials. Thus, there is infrastructure in place in the city for filmmaking and potential commercial work for industry professionals. This is a key enabling condition because it creates a situation where film industry professionals can be constantly working on screen media, even if they cannot be working on fiction or creative projects. Another key feature of the city for sustaining Nairobi-based female filmmakers, is the local presence of international cultural institutions, and more specifically the Goethe-Institut and the Alliance Française. The Goethe-Institut sometimes provides funding for films – the Pan-African projects "Latitude – Quest for the Good Life" and "African Metropolis" are the most important – but the more significant role of these institutions is that they provide exhibition spaces. The auditoriums of the Goethe-Institut and Alliance Française, alongside the art center Pawa 254, are the most central spaces – both in terms of being spatially located in the center of town and in terms of importance – for local films to be exhibited (almost always for free) and are also the dominant spaces for screening art cinema and documentary films in the city. Nairobi does have conventional cinemas, but they tend to screen locally produced content only on an ad hoc basis in favor of focusing on Hollywood and sometimes Bollywood films, so the presence of transnational cultural institutions is essential to the local circulation of films by Nairobi-based female filmmakers.

The career of filmmaker Judy Kibinge has emerged as a result of many of these most important shifts in Nairobi-based filmmaking in the last 15 years. Before embarking on a career as a filmmaker, Kibinge had a successful career in advertising – she was Creative Director of McCann Erickson Kenya. She has a Bachelor of Arts in Design for Communications from Manchester Polytechnic, but never attended film school. In 1999, she left advertising to become an independent filmmaker and began directing commercial documentaries for the American multinational agricultural giant Monsanto. Subsequently, she made her first fiction film – the short *The Aftermath* (2002) – with M-Net New Directions, a project that is part of M-Net Cares, the corporate social investment group of the transnational media corporation. The project is for "emerging directors and scriptwriters" and it "solicits proposals from first-time directors and writers." It then mentors the film-makers and refines the projects to create 30-minute dramas it then broadcasts (Tomaselli and Shepperson 2014, p. 121). New Directions initially operated exclusively in South Africa, but it expanded in 1999 to include Zimbabwe, Tanzania, Kenya, Ethiopia, Ghana, and Nigeria and became known as New Directions Africa (Saks 2010, p. 74). Many high-profile Nairobi-based female filmmakers have been part of this project including Wanuri Kahiu who used it to make her short film *Ras Star* (2007).

Kibinge's breakout moment came when Executive Producer Njeri Karago asked her to direct *Dangerous Affair*, a project that sparked a great deal of excitement because Karago, who had worked as a producer in Hollywood, had raised the money for the film (Kibinge, 2015).[8] Furthermore, the film also received a great deal of press attention because so few films were being made locally at the time (Kibinge, 2015). *Dangerous Affair* was shot on the professional videocassette technology Betacam (Kibinge, 2015) and was distributed through Karago's company Baraka Films. Unlike Ghana where "no Ghanaian women had directed or produced a documentary or feature film before the advent of video movies" (Garritano 2013, p. 17), women like Anne Mungai, Wanjiru Kinyanjui, and others had produced films on celluloid, yet, for the first decades of production these films were few and far between. Much like other ventures from across the continent signaling a technological revolution, in Nairobi "equipment became cheaper, so barriers to entry were lower" (Kamau, 2015), but unlike Nigeria and Ghana "viable" local production would only emerge after *Dangerous Affair* (McNamara 2016, p. 24).

A romantic comedy about the loves, marriages, and affairs of young urban professionals, *Dangerous Affair* explored a subject not yet taken up in Kenyan cinema. The central protagonist Kui opens the film, returning home to Nairobi after working in New York City. The film is set in a middle-class milieu and its dominant locations are upscale bars, parties, and homes where a class of stylishly dressed young professionals unaffectedly discusses sex and romance. The technical quality of the film is uneven – the sound varies in volume and occasionally cuts out completely and the editing between scenes sometimes disrupts locational continuity – but these flaws are transcended by the bold honesty of its characterization. The characters are imagined as modern subjects – equally at home in "traditional" marriage rituals as in Christian Dior gowns and business suits – and the film sees the metropolis not as a space of immoral danger (as it is in *Saikati*) but simply as home. The film depicts what Anthropologist Rachel Spronk calls Nairobi's young professionals (2012. 2014). These young professionals are generally born and raised in Nairobi with only weak ties to their families' rural homes (Spronk 2014, p. 101). They are cosmopolitan and seek to connect with the world outside Kenya and they "see themselves as the frontrunners of a contemporary identity in which professional pride, progressive attitudes, and a fashionable outlook are important

markers" (Spronk 2014, pp. 107–108). As Spronk notes, "every generation perceives itself as modern: the interesting issue is how they do so" (2014, p. 107). In
Saikati, progressivism meant women holding on to their rural roots while also
becoming educated, whereas for the young professionals in *Dangerous Affair* there
is no disjuncture between African authenticity and urban cosmopolitanism.

Kibinge has continued to work on commissioned projects, including corporate
documentaries, because it has not been financially feasible to sustain her career
making only fiction films. In her words: "I've never made any money on any
drama. I've never paid rent off any dramatic film. In fact it costs you" (Kibinge
2015). In these circumstances, making corporate documentaries is a way of
continuing to work as a filmmaker; yet even in these conditions, she found ways to
explore the possibilities of storytelling. In her approach, corporate videos do not
have to be "boring" and "any story, even corporate videos, can be proper feature-
length documentaries that are gripping" (Kibinge, 2015). She brought this philosophy to her Transparency International film *A Voice in the Dark* (2005) (which was
cut down to *The Man Who Knew Too Much* (2007)) and she continued this approach
in her 60-minute documentary *Headlines in History* (2010) where she transformed
a story about the corporate history of the Nation Media Group into "the story of
Kenya seen through the eyes of the journalists who wrote the headlines about the
nation" (Kibinge, 2015). *Headlines in History* blends archival footage and interviews,
but transcends this educational and expository style of documentary making
through a careful focus on character and Kibinge's unique ability to find drama in
seemingly ordinary situations.

Like many Nairobi-based female filmmakers, Kibinge also runs a small production company called Seven Productions. She describes Seven as "really just me and
my computer" (Kibinge, 2015), but she has produced a number of films through
Seven. She made the 40-minute noir thrill *Killer Necklace* (2008) in partnership with
M-Net New Directions and two documentaries: *Peace Wanted Alive* (2009), about
the 2007/2008 Kenyan post-election violence and *Scarred: The Anatomy of a
Massacre* (2015), about the 1984 massacre of Somali men at the Wagalla airstrip in
the Wajir county of North Eastern Kenya.[9] *Scarred* is a passion project she developed over the course of four years after she met survivors of the massacre. She
received financial support from the Open Society Initiative for Eastern Africa
(OSIEA), the Nairobi-based branch of the American Open Society Foundation to
make the film, but acted as the director, producer, and researcher.[10] *Scarred* is a particularly interesting example of her work. Based on her advertising background
she wanted to have a "visual hook" running through the film and consequently she
decided to photograph the scars of Wagalla survivors in a manner reminiscent of
a fashion photo shoot (Kibinge, 2015).[11] The result of this unusual approach is dig-
nified scar portraits. Each portrait is a close up black-and-white photo against an
opaque background and the scars are the focal point. While the idea to have an
anchoring visual theme in the film was drawn from her advertising background,
the images themselves avoid merely aestheticizing or sanitizing the violence.

The portraits depict various body parts, but most include the victims' faces, and these portraits are especially evocative because the survivors look directly into the camera in an accusing demand for recognition. The portraits thus work to establish a human connection between victim and viewer, which is especially important given that the massacre has long been officially denied. The portraits thus boldly challenge the Kenyan government to recognize the Wagalla atrocity through showing the embodied evidence of wrongdoing provided by the scars. This sort of creativity and boundary pushing has been evident throughout her career regardless of the genre or medium used to tell a particular story.

As the example of Kibinge shows, binary categorizations of African screen media do little to explain trends in filmmaking because the filmmakers themselves work across these divisions (cf. Dovey, 2010).[12] As has been shown, much of the work of Nairobi-based female filmmakers shifts between formats and shows a diverse way of working that cannot solely be confined to "festival" work. Acclaimed "festival" filmmaker, Wanuri Kahiu, is notable here because while her international reputation is due to her fiction films (*Pumzi* (2010) and *From a Whisper* (2009) most notably), throughout her career she has moved between feature and short fiction films, documentaries,[13] television,[14] production,[15] and writing. In her words:

> I wouldn't have said that I would do documentaries but I started doing them because those were the jobs that were available … I mean all of it is storytelling and I love all of it, it's just that I really did think that I'd be doing more feature films and shorts than documentary projects. (Kahiu, 2015)

This format shifting is not a matter of artistic compromise – Kahiu made it very clear that she loves the storytelling afforded by documentary filmmaking – but an adaptation to a constantly evolving market.[16] Kahiu is but one example of this trend, and indeed this form of working is completely typical of women operating in film in Nairobi today.

The examples of Kibinge and Kahiu are among wider convergences taking place in African screen media production. In Nigeria and Ghana, where most films are viewed on television rather than in cinemas, the distinction between "film" and "television" is often blurred. As Moradewun Adejunmobi has explained, "cinema" and "television" are meaningfully differentiated not by the "specifics of the platform or the site of spectatorship" (2015, p. 124), but by their "potential for televisual recurrence," which she defines as "the ability to attract similarly constituted publics to the same or similarly themed and styled audiovisual texts on a fairly regular and recurrent basis" (2015, p. 121). This shift happened within the twenty-first-century context of detheatricalization across Africa and the expansion of the popularity of television viewership (Adejunmobi 2015, p. 124). Conventional differentiations between film and television are no longer sufficient within this context. Nairobi-based filmmakers also seek to have their films broadcast on television, but for broadcasters to buy films instead of conventional television series "the quality of the movies will have to be consistent and will need to come in numbers" (Overbergh 2015, p. 110). While Nairobi-based female filmmakers are rarely disadvantaged because of the technical quality of their films (unlike the Riverwood[17] filmmakers Overbergh examines), they face the difficulty of generating the consistent quantity of films required to carve out a space for their films on television.

Nairobi-based filmmakers work in multiple formats (as previously mentioned), and this multi-format convergence helps explain why even despite a lack of state and social support a vibrant screen media industry of international caliber has developed in Nairobi. Working across formats can lead to new and innovative business models for making screen media content. A key example of this is Zamaradi Productions, led by veteran film producer Appie Matere. Zamaradi undertook a bold filmmaking experiment when they attempted – successfully – to produce 56 60-minute films for South African pay television company M-Net in a five-month period. All the films were shot at Zamaradi's studio, which consists of a large bungalow on an expansive property in a leafy suburb in North West Nairobi where they constructed a variety of interchangeable indoor and outdoor sets. While sitting outside the bungalow by a dilapidated pool that would soon become the set of a television show about a hotel under renovation, Matere described the process of shooting the 56 films as follows:

> It was so crazy because all the interiors had to be in this house for the films so that we can be able to work within the budget and within the timeframe … we had to build sets here for all of them. So this room now … could be a restaurant, in another half an hour you come back and it's a classroom. And the *fundis* [handy men] are on standby waiting to paint or whatever it was. … It was crazy. (Matere, 2015)

The pace of the shoot is reminiscent of Nollywood-style filmmaking, but the interesting element lies in the fact that Matere was able to adapt this mode of filmmaking to make television movies of the standard required by a major cross-continental broadcaster. She brought her skills, gained in the production of slick and successful local films like *Project Daddy* (Kibinge, 2004) and *Killer Necklace* (Kibinge, 2008), to the production of films in another format, and subsequently used the model developed through this project to shoot three television shows simultaneously.

Adejunmobi's theory provides a space to think of all of Matere's modes of production together, of both television and made for television movies as other aspects of filmmaking and vice versa. Adejunmobi discusses convergence in modes of viewing, and argues that film and television can no longer be meaningfully differentiated based on where and how they are watched. But this convergence is also happening at the level of production, where the same models can be employed, as the example of Matere demonstrates, to make both film and television. Thus, an in-depth examination of her work, and that of other Nairobi-based female filmmakers, shows that conventional definitions of "African cinema" as only embracing film need to give way to the much wider concept of "African screen media" so as to be cognizant of the vital interplay between formats and modes of production happening in Nairobi today.

Re-emergence of "Festival" Films

Although there are exceptions, Nairobi-based femalefilmmakers have attracted attention largely because of their feature-length and short fiction films that have received acclaim on the international film festival circuit. Key examples include Anne Mungai (*Saikati*, 1992), Wanuri Kahiu (*Pumzi*, 2010), Hawa Essuman (*Soul Boy*, 2010), Ng'endo Mukii (*Yellow Fever*, 2012), and Judy Kibinge (*Something Necessary*, 2013), of which *Pumzi* is perhaps the most notable. It depicts a dystopian future and a postwar apocalyptic landscape where humankind lives in an underground colony. The colony is one of scarcity, powered by the kinetic energy inhabitants produce, where water is prized and all bodily fluids, including sweat and urine, must be recycled into drinking water. The narrative arc consists of the protagonist Asha, a worker at the virtual natural history museum, escaping the colony with a tree seed and sacrificing herself to plant it so that life can once again grow outside. The message of human impacted environmental destruction is clear, and the film participates in a long history of cautionary science fiction.[18] Yet, the film gives equal weight to the pleasurability of the viewing experience as it does to its eco-political message because of Kahiu's intentional strategy of composing the film of precisely framed photographically beautiful images (Kahiu, 2014). *Pumzi* is thus part of a longstanding film tradition, going back to the earliest African films, where pleasure and politics are "deeply imbricated with one another" (Dovey 2010, p. 3).

   The contemporary filmmaking landscape Nairobi-based female filmmakers must navigate is one marked by the worldwide proliferation of film festivals. Film festivals have played a crucial role in bringing these filmmakers to international attention, and as such, using Dovey's definition of "festival" filmmakers as a tool for understanding Nairobi-based female filmmakers can be illuminating. She argues that "festival" filmmakers generally "come from middle class or upwardly mobile social environments, have had access to professional film training, and have traveled widely" (2015a, p. 6). These filmmakers also have international perspectives and desire "for their films to *travel* beyond their local contexts" while nevertheless remaining "marked" by those contexts (Dovey 2015a, p. 7). She argues via De Valck that another characteristic of "festival" filmmakers is the way they value artistry and creativity over commercial concerns (Dovey 2015a, p. 8), while also maintaining that "art" and "commerce" are always imbricated (Dovey 2015a, p. 5). Similarly, while the need to grow a local market for their films was continually mentioned in my interviews with them, Nairobi-based female filmmakers generally make films first as a way of sharing their art and their ideas with the wider world and only second as a profit driven venture. Dovey's concept of "festival" filmmakers can capture emerging filmmakers, not just those who have already gained acclaim on the festival circuit, because its focus includes character traits and the personal background of filmmakers. As such, it is applicable not only to well-known Nairobi-based filmmakers, but also to "rising" stars.

"Festival" filmmakers tend to "spend their lives moving between their homes in Africa and elsewhere" (Dovey 2015a, p. 6). This is true of Nairobi's "festival" filmmakers who continually travel outside the country to study and work. This leads to Julien's important question: "What impact does residence abroad – or the continual shuttling between host country and homeland – have on literature and film by Africans?" (2015, p. 18) The mobility of "festival" filmmakers may be a sign of "these filmmakers' inability to convert symbolic capital accrued outside of the continent into other kinds of capital, particularly back home in Africa" (Dovey 2015a, p. 7). While promoting her now classic science-fiction short film *Pumzi*, Wanuri Kahiu said "I am a filmmaker when I'm outside the country – in Kenya, I'm a hustler" (Kermeliotis, 2010).[19] At this point Kahiu had not only released an innovative and highly regarded new film, but had also received 12 nominations and won five awards at the African Movie Academy Awards in 2009 for her film *From a Whisper*. Her statement reflects, in Dovey's terms, a failure to make the symbolic capital gained from success in prestigious international circuits "operative" (2015a, p. 5) back home in Kenya. A filmmaker may receive symbolic capital from attending or winning at prestigious festivals and awards, but a lack of recognition of that achievement within Kenya leads to a failure to find financial backing within the country to continue making films.[20]

The transnational mobility of filmmakers also impacts the content they produce. In a statement that typifies the experience and perspective of many Nairobi-based female filmmakers, Hawa Essuman (director of films such as *Soul Boy* (2010)) said:

> I would consider myself an African middle class individual … And there are so many people who would consider themselves as such … I mean, we crave art like most first world cities, I think it's because we've spent time in them. We care about the quality of life, we care about food, we care about fashion … It's a very interesting hybrid between – it's not actually, *it's not even a hybrid, it's just who we are*. Our education has been all over the world, sometimes predominantly the West. Our roots are very much continental, and we are looking for ourselves in the middle. (Essuman, 2015, my emphasis)

Essuman points to the vital influence travel and living between multiple spaces has on screen media production. A particularly cogent example of transnational mobility shaping a film is Ng'endo Mukii's documentary animation short *Yellow Fever* (2012). It explores a global hierarchy of female beauty standards that positions whiteness at its pinnacle and the psychological impact this has on African women. In a particularly evocative sequence, Mukii interviews her young niece – depicted in animated form – and her niece plainly states "I really want to be American instead of a Kenyan. If I was American I would be white, white, white, white and I love being white" (see Figure 14.1). Animated interviews such as this are placed throughout the film and interspersed with live action female modern dancers who contort their bodies to depict the existential discomfort of trying to conform to unrealistic beauty standards. Mukii made the film while she was a student at the Royal College of Art in London, but the inspiration for her incisive critique of race and representation was her return to Nairobi after studying at the Rhode Island School of Design and living in the United States. The circular motion of travel and return opened her to a new perspective on issues she had never originally questioned while living in Nairobi and she began "looking at this issue of race and representation in media and trying to figure out where this added value of whiteness had come from in African countries" (Mukii, 2014).

Filmmakers are led to "festival" filmmaking through various trajectories. Some through film school training – Wanuri Kahiu did a Masters in Film Directing at UCLA and Ng'endo Mukii trained at the Rhode Island School of Design and the Royal College of Art in London for instance – but others through a "learning on the job" in Nairobi approach. A key example of this second trend is Hawa Essuman. She began her career in production before realizing she wanted to be a creator. At this point she joined the local television drama series *Makutano Junction*[21] in the directing department and worked there for four seasons (Essuman, 2015). She had the opportunity to make her first film *Selfish?* (2008) when she approached the local Nollywood-style[22] production house Jitu Films – which made "really low budget films" – about creating a film for them. There was "barely a script" and it

Figure 14.1　An animated interview in *Yellow Fever* (Ng'endo Mukii, 2012). Image courtesy of Ng'endo Mukii.

was shot in six days and the film has "so many problems it's ridiculous," but she described making the film as "a good education" (Essuman, 2015). Subsequently she experimented with short films, filmed with the help of friends, so she could discover what her "own filmic voice looked like" (Essuman, 2015). Following this she was accepted by One Fine Day Films[23] to direct *Soul Boy*, and at this point her career changed.

Soul Boy is a simple story of magical realism that follows a fairy-tale quest format; in this instance a young boy must complete a series of tasks to save his father's soul. It is set in Nairobi between the "slum" Kibera and upscale suburb Karen, and it shows both parts of the city – the richest and poorest – in the same bright color and their respective residents with the same depth and agency.[24] *Soul Boy* had its world premiere at the International Film Festival Rotterdam (IFFR) where it went on to win the Dioraphte Award (worth €10,000), and subsequently went on to win various awards at the African Movie Academy Awards, the Kalasha Awards (based in Nairobi), and the Zanzibar International Film Festival, to name only a few, and to screen at "virtually every other festival worldwide" (Wenner 2015, p. 189). *Soul Boy* was validated on an international film festival circuit, but its popularity within Nairobi (and specifically in the "slums" of Kibera and Mathare) shows the limits of "any easy dichotomy of festival cinema and popular film" (Dovey 2015b, pp. 131–132). After *Soul Boy's* successful festival run Essuman won the Director's Eye Prize at the African Film Festival of Cordoba (FCAT) in 2012 – worth €25,000 – to write a feature screenplay, and she is in the process of co-directing two documentaries, both of which have received prestigious international film festival support.[25] Essuman had a diverse career in production, television, and "video film" before *Soul Boy*, but it was unquestionably this film that launched her international career and gave her the status of a "festival" filmmaker.

Soul Boy is but one example of a wider trend in Nairobi-based filmmaking where female filmmakers receive funding (or a combination of funding and mentoring) from transnational partners. Similar dynamics can be observed with the participants of the Focus Features Africa First program. This program helped Wanuri Kahiu make *Pumzi* and also provided a grant for Ng'endo Mukii's film *The Teapot* (in production). "Deliberately inscribing itself in an artcinema context, cultivating a sense of cool cosmopolitanism, and invested in global auteurist cinema discourse," Africa First explicitly intended to make films for the festival circuit and related highbrow outlets (Sanogo 2015, p. 142). Its goal was to "produce first-rate short fiction films from Africa by discovering or enabling film directors early in their careers" (Sanogo 2015, p. 142). Yet, while these circuits have worked to the benefit of many Nairobi-based female filmmakers, this may only be for a time. Essuman spoke with particular clarity on the subject:

> In the international arena I think it is possible for you to find funding for your first and second feature. After that, there is a hope that you know how to do it by now …

but if you know how to work a system that is finite you are not equipped to handle another system. You have to find a way to invent a new one. (Essuman, 2015)

Of critical importance here is the issue of sustainability: Many of the funding structures Nairobi-based female filmmakers have used to make their films are for *emerging* filmmakers (Africa First and New Directions are explicitly for emerging voices). Thus the need to make films for Kenyan audiences was repeatedly emphasized by Nairobi-based filmmakers in our discussions just as they seek prestige, audiences, and funding in other markets.

Many films by Nairobi-based female filmmakers have found success internationally, yet locally distribution is the biggest challenge the industry faces. There is essentially no distribution system in place that would enable an upmarket film to make a profit, and it is very difficult to even access many locally made films.[26] Nairobi's few cinemas almost exclusively screen foreign films and there is a pervasive culture of film piracy across the city. It is possible to buy a 50 KES (¢50 US) DVD of the latest release of films and television shows from around the world almost anywhere in the city. Furthermore, broadcasters in Kenya pay little for local content because they have a very cheap way of filling airtime in the form of imported content (Ghettuba, 2015). Although there is cautious optimism, this broadcast situation might change and lead to a boom in locally produced content since President Kenyatta announced, in 2013, that "the required quota for local content on television will be increased from 40 to 60 per cent," which would result in broadcasters having to commission more local productions or make more in-house productions, that is, if the law is enforced (Overbergh 2015, p. 109). The market for locally produced films is very small in Kenya, making international markets both on the continent and farther afield vitally important.[27]

Conclusion

This chapter participates in ongoing projects of "re-thinking" taking place in contemporary African screen media studies. The re-evaluation of existing ways of thinking about African film has always been at the heart of Nollywood and video film studies, and is exemplified in the entire corpus of Jonathan Haynes, *African Video Movies and Global Desires: A Ghanaian History*, and the seminal text *Viewing African Cinema in the Twenty-First Century: Art Films and the Nollywood Video Revolution* (the first attempt to bring the divergent fields of video and celluloid film scholarship into close conversation). Re-conceptualizing ideas of "African-ness" is another core debate in African film studies and the recent essay collection *Rethinking African Cultural Production* is exemplary for proposing new models for understanding the creative production of Africans when many of them "do not live in Africa" but rather live in other countries or "travel between Africa and elsewhere" (Ekotto and Harrow 2015, p. 1). The case of Nairobi-based female film-makers contributes to moving both of these important scholarly debates forward as it proposes new ways of thinking about screen media and African-ness.

Nairobi-based female filmmakers' work is daring and innovative and challenges many of the stereotypes that govern the study of women in filmmaking. Their diversity in switching between formats and genres reflects the struggles they face financing films in Nairobi, but even more than that it shows that their creativity and artistry cannot be limited to only one format. Ultimately, this chapter has shown that understanding the emergence of a unique industry led by women in Africa requires new ways of looking – specifically arguing for an approach that looks at transnational connections while remaining firmly grounded in local spaces – and that these "new looks" can illuminate the entire field of African screen media studies.

Notes

1   A core source of discontent among filmmakers is that the Kenyan government has no system for granting funding to filmmakers. They have a loan – called "Take 254" – that is offered through the Youth Enterprise Development Fund. Through Take 254, film-makers can borrow up to 25 million shillings (approximately US$250,000) if they are under 35 (or part of companies where 70% of the employees are younger than 35). The loan has an interest rate of 8%, which must be repaid in full (with interest) in six years, and, depending on the size of the loan, the filmmaker gets a 2–3 month grace period and the project has to be completed within 4–6 months. The loan is widely considered laughably impractical because of its unrealistic timeframe for film completion and loan repayment, and veteran film and television producer Isabel Munyua went so far as to describe the loan's conditions as "insane" (2015).

2   Curiously, scholars have so far neglected this aspect of the careers of Nairobi-based female filmmakers. The work that does exist focuses on textual analysis of their fiction films (cf. Mukora, 2003; Omelsky, 2014; Giruzzi, 2015) or consists of short, and highly incomplete, descriptive surveys of industry trends (Kinyanjui, 2014; Okioma and Mugubi, 2015).

3   Mungai had made "short and medium-length documentaries on a number of topics dealing with women, health, youth, religion, agriculture, and education" all for televi-sion (Cham and Mungai 1994, p. 99) prior to *Saikati*, but this was the pivotal film in her career and her reputation as a filmmaker is almost entirely based on this production. Her subsequent films – like *Tough Choices* (1998) and *Promise of Love* (2000) – are almost entirely unknown.

4   Wanjiru Kinyanjui trained in screenwriting and directing at the German Academy for Film and Television Berlin (DFFB).

5   Since 2011, KIMC has been a Semi-Autonomous Government Agency (Kenya Institute of Mass Communication, 2017).

6   The Friedrich Ebert Foundation is a political foundation affiliated with, but independent from, the Social Democratic Party of Germany.

7   While KIMC once had a lab equipped to process 16 mm film, the equipment is no longer functional and it is not currently possible to process celluloid film in Kenya (Kinyanjui, 2015).

8   Subsequently, Karago and Kibinge collaborated on another urban romantic comedy called *Project Daddy*, which was similar in theme, aesthetics, and production style to *Dangerous Affair*.

9   In February 1984, the Kenyan Army forcibly gathered up to 5,000 Somali men from the Degodia clan and took them to Wagalla airstrip. This location then "became the scene of the worst atrocities and slaughter to be witnessed in Kenya's modern history" after four days of interrogation left hundreds dead (Anderson 2014, p. 658). The official position is that 57 died, but survivor testimonies account for almost 1,000 dead with perhaps 2,000 additional people missing (Anderson 2014, pp. 658–659). The exact death toll remains unknown.

10   Half the proceeds from DVDs sold go to the Wagalla Massacre Foundation. The film has had limited distribution, mostly consisting of free screenings in various parts of Kenya, after it premiered in Nairobi to a packed audience at the Louis Leakey Auditorium of the National Museum in February 2015.

11   Kibinge described the process as follows: "We set up a proper photo shoot and then when we started the photo shoot it was just pushing it a little bit more. Can you look in the camera lens? Which is something a bit strange to ask a victim of a massacre, show us your scars and look in the camera. It's almost like a fashion shoot" (Kibinge, 2015).

12   In defining the parameters of his *Dictionary of African Filmmakers*, film scholar Roy Armes chose to include only feature length films made or distributed on celluloid (2008, p. 3). The limitations of this technological division between "film" and "video" is clearly apparent in the entry on Kenyan film. Armes lists only three feature films and three filmmakers in Kenya's *entire history* (Sao Gamba, Anne Mungai, and Wanjiru Kinyanjui). He accounts for all other screen media production in a note, stating "a number of feature-length videos have been shot in Kenya in the 2000s" and an incomplete list of films, including shorts and documentaries, with no account of their importance (Armes 2008, p. 217). The fundamental transformations happening in Nairobi-based screen media industries in the new millennium are entirely obscured through this approach.

13   Wanuri Kahiu directed *For Our Land* (2009) for M-Net's "Great Africans Series" and is currently in-production on a number of documentary projects.

14   Wanuri Kahiu made one season of a TV show called *State House* (2014) for the East African pay-TV network Zuku.

15   Wanuri Kahiu runs a production company called Awali Entertainment with Rebecca Chandler. She is also credited as a producer on the African Metropolis short film *Homecoming* (Chuchu, 2013).

16   Wanuri Kahiu's frontiers are continually expanding and she is now working with the South African Triggerfish Animation Studios Story Lab project to make a feature film called *The Camel Racer* with Nnedi Okorafor.

17   Nairobi has a video film industry named Riverwood. Riverwood films, in opposition to the films of Nairobi-based female filmmakers, are ultra-low-budget, being made on budgets of 20-30,000 KES (US$200–300), DVD movies that circulate around River

Road on the East side of downtown Nairobi alongside music and "Hollywood, Bollywood or Nigerian filmfare" (Overbergh 2015, p. 99).

18 *Pumzi* has been noted most predominantly because of its unusual genre: Science fiction. It is cited by Kenneth W. Harrow as an example of the new "kinds of films that are now emerging" that demand "new kinds of critical approaches" (2015, p. 14). Other scholars have suggested *Pumzi* "provides a never-before-seen image of high-tech Africans in the future" (Womack 2013, p. 135) and displays a "new use" of film genre (Higgins 2015, p. 85).

19 This expression struck me, and throughout my research I asked each filmmaker I met what they thought of Kahiu's articulation – whether or not filmmaking in Nairobi is "a hustle." In response I received an almost unanimous, immediate, and enthusiastic yes.

20 The extent of this problem is demonstrated by the pervasive idea in Kenya that film-making is not a "real job."

21 Notably, while *Makutano Junction* is made in Kenya, it is produced by a global charity called Mediae that works to use entertainment for education, and the show has been on air since 2007.

22 The term Nollywood, while often used as shorthand to describe a particular genre of video film, actually refers to a specific industry in Southern Nigeria. Garritano cautions against using the shorthand since it obscures complex regional dynamics and differences between video industries (2013, p. 3) including intense competition (also see Haynes 2007b, p. 4). "Nollywood-style" is perhaps the more appropriate term.

23 One Fine Day Films (OFDF) is a German organization started by husband and wife team Marie Steinmann and Tom Tykwer that grew out of their existing Nairobi-based arts NGO One Fine Day e.V. (Slavkovic 2015, p. 205). It "is supported by the German-based DW Akademie, a media capacity building cooperation development group, and British-funded Nairobi-based organisation Ginger Ink Films" (McNamara 2016, p. 26). OFDF's first film *Soul Boy* (2010) was made with the system of using foreign professionals to mentor local talents – for instance Tykwer mentored the director Hawa Essuman. Following the success of *Soul Boy*, OFDF expanded to run a two-part project consisting of a workshop or "two week class-room-like 'mini film school'" (One Fine Day Films, 2016) whose participants are experienced filmmakers from across the continent and a film (whose participants would ideally be drawn from that workshop). This model produced *Nairobi Half Life* (Gitonga, 2012), *Something Necessary* (Kibinge, 2013), *Veve* (Mukali, 2014), and *Kati Kati* (Masya, 2016).

24 The film is thus in rather direct contrast to dominant images of Kibera as gray and dirty and its inhabitants as desolate – a difference that likely contributed to the film's local popularity. Kibera residents also praised it for its creativity (Dovey 2015b, p. 131).

25 Hawa Essuman is co-directing a documentary with Malou Reymann supported by a development grant from CPH:LAB (a project of the Copenhagen International Documentary Festival) and another, called *Silas*, with Anjali Nayar, which has received financing from the International Documentary Film Festival Amsterdam (IDFA) Bertha Fund. *Silas* is set to premier at the 2017 Toronto International Film Festival (TIFF).

26   Interestingly, distributions and sales problems are also pervasive in Riverwood. The
      type of filmmaking practice in Riverwood is reminiscent of Nollywood-style
      filmmaking because the films are made cheaply and quickly. However, the crucial dis-
      tinction here is that unlike Nollywood Riverwood "does not seem to be widely viewed
      and is not hugely profitable" (Overbergh 2015, p. 100 via McNamara p. 2010) aside
      from the small core group of "successful comedians" (Overbergh 2015, p. 106), who
      were Riverwood's pioneers.
27   This transnational turn has countless precedents in film industries around the world
      (for instance post-Revolutionary Iranian cinema and Chinese Fifth Generation cin-
      emas). In circumstances where the state can no longer support creative filmmaking
      (or chooses not to) filmmakers have looked to transnational sources of funding and
      circulation. Nairobi-based female filmmakers are no different.

References

Adejunmobi, Moradewun. 2015. "African Film's Televisual Turn." *Cinema Journal* 54, no. 2:
      120–125. doi: 10.1353/cj.2015.0002
Adesokan, Akin. 2014. "African Film." In *Africa, Fourth Edition*, edited by Maria Grosz-
      Ngaté, John H. Hanson, and Patrick O'Meara, 233–249. Bloomington and Indianapolis:
      Indiana University Press.
Armes, Roy. 2008. *Dictionary of African Filmmakers*. Bloomington: Indiana University Press.
Anderson, David M. 2014. "Remembering Wagalla: State Violence in Northern Kenya,
      1962–1991." *Journal of Eastern African Studies* 8, no. 4: 658–676. doi.org/10.1080/1753
      1055.2014.946237
Bisschoff, Lizelle. 2012. "The Emergence of Women's Film-making in Francophone Sub-
      Saharan Africa: From Pioneering Figures to Contemporary Directors." *Journal of
      African Cinemas* 4, no. 2: 157–173. doi: 10.1386/jac.4.2.157_1
Cham, Mbye, and Anne Mungai. 1994. "African Women and Cinema: A Conversation with
      Anne Mungai." *Research in African Literatures* 25, no. 3: 93–104.
De Lame, Danielle. 2010. "Grey Nairobi: Sketches of Urban Socialties." *Nairobi Today: the
      Paradox of a Fragmented City*, edited by Hélène Charton-Bigot and Deyssi Rodriguez-
      Torres, 151–198. Dar es Salam, Tanzania: Mkuki na Nyota Publishers, in association
      with French Institute for Research in Africa (IFRA).
Dennison, Stephanie, and Song Hwee Lim. 2006. "Situating World Cinema as a Theoretical
      Problem." In *Remapping World Cinema: Identity, Culture and Politics in Film*, edited by
      Stephanie Dennison and Song Hwee Lim, 1–15. London: Wallflower.
Dovey, Lindiwe. 2010. "African Film and Video: Pleasure, Politics, and Performance."
      Journal of African Cultural Studies 22, no. 1: 1–6.
Dovey, Lindiwe. 2012. "New Looks: The Rise of African Women Filmmakers." *Feminist
      Africa* 16: 18–36.
Dovey, Lindiwe. 2015a. *Curating Africa in the Age of Film Festivals*. New York: Palgrave
      Macmillan.
Dovey, Lindiwe. 2015b. "Through the Eye of a Film Festival: Toward a Curatorial and
      Spectator Centered Approach to the Study of African Screen Media." *Cinema Journal*
      54, no. 2: 126–132. doi: 10.1353/cj.2015.0005

Ekotto, Frieda, and Kenneth W. Harrow Eds. 2015. *Rethinking African Cultural Production.* Bloomington and Indianapolis: Indiana University Press.

Ellerson, Beti. 2010. "The Evolution of Women in Cinema." In *Through African Eyes Vol. 2: Conversations with the Directors*, edited by Mahen Bonetti and Morgan Seag, 121–124. New York: African Film Festival Inc.

Essuman, Hawa. 2015. Recorded interview over Skype, 4 May.

Garritano, Carmela. 2013. *African Video Movies and Global Desires: A Ghanaian History.* Athens, OH: Center for International Studies, Ohio University.

Ghettuba, Dorothy, and Ndanu Kilonzo. 2015. Recorded interview, Nairobi, 3 June.

Giruzzi, Clara. 2015. "A Feminist Approach to Contemporary Female Kenyan Cinema: Women and Nation in *From a Whisper* (Kahiu, 2008) and *Something Necessary* (Kibinge, 2013)." *Journal of African Cinemas* 7, no. 2: 79–96. doi: 10.1386/jac.7.2.79_1

Harrow, Kenneth W. 2015. "Manthia Diawara's Waves and the Problem of the 'Authentic'." *African Studies Review* 58, no. 3: 13–30. doi: 10.1017/asr.2015.74

Haynes, Jonathan. 2007a. "Nollywood in Lagos, Lagos in Nollywood Films." *Africa Today* 54, no. 2: 131–150.

Haynes, Jonathan. 2007b. "Video Boom: Nigeria and Ghana." *Postcolonial Text* 3, no. 2: 1–10.

Higgins, MaryEllen. 2015. "The Winds of African Cinema." *African Studies Review* 58, no. 3:77–92. doi:10.1017/asr.2015.76

Higson, Andrew. 2006. "The Limiting Imagination of National Cinema." In *Transnational Cinema: the Film Reader*, edited by Elizabeth Ezra and Terry Rowden, 15–25. London and New York: Routledge.

Julien, Eileen. 2015. "The Critical Present: Where Is 'African Literature'?" In *Rethinking African Cultural Production*, edited by Frieda Ekotto and Kenneth W. Harrow, 17–28. Bloomington and Indianapolis: Indiana University Press.

Kahiu, Wanuri. 2014. Recorded interview, Nairobi, 27 October.

Kahiu, Wanuri. 2015. Recorded interview, Nairobi, 6 March.

Kamau, Toni. 2015. Recorded interview, Nairobi, 6 March.

Kenya Institute of Mass Communication. 2017. "History." Accessed 1 June. www.kimc.ac.ke/index.php/about-us (accessed 30 March 2018).

Kermeliotis, Teo. "Wanuri Kahiu: 'In Kenya, I'm a Hustler'." *CNN.* 30 March 2010. http://edition.cnn.com/2010/SHOWBIZ/Movies/03/26/wanuri.kahiu.pumzi/ (accessed 14 January 2016).

Kibinge, Judy. 2015. Recorded interview, Nairobi, 13 May.

Kinyanjui, Wanjiru. 2014. "A Historical Voyage through Kenyan Film." In *African Film: Looking Back and Looking Forward*, edited by Foluke Ogunleye, 69–74. Newcastle-upon-Tyne: Cambridge Scholars Publishing.

Kinyanjui, Wanjiru. 2015. Recorded interview, Nairobi, 24 March.

Matere, Appie. 2015. Recorded interview, Nairobi, 6 May.

McNamara, Joshua. 2016. "The Culturalisation of Development in Nairobi: A Practice-based Approach Toward Understanding Kenya's Urban Audiovisual Media Environment." PhD diss., SOAS, University of London.

Mukii, Ng'endo. 2014 Recorded interview, Nairobi, 2 November.

Mukora, Beatrice Wanjiku. 2003. "Beyond Tradition and Modernity: Representations of Identity in Two Kenyan Films." In *Women Filmmakers: Refocusing*, edited by Jacqueline Levitin, Judith Plessis, and Valeria Raoul, 219–228. Vancouver: UBC Press.

Mungai, Anne. 1996. "Responsibility and Freedom of Expression." In *African Experiences of Cinema*, edited by Imruh Bakari and Mbye Cham, 65–66. London: British Film Institute.

Mungai, Anne. 2015. Recorded interview, Nairobi, 5 March.

Munyua, Isabel. 2015. Recorded interview, Nairobi, 29 May.

Okioma, Nicodemus, and John Mugubi. 2015. "Filmmaking in Kenya: the Voyage." *International Journal of Music and Performing Arts* 3, no. 1: 46–61. doi 10.15640/ijmpa.v3n1a5

Omelsky, Matthew. 2014. "'After the End Times': Postcrisis African Science Fiction." *Cambridge Journal of Postcolonial Literary Inquiry* 1, no. 1: 33–49. doi:10.1017/pli.2013.2

One Fine Day Films. 2016. "About Workshop." http://onefinedayfilms.com/workshop/about-workshop.html (accessed 28 April 2016).

Overbergh, Ann. 2014. "Technological Innovation and the Diversification of Audiovisual Storytelling Circuits in Kenya." *Journal of African Cultural Studies* 26, no. 2: 206–219. doi: 10.1080/13696815.2013.870028

Overbergh, Ann. 2015. "Kenya's Riverwood: Market Structure, Power Relations, and Future Outlooks." *Journal of African Cinemas* 7, no. 2: 97–115. doi: 10.1386/jac.7.2.97_1

Sanogo, Aboubakar. 2015. "Certain Tendencies in Contemporary Auteurist Film Practice in Africa." *Cinema Journal* 54, no. 2: 140–149. doi: 10.1353/cj.2015.0011

Saks, Lucia. 2010. *Cinema in a Democratic South Africa: The Race for Representation*. Bloomington: Indiana University Press.

Şaul, Mahir, and Ralph A. Austen Eds. 2010. *Viewing African Cinema in the Twenty-First Century: Art Films and the Nollywood Video Revolution*. Athens: Ohio University Press.

Slavkovic, Milica. 2015. "Filmmaking in East Africa: Focus on Kenya, Tanzania, and Uganda." In *Small Cinemas in Global Markets: Genre, Identities, Narratives*, edited by Lenuta Giukin, Janina Falkowska, and David Desser, 189–214. London: Lexington Books.

Spronk, Rachel. 2012 *Ambiguous Pleasures: Sexuality and Middle Class Self-Perceptions in Nairobi*. New York: Berghahn Books.

Spronk, Rachel. 2014. "Exploring the Middles Classes in Nairobi: From Modes of Production to Modes of Sophistication." *African Studies Review* 57, no. 1: 93–114.

Taylor, Peter J. 2004. "The New Geography of Global Civil Society: NGOs in the World City Network." *Globalizations* 1, no. 2: 265–277. doi: 10.1080/1474773042000308604

Thackway, Melissa. 2003. *Africa Shoots Back: Alternative Perspectives in Sub-Saharan Francophone African Film*. Oxford: James Currey.

Tomaselli, Keyan, and Arnold Shepperson. 2014. "Transformation and South African Cinema in the 1990s." In *Critical Approaches to African Cinema Discourse*, edited by Nwachukwu Frank Ukadike, 107–134. Lanham, MD: Lexington Books.

Wenner, Dorothee. 2015. "Post-colonial Film Collaborations and Festival Politics." In *Gaze Regimes: Film and Feminisms in Africa*, edited by Jyoti Mistry and Antje Schuhmann, 188–200. Johannesburg: Wits University Press.

Womack, Ytasha. 2013. *Afrofuturism: The World of Black Sci-fi and Fantasy Culture*. Chicago: Lawrence Hill Books.

Filmography

A Voice in the Dark. 2005. Dir. Judy Kibinge. Transparency International. Short documentary.
Dangerous Affair. 2002. Dir. Judy Kibinge. Baraka Films. Feature fiction.
For Our Land. 2009. Dir. Wanuri Kahiu. M-Net. Feature documentary.
From a Whisper. 2009. Dir. Wanuri Kahiu. DADA Productions. Feature fiction.
Headlines in History. 2010. Dir. Judy Kibinge. NTV. Feature documentary.
Homecoming. 2013. Dir. Jim Chuchu. African Metropolis. Short fiction.
Kati Kati. 2016. Dir. Mbithi Masya. One Fine Day Films. Feature fiction.
Killer Necklace. 2008. Dir. Judy Kibinge. M-Net New Directions and Seven Productions. Short fiction.
Makutano Junction. 2007-present. Various directors. Mediae. Television series.
Nairobi Half Life. 2012. Dir. David "Tosh" Gitonga. One Fine Day Films. Feature fiction.
Peace Wanted Alive. 2009. Dir. Judy Kibinge. Seven Productions. Short documentary.
Project Daddy. 2004. Dir. Judy Kibinge. Baraka Films. Feature fiction.
Promise of Love. 2000. Dir. Anne Mungai. Good News Productions. Feature fiction.
Pumzi. 2010. Dir. Wanuri Kahiu. Inspired Minority Pictures and One Pictures. Short fiction.
Ras Star. 2007. Dir. Wanuri Kahiu. M-Net New Directions. Short fiction.
Saikati. 1992. Dir. Anne Mungai. Copyright Friedrich Ebert Stiftung. Feature fiction.
Scarred: The Anatomy of a Massacre. 2015. Dir. Judy Kibinge. Seven Productions. Feature documentary.
Selfish? 2008. Dir. Hawa Essuman. Jitu Films. Feature fiction.
Silas. 2017. Dir. Hawa Essuman and Anjali Nayar. Ink & Pepper, Big World Cinema, and Appian Way. Feature documentary.
Something Necessary. 2013. Dir. Judy Kibinge. One Fine Day Films. Feature fiction.
Soul Boy. 2010. Dir. Hawa Essuman. One Fine Day Films. Feature fiction.
State House. 2014. Dir. Wanuri Kahiu. Zuku. Television series.
The Aftermath. 2002. Dir. Judy Kibinge. M-Net New Directions. Short fiction.
The Battle of the Sacred Tree. 1995. Dir. Wanjiru Kinyanjui. Birne-Film. Feature fiction.
The Man Who Knew Too Much. 2007. Dir. Judy Kibinge. Visual Edge. Short documentary.
Tough Choices. 1998. Dir. Anne Mungai. Daystar University and Good News Productions. Feature fiction.
Veve. 2014. Dir. Simon Mukali. One Fine Day Films. Feature fiction.
Yellow Fever. 2012. Dir. Ng'endo Mukii. Short documentary animation.

Part VI
Genre / Poetics / Gender

15

Darker Vision
Global Cinema and Twenty-first-Century Moroccan Film Noir

Suzanne Gauch

Regardless of the generic forms they adopt, their aesthetic approaches, their auteurist signatures, their production values, or their intended exhibition venues, Moroccan films are inevitably assessed for their social realist content. While there are legitimate and complex historical reasons for this focus on social realism, it also tethers Moroccan films and their audiences in place. Looking predominantly at social realism neglects the importance of genre, style, and aesthetics in the domestic and international success of Moroccan films, and forecloses the possibility of examining how Moroccan cinema contributes to the evolution of various cinematic genres, styles, and aesthetics writ large. Above all, privileging social realism over the cinematic encourages a certain developmental, often Orientalizing, logic, positioning Moroccan cinema as a latecomer whose role within the arena of global cinema is to reflect local, forever exotic, realities. Since the late twentieth century, however, Morocco has seen not just a surge in film production, but also a swell of box-office record making and festival audience-pleasing crime dramas, thrillers, and portraits of life in urban underworlds that assert their generic and cinematic qualities. Consciously noir in style, tone, and form, these films have taken a globally popular genre with multiple origins, and wide-ranging and varied identifying features, and have at once highlighted its provincial origins and refashioned it into a uniquely global Moroccan genre.

Tracing the genealogy of Moroccan noir in his magisterial study of the emergence of thrillers and police procedurals in Morocco, Jonathan Smolin (2013) tracks its rising popularity to the Moroccan state's revamping of its image in the waning years of the twentieth century and King Hassan II's rule. In news stories by turns lurid and hard-hitting, Smolin argues, the police were recast as servants of the public good, at least ideally, rather than as minions of the *Makhzen*, or powerful elites of the regime.[1] Tabloid-style journalism drew new readers, its break with decorum signaling a transition from newspapers as mouthpieces of the king's state, their veiled criticisms legible only to those highly schooled in reading between the lines, to tools of civil society, occupied with relating news about and for the public. Smolin's attention to socio-political context is consonant with the approach of theorists who find in classical film noir reflections of anxieties generated by the destabilization of social institutions in the post-World War II United States (Dixon, 2009), yet his focus on local media's conscious shaping of Moroccan noir with an eye to American and European print and visual media trends nuances that understanding. Certainly, late twentieth-century Moroccan noir might more properly be described as neo-noir, a self-reflexive form of noir commonly dated to the 1970s (Naremore, 2008). Equally significant, however, are the divergent ideological backdrops to American and Moroccan noir. Mark Osteen examines how classical films noir, in which characters' "defeat or death often seems fated," highlight and challenge the American dream, characterized by an "ideology of individualism [that relies on] the belief that personal effort enables one to determine one's own destiny and character; throw off the fetters of history; overcome class, gender, and racial barriers; and gain wealth and prestige" (Osteen 2012, p. 2). In Morocco, by contrast, fated defeat predominated during the reign of Hassan II, the ideology of individualism arriving only as part and parcel of the neoliberalism of the late twentieth century.

Smolin identifies Nabil Ayouch's 1997 *Mektoub*, which outstripped even the global hit *Titanic* at the Moroccan box office, as the film that first notably capitalized on the new sensationalist and critical style of reporting and narrating Moroccan social reality. Based loosely on a real case that rocked Morocco in the 1990s and revolutionized journalistic coverage of trials and crimes, *Mektoub* details a young, modern, well-to-do couple's search for justice after the wife is kidnapped and ritualistically raped by a corrupt police inspector and his gang of powerful men.[2] By turns a thriller, road movie, action film, and social drama, *Mektoub* foregrounds the varied social milieux and landscapes of Northern Morocco, concluding on a guardedly optimistic note grounded in a commitment to justice exemplified by the most modest Moroccans the couple encounters along the way, and shared by a new generation of police officers (Gauch, 2016). Just over ten years later, however, the focus, stories and outcomes of Moroccan film noir have evolved in significant ways, though not without nods to this genealogy. These more recent films follow younger, urban, largely uneducated yet street-smart protagonists as they attempt to twist in their favor the intertwined, local, transnational, and global networks of economic power and status. Targets of daily humiliations and banal exploitations, rather than victims of any single, shocking crime, these young women and men ambitiously, hopefully, and cynically navigate a world characterized by suspicions, wariness, doubts, and fears. Neat resolutions remain elusive in the urban worlds through which these

anti-heroes move. Good and evil are no longer (or never were) starkly differentiated. Mobility is promised yet pathways are blocked. The legitimate is deeply
imbricated with the illegal, and morality is ever shifting.

Consider how the opening scenes of four Moroccan neo-noir films made in the
past decade introduce their protagonists. Leila Kilani's *On the Edge [Sur la planche]*
(2011) presents a frontal close-up of its young female lead, framed by darkness, as
she stares with determination at a point somewhere above the camera. She runs
forward, falls back, and runs forward again, accompanied by a fiercely whispered
voiceover: "Pride lies. And is right to do so. Better to stand upright supported by
one's lies, than lie down, crushed, by others' truths. I don't steal: I reimburse
myself. I don't burgle: I recover. I don't deal: I do business. I don't prostitute myself:
I invite myself. I don't lie: I'm already what I will be. I'm just ahead of the truth,
my truth." Rapid-fire and striking, Badia's monologue vies for attention with the
film's images, which depict her repeatedly jumping at something above the camera,
though it is impossible to apprehend the object of her motions. It is only when the
film, in true noir fashion, circles back to this scene near its conclusion, this time
from a side rear-angle medium long-shot, that we see how Badia is doggedly trying
to run up a wall outside the Tangier shrimp factory where she works. By that time,
the urgent context of her words and behavior has become explicit, and one wishes
she might actually succeed in redefining the material, relational, and physical possibilities available to her. Yet prior to the film's flashback, Badia is shown being
dragged by a silent police officer into a waiting police van, from which she stares
through the window at a gathering crowd. Conventional morality has caught up
with her, though at that point, viewers know that her arrest only perpetuates,
rather than resolves, injustice.

A climax scene at the outset of Nour Eddine Lakhmari's Moroccan box-office
smash *Casanegra* (2008) also captures its anti-heroes in the aftermath of a presumably criminal act. After a leisurely credit sequence where names and titles appear
as neon signs on the façades of Casablanca's art deco buildings, languid saxophone
music cedes to an up tempo drum flourish as two young men run full tilt toward
the camera on a dimly lit street. Pursued by an orderly line of police officers, the
two, Karim and Adil, exchange words, Karim insulting Adil with a slew of vulgar-
ities in Casablancan colloquial Arabic, and Adil protesting in equally colorful language that he just laid eyes on an unbelievable stash of money moments before the
police arrived. Two successive freeze frames break up the rapid tempo, each 20-
something young man identified in turn by means of a brief, rap-sheet-like text
that lists his name, age, and profession: Unemployed. When the action resumes,
Karim asks for details about the money. Adil supplies them, and the two simultaneously look back at the pursuing officers as the scene again freezes, holding the
characters in center frame. If Lakhamri's film opens on a more hopeful note than
Kilani's because the police fail to collar Karim and Adil before the flashback, it
nonetheless presents youthful protagonists just as shady, and just as determined to
break through limitations on the possible, and legal, in hopes of a payoff.

Much less frenetic, Lakhmari's also quite successful *Zero* (2012) takes its time in introducing its eponymous protagonist, the only one of those discussed here to hold a proper job, and as a police officer no less. A drawn out, sung lament accompanies a slow moving camera that first takes in a lace curtain billowing over a window open to the night, and then pans to a rear view of Zero sitting in a wheelchair in an unlit room, facing a blank wall dappled with blue-tinted shadows. Reversing directions, the next shot frames his face as he stares fixedly ahead, chin in hand. After a moment, he rises easily, grabs a pail, and begins scrubbing the walls as the camera moves above, to the rear, and around the room in series of time lapse shots. A repetition of the initial lament creates a sound bridge to a daytime, close-up shot of a watch-cap wearing Zero sneering against a backdrop of street traffic sounds. An eyeline match reveals the object of his scrutiny, a young, made-up woman stepping out of the door of a European-style apartment building arm in arm with an older man dressed in a business suit. A moment later, Zero walks up to their car, raps on the window, shows his badge, and announces "police." In the course of questioning the older man, he "recognizes" the woman as an underage runaway, and taxes her companion with perversion in a diatribe cut short by a scene change. Following the cut, Zero hands his prostitute accomplice, Mimi, her share of the cash from the shakedown, while she rebukes him for the moral tirades he addresses to their targets. Though the opening scene is not explicitly framed as a flashback, *Zero* returns to the darkened, empty room late in the film, after it has established that despite his position as an agent of law and order, Zero is no less than his cinematic counterparts disillusioned, disempowered, and determined to get his due in a corrupt system where the deck is stacked against him.

By contrast with these three films, Faouzi Bensaïdi's *Death for Sale* (2012), offers a more tonally ambiguous introduction to its three protagonists in a film that pays tribute to classical noir while balancing cinematic experimentation with narrative tension. An initial shot of a young man, Malek, appears in three-quarter close-up. It holds steady as he takes a drag on a cigarette, traveling to the left as he passes the cigarette to Soufiane, a tall youth hulking in a peacoat buttoned over a red track suit. Pulling forward, ignoring a blurred figure that walks through the scene, the camera pauses again on Malek and Soufiane, standing hunched against the cold on a broken sidewalk in front of a high stone wall. When it tracks forward anew, Allal's father appears in the foreground and to the right. He looks back at the two youths, and Malek drops his gaze while Soufiane stares back. When Allal emerges from a small door set in the imposing stone archway of the civil prison, the camera stays back as Allal's father advances and awkwardly embraces his son. Allal permits the embrace, but holds his bags stiffly in either hand, meeting his buddies' eyes over his father's shoulder. Malek and Soufiane dash forward, grab his bags, and move to the opposite sidewalk. Allal turns silently from his father and joins them. A backdrop of pop-style music sets the tone of their reunion, conveyed via an extended traveling shot that follows the three friends through Tetouan, the film's credits appearing discreetly in the background. While it offers few hints of the convoluted, very dark, intrigue to come, this introduction unmistakably signals the protagonists' petty criminality as much as their flaunting of deeply held social values. As is the case with the protagonists of the other films described above, Malek, Soufiane, and Allal alternately reject and are rejected by the status quo in ways that make them at once shocking and likable.

These four films show how in the twenty-first century, Moroccan film noir has come to feature resourceful, wary, young protagonists striving to take control of their destinies from within competing structures of domination. Entwining bursts of desperate action with snapshots of a bleak quotidian, the four films, all of which went into production before the North African uprisings of 2011, now seem prescient. To be sure, in certain ways, they are legible through noir genre conventions as reflections of familiar psycho-social anxieties, even without much knowledge of social context. True to noir form, each film features flawed protagonists, often circular, byzantine plots, stark lighting and heavy shadows, double dealing, shadowy criminal networks, and bursts of violence that veer toward madness. Sometimes they gesture explicitly and sometimes implicitly toward well-known classic or neo-noir films; for example, Lakhmari's *Zero* evokes Niels Arden Oplev's 2009 *The Girl with the Dragon Tattoo* and the classic noir films of Jean-Pierre Melville, among others. Nevertheless, all of the films are also imbricated with Moroccan cinematic history and the country's socio-economic realities. Lakhmari's *Zero* seemingly develops the story of the minor character of a downwardly mobile, drug-addicted, drunkard police officer from *Mektoub*, and the film's storyline shadows that film to some extent. For his part, Bensaïdi, who as an actor played the role of that drug addled police officer in *Mektoub*, creates the composite character of Inspector Debbaz, a contemptible alcoholic at once powerful and viciously perverse, in *Death for Sale*. Still, the police recede further into the background in *Death for Sale* than was ever possible in *Mektoub*, while in *Casanegra* and *On the Edge*, the police are only one among several networks of power, including traffickers of pirated goods, drugs, and people, and recruiters for jobs in the factories of transnational businesses headquartered in the Global North. In a shift from the cautious embrace of neoliberal promises of Ayouch's film, these twenty-first-century noir films showcase the instability, deceptions, and shortfalls entwined with neoliberalism's possibilities.

Unlike the upwardly mobile, educated couple at the center of *Mektoub*, the protagonists of Kilani, Lakhmari, and Bensaïdi's films have nothing to lose. Several are urban migrants or members of urbanized families clinging to the trappings of respectability while slipping toward a poverty that is de facto criminalized; all get by on streets smarts and seem to have had little formal education. Each character's precarious social status is showcased through the use of crude, locally specific, vernacular language, the ubiquity of alcohol and drugs, their disaffected manipulation of appearances and rituals of social respectability, their mistrust, and their experience of daily humiliations. *Zero* and the terrorist subplot of *Death for Sale* aside, these twenty-first-century films portray crimes that are largely economic, if overlaid with morality, various forms of theft, scams, prostitution, loan-sharking, and bet rigging to which the protagonists are drawn in the hopes of accessing that universally recognized source of power and respect, money. Significantly, their petty crimes always occur against the backdrop of greater, larger-scale theft, brutality, violence, and exploitation perpetuated by organized crime networks, international conglomerates, and/or local authorities. Highlighting the distinct local particularities of their urban settings of Tangiers, Casablanca, and Tetouan, all four films train their lenses on these milieux as nodes in networks of global, neoliberal forces that are also reshaping them and further engendering competing networks of influence and power.

Although varied in pacing, sometimes veering toward hyperbole, dark comedy, or affective flatness in tone, Kilani, Lakhmari, and Bensaïdi's films feature characters driven by varying degrees of muted rage. Fueled by the frustration that results from the gap between the promises of neoliberalism, new forms of oppression, and the reality of intensified global divisions of labor and renewed social stratifications, this rage has several points of commonality with the Black rage defined by Manthia Diawara in his classic essay on Black noir, a rage "induced by sense of frustration, confinement, and White racism" (Diawara 1993, p. 528). Each film, for example, emphasizes particular checks on its protagonists' mobility that result from social prejudice, stereotypes of Arab men or women, or global hierarchies. Badia dreams of working in the factories located in the free trade zone of Tangiers but lacks the papers to do so; Adil – his family, like that many of the other characters, already urban migrants – wants nothing more than to leave Casanegra for Sweden, but has little hope of obtaining a visa; Karim and Zero cannot cross the lines of social class to become suitable lovers for women from the upscale milieux of Casablanca; and the three protagonists of *Death for Sale* are variously barred from social institutions, obliged to flee Tetouan, and thwarted in their attempts to escape the city. All but *Zero* feature factories of multinational enterprises as reminders of the kind of participation in globalization that is expected of the characters and those similarly marked by race and social class. Yet the four films depict relatively little of the eroticized or explosive violence that Diawara finds in Black noir, focusing instead on the characters' efforts to navigate persistent structural violence. Not simply Moroccanized versions of a wildly popular, if amorphous genre, Kilani, Lakhmari, and Bensaïdi's films employ the codes of noir to stretch the possibilities of and for Moroccan cinema, and those of Moroccan social realism to redefine noir in the era of neoliberalism's global reach.

Homing in on the crucible where the multiple forces and counterforces of economic and cultural globalization meet and refashion social possibilities and expectations, as well as cinematic ones, the stylistically distinct noir films of Kilani, Lakhmari, and Bensaïdi reflect a Morocco where social realities echo those elsewheres likewise being molded and convulsed by neoliberal globalizing and antiglobalizing forces. They produce a Moroccan cinema that is not an exemplar for inclusion in prefabricated catalogues of global cinema, but that exacts reconsideration of what global cinema is and how it is formulated. In an interview with Olivier Barlet of *Africultures* (2006) after the release of his 2006 pastiche film *WWW: What a Wonderful World*, Faouzi Bensaïdi explains his narrative and stylistic shifts away from the social realism of his first feature film, *A Thousand Months* [*Alf Shahr*] (2003): "Everybody knows thriller codes, but not those of North African social realist films; thus that [the social realist thematic tropes of *A Thousand Months*] remained a marginal approach." Because of Hollywood's global reach, the codes of thrillers, and film noir, are easily legible worldwide as more or less successful models of a broadly reproducible genre. By contrast, North African social realist films are perceived as shaped first and foremost by exotic, localized social realities that elude generic codification; consequently, they are presumed to be truer to reality than genre films by those unacquainted with those codes. Yet Bensaïdi's ostensibly straightforward observation underscores an additional point, namely that while some of these codes are bound up with local realities of state and soft censorship that necessitate the modulation of criticisms of power, others are simply obscured by over-investment in authenticity. The work of Kilani, Lakhmari, and Bensaïdi chips away at this politics of authenticity by multiplying the shadows that make noir so compelling and which social realism strives to keep at bay.

Bensaïdi concludes this same interview (2006) with the observation that crime has become banal everywhere, "le monde est devenu plus noir." Playfully equating noir with social realism, he suggests that the conventions of noir – a mood, themes, and narratives that are all about unease, liminality, transgression, mistrust, and the underbelly of modernity, adjusted in these instances to reflect the underworlds of globalization – are also recognized worldwide as realistic reflections of the contemporary era. Consequently, despite frequent critical celebrations of them as taboo-breaking, Moroccan noir films do much more than employ a popular genre to push the limits of what Moroccan films may acceptably show. Rather, they provincialize noir to stretch what the genre can show, how it is defined, and where and to whom it belongs. A convergence of generic codes comes into focus from the very first scenes of each film, establishing expectations for the narrative to come, as much as setting up small and large departures from various anticipated scripts, characters, tones, and moods. The results expose and trouble the geographic division of labor and associated differential valuation of cinematic production in formulations of global cinema.

Read according to the codes of Moroccan social realism, the opening of Kilani's *On the Edge* introduces its protagonist Badia as a victim of presumably Moroccan, sexist social forces: Here is a young woman waging a fierce, internalized struggle for agency in the language of the uneducated; no sooner has she forcefully, if privately, asserted her agency than she is wrestled from the private space of a shower (though she is fully clothed) and arrested by male agents of social order. Yet it quickly grows clear that the film is not going to tell this familiar story: Its framing is too tight, never expanding to convey the structural causes of Badia's oppression.

Furthermore, her opening internal monologue not only details but claims a list of acts broadly criminalized by societies in the Global North. When the film offers an eyeline match as Badia sits in the police van, it reveals that the objects of her gaze are three other young women who look back at her from distinct points in the crowd with varied expressions, the ensuing shot-reverse-shots signaling a betrayal among criminal co-conspirators rather than a direct struggle against representatives of repressive mores. Her appearance of defeat in these opening scenes notwithstanding, Badia dominates the remainder of the film in a manner both unique and unusual for a female character in film noir, where as Yvonne Tasker (2013) notes, women have long been recognized as central yet are always held at a certain distance, never guiding the film's action and perspective (Mulvey, 1975). Neither spectacle, nor femme fatale, Badia not only steers, but determines the intrigue, constantly in the audience's faces.

Strikingly, Badia is never sexualized despite the film's intense, tight framing and repeated bathing scenes. Rather than tracking her, the camera seems to partake of her wariness, nervous energy, self-projections, and paranoia, to the extent that other characters remain underdeveloped. This absence of voyeuristic undertones has the effect of bringing to the fore the audience's assumptions about and judgments of Badia. As the film progresses, this tight framing sometimes feels claustrophobic, as it neither allows for any personal history that might illuminate Badia's temperament or behavior, nor for the kind of distance that would allow one to question the legitimacy of her paranoia. From the outset, when she rebukes her co-worker and co-conspirator Imane for speaking with the other women at the shrimp factory where they both work peeling shrimp, Badia comes across as something of a bully, an impression that only builds as Badia's consistent and calculated lies to her closest friend grow increasingly obvious. Unblinkingly amplifying her ambition, shrewdness, and mistrust, *On the Edge* leaves no room for the development of melodrama, a fixture of both Moroccan social realism, and as James Naremore (2008) contends, frequently of classical film noir. Far from signaling its failure, however, this absence of melodramatic overtones merely heightens the film's successful challenge of viewer expectations. For *On the Edge* is itself manipulative; not, as expected, of audience emotions, but rather of the social realist mechanisms of spectator distancing fed by senses of moral, intellectual, social, and civilizational superiority, and which obscure the disturbing presence of the unknowable.

Badia's rejection of convention always occurs proximately against the backdrop of the stunning, fluorescent whiteness of the shrimp factory where she works in the daytime: She obsessively counts how many shrimp are in the kilo by which she is paid in an effort to make sure that she is not being short changed; she works with her mask lowered amid the stench of fish; she rejects the sociability of her coworkers; and she repeatedly refuses a promotion to recruiter. At night, however, when she and Imane prowl cafes on the lookout for dates to rob, she claims to work in the textile factories of Tangier's heavily guarded freetrade zone, where female laborers assemble a ceaseless stream of brand-name clothing for consumers in the Global North. Far less smelly than shrimp peeling, textile work leaves fewer traces on the body and is located in an extraterritorial zone accessible only with identity papers and clearances that are out of Badia's reach. Not a victim of her society, but also not easily labeled victim of globalization's gendered divisions of labor, Badia tries to game several exploitative systems, only to find herself betrayed as a result of those systems' greater power, depth, and breadth. All while *On the Edge* taps into domestic anxieties about the social ramifications of Morocco's insertion into the global economy, the film never reads as a cautionary tale about the vulnerability of women in the labor force or of women's labor as destabilizing the family. Instead, it confronts audiences with a flawed, sometimes unlikable, character who rejects morality as a tool of social control, breaks the law, and ends up in prison, but whose transgressions are born of a need to survive. Not least, they target an organized crime family and trafficked, likely pirated, goods. In this, Kilani's film compels audiences to see and read across the lines everywhere bisecting formulations of global material and cultural production, without offering them a femme fatale whose defeat would offer at least symbolic resolution to the anxieties upon which the film builds.

In failing to deliver on expectations of what a film featuring a poor, young Moroccan woman should do, *On the Edge* draws attention to those expectations while clearing the way for films that are newly challenging for all audiences. Put simply, Kilani's film presents a new kind of female Moroccan character at the same time that it presents a new kind of woman-centered noir. Badia is realistically Moroccan not in the sense that she is a long-suffering victim of a society presumed to be sexist at its core, as are the heroines of so many internationally acclaimed North African films, but because she quickly grasps the twinned opportunity and exploitation in factory labor, much as she does in her casual after-hours prostitution, determining to reap maximum benefits from both before they consume her in turn. In his review of *On the Edge* in *Le Monde* (2012), Jacques Mandelbaum describes it as a Tangier-based *A bout de souffle*, reminiscent of John Cassavetes' 1960 *Shadows*, Barbara Loden's 1970 *Wanda*, and Luc and Jean-Pierre Dardennes' 1999 *Rosetta* in its "desirable imperfection." Unsurprisingly, Mandelbaum draws comparisons to films from earlier decades, reinforcing the idea that Moroccan cinema is eternally engaged in a game of catch-up. Equally significant, however, is that none of his choices similarly targets neoliberal discourses that equate (Arab) women's entry into the labor force with emancipation and rights advancement, glossing over the ways in which those opportunities for salaried work depend on and exacerbate local and global gendered, social, and economic inequities. Kilani's promotion of Badia's perspective, as a woman from the Global South, within a narrative that explores the possibilities and limitations of this feminized labor force upon which globalization relies, with all the insecurities, suspicions, and moral uncertainties that result from it, is what makes of *On the Edge* a new kind of film noir with a global reach.

Lakhmari's protagonists in both *Casanegra* and *Zero* stand in stark contrast to Badia in terms of immediate likability. Karim, Adil, and Zero are rendered sympathetic through careful management of point-of-view shots and social-realist and noir cinematic framing conventions, as well as savvy negotiation of competing ideals of masculinity, with the result that empathy for their socio-economic struggles overwhelms any moral condemnation of their crimes. All three anti-heroes stand out as slightly varied paradigms of the sensitive North African family man – respectful to a fault of his mother, champion of women, and protector of the weak – who adopts a tough façade to survive in a cruel, corrupt, and unjust world. Riffing on genre, *Casanegra* at times borrows tropes from Moroccan and global picaresque film, while the opening notes of *Zero*'s soundtrack cry melodrama. Yet unlike Kilani's *On the Edge* or Bensaïdi's *Death for Sale*, whose innovative framings expose the unheard and unseen that underpin narrative and visual tropes, *Casanegra* and *Zero* revel in recombining genre conventions. Raw and real as Karim and Adil's Casablancan colloquial Arabic may be, the duo's first on-screen appearance follows the script of comedic pairings: Karim's stream of invective excoriates Adil for leading them into this mess, while Adil, still swept up in hopes for a payday, naïvely ignores their present predicament. Dressed in a suit and tie, Karim projects an aura of responsibility, intelligence, and seriousness, while Adil's jeans and leather jacket present him as the none-too-sharp street thug of this youthful couple who, though good at heart, find trouble as a result of foolish decisions and happenstance.

No less true to cinematic convention, albeit different ones, *Zero* introduces its protagonist as a shadow-shrouded victim of tragic fate. When he suddenly rises from his wheelchair and begins energetically scrubbing the walls, he seemingly morphs from victim to perpetrator erasing evidence of his crime. But not really. For not only does the film quickly clarify that the wheelchair belongs to Zero's father, it also portrays that father in such a way that viewers would hardly condemn Zero even if he had killed him. Instead of resorting to murder, however, Zero evidences a dutiful, even masochistic, devotion to his father, enduring daily insults and humiliations. Notwithstanding the starkly different tones of the two films, presentation of the protagonists follows exactly the same pattern in *Zero* and *Casanegra*. First, Zero, Karim, and Adil appear in the aftermath of an apparent crime. Second, flashing backwards in time, each film contrasts their profession or self presentation with their thuggishness or criminal endeavors. Third, scenes of their home lives reflect both hardships and filial devotion. Finally, their respect for women is featured either in scenes involving mothers and sisters (Adil, Karim) or through a romance with a more educated, upper-middle class woman (Karim and Zero). Fathers, interestingly, are either mute, disabled shells as a consequence of a lifetime of exploitative under-remunerated work (Karim), or angry, intoxicated, violent abusers (Adil), or a combination of both (Zero). Throughout, both films develop an opposition that elevates the powerless scoundrels Adil, Karim, and Zero to a higher moral ground than the decadent, exploitative, sexist, and perversely violent men they encounter at all turns, much of the distinction revolving around the characters' devoted and respectful treatment of women and those weaker than them. As a result, both films flirt constantly with the melodramatic conceit of the fundamentally well-intentioned youth sacrificed by a corrupt, morally bankrupt society that treats them with violence, even though their outcomes are quite distinct, if both more than a little implausible according to social realist and even noir standards.[3]

In 2008, when *Casanegra* smashed box-office records, older movie theatres in Morocco had long developed a reputation as places of ill repute populated mainly by young men up to no good. Attending a screening of a stylistically accomplished and narratively compelling film about two young men from this underclass in a Moroccan movie theatre may have been a show of solidarity and reclamation, but it was also a confirmation of Moroccan cinema's new (global) worthiness.[4] Consistently lauded as taboo-breaking, the film's success, as much as that of *Zero*, was nevertheless due more to its skillful manipulation of social realist and genre codes than to any transgression of moral codes. This conformity to the character, narrative, and pictorial conventions of not just Moroccan realism, but also contemporary global neo-noir, picaresque, and buddy films, is likely one, if not the principal, reason that *Casanegra* met with such public enthusiasm, particularly among Moroccan youth. Lakhmari, who resides in Norway and has acknowledged his debt to dark Scandinavian cinema, has largely escaped the kinds of charges of inauthenticity and opportunism lobbed at other successful Moroccan directors dividing their time between Morocco and abroad, in part by stressing his commitment to sociological study of the milieux his films feature (Bahmad, 2013). Following a host of critics and scholars, Jamal Bahmad lauds this sociological approach, characterizing *Casanegra* as a model of affective realism where "the spectator is plunged into the lived experience of Casablanca's disaffected youth" (2013, p. 31).[5] Yet, like many others, Bahmad concentrates on the film's visceral portrayals of structural and physical violence, neglecting entirely the humor and abundant visual and stylistic tributes to well-known global films that constitute much of its appeal.[6] For by explicitly borrowing from globally popular neo-noir films such as *Pulp Fiction* and combining those influences with Moroccan social realism and comedy, Lakhmari's *Casanegra* does not simply bring relatively neglected perspectives to the screen, but also engages audiences as knowing and discerning critics of global cinema and culture.

In a recent essay, David Desser (2012) tracks the emergence of global neo-noir to the 1990s in the wake of the international success of the cinephilic *Pulp Fiction*. Such cinephilia, Desser argues, is both a condition and hallmark of global noir:

> The impulse toward cinephilia – that is, the ability and necessity of acknowledging the intertextual chain of references, borrowings, and reworkings – may be at the heart of global noir. For it involves filmmakers and film audiences in a circuit of acknowledgments – the ability of filmmakers to make references and their confidence in the audience's recognition of them. (p. 640)

All while celebrating the American-led advent of global genre fluency, however, Desser allows that it might be Americans who came late to this game. Acknowledging that Tarantino borrowed much in his neo-noir films, especially in his earlier neo-noir *Reservoir Dogs* (1992), from Asian and particularly Hong Kong cinema of the 1980s, he points to the existence of an influential global noir well before the 1990s. For his part, Naremore (2008, p. 245) highlights the influence of Black film noir on *Pulp Fiction* in his sweeping study of the multiple and shifting characteristics and contexts of noir. Absent from both accounts, however, is any recognition that familiarity with a broad range of international films, genres, and styles, and media more generally, is a fact of life for African media consumers, much as it is for many around the world. Moroccans, like many who hail from places that do not produce media that reaches global satellite and cable providers, regularly consume a far broader, more international, range of film and media images than does the average American. Lakhmari's films acknowledge and celebrate that familiarity while showing things and telling stories that global neo-noir films from elsewhere cannot possibly see from this particular angle.

So, too, does Bensaïdi's *Death for Sale*, but in a manner that solicits recognition of Moroccan social realist and film noir tropes only to pull them apart, exposing and leaving unresolved the persistently unknowable that informs the anxieties with which noir toys. Although Bensaïdi's film also introduces lead characters that could read as unlikable according to dominant moral codes, its oblique visual and narrative approach works to destabilize viewer judgment throughout the film. Accordingly, their lack of respect and consideration for Allal's father at the film's opening establishes the trio as obnoxious n'er do wells, while Soufiane and Allal's harassment of Malek's new love interest, Dounia, a few scenes later, begins to pit the two against Malek's presumably more sensitive character in true noir fashion. Glimpses of Malek and Allal's home lives and Soufiane's dorm draw upon and scramble presuppositions about the relation of family structure and socio-economics to their criminal behavior and subsequent actions. Narratively, the film's treatment of its three leads is unbalanced, concentrating on Malek and to a lesser degree Soufiane, subtly prompting audiences to bridge the missing information. At the same time, *Death for Sale* sets social interactions against striking backdrops, minimizes dialogue, and draws attention to its framing through off-center and oblique shots, unexpected camera movements, meta-framing of characters through windows and doorways, and attention-grabbing, gravity defying, artful compositions, as well as pastiches of classical and commercial scenarios, and contrapuntal pairings of image and music. As artful and visually rich as it is, *Death for Sale* nonetheless exacerbates the sense that something is missing.

Unlike *On the Edge*, *Casanegra*, and *Zero*, *Death for Sale* does not feature a circular narrative that hints at its characters' fate in its opening scenes. Rather, by juxtaposing and transforming visual and narrative tropes, the film plays with filmgoer impulses to assemble meanings from familiar visual, aural, and narrative cues. Early on, *Death for Sale* highlights this process in a resonant scene where Malek spots Dounia on a Tetouan street and passes his Coca-Cola bottle to her as they stand against a spectacular mountain backdrop. In a film from the United States, this detail would pass as an unremarkably successful bit of product placement, but the explicit use of television commercial framing at the scene's conclusion empha-sizes the implausibility of imagining for even an instant that a Moroccan film would interest a global brand, even one purportedly championing diversity, as an advertising platform. This sly reference to its own status in the global hierarchy of cinema merges with the knowledge, confirmed by Dounia's expression of surprise at the liquid's taste, that the three protagonists had earlier filled Coke bottles with cheap wine, employing the well-known container as cover for their illicit behavior. Such subversion and trafficking of global brands threads through the film, as Malek's family supplements their income by selling luxury brand labels stolen from the clothing assembly factory that employs his sister, raising uncomfortable issues of ownership, theft, creativity, and value, among others. Amidst these mul-tiple levels of signification, it passes unnoticed that Dounia's character remains crucially underdeveloped, revealed only through the distancing mechanisms of cinematic conventions that feature women as objects of romantic interest only by way of developing male characters. True to the best of cerebral noir films, *Death for Sale* not only portrays the miscalculations, bamboozlement, and entrapment of its protagonists, but also ensnares viewers in their own misjudgments.

At least one scholar has faulted Bensaïdi's film for deviating too far from the classic noir script to which it pays tribute. In his recent analysis of the film, Roy Armes (2015, pp. 152–153) details how the action should have unfolded had it stuck to the conventions of noir, before heaping praise on it for its wonderfully realistic portrait of youth just prior to the Arab uprisings of 2011. More than the other films discussed here, however, Bensaïdi's film probes the conventions of such social realism by means of film noir, itself an elusive genre since its emergence as a genre in the work of French film critics studying American films made by immi-grant directors in the 1940s and 1950s (Naremore, 2008). In her study of the dom-inance of realism in fiction, Catherine Belsey asserts that, "in order to pass for realism mimetic fiction has to put forth an analysis of the world that confirms – or at least accords with – the reader's existing convictions," with the result that "realism broadly corroborates what we already think we know" (Belsey 2011, p. 64). Belsey's observations apply to no less to Moroccan social realism, whether viewed by Moroccan or international audiences. While it plays to audience cer-tainties regarding the dissolute youths of this Moroccan border city, however, *Death for Sale* time and again introduces unexpected views where one expects to find only confirmation, its quirky framing of each scenario emphasizing the ines-capability of uncertainty and the unknowable. At the same time, paying tribute to classical noir in an era of new societal transformations occasioned by economic and cultural globalizations, Bensaïdi's film sidesteps the motif of the discoverable that classical noir deploys. For *Death for Sale* highlights not just the unknown, but presents it as unknowable, with all the attendant anxieties that suggests, not so much showing the social upheavals occasioned by neoliberal realities and ideals, as decentering the narratives, social and cinematic, that normally emerge to make sense of and evaluate these upheavals.

From the moment that Malek lowers his eyes instead of meeting the gaze of Allal's father, he appears as the most sensitive of the three young men, clearly poised to become the louche, romantic hero. This impression seems cemented shortly afterwards, when he falls head over heels for Dounia at first sight. That Dounia labors as a sexworker only cements Malek's persona as a sensitive protector, and in each of their encounters, the romantic charge outweighs narrative and visual contradictions signaling that his view of things is somehow skewed. The spectacular mountain vista of their first meeting, for example, overlooks a garbage dump, while the streams of celluloid cascading around them, tossed upwards by young boys searching the dump for saleable items, read as affirmations of the cinematic worthiness of their romance, rather than as signs of clichés or dissimulations. As he behaves more and more reprehensibly toward his family, however, inconsistencies in Malek's character multiply. He refuses to help his stepfather in the family bakery though his skills could help turn the business around. He takes all the money from the sale of the designer labels that his beloved sister Awatef has smuggled out of the textile factory, where she works from pre-dawn to post-dusk to support the family, and blows it on alcohol and dates for himself and his friends. When Awatef's wealthy suitor dumps her just as her family learns of the scandalous affair, Malek is too focused on Dounia to intervene in the resulting fight; when Awatef kills herself in despair, Malek blames his stepfather for her death. Finally, without regard for his mother's welfare, he sells out his stepfather, now the family's sole provider, to the unpredictable, sadistic police Inspector Debbaz, in return for Dounia's release from prison.

Finally, after transgressing multiple norms of social propriety, morality, and filial piety, Malek violates the codes of male solidarity and thieves' honor by turning police informant and leaking the details of the jewelry store heist he, Allal, and Soufiane have planned. Self-absorbed and enthralled by a fantasy scenario where he and Dounia escape with their share of the money to live happily ever after, Malek fails to notice his own progressive blinding by a confluence of assumptions about the fixity of gender roles and romantic love, and investments in picaresque David and Goliath narratives where the clever criminal defeats the infinitely more corrupt and exploitative networks of power. He, and we, fail to notice that Dounia is no helpless victim, that the drunken Debbaz is far more dangerous than his shows of affection allow, and that Soufiane is far more serious about his newfound, garbled religio-political convictions than he is about Allal's plan for wealth and power. On the day of the heist, Malek steps over the body of Allal, shot dead by Debbaz the moment he emerges on the roof of the jewelry store with the loot, grabs the bag and runs away, dodging bullets. Meanwhile, the film returns for a moment to the storefront, from which a blood soaked Soufiane emerges as if in a trance, quickly encircled by a SWAT team. Malek finds Dounia waiting for him at the central bus station, only to lose her moments later, when she runs to the bath-room under the pretext of hiding the money, instead fleeing out a backdoor. Disconsolate, less the victim of a femme fatale than of ingrained prejudices that cloud his ability to see and understand the power dynamics in which he is enmeshed, Malek stumbles from the bus depot, police officers with guns drawn visible at the edge of the screen, and climbs atop a wall as the film illustrates the metaphorical inversion of his world by flipping the image upside down.

Much as do Bensaïdi's previous films, *Death for Sale* highlights the invisible, providing just enough material to maintain narrative meaning on the edge of incomprehensibility. Dialogue is sparse, off-screen sound significant, and images resonant with multiple meanings. Amidst those meanings, however, something crucial remains out of sight and unspoken. Like Kilani's *On the Edge*, *Death for Sale* is an intellectual film, one whose self-conscious cinematic-ness thwarts the kinds of reception that has often been the lot of Moroccan films, a reception that treats films as mirrors of local realities that perform a kind of public service by returning those realities to domestic audiences somehow incapable of seeing, or at least acknowledging, them unaided. Instead, Bensaïdi and Kilani's films create unaccus-tomed gaps for viewers to fill in, promoting unease about the inevitable reductions and misdirections behind any popular or filmic representation of complex socio-economic realities. It is no coincidence that both Kilani and Bensaïdi have made films – he his first feature, *A Thousand Months*, and she a celebrated documentary, *Our Forbidden Places* (2008) – that treat Morocco's still recent era of political vio-lence known as The Years of Lead – a period marked by the suppression of free speech and dissent, and torture and disappearances – that explore its legacies of self-censorship and internalized violence.[7] In distinct ways, the slow, carefully com-posed, off-center scenes of *Death for Sale* and the cramped shots and amped up pace of *On the Edge* both convey the impression that something critical is being withheld. In their refraction of Moroccan social realism through the lens film noir, the two films also expose the ramifications of neglecting to venture into these uneasy recesses of the unknown.

This emereges most saliently in Soufiane's trajectory from petty criminal to rad-icalized warrior of the faith, rendered in a realism by turns gritty, oblique, and magical, and functioning as a shadow plot to the more conventionally noir trajec-tories of Allal and Malek. On the surface, Soufiane's story follows a familiar arc: Younger than the others, he lives in a crowded, squalid dorm while attending school, though he spends more time on the street purse-snatching, drinking, and getting high with his buddies than he does in the classroom. After Allal goes into hiding and Malek becomes infatuated with Dounia, Soufiane is left to struggle on his own. Caught and brutally tortured by schoolboys after a failed purse-snatching, he is radicalized by the group of solemn Islamists who come to his rescue. Images of the process of this radicalization are few and notional: The flicker of a possibly extremist video on a video screen, and groups of youths running and practicing martial arts moves in the mountain sanctuary where Soufiane is taken and nursed back to health. In their place are scenes that wordlessly emphasize care, regard, and thoughtfulness: An old man gently tends to Soufiane's wounds in his room, and the cell's leader speaks to him in fatherly tones, sending him back Tetouan with DVDs to sell cheaply at mosques and telling him to keep the proceeds. In sharp contrast, Malek and Allal abandon him to pursue their own interests, and Allal bullies and belittles the newly radicalized Soufiane when he appears less than enthusiastic about their planned heist. Surprisingly alone among these four recent noir films in depicting radicalization as an outcome for its protagonists, *Death for Sale* counts on its audiences's familiarity with such narratives to fill in the details that it omits, while subtly recasting the affective valences associated with Soufiane's transformation. This at once (mis)directs audience attention away from the inevitable outcome of Soufiane's newfound religious extremism, and subsequently heightens anxieties by raising the specters of radicalization's complexity, unpredictability, and potentially vast audience.

Later, the film at once intensifies and modulates this disquiet by transposing the depth of Soufiane's religio-ideological transport into an aesthetically stunning sequence. Following the trio's reunion on a forested hillside, where Allal details his plans to rob a jewelry store owned by an elderly Christian, Soufiane runs away from his friends after they mock his declaration that Christians are their eternal enemies. Seated on a stony outcrop at edge of the forest, Soufiane falls into a trance, and in what follows, the film seems to dip disconcertingly into his consciousness. Rising, Soufiane stares up at the darkening sky, arms outstretched at his sides and palms open, against a soundscape of Sufi-esque chanting and steady drumbeats. After a cutaway, he reappears circling from behind a burning tree, naked, a flaming torch in each hand. Enraptured by the flaming tree, Soufiane throws the torches to the ground and approaches it, arms outstretched, while the camera rotates around him. Another cutaway shows Malik and Allal walking down the hillside on a dirt road, pausing and exclaiming in disbelief as they spot flames on the mountainside. Arrestingly poetic – irreducible to a simple meaning and out of sync with the surrounding narrative and aesthetics of *Death for Sale* – the magical realism of this sequence suggests not only the inadequacy of the clichés usually employed to account for radicalization but also that its lure cannot be accounted for through rational, intellectual explanations or the tropes of Moroccan social realism. Using the device of Malek and Allal's disbelief, *Death for Sale* gracefully backs away from this potentially destabilizing moment and returns to the more familiar deceptions of classical film noir.

Writing of classical noir cinema, Naremore (2008) notes the crucial role played by border and liminal spaces in the Hollywood noir films of the 1940s and 1950s, liminal spaces that include "the Casbah" and certainly a number of Moroccan settings, and which depend on racist and Orientalist tropes even as they challenge a Western modernity portrayed as fundamentally dysfunctional or rotten. Kilani, Lakhmari, and Bensaïdi's films explicitly inhabit such liminal zones, liminal, urban, spaces no longer maintained by a colonial power but reshaped by forces of globalization from which elites and rulers benefit, taking ownership of and "homing" them. They depict the margins on which economic globalization relies even as it vaunts the abolition of borders and such concepts of margin and center, while asking just what is global about global cinema. Luring audiences with the promise of insights into Moroccan lived realities, before disrupting that promise through their skillful manipulation of genre conventions, Kilani, Lakhmari, and Bensaïdi unsettlingly foreground what is at stake today in Moroccan cinema. If noir first emerged as a critical genre in the sense that it was first labeled a genre by film critics rather than filmmakers, the films of Moroccan noir retain that element of critical searching, always scrutinizing how the genre both reflects and covers up something essential about the societies from which it first emerged, those that have appropriated it, and the ties among them.

In the twenty-first century, the films of Moroccan noir reflect public anxieties not just about the accelerating and increasingly visible signs of economic and social change, but also about economic, social, and political justice not just in Morocco, but for Moroccans in a global world, as much as for global audiences. Lakhmari, Bensaïdi, and Kilani's use of noir tropes and stylistics becomes a means for audiences to watch Morocco and Moroccans through the lens of a globally familiar and beloved genre to which they have historically been a shadowy backdrop. At the same time, the conventions of film noir allow for an expansion of Moroccan films' audiences and the foci of Moroccan cinema. For while civil society has made considerable gains in Morocco, much about both global and domestic networks of power remains illiberal and opaque. Periods of growth in press freedoms, groundbreaking print and electronic publications, and enthusiastic use of social media for previously unimaginable forms of critique and exposure have been punctuated by new crackdowns, approaches to censorship, and prosecutions for lese majesty. Similarly, renewed public protests, especially since 2011, have led not only to new gains but also to sometimes severe repression. Nor has this been the case only in Morocco. Dixon (2009) characterizes noir as a cinema of paranoia more suited than ever to the United States of the twenty-first century, where he contends it has proliferated across media forms. Suspicion of government, politicians, and wealthy elites, alongside skepticism and apprehension in the face of neoliberalism and globalization, protracted and proliferating wars, security concerns, and a climate of ever-present threat are not limited to Morocco and the Global South, and present perfect fodder for noir, where a climate of mistrust prevails and secret double dealing, or impressions of it, drives plots. In this era of globalization, Moroccan anxieties are global anxieties, and Moroccan noir is global noir.

Of course, when it comes to global relations, the power to intervene in, respond to, or escape such threats and conditions is not evenly distributed, and these films reflect anxieties raised by new restrictions on visas for Moroccans, ever tightening borders between Global South and Global North, limited opportunities for Moroccan youth in much vaunted global industries and trade, the spread of extremist Islamist ideologies, multiple forms of terrorism, and constant pressures to self-censor and recalibrate images in an effort to mitigate globally circulating pejorative images of Arabs, Africans, and Muslims. From beneath this crush of stereotypes that impedes free circulation of ideas and images as much as people, a new cinematic scrutiny has emerged, one that explores the power dynamics of images alongside the uncertainties that drive their proliferation and their mobility. With vertiginous urgency or exaggerated slowness, the films of Kilani, Lakhmari, and Bensaïdi attempt to peel back these layers of presupposition about what Moroccan films can do, what audiences they address and how they participate in the construction of global cinema. If you think you have already seen these films, you are missing something.

Notes

1 *Makhzen* is a term from Moroccan Arabic that is employed to refer to the network of ruling elites, all presumably tied in one way or another to the king.
2 Smolin (2013) offers details of the original case in, "Police on Trail: The Tabit Affair, Newspaper Sensationalism, and the End of the Years of Lead," pp. 14–46.
3 In *Casanegra*, Adil and Karim somehow escape the cops and are shown back on the street a few days later, Karim in a new suit and Adil claiming to have traveled to Norway. Meanwhile, in *Zero*, the hero has broken up the sex-slavery ring and seems poised for happiness when a tattoo artist he had confronted earlier appears out of nowhere and fatally stabs him.
4 I was fortunate enough to see this film in a movie theatre in Rabat shortly after it opened. Attending a screening was clearly part of its appeal, and audience participation was vocal and frequent.
5 Similarly, the Moroccan French language weekly *TelQuel* (no. 356, 2009) featured the film on its cover, in its editorial, and in a substantial feature story, praising its unflinching look at neglected social realities.
6 Despite obvious points of commonality with *Pulp Fiction*, Florence Beaugé, reviewing *Casanegra* for *Le Monde* (2009), characterizes Lakhmari's film simply as hyper-realist and omits any references to its cinematic qualities, praising it instead for exploding taboos.
7 The Years of Lead broadly encompass the years of King Hassan II's reign, from 1961 to 1999. During these years, perceived political opponents including Marxists and Islamists, as well as feminist and Amazight activists, were routinely arrested, tortured, and disappeared, and the press and media were heavily censored. State repression began to ease somewhat in the 1990s, with some former opponents of Hassan II's government even appointed to state ministries. Sweeping changes, however, set in only after the king's death in 1999.

References

Armes, Roy. 2015. *New Voices in Arab Cinema*. Bloomington: Indiana University Press.

Bahmad, Jamal. 2013. "From *Casablanca* to *Casanegra*: Neoliberal Globalization and Disaffected Youth in Moroccan Cinema." *Middle East Journal of Culture and Communication* 6: 15–35. DOI 10.1163/18739865-00503002.

Beaugé, Florence. 2009. "*Casanegra*: Film vérité sur Casablanca, dévoile la face sombre du Maroc" *Le Monde*, 27 January. Accessed 27 January 2017. www.lemonde.fr/afrique/

article/2009/01/27/casanegra-film-verite-sur-casablanca-devoile-la-face-sombre-du-maroc_1147066_3212.html

Belsey, Catherine. 2011. "Realism: Do We Overrate It?" *A Future for Criticism*. Malden, MA: Wiley-Blackwell: 54–71.

Bensaïdi, Faouzi. 2006. "Pourquoi un Marocain ne pourrait-il faire du polar?" Interview with Olivier Barlet. *Africultures*, 19 October. Accessed 29 January 2017. http://africultures.com/pourquoi-un-marocain-ne-pourrait-il-pas-faire-du-polar-4599/

Desser, David. 2012. "Global Film Noir: Genre Film in the Age of Transnationalism." In *The Film Genre Reader IV*, edited by Barry Keith Grant, 628–648. Austin, TX: University of Texas Press.

Diawara, Mathia. 1993. "Noir By Noirs: Towards a New Realism in Black Cinema." *African American Review* 27(4): 525–537.

Dixon, Wheeler Winston. 2009. *Film Noir and the Cinema of Paranoia*. Edinburgh: Edinburgh University Press.

Gauch, Suzanne. 2016. *Maghrebs in Motion: North African Cinema in Nine Movements*. New York: Oxford University Press.

Mandelbaum, Jacques. 2012. "*Sur la planche*: A Tanger, le *A bout de souffle* de quatre rebelles," *Le Monde*, 31 January. Accessed 29 January 2017. www.lemonde.fr/cinema/article/2012/01/31/sur-la-planche-a-tanger-le-a-bout-de-souffle-de-quatre-rebelles_1636875_3476.html.

Mulvey, Laura. 1975. "Visual Pleasure and Narrative Cinema." *Screen* 16(3): 6–18.

Naremore, James. 2008. *More Than Night: Film Noir in its Contexts*. Berkeley, CA: University of California Press.

Osteen, Mark. 2012. *Nightmare Alley: Film Noir and the American Dream*. Baltimore, MD: Johns Hopkins University Press.

Smolin, Jonathan. 2013. *Moroccan Noir: Police, Crime, and Politics in Popular Culture*. Bloomington: Indiana University Press.

Tasker, Yvonne. 2013. "Women in Film Noir." In *A Companion to Film Noir*, edited by Andrew Spicer and Helen Hanson, 353–368. Hoboken, NJ: Wiley-Blackwell.

Filmography

Ayouch, Nabil. (1997) *Mektoub*. Morocco, France: Shems, Playtime.

Bensaïdi, Faouzi. (2003) *A Thousand Months*. Morocco, Belgium, France, Germany: Agora Films, Entre Chien et Loup, Gloria Films.

Bensaïdi, Faouzi. (2012). *Death for Sale*. Morocco, Belgium, France, Germany, UAE: Entre Chien et Loup, Liaison Cinématographique, Agora Films.

Kilani, Leila (2008). *Our Forbidden Places*. Morocco, France: Catherine Dussart Productions.

Kilani, Leila. (2011). *On the Edge [Sur la planche]*. Morocco, France, Germany: Aurora Films, Socco Chico Films, Institut National de l'Audiovisuel.

Lakhmari, Nour Eddine. (2008). *Casanegra*. Morocco: Sigma, Soread-2 M

Lakhmari, Nour Eddine. (2012). *Zero*. Morocco: Timlif.

Oplev, Niels Arden. (2009) *The Girl with the Dragon Tattoo*. Sweden, Denmark, German, Norway: Yellow Bird, ZDF Enterprises, Sveriges Television.

Tarantino, Quentin. (1994). *Pulp Fiction*. USA: Miramax, A Band Apart, Jersey Films.

16

From Ethnography to Essay
Realism, Reflexivity, and African Documentary Film

Rachel Gabara

Renowned French anthropologist, Marcel Griaule, was a pioneer in the domain of European ethnographic filmmaking. In the late 1930s, Griaule produced two short films in the context of his research on the Dogon in what is now southeastern Mali. He described his documentary process as follows:

> The shooting was all done live like real newsreels. You cannot ask the natives to do a reenactment or even a rehearsal. For them everything is spontaneous and if you burden them with details, all is lost … The documents recorded by our camera are therefore precise and faithful accounts and unquestionably authentic. (Leprohon 1945, p. 185)[1]

Griaule's simplistic conception of filmic realism and the racism on which it relied ally his work with a tradition of French colonial documentary dating back to newsreels shot in the first years of the twentieth century. And in the decades following the release of Griaule's *In the Land of the Dogon* (1935) and *Under the Black Masks* (1938), even as many documentary filmmakers working in Europe and North America began to experiment with form as they questioned conventional conceptions of objectivity and realism, representations of Africa and Africans in nonfiction films remained for the most part the same. Immediately following independence, African documentarists were eager to counter colonial stereotyping in films that would represent their continent and cultures from the inside. A second generation of nonfiction filmmakers adopted a reflexive approach to personal and political African histories and realities, rejecting not just colonial content but also its form. In what follows, after tracing in more

A Companion to African Cinema, First Edition. Edited by Kenneth W. Harrow and Carmela Garritano.
© 2019 John Wiley & Sons, Inc. Published 2019 by John Wiley & Sons, Inc.

detail this history of documentary film in Francophone West and Central Africa, I will argue for the inclusion of their films in a global category of reflexive documentary and the essay film in particular.

Documentary filmmakers for both private studios and governmental agencies worked in the service of French colonialism. European cameramen appeared in sub-Saharan Africa soon after colonial armies, eager to record images of newly acquired assets. As early as 1905, Pathé, Gaumont, and other major French studios, competing with companies from Great Britain, Belgium, and the United States, began sending cameramen south of the Sahara Desert for documentary footage in the form of newsreels or *actualités*. Alfred Machin called himself and other European cameramen "image hunters" (Machin 1909, p. 9), and Pathé released, among others, his *Hippopotamus Hunt on the Blue Nile* (1908), *Panther Hunt* (1909), and *Elephant Hunt* (1911). Machin, who published articles about his expeditions with titles that included "The Cinematograph and the Conquest of the World" (1909) and "Shooting Guns and Film Across Central Africa" (1911), was capturing animals and Africa on film. From its beginnings, colonial film claimed to offer spectators back in the metropole what G. Dureau, the editor of *Ciné-Journal*, described as "a living illustration of all of the corners of the world where the French flag flies." The cinema, Dureau continued, "is the exact representation of the nature and the people we cannot all go see. It evokes the distant lands of which an atlas or the words of a teacher can give only a confused and usually false idea" (Dureau 1913, p. 1).

Looking back at these earliest years of colonial filmmaking, André Liotard and Samivel in 1950 stressed the importance of the advent of what they called a "cinema of exploration." Prior explorers, Europeans whose self-proclaimed profession consisted of travel in areas of the world they considered to be premodern or uncivilized, had produced drawings and photography that Liotard and Samivel deemed "rare and episodic documents." Film, they contended, would by its very nature provide "impartial testimony" in support of colonialism; "it was life itself that [cinema] was henceforth going to be able to collect in canisters…thus began a new era of the conquest of the Earth, that of the camera" (Liotard et al. 1950, pp. 7–8). Machin and his colleagues had inaugurated a tradition of documentary whose assertions of objectivity and a perfect match between reality and representation denied its colonial and racist bias, and although their films focused on landscapes, flora and fauna, they also began to highlight the customs of the African peoples encountered along the way. Marc-Henri Piault argues that ethnography and the cinema were born at the same time not by accident, but as the "twin children of a common endeavor of discovery, or identification, or appropriation" (Piault 2000, p. 10). Manifestations of a desire for scientific observation "in the field," both grew out of expansions of enterprises for which colonial conquest was critical (Piault 2001, p. 6). Over the course of approximately 40 years, ethnography would move steadily to the forefront of French colonial documentary cinema.

Between 1913 and 1928, Gaumont Actualités released a number of films in a program entitled "Educational Series, Geography, Africa." *In West Africa* (no. 4355), subtitled "Trades, Types, and Customs," opens with images of a tailor working on his sewing machine, after which we see women with elaborate hairstyles, men getting haircuts, women cooking dinner around a fire, artisans working, fishermen going out to sea, and women pounding millet. *Through French Equatorial Africa* (no. 6022) shifts seamlessly from indigenous animals to the daily activities of local peoples:

> A river in Africa. Ducks take flight. Hippopotamus heads rise from the water. Shots, a hippopotamus is dead…A village in the savanna, huts with straw roofs. The local population, the women walk swaybacked, wearing cloths around their waists… Daily activities in the village. The women carry baskets on their heads. A group of women and children. Men working: they arrange tree trunks in a grotto, others carry bricks dried in the sun on their shoulders.

This Gaumont summary concludes with four keywords – "Customs. Traditions. Landscapes. Fauna" – not merely claiming to introduce the spectator to Africans as well as Africa but giving first billing to the newsreel's ethnographic attractions. According to *Cinémagazine*, the cameraman with the Vandenbergh expedition in Central Africa recorded "the bizarre habits and customs of Negro peoples" such that, "thanks to the cinema, a voyage to African lands could be completed without fatigue" (Anon. 1923, p. 243).

Swedish cameraman Oscar Olsson's *In the Heart of Savage Africa* (1922) was a huge success in Paris, and critic Georges-Michel Coissac considered it to be a "great documentary," one that "calls documentary films into question and shows how captivating they are, even awe-inspiring, as long as they are real." Describing the film, Coissac asserted that, "For the first time, the audience was transported to a place until now known only to audacious explorers, among the savannas, the virgin forests and their wild animals, the Negro peoples and their customs" (Coissac 1922, p. 516). Landscapes and animals were again paired with people and their customs, and Coissac, like Dureau, Liotard, and Samivel, stressed the self-evident, unquestionable realism of the film's representation of all of these as its most powerful quality. In 1926, two major French documentary film productions shot in sub-Saharan Africa were released: Léon Poirier's *Croisière Noire*, a feature-length recording of the Citroën expedition in Central Africa, and Marc Allégret's *Voyage to the Congo*. Both offered ethnographic images and information as part of their travelogues, and Allégret's filmed journey with writer André Gide was subtitled "Scenes of Indigenous Life in Equatorial Africa." Even Marcel Carné, who would go on to direct the masterpieces of French poetic realism *Port of Shadows* (1938) and *Daybreak* (1939), praised colonial documentaries, including those of Olsson, Poirier, and Allégret, in the same terms as Machin in an article entitled "The Cinema Out to Conquer the World" (Carné 1930, pp. 9–10).

French documentary images of Africa were from the beginning conceived of and deployed as propaganda, designed to rally support for the colonial project, and particularly so in the years during and after World War I.[2] The Cinematographic Section of the Armies (SCA) was established in 1915 and soon produced and distributed *The Colonies' Aid to France* (1918), which begins by showing the metropolitan viewer, in two contrasting maps introduced by intertitles, the expansion of French colonial possessions between 1870 and 1912 credited to the vision of Jules Ferry. Traveling first from Morocco to Indochina to display the contributions of the colonies to the war effort in the form of food and ammunition, the film's emphasis then shifts to the accomplishments of the *tirailleurs sénégalais*, colonial troops forced to fight in Europe, with a section devoted to their "games and dances" (Figure 16.1). Like the studio newsreels and travel films, then, the films made by the SCA often included ethnographic details. In *Toward Tchad* (1922), after a series of images of European adventurers traveling through North and then sub-Saharan Africa and accompanying shots of landscapes and wild animals, the intertitle "Small Trades" appears, followed by images of women spinning thread, a weaver at work, the dying of cloth, a wrestling match, traditional wrestling, dancing, and drumming.

Figure 16.1 *L'aide des colonies à la France,* Henri Desfontaines, 1918, Section cinématographique des armées.

The Committee of Colonial Propaganda by Film was created in 1928 to produce a collection of newsreels glorifying the French colonies for the upcoming Colonial Exhibition, "a visitor's book in moving images that will evoke the glorious past, show the laborious present, and announce the fertile future" (Anon. 1928, p. 23). The number of documentaries shot in the colonies quickly increased, some for the first time had sound, and at least 300 were projected at the Exhibition in 1931 (Bloom 2008, p. 130). Such films, including *The Colonial Expansion of France* (1930) and *History of Greater France* (1931), praised France's "civilizing mission" across the centuries. According to Coissac, they provided for a kind of virtual tourism that would encourage spectators to extract resources from the colonies; "Thanks to films, we wander through any and all lands, not as tourists but as prospectors; they open themselves up to us in all of their features and with all of their resources and possibilities" (Coissac 1931, p. 387). And even after World War II, the SCA's *From Trêves to Abidjan* (1946) includes a brief ethnographic pause amid explanations of military training maneuvers underway in French West Africa. French pilots bargain for their purchases at Bamako market, after which they and the film's spectators are treated to a performance of the Dogon masks.

I began this chapter with Marcel Griaule, an academic anthropologist who studied the Dogon and in whose filmic work of the late 1930s ethnography became the primary and not an auxiliary project. In the second half of the twentieth century, Griaule's disciple Jean Rouch brought French ethnographic filmmaking in Africa to the forefront and to a global audience. Rouch was not working alone; the Committee on Ethnographic Film within the Museum of Man in Paris, which he co-founded with André Leroi-Gourhan in 1952, sponsored a large number of ethnographic undertakings by self-proclaimed filmmaker-anthropologists, including Serge Ricci, Guy Le Moal, and Georges Bourdelon. Ethnographic documentaries were also funded by the French National Center of Scientific Research (CNRS), the Ministry of National Education, the National Pedagogical Institute, and the Cinémathèque of Public Education. Although Leroi-Gourhan took pains to distinguish the ethnographic documentary from colonial propaganda and exotic documentary films (Leroi-Gourhan 1948, pp. 42–43), most of these films, in both their content and style, perpetuated the colonial representations of Africa and Africans of the newsreels, travel and adventure, and army films that preceded them. In Ricci's *Water Wedding* (1953), for example, a French voice-over describes life along the river among the Bobo in what is now Mali and western Burkina Faso as we see men weaving nets and fishing, women gathering and smoking fish, selling the fish at market, and singing and dancing. When we hear the voices of the people on screen, they are muted and neither synched nor translated. Only Rouch, the most prolific of the group, would substantially diverge from this model.

With *Jaguar* (1955/1967) and *I, A Black Man* (1958), Rouch began to transform his documentary and ethnographic practice, allowing his African subjects to become actors and contribute, often in their own French, to the voice-overs of his films. He trained many of his actors to become filmmakers themselves and established the first film production facilities in Africa. Rouch called this method "shared anthropology" and these films "ethno-fictions," claiming, contrary to Griaule, that he saw "almost no boundary between documentary film and films of fiction" (Rouch 2003, p. 185). He continued to narrate his films, but his voice became less authoritative and more speculative, and African voices were for the first time telling at least part of the story. This transformation was more dramatic in *Little by Little* (1969), filmed almost ten years after the end of the colonial era, in which the character of Damouré visits Paris to see "how people live in houses with many floors." Damouré, like the cameramen sent by Pathé and Gaumont and the Museum of Man, is on a mission to learn "geography, habits, customs," but he reverses their route to travel from Africa to Europe. In Rouch's later films, Africans were not only objects of documentary, though Senegalese filmmaker Ousmane Sembene nonetheless famously accused Rouch of filming Africans as if they were insects. Rouch could perhaps never escape the formative influence of Poirier's travel documentary, which he had seen as a child. His memories of the film were so strong, in fact, that when he arrived in Niamey for the first time, he could not see the African reality before his eyes; "it was these views from *Croisière noire* that, fifteen years later, welcomed me on this plateau of dusty laterite above the valley of the Niger River" (Rouch 1957, p. 32).

During and after the wave of independence from France in the late 1950s and early 1960s, West and Central African filmmakers sought to reclaim the cinema and their cinematic image from their former colonizers. Many new African governments established national cinema services, which funded inexpensive and straightforward educational films that were often co-sponsored by the French Ministry of Cooperation and the International Audiovisual Consortium (CAI) in Paris (Tapsoba 1996, p. 50). Togo, for example, according to François Kodjo, emphasized "creation toward a goal and not for artistic pleasure" (Kodjo 1979, pp. 608–609). Aside from such productions, most early African film was not documentary, but historical fiction film, and many well-known directors, including Souleymane Cissé (Mali) and Idrissa Ouedraogo (Burkina Faso), got their start with short documentaries and then shifted to feature films as quickly as their funding permitted. Pioneering Senegalese filmmaker and film critic Paulin Soumanou Vieyra, one of only a few filmmakers of his generation to work consistently in documentary, responded to Griaule, Rouch, and their colleagues with what he called social anthropological or sociological films (Vieyra 1990, p. 128). Vieyra is best-remembered for his pre-independence docu-fiction *Africa on the Seine*, shot in Paris in the mid-1950s, but he returned to Senegal to direct *A Nation is Born* (1960), a celebration of independence from France, *Lamb* (1963), a humorous study of Senegalese traditional wrestling, and *Môl* (1966), a representation of the life of a fishing village near Dakar via the story of a young man.

Vieyra was at the origin of a revolution within a global documentary cinema whose relationship with Africa had been one of exoticization, oppression, or neglect. In a first wave of West and Central African documentaries, from the early

1960s through the early 1980s, Blaise Senghor (Senegal), Moïse Zé (Cameroon), Pascal Abikanlou (Benin), Tidiane Aw (Senegal), Safi Faye (Senegal), Timité Bassori (Côte d'Ivoire), Momar Thiam (Senegal), and others joined Vieyra to challenge the so-called realism of colonial film. In Vieyra's words, and in documentaries as much as in feature films, "African cinema is reestablishing the truth about Africa because Africans themselves have taken charge of their cinema. The vision becomes an interior one" (Vieyra 1990, p. 132). Many of these early African documentary films can be described as autoethnographic, a term used by Mary Louise Pratt to describe "instances in which colonized subjects undertake to represent themselves in ways that *engage with* the colonizer's own terms" (Pratt 1992, p. 7). Working against the French tradition that preceded them, filmmakers began with an inherited style, in which footage of rituals, customs, and traditional occupations was accompanied by an authoritative, explanatory voice-over. Their films were in many cases funded by the same Paris-based institutions that had supported and continued to support French ethnographers working in Africa.

The narrator of Blaise Senghor's *Great Magal to Touba* (1962) details for the spectator the stages of the yearly Mouride pilgrimage to the mosque in Touba, Senegal. The 20-minute film, which was awarded the Silver Bear at the Berlin Film Festival, begins with a map identifying Dakar and Touba, after which an on-screen text and formal third-person voice-over commentary in French first describe and then follow the pilgrims' journey. Although Senghor was Senegalese, he was criticized by fellow Africans for depicting the ritual from the outside, as had European documentarians (Haffner 1984, p. 32). Moïse Zé, in his 15-minute *The Mvet* (1965/1972), chose instead to narrate his representation of Cameroonian musical traditions and rituals in the first-person singular and plural and to share his voice-over with a woman, Jackie Maman. Zé asserted that his deep knowledge of his topic and his use of the first person allowed him to break away from a "traditional ethnographic cinema" that he described as "an abusive enterprise," for which foreign filmmakers arrive with a foreign crew to film local populations who neither contribute to the finished product nor profit from it (Sormery 1974, p. 8). As independent African filmmakers continued to work in documentary, many would join Zé in breaking away from conventional ethnography, for the most part by experimenting with multivocal and multilingual voice-overs and by challenging Griaule's insistence on the production of a "precise and faithful account."

I labelled *Africa on the Seine* a docu-fiction and, as Frank Ukadike, Jude Akudinobi, and Maria Loftus have noted, a number of African directors since Vieyra have combined nonfictional and fictional strategies in their portrayals of previously misrepresented African realities (Ukadike 1995, p. 91; Akudinobi 2000, p. 346; Loftus 2010, p. 37). Whereas Sembene as early as *Borom Sarret* (1963) reached toward nonfiction in his portrayals of fictional characters, early African documentary filmmakers reached toward fiction, as had Rouch. They reacted against the inaccuracies, racism, and condescension of the European documentary tradition by entangling fiction and nonfiction, questioning the purportedly uncomplicated

realism of colonial ethnography while also pointing to the absence of ethnographic evidence filmed from an African point of view. Pascal Abikanlou both
fictionalized and personalized the poetic voice-over narration of *Ganvié, My Village*
(1967), in which a man returns to his home village in Benin and describes the daily
lives of its inhabitants in the first person. Safi Faye, who had acted for and trained
with Rouch, studied filmmaking in Paris, where she also undertook doctoral work
in ethnology. Like Abikanlou, she chose to blur the boundaries between fictional
and nonfictional narrative strategies in her films *Kaddu Beykat* (1975) and *Fad'jal*
(1979), both of which portray the lives of the inhabitants of a traditional Serer
village who face very contemporary social, cultural, and economic pressures. Faye
asserted that "For me all these words – fiction, documentary, ethnology – have no
sense… At the end of my films people wonder if there is mise en scène or not"
(Martin 1979, p. 18) (Figure 16.2). Complicating Coissac's "as long as they are real,"
she has described her films as "reenacted documentaries" (Faye, 2010).

A new generation of African filmmakers turned to documentary in the early
1990s, building on the work of Vieyra, Zé, Faye, and others. They have mixed documentary and fictional modes in their representations of African social and political
histories and realities but have rejected autoethnography in favor of experimental
films that foreground first-person narrative strategies. In films like *Allah Tantou*
(David Achkar, Guinea, 1991), *Africa, I Will Fleece You*, and *Vacation in the Country*

Figure 16.2 *Fad'jal*, Safi Faye, 1979.

(Jean-Marie Teno, Cameroon, 1992 and 2000), *The King, the Cow, and the Banana Tree* (Mweze Ngangura, Democratic Republic of the Congo, 1994), *Dakar Bamako* and *Letter to Senghor* (Samba Félix Ndiaye, Senegal, 1992 and 1998), *Rostov-Luanda* and *Life on Earth* (Abderrahmane Sissako, Mauritania/Mali, 1997 and 1998), *Bye Bye Africa* (Mahamat-Saleh Haroun, Chad, 1998), *Open Window* (Khady Sylla, Senegal, 2005), *Si-Gueriki* and *Indochina: Traces of A Mother* (Idrissou Mora Kpai, Benin, 2003 and 2011), and *Black Business* (Osvalde Lewat, Cameroon, 2009), they have continued to challenge outsider claims to unquestionable authenticity as they work to transform the language of realism on which colonial documentary, from newsreels to ethnographies, relied. Ndiaye, whose extraordinary documentary career spanned four decades, when asked "Do you often use your camera to explore sociocultural traditions, as did the Senegalese director Safi Faye?" answered with a straightforward "No." Asked if the first-person voice-over in his films meant that they lacked objectivity, he denied the claim of any documentary film to objectivity; "Your reality is not the reality of your neighbor!" (Pfaff 2010, pp. 167–168).

The films I have listed are often described in French as "creative documentaries" (*documentaires de création*), but they also fit the more specific description of the essay film, a subset of reflexive documentary that has been defined and examined by a number of British and North American film scholars. African cinema, however, has been notably absent from these debates. It is significant that the only films with any connection to Africa that are repeatedly cited in overviews of reflexive documentary are Trinh Minh-ha's *Reassemblage* (1982) and Chris Marker's *Sans Soleil* (1982), both shot only partially on the continent and neither by an African filmmaker. Catherine Russell analyzed both in *Experimental Ethnography*, an impressive study of films that question the colonial realism of the documentary enterprise, or "radical film practice within a specifically ethnographic milieu" (Russell 1999, p. 4), but neglected to mention even a single African director. African films are equally lacking in Hamid Naficy's *An Accented Cinema* (2001), a study of reflexive films made by postcolonial directors in exile that similarly included both Trinh and Marker.

In the late 1970s, Jay Ruby distinguished between reference, reflection, and reflexivity in documentary film, concluding that "to be reflexive is to reveal that films … are created, structured articulations of the filmmaker and not authentic, truthful, objective records" (Ruby 1988, p. 75). More recent discussions have been guided by Bill Nichols' analysis of what he calls the reflexive mode of documentary, which "arose from a desire to make the conventions of representation themselves more apparent and to challenge the impression of reality which the other three modes [expository, observational, and interactive] normally conveyed unproblematically" (Nichols 1991, p. 33). The reflexive filmmaker, Nichols continues, engages in "metacommentary" and speaks about "the process of representation itself" (p. 56). Reflexive documentary works to break what Roland Barthes called the referential illusion, the sense that a text embodies the reality it is attempting to represent, a sense fully present, as we have seen, in French colonial documentary. Barthes argued that the would-be objective historian strives to sustain this illusion in part by avoiding the use of the first-person pronoun, "so that history seems to tell itself" (Barthes 1986, pp. 131–132). Reflexive documentary filmmakers may deploy a first-person filmic voice precisely to break the illusion of objectivity, emphasizing, as did Ndiaye, that even a nonfiction film is a partial narrative told from a particular point of view.

In the early 1990s, Michael Renov analyzed Jonas Mekas' *Lost, Lost, Lost* (1976) as both a diary film and a reflexive essay film, citing an early review of the film written by Alan Williams. Renov outlined a history of the essay from Michel de Montaigne in the late sixteenth century to Roland Barthes and then to Mekas, contending that the essay film is doubly reflexive, "a mode of autobiographical practice that combines self-examination with a deeply engaged outward gaze" (Renov 2004, p. 69). Nora Alter returned to Montaigne 15 years later to find "essayistic tendencies" in film going back to Dziga Vertov's *Man with a Movie Camera* (1929). Alter, like Renov, points to the hybrid nature of essay films, emphasizing the ways in which they "fus[e] the two long-established categories of film: fiction and documentary" and also "self-reflexively offer their own film criticism" (Alter 2007, p. 44). Laura Rascaroli retains Renov's focus on a personal and first-person voice to argue that filmic essayists are "strong auteurs," inheritors of an avant-garde tradition dating back to the French New Wave (Rascaroli 2009, p. 7). And Timothy Corrigan argues that the essay, both written and filmed, is both fiction and nonfiction, narrative and non-narrative, verbal and visual (Corrigan 2011, p. 3). Unlike Rascaroli, however, Corrigan stresses the incoherence of the essayistic subject, who is expressed in but also produced by film.

Although Rascaroli argues that the essay films she examines "form a diverse, paradoxical, heretical body of work," her list of filmmakers contains only the most celebrated European and, to a lesser extent, North American auteurs: Mekas, Jean-Luc Godard, Chris Marker, Pier Paolo Pasolini, Michelangelo Antonioni, Agnès Varda, Harun Farocki, Chantal Akerman, and Ross McElwee (p. 2). She uses the term "transnational" to refer to her inclusion of North America films, and the cinemas of other continents are completely absent (p. 193, n.6). Corrigan, after describing what he calls the five modes of the essay film, states that although "virtually every country in the world produces essay films," he has excluded non-"Western" film from his purview, "in large part because of the historical and cultural origins and evolutions of the essay," which he traces back, per his title and like Renov and Alter, in writing to Montaigne and in film to Marker (p. 7). Yet even if the genre of the written essay has its origins in France, it has been widely adopted and adapted around the world. A documentary filmmaker from a formerly colonized and currently "underdeveloped" region would seem to be ideally situated to perform what Corrigan describes as "the simultaneous enactment of and representation of a destabilized self...a self whose place in a public history is at best on its margins or in some cases in an excluded or inverted position" (p. 80).

European and North American film critics and historians, like their colleagues in literary fields, have tended not to recognize reflexivity within African cinema, preferring to read African films as informative ethnographic documents rather than works of art. Although Rascaroli mentions in passing that Fernando Solanas and Octavio Getino included the essay film as a potential "militant form of expression" in their 1969 manifesto "Towards a Third Cinema" (p. 29), both she and Corrigan neglect this tradition, one which, along with the European avant-garde and local narrative traditions, has nourished experimental subjective and political films in Africa as well as Latin America. As we have seen, African filmmakers had particular reasons to challenge both authoritative third-person voice-overs and unproblematized documentary representations of reality, strategies that carry a particular resonance in colonial and neo-colonial contexts. African essay films, both intimate and political, continue the process of reappropriating documentary for and from Africa, often from a position of partial exile and at least partially in French. They constitute a powerful argument against the exclusion of African film from the documentary canon and from studies of reflexive filmmaking, enacting and representing destabilized selves as they engage in an international filmic conversation about the methods and goals of documentary realism. In order to support my case not only that African essay films exist, but that they enrich our understandings of both the essay film and contemporary African cinema, I will focus on Mahamat Saleh Haroun's *Bye Bye Africa* (1998), a film that in many ways exemplifies the essay film as described by Renov, Alter, Rascaroli, and Corrigan.

Born in 1961 in Abéché, Chad, Haroun was wounded during the civil war in his late teens and escaped first to Cameroon, then to China and Europe. He went on to to study both filmmaking and journalism in France. Haroun's first films were short fictions, *Tan Koul* (1991), *Maral Tanié* (1994), and *Goi Goi the Dwarf* (1995), after which he released two mid-length documentaries, *Bord'Africa* (1995) and *Sotigui Kouyaté: A Modern Griot* (1996). Haroun has maintained his Chadian nationality even though he is based in France, and *Bye Bye Africa*, his first feature-length film, was also the first feature-length film from Chad. Over the course of his career, Haroun has become one of few filmmakers from Africa to gain recognition at prominent festivals both on the continent and abroad. *Bye Bye Africa* was awarded the prizes for Best First Film at the Venice Film Festival and Best Film at the Amiens International Film Festival. *Abouna* (2002) won for Best Cinematography at the 2003 FESPACO biannual African film festival and was selected for the Director's Fortnight at Cannes. *Daratt* (2006) won the Bronze Stallion at FESPACO and the Special Jury Prize at the Venice Film Festival. *A Screaming Man* (2010) won the Silver Stallion at FESPACO, the Jury Prize at Cannes, and the Robert Bresson Prize at Venice. As a result of these successes, the government of Chad sponsored the renovation of the Normandy theatre in the capital of N'Djamena, announced plans to open a national film school, and funded Haroun's *GriGris* (2013), which was then selected for the Official Competition at Cannes. Haroun has made several mid-length documentaries, including *Sotigui Kouyaté, A Modern Griot* (1996) and *Kalala* (2005), but *Hissein Habré: A Chadian Tragedy* (2016), projected at a special screening during the Cannes Festival, is Haroun's first feature-length documentary since *Bye Bye Africa*.

In *Bye Bye Africa*, Haroun acts, narrates, and films central character Mahamat-Saleh Haroun's return to Chad after ten years in France. The story of an individual who goes home after the death of his mother, the film also becomes a commentary on the situation of the cinema in Chad and on the African continent. *Bye Bye Africa* is both autobiographical and staged, personal and political, and from the start avowedly reflexive. The film has variously been called documentary, documentary-fiction, fictional documentary, docu-fiction, docu-drama, and, on the website for Haroun's production company Pili Films, "a fiction that imitates a documentary style." Haroun has said that the film "constantly goes back and forth between fiction and reality" (Barlet 2002, p. 22), and an uneasy relationship between film and reality is not just one of the film's characteristics, but one of its major themes.

Bye Bye Africa begins with Haroun, asleep in his bed in France, waking up to the ringing of a telephone call that will announce his mother's death. He will leave France for N'Djamena, Chad, spend time with his father, grandmother, and nephew, reunite with an old friend, and start the preparations for a film to be entitled "Bye Bye Africa." Just over 15 minutes into the film, Haroun's character describes the film he is planning to make as "a multi-layered task [*exercice à tiroirs*]. It's about cinema, exile, family, love, life. How to film life, that's the question I ask." Haroun is the director of "Bye Bye Africa" as well as *Bye Bye Africa*, then, and this film-within-the-film theme creates a mise-en-abîme typical of reflexive art. The majority of *Bye Bye Africa* consists of scenes in color in which the spectator sees Haroun on screen as a character who often films the world and people around him. Other scenes, in black and white, consist of images ostensibly filmed by his character's video camera. The reflexive trope of the man in a movie with a movie camera, of filming within a film, goes back to Dziga Vertov, and Yifen Beus notes that Haroun's manner of filming N'Djamena evokes *Man with a Movie Camera* (Beus 2011, p. 142), identified by Alter as the first essay film.

The life Haroun is filming, in "Bye Bye Africa," and has filmed, in *Bye Bye Africa*, is in part and in many senses his own. Years of exile have distanced his character from his family and his compatriots, few of whom understand or approve of his chosen career. In the first of many voice-overs, Haroun announces, "And so, I will never see my mother again. She died yesterday, over there. Very far away. And suddenly I feel alone. Very alone." His parents have never met his children, who were born in France, and Haroun suggests that this is because his French ex-wife does not want them to travel to Chad. After he arrives in N'Djamena, Haroun shows how out of touch he is with the reality of his homeland by asking his taxi driver, "So, how is this country doing?" One of the goals of the film is to answer this question, and Haroun and the driver commiserate about the heat and the price of gas. Haroun also shows us, without explicit commentary, the presence of the military in the city as a result of Chad's longstanding civil war; a soldier stops the taxi and refuses to accept a bribe to let them pass. Over the course of both *Bye Bye Africa* and "Bye Bye Africa," Haroun shows us the varied landscapes of N'Djamena as well as glimpses of its inhabitants, but without describing what we are seeing nor explaining who these people are or what they are doing and why. His commentary, in a strong first-person voice-over, instead provides information about both his character's thoughts and feelings and the state of the cinema in Africa, combining, to return to Renov's words, "self-examination" and "a deeply engaged outward gaze."

Haroun's father watches him pick up his video camera to film boys playing soccer in the streets and complains, speaking in Chadian Arabic, "Cinema! Cinema! We don't understand what you do. You sent a tape. We didn't understand. Just blabla. It was about a European." Haroun explains that the film was about Freud, and his father asks if this is one of his friends. Haroun's father then continues, "Your films are not made for us. They are for the Whites... If only you had become a doctor, you could have helped your mother. Being a doctor is useful. But what's the use of cinema?" Haroun offers the beginnings of a response to this question when, back at home, he and his father watch home movie footage of his mother. Over the clicking of the 16mm projector, Haroun's father exclaims, "Good God! It's your mother! I remember this." Haroun switches to French to answer that "You see, it's for memory that I make films. A great man named Jean-Luc Godard said 'Cinema makes memories'." After this second invocation of a canonical European, Haroun's father again asks if this is one of his friends. This time, although a friendship would not be chronologically impossible, Haroun's smile and shake of the head is evidence of the chasm not just between son and father, but also between two residents of France, the eminent and reclusive co-founder of the French New Wave and the African filmmaker just beginning his career. Despite his father's distaste for his chosen profession, Haroun's voice-over, inspired by Godard, then creates a link between cinema and his family, stating that, "to kill my sorrow, I will make a film in memory of she who gave me life."

Haroun visits an old friend of his, Garba, who is connected to African filmmaking at both a private and a public level. Haroun informs us that Garba, who shot the footage of Haroun's mother at a wedding years earlier, used to work as a projectionist at the Normandy movie theatre. The two go out for what will be one of many joint motorbike rides around the city, Garba steering and Haroun filming the streets around them. Garba reminds Haroun that his films, and African films in general, are not shown in Africa, and Haroun, instead of responding to Garba, addresses the spectator in a voice-over; "Yes, I know. Nobody sees my films here. I ask myself, then, for whom I make them. It's one of the reasons Garba doesn't want to work in the cinema anymore." Engaging the question of how and why to make films in Africa first by examining the current state of film exhibition, Haroun and Garba ride to the Normandy, which has been transformed from the lively social center of Haroun's childhood to a scarred, dilapidated symbol of neglect.

Haroun then takes us on a tour of other crumbling movie theatres in N'Djamena, the Shéhérazade, the Rio, the Vog, and the Étoile, all destroyed by decades of war and emptied of their audiences. Haroun wonders if a Godardian association of cinema and memory can remain valid in this context; "How can one believe in the cinema in a country where war has become a culture? The war has caused so much damage that N'Djamena seems to elude all memory." Yet the owner of the Étoile, whose father opened the theatre in 1946, is working to obtain the funds to undertake a renovation, to "bring the cinema back to life in my country," and she encourages Haroun to continue making films in order to participate in this endeavor.

Bye Bye Africa, then, is not only the story of the return of an individual exile, but also a political commentary about the present and future of Africa and of African cinema. Because of struggles for funding and a lack of exhibition within Africa, Haroun has argued elsewhere, "the African cinema becomes foreign on its own continent" (Haroun 2004, p. 146). And we watch Haroun's character as he listens to a speech on the radio about Africa's need to counter imperialism by refusing to rely not only on imported food, but also imported cultural products. The announcer reveals that the speaker, ten years prior, was anti-neo-colonial hero Thomas Sankara. Haroun thus links his exile from Chad, both temporally and thematically, to the death of Sankara, the leader of a popular revolution in Burkina Faso who became President in 1983, then was assassinated in a 1987 coup after which his deputy Blaise Compaoré took power for a reign of 27 years. The urgent need for self-reliance, for a cinema produced by Africans, is echoed later in the film in a letter that Haroun receives from friend and fellow African filmmaker David-Pierre Fila, sent from Brazzaville, another African city damaged by war. Fila speaks in a voice-over, adding his voice to Haroun's commentary on the cinema in Africa and concluding with a quote from another pan-African hero, Aimé Césaire; "The culture that is strongest on the material and technological levels threatens to crush all weaker cultures. Especially in a world in which distance is no longer an obstacle."

Haroun argues that the link between technological and cultural imperialism extends to the kinds of films we expect African filmmakers to create. The Chadian producer to whom he pitches "Bye Bye Africa" likes the story and wants to fund the film but tells Haroun he will need to shoot on video instead of celluloid to cut costs. Outraged at this suggestion, Haroun refuses, insisting that he wants to make "real cinema." *Bye Bye Africa*, however, was shot on video (Beta SP) and then transferred to 35mm film. Haroun has described it as an "emergency movie...we shot it on video in fifteen days, because I really had this urgency to say something and show that this is my place in Chad – my territory" (Scott 2003, p. 90). This accomplished, Haroun went on to shoot all of his subsequent features in Africa and on 35mm, including his feature-length documentary about Hissein Habré's reign of terror. He argues against the widespread idea that the future of African filmmaking lies with video, stating that this "African exception" is the result of a condescending attitude and that "on no other continent has it been said that digital video would be synonymous with quality" (Haroun 2011, p. 74). Visiting the Shéhérazade theatre, Haroun is told that, if movie theatres had new projectors and new film prints, they would also have an audience. Haroun's interrogation of the state of the cinema in Chad leads him to exhort African filmmakers to reject the politically, economically, culturally, and cinematically marginalized position to which the rest of the world wants to relegate them, to make films that Africans could watch at the Normandy, the Shéhérazade, and the Étoile.

While Haroun is standing in front of the Shéhérazade theatre, a man attacks him and grabs his video camera, yelling "He's stealing our image! Thief! Why film us? He's a foreigner." Garba attempts to explain the man's reaction, one he believes Haroun has been abroad for too long to understand; "Here people don't trust the camera. We have a huge problem with images. We can't distinguish between fiction and reality." The proof, Garba says, is the case of Isabelle, an actress who played the role of a woman with AIDS in one of Haroun's earlier films and is now a pariah because everyone believes she, like her character, is sick. When Haroun sees Isabelle again for the first time in ten years, he immediately begins to film her, but she covers the lens with her hand. Isabelle then, like the man in front of the Shéhérazade, takes the camera from Haroun. Unlike the man who called Haroun a thief, however, she takes his camera to turn it on him, and for the first time in *Bye Bye Africa* we see Haroun in black and white. Haroun and Isabelle rekindle a love affair, but he does not want to take her back to France with him. Abandoned, she again takes his camera, this time to record her suicide note.

According to Garba, Isabelle's life has been destroyed by an African confusion of fictional images and reality, but Haroun has carefully led his spectators toward the same confusion. *Bye Bye Africa*'s imitation of a documentary style, and particularly the use of black-and-white footage to represent what has been filmed by Haroun's camera, achieves what Olivier Barlet calls the "impression of spontaneity" characteristic of a genre he designates "documentary-fiction" (Barlet 2000, p. 114). Thanks to Haroun's unifying voice-over and physical presence within the film, acting the part of himself, we are drawn into his story with Isabelle so much that we risk forgetting that Haroun has never made a fictional film about a woman with AIDS. Yet Haroun, by means of the various reflexive strategies deployed throughout *Bye Bye Africa*, never quite lets us believe in what Rascaroli calls a "strong auteur" persona, reminding us, like Corrigan, that his essayistic subjectivity is as much created by as represented in his film. When Haroun discovers Isabelle's dead body, we see behind him a large poster for Clint Eastwood's *Pale Rider* (1985), a film in which the director plays the role of a clearly fictional protagonist. The invented character of Isabelle (played by Aïcha Yelena) is on the fictional side of this docu-fiction. Her story, one that thematically gestures toward the idea that the cinema, as Isabelle tells Haroun, "is stronger than reality," is not real, and Haroun's audience is forced to reflect upon how the conventions of filmic representation create what Barthes called the "referential illusion" and Nichols the "impression of reality." We remember, for example, the other cameraman, the one we do not see, but who is filming Haroun in color as he acts out his autobiographical role.

Haroun, more explicitly than had Safi Faye, forces his audience to wonder whether, and where, there is mise en scène or not. The only major characters playing themselves in *Bye Bye Africa* are African filmmakers: Mahamat-Saleh Haroun, David-Pierre Fila, and Issa Serge Coelo, who is younger than Haroun and was at the time his only Chadian colleague. The character of Garba, like that of Isabelle, has been invented for the film. Actor Garba Issa is not a former projectionist and played very different roles in Haroun's later films *Abouna* and *Daratt*. The role of Haroun's father is played not by Haroun's father, but by Khayar Oumar Defallah, who also played the role of Atim's grandfather in *Daratt*. In the home movie footage that Haroun watches with the character of his father, the character of Haroun's mother is played by actress Hadje Fatima N'Goua, who went on to act in *Daratt* and *A Screaming Man*. The status of the various interviews that Haroun conducts in N'Djamena, such as that with the owner of the Étoile theatre, is impossible to determine from the evidence we have in the film. Haroun's citation of Godard after watching the footage of the actress playing the role of his mother is therefore particularly appropriate, since his cinema has as much made memories as recorded them.

Speaking more than ten years after *Bye Bye Africa* about his decision to cite Aimé Césaire in the title of *A Screaming Man*, Haroun explained, as had Paulin Vieyra in the 1960s, that "We must not forget that the original sin comes from the fact that Africa was first filmed by others. This representation is so distorted that our cinema works to counteract this vision" (Barlet, 2010). Although Haroun has lived outside of Chad for his entire adult life, he sets and shoots his film in his native land "through solidarity and because I feel a responsibility not to leave this country invisible" (Topping, 2013). Yet this desire to film Africa, and specifically Chad, differently from how it was filmed by colonial others, is not anthropological, and Haroun's "deeply engaged outward gaze," as we have seen in *Bye Bye Africa*, is not an ethnographic one. At the turn of the twenty-first century, Haroun was associated with the African Guild of Directors and Producers, a group of young African filmmakers based in France that included Jean-Marie Teno and Abderrahmane Sissako. Their manifesto declared that "Far from an ethnographic cinema that records habits and customs, the new cinema must quite simply bring us closer to the great family of cinema" ("Guilde" 2005, p. 269). This family is a global one, composed of a variety of styles and genres including the essay film, of which *Bye Bye Africa* is an important member.

Reaching for "the great family of cinema," Haroun is very conscious of both his African and non-African cinematic influences. In one interview, he remembers the close-up of a woman's face in an Indian film that he saw as a child in Chad and then mentions his admiration for François Truffaut's Antoine Doinel films (Higuinen 2003, p. 85). In another, he starts with the Charlie Chaplin films that he saw as a child, continues with his adolescent discovery of Roberto Rossellini's *Rome, Open City* and the films of Wim Wenders, and concludes with his admiration of the work of Yasujiro Ozu, Akira Kurosawa, Robert Bresson, and Ousmane Sembene

(Malausa 2010, p. 45). Other auteurs in Haroun's canon include John Ford, Abbas Kiarostami, Takeshi Kitano, Hou Hsiao-hsien, and Idrissa Ouedraogo. It is not surprising, then, that *Bye Bye Africa* would participate in a global tradition of reflexive, experimental documentary. But instead of influence, art historian Robert Nelson has reminded us, we can speak about appropriation (Nelson 2010, p. 172). Haroun brings from Africa to the essay film a particular regional filmic and political history, a particular complex exilic subjectivity, and a particular interweaving of aesthetic and narrative traditions. The penultimate scene of *Bye Bye Africa* consists of a fixed long shot in black and white of Haroun's grandmother walking across the courtyard of the compound, across the frame, accompanied by Haroun's voice-over, which says "This is the woman who raised me. This is the woman who taught me how to tell stories. I often think about her when I'm far away from here. Then it's enough to lie down and close my eyes and I hear her soft voice." And despite his character's uneasy position as a returned exile with a movie camera, despite the history of documentary film in Africa, Haroun describes *Bye Bye Africa* as drawing from an African narrative tradition: "there is a structure in the screenplay, but I wanted a story told in the oral tradition…counting the seconds and then moving in another direction" (Scott 2003, p. 90). The essay, like reflexivity itself, is not only European.

Reviewers outside of Africa, however, have not always been willing to acknowledge this. The world continues to expect ethnography from films set in Africa, documentary information rather than essayistic commentary. Although the reception of *Bye Bye Africa* both in Africa and abroad was for the most part positive, *Variety* warned that "viewers not already schooled in the region's history and cultures won't gain much enlightenment here" (Harvey, 2000). Even more telling, the *Chicago Reader* praised Haroun's "feel for life and customs in the alleys around his family home," but claimed that Haroun "veers into precious intellectuality, and the talk turns to cultural crisis and cinema being 'stronger than reality' – it's as if Godard had suddenly injected himself into a documentary about a former French colony" (Shen). The use of the word "injected" implies not only that Haroun has no right to Godard's words, but that Godard and Haroun exist in different worlds, that only ethnographic film, and not the auteurist essay, can thrive in a former French colony. Yet *JLG/JLG: Self-Portrait in December*, Godard's fragmented autobiographical documentary about filmmaking, appeared in 1995, while Haroun was living in France, and could be understood as an important precursor of Haroun's 1998 film.

Chadian film history, in its scarcity, provides the perfect mirror for the condensed history of documentary film in West and Central Africa that I have traced here. I stated that *Bye Bye Africa* was the first feature-length film from Chad, but if we go back 20 years we do find African predecessors to Haroun's short films from the early 1990s. Chadian cameraman Edouard Sailly, who trained in Paris with the Actualités françaises, made a series of short films in the 1960s and early 1970s, all between 5 and 35 minutes long and for the most part ethnographic. In *The*

Fishermen of Chari (1964) funded soon after independence by the Chadian Ministry of Information, a French-language voice-over praises the beauty and power of the Chari river and then describes the fishing customs and economy of the men, women, and children of the region. Sailly continued with *Lake Chad* (1966), *The Slaughterhouses of Forcha* (1966), *Child of Chad* (1969), and *To Discover Chad* (1972), among others. Sailly's *The Third Day* (1967), a wordless film, with no voice-over at all, about a young fisherman whose mother has died, has been restored and was included in the 2010 "Where is Africa?" program at the International Film Festival of Rotterdam (Dovey 2015, p. 70). And before Sailly, what is now Chad was filmed in a number of early French newsreels, including Gaumont's *Through French Equatorial Africa* (1920) and the SCA's *Toward Chad* (1922). Several decades later, the voice-over of Pierre Ichac's post-World War II, pre-independence ethnography *Watching Chad Pass By* (1958), which identifies Lake Chad as a "blue stain in the center of the black continent," provides its French audience with information about the animals and peoples of this "vast" region, from the camels in the north to the elephants in the south, from the Arab Muslims in the north to the black "animists" in the south. Garba's assertion that in Chad "people don't trust the camera" may have more to do with film history than with an inability to distinguish fiction and reality.

In *Bye Bye Africa*, Haroun's young nephew Ali becomes so enamored of the idea of filmmaking that he asks Haroun to give him his camera. When Haroun refuses, Ali makes himself a toy camera out of cardboard and cans (Figure 16.3). Haroun eventually decides to take Ali to his friend Serge Coelo's film shoot so he can watch and learn and, just before leaving to return to France, he gives Ali his camera, cautioning him to "pay close attention to what you will film." As Haroun gets into the taxi that will take him to the airport, Ali lifts the camera to his shoulder and begins to film. We see his first images in black and white, the camera bouncing up and

Figure 16.3　*Bye Bye Africa*, Mahamat Saleh Haroun, 1998, Pili Pili Films.

down with his steps, and hear Haroun's last voice-over, "In a few hours, I will be in France, I will return to my little life of an exiled filmmaker." Ali catches up with the taxi, and we for the second time see Haroun in black and white, filmed by his own camera, while Haroun's voice concludes, "Leaving, I am calm. I know I will come back soon, very soon, to shoot 'Bye Bye Africa.'" Ali follows Haroun with his camera, in a nod to the conclusion of Ousmane Sembene's *Black Girl* (1966), when Diouana's younger brother, African mask over his face, pursues her former French employer as he leaves the neighborhood. Yet while Sembene's boy is chasing away the neo-colonial, Haroun's boy-filmmaker is both a protégé and a call to return.

Notes

1   Unless otherwise noted, all translations from the French are mine. It is ironic that Griaule's racism led him to a conclusion contrary to that of Michel Heroin, whose later but equally racist opinion was that Africans were "born actors" (Heroin 1953, p. 53).
2   Peter Bloom, in *French Colonial Documentary*, and Alison Murray Levine, in *Framing the Nation*, examine at length the history of the strategic use of film to convince French citizens of the value and importance of the colonial enterprise.

References

Akudinobi, Jude. 2000. "Reco(r)ding reality: representation and paradigms in nonfiction African cinema." *Social Identities*, 6: 345–367.
Alter, Nora. 2007. "Translating the essay into film and installation." *Visual Culture*, 6.1: 44–57.
Anon. 1923. "Les grands films documentaires, L'expedition Vandenbergh dans le 'Centre Africain'." *Cinémagazine*, 19: 243–246.
Anon. 1928. "La propagande coloniale par le film." *Cinéducateur*, 3: 23.
Barlet, Olivier. 2000. "Les nouvelles écritures francophones des cinéastes afro-européens." *Cinémas*, 11.1: 113–133.
Barlet, Olivier. 2002. "Une relation d'amour avec le spectateur: entretien avec Mahamat Saleh Haroun." *Africultures*, 45: 22.
Barlet, Olivier. 2010. "Plus l'Afrique est oubliée, plus il faut la ramener au souvenir du monde." *Africultures*. Accessed 17 September 2015. www.africultures.com/php/index.php?nav=article&no=9501
Barthes, Roland. 1986. *The Rustle of Language*. Berkeley: University of California Press.
Beus, Yifen. 2011. "Authorship and criticism in self-reflexive African cinema." *Journal of African Cultural Studies*, 23.2: 133–152.
Bloom, Peter. 2008. *French Colonial Documentary: Mythologies of Humanitarianism*. Minneapolis: University of Minnesota Press.
Carné, Marcel. 1930. "Le cinéma à la conquête du monde." *Cinémagazine*, 9: 9– 11.
Coissac, Georges-Michel. 1922. "Un très beau film d'enseignement." *Cinéopse*, 34: 516–517.
Coissac, Georges-Michel. 1931. "Vacances et exposition coloniale." *Cinéopse*, 145: 385–387.

Corrigan, Timothy. 2011. *The Essay Film: From Montaigne, After Marker*. New York: Oxford University Press.

Dovey, Lindiwe. 2015. *Curating Africa in the Age of Film Festivals*. New York: Palgrave Macmillan.

Dureau, G. 1913. "La cinématographie coloniale." *Ciné-Journal*, 257: 1, 4.

Faye, Safi. 2010. "Leçon de cinéma." Accessed 30 June 2016. www.dailymotion.com/video/xcmkn9_la-lecon-de-cinema-de-safi-faye_creation

"Guilde, La." 2005. "Pour un nouveau cinéma africain." In *Afriques 50: singularités d'un cinéma pluriel*, edited by Catherine Ruelle, 269–270. Paris: L'Harmattan.

Haffner, Pierre. 1984. "Quatre entretiens avec Paulin Soumanou Vieyra (III)." *Peuples Noirs, Peuples Africains*, 40: 26–40.

Haroun, Mahamat-Saleh. 2004. "From militancy to schizophrenia." *African Geopolitics*, 13: 143–150.

Haroun, Mahamat-Saleh. 2006. "Nous avons fait des enfants au français." *Cahiers du cinéma*, 611, supplement: 6.

Haroun, Mahamat-Saleh. 2011. "Une promesse non tenue." *Cahiers du cinéma*, 664: 74–75.

Harvey, Dennis. 2000. "Bye Bye Africa." *Variety*, May 8. Accessed 5 February 2015. http://variety.com/2000/film/reviews/bye-bye-africa-1200462452/

Heroin, Michel. 1953. "Étude sur l'éducation de base et les moyens audio-visuels dans leurs applications au cinéma." *IDHEC*, 53: 43–61.

Higuinen, Erwan. 2003. "Rencontre/Mahamat-Saleh Haroun." *Cahiers du cinéma*, 577: 85.

Kodjo, François. 1979. "Les cinéastes africains face à l'avenir du cinéma en Afrique." *Tiers-monde*, 20.79: 605–614.

Leprohon, Pierre. 1945. *L'exotisme et le cinéma*. Paris: J. Susse.

Leroi-Gourhan, André. 1948. "Cinéma et sciences humaines: le film ethnologique existe-t-il?" *Revue de géographie humaine et d'ethnologie*, 3: 42–50.

Liotard, André F., Samivel, and Jean Thévenot. 1950. *Cinéma d'exploration, cinéma au long cours*. Paris: Chavane.

Loftus, Maria. 2010. "The appeal of hybrid documentary forms in West Africa." *French Forum*, 35.2–3: 37–55.

Machin, Alfred. 1909. "Le cinématographe et la conquête du monde." *Ciné-Journal*, 36: 9–10.

Malausa, Vincent. 2010. "Un cinéaste tchadien: entretien avec Mahamat Saleh Haroun." *Cahiers du cinéma*, 660: 43–46.

Martin, Angela. 1979. "Four film makers from West Africa." *Framework*, 11: 16–21.

Murray Levine, Alison. 2010. *Framing the Nation: Documentary Film in Interwar France*. New York: Continuum.

Naficy, Hamid. 2001. *An Accented Cinema: Exilic and Diasporic Filmmaking*. Princeton, NJ: Princeton University Press.

Nelson, Robert. 2010. "Appropriation." In *Critical Terms for Art History*, second edition, edited by Robert Nelson and Richard Shiff, 160–173. Chicago: University of Chicago Press.

Nichols, Bill. 1991. *Representing Reality*. Bloomington: Indiana University Press.

Pfaff, Françoise. 2010. *A l'écoute du cinéma sénégalais*. Paris: L'Harmattan.

Piault, Marc-Henri. 2000. *Anthropologie et cinéma*. Paris: Nathan.

Piault, Marc-Henri. 2001. "L'exotisme et le cinéma ethnographique: la rupture de *La Croisière noire*." *Journal of Film Preservation*, 63: 6–16.

Pratt, Mary Louis. 1992. *Imperial Eyes: Travel Writing and Transculturation*. New York: Routledge.

Rascaroli, Laura. 2009. *The Personal Camera: Subjective Cinema and the Essay Film*. London: Wallflower Press.

Renov, Michael. 2004. *The Subject of Documentary*. Minneapolis: University of Minnesota Press.

Rouch, Jean. 1957. *Connaissance de l'Afrique noire*. Paris: Le Livre de Paris.

Rouch, Jean. 2003. *Ciné-Ethnography*. Minneapolis: University of Minnesota Press.

Ruby, Jay. 1988. "The image mirrored: reflexivity and the documentary film." In *New Challenges for Documentary*, edited by Alan Rosenthal, 64–77. Berkeley: University of California Press.

Russell, Catherine. 1999. *Experimental Ethnography*. Durham, NC: Duke University Press.

Scott, A.O. 2003. "Taking what you need to refresh." In *Through African Eyes*, 87–92. New York: African Film Festival, Inc.

Shen, Ted. "Bye Bye Africa." Accessed 5 February 2015. www.chicagoreader.com/chicago/bye-bye-africa/Film?oid=1074386

Tapsoba, Clément. 1996. "Filmer l'Afrique." *Ecrans d'Afrique*, 16: 45–54.

Topping, Alexandra. 2013. "Mahamat-Saleh Haroun brings Chad to the world, and vice versa, through film." *The Guardian*, 25 February. Accessed 22 May 2013. www.guardian.co.uk/world/2013/feb/25/mahamat-saleh-haroun-chad-film

Ukadike, Frank. 1995. "African cinematic reality: the documentary tradition as an emerging trend." *Research in African Literatures*, 26.3: 88–96.

Vieyra, Paulin Soumanou. 1990. *Réflexions d'un cineaste africain*. Bruxelles: OCIC.

Filmography

Haroun, Mahamat-Saleh. (1998). *Bye Bye Africa*. Chad-France: Productions de la Lanterne.

Senghor, Blaise. (1962). *Great Magal to Touba*. Senegal: Films Pierre Remont, UCINA.

The Colonies' Aid to France (1918). France: Section cinématographique des armées.

Zé, Moïse. (1972). *The Mvet*. Cameroon: Mozes Films.

17

New Algerian Cinema
*Portrayals of Women in Films Post-*Les années noires

Valérie K. Orlando

In the 2000s, in the wake of the Algerian civil war –now known as the Black Decade, or in French as *la décennie noire*, and sometimes, *les années noires* (1990–2005)– Algerian women on screen and behind the camera are defining and depicting new female roles in society, culture, and politics. The first decade of the post-*années noires*, depicted in films such as Lyès Salem's *Masquerades* (2008), Yamina Bachir-Chouikh's *Rachida* (2003), Djamila Sahraoui's *Barakat!* (*Enough!*, 2006) and *Yema* (2012), Nadir Moknèche's *Viva Laldjérie* (2004), and Merzak Allouache's *Les terrasses* (*The Rooftops*, 2013), explore the important roles that women are taking and making to heal the wounds of contemporary Algeria. Philosophically, as Cameroonian philosopher Achille Mbembe's suggests referring to the roles of women in African millennial societies, Algerian women as social-activists engender, much like their African sisters, "the promise of another body and of another life" (Mbembe 2006, p. 171). Mbembe's philosophy, dedicated to exploring the agency of women as contributors to the socio-cultural and political challenges and changes that must take place in African societies across the continent in the new millennium, rings true for Algeria in the 2000s (Mbembe 2006, p. 171). In general, his feminist views as expressed in his work *De la postcolonie: essai sur l'imagination politique dans l'Afrique contemporaine* (2000, translated as *On the Postcolony*, 2006a) and a later article, "On the Postcolony: A Brief Response to Critics," published in 2006, stress the importance of women's active participation in African society as a means to advance new socio-political agendas in African nations in today's contemporary globalized world. These agendas contribute to what Mbembe stipulates are "other historical alternatives" to postcolonial master narratives of postcolonial states (2006, p. 172).

A Companion to African Cinema, First Edition. Edited by Kenneth W. Harrow and Carmela Garritano.
© 2019 John Wiley & Sons, Inc. Published 2019 by John Wiley & Sons, Inc.

Mbembe's framework promoting alternative narratives for African postcolonial nations is propitious for analyzing the cultural production of Algeria in the wake of the 1990s civil war. With respect to the roles created for women in films made since 2000, the films discussed in this chapter demonstrate anew, what Mbembe defines as, "[an] idiom of female power," in the aftermath of the incessant violence witnessed in the 1990s and early 2000s in Algeria. The roles women play on screen exemplify that women today in Algeria can no longer be "reduced to the position of object," as they more often than not have been in earlier films where they were silenced mothers or martyrs for the state (Mbembe 2006, p. 171). Women's noticeable presence on the screen in recent Algerian films has also influenced in the 2000s the way filmmakers are depicting the other, alternative stories of Algeria which were often sidelined, or simply left untold: Primarily those of ethnic minorities (particularly Berber communities in rural areas) and youth, silenced in the cinematic and historical past.[1]

Algerian post-civil war films today challenge the overdetermined, masculine narratives of post-revolutionary cinema written immediately after independence in 1962. They also wrestle the art form from the nation's ruling, one party, dogmatic Front de Libération Nationale's (FLN) Master Narrative which dictated the storylines of Algerian cinema for decades, sidelining the inherent ethnic and linguistic diversity of the country. Contemporary films challenge postcolonial "mechanisms of representation" that were constructed immediately after Algerian decolonization (Khanna 2008, p. 12). Women have become the linchpin for progress and social change both on screen and behind the camera as they challenge the "construction of the Nation-Image" that held them hostage to the patriarchal status quo in the 1970s, 1980s and even the 1990s; a status quo that defined all "gender relations in Algeria" (Hadj-Moussa 2014, p. 156). In films of this century, women are no longer depicted as reproductive-agents and "the guardians of deeper Arab-Islamic values" (Hadj-Moussa 2014, p. 156); rather they are, in this rebuilding moment of Algerian cinema, questioning what Mbembe states is "the phallus … and the birthing of manhood," rooted in the "birthing of the nation" in the narratives of African postcolonial states (Mbembe 2006, p.174). Like Western feminists of the past, a new generation of Algerian women social-activists in the post-années noires years are questioning the phallocentric frameworks of Algerian national cinema. Recent twenty-first-century films such as Djamila Sahraoui's *Barakat!* (*Enough!*, 2004), Sofia Djama's *Mollement, un samedi matin* (*Softly One Saturday Morning*, 2012), Mina Kessar and Nadia Cherabi's *L'Enfer du miroir* (*The Hell of the Mirror*, 2007) and Fatma-Zhor Zamoun's *Zhar* (2009), all announce a new generation of Algerian women cineastes who are making groundbreaking films that move women into the forefront of social progress and, at the same time, document the socio-cultural taboos they still face. Underscoring the hurdles and mixed messages women come up against in contemporary Algeria, 33 year-old, filmmaker Sofia Djama notes, "The rights of women in Algeria are such that you can't be feminist in the traditional sense. There are things you can't even discuss or negotiate … On one hand, I consider myself totally free…I have a right to wear a skirt, to go to the beach – the law doesn't ban me from doing so. If I don't want to fast during Ramadan, the law doesn't oblige me to. But from the perspective of social morality, it's absolutely forbidden."[2]

This chapter uses two films, *Rachida* (2003) and *Masquerades* (2008), as salient examples of the conflicted and complicated roles Algerian women have had to negotiate in contemporary society during the civil war and in the post-années noires. The films themselves emerge as a response to the Black Decade – its silences and its violence. They are interesting for what they communicate about the civil war years with respect to women's roles as first victims who survive and persevere (*Rachida*), and second as negotiators of their own identity in a country whose future is ambiguous (*Masquerades*). Although these films were made in the first decade of the twenty-first century, each evokes interesting possibilities for women as well as symbolically and metaphorically for the nation of Algeria as the country moves forward in the new millennium. Despite the socio-cultural and political adversity which compromises women's total enfranchisement in Algerian society, both films demonstrate their heroines' resolve and commitment to building a livable country for the future. In general, millennial Algerian films also mark a significant break with the highly masculinized and dogmatic themes of the past that grounded cinema of the 1960s–1990s. Contemporary films give birth to a new Algerian cinema that has emerged from the trauma of the 1990s; a timeframe during which cinema was "overwhelmed by the social, political and human events of the civil war that destroyed in a tragic manner the entire country" (Tesson 2003a, p. 5). The rebuilding of the cinema industry in Algeria has also led to the rethinking of the genres held dear by filmmakers immediately following the revolution. The most important of these genres was the "cinema of the mujahidin" known for its overarching trope of the hyper-masculinized, freedom fighter who liberates the nation from the colonizer. As explained in this chapter, this particular genre contributed to maintaining the one-sided story of the Algerian postcolonial nation for decades after independence.

This chapter considers *Rachida* and *Masquerades* not only for the strong roles they promote for women, but also as examples of a new Algerian cinema that is responding to the silence of the Black Decade. They are part of a body of cinematic work that disassociates itself from the FLN's hyper-masculinized, didactic, and dogmatic themes of the past in order to present a truer picture of Algeria as a country that is multifaceted, diverse and inclusive.

The Masculine Stories of the Mujahidin: The FLN's Master Narrative on Screen

The challenged development of Algerian cinema since independence has been well articulated in a plethora of works by scholars in the field of Maghrebi cinema studies. Scholarship has generally contextualized early Algerian films from the

1960s as overtly nationalist, used by the newly minted postcolonial FLN-led state to further the cause and primary objectives of the nation. These objectives were packaged in "nationalist imaginary" devoted to mythological scenarios that grounded the *"cinéma moudjahid* or 'freedom fighter' cinema of the 1960s," glorifying the men who contributed to the revolution (Austin 2011, p. 196). In his 1971 work, *Naissance du cinéma algérien (The Birth of Algerian cinema)*, one of the first dedicated to Algerian film in the postcolonial era, Rachid Boudjedra emphasizes that Algerian films were conceptualized purely as a tool for revolutionary propaganda: "Il était impossible de faire une étude sur le cinéma algérien sans faire intervenir un élément fondamental: la guerre de libération" [it is impossible to study Algerian cinema without engaging with a fundamental element: The war of liberation] (p. 7). Boudjedra's work enunciates to what extent early Algerian cinema contributed to the "monolithic identity-formation of the state" after independence that sought to centralize unity bound in the revolutionary tenants of the FLN: "Islam is my religion, Arabic is my language, Algeria is my nation." In his account of the revolutionary war, *On nous appelait fellaghas (We Were Called Rebels*, 1976), Rabah Zerari, known as Commandant Si Azzedine a leading commandant of the rebel *maquis*, underscores the fact that "tous les Algériens devaient se sentir fraternellement unis au sien d'une même nation" [all Algerians were to feel fraternally unified within the same nation] (Zerari 1976, p. 16). This unifying message from the outset of the postcolonial period marginalized three "particular identities" to the sidelines: Berber, women and youth (Austin 2011, p. 196).[3] Historian Benjamin Stora (2014) underscores that the FLN's narrative was responsible for effacing any dissent from minority groups or competing, alternative stories. In essence, it was a "histoire-fiction" (literally fictitious history), "where the military played a central role" and demanded that "people forget some moments of the partisan history of Algerian nationalism" such as

> the intervention of the peasant masses (August 1955), urban uprisings (December 1960), the role of immigration, and thus the National Federation of France branch of the FLN, and finally the leveraging of international relations in order to win the war…This "writing of history" starts in June 1966 when it was decided to implement a measure of sovereignty by "nationalizing", through Arabization, the teaching of history. (Stora 1994, p. 57)

Films made in the wake of the famous neorealist film, *The Battle of Algiers* (1965) by Italian, Gillo Pontecorvo, considered one of the first films to celebrate Algerian "male heroes as the martyrs of the revolution," as well as the unifying messages of FLN dogma, fostered a stylized masculine-centered narrative that was reified constantly during the late 1960s and early 1970s in films such as Tewfik Fares's *Les hors-la-loi (Outlaws*, 1968), Ahmed Rachedi's *L'opium et le bâton (Opium and the Stick*, 1969), Mohamed Lakhdar-Hamina's *Le vent des Aurès (Wind of the Aurès*, 1966) and the later *Chronique des années de braise (Chronicle of the Years of Embers*, 1974) (Sharpe

2015, p. 450). This era is known mostly for "how directors … represent male identity in mythical, hagiographic and demiurgic terms" and, consequently, how they repeatedly disavowed any questioning of "patriarchal ideology" as the mainstay of the one-party state (Sharpe 2015, p. 450). Algerian film scholar Lofti Maherzi in *Le cinéma algérien: institutions, imaginaire, idéologie (Algerian Cinema: Institutions, Imaginary, Ideology*, 1980) identifies three masculine roles that typify the character typology of this time that contributed to the "structures profondes de l'imaginaire collectif" [profound structures of the imaginary collective] (1980, p. 244): the *moudjahid* (freedom fighter), the *peasant (fellah)* and the *intellectual* (1980, p. 245). All three roles fuse into narratives that highlight the rebels of the *maquis* as nationalist leaders, unified and organized in their efforts to throw off the yoke of colonialism during the war for independence (1954–1962). At no time do these early films deviate from the one, national narrative which depicts the maquis as fighting for the land and its people. At this juncture,

> it was necessary both to articulate the three structures – state, army, and FLN – with one another to make them a functional triangle, and to "nationalize" them to make people forget their original illegitimacy … people were encouraged to produce episodes in revolutionary *chanson de geste* that projected the mythic image of a Manichaean universe, with the roles of heroes and traitors, liberators and oppressors, well defined. (Stora 2001, pp. 172–173)

Films such as *Le vent des Aurès* and *Les hors-la-loi*, coopted rural, Amazigh culture into an overarching masculine narrative code that "embellished masculinity as a method of dramatizing the emergence of national sovereignty" (Sharpe 2015, p. 455). By the end of the 1960s, the homological association between Amazigh traditional, masculine, ritualized culture and the nationalist urban, FLN elites had been forged. The all-encompassing rebel fighter of the maquis represented the revolutionary-hero ideal equally for the rural enclaves of the poor and downtrodden, victimized by years of French colonial rule that had dispossessed them of their lands, as well as the urban ideologue. The country's narrative, featuring this rebel fighter icon, cast him as savior or, in the case of his death, as martyr for the people.[4]

Although Rachid Boudjedra wonders in his study if cinema was capable of promoting debate between the objectives of the National Liberation Front and the socialist revolutionary ideals it hoped to propagate at the dawn of the independence, the films of the 1960s do attest to the galvanizing possibilities the medium presents for shaping nationalist state identity (Boudjedra 1971, p. 20). At no time in these films, or in popular intellectual discourse, is the authority of the FLN and its military wing the ALN (Armée de Libération Nationale), questioned. Of course, as scholars and historians have noted, the FLN's Master Narrative was fabricated on completely false conceptions of cultural unity, as widespread disagreement and power grabs characterized the "anti-democratic militarism and authoritarianism" of the early years of post-independence under first president, Ahmed Ben Bella (Malley 1996, p. 2). "Despite talk of the nationalist-revolutionary aspirations" of Third World movements and Algerians "being regarded almost as supermen by the radical nationalists of the Third World" (Malley 1996, pp. 2–3), a climate fueled by divisions, camps and factions, coined "the phrase 'enemy brothers' to describe feuding Algerians, [and] by midsummer 1962 it was already clear that these feuds would be the undoing of revolutionary Algeria" (Humbaraci 1966, p. 2).

In early films, women were cast in the background, silenced and passive, despite their heroic depictions in Pontecorvo's *The Battle of Algiers* as active members of the maquis (participating as *les porteuses de bombes*), tortured by the French military, and ultimately responsible equally with men for helping to bring the war effort to its fruition. In indigenous Algerian films, however, 1960s and 1970s scenarios depicted women overwhelmingly as mothers and wives of men lost in the war; victims without voices. Even Pontecorvo's film cast women in ways that made it difficult to find alternative representations in film scripts later in the decade (Khanna 2008, p. 124).

Cinema of the 1970s associated women and agrarian reforms as responsible for building the nation according to a strict, socialist model. This model became the norm for President Houari Boumediene's postcolonial state in which women were "considered an active part of the economic process for development" (Discacciati 2008, p. 37). In films such as *Al-Faham* (*Le Charbonnier, The Charcoal Burner*, Mohamed Bouamari, 1972), a woman rejects "her traditional role as a housewife" in order to become more socio-politically engaged. This change is "for reasons linked to an economic change" as women in Algeria during the 1970s were encouraged to contribute to the national economy (Discacciati 2008, p. 37). One of the first films to counter the staid depictions of women as silenced and victimized was the stylized documentary *La Nouba des femmes de Mont Chenoua* (*The Nouba of the women of Mount Chenoua*) made by celebrated author and member of the Académie française, Assia Djebar. Her 1977 film took two years to make and traces the forgotten voices of women who participated in the struggle for independence in the rural mountain communities of Algeria. Fragmented by numerous stories told from different perspectives, the film leaves audiences perplexed about the outcomes of women's post-revolutionary lives. The nebulous female accounts portrayed mirror the socio-political confusion of the postcolonial Algerian nation which offer no "unifying theme" but rather a "universe that ... invites us to contemplate...a world in progress, in gestation" (Bensmaïa 2003, p. 84). Djebar's early films, such as *La Nouba* and the later *La Zerda, ou les chants de l'oubli* (*Zerda and the Songs of Forgetting*, 1982), began to mark a slow break with the nationalist, overly masculinized *histoire-fiction* of the 1960s "mujahidin cinema" genre as more women filmmakers contributed films to the nationalized Algerian film industry.[5]

The social discourse of Algerian films changes in the late 1970s-early 1980s to focus on women who rebel against paternal authority in order to pursue individualistic goals of education and emancipation. Films like *Rih al-Janub* (*Wind from the*

South, 1975) by Mohamed Slim Riad and the later *Houria* by Sid Ali Mazif (1986), are viewed as offering positive social commentaries on women wanting to pursue individual betterment for themselves as well as the "economic development needed to emancipate and educate [them]" in general (Discacciati 2000, p. 37). Ironically, these emancipatory films furnished alternative scenarios for women in a decade which was marked by the repressive reform of the 1982 Algerian Family Code; legislation that greatly restricted women's rights in public and domestic space in Algeria (Lazreg 1994, p. 151). The Family Code was a legislative concession to the rise of Islamic fundamentalism that had been steadily increasing since the late 1970s. Islamists called for strict adherence to *Shari'a* law as a means to thwart what was perceived as the growing Westernization of the country. Nineteen eighty-eight was "a watershed year" for the social unraveling of the country during which the people lost faith in the narrative of the nation and its ideologues of the FLN (Austin 2012, p. 13). This loss of faith escalated the easy rise of the Islamic front known as the Front Islamique du Salut (FIS):[6] "The disjuncture between the Algerian people and the state reached a nadir in Black October of 1988, the autumn of 600 dead. For the first time in the history of independent Algeria, the violence of the regime became undeniably explicit as the army fired on the people, with hundreds of protestors killed and many survivors tortured in incarceration" (Austin 2012, p. 13–14). Since most of those slaughtered were the young of Algeria, born after the revolution, the significance of their deaths had a lasting impact on the psyche of the nation, as journalist Benamar Mediene notes: "In October 1988 [the deaths of] Algerian youth neutralized or cancelled out the founding, legitimizing sign of nationalist power, its symbolic payment, namely the 'blood of the martyrs', was paid by its own blood" (cited in Austin 2012, p. 14).[7] The FLN-led state's slaughter of hundreds brought the FIS to power. Their legitimate win in elections in 1992, followed with the suspension of these same elections and the declaration of a state of emergency during the following years as the civil war escalated. At the end of the bloodshed in 2005, when an Armistice with the FIS was signed, by some estimates 200,000 people had been killed (Austin 2012, p. 119). The films of this period depict women as victims of repression – social, political, and cultural. Mohamed Rachid Benhadj's *Touchia* (1992) and the earlier *Al-qal'a* (*The Citadel*, 1988) by Mohamed Chouikh reflect the tense climate of the era. Filmmaking in Algeria in the 1990s was impacted by the social unrest raging in the country as the civil war escalated. Merzak Allouache's 1994, *Bab el-Oued City*, reflects the growing chaos evident in the socio-political spheres of Algeria at the time and also articulates the particular repression against women who were cowed by men coopted into Islamic radicalization. Nadir Moknèche's *Viva Laldjérie* (2004), raw and brutal in its depiction of women living on the edge of a psychological abyss caused by the violence reigning in Algeria as the civil war came to a close, was one of the first films to be filmed in Algiers immediately following the unrest.

Without a doubt, the civil war impacted the film industry artistically and commercially. Algerian filmmaking "entered a crisis in the late 1980s … resulting both from a reorganization of the film sector in a privatizing direction and the outbreak of civil strife in the early 1990s" (Tazi et al. 2004, p. 9).[8] In addition, the spreading violence across the country also engendered the "disengagement of the state, the impoverishment of the population, the increase in corruption and the contestation of power by Islamist movements" (Bonner et al. 2005, p. 14). In 1988, the FIS wielded its power influencing state institutions to denounce cinema "as a forbidden and unholy pastime." Armed Algerian-Islamist groups targeted cinemas, film-makers, and moviegoers. It became increasingly difficult for directors to shoot in the streets, leading many to flee the country after a number of "Algerian cineastes [were] sentenced to death by the Islamists" (Shafik 2007, p. 43). Boujemaa Karèche, director of the Algerian Cinémathèque, noted that by the end of the 1990s, "Algerian cinema [had] zero production, zero film theatres, zero distributors, zero tickets sold" (Armes 2005, p. 68). In fact, "between 1997 and 2002 not a single fea-ture film was made in Algeria. The country [ultimately] risked cinematic amnesia" (Austin 2010, p. 24). The growing Islamic radicalism in the streets meted out by devotees of the FIS, particularly targeted women. "The psychological and physical violence" of the time was viewed most definitely as "an obstacle to women's progress in society" (Discacciati 2000, p. 37).

Films by Algerian women filmmakers in the late 1990s–early 2000s have been particularly successful at telling undocumented stories from the recent past, certainly during the *années noires* up to the present. *Algérie, la vie quand même* (*Algeria, Life all the Same*, 1998, Djamila Sahraoui) documents the filmmaker's return to Kabylia whereupon she gives the camera to her cousin in order to give a voice to disenfranchised youths. Habiba Djahnine's 2008 film-documentary, *Lettre à ma sœur* (*Letter to My Sister*), tells the story of the filmmaker's sister, Nabila Djahnine, a feminist civil rights advocate working in Tizi-Ouzou who was killed in 1996 by Islamists. Djamila Sahraoui's *Barakat!* (2006) and her later, *Yema* (2012) also depict the civil war and how the atrocities committed during the conflict affected women's lives.

One of the most commercially successful films to portray the raging civil war of the 1990s, made with the hope of generating some sort of healing process about a period that has virtually gone undocumented or scrutinized socio-politically as well as psychologically, is the film *Rachida* (2003). The later *Masquerades* (2008), is the first comedy made in the post-Black Decade and offers a compelling script of hope for the youth of Algeria. These films are important for what they say with respect to undocumented trauma and how it has affected women psychologically (*Rachida*), and also for contextualizing potential hope and investment in the future (*Masquerades*). Both films depict women as the fulcrums of socio-cultural and political transformation. Women here are key components in the healing process of the new era. As mentioned above, these films, as well as many others made in recent years, have also resurrected a cinematic industry that had virtually been halted for over a decade.

Post-civil War: Victims Who Survive and Persevere

In the post-*années noires*, filmmakers have come back to reformulate the cinema industry as they denounce Algeria's socio-political deterioration, as well as offer new narratives for the contemporary era. Increased international investment in film has aided in boosting the millennial Algerian cinema industry. Indeed, most films today are made with international funding from France, Belgium and the United States.[9] In contemporary films, Algeria is often a country on the verge of implosion as very graphically depicted in Merzak Allouache's *Les terrasses* (2013), one of the most recent films to transmit this singular message. In recent years, as the works of filmmakers such as Allouache and Tariq Teguia (*Rome plutôt que vous* (*Rome Rather than You*), 2006) demonstrate, the filmic text has become a means to challenge official definitions of the Algerian nation and the failures of its post-independence mandate. Recent films of the millennium ignore the boundaries imposed by Algeria's national history and interests of the state in order to reveal what has not (but should) be said, offering insight into how to heal a country that has been torn apart. Not only are films of the 2000s challenging the silence surrounding the civil war of the 1990s; they are also engaging to overturn the hyper-masculinized Master Narrative of the FLN, marking a new era in Algerian cinematographic storytelling. In addition to rethinking genres and styles, film critic Ahmed Bedjaoui notes that "filmmakers have organized themselves into production companies and are trying to find the financing that the film market is incapable of generating" at the state level (2015, p. 136). Attesting to this transformation of Algerian cinema at all levels, a recent article entitled, "Algerian Cinema: A New Wave" is Emerging, published in *The Guardian*, focuses on new and upcoming cineastes, many of whom are women. The author notes that "this new generation of self-taught Algerian filmmakers ... [grew] up without ever having seen the inside of a cinema. Their enthusiasm for cinema has paid off with some already making breakthroughs in the festival circuit, and they all wish to see Algeria's once-celebrated cinema flourish again."[10] Increasingly, Algerian filmmakers coming of age in the new millennium are working across mediums, genres, and styles with diverse funding possibilities. Young cineastes such as Yasmine Chouikh (daughter of Yamina Bachir-Chouikh), born in the early 1980s, are multi-talented, working as writers, journalists, and film directors. Absence of style, of genre and training lead most of all to a free-flowing concept of what cinema should be and do in Algerian society, thus opening up new channels, unfettered by traditional cinematic paradigms. Film has become, therefore, the perfect borderless milieu in which to scrutinize the civil war for what has not been said or admitted to by either the government or members the Islamic Salvation Front since the armistice charter was signed in 2005.

Rachida

Yamina Bachir-Chouikh's *Rachida* (2003)[11] depicts women's resistance to Islamic fundamentalism wielded by the FIS in in the 1990s. Told from Rachida's point of view, the young schoolteacher is the victim of a gunshot to the stomach in the streets of Algiers by members of a local terrorist band. One of the gang who shoots her is her former student. Rachida is shot because she refuses to carry the terrorists' bomb to the school for their radical Islamic cause. Subsequently, she and her mother, Aïcha, escape to a remote village so that she may recover psychologically from the post-traumatic stress resulting from her experience. Rachida's perseverance as a woman who refuses to wear the *hijab* (veil), and who, after deciding to remain in the village indefinitely to teach grade school, determined even more to instruct the little girls there, becomes a symbol for justice for so many Algerian women who were silenced and even killed during this time (Brahimi 2009, p. 154–155).[12] In the DVD extras included with her film, filmmaker Bachir-Chouikh makes the following statement about how important Rachida's perseverance on a national level is to the healing process of the country in the wake of the civil war, as well as the contribution the film makes to resuscitate an industry that had gone dormant during the 1990s:

> The Algerian cinema industry was brought to an abrupt halt by the government at a moment when the population was going through a terrible tragedy. The blank movie screens and the suffocating atmosphere planted in me the wild idea of making a film that went totally against the tide. Perhaps, so as to never forget this period of time, perhaps simply out of pain, I wanted to embed in the rolls of film the helplessness of ordinary citizens, up until then, considered as nothing more than faceless casualties amid the atrocities. A people held hostage between a violence that was said to be justified and one that was obviously barbaric, and a youth who had lost all points of reference, who was humiliated and ready to join any extremist faction.
>
> *Rachida* is my hymn to peace, tolerance and the courage of the countless 'anonymous' faces in my country. It is perhaps, but a tiny contribution, on my part, towards the healing of the deep wounds of my people. If, in the film, I cast every day, ordinary people, and portrayed them in violent confrontation with each other, it is my hope that the audience will judge these portrayals and situations honestly.
>
> I chose, for the main character, the 'perfect' victim: a woman, a young schoolteacher. The choice permitted me to point out the debasement of an education system that has become the breeding ground for a culture of hatred. In spite of the dismemberment of the cinema industry in Algeria, and the difficulties and risks of making a first film, the story of Rachida imposed itself on me; today, it exists as a film. This was not an easy feat.

Bachir-Chouikh is one of the first cineastes to go on record as specifically articulating the role of film in national healing as well as documenting the civil war. She remarks in a 2003 interview that *Rachida*, struck a chord with whole families who went to see it: "Cela n'était pas arrivé depuis *La Bataille d'Alger*, depuis 1965.

C'est le même phénomène: des gens viennent voir leur histoire, la première représentation des dix dernières années de leur vie. Plus de dix ans en fait car on est dans cette violence depuis 1988" [That hasn't happened since *The Battle of Algiers*, in 1965. It's the same phenomenon: People came to see their history, the first representation of the last ten years of their lives. In fact, for more than ten years because we have been in this violence since 1988] (Lequeret and Tesson 2003, p. 31). Bachir-Chouikh emphasizes that *Rachida* "n'est pas une histoire sur le terrorisme. Mais … j'ai fait un film sur une violence, un peuple, sur le non-sens de la violence, et sur ce qui la nourrit" [is not a story of terrorism. But … I made a film on violence, a people, on the nonsense of violence and what nourishes it] (Lequeret and Tesson 2003, p. 31).[13] Despite risking the lives of her crew and her own as they filmed in the streets of Algiers, Bachir-Chouikh persevered and added that she also achieved the film with no help from official state funding sources (Lequeret and Tesson 2003, p. 31).

The release of *Rachida* in early 2003 also marked the resuscitation of a dormant Algerian cinema. Reporting on the film's debut in Algerian movie houses, film critic Charles Tesson notes, "in Algiers, next to the Grande Poste, *Rachida* was shown three times a day … its first week gleaned 13,600 tickets sold, more than 2,000 people per day" (Tesson 2003b, p. 14). The film's release was monumental on many levels; it was the first to be shown widely in the country as the civil war waned, it was viewed not only by men (who had been up to the time the principal moviegoers in the nation), but also by young women, and was shown in a cinema that had been completely renovated in terms of "entrance, seats, and projection" (Tesson 2003b, p. 14). Tesson remarks that *Rachida* was the film that prompted a phrase heard in cultural circles: "L'Algérie ne tourne plus le dos au cinéma" (Algeria will no longer turn its back on cinema) (p. 14). This looking forward meant the state returned to its system of subventions (much like the French national cinema funding program known as *l'avance sur recettes*), cultivated connections with filmmakers in the Algerian diaspora, encouraging them to come back home to shoot films, and cautiously stepped around harsh censorship (Tesson 2003b, p. 14). One of the leading debates plaguing the revival of Algerian cinema was couched in the tension between which entities would fund film: The state or the private sector. Many filmmakers accused the state of hiding state owned equipment used to shoot films in the country before the civil war. These accusations were also linked to filmmakers feeling the pressure of a state-run cinema that would, once again, censor the themes it did not want projected on the screen. The debates surrounding how much the state should be involved in filmmaking in the new millennium are still on-going.[14]

Rachida is an interesting film on many levels, certainly as noted above for what it says about how cinema and the heroines portrayed in films in the 2000s will reflect the socio-political and cultural realms of a post-civil war Algeria. Denise Brahimi called the film a "tragedy" for its portrayal of a "heroine overtaken by the events of the time which overwhelm her" as she flees one violent space for another (2009, pp. 153–154). Rachida is also lauded for her resistance as she "revolts against her victimization" by returning to teach the day after the massacre in the village (Brahimi 2009, p. 155). The film's ending suggests that Algeria will come out of the violence to see a better day. This sentiment is conveyed in the last minute of the film when, in front of her class of students who have obediently taken their seats in the ransacked classroom, Rachida writes on the board "today's lesson" in Arabic and then looks directly into the camera with a face filled with resolve.

Bachir-Chouikh's most daring messages evoked through dialogues between the women in the film center around several salient messages. First, that obscurity surrounding perpetrators – who is killing whom (*qui tue qui?*) a question constantly asked by authors, journalists, filmmakers, and the Algerian people during the 1990s– is a piece of the civil-war puzzle that remains unsolved. The filmmaker is careful to at no time name killers by faction. Those who wield guns and terrorize are simply called "terrorists," thus implying butchers can come from all sides – the Front Islamique du salut and also the government's military which is now known to have used the excuse of combating the FIS in order to subjugate communities it viewed were dangerous (certainly those in Berber Kabylia). Distrust of the state is a constant platform in the conversations Rachida has with her mother, Aïcha, and Yasmina, in whose family village home they hide, as they listen to news reports of the killing taking place across the country. After hearing about the slaughter of 11 Franciscan friars (the Tibhirine friars) as well as "80 muftis, Imams and Muzzins … and in Mitijida where 22 people had their throats cut, 4 girls were kidnapped," Yasmina ironically, perhaps even overly hopeful, notes, "the state claims that terrorism is coming to an end." Rachida, however, places all killers in the same basket, remarking "where was this hate buried, this cruelty? This barbarity? … these hearts deserted by all humanity … from time immemorial there has never been so much crime … Raped women, babies with slit throats." The difference in how the women come to terms with the violence is generationally stratified. Yasmina and Rachida's mother, of the older generation, urge forgiveness as a means to heal the country. However Rachida, speaking as a young victim, sees very little possibility of pardon "… for the state who humiliates its youth," forcing "young men to choose to take up guns to kill innocents." Reference to the thousands of young men with no jobs or prospects, who ultimately decided to join the FIS out of desperation, is a leitmotif of the film that cannot go unnoticed. These young men are the *hitistes*, a term derived from the Algerian Arabic word for "wall." In the postcolonial era, the word became popularized in songs and popular culture across the Maghreb to characterize the lack of opportunities for young men, standing around in the streets, often with their backs against the walls of buildings, holding them up, as they hang out with nowhere to go. As one Algerian blogger notes,

Yes, the definition of this term designates a no name Algerian male, between 17–30 who spends his day holding up the walls in Algeria, Oran, Bou Ismaïl or other places dotted with buildings or simply houses. Finally, we realized that they are leaning against walls and contemplating social life like a tribunal president judges the condemned.[15]

These are the men Rachida passes as she walks to her teaching position at the school. Indeed, the women depicted in the streets are always walking somewhere to do something, contrasting sharply with the wayward, primarily young men doing absolutely nothing, idly watching and harassing them. Women are a force against the inertia of the country, yet they are still the primary targets in public space, which is the case for Rachida when she is shot. In her film, Bachir-Chouikh emphasizes constantly the powerful agency of women, since during the civil war they were barred de facto from public places and spaces by Islamists. This aspect of Islamic religious fundamentalism is not new and has been documented by Arab feminists for years. Algerian Islamists, like those in Pakistan and Iran, have for decades targeted women in the streets making it their primary aim to efface them from public space. Feminist scholar Leila Ahmed's descriptions of women's curtailed liberty in the streets immediately following the Iranian revolution, is reified in Algeria during the 1990s: Islamist groups always seek to "deprive[] women ... of their most hard-earned civil rights and ... reduce them to the status of privatized sex objects required by their religious order to be at the disposal of their husbands at all times ...Their mere presence in public was described as 'seditious' and they were required to don the Islamic hijab, covering themselves from top to toe and to return to the home" (1992, p. 232).

Despite her physical victimization, Rachida refuses to give up on her country. Bachir-Chouikh makes a third point about the extent to which people were invested in staying in Algeria, despite the violence raging around them. Rachida even professes that she prefers shoes "made in Algeria," rather than Europe. When hiding out in the village, her only means of entertainment to take her mind off her situation is to listen to popular Raï music, which at the time was banned by the FIS for its sexually suggestive themes. It is known as music listened to clandestinely and is present in films such as *Bab el-Oued City* (*Allouache*) as a symbol for resistance. In *Rachida*, Bachir-Chouikh blends traditional and modern scores. Cheb Hasni, Cheb Akli, Reinette l'Oranaise, S.O.S., and El Anka (popular groups and singers of the 1990s Raï scene), give Rachida the sustenance to continue living. Music and dance performed by women; either Rachida by herself in her garden, dancing to her radio, or women dancing at a wedding held in the village despite the turmoil, all are performances of resistance to the staunch hardline dogma of the FIS.

A fourth salient point the filmmaker transmits is the clear demarcation between the FIS's corruption of Islam and a notion of the religion as real, pure, and without reproach. Rachida's secular views and individualism are contrasted to her mother, Aïcha's, devout beliefs rooted in the pure tenants of Islam. When Rachida is shot, Aïcha runs out into the street, screaming "what is this religion that allows them to kill people?" Yet at no time does her pious commitment to true Islam waver. She is seen praying five times a day and emphasizes to Rachida that to heal they must all forgive using the parameters of spirituality. With the daily killings listed in reports on the radio, including the one depicting the 1996 slaughter of 11 French monks (who had lived at the Atlas Abbey of Tibhirine, near Médéa, for over a century and were allowed to stay after 1962), it is not only Muslims who are victims but also Christians and innocent villagers caught in the crossfire.[16]

The most poignant message Bachir-Chouikh makes in her film, is about the variety of women present in the country, as she notes in an interview, "I wanted to show the diversity of women in the country. Women with the hijab and without" (Lequeret and Tesson 2003, p. 30). However, we cannot discount the staunch feminist interpretations of socio-political realms that are constants throughout the film. At no time does Rachida brush aside her commitment to secular and emancipated views. She refuses to wear the hijab, even when threatened, and jokes to women in the village with whom she teaches that she does not need it to "buy a husband." The young woman is sensual and will not comply with the radical Isalmicization influencing women's dress codes taking place in Algiers and later in the village. In the opening scenes of the film, the camera focuses up close on her lips as she carefully applies bright red lipstick. The young woman's hair is wildly beautiful and full, curly and worn loose most of the time to accent to what extent she is corporeally free in public space. Played by Ibtissem Djouadi, appearing here in her first film, Rachida walks defiantly in the Algiers' streets. She wears pants and tight fitting skirts which accent her willowy frame, refusing to kowtow to the traditionalism of the hijab and severe interpretations of the Qu'ran. When the village school's principal gropes and harasses her by demanding "what's a beautiful, young single girl from the city doing in a village?," she shrugs him off and defiantly states "all children have a right to an education." The very idea of locking women up behind doors and interior spaces is also constantly challenged in Bachir-Chouikh's scenario. Rachida's mother even goes so far as to say, once they are in the village, that "if we stay locked up, we'll look suspicious."

Once recovered from her gunshot wound, Rachida briefly returns to Algiers to see her fiancé who has had no news of her. They swim freely in the ocean, and lie in the sun on the beach. Their relationship is "modern" and unencumbered for a brief moment by the war raging around them. However, despite his wishes, Rachida refuses definitively to come back to the city to marry him. Their relationship is left open-ended. The young woman's first and foremost concern is for the children whom she teaches. Bachir-Chouikh's overall focus on the protection of children as necessary for the future hope of the country is constantly reified in scenes throughout the film. There is innocence to be found in the ruins of war, thus caring for children, whose "mothers are in prison, and fathers are terrorists," becomes the mission of all the women in the village. "Those kids didn't choose their parents," Rachida quips, suggesting that the hundreds of orphans of the war will have to be taken care of if the future is to be brighter. After the massacre in the village, it is the children who defiantly return to the school with Rachida to begin a new beginning.

In 2003, Bachir-Chouikh's film marks a cautious opening to the period of healing that has continued in Algeria to this day. In the early 2000s, Rachida is left standing looking defiantly into the camera. In 2005 an Armistice with the FIS was signed with the FLN government.[17] *Rachida* encapsulates the first stage in a process of cultural healing that five years later is contextualized in very different terms in Lyès Salem's comic film, *Masquerades*.

Masquerades

Lyès Salem is known for pushing the envelope of the Algerian nation's official narrative regarding its past.[18] His recent film, *L'Oranais* (*The Man from Oran*, 2014), has been characterized as "piercing the taboos of the post-liberation period and the 'storytelling' which the Algerian State continues to use in order to crush all dissident voices and prolong a regime that is at the end of its rope."[19] The filmmaker notes that "with this film [*L'Oranais*], I wished to present human beings and not the smooth and unblemished characters that have been presented to us incessantly through the old *moudjahid*."[20] True to his word, his first feature-length film, *Masquerades* (2008), also reflects these views. Salem in several interviews does not hide the fact that he seeks out stories about Algerian identity that will allow for processing the dark years of the civil war.

As a light comedy, *Masquerades* contrasts sharply with *Rachida*. However, Salem still manages to drive home some significant socio-political points about Algeria in the post-civil war 2000s. Effaced completely in the stark, arid landscape of the village in which the action takes place, is any trace of the bloody massacres of the 1990s. Salem sets the film's action on the edge of the Rif Mountains in the Sahara and uses non-trained actors from the village in which the story takes place. Confessing that he had never lived in a village, Salem thought it best to go to the source. For the comic fable to work, he notes, "I needed a close, small community."[21] Although the village is a backwater, it is as vibrant as it is poor and relatively sleepy. Lead protagonist, Mounir, played by Salem himself, underscores the dire straits of the villagers when he quips to his wife, "I break my back trying to get us food." The village poverty is noticeable everywhere except for the occasional huge, sleek black cars owned by the "Colonel," the wealthiest man in the area who rents them out to drunken wedding parties. These cars' chauffeurs drive insanely fast around the village square, but are never seen. The bright flower arrangements on their hoods, boldly stating in English "Love you forever" comprise a generic phrase used by every unidentified wedding party. From and to where these parties are going is never indicated to viewers (either in the village, or in the cinema audience). Dissatisfied Mounir, gardener (or "horticultural engineer" as he likes to refer to himself) to the obscure Colonel, aspires to make something more of life. Although he is married to the perfect wife, Habiba, has a young son, Amine, and lives with an adoring sister, Rym, his aspirations exceed the potential of the village. He also is burdened by the unending problem of Rym's narcolepsy which precludes her from finding a husband, or so he thinks.

Secretly, though, Rym is meeting with Mounir's best friend, Khliffa, and they are passionately in love and want to get married. Unfortunately, Khliffa is too scared to go against the wishes of his overbearing best friend who wants to marry Rym to a "prince." Mounir is macho and easily succumbs to village gossip about his sister and her lack of prospects. One night, drunk in the village square, he shouts that Rym is "now engaged" to a wealthy suitor whom he has found to take her hand. The next day, upon interrogation by his wife and sister, he admits that he made it up. In order to rectify the fib, though, Rym must "refuse the rich husband." The family decides to perform this stage of the story by going to a four-star hotel in Algiers in order to "be seen" closing the deal of the marriage (during which Rym will refuse her intended on some pretense). While at the hotel, an important Westerner passes by, unseen to the audience, but mobbed by photographers and journalists and keenly observed by Rym and her nephew. When the family gets back to the village the "telephone Arab" has worked well, since all inhabitants are *au courant* as to the family's doings. All would have gone as planned, if Rym had not changed her mind in mid-sentence as she and Habiba were supposed to report her marriage refusal to the village women gathered outside their house. Seeing Khliffa hiding behind a wall, Rym decides to make him jealous, forcing him to ask Mounir for her hand. She amplifies the story even more, noting that she is "now engaged to William Vancooten" a famous "American…who has blond hair and blue eyes." Through amplification of the fabricated story, Vancooten becomes the promised savior of the village which longs for European/American/Western investment (the tycoon's own identity oscillates from "American" to "Australian" to "Canadian"). Realizing that such a match would drastically increase his social standing in the village, Mounir plays along, deciding to milk the story for as long as he can. In the meantime, Rym tells Khliffa the story is not true and tries with Habiba to keep the whole narrative from spiraling out of control. Eventually, love conquers all, Rym tells Khliffa that "it's silly having to hide with all the sunshine we have here …" and when a mufti (holy man) suddenly appears in the village out of nowhere, the couple trick him into marrying them in a hasty backyard ceremony without fanfare and traditions to hinder them.

The lighthearted comedy-romance "could take place almost anywhere … *Masquerades* contains stock elements of romantic comedies and fairy tales while the characters of Mounir and Habiba recall the clueless or frustrated blue-collar worker and his good-humored wife that have been developed to popular acclaim in US sitcoms from the *Honeymooners* to *Everybody Loves Raymond*" (Gauch 2016, p. 96). The film is, thus, atypical for Algerian filmmaking and marks the global outlook increasingly promoted by filmmakers who live both in and outside Algeria (such as Merzak Allouache, Tarik Teguia, and Nadir Moknèche). The film's interesting "anywhere scenario" resonates well with Molière and Shakespeare enthusiasts who easily recognize conventional tropes featuring a universal focus on the human condition. Individuals everywhere are subjected to humanity's quotidian emotions – jealousy, envy, love, sadness. These universalisms make the film accessible to global, particularly Western, audiences. Indeed, it is one of the only Algerian films to obtain U.S. distribution and has been shown widely in festivals (Gauch 2016, p. 96). The film also celebrates the originality of Algerian village culture, the beauty of the Algerian natural landscape, and traditional music (the film's score is original) integrated at times with a more world music beat. These qualities make it a film that transcends nations, languages and origins. It also, though, resonates locally as Salem affirms in an interview: "I think ... the Algerian audiences recognized themselves in the film. It doesn't happen very often these days – either because of the quality of the movie or the acting or the script, or because the films ... are made for a western or European audience. These movies are usually in French, not in Arabic. This film is in their own language, and I think they can recognize themselves and their own humor when they watch it."[22]

In general, the few scholars who have published on *Masquerades* (Roy Armes and Suzanne Gauch) weigh in on both sides of how good a job it does in presenting the socio-cultural and political messages of the post-civil war era. Although glib at times, the film draws on archetypal hyper-masculine character portrayals of the Algerian mujahidin cinema of the past in order to subvert them for a newer brand of Algerian man who is sensitive, caring, and invested in country and clan. Mounir seems to be stuck between the past mujahidin hero and the sensitive, younger Khliffa who is of the millennial generation. Mounir constantly fights with the macho image he thinks he is supposed to play in the village and with his family. In the earlier scenes of the film, he tells his son Amine to stop torturing a beetle, stating "how would you like that done to you ... it's got a mother too." However later, as the prestige and possibility of power through the Vancooten-Rym match go to his head, Mounir tells Amine (who has been beaten up by his classmates because he wanted to save a toad from being forced to "smoke") that "you rally around the strongest ... you join the others or you die." When Amine professes that the toad "was going to die," his father quips: "It's just a toad, what do you care? You quarrel with your clan about a toad you don't even know? They decided to make him smoke ... He was there, too bad for him ...That's democracy, right?" Whether to go along with the clan or be an individualist is one of the most striking messages of the film. In a larger context, Salem compels his audiences to think about the consequences of "going along" with the purviews of others, even when they are not right and just. In the wake of the civil war and the genocide that took place, the question of succumbing to the will of fanaticism has continued resonance.

What the film says about the roles and places of women in contemporary society is also telling. Both Rym and Habiba refuse to wear the hijab at any time. When Mounir asks Habiba "where's your scarf?," she retorts, "I lost it." This declaration is supported by Rym who states, "mine's with hers." They are women who are free agents and who speak their minds on all subjects unencumbered by headscarves and dress codes. Needless to say, bucking rigid and static traditions is a constant challenge. Salem remarks that both genders are subject to wearing masks in order to survive being stuck between modernity and the overbearing socio-traditional frameworks in which they must live:

> The word "masquerades" evokes both the hypocrisy of certain behaviors and the role playing in society which fools no one: this word describes Mounir's trajectory and the attitude of part of the village residents. Also it evokes the lightness of comedy and the gravity of criticism. This ambivalence between the two pleases me, and is underscored by the title in French which is in the plural form. In Arabic, the title is in the singular –it sounds better – but the sense is pretty much identical, even if it means less the idea of a mask.[23]

In several interviews, Salem also underscores to what extent the comedy functions as a necessary social criticism on the post-civil war climate of Algeria. Rym's narcolepsy is symbolic for a country that keeps falling into a deep sleep as its reality swirls around it. Decreasing petrol prices, continued housing shortages, high unemployment, as well as a huge population of young people with few prospects, are the contemporary challenges the Abdelaziz Bouteflika government refuses to address. The subtle political commentary of Salem's film is even more telling in 2016 as the Bouteflika presidency has come under increasing criticism for being virtually unseen (many think the president is actually dead and his henchmen are the ones running the country). Bouteflika, known as "l'homme de paille" (the man of straw),[24] is the butt of jokes, considered to be a puppet of the oligarchs and capitalist movers and shakers behind the scenes who are really running the country. The phantom Colonel, whose sleek, black cars symbolize his local power in the village, alludes to Algeria's corrupt underbelly. Layers of dubious, shadowed authority are construed and run by the rich, powerful, and well-connected who are the root cause of "the collision of neoliberalism, the ruins of post-independence ideology, and an autocratic state" (Gauch 2016, p. 97).

On subjects such as corruption and traditional taboos, Salem seeks to "render people less fearful, to free up their speech." The filmmaker emphasizes that comedy is the best way to tackle issues "that have never been permitted to be uttered in Algeria."[25] Down to how the couple is presented in his film is something of a novelty. Mounir and Habiba live in a traditional, conservative village, yet they are very egalitarian in how they negotiate their relationship. Their marriage was forged out of love and they hint that they did have sex before their wedding. Although Mounir strives to play the role of an overbearing, macho man, in the end, he proves to be a softy, as Habiba convinces him that Rym and Khliffa "love each other" and resemble them in their younger days.

Khliffa and Rym's relationship is also depicted as one construed by two young people seeking to go against the grain in order to question the taboos that poison young people's lives: Mainly that sex before marriage is forbidden, and the right to leave and go elsewhere away from family and clan is not an option. Salem underscores the fact that today many more young men identify with Khliffa rather than

Mounir. Khliffa is a dreamer, who aspires to establish his own video rental business, love Rym, and take care of his aging mother. He is also pious, praying daily, but this does not keep him from living a modern life. Salem affirms that juxtaposed to Khliffa, "among the people who resemble him, Mounir stands for someone who just doesn't get it: that's rather a good sign."[26] Despite the hurdles the couple faces, bucking tradition and family ties, they look to find happiness in their own country, not elsewhere abroad in Europe or other places in the West. This is a particularly poignant message voiced by Rym. As she and Khliffa discuss their honeymoon plans, going far away abroad is not what the young woman desires. Her wish is to see Algeria: "It's a big country ... Mostaganem... on the seaside. ... I want to swim in Jiiel, spend the night in Timimoun, and have breakfast in Algiers." Khliffa answers her, remarking: "But before you have breakfast in Algiers, I'll take you to bathe in Menâa," a village in the high mountains of the Aurès. He thus displaces what is normally considered a preference for the urban, more modern, environment of the city, for the rural and culturally rich Berber enclave. Rym responds, "Every minute counts, we're capable of anything." When she confesses she wants to be a pilot to "go everywhere" but is disappointed, knowing she can't because of her narcolepsy, Khliffa is supportive, telling her that her affliction "might not last forever." The young couple desires the right to free circulation and to wander without fear of violence in their home country. Their investment in the future will begin at home, occupying and possessing the land as free agents; a land that has been so hostile to Algerian young people for years.

In the closing scenes, as Khliffa and Rym make their getaway in his dilapidated car, Rym discovers that her narcolepsy has disappeared. Perhaps, she thinks, it is because she "is in love." As they drive out of the village after sleeping together in Khliffa's video store, Mounir chases after them, more out of performance for the village, than out of conviction. He yells to Khliffa, "if you scratch her..." His sentence is left unfinished just as the couple's ultimate destination is left undisclosed. Mirroring the socio-political climate of the Algeria of his era, Mounir cannot control outcomes or predict how the changing country, its challenges and its successes, will help or hinder it from healing in the post-civil war century. This sentiment is echoed by Lyès Salem in an interview: "More generally, during the entire film, it is a question also of showing another side of Algeria. I wanted to make a film that doesn't rely on any victimization; a film that refuses a certain tendency here in North African film, to always show how difficult it is to be Algerian. The political ambition of the film is also there."[27]

Rachida and *Masquerades* mark a new era in Algerian filmmaking. Not only do these films probe the untold stories of women during the civil war, but they also reveal the healing process that can take place in a country that must find ways to negotiate the traumas of the past if it is ever to assure the future for generations of young people who are facing the challenges of our globalized era. In the past, the nationalism of the emerging postcolonial nation conceptualized, as Mbembe states, "power as a masculinist prerogative ... firmly inscrib[ing] resistance in the framework of a war between men" (Mbembe 2006, p. 171). The FLN's Master Narrative allowed for only one story, thus sidelining the many others that should be told as the country seeks to rebuild itself in the post-civil war era. The insular, singular script for the nation's revolutionary and postcolonial history is no longer applicable for the international pressures of global markets, nor can it accommodate calls for equality and recognition of Algerian diversity. Algeria, as elsewhere on the African continent, must form new ways of thinking about its national representation in its cultural production of the twenty-first century. Additionally, filmmakers' conception of cinema as representing the actuality of their time, means both challenging the socio-political nepotism of state authorities, as well as giving voice to the voiceless of the country: Women, children, and Berber communities. Algerian films in the post-*années noires*, are documents of witnessing the past and harbingers of the "what ifs" and the "could bes" of a new generation.

Notes

1   International, critical acclaim for the now iconic Berber films from the late 1990s, *La colline oubliée* (*The Forgotten Hill*, 1997) by Abderrahmane Bouguermouh and *La montagne de Baya* (*Baya's Mountain*, 1997) by Azzedine Meddour, has led to historically silenced groups in Algerian film becoming more visibly present in films of the 2000s. Other Berber films include: *Machaho* (1994) by Belkacem Hadjadj, and the more recent, *La maison jaune* (*The Yellow House*, 2008) by Amor Hakkar and *Mimezrane* (2007) by Ali Mouzaoui.

2   www.theguardian.com/film/2012/aug/26/new-africa-film-maker-feminism-algeria

3   There are four Berber groups in Algeria: Kabyle, Chaoui, Mozabite and Toureg.

4   Algeria's nationalist leaders developed an official narrative which extoled "one million martyrs" lost in the war of liberation. According to French army records the French military lost 24,614 men. Nineteen thousand French and Algerian civilians were killed by FLN "terrorism," between 1954–1962, whereas, it is estimated that between 55,000–65,000 Algerian civilians died at the hands of the French (Evans 2012, p. 337).

5   In addition to Assia Djebar, from the late 1970s onward, women contributed films to Algeria's cinematographic industry. Yasmina Bachir-Chouikh and later, Fatma Zohra Zamoun, Djamila Sahraoui, and the young, documentarist, Safinez Bousbia have all added films to the growing oeuvre of female works.

6   Founded in 1989, the Front Islamique du Salut (FIS) won regional and local elections in June 1990 and the first round of parliamentary elections in December 1991. Before the second round of elections, scheduled for January 1992, the oligarchic *pouvoir* (military and technocratic power establishment) deposed President Chadli Benjedid and terminated the elections. In March, the government declared the FIS an illegal party. These events provoked civil strife that claimed by some estimates 150,000–200,000 Algerian lives. The FIS's military wing, the Armée Islamique du Salut (Islamic Salvation Army [AIS]) disbanded, taking advantage of the government's 1999 Civil Concord Law's amnesty program.

7   Benamar Mediene, "Un état déconnecté," *Le Nouvel Observateur*, Collection Dossiers, 9, "La Guerre d'Algérie trente ans après" (1992): 72–73.

8   In 1986, there were approximately 400 cinemas operating in Algeria. By 2004 only ten remained to screen films. During the civil war period, audience attendance fell dramatically from 40 million annually to only 50,000 (Dwyer and Tazi, p. 10). Since the end of the civil war, cinemas have been renovated, and Dolby Digital systems installed. El Mougar, Ibn Zeydoun, and ABC theatres in Algiers, as well as one cinema in Tizi Ouzou, are of top quality. However, as Bachir-Chouikh noted in 2003 in an interview, these "newly renovated cinemas are empty because there aren't any films to show in them" (Lequeret and Tesson 2003, p. 31).

9   Particularly Merzak Allouache and Rachid Bouchareb are now internationally recognized names in filmmaking. Bouchareb has made films in English and French whose scripts are set in places all over the world. *Little Senegal* (2001) takes place in Senegal and the United States. *London River* (2009) is set in London and his most recent *La voie de l'ennemi* (*Two Men in Town*, 2014) features well-known American actors, Harvey Keitel and Forest Whittaker, in a scenario that takes place in New Mexico.

10   www.middleeasteye.net/in-depth/features/cinema-algerias-new-wave-emerging-1385200367

11   Bachir-Chouikh has for many years been married to famous filmmaker Mohamed Chouikh.

12   During the civil war, the FIS slaughtered many women schoolteachers, most particularly those who refused to wear the hijab.

13   Bachir-Chouikh's own brother was killed by assassination.

14   See, the special edition of *Cahiers du cinéma*: "Où va le cinéma algérien?," February–March 2003.

15   www.bahdja.com/point-de-vue/item/260-les-hitistes-une-production-made-in-alg%C3%A9ria-quil-faudra-assumer.html

16   Mention of this incident is particularly noteworthy since mystery has surrounded it for years. As reported in the French and Algerian press, the circumstances of the monks' kidnapping and subsequent killing are controversial. It was first believed and reported in the 1990s, that the Armed Islamic Group (*Groupe Islamique Armé*, GIA) wing of the FIS claimed responsibility for both. However, in 2009 then retired General François Buchwalter reported that the monks had been accidentally killed by the Algerian army. Again, the anomalies between accounts demonstrate to what extent reporting on the details of the civil war, as well as getting at the truth, needs to be rectified.

17   By the time the exhausted country approved the Charter for Peace and National Reconciliation in 2005, the violence had significantly waned (although Algiers suffered bombings in 2007). The FIS remains an illegal party, although moderate Islamist parties are permitted.

18   Lyès Salem was born in 1973 in Algiers, but since the age of 15 has lived in Paris. He studied at the Sorbonne and at L'École de théâtre national de Chaillot and the Conservatoire national d'art dramatique in France.

19   www.mediapart.fr/journal/international/091214/lyes-salem-realisateur-de-l-oranais-nous-vivons-le-dernier-baroud-du-regime-algerien

20   www.mediapart.fr/journal/international/091214/lyes-salem-realisateur-de-l-oranais-nous-vivons-le-dernier-baroud-du-regime-algerien

21   Interview with Rob Avila, Global Film Initiative.

22   www.austinfilm.org/page.aspx?pid=3889

23   www.cinemaotions.com/interview/36511
24   www.youtube.com/watch?v=5_FoXu0_OmY. The president has not been officially
     seen since May 2012. He has also been called the phantom president due to his limited
     appearances since being declared ill over five years ago.
25   www.cinemotions.com/interview/36511
26   www.cinemotions.com/interview/3611
27   www.cinemotions.com/interview/3611

References

Ahmed, Leila. 1992. *Women and Gender in Islam: Historical Roots of a Modern Debate*. New
     Haven, CT: Yale University Press.
Armes, Roy. 2005. "Algeria." *Variety International Film Guide 2005*. Los Angeles: Silman-
     James Press.
Armes, Roy. 2015. *New Voices in Arab Cinema*. Indianapolis: Indiana University Press.
Austin, Guy. 2010. "Against Amnesia: Representations of Memory in Algerian Cinema."
     Journal of African Cinemas 2(1): 27–35.
Austin, Guy. 2011. "Spaces of the Dispossessed in Algerian Cinema." *Modern & Contemporary
     France* 19(2): 195–208.
Austin, Guy. 2012. *Algerian National Cinema*. Manchester: Manchester University Press.
Bedjaoui, Ahmed. 2015. "Sixty Years of Algerian Cinema." *Black Renaissance/Renaissance
     Noire* Spring/Summer 15(1): 126–139.
Bensmaïa, Réda. 2003. *Experimental Nations: Or, the Invention of the Maghreb*. Princeton, NJ:
     Princeton University Press.
Bonner, Michael David, Megan Reif, and Mark A. Tessler. 2005. *Islam, Democracy and the
     State in Algeria: Lessons For the Western Mediterranean and Beyond*. Abingdon: Routledge.
Boudjedra, Rachid. 1971. *Naissance du cinéma algérien*. Paris: Maspero.
Brahimi, Denise. 2009. *50 ans de cinéma maghrébin*. Paris: Minerve.
Discacciati, Leyla. 2000. "The Image of Women in Algerian and Tunisian Cinema."
     ISM Newsletter 5/00. "Visual Arts": 37. www.library. cornell.edu/colldev/mideast/
     cinmwmn.html (accessed 31 March 2018).
Evans, Martin. 2012. *Algeria: France's Undeclared War*. Oxford: Oxford University Press.
Gauch, Suzanne. 2016. *Maghrebs in Motion: North African Cinema in Nine Movements*. Oxford:
     Oxford University Press.
Hadj-Moussa, Ratiba. 2014. "The Past's Suffering and the Body's Suffering: Algerian
     Cinema and the Challenge of Experience." In *Suffering, Art and Aesthetics*. Eds. R.
     Hadj-Moussa and M. Nijhawan. New York: Palgrave: 151–176.
Humbaraci, Arslan. 1966. *Algeria: A Revolution that Failed: A Political History since 1954*.
     London: Pall Mall Press.
Khanna, Ranjana. 2008. *Algeria Cuts: Women and Representation, 1830–Present*. Stanford, CA:
     Stanford University Press.
Lazreg, Marnia. 1994. *The Eloquence of Silence: Algerian Women in Question*. New York:
     Routledge.
Lequeret, Elisabeth and Charles Tesson. 2003. "Yamina Bachir-Chouikh." *Cahiers du cinéma*.
     Éditions spécial, "Où va le cinéma algérien?" Feb–Mar: 26–31.

Maherzi, Lofti. 1980. *Le cinéma algérien: institutions, imaginaire, idéologie*. Algiers: Société National d'Edition et de Diffusion.

Malley, Robert. 1996. *The Call from Algeria: Third Worldism, Revolution and the Turn to Islam*. Los Angeles: University of California Press.

Mbembe, Achille. 2000. *De la postcolonie: essai sur l'imagination politique dans l'Afrique contemporaine*. Paris: Karthala. 2001. Trans. *On the Postcolony*. Berkeley: University of California Press.

Mbembe, Achille. 2006. "On the Postcolony: A Brief Response to Critics." *African Identities* 4(2): 143–178.

Mediene, Benamar. 1992. "Un état déconnecté." *Le Nouvel Observateur*, Collection Dossiers, 9: "La Guerre d'Algérie trente ans après": 72–73.

Shafik, Viola. 2007. *Arab Cinema: History and Cultural Identity*. Cairo: American University of Cairo University Press.

Sharpe, Mani. 2015. "Representing Masculinity in Postcolonial Algerian Cinema." *The Journal of North African Studies* 20(3): 450–465.

Stora, Benjamin. 1994. *Histoire de l'Algérie depuis l'indépendance*. Paris: Éditions La Découverte.

Stora, Benjamin. 2001. *Algeria 1830–2000: A Short History*. Ithaca, NY: Cornell University Press.

Stora, Benjamin. 2014. "The Algerian War: Memory through cinema." *Black Camera* 6(1) Fall: 96–107.

Tazi, Mohamed Abderrahman and Kevin Dwyer. 2004. *Beyond Casablanca*. Bloomington: Indiana University Press.

Tesson, Charles. 2003a. "L'état des lieux." *Cahiers du cinéma*. Édition spécial, "Où va le cinéma algérien?" February–March: 5.

Tesson, Charles. 2003b. "Algérie année zéro." *Cahiers du cinéma*. Édition spécial, "Où va le cinéma algérien?" February–March: 14–17.

Zerari, Rabah (Si Azzedine). 1976. *On nous appelait fellaghas*. Paris: Editions Stock.

Ziad, Sofiane and Guy. 2011. "Mapping Algerian Cinema." www.mcc.sllf.qmul.ac.uk/?p=550 (accessed 31 March 2018).

Filmography

Allouache, Merzak. (2013). *Les terrasses (The Rooftops)*, Algeria / France: JBA Production.

Bachir-Chouikh, Yamina. (2003). *Rachida*, Algeria: Global Lens.

Djahnine, Habiba. (2008). *Lettre à ma sœur (Letter to My Sister)*, Algeria: Etouchane, Momento!, Polygone Étoilé.

Moknèche, Nadir. (2004). *Viva Laldjérie*, Algeria: Film Movement.

Sahraoui, Djamila. (2006) *Barakat! (Enough!)*, Algeria: Global Film Initiative.

Sahraoui, Djamila. (2012). *Yema*, Algeria: Néon Productions.

Salem, Lyès. (2015). *L'Oranais (The Man from Oran)*, Algeria: Haut et Court.

Salem, Lyès. *Masquerades*. (2008). Algeria: Urban Distribution International.

Teguia, Tariq. (2006). *Rome plutôt que vous (Rome Rather than You)*, Algeria: Flying Moon Film Production.

18

"Qu'elle aille explorer le possible!"
Or African Cinema according to Jean-Pierre Bekolo

P. Julie Papaioannou

Amidst various socio-political, institutional, theoretical crises, and "deaths" in recent world history – from the theoretical death of the author to dead revolutions and socio-political negotiations, dead cultural and racial interactions, or economic crises – Stefan Helgesson's suggestion (2011) that a "form of exit may also be historical and political rather than spatial: at a given moment, it becomes necessary for a society to leave its long-established forms of governance, production, and discourse behind" (p. ix), resonates with Jean-Pierre Bekolo's appeal in the mid-1990s to a "dead" African cinema. Since the early 1990s, there has been a continuous strife for a new aesthetic approach in African filmmaking to exit the dead-end of cultural determinism that derived from interpretations of African reality based on the dichotomy of a sterile rehabilitation of traditional cultural practices and the project of modernity in post-independence times. Influential filmmakers such as Jean-Pierre Bekolo, Jean-Marie Teno, and Abderrahmane Sissako began their artistic career with the objective, often considered controversial, to break new ground in African film aesthetics by adopting, yet challenging the militant auteur-oriented approach, and critical investigation within the postcolonial and post-modern framework. Third Cinema theorization initially appeared to offer the necessary critical tools to address African cinematic production in the divisive relationship of an illusionistic Hollywood-like reproduction of reality, and the cultural impression of reality in non-Western films. The critical focus on the connection between culture, narrative, and ideology was predominant in Teshome Gabriel's Third Cinema aesthetics (1989) that aimed at amalgamating popular memory via the visual sign, but conflated culture and ideology. Along with the objective to reinstitute cultural memory, Gabriel's systematic codification of cultural signs in

A Companion to African Cinema, First Edition. Edited by Kenneth W. Harrow and Carmela Garritano.
© 2019 John Wiley & Sons, Inc. Published 2019 by John Wiley & Sons, Inc.

African films also created the expectation of certain "African" aesthetic orientations that were primarily formed as a critical response to Hollywood and Western cinema. However, with the expansion and combination of genres and styles, modes of production and co-production, and the rise of new technologies in the globalized world, new critical approaches have been emerging, shifting, and forging the given theoretical paradigms not only to contest the old approach of an all-encompassing aesthetic formula to African film, but most importantly to question the way these theoretical and critical tools have been perceived with regard to the medium, and its aesthetic capabilities. The relevance of a postcolonial, postmodern Third Cinema that emerged about 25 years ago, has offered an appealing and laudable critical response to the hierarchization of theories and marginalization of "other" cinemas, as well as the theoretical ground to think about bridging binary gaps in order to address the question of a contemporary African film aesthetic. As Kenneth Harrow (2013) in *Trash: African Cinema from Below* states: "Art and politics remained at loggerheads as long as the issues surrounding their exigencies were addressed in frozen terms of aesthetics and political commitment, or commercial versus serious cinema" (p. 31). Seeking to redefine conceptual binaries such as "art" and "politics," and the relationship of "high" to popular art through the trope of trash, or rather "the economics of trash," Harrow asks anew the necessary critical question as to *how* to locate, problematize, and analyze questions that have been neglected in "the blurring of boundaries between documentary cinema and fiction" (pp. 31–32), and its requirements of "authentic" cultural representation.

Along these lines of theoretical investigation, Jean-Pierre Bekolo's filmmaking has long been considered exemplary in eluding an "authentic" cultural element, particular genres, and prescriptive categorizations. Bekolo has been experimenting with the potential of the medium within discursive and critical contexts since his *Quartier Mozart* (1992), and has continued to question binary oppositions and their bridging with *Aristotle's Plot* (1996), and *Les Saignantes* (2005). Viewed as artistically subversive, yet political toward critical questions of African film aesthetics, Bekolo has scrutinized, and attempted to stretch and reshape the boundaries of major concepts that are particular to the art of filmmaking. By challenging Third Cinema concepts, as well as epistemological ideas with regard to narrative, identification, and representation, Bekolo does not propose a "dead" African cinema by starting back at "zero," which would historically re-determine the medium, but instead he suggests a "zoom in and out" approach on the question as to what is considered "African" filmmaking and its aesthetics.

In this work, I consider *Quartier Mozart, Aristotle's Plot,* and *Les Saignantes* as a trilogy that bridges past beginnings and future endings in an attempt to address the question of African film aesthetics in its temporal relevance and spatial fluidity from one century to the next. I would argue that Bekolo's eclecticism in the making of his films derives from the desire for a filmic "pro-creation" as the possibility of artistic resistance to existing forms of representation, as well as the possibility of perceptual and cognitive changes in the world with the power of the visual, and imagination. I discuss the ways that Bekolo's critical project of *mantisme* (2009) has built an aesthetic direction for the *new* of the "new Africa," a sort of *contemporary cinéma engagé* with feminist overtones, which has also profoundly shaped the narrative of each one of his films, and attempted to take his filmmaking beyond the postmodern, postcolonial hybrid model that Cinema declares in *Aristotle's Plot:* "we take what we can get, if it is old and good fine, if it is new and it fits, excellent." Bekolo has traced a new path to African film aesthetics, and in doing so, he opened numerous possibilities for thinking about African film in connection with the world.

More precisely, his trilogy that began with a *fin-de siècle* appeal to a new contemporary African film aesthetics in mid-1990s, has created not only its own trajectory of an upbeat contemporary style, but also a critical proposal that aims to free African filmmaking from the impasse of a culturally determined representation. In other words, Bekolo detaches the "African" from "filmmaking" so that he can bring anew these terms together in a strong artistic and aesthetic connection. This trajectory begins with *Quartier Mozart* (1992) asking seminal questions about identification, the gaze and embodiment of the "other," and continues with *Aristotle's Plot* (1996) and the confrontation between the monopoly of Hollywood films and African film productions. Narrative modes, and processes of production, marketability, distribution and exhibition clash, and the shootout that ensues at the end of *Aristotle's Plot* calls for *Les Saignantes* (2005) to bury the "dead." Based on concepts already explored in *Quartier* and *Aristotle*, *Les Saignantes* provides a more solid redefinition of the medium's potential to go beyond the notion of cinema as a capitalist venture that dictates norms of representation, and become an artistic force that incorporates a feminine / feminist side in the process of creating images. However, in *Les Saignantes*, the pessimistic tale with a rather happy ending, the old SGCC (*Secrétaire Général du Cabinet Civil*) is missing the head, and the wake of an important person (WIP) that is staged as a red carpet ceremony in the manner of Hollywood is still under way at the end of the film. Interestingly, the allegory of the headless corps of SGCC is replicated in *Le président* (2013) when it is announced on reality TV that the Head of State is missing. The President is not declared dead but absent, yet his "absence" implies a spectral "presence" and exercise of power. If, from a pessimistic standpoint, Bekolo suggests that the burial of political agendas and ideologies of the past has not yet taken place within the context of African filmmaking, his documentary *Les choses et les mots de Mudimbe* (2015), an homage to the philosopher and scholar V. Y. Mudimbe, attempts to highlight the spectrality of philosophical and critical notions that inform our understanding of art. His latest film *Naked Reality* (2016), a highly aestheticized quest for identity via a futuristic rendition of an identity theft case, reconnects with his trendy and upbeat trilogy, *Quartier*, *Aristotle*, and *Les Saignantes*, and in an experimental, feminist, albeit at times surrealistic approach, Bekolo proclaims an Afrofuturistic film aesthetics that delves simultaneously in the present, and future.

Bekolo's book *Africa for the Future: sortir un nouveau monde du cinéma* [*Africa for the Future: Making a new world out of cinema*, my translation], published in 2009 after the completion of his first three films, lays out his transdisciplinary project to redefine the purpose of African cinema, and redirect the spectator's gaze to question the *status quo*, both through and beyond the pleasure of looking at stories. In this work, Bekolo introduces the concept of *lingua mantis* that he explains as a mental language, or mediate soothsaying, "le langage de la pensée" (p. 22), a language that expresses understanding and communication within a social locale, and the world at large. Bekolo proposes a system of thought that he calls *mantisme*, and he describes it as:

> Une manière d'appréhender le monde [selon] mon expérience, mon éducation, ma culture et mon environnement. Le *mantisme* est le système de pensée qu'on assimile quasiment à un langage qui est unique à chaque individu. Un langage que je "négocie" en permanence avec le langage de l'autre, cet autre avec qui je partagerais une expérience, une éducation, une culture ou un environnement similaire. (p. 22)

> [A way of apprehending the world based on my experience, my education, my culture and my environment. *Mantisme* is a system of thought that we virtually assimilate to a language that is unique to each individual. A language that I permanently "negotiate" with the language of the "other" with whom I would share an experience, education, culture and a similar environment.] (my translation)

The term *mantisme* finds its stem in the Greek noun μαντεία/*mantēa*, and μαντική/*mantikē* that appear in the suffix *-mancie* (-mancy) as in *cartomancie* (cartomancy, card reading) or *chiromancie* (palm reading), and incorporates temporal notions of a virtual and imagined reality, the desire to predict the future, as well as the instant gratification to be able to make use of future predictions in the present in a sort of divine approximation. Bekolo's discursive tropism to *mantisme* is a foretelling that implies the desire for an imagined future that is projected in multiple *mises en abîme*, and a constant negotiation with the self and the world in the understanding of present. It is also an attempt to break even with the space of similarity rather than otherness in the language of "similar other," and reconcile dichotomies that have long beguiled the African cinema critical discourse. By creatively attracting, incorporating, re-layering, and overlapping diegetic elements that pertain to the trajectory of African film and criticism, Bekolo establishes a narrative interconnectivity from *Quartier* to *Les Saignantes* in a subversive adaptability of tropes. His tropism toward *mantisme* for a new, *contemporary cinéma engagé* attests to the filmmaker's desire to actively proclaim the "death" of African cinema as such in *Aristotle*, only to have it rise from below, to use Harrow's reference (2013), in a fantasy world of tropes in worldbuilding mode. In popular fiction writing or videogame development, the worldbuilding connection of elements suggests a localized eco-mediatized imaginary world that develops piece by piece according to the developer's production and planning. In *Africa for the Future*, the notion of

worldbuilding – although Bekolo does not name it as such – relates to a new understanding of building an imaged locality within the globalized world through the
medium of cinema.

Bekolo's configuration of patterns of imagination and cognition in a designed
locality, parallels Arjun Appadurai's claim (2013) of "production of locality" in
social anthropology. According to Appadurai, the "production of locality" relies
on a complex project of people working through social resources and connections
on a daily basis to produce their environment:

> while human beings exercise their social, technical, and imaginative capacities,
> including the capacity for violence, warfare, and ecological selfishness, they literally
> produce the environments within which they function, including the biological and
> physical nature of these environments. (p. 66)

Appadurai argues that the notion of "production of locality" is inextricably linked to
the concept of predictability as a viable response to existing forces that support
difference, and exclusion. To that extent, Bekolo situates African cinema into a
pattern of localized productions that, along with the approach of *mantisme* as a
notion of predictability for its future, he attempts to connect it with the complexities
of the global world. As the medium preserves its exteriority/interiority in the process of creating an imaged locality and imagined reality, it allows the filmmaker to
maintain both a distance and close proximity in relation to the filmic object and its
locale. Bekolo's imaged locality and imagined reality (2009), as well as the relations
that develop between them, connect through the desire to create and project an
extra-ordinary place of imagination, a utopic place that may be contemporaneous
both to a local collective and social reality, and to communities around the world:

> Je vais donc me servir de ce support extérieur de la vie qui me permet de prendre du
> recul, de voir loin et près en même temps *versehen* en allemand, une *télé-vision*. Voir
> comment je m'attache à des motifs produits par mon imagination et qui finissent par
> devenir le prisme par lequel j'appréhende le monde et essaye de lui donner un sens.
> Je veux faire ce que fait le cinéma qui est à la fois un support et une sémantique pour
> nos utopies, je veux créer cet endroit dans lequel on pourra géographiquement
> situer cette société exemplaire. Parce qu'il est un support de la métaphore, le cinéma
> représente assez bien la forme mentale et rhétorique de mon colonialisme imagi-
> naire qui sert à la fois à *projeter* mon imaginaire sur la réalité extérieure de notre so-
> ciété et à extérioriser mes rêves enfouis sur des lieux jusqu'ici inaccessibles. (p. 49)

> (I am going to use this exterior support in life [the art of cinema] that allows me to
> step back, to look from a distance and up close at the same time, *versehen* in German,
> a *tele-vision*; to look how I get attached to motifs that are produced by my imagina-
> tion, and become the prism through which I apprehend, and try to assign meaning to
> the world. I want to do what cinema does, which is both a support and a semantic
> field for our utopias; I want to create this place in which we will be able to situate,
> geographically speaking, this exemplary society. Because cinema that supports

metaphor, represents quite well the mental and rhetorical form of my imaginary colonialism, which in turn serves to *project* my imaginary on the external reality of our society, and at the same time, externalize my dreams, hidden up to now in inaccessible places). (my translation)

The interplay that ensues in this creative process offers an extra-cinematic space, which often has been claimed by a predictable ideological engagement in African film aesthetics, and an anticipated contestation of the language of the "other," namely Hollywood and the commercial cinema of the West. From *Quartier* to *Les Saignantes*, the urgency of burying the old "dead" political commitments in the understanding and negotiation of difference and exclusion of African cinema is straightforward, all the more so if we consider the ever shifting cultural flow that creates new forms of political activism.

At the opening of *Les Saignantes*, the first billboard reads: "Comment faire un film d'anticipation dans un pays qui n'a pas d'avenir?" [How can you make an anticipation film in a country that has no future?], and the voice-over continues: "It *was* the year 2025, and nothing much had changed" (my emphasis). The use of a past tense in narrating the future pinpoints Appadurai's suggestion (2013) that in the era of globalization there is a new development in understanding relations within cultural flows, whatever these cultural flows may be, because they have "a curious inner contradiction" (p. 65) that may impede the freedom of their movement in the present and future. Bekolo's commitment to artistic activity questions the legitimacy of political, social, and critical structures in place, in order to define new relations and connections that would free African cinema and its value, be it aesthetic or commercial, from existing contradictions. To that extent, Bekolo has been characterized as revolutionary and *engagé*, because he maintains a critical distance toward any given local and social reality, yet he remains close to what Amílcar Cabral (1973) considers the struggle for liberation to be: "A mass character, the popular character of the culture," and for this reason "those who lead the movement must have a clear idea of the value of the culture in the framework of the struggle and must have a thorough knowledge of the people's culture" (p. 44). Clearly, Bekolo demonstrates not only a creative understanding of the potential of the medium as such, but also its potential in relation to mass culture in terms of cultural capital transmission, and cultural capital reception in a global perspective. With *Quartier Mozart*, Bekolo has transformed the landscape of African filmmaking by building from bottom up, looking imaginatively at a small urban neighborhood that finds its global resonance, because the visual text is consistently altering the relation between cultural transmission and reception. In other words, Bekolo values the filmic depiction of local cultural elements in global proportions via a witty appropriation of contemporaneous Western popular signs in global circulation: for example, references to Michael Jackson, Denzel Washington, or Lady Di for standards of sexuality or elegance in the neighborhood in *Quartier*; ET, Cobra, Nikita, Terminator in *Aristotle*, and the choreographed karate gestures in *Les Saignantes* as references to popular karate films and glossy Hollywood action movies, decentralize the main elements in the artistic process – namely the film narrative, representation, and identification – by the desire to both incorporate and express the "other" in order to open African cinemas to circuits of global connectivity, and circulation.

According to Bekolo (2009), the potential of the medium to virtually link to *everyone*'s story through identification has been overlooked since cinema was primarily linked to its commercial adaptability and capacity. As *pessimiste actif*, an active pessimist, Bekolo also questions what connects the value of cinema to economic capital, and its narrative of modern progress: "*Cette narrative réductrice* que génère l'argent à la vie" [this simplistic narrative that money assigns to life, my translation] (p. 72). However, if Bekolo aims at redefining African cinema, and its local and global value, it is not because he wishes to escape the commercial appeal of the medium which ensures its viability, or attack ideology as such, but first and foremost it is because he aims to bring to the foreground its connection with aesthetics and identification. He explains in *Africa for the Future*:

> Il convient de garder à l'esprit que le cinéma n'a jamais été véritablement défini parce que, dès sa naissance, son potentiel a fait qu'il a été accaparé, confisqué et enfermé dans la dimension commerciale, rendant quasiment accessoires ses autres dimensions, dont celle de *l'identification* qui ouvre le champ à une étude quasi scientifique sur l'Homme. (p. 46)

> [It is important to keep in mind that cinema has never truly been defined because, since its birth, its potential allowed it to be monopolized, confiscated, and limited in its commercial dimension, reducing virtually its other dimensions into supplements, amongst which that of *identification*, which opens the field to a virtual scientific study of Man.] (my translation)

If the visual and virtual properties of the medium, this quasi-utopian space in the magical connection of cinema's two-dimensional virtual reality on the screen with the spectator's three-dimensional local reality, have been primarily explored in their commercial value, Bekolo argues that the reconceptualization of this space of representation, and the process of identification are open for a new discussion. "A virtual scientific study of Man" through the art of filmmaking situates anew these questions as modern and political, but not forcibly or solely as ideological and cultural. African cinema has been declared "dead," precisely because it has come to an impasse in its dialectical contestation against its own "other," be it entertainment cinema, Hollywood, or the cinemas of the West that have long guided its aesthetic orientation towards a cultural or political cinema. As Harrow suggests in *Postcolonial African Cinema* (2007), "it is the retreat into safe and comfortable truisms that must be disrupted by this new criticism" (p. xi). In his trilogy, Bekolo always already articulates a new critical project to bring to focus the theoretical, and critical conventions that help us comprehend signs and codes to make meaning. In his most recent work *Naked Reality*, the futuristic narrative supports the notion of *mantisme*, and in the story of identity theft the "same" and "other," the "real" and "fake" face off to disrupt the processes of identification and representation. Bekolo argues that the immediate and mediated (*l'im-médiat*) space in filmmaking facilitates this disruption because the art of filmmaking itself addresses the question of meaning (*le sens*), and the meaning of life (*le sens de la vie*) (p. 48), the existent and the possible.

To that extent, it appears that Appadurai's notion of the *contemporary* (2003) that relies on the effect of *l'im-médiat*, the immediate and momentous shared situation or exchange, along with the existing notion of *cinéma engagé* that may inherently carry an archival critical and structural engagement as a different, or counter cinema to a modern dominant cinema of the West, conjure up a framework of "disjuncture" that comes as a destabilizing interaction to any prior causality. Appadurai's anthropological approach of "disjuncture" that explains an ad hoc reaction to reality, may be of great importance in this analysis, and the consideration of Bekolo's tropism to *mantisme*. Appadurai notably argues in an interview that:

> The kinds of causalities [that underlie Marxist thinking] about the relations among, for example, technology, production, and ideology not only have to be reconsidered but have to be reconsidered in an ad hoc manner depending on the situation. In other words, one cannot come to a given situation with a strong prior sense about how the causal flows work. That for me is what the word "disjuncture" captures. I use "relations" to refer to the strength of the Marxist approach, to say that these things are not simply randomly happening, that there are structured interactions between them. However, the forms of dispersal of these forces – ideological, technological, and social – make it difficult to have a general a priori sense of how they relate to one another. I would say a further word about the "new or contemporary" by going to the question on "the modern and the contemporary." The way I would make the distinction between the modern and the contemporary, which is a very generic way, is to say that modernity is a project whereas the contemporary is a condition. (p. 45)

For example, Bekolo's contemporary approach to *cinéma engagé* is disconnected from the marginal African *cinéma engagé* of the 1960s, because it has to be considered ad hoc, and on the spot, not in a symmetrical, complimentary, or oppositional relation to its previous political and ideological engagement. Bekolo (2009) has a similar stance with regard to the "virtual scientific study of Man" that may find its basis in an *ad hoc* shared human experience, not in an *a priori* Europeocentrist or antieuropeocentrist relation, but in a cognitive, mental construction in *lingua mantis* or *mentalais* (p. 22) that takes place in a locality and temporality without recourse to preconceived notions or structural relations. In addition, the notion of a "similar other" shifts the focus from the "other," and the global flow of cultural difference, to "similar" as a contemporary condition of what makes sense both physically and mentally in the process of identification. The notion of similarity in our humanity, as inextricably linked to the understanding of difference and its conceptualization in modernity, plays a pivotal role in support of Bekolo's idea of a "virtual study of Man." Understanding our own humanity and the world, leads also to the question of what constitutes the space of intersection in the common, shared human response. Harrow (2013) also raises these questions in his analysis on Jacques Rancière's notions of politics and aesthetics and the discussion of the "sensible" that link with Bekolo's *cinéma engagé* and its *contemporary* condition:

> what do we perceive as piecing together the fabric of the world that we experience in common, what comes to constitute the *"sensible,"* that is, the world of what is apprehended by our senses, the material words and things that together create a familiar regime. (p. 36)

Without promoting a regime of homogeneity in the narrative of "our" stories, Bekolo investigates the particular individual, or group elements as a common shared experience that "makes sense"; these narrative elements are summoned around the notion of the desire to speak, write, and act in connection with cinema in general, and African cinema in particular. Bordering the Deleuzian notion of sense that attempts to evade "the immanence of sense to language itself," and free "the condition of possibility of expression" (Poxon and Stivale 2011, p. 70) by organizing and instantiating the actual and virtual realms in a series and repetitions, Bekolo's *mantisme*, with its immediacy, as well as futuristic elements appears to be crucial to the circulation, repetition, and the ritual of exchanging imaged stories via the medium of cinema. Based on the human desire to project dreams both geographically and imaginatively onto a locale and into the future, the relevance of repetition and exchange of words and images to avoid "the pitfalls of representation within which difference is tamed by the mechanisms of resemblance, identity, analogy and opposition" (Poxon, and Stivale 2011, p. 70) becomes for Bekolo a desire for everyday knowledge of life, a school of life that focuses on elements of feel, and sense to treat difference and similarity. In *Africa for the Future*, for example, Bekolo's story of his effeminate uncle Claude, and tomboy cousin Claude plays and attracts their similarity around their proper name, their difference by sex and gender, and highlights the false truism in thinking of either Claude's identity by their sexual difference that is incongruous with their personality, desires, gender characteristics, and identification at different instances in their lives.

In fact, *Quartier Mozart* is based on such an allegory, with Queen of the Hood and My Guy incarnating the same gender qualities because of the desire to sense, and understand the world both physically and mentally from the point of view of the "other." The transformation of the Queen of the Hood into My Guy, the desire to undergo a virtual transgendered transformation to embody the "other," allusively sustains Bekolo's virtual space of understanding representation and identification not in antithetical terms but in a form of "disjunctive" contemporariness through the medium of cinema, and its potential to circulate words and images, visual, and virtual expressions of desire and imagination. From *Quartier* to *Les Saignantes*, and *Naked Reality*, Bekolo's project of *mantisme* as a contemporary critical and aesthetic engagement of projected desire increasingly becomes a sexy visual interplay of senses. In *Naked Reality*, for example, it culminates in the artist's orgasmic moment of inspiration that gets to be recreated in the "writing" of pleasure on the body of his muse. This act of writing is as real in gesture – we see the man write with a quill on the body of his angel without leaving any marks – as it is virtual, allusive, and imaginary because it is not traceable but only "projected" on the body. The aesthetic moment of Bekolo's *mantisme* is fashioned by desire in libidinal immediacy and futuristic projection. As the opening sequence of *Les Saignantes* suggests, Majolie's treacherous love affair with the SGCC invites desire as the expression of basic instincts, and the *eros* and *thanatos* of the old model of representation. It also invites identification through the gaze and pleasure of looking; yet, it provides a space for the imagination to be lifted, flip and float in space like Majolie in the harness. The creative process of filmmaking proliferates in its possibility to break down or alter narrative and visual elements in the name of virtual reality.

The embodiment of the "other" in *Quartier Mozart* with Chef du Quartier in the body of My Guy, the confrontation between Cinéaste and Cinema in *Aristotle's Plot*, and Majolie's and Chouchou's encounters with the network of political power in *Les Saignantes* articulate Bekolo's new creative project of *contemporary cinéma engagé* as an aesthetics that is conditioned by the filmmaker's own desire and seduction with the medium, and its potential of myriad possibilities of manipulating, and refashioning reality.

"Qu'elle aille explorer le possible!" – the possibility of a *she* cinema

All three films under discussion, *Quartier Mozart*, *Aristotle's Plot*, and *Les Saignantes*, propose a virtual critique of an African cinema stuck in aesthetics that does not make "sense," but more importantly, they explore a new territory in understanding a shared humanity in a creative exchange in the world. Bekolo (2009) argues, "le cinéma est un support qui nous permet de vivre les événements 'théoriques' comme si on les vivait dans la réalité" [Cinema is a support system, an aid that allows us to live 'theoretical' events as if we were living them in reality, my translation] (p. 48). Theory and praxis come virtually together; the magic of the visual finds its approximate interpretation in the notion of the virtual as a support system of understanding humanity in "a virtual scientific study of Man" (p. 46) in a secret rendez-vous in the dark to experience the treacherous pleasure of the "real" on the screen. As I have discussed, Bekolo's trilogy implies that this secret rendez-vous is immediate (*im-médiat*) like any other story projected on the screen; however, it remains elusive, and deceitful because the "real" provokes its own collapse into nothingness at the end of screening. The meaning of the story is disseminated, and deferred into the future, and according to Harrow (2011):

> It was only a game, a Freudian *Fort-Da* game, in which what seems to be here is soon gone; and if it is to be recovered, it is only because that which is recoverable is susceptible to loss, to absence, to lack, to deferring, dissemination, and difference. (p. 53)

Interestingly, however, in *Les Saignantes*, Bekolo's *mantisme* brings us up to speed with the year 2025 in a projection of an ever fleeting present into the future; this past of the future in *Les Saignantes* is located in our present, which retrospectively formulates the future of *Quartier Mozart* about 25 years ago. Along these lines, Bekolo attracts our attention to the "real" in its exclusivity as virtual reality of the future, and not the real as an "authentic" representation. His balancing of discursive tropes, and juggling of critical notions operates much like a fine-tuned throw of a boomerang that spins in time, and spirals in space much like Majolie's body in an erotic dance inviting the power of the SGCC, the "old wise role model" to its death-driven pleasure; the return to the initial spot, that of a *cinéma engagé*, is never the same, since the spinning and turning have already assigned to its move a new force that ensures its contemporariness. The two-dimensional *fort-da* game follows a spiraling motion, an operation in "disjuncture," like a helix of DNA, or Majolie hanging in a harness, who upon her stepping down assumes the position of a shooter, her arms and hands put together as if to point a gun to her sexual partner in a strong metaphor of the camera-weapon and *cinéma engagé* that deals with its own past in its contemporary and futuristic rendition. Bekolo's critical project on the role and function of African filmmaking and its aesthetics shares the Deleuzian project of difference and repetition in terms of a perpetual critique to expose the project of modernity. According to Melissa MacMahon (2011):

> In this movement, difference and repetition, in and for themselves, would be appreciated as the ultimate elements and agents of a thought "of the future": not a historical future, but the "future as the essential object of a vital and liberated philosophy" that would escape the "transcendental illusion" (the term comes from Kant). (p. 44)

In the laborious process of artistic and critical expression that propels itself in a non-linear historical time, this notion of the future incorporates *mantisme* and predictability, a projected dream that finds a path to strategically contest and negotiate the "old model" in place. This process systematically relates to the filmmaker's investigation of his own position, and the construction of narrative:

> I started my search at the root of European storytelling. Aristotle's *Poetics*.
> I needed a good story. The setting contemporary Africa. The protagonist, the filmmaker: Essomba Tourneur; ET we call him. When ET graduated and came home from France ... he refused to be "imperfect." He was *artiste maudit*. He thought he was an angel, but he was a spirit, an African spirit. (*Aristotle's Plot*)

In *Aristotles' Plot* the filmmaker is an alienated angel with an African spirit who refuses to see his art as a "different," "imperfect," and "illegitimate" copy of an ideal Hollywood-like filmmaking that substantiates itself by fundamental dualisms. In *Quartier*, this spirit transforms the Queen of the Hood into My Guy, and in *Les Saignantes*, this creative spirit, a dream of a robust and sexy African cinema in the future, descends as harnessed Majolie spiraling above the SGCC's body. Not surprisingly, this African angelic spirit is the driving force in the opening sequence of *Naked Reality*, unlocking the aesthetics of *mantisme*, and the idea of repetition, and multiplicity in an imagined future, not as a copy, replica, or simulacrum of what is essential, and therefore eternally developing, but what is potential and possible in its own multiplicity, and virtually escapes control in a locality and production of desire. In *Aristotles' Plot*, Bekolo's voice-over asks: "Why are African filmmakers young, upcoming, promising, emerging, developing, until they are 80 years old and then suddenly they become the ancestors, the fathers the old wise role model?" For Bekolo (2009), the medium's potential of the virtual and visual converges around the notion of externalizing an instinctive space, the desire to attain the "dreams hidden up to now in inaccessible places" (p. 49, my translation); supported by the metaphor of cinema, they can transform boundaries, challenge taboos, question and criticize both the real and imaginary, and most importantly connect with different communities in futuristic repetitions on a local scale with global affinities.

Quartier Mozart begins with the preamble that it "uses traditional Cameroonian folk beliefs to explore the sexual politics of an urban neighborhood," which summarizes at the outset the filmmaker's project to tackle questions that have preoccupied African cinema's creative expression, namely traditional oral storytelling, urban modernity, and identity. Rooted in a particular but relatable place and time, "an urban neighborhood" and Cameroonian folk beliefs, the narrative wittily spins around sexual politics as a metaphor for the art of filmmaking. Like Atango's sewing machine, the stylish elitist tailor who carries the nickname *Bon Bon des jeunes filles* because he attracts women by promising them to produce the Western-type dresses of their dreams, the film projector "stitches together" the moment of magic for Queen of the Hood, who has expressed her desire to transform into My Guy. Queen of the Hood, a girl in a young man's body, incarnates the spirit of a dynamic African cinema that will have to seduce Samedi, the daughter of the police commissioner Bad Dog in an allusive story of state control, sexual politics, and attraction as entertainment, as well as through the gravitational force of sex appeal and pleasure. Sexual politics in *Quartier* play out relations of power that echo Foucault (1978) in *History of Sexuality*:

> Sexuality is not the most intractable element in power relations, but rather one of those endowed with the greatest instrumentality: useful for the greatest number of maneuvers and capable of serving as a point of support, as a linchpin, for the most varied strategies. (p. 103)

In *Quartier*, sexual politics strategically operates as the "cheat sheet" for the narrative and form. If Samedi is unattainable because of Bad Dog's paternal authority and official power, Atango suggests that Queen of the Hood/My Guy try his Westernized mannerisms and strategies: "Tu gères Samedi?" [Do you manage Saturday? Do you seduce Saturday? my translation], Atango asks him at the soccer field. To seduce Samedi, My Guy has to confront the young boys of Mozart neighborhood in a soccer game; unable to keep up with the sport, he is "beaten up" both metaphorically and literally when he loses the game. However, in the evening at the same soccer field, the place of dreams and aspirations for the young boys in Mozart, Samedi has a date with Queen of the Hood/My Guy that is filmed in a telenovela fashion. My Guy is a *she*, and the form of the telenovela, suitable for mass entertainment like soccer, creatively alters the form of the film, and captivates audiences with its popular and romantic appeal. At the same time, if My Guy is considered as the young emerging cinema with new sensibilities, he has to compete against popular desires at the soccer field, Atango's Westernized practices, and Mad Dog's state power. In *Les Saignantes*, sexual politics are expressed by Majolie's treacherous and seductive maneuvers as the strategy to virtually maintain power and control against official networks, whereas in *Aristotle's Plot* the attraction/repulsion of the "similar other" is presented within the narrative of Cinéma and Cinéaste locked in handcuffs, controlled and mediated by the policeman: story and form, aesthetics and politics, commercial and auteuristic formulas are locked together in a relationship without a future. When Cinéma and Cinéaste compete for the control of movie theatres, they represent the uneven battle and power relations between commercial and artistic cinema, as well as the monopoly and control over film distribution and exhibition. Nonetheless, when they emerge intact at the end of the shootout, after they had "died," they express the filmmaker's undeniable admiration for the virtual power of the medium over our imagination and understanding of the real. In addition, the ending of *Aristotle* implies the potential virtual "death" and "rebirth" of African cinema, and its redefinition by similarities rather than oppositions.

The trilogy from *Quartier* to *Les Saignantes* proposes a space for African cinema that carries its moment of possibility to evade prescribed formulas, while at the same time it justifies this entire process of reproducing "real" images of Africa in as much as they are virtual and imagined. Bekolo claims a libidinal character to this space for African cinema, and assigns to it a futuristic appeal by virtue of desire in terms of virtual and visual gratification, and attraction of the gaze in an interplay of wishes and fears, of what makes sense in a certain place at a certain time. In this process, however, Harrow (2013) asks, "whose voices are heard and whose presence is attended to?" (p. 36). Whose libidinal space does Bekolo's cinema claim? When considered as a trilogy, Bekolo's first three films allow us to understand the space of *mantisme*, the mediation of filmmaker's *lingua mantis*, in terms of a feminine, maternal, and sexual, yet virtual space in a spiraling of notions around a contemporary non-antithetical conceptualization of a "similar other." In *Quartier*, for example, Maman Thecla performs Queen's of the Hood gender transformation before she transforms herself into Panka to cast spells to humble arrogant men by shaking their hands and making them lose their genitalia. In *Les Saignantes*, Majolie and Chouchou, celebrate their secrets, youth and femininity in Mevoungou, the mystical old ritual of Beti women. In-between these two films, *Aristotle* investigates the poetics of a good story:

> Crisis, confrontation, climax, and resolution.... Is there anything in this cinema which is not African? Fantasy, myth, we got. Walt Disney, we got. Lion King, we got. Sex, action, violence, we got. Massacres, we got. Comedians, music, we got. Paul Simon, we got. Aristotle, catharsis, kolanut, we got. (*Aristotle's Plot*)

In a Mevoungou-like moment, Bekolo continues in a voice-over: "Life or cinema? Because when cinema becomes your life, you're dead. It's dead. We are all dead." (*Aristotle's Plot*). If the real and virtual in filmmaking rely on the storyline (the plot), then what sort of conspiracy (plot) controls the visual in African filmmaking, and makes it only depend on reality? *Les Saignantes* provides answers as a "cautionary tale" (Bekolo 2009, p. 173) for the future: The metaphorical death of the "old papa" and the artistic expression that relied on old formulas of narrative and representation, as well as the attempt to build a new contemporary aesthetic approach at present would prevent African films from asking the same questions in 2025, in a never-ending WIP with a dead body that is "managed" and dismembered, still missing the head. In the opening scene, a sultry voice-over forewarns us about the prophetic, yet undefinable, and unexpected spell of the Mevoungou: "Mevoungou nous apparaît; il avait posté son dévoulu sur nous. Qu'on s'approprie, qu'on s'en serve" [Mevoungou appears to us; it has put a spell on us, captivated us; let's appropriate it, let's make use of it, my translation]. Majolie and Chouchou remind us that the old "dead" body of ideas has been circulating, as the forgotten corps of SGCC on the pavement, at the butcher's to be dissected as "du boeuf SGCC" [the Head of State beef], and "du boeuf virtuel" [virtual beef, my translation], or at the morgue. As a cautionary tale, then, *Les Saignantes* allegorically depicts the story of a "dead" African cinema that virtually circulates on state TV, in film festivals as images of particular geographies, or is stored in the vault of film museums. By keeping the head and dispersing the rest, Majolie and Chouchou negotiate the Deleuzian notion of "disembodied Ideas, and difference" that are not constricted "within the Same, that is, within common sense or representation" (Poxon, and Stivale 2011, p. 69), but within the difference of substitution. To that extent, the space of a new exciting cinema assigns a new "body" of ideas, in repetition, substitution, and manipulation of signs in the process of representation.

Moreover, *Les Saignantes* describe African cinema by the usage of the adjective *saignantes* in the plural of the feminine form to describe a condition in its contemporariness.

According to Judith Poxon, and Charles Stivale (2011), there is the Deleuzian notion that:

> bodies are dynamic and self-causing, while events, including Ideas, are caused by bodies. Linguistically, bodies are associated with nouns, while events are verbs, in particular infinitive forms of verbs. Bodies exist in the pure present, in being, while events subsist in both the past and the future, in becoming. (p. 69)

Majolie negotiates her condition as a bleeding body, a *saignante* "qui voit la lune" (that sees the moon) as a metaphor for menstruation, and periodic bouts of lunatic sense. As Majolie describes to Chouchou in their nocturnal wondering, *saignante* is the condition of the bleeding body that undergoes its deterritorialization, much like the bleeding mask-projector in *Aristotle's Plot*. Aesthetic expectations around notions of African tradition and reality make Majolie and Chouchou chant: "Not my clit, clit, clit" to Chouchou's mother in an allusion of Mevoungou rituals to refuse excision, and virtually decline the adjective *saignante*, and the process of their bodies' deterritorialization. As adjectives modify and describe bodies, ideas, and conditions, the title of *Les Saignantes* in the plural of the feminine form show-cases the potential of multiple possibilities in a *she*/cinema. Majolie is *saignante* in emotional pain and distress for the death of her mother, and her dreamlike fantasy of her own death wearing the exact same dress as her mother; at the same time, she is *saignante* in the karate scenes and cyborg attitude that describe Majolie's toughness: "Nous nous étions promises" Majolie and Chouchou state, "mais pas soumises" [We were hopeful, but not submissive, my translation]. At the end, the two women create the conditions to beat, cheat, and appease the moment of archival dualisms in African cinema, in order to make them dance and dream together "in technicolor": "Nous avions peut-être neutralisé la bête ... nous étions déjà mortes rien de pire ne pourraient nous arriver" [We had perhaps neutralized the beast ... we were already dead, nothing worse could possibly happen to us, subtitles in *Les Saignantes*).

The *mise en scène* in the opening sequence of *Les Saignantes* sets up "the machinic process," the moves and maneuvers of desire that break a taboo on the African screen by harnessing together the voyeuristic appeal of a sex scene in close ups of Majolie's naked body, and the repulsive attraction of SGCC's power. According to Kenneth Surin's discussion (2011) on Deleuze and Guattari's notion of "machinic process," this process "is a mode of organization that links all kinds of attractions and repulsions, sympathies, and antipathies, alterations, amalgamations, penetrations, and expressions that affect bodies of all kinds in their relations to one another" (27). In her sexual encounter with the SGCC, Majolie's body becomes the agent of this "machinic process," a force that expiates the past in a mimetic attempt to "appropriate" the phallus – to have it rather than be it – and mediate notions of patriarchy and state power. Upon the realization that the "papa" born in 1939 is dead, Majolie immediately calls her friend Chouchou to the rescue, and while Chouchou has to break away from her mother and women that await her for her virtual Mevoungou via her cell phone, Majolie "appropriates" the phallus once again when we see her urinate standing up, drunk in front of a group of men. "Comment reconnaitre mevoungou dans un pays ou les morts et les vivants se confondent" [How does one recognize Mevoungou in a country where it's impossible to separate the living from the dead? *Les Saignantes*] asks the voice-over. The living and the dead, ideas, actions, conditions are under the scrutiny of *mantisme*, and the desire to make sense out of them depends on the circumstances.

Discussing Deleuze and Guattari, Stivale explains that "it is desire, which is always social and collective, that makes the gun into a weapon of war, or sport, or hunting, depending on extant circumstances" (Stivale, p. 28). For Chouchou and Majolie, notwithstanding the circumstances, the libidinal space is their own to claim. Chouchou often calls Majolie Guy, an indirect reference to My Guy in *Quartier*, peeks through to see Majolie's naked body, and shares a bed with her, as we see them waking up together arm in arm.

Majolie and Chouchou designate the current state of African cinema that is double-bound by its colonial past and postcolonial condition, in parallel with any feminist discourse that would describe the voiceless "other," the condition of the woman as a double-bound subject by patriarchal order and its postcolonial condition. However, in an attempt to replace the dead body at the morgue, so that he might virtually be buried, the two women undertake an ironic critique of any process that decontextualizes relations without reterritorializing them. Majolie's and Chouchou's friendship builds the active moment amidst a pessimistic science-fiction tale, and since they still hold on to "the head," the knowledge, the science of making movies, they reclaim "the body," the story, the fiction, the dream of exhibition. In the karate scenes, they claim the body of a market that has been denied to them, as well as their own bodies in a coordinated choreography of sexual moves. If in the final sequence of *Les Saignantes*, Majolie and Chouchou exit a movie theatre onto the street laughing, it is to dissuade us from having (Afro) pessimistic thoughts about the future of African cinema: "Nous vivions en 2025 pas de place pour le désespoir" [We were living in the year 2025, no place for pessimism or despair, my translation].

The understanding that it was a dreamlike story for the purpose of making a film connects *Les Saignantes* with the opening statement in *Africa for the Future*: "Au commencement il y a toujours une histoire" [At the beginning, there is always a story, my translation] (Bekolo, 2009, p. 13). For Bekolo, the universal power of storytelling that clearly informs any filmmaker's work, builds around the importance of telling one's story through the shared moment of "sensing" the other, acting, and speaking in familiar interactions within the story, a relatable moment which unfolds with the greetings and hugs every time upon his return to his village. From *Quartier* to *Les Saignantes*, story and form alternate, attract, and complement each other for the subtext to make "sense," "pour neutraliser la bête et se débarasser de mevoungou" [to neutralize the beast and get rid of Mevoungou, *Les Saignantes*]. Bekolo's subversive and artistic interpretation of a libidinal, futuristic, and feminist space in his films traces the possibility of understanding anew questions of representation and identification in African filmmaking. Bekolo's seduction with image and imagination, real and virtual, and the appropriation of the sign of "self" and "other" in a unique production of a contemporary condition of *mantisme*, sense, sensibility, sensuality and sexuality reclaims or rather reterritorializes the "body" of African cinema aesthetics. In the process, the ultimate goal is to reconnect cinema with the power of fiction, and express the desire of the young and young at heart with the upbeat and fashionable circulation of contemporary elements in a continuous critical engagement with the politics of *mantisme* as an immediate response to mediation. The notion of desire and attraction, the force of a sex appeal that draws together the action of creativity, and imagination is expressed in Bekolo's idea (2009) of a future launch of "une Africaine dans l'espace" [an African woman in space, my translation] (p. 141); however, Queen of the Hood, Majolie, and Chouchou have already been launched into space in a time capsule to become Wanita in the Afrofuturistic *Naked Reality*. Bekolo has answered the questions he was asking in *Quartier Mozart, Aristotle's Plot*, and on billboards in *Les Saignantes* with one simple answer to all: "Qu'elle aille explorer le possible!" [She can explore the possible!, my translation] (p. 144), and in his latest film, Wanita undertakes this exploration in a highly mediatized world.

References

Appadurai, Arjun. 2003. "Illusion of Permanence: Interview with Arjun Appadurai." *Perspecta*, 34: 44–52. www.jstor.org/stable/1567314 (accessed 31 March 2018).

Appadurai, Arjun. 2013. *The Future as Cultural Fact: Essays on the Global condition*. London and New York: Verso

Bekolo Obama, Jean-Pierre. 2009. *Africa for the Future*. Achères, France: DAGAN &Yaoundé, Cameroon: Medya

Cabral, Amílcar. 1973. "National Liberation and Culture." In *Return to the Source*, edited by Africa Information Service, 39–56. New York and London: Monthly Review Press with AIS.

Foucault, Michel. 1978. *The History of Sexuality* (vol. 1). New York: Random House.

Gabriel, Teshome H. 1989. "Third Cinema as Guardian of Popular Memory: Towards a Third Aesthetics." In *Questions of Third Cinema*, edited by Jim Pines, and Paul Willemen, 53–64. London: BFI Publishing.

Harrow, Kenneth. 2007. *Postcolonial African Cinema*. Bloomington: Indiana University Press.

Harrow, Kenneth. 2011. "Let Me Tell You About Bekolo's Latest Film, *Les Saignantes*, But First …". In *Exit: Endings and New Beginnings in Literature and Life*, edited by Stefan Helgesson, 45–55. Amsterdam, New York: Rodopi.

Harrow, Kenneth. 2013. *Trash: African Cinema from Below*. Bloomington: Indiana University Press.

Helgesson, Stefan. 2011. "Introduction: Exit." In *Exit: Endings and New Beginnings in Literature and Life*, edited by Stefan Helgesson, ix–xiii. Amsterdam and New York: Rodopi.

MacMahon, Melissa. 2011. "Difference, Repetition." In *Gilles Deleuze: Key Concepts* (2nd edition), edited by Charles J. Stivale, 44–54. Durham: Acumen.

Poxon, Judith L., and Charles J. Stivale. 2011. "Sense, Series." In *Gilles Deleuze: Key Concepts* (2nd edition), edited by Charles J. Stivale, 67–79. Durham: Acumen.

Surin, Kenneth. 2011. "Force." In *Gilles Deleuze: Key Concepts* (2ndeEdition), edited by Charles J. Stivale, 21–32. Durham: Acumen.

Filmography

Bekolo, Jean-Pierre. (1992). *Quartier Mozart*. Kola Case, Cameroon Radio Television. Cameroon.

Bekolo, Jean-Pierre. (1996). *Aristotle's Plot*. JBA Production, BFI. France, Zimbabwe.

Bekolo, Jean-Pierre. (2005). *Les Saignantes*. Quartier Mozart Films, é4 Television. France, Cameroon.

Bekolo, Jean-Pierre. (2013). *Le président*. Cameroon, Germany.

Bekolo, Jean-Pierre. (2015). *Les choses et les mots de Mudimbe*. Cameroon.

Bekolo, Jean-Pierre. (2016). *Naked Reality*. Cameroon.

Part VII

Movement / Fluidity and Aesthetics / Migration

19

Relational Histories in African Cinema

Sheila Petty

In an era of slippage between borders and hybridization of cultures, narratives, and aesthetic constructs through film art, it seems inevitable that Eurocentric linear configurations of nation and history are subsumed by newer paradigms of postcoloniality and globalization. However, this is not a process without challenge. In discussing "the relationship between globalization and postcoloniality," Simon Gikandi asks if these terms emerge from "a general state of cultural transformation in a world where the authority of the nation-state has collapsed or are they codes for explaining a set of amorphous images and a conflicting set of social conditions" (2001, p. 628). Has, as Gikandi contends, "the failure of the nationalist mandate," created a void where irreconcilable impulses are destined to compete without resolution? Or are there other ways of viewing the cultural transformations resulting from globalization that escape the uotpia/dystopia binary so often associated with this process? (p. 630).

Cinema in most areas of the African continent developed as a postcolonial industry,[1] born alongside nations' independence. In French-colonized areas, the major production imperative during the 1960s and 1970s was the reversal of the colonist's gaze and the reappropriation of African cultural space, ideology, and images. A fractured, often convoluted association emerged between France and its ex-colonial African territories, fueled by opposition to the so-called "mission civilisatrice" that disparaged indigenous cultures and languages of its colonies by valorizing all aspects of French culture. Present-day discourses in France surrounding issues of sub-Saharan African and North African immigration and migration still echo with the racism and exclusion that characterize the tension of a nation uneasy with cultural difference but dependent on the profit immigrant labor

provides. Arising out of this conflicted cultural terrain, African filmmakers north
and south of the Sahara as well as in the diaspora create filmic works that probe
what it means to be African in such globalized contexts.

In his 2013 *Africa and France: Postcolonial Cultures, Migration, and Racism*, Dominic
Thomas argues that "since at least the 1970s, Africa and African-centered films
have successfully evaded simple categorization" and have contributed significantly
to the "expansion and decentralization of the parameters of French-language film
production itself" (p. 8). Thomas further argues that the transnational, globalized
geographic spaces and contexts of African films have "also been accompanied by a
thematic evolution" reflecting the concerns of transnational populations (pp. 7–8).
Gikandi contends that, "the most powerful signs of globalization" can readily be
seen in "works of art" that take "a frame of reference" from contexts informed by
transnational impulses (p. 632). For filmmakers north and south of the Sahara
whose works draw from global contexts, a new type of film poetics is emerging
that moves beyond the oppositional to probe relational, rather than static, binary
interactions between flows of race, religion, histories, and events. As Chielozona
Eze posits, "identity is no longer shaped exclusively by geography or blood, or
culture understood in oppositional terms. ... identity is now relational ... fluid ...
and now shaped by ... cultural and racial intermixing" (p. 235).

Thomas mainly asks what it means to be French and African, exploring the role
France has played in Africa, the influx of Africans to France, and their influence on
French history (p. 7). This chapter proposes an entry into the exploration of this
complicated terrain by looking at how relational identities are constructed in two
films made by French-Maghrebi-French-Africans on the continent and in the diaspora. More specifically, I will focus on the work of Alain Gomis (*L'Afrance*, Senegal/
France, 2001) and Rachid Djaïdani (*Rengaine*, France, 2012) who are both searching
for a new cinema aesthetic to reflect journeys, relational movement and identity
construction. Their films underscore that "place and origin are no longer exclusive
markers of identity, even if they still play vital roles in many people's self-reading"
(Eze 2014, p. 238). They employ cinematic techniques that create delocalized, fluid
spaces in which character identities are shaped by selective and multiple affinities
to colonial culture, ancestral culture, and adopted cultures. Identities are no longer
constructed in opposition to, or in reaction to another force. The relational model
of identity is highly-inflected with openness to diversity and dialogue.

From Here to There (or There to Here)

How do we get to the relational? What kind of journey is required to get from here
to there? One of the foremost thinkers of the concept of relation is the Martinican
Édouard Glissant who invoked a metaphorical journey of sorts as he was working
through his theory of "poetics of relation." Famously declaring, "Where histories

meet, History comes to an end," he denounced dominant hierarchical European history as an oppressor of more local and plural histories. These latter histories, along with their participants, are the products of cultural interactions operating on global levels (2010, p. 199). Slavery and colonialism wrought dispossession and disjunction from self, and the antidote to this is an exploration of all forms of oral and written storytelling, multilingualism, travel and migration, and defiance of established boundaries. Unpredictable combinations and re-combinations of travel, movement and interactions allow for the emergence of innovative artistic and cultural practices.

What links art-making, cinema and filmmakers of the African continent and the diaspora? Is it geography alone, whereby a filmmaker "belongs" to the category by virtue of her or his (or their parents) birth on (or off) African soil? But then what can one do with all the languages, cultures and ethnic groups from Cape Town to Algiers and across the continent from Dakar to Mogadishu? French colonialism provides the major link between sub-Saharan African and Maghrebi cinemas. However, the contexts are quite different in terms of colonial legacy, history, politics, cultures, and ethnic composition. I believe it is valuable to consider the origins of the Algiers Charter of African Cinema, adopted at the Second Congress of the FEPACI (Fédération Panafricain des Cinéastes) in Algiers, January 1975. The Congress brought together filmmakers from around the continent keen to build viable film industries in the wake of independence. The Congress and Charter clearly recognized the continental link of common oppression through various histories of colonization. The Charter describes cinema as a "stimulus to creativity," but when writing about African film, critics often gloss over this factor in favor of describing how the films promote the pedagogical goal of conscious-ness-raising (Bakari and Cham 1996, p. 25). This overwhelming focus on the educational imperative had a significant impact on the direction that African film criticism would take for several years.[2] The point I am trying to get at here is that freedom of expression was encouraged to take root in all directions, not just in one way or one direction: The roots of oppression were common and filmmakers' concerns for means of production, distribution, and exhibition were shared north and south of the Sahara, but the outcomes of expression were meant to be myriad, fluid, reconfigured, and remediated into multiple journeys, not one-way dead-ends.

The work of Achille Mbembe is useful here because he has held that "fixed identity is the source of cultural death" (*Africultures*, 5 September 2007) and the "movement of worlds" as he describes it, creates histories that must be understood as "cultures of mobility" emerging in response to internal and external contacts (*Africultures*, 26 December 2005). Yet, the fact that France has never been able to relinquish its hold, psychologically, politically and economically on its Empire has had serious impacts on directions and paths taken by filmmakers of African ancestry. With no national funding structures in place following independence, most filmmakers were forced to look to Paris and the early decades of African filmmaking were marked by productions that profited from French funding but espoused national and cultural autonomy (Barlet 2015, p. 318). In later years, before digital filmmaking took hold, filmmakers of African ancestry in France were forced to shoot their films in Africa if they wanted to benefit from French Coopération funding (p. 319). Subjectivity risks being washed away in a flood of terms and categories brandished by France since the 1980s as it struggles to come to grips with a rapidly-changing population who is challenging the nation's myth of universal Republicanism and integration. These categories, argues Caroline Trouillet, are constructed according to specific historical, social, and economic contexts and the politics of hospitality (2014, p. 84). These categories or labels are built to be static and fixed, with spaces and distances set up in Manichean fashion between "French" and "not really French" and "immigrant" and "not really immigrant." The spatial and social segregation created by these polarities forces occupants back into static spaces of ethnic origin and sets up the desired category of belonging (appartenance as a "Français de souche") to the French nation as the immigrant's (Français issu de l'immigration) ultimate achievement (pp. 86–88).

How then to move beyond the fixity of origin toward fluidity and movement, reconfiguration and remediation? In their article, "Remediation," Jay Bolter and Richard Grusin argue that "in the case of hypermedia, the subject is defined as a succession of relationships with various applications or media. She oscillates between media … and her subjectivity is determined by those oscillations … and insofar as we are mediated, we are therefore remediated, because in each case we also understand the particular medium in relation to other past and present media" (1996. P. 355). Is this a way, therefore, to "mobilize fluid identities" as Mbembe would have it, and forge new ways "for speaking about postnational human communities"? (Mbembe cited in Werbner and Ranger 1996, p. 1; Nimis 2014, p. 48).

One of the major contemporary theorists of movement within the African diaspora, Paul Gilroy, has described the crisscrossing movements of Africans across the Atlantic as a journey of peoples who are not only commodities through slavery, but are also engaged in various struggles toward emancipation, autonomy and citizenship. He sees these journeys as creating a means in which to reexamine the problems of nationality, location, identity, and historical memory (1993, p. 16). In fact, he lays claim to an "identity of passions between diverse black populations" (1996, p. 18). Thus, for Gilroy, diasporic experience transcends nation and cultural specificity of origin because the struggles to maintain identity in the face of dispersal creates a common, perhaps even overwhelming bond. There is some persuasive support for Gilroy's construct. Consider, for example, the case of Fanon whose identity is a culmination of several journeys, i.e. Martinique + France + Algeria = Fanon the transnational. And if one were to discuss Fanon as only Martinican, or Algerian, without discussing his relationship to France, you would only be examining narrow layers of his total identity. In a sense, Fanon's writings were generated by the interstitial spaces or relationships between his various journeys and were, in part, a reaction to the transcontinental movement known as Negritude which glorified an untouched Africa, rooted in a distant lost past. Fanon was critical of Negritude because he saw in it an impossible journey to a nostalgic place that does not reflect change, but instead merely reverses the colonizer/colonized binarism.

To be fair, Gilroy is not valorizing the essence of African origin, but rather, similarities of black diasporic experiences. Edward Said would disagree with the valorization of exile as a positive experience and has described exile as "the unhealable rift forced between a human being and a native place, between the self and its true home" (1990, p. 357). Said argues that exile is "unbearably historical" and its scale in contemporary times prevents it from ever being viewed as humanitarian as "it has torn millions of people from the nourishment of tradition, family and geography" (pp. 357–358). Unlike Gilroy, Said perceives flows of exiles to be linked primarily by historical circumstances rather than by the experience of exile itself – thus, each experience of exile is separate and the African diaspora is a patchwork of experiences generated on the basis of separate and individual historical imperatives. Said suggests that exiles have an urgent need to reconstitute broken lives and cultures and in order to bear the pain of dislocation, create political structures within which to view their cause as just, and to provide a sense of identity in a world of otherness. Gilroy focuses on similarities of experiences while Said is more concerned with differences of experiences, but both views add value to the ever evolving debate.

The term "Afropolitan" has been proposed to foreground the notion that identity is always in motion, with one of its key proponents, Achille Mbembe, defining this state as "a way of being 'African' open to difference and conceived as transcending race" (*Eurozine* 1 September 2008). Mbembe considers this process to be incomplete, and subject to "tensions and contradictions," but sees this as a present and future state that will redefine how the world sees Africa and, in turn, how Africa sees the world (*Eurozine*, 1 September 2008). Eze would also agree here claiming that the situation is not perfect, but that Afropolitanism does allow one to "grasp the diverse nature of being African or of African descent in the world today" (p. 2014, 239). Here, the Afropolitan circulates within the larger cosmopolitan context of humanity, bypassing in a sense the politics of location and specific geographies – is there an inherent danger here of glossing over specific histories of oppression, but also histories of achievement, allowing others to index lives? Eze's insight into Afropolitanism within the more global movement of cosmopolitanism opens a fruitful space for considering the films *L'Afrance* and *Rengaine*. Borrowing the term, "moral topography" from Charles Taylor, Eze opens up its use beyond the ways in which Taylor saw the "Western sense of self" evolving over time, to now include a sense of becoming and interconnectedness with others beyond skin color: "The African interconnected moral self. ... is the self in conversation with the other" (p. 244). Eze still sees Afropolitans as rooted geographically and through specific communities, but now these communities are "polychromatic, polymorphic, diverse, and open" (p. 245).

Other recent frameworks for describing experiences and states of being African-European (Afro-European) include "migritude" and "Afropeanness," terms deployed most often within the context of literary production. Afropean authors, for example, write in French and deal with the thorny issue of navigating both African and European spaces, identities and thought patterns. As John Nimis has argued:

> the term Afropean has become useful given that it incorporates the term European – which designates a postnational economic community (the EU) – while also referring to "whites" as a racial category. For the prefix "Euro" is substituted "Afro," which like Euro, refers to both a continent (i.e. a larger than "national" formation) *and* a racial category. Afropeanism is thus more grounded in this duality than more universalizing terms such as *négritude* or the more recent "Afropolitan." (2014, pp. 48–49)

Nimis further elaborates that being Afropean involves seamless mixing and movement across spaces and distances, but also "across imagined categories of humans" (black and white) (p. 49). Sub-Saharan African-born authors such as Fatou Diomé (Senegal), Lauren Ekué (Togo), and Alain Mabanckou (Republic of Congo) grapple with themes pertaining to their communities in France but always from different gender, class, or national perspectives making it impossible, according to Dominic Thomas, to apply any sort of schematic to the overall corpus of work being produced (2014, p. 22).

Is there a way past the hyphenated identity of Afro-this or that – indexes deemed threatening, as Nicki Hitchcott describes it, to European national identities? (2014). Gilroy provides yet again some insight when he opines that "we need to conjure up a future in which black Europeans stop being seen as migrants. Migrancy becomes doubly unhelpful when it alone supplies an explanation for the conflicts and opportunities of this transnational moment in the life of Europe's polities, economies, and cultural ensemble" (2004, p. xxi). However perceptive this is, there is an undercurrent of double consciousness which ultimately always leads back to the necessity and negotiation of two states of being. The Canadian George Elliott Clarke coined the term "poly consciousness" to express the process and ramifications of negotiating multiple identities by blacks in Canada where reference points are the homeland (for recent arrivals), African Americans, and indigenous black Canadians, all of which must be negotiated within the frame of Canadian multicultural politics (1998, p. 17).

It would seem here that migritude might provide a useful entry point to the dilemma of identity construction in transnational contexts. Dominic Thomas has pointed out that there are "critical and theoretical precursors to Afropeanism," most notably migritude which seems to bundle together notions of both immigrant and expatriate belongings. Thomas attributes the term to Jacques

Chevrier (2004) who first used it to explain how the early-twentieth century cultural and philosophical precepts of "negritude" could be linked with African migration to France later in the same century (Thomas 2014, p. 21). This concept, however, along with that of "Afrique sur Seine" deployed by Odile Cazenave in 2005, to denote immigrant sub-Saharan African authors who have turned their focus away from their continent of birth toward France almost exclusively, seem to place most emphasis on the expatriate status of the authors. I would argue that these tropes, although important for the framing and exploration of much literary production, fall short of fully describing and assessing the relational spaces and positions occupied by ALL "afrodescendants" (persons of African ancestry) in Europe. They all posit Africa as source, but they seem to only designate persons of sub-Saharan African or Caribbean origin, thus privileging blackness as a category and striving for a black French presence fully recognized by the French nation-state. Furthermore, migritude conjures up notions of roaming and wandering like a flâneur, as if the protagonist is not sure which direction he or she should take, an aimless wanderer, so to speak, with the luxury of living a nomadic lifestyle. I do, however, agree with Thomas that Afropean literary production has been successful in,

> the vibrancy, ingenuity, creativity and capacity of protagonists to imagine the contours of a diverse and inclusive France, and … the ways in which the concerns and objectives of Afropeans are inseparable from the broader project of Europeanization, and of Europeans' own reckoning with colonial history, its legacy and the multiple configurations of expanded twenty-first-century identities. (2014, p. 28).

The terms keep evolving into ever-new descriptions of experiences which in, and of themselves, are not new. Racial discrimination as a result of French colonialism is a constant reminder and a constant marker of what one is not, regardless of which name one takes on. Here, the work of Moroccan thinker Abdelkébir Khatibi might help provide another way forward. His work links very closely with that of Édouard Glissant since it deals with "cultural plurality and relationality created by colonialism" but he cautions that "multiple differences" must necessarily result from varying "engagement with the effects of colonialism in the Maghreb" (Hiddleston 2009, p. 126). Khatibi conceives of a "plural Maghreb," which he imagines as a layering of Derrida's thinking on deconstruction with that of decolonization to account for multiple differences and multiple languages (linguistic relationality) within the Maghreb. In his landmark study entitled, *Maghreb pluriel* (1983), he maps out his idea of plural thinking and "pensée-autre" to explore what he considers the multiple differences which constitute the Maghreb. He proposes a dismissal of European society from the Maghreb (reminiscent of Fanon) and argues for a process of identity construction that always calls itself into question while acknowledging: The limitations of simply embracing Western influence, the undesirability of a return to source, and the necessity of exploring the rich multi-plicity of differences that constitute the Maghreb. Khatibi names three schools of thought that he claims have impeded the evolution of philosophical and cultural thinking in the Maghreb: Rationalism and its limitations; traditionalism and the embracing of hard-line concepts of theological doctrine; and Salafism with its simultaneous inability to move beyond strict binarisms of self and other, or us and the enemy (much like colonialism). Khatibi's thinking has proven prescient 30 years after its publication. Consider, for example, the recent documentary film, *Salafistes* (France/Mauritania, 2016) by François Margolin and Lemine Ould Salem in which several high-profile Salafi leaders and theorists are interviewed, with one proclaiming that Mohammed Merah, the 23-year-old French man (described as Franco-Algerian in most of the press) who shot and killed seven people (including three children at a Jewish school in Toulouse) in March 2012, was "a fruit with thorns that France cultivated with its colonial politics. France is the real terrorist." It seems there is no middle ground. The word "Salafi" is derived from the Arabic, "as-salaf as-saliheen," which refers to the first three generations of Muslims known as the Pious Predecessors. Salafis are fundamentalists within Sunni Islam who pro-mote a return to practicing the religion's early ways including an eye for an eye and a life for a life. Indeed, *Salafistes* shows many images of these practices in and around Timbuktu, including footage of preparations for the execution of a cattle herder who allegedly killed a Bozo fisherman and an interview with the judge involved in the case. Interestingly, the film's directors claim that Abderrhamane Sissako's film *Timbuktu* (2014) was actually inspired by events in *Salafistes*, espe-cially the first 20 minutes of footage.

Ultimately, Khatibi champions a process of bilingualism as an open-ended exchange between cultures and languages, but which carries with it something of the untranslatable. He is firm in his belief that there is no linear continuity between classical and modern Arabs and that it is impossible to essentialize Arab identities (1983, pp. 179–207). Although Khatibi's work is extremely illuminating and provocative, and moves beyond thinking that essentializes Arab and North African identities, it is nevertheless grounded in the specific region of the Maghreb. What happens then when we gather all the threads of diaspora, exile, migritude, Afropeanness, Afropolitanism, relationality and pensée-autre together? Can we create a framework for understanding creative relationalities of being Afro-Arabo-pean in present-day France, and perhaps by extension, the globe? Valérie K. Orlando (2013) has very aptly extended the work of Khatibi and others in her analysis of the Afropolitanism in the writings of Moroccan authors, Youssouf Amine Elalamy and Fouad Laroui. She argues that they espouse a "being-in-the-world" which promotes "movement forward, to engage in *becoming* something other than the pessimistic stereotype associated with Morocco as well as the African continent" (2013, p. 275). Orlando, building on Khatibi, sees cultures as fluid and relational and this analysis helps steer the debate in the direction of fluidity and movement in twenty-first-century "being-in-the-world."

Twenty-first-Century Ambiguous Adventures: *L'Afrance*

Olivier Barlet has argued that cinema based on the experience of the rising African presence in France has existed for some time and is in constant evolution (Barlet 2015, p. 315). The two films chosen for this chapter provide excellent examples of Barlet's assertion. In both films, the main protagonists undergo a sort of initiation journey and experience identity crises set in motion by racism (on the part of others, or the protagonist himself) – from the student turned sans-papier (clandestin) El-Hadj in *L'Afrance* to second-generation Afro-Arabo-pean Slimane in *Rengaine*. Both are transformed by the end of the films as a result of their own personal journeys.

In *L'Afrance*, Alain Gomis explores the fluid spatial and psychological dynamics between France and Senegal. The central protagonist, El-Hadj Diop is a young Senegalese student in Paris, attempting to complete his DEA (Diplôme d'Études Approfondies) in History and has declared his intent to return to Dakar to teach where his family and fiancée, Awa, reside. Although it is unstated in the film, the requirement to return to teach in Senegal would likely have been a condition of his government's bursary funding. He meets a young white French woman, Myriam, with whom he begins a romantic liaison. He allows his carte de séjour (identity card) to expire and when he tries to renew it he is immediately arrested, physically abused, and held in custody in a detention center for several days. Upon his release and the restoration of his carte de séjour, he is faced with the dilemma of whether to stay in France or return to Senegal.

In between France and Africa ... in the process of becoming ... this state of existence embodied by El-Hadj is the reason Alain Gomis decided to title his first feature film, *L'Afrance*, a sort of métissage of the two geographical, cultural, and psychological spaces. But it is really so much more than that; Gomis himself was born in France to a Senegalese father and French mother. After studying art history and obtaining a Master's degree in film (Paris I – Sorbonne), he taught video workshops for the municipality of Nanterre. During the time he held this position, he directed several media reports focusing on youth like himself who are the off-spring of immigrant parents. After directing several short films, he made his debut in feature filmmaking with *L'Afrance* in 2001. He has since directed *Andalucia* (2007), *Tey (Today)* (2012), and *Félicité* (2017).

L'Afrance is groundbreaking not only for its story, which probes complicated ideological and psychological terrain, but also for its visual and narrative aesthetics. The film opens with a sustained (1 minute and 12 seconds) extreme close-up shot of a young African man, who we eventually learn is El-Hadj. He is positioned so far left in the frame that the right side of his face is cut off by the frame's edge, leaving almost half the frame on his left (screen right) empty. This is an extremely fascinating composition for the opening of any film, but especially an African film, where characters, at least up until this point in African film history, have almost always been defined within the frame of landscape and community. Naysayers could argue that this is because Gomis is not African-born but French-born through immigration![3] As a director, however, Gomis's choice of a loosely-framed extreme close-up in closed form denotes a blending of so-called Western and African aesthetic tropes. Visually, he begins setting up a space in-between, a space of migritude which will thread throughout the film. The framing of this extreme close-up does not immediately allow the viewer to situate the physical geography of the diegesis. Is El-Hadj in France, in Senegal, or somewhere else? Gomis forces the viewer to concentrate on the emotion of the image as El-Hadj gazes off-screen left. Incredibly, movement in this frame space appears dynamic as El-Hadj shifts his gaze around the frame while barely moving his head. At one point, he reacts to a flash of light (a camera?) and smiles. He closes his eyes, still smiling as rain drops begin to gently caress his face. Sound layered over image, Gomis stitches together the fragments that establish the two geographical spaces germane to the film's narrative: Senegal and France. Sathya Rao has written astutely that through "la magie du montage" (magic of editing) Gomis depicts El-Hadj experiencing the emotion of nostalgia, blending sounds of crickets and birds chirping, an outdoor market, cars honking, children playing and rain drops falling so that metaphorically France and Senegal intermingle in his mind, creating a new space, that of *L'Afrance* (2011, p. 111). By deliberately leaving the right side of the frame blank, Gomis is indicating that the whole story has yet to be written/filmed. This is an in-the-process-of-becoming story. It is El-Hadj's story, but it is also, in part, his father's story we learn at the end of the film, and ultimately, the wending story of all migrants. Gomis eschews linear time and space and immediately draws the spectator in to the process of relation whereby she must imagine the "lines of force" interacting and then participate in their shaping and re-shaping (Glissant 1997, p. 131). Is it up to the spectator then to create this new space called "L'afrance" after sifting through all the elements presented by the filmmaker?

Indeed, the end of the opening shot with rain streaming down El-Hadj's face, almost gives the impression that he is weeping and smiling simultaneously, adrift in daydreams. This image gives way to point-of-view long shots of a boat navigating through water, only the bow visible. The film's title appears as the boat pushes forward. This is clearly a film about journey and traveling. A male's voice begins in Wolof, "El-Hadj, I hope this cassette finds you in good health." In the audio cassette letter, his father in Dakar imparts news of the family business, the mourning period for his recently-deceased grandfather, and implores El-Hadj to study hard and call home more often so his mother and fiancée will worry less. Brief flashback images depict El-Hadj as a youth in a Dakar classroom reciting a key passage from Cheikh Hamidou Kane's landmark 1961 novel *L'aventure ambiguë*, as his adult voice merges with that of his childhood. This is a highly intertextual film with El-Hadj embarking on the same journey to France for "colonial education" and to experience "la théorie se heurte à la réalité" (theory clashes with reality) as did Samba Diallo in the Kane novel. Like Samba's family, El-Hadj's is deeply religious, practicing a tolerant version of Islam. One of the opening sequence's flashbacks is a medium two-shot of El-Hadj as a child and his father praying together. There is also an important moment of "opening" in the father's letter that demonstrates a tolerant Islam: El-Hadj's father asks him to think of his sister who will soon make the same journey to France for her studies. Women as well as men in this family are encouraged to pursue higher education. As his father speaks of his sister's impending journey, we see the first of the shower scenes that will punctuate the film throughout, depicting moments of emotional breakdown.

The two geographical spaces germane to the film's narrative – Senegal and France – are laid out in the opening sequence and enter into a sort of competition as extreme high angle crane shots of busy Dakar streets are intercut with bird's eye view shots of Place de Trocadéro in Paris, exploding with movement in all directions. A mechanical bird, the type sold by African immigrants to tourists, flies over the heads of tourists in the Paris shots, eventually crashing to the ground in the square in front of El-Hadj, foreshadowing his impending crisis of conscience and identity. Both Samba Diallo and El-Hadj must navigate two countries, two cultures, and two languages (three if Arabic is included). Samba Diallo's quest ends in tragedy but what of El-Hadj? Does he manage, through migritude, to move beyond the spaces of both his culture of origin and the receiving culture of France to a new space of L'Afrance? At the beginning of the film he is firmly anchored in Senegalese space and identity as evidenced by his mental flashbacks to his family, Awa and life in Dakar. When he meets Myriam at a wedding and then joins her at her art restoration workshop, he declares, "J'en ai marre d'être black. Je suis Senegalais!" (I'm fed up with being "Black." I'm Senegalese). Here, he resolutely stakes a claim in Afropeanness wherein his blackness is less of a color and racial identification and more of an experienced identity.

The film's inciting incident occurs when El-Hadj attempts to renew his expired carte de séjour. "It's expired by only six days!" El-Hadj exclaims to the clerk at the Préfecture de Police who promptly alerts the police who forcefully arrest him. Although the film does not delve into the intricacies of how his carte is eventually renewed, the fact that his carte de séjour has expired means that his visa has likely also expired, and thus probably his student bursary as well (although we do see El-Hadj attempt to gain both licit and illicit employment), so the complications multiply as they do for all "sans papiers" (those without identity cards). Between 1982 and 2006, the government had allowed the legalization of over 200,000 "sans papiers," but in 2006 la Loi Relative à l'Immigration et à l'Intégration abolished the automatic process of legalizing immigrants who had lived in France without cartes de séjour for ten years or more. Nicholas Sarkozy, then Minister of the Interior, also announced plans to increase the number of deportations from France and the nation that was once seen as a so-called beacon of liberty and justice for all, thus began the practice of "immigration choisie" (selective immigration) whereby only highly-skilled foreign workers would be chosen to enhance France's image. (Engler, 2007). Many human rights organizations denounced this practice because it focuses on economics and not society and reinforces what Ginette Verstraete has aptly described as Fortress Europe, that is, a "Europe that wants to be connected economically and technologically but not yet socially" (2007. p. 120).

The film *Afrique sur Seine* (1955, Vieyra, Sarr, Caristan and Mélo Kane) comes to mind as El-Hadj is transported to the detention center by police van. In fact, it is *Afrique sur Seine* in reverse but with the same outcome. The van drives along the Seine passing by France's greatest historical monuments and symbols of liberty, but this time, rather than tracking shots that present like a travelogue, Gomis forces the viewer to glimpse the scenery through the barred windows of the van. El-Hadj, in extreme close-ups reminiscent of those at the beginning of the film, faces inward, hunched toward frame right. Paulin Vieyra and Mamadou Sarr's commentary from *Afrique sur Seine* is as relevant in 2001 as it was in 1955. The voice-over is upbeat to begin with as it describes being full of hope at discovering Africa on the Seine, civilization and all of Paris's monuments to its past and present greatness. The tone changes as the commentary bitterly describes a Paris of days without bread and without hope. Will El-Hadj's journey be the same?

Sathya Rao demonstrates convincingly how El-Hadj experiences a form of psychological exile which begins from the moment he is humiliated during the prison strip search and all through his brief incarceration (2011, p. 112). Medium close-ups and extreme close-ups drive the emotional arc in this film and are used to portray El-Hadj in interior conflict with his very existence. He effects a process of relationality as he negotiates with himself the value of all his learning. Gomis stages montages of photos and footage of Patrice Lumumba's arrest, incarceration, and assassination at various intervals in the film to correspond with El-Hadj's increasing isolation and breakdown. At one point in the shower, El-Hadj mouths the words of one of Lumumba's speeches, yet it is Lumumba's voice we hear as though they are taking a similar journey, 40 years apart. Events are delocalized, but Gomis "recasts the narrative of postcoloniality into the model of relationality" (Eze 2014, p. 238). Thus, by rejecting linear time and space, and through the layering of images and sounds, Gomis references the cultural plurality made possible by the many influences of colonialism, migration, and globality. Unlike Lumumba, El-Hadj is not acting in opposition to colonial constructs, he is learning from the leaders of the postcolonial movements and valorizing the interaction of all processes and cultures to create a path that allows him to survive and thrive (unlike Samba Diallo). It is this "mutual interference" as Glissant would have it, which evokes relation (Hiddleston 2009, p. 146).

As much as this film is about El-Hadj's personal journey, it is also a history lesson and moral topography. El-Hadj exclaims to Myriam, "L'Afrique écrira son histoire" (Africa will write its own history) when he explains to her that his thesis topic is: "Sékou Touré: des origines de l'action syndicale à l'emancipation nationale" (Sékou Touré: From his Beginnings in Union Activism to National Emancipation) because Touré, elected the first President of the newly independent Guinea in 1958, was the only sub-Saharan African leader to refuse a union-partnership with France when offered by De Gaulle, and opted for full independence. How independence was gained is a much-debated topic amongst African students in France. Khalid, the Algerian student living in the same residence as El-Hadj, takes a jab at Senegal, when he declares, "we weren't given our independence; we took it in blood," making obvious reference to the Algerian War of Independence (1954–1962) which claimed the lives of many Algerians. Senegal, by contrast, "gained" independence when Léopold Sédar Senghor, a socialist deputy for Senegal in the National Assembly in Paris since 1946, signed the transfer of power agreement with France in 1960 and became Senegal's first President. Many, including renowned filmmaker Ousmane Sembène, remained bitter over the events. Senghor, one of the founders of Negritude, and a member of the Académie Française since 1983, died in 2001 and not one senior French politician bothered to attend his state funeral in Dakar (Gondola 2009, p. 153).

El-Hadj finally decides to return to Senegal telling Myriam, in a slightly high angle medium two-shot, that he will come back to her. The angle of the shot compels the viewer to ponder whether or not his intent will be realized. In Senegal, he reaffirms to his father that he will teach, but not "here." Within the Afropolitan frame, as Eze would have it, El-Hadj cannot be considered a victim, existing in marginalized space on the sidelines. He now has a voice that he must use, to write his history and that of Africa, in relation to others in his world (2014, p. 245).

The Frame is Not Enough: *Rengaine*

In 2012, ten years after the release of *L'Afrance*, Rachid Djaïdani completed his first feature film *Rengaine* (Refrain), which took nine years to make on a shoestring budget. The film was described by Rémi Yacine in *El Watan* (20 November 2012) as the Barbès version of *Romeo and Juliet* but I believe it is really a modern-day tale that goes beyond a love story to probe the right to social, political, and cultural self-determination as well as personal responsibility within integration in contemporary French society. Ostensibly focused on the couple of Dorcy, a young, black African actor struggling to survive through his art, and Sabrina, a French-Maghrebi woman, the film depicts their resolve to marry despite varying opposition from members of their respective Catholic and Muslim families.

This mixed cultural terrain is not unfamiliar to Djaïdani, himself the product of a Soudanese-Algerian mother and Algerian father, who grew up in the Yvelines area outside Paris. At the age of 15 he became a mason. At the age of 20 he worked as security guard on the set of Mathieu Kassovitz's *La Haine*. After a successful boxing stint, he began a career in acting, which included a five-year world tour with Peter Brook's theatre troupe. He wrote three novels and produced documentaries before directing *Rengaine*.

With *Rengaine*, Djaïdani is committed to exploring the relational interplay between French, Maghrebi, and African imperatives, staking out an "affiliative" and relational narrative structure in which each of the characters evidences an individual engagement with their culture, history and global influences. This works to foreground "forms and idioms" that are "mobile, reversible, and unstable" (Mbembe 2002, p. 272). Djaïdani's relational affiliation with France and Africa serves to shape his depiction of events in a specific fashion. According to Kamel Zouaoui, one of the film's actors, Djaïdani's goal was to portray his own personal experiences of racism in France. Arabs would tell him that his mother is black and blacks would tell him that his father is Arabic and Djaïdani wanted to show that intra-community racism is alive and well (Barlet 2014, p. 185).

The film's narrative structure provides a case in point for relationality. The film begins very unconventionally with a hand-held POV shot in high angle close-up on what appears at first to be a tricycle, but is really a battery cart being pushed. The next shot is a medium two-shot (eye-level angle) of Dorcy, a young African man proposing marriage to Sabrina, a young French-Maghrebi woman. The film then cuts back to a high angle close-up of the battery cart as the camera tilts up and reframes to reveal Slimane in close-up profile as he pushes the battery cart. In the next shot, Sabrina accepts Dorcy's proposal. The film's title, *Rengaine (Refrain)* appears over an extreme close-up of the battery cart and then the camera zooms in to an insert shot of the cart before tilting up and reframing to an extreme close-up of Slimane in reverse profile as he gets his car battery to start. This is followed by insert shots of Slimane's and a woman's mouths and eyes as they list and count his 39 brothers. Over a punch-in shot of a black screen, we hear the woman say, "now, come and eat." The next shot of the film is the inciting incident; Slimane is framed in extreme close-up, profile screen left as he drives his car and answers his cell phone; an anonymous caller is telling him something he does not want to hear judging by his shocked reaction. We learn subsequently that the caller is informing him that his Muslim sister intends to marry a Catholic black African.

The major story/narrative strands and thematic issues are laid out in this short exposition of about two and a half minutes: First, second- and third-generation Maghrebi and sub-Saharan African immigrants as workers in the Metropole; second, mixed marriage discourse, including how, as Michel Cadé puts it, "to distinguish between religious values and what is simply a matter of tradition" (2011, p. 44), and third, integrationist discourse, including the interplay of ethnic origins in a purportedly egalitarian Republic such as France. These strands appear simple in and of themselves, but in fact, are woven very tightly together in the film underscoring what Will Higbee has argued occurs in Rabah Ameur-Zaïmeche's film, *Le dernier maquis*, notably, "the impossibility of separating personal religious belief from individual and collective interaction in the socio-economic sphere" (2012, p. 178).

The rise of the working class in France was bolstered by immigration during the nineteenth and twentieth centuries. During its economic crisis in the 1970s, France allowed a significant influx of immigrants to permanently settle and obtain citizenship. One result of this in the larger urban areas was high unemployment rates amongst immigrants. Nadia Kiwan has shown that in contemporary France from 2002 to 2005, cultural discrimination is more of a determining factor in higher unemployment trends of Algerian-origin youth than those of other cultural groups because of lingering memories of the Algerian War of Independence as well as a general discomfort with Islamic cultures (2007, p. 159). *Rengaine* is set in the mid-2000s and Slimane and his brothers appear for the most part to be gain-fully employed as mechanics, taxi drivers, shop workers, a detective, etc. It is Dorcy who is unemployed and searching for work as a theatre and film actor, a profession likely less popular amongst immigrants 20 to 30 years ago. However, the main characters in the film are not first-generation immigrants. They are French-born. But are they "integrated"?[4] Dorcy is portrayed in a variety of humiliating parts as he auditions for role after role, the most demeaning of which occurs when he is covered in white shaving cream and positioned in the frame in a crucifix position while he is told by the white woman filming him for her performance art project that he is "nice and white." This is a subtle form of racism and serves as a performance of exclusion reinforcing common assumptions and images of a white Jesus Christ, for example. Dorcy could never perform this role without being overhauled to fit into dominant, white French culture.

When Slimane, the eldest of the brothers, receives the anonymous phone call, he sets out immediately on a frantic inquisition to verify the information and per-suade his brothers to join his crusade against the marriage. Slimane, however, whose character acts as the major blocking force to the young couple's quest to get married, is confronted by a blocking force to his own actions: Many of his brothers seem to have "integrated" and are imbued in varying degrees with values of lib-erty and free choice and are not interested in preventing Sabrina's marriage. Dorcy also encounters resistance from his family who considers Sabrina, "white" and a foreigner. Thus, two communities live side-by-side but rarely mix or intermarry, individual desire eclipsed by collective will. This "touche pas à ma soeur" attitude is underscored with irony in an early scene in which one of Sabrina's brothers breaks the Ramadan fast with his black friend and explains the family's "dilemma" expecting his friend to understand. The scene begins as the two young men repeat the Maghreb prayer to break the fast: "Oh Allah! I fasted for You and I believe in You [and I put my trust in You] and I break my fast with your sustenance." The mood at the beginning of the scene is one of easygoing camaraderie with Sabrina's brother teaching his friend the prayer in both Arabic and French and then sharing his dates as they break their fast. The tone begins to shift as her brother describes Dorcy as "one of yours?" The friend is incredulous at the implication that because he himself is black and of sub-Saharan origin, he should therefore know Dorcy: "Africa is a continent, not a country." Sabrina's brother retorts, "Why did she have to choose a black? Know what I'm saying?" He goes on to complain that because Dorcy is a non-Muslim black he would not be presentable to the family. His friend begins to turn away in disgust exclaiming, "Who did you eat with last night? Who showed you hospitality?" Sabrina's brother retorts, "It's not the same. Your family's different. It's not their color, it's their heart." The argument escalates as the friend asks, "And if I wanted to marry Sabrina, what would you say?" Sabrina's brother exclaims, "Nothing to say, the answer's no." The friend walks away in disgust ordering Sabrina's brother to move in the opposite direction, the latter whining, "No need to get in a sweat." Cinematically, the friends are depicted in medium and medium close-up two shots and framed either side-by-side facing the camera, or in over the shoulder shots. Thus, character space is linked here, but disrupted by the mobile camera which hovers like a nervous hummingbird moving back and forth between the two friends, beginning in mostly low angle as though it is trying to perch on their shoulders, but ending in a slightly high angle long shot of Sabrina's brother, back to the camera, walking slowly into the cityscape. Is Djaïdani suggesting that this unresolved interaction is the "refrain" of the film's title: Simply the same old story of racism? This scene cleverly frames the exclusionary practices at work in French nation and identity-building.[5] Djaïdani further complicates his narrative with layers of irony by exposing the relationship of Slimane with his Jewish girlfriend, Nina, whom he considers the love of his life and whom he has promised to marry. Kept secret for fear of reprisal by his brothers on religious and racial grounds, Slimane's relationship and attitude embodies perhaps the most hypocritical stance of the whole film: "You are Arab when you want to be!" exclaims Sabrina to one of her other brothers who also opposes her marriage.

The film's episodic narrative structure, with each shot or sequence loosely assembled, contributing to the rising action all the while refusing a "fixed linearity of time," creates a poetics of relation whereby static positions are subverted (Glissant, 1997, pp. 29, 27). Economy of narrative is eschewed in favor of an oral storytelling form in which the forward timeline is replete with digressions and plays on words. Interestingly, this structure conforms to Djaïdani's shooting methodology. According to Kamel Zouaoui, there was no written screenplay. Djaïdani had ideas in his head and would simply suggest key words and then let the actors (who were mostly non-professional) improvise at will with each other (Barlet 2014, p. 187). This methodology allowed for relational interaction of actor/character belief systems with viewers subsequently participating by weighing the relational implications advanced by each character/ideological position. The climax and resolution of the film demonstrate this principle. After seeking out the support of all his brothers except one, Slimane goes to visit his estranged brother, ostracized for 30 years because of his homosexuality. He, in fact, is the eldest brother, who sought support from Slimane when he was persecuted as a youth. He tells Slimane that he knows all about his life (implying his life with Nina) and Slimane pulls a gun on him while he implores Slimane to shoot, "I'm already dead. I can't die a second time." Slimane cannot pull the trigger and the words of his brother, "Tonight is the night of destiny. The gates of heaven are open. I'll pray for you," continue to haunt him as he wanders through a night circus fair close to Sacré Coeur. Dorcy, who just happens to be standing in front of the Sacré Coeur, makes the sign of the cross and leaves, eventually mounting a Montmartre staircase where he runs into Slimane. They both pause and Slimane asks if he's Dorcy. When Dorcy says yes, Djaïdani renders the connection between the two in visual terms through an over the shoulder medium close-up two-shot and then extreme close-ups with eyeline matches as the two lock eyes. Slimane begins to recite *Surat al Fatiha*, the opening sura from the Qu'ran: "In the name of God, the all merciful. Praise be to God, Lord of the Worlds. The all beneficient, the ever merciful. Master of the day of judgment. Thee alone we worship. Thee alone we ask for help. Show us the path of righteousness. The path of those who have won Thy favor, not Thy wrath. Or who have gone astray." The eyeline match is carried through as Slimane asks for Dorcy's forgiveness. After a barely perceptible nod, Dorcy, visibly moved, turns and walks away, looking back once over his shoulder. The film ends on an extreme close-up profile low-angle shot of Slimane looking down, deep in thought, exploring his moral topography, and realizing that his self has evolved, in relation to the other.

The film begins and ends with shots of Slimane. Religious and racial intolerance enslave him at the beginning of the film. Yet he draws on religion to liberate him at the end. By reciting this particular sura, he is giving his blessing to the marriage and embracing a tolerant form of Islam with subtle traditions. The silence of both men after Slimane asks for Dorcy's forgiveness and the fact that the shots are rather static, allow a rest at the closure point for spectators to weigh the ideological merits of all the character positions presented in the film. Zouaoui considers the film, as well as Djaïdani's working methodology, to be democratic because at the end of the process everyone is free to carry on and construct her own story/history (p. 186).

Eschewing the didactic filmmaking of social realism, *Rengaine* is a work of montage, featuring a mobile, almost frantic camera ("c'est la vie qui bouge" selon Djaïdani), replete with grainy footage, jump cuts, extreme close-ups, because, as Djaïdani has revealed, he chose to film in close-up so that "for once, the spectator would be forced to look at us face-on" (Yacine p. 2012). Zouaoui adds that with the camera so close to the actors, the actors themselves became the landscape and sets (Barlet 2014, p. 187). The camera is not content to simply record, but is an active participant, moving and shifting with the characters, as though the frame is too restricting for the story space.

Conclusion

L'Afrance and *Rengaine* evidence an interesting blend of the relational and auteurism where the personal is the standard of reference in a creative work. Two of the most important corollaries of auteurism or authorship, can be extended to the work of Djaïdani and Gomis. First, there is the personal relationship between artist and viewer; and second, auteurism carves out a space for a dialectics of the artistic process demanding an active audience, posing questions and forcing the viewer to think. They require several viewings to peel back the meaning, and all of this is achieved ultimately through a relational process in which the film or an artwork becomes a new force out of many elements that the viewer must think through and engage with. Films are never static artworks: How they are read or experienced by an audience or critic depends upon the relationship between the present historical/political/cultural context of the spectator and the historical/political/cultural context of the film. *L'Afrance* and *Rengaine* are less about conclusions and more about the journeys of construction (Reeck 2011, p. 144). The relational interplay created by the films' directors and characters, seeks to raise debate across a wide range of spectators-in-the-world and poses complex questions of responsibility, and in doing so connects worlds and histories.

Glissant reminds us that the poetics of relation are always "conjectural … multilingual in intention" and always "directly in contact with everything possible" (1997, p. 32). The effects of colonialism and globality on the African continent, in the diaspora, in the French metropolis and everywhere in-between, mean that relational histories are not simply about self-identifying as French and African or French and Maghrebi or about selection of language or territory, but are about liberty and the freedom of choice to create and innovate through unfettered imagination, forever in construction.

Acknowledgements

The author wishes to thank the Social Sciences and Humanities Research Council of Canada for providing funding and support for this research, as well as Brahim Benbouazza for his advice.

Notes

1   Many would contend that there is no such thing as an African film industry since most of the apparatus is located off-continent, and mostly in Europe. The Paris-based Mauritanian filmmaker Med Hondo, for example, recently stated that there are African filmmakers, but there is no such thing as an African cinema! (Carleton University, Ottawa, 27 February 2016).

2   See especially Manthia Diawara, *African Film: Politics and Culture* (1992), N. Frank Ukadike, *Black African Film* (1994) and Ferid Boughedir, *Le cinéma africain de A à Z* (1984).

3   Sathya Rao's term "French cinema of the postcolony" is useful and thought-provoking (2011, p. 107).

4   Laura Reeck writes that when the children of North African immigrants marched alongside Jacques Lang and Cardinal Lustiger in the 1983 March for Equality and Against Racism, they were seen to be "integrat-*able*" (2011, p. 131).

5   Interestingly, the 2009 National Identity Debate, rather than fostering a national identity consciousness, actually served to aggravate tensions between populations (Thomas 2014, p. 19).

References

Bakari, Imruh and Mbye Cham (eds.). 1996. *African Experiences of Cinema*. London: British Film Institute.

Barlet, Olivier. 2015. "Cinéma: évanescente diaspora." *Afropéa, un territoire culturel à inventer. Africultures*, 99–100: 314–329.

Barlet, Olivier. 2014. "Être des guerriers du quotidien. Entretien d'Olivier Barlet avec Kamel Zouaoui." *Africultures: La Marche en heritage*, 97: 184–189.

Bolter, Jay David and Richard Grusin.1996. "Remediation." *Configurations* (4.3): 311–358.

Boughedir, Ferid. 1984. *Le cinéma africain de A à Z*. Brussels: OCIC.

Cadé, Michel. 2011. "Hidden Islam: The Role of the Religious in *Beur* and *Banlieue* Cinema." In *Screening Integration: Recasting Maghrebi Immigration in Contemporary France*, edited and with an introduction by Sylvie Durmelat and Vinay Swamy, 41–57. Lincoln and London: University of Nebraska Press.

Cazenave, Odile. 2005. *Afrique sur Seine: A New Generation of African Writers in Paris*. Lanham, MD: Lexington Books.

Chevrier, Jacques. "Afrique(s)-sur-Seine: autour de la notion de 'migritude'." *Notre Librairie*, Vol. 155–156 (July–Dec. 2004): 96–100.

Clarke, George Elliott. 1998. "Contesting a Model Blackness: A Meditation on African-Canadian African Americanism, or The Structures of African Canadianité." *Essays on Canadian Writing* 63 (Spring): 1–55.

Diawara, Manthia. 1992. *African Cinema: Politics and Culture*. Bloomington: Indiana University Press.

Engler, Marcus. 2007. "France." *Focus Migration*. No. 2 (March). Accessed 14 December 2014. http://focus-migration.hwwi.de/France.1231.0.html?&L=1

Eze, Chielozona. 2014. "Rethinking African Culture and Identity: The Afropolitan Model." *Journal of African Cultural Studies*, 26.2: 234–247. DOI: 10.1080/13696815.2014.894474

Gikandi, Simon. 2001. "Globalization and the Claims of Postcoloniality." *The South Atlantic Quarterly*, 100.3 (Summer): 627–658.

Gilroy, Paul. 1993. *The Black Atlantic: Modernity and Double Consciousness*. Cambridge, MA: Harvard University Press.

Gilroy, Paul. 1996. "Route Work: The Black Atlantic and the Politics of Exile." In *The Post-Colonial Question: Common Skies, Divided Horizons*, edited by Iain Chambers and Lidia Curti, 17–29. London and New York: Routledge.

Gilroy, Paul. 2004. "Migrancy, Culture, and a New Map of Europe." In *Blackening Europe: The African American Presence*, edited by Heike Raphael-Hernandez, xi–xxii. London and New York: Routledge.

Glissant, Édouard. 1997. *The Poetics of Relation*. B. Wing (trans.). Ann Arbor, M.: University of Michigan Press.

Gondola, Didier. 2009. "Transient Citizens: The Othering and Indigenization of *Blacks and Beurs* within the French Republic." In *Frenchness and the African Diaspora: Identity and Uprising in Comtemporary France*, edited by Charles Tshimanga, Didier Gondola, and Peter J. Bloom, 146–166. Bloomington: Indiana University Press.

Hiddleston, Jane. 2009. *Understanding Postcolonialism*. Stocksfield, UK: Acumen.

Higbee, Will. 2012. "Le cinema maghrébin vu de l'autre côté de la Méditerranée: cinema national/transnational/diasporique." In *Les cinemas du Maghreb et leurs publics*, edited by Patricia Caillé and Florence Martin, 102–114. Paris: L'Harmattan.

442 *Sheila Petty*

Hitchcott, Nicki and Dominic Thomas. 2014. "Introduction: Francophone Afropeans." In *Francophone Afropean Literatures*, edited by Nicki Hitchcott and Dominic Thomas, 1–13. Liverpool: Liverpool University Press.

Khatibi, Abdelkébir. 1983. *Maghreb pluriel*. Paris: Denoël.

Kiwan, Nadia, 2007. "Equal Opportunities and Republican Revival: Post-Migrant Politics in Contemporary France (2002–2005)." *International Journal of Francophone Studies*, 10.1–2:157–172. DOI: 10.1386/ijfs.10.1and2.157/1

Mbembe, Achille. 2002. "African Modes of Self-Writing." Steven Rendall (trans). *Public Culture*, 14.1: 239–273.

Mbembe, Achille. 2005. "Afropolitanisme." *Africultures*, 26 December 2005. Accessed 14 August 2009. www.africultures.com/index.asp?menu=revue_affiche_article&no=42 48&section=rebonds

Mbembe, Achille. 2007. "France-Afrique: The Idiocies that Divide Us." *Africultures*, 5 September 2008. Accessed 14 August 2009. www.africultures.com/index.asp?menu=affiche_article&no+6864

Mbembe, Achille. 2008. "What is Postcolonial Thinking? An Interview with Achille Mbembe." *Eurozine*. 1 September 2008 John Fletcher (trans)9 January 2008. Accessed 14 August 2009. www.eurozine.com/articles/2008-01-09-mbembe-en.html

Nimis, John. 2014. "*Corps sans titre*: 'Fleshiness' and Afropean Identity in Bessora's *53 cm*." In *Francophone Afropean Literatures*, edited by Nicki Hitchcott and Dominic Thomas, 48–63. Liverpool: Liverpool University Press.

Orlando, Valérie K. 2013. "*Being-in-the-World*: The Afropolitan Moroccan author's worldview in the new millennium." *Journal of African Cultural Studies*, 25.3: 275–291. DOI: 10.1080/13696815.2013.818917

Rao, Sathya. 2011. "Mythologies et mythoscopies de l'exil dans les cinémas Africain Francophone et de la Postcolonie." In *Images et mirages des migrations dans les littératures et les cinémas d'Afrique francophone*, edited by Françoise Naudillon and Jean Ouédraogo, 103–117. Montréal: Editions Mémoire d'encrier.

Reeck, Laura. 2011. *Writerly Identities in Beur Fiction and Beyond*. Lanham, MD: Lexington Books.

Said, Edward. 1990. "Reflections on Exile." In *Out There, Marginalization and Contemporary Cultures*, edited by R. Ferguson et al., 357–366. Cambridge, MA: MIT Press.

Thomas, Dominic. 2013. *Africa and France: Postcolonial Cultures, Migration, and Racism*. Bloomington: Indiana University Press.

Thomas, Dominic. 2014. "Afropeanism and Francophone Sub-Saharan African Writing." In *Francophone Afropean Literatures*, edited by Nicki Hitchcott and Dominic Thomas, 17–31. Liverpool: Liverpool University Press.

Trouillet, Caroline. 2014. "Les dérives sémantiques de l'immigration." *Africultures: La Marche en héritage*, 97: 83–93.

Ukadike, Nwachukwu Frank. 1994. *Black African Cinema*. Berkeley: University of California Press.

Verstraete, Ginette. 2007. "Women's Resistance Strategies in a High-Tech Multicultural Europe." In *Transnational Feminism in Film and Media*, edited by K. Marciniak, A. Imre, and A. O'Healy, 111–128. New York: Palgrave Macmillan.

Werbner, Richard and Terence Ranger, eds. 1996. *Postcolonial Identities in Africa*. London: Zed Books.

Yacine, Rémi. 2012. "Le film Rengaine: tabous et certitudes bousculés." *El Watan*. 20 November 2012.

Further Reading

Glissant, Édouard. 2010. *Poetic Intention*. N. Stephens (trans.). Callicoon, NY: Nightboat Books.

Filmography

Ameur-Zaïmeche, Rabah. (2008). *Le dernier maquis (Adhen)*. France/Algeria: Sarrazink Productions, Région Île-de-France, Centre National de la Cinématographie.

Djaïdani, Rachid. (2012). *Rengaine (Refrain)*. France: Or Productions, Arte France Cinéma.

Gomis, Alain. (2001). *L'Afrance*. France/Senegal: Centre National de la Cinématographie, Mille et Une Productions.

Gomis, Alain. (2007). *Andalucia*. France: MLK Producciones, Mallerich Films, Mille et Une Productions.

Gomis, Alain. (2012). *Tey (Today)*. France/Senegal: Granit Films, Maïa Cinéma, Cinekap.

Gomis, Alain. (2017). *Félicité*. France/Belgium/Senegal/Germany/Lebanon: Andolfi, Granit Films, Cinekap.

Kassovitz, Mathieu. (1995). *La Haine (Hate)*. France: Canal+, Cofinergie 6, Egg Pictures.

Margolin, F. and Ould Salem, L. (2016). *Salafistes (Salafists)*. France: Margo Cinema.

Sissako, Abderrahmane. (2014). *Timbuktu*. Mali: Les Films du Worso.

Vieyra, P. and Sarr, M. (1955). *Afrique sur Seine (Africa on the Seine)*. France: Groupe Africain.

20

Crossing Lines

Frontiers, Circulations, and Identity in Contemporary African and Diaspora Film

Melissa Thackway

La première chose que l'indigène apprend, c'est de rester à sa place, à ne pas dépasser les limites. C'est pourquoi les rêves de l'indigène sont … des rêves d'action … Je rêve que je saute, que je nage, que je cours … que je franchis le fleuve d'une enjambée…
(Fanon 1961, p. 82)[1]

Frontiers, borders, lines – be they geographic, imaginary, mental, visible or invisible – traverse the history of African and diaspora auteur film with the striking constancy and recurrence of the leitmotif. Ever since the first works of pioneers Paulin S. Vieyra (*Afrique sur Seine*, 1955) and Ousmane Sembène (*Borom Sarret*, 1962), film protagonists have crossed, re-crossed, or their movement been hindered by national borders and the unspoken, invisible, yet no less real lines that compartmentalized the colonial, and later the postcolonial city; the "lines of force" that Fanon describes (p. 37), creating distinct spaces of belonging or exclusion.

In today's postcolonial, globalized world where discourses of free circulation, of the free flow of ideas, of "the death of distance," stand in stark and awkward contrast with the realities of increasingly rigorous and hostile border controls and even the construction of walls destined to stem the flow of certain populations in what Achille Mbembe terms as a "race towards separation and *unbonding*"[2] (2016, p. 8), a range of contemporary films offer striking questions and representations of the frontier and its corollaries: Itinerancy, migration, circulation, de- and reterritorialization.[3] Exploring actual journeys, crossings, displacements and exile, these filmic journeys are symbolic of quests too: Quests for identities, as both an individual and part of a wider family or a community; quests for a sense of belonging and for an understanding of one's place in the world.

While the theme of exile and the concomitant exploration of frontiers and borders have been prevalent in African filmmaking from the outset, the contemporary transnational films discussed in this chapter – Jean-Marie Teno's *A Trip to the Country* (Cameroon, 2000); John Akomfrah's *The Nine Muses* (UK, 2010); Zeka Laplaine's *Kinshasa Palace* (DRC, 2006); and Mati Diop's *A Thousand Suns* (France, 2013) – are notable for their aesthetic explorations and crossing of lines too. Self-reflexive and often experimental, they, like their filmmakers, whose belongings are often multiple and lifestyles itinerant or exilic, indeed resist easy categorization. All are at the intersection of, and often blend, several forms: (First-person) documentary, (auto)fiction, art and experimental film. Moving between genres and styles, moving through places and histories – both personal and collective – crossing spatiotemporal lines to reinvent filiations and genealogies, they question and explore memories and identity, not as "a fixed essence," to cite Stuart Hall, but as "a *positioning*." (1989, p. 226) In a moving world, they seek "points of identification" (Hall 1989, p. 237) between the local and global, the ebb and flow, the pull of roots, of filiations, of origins, and the freedom to go forth and forge new belongings. Without attempting to artificially pin these works down, then, or to conflate their styles and themes, without attempting to group them together in a wave, and even less a genre, I simply wish here in an otherwise heterogeneous body of works, to point to some striking commonalities that seem symptomatic, perhaps, of belonging, as Paul Gilroy describes it, to "part of a same historic moment or conjuncture … to a common present" (2016).

But before looking at the films themselves, at their embracing of circulations, it is worth considering a few reflections on the notion of the frontier in the sub-Saharan and diaspora contexts and what they seek to regulate or control: Movement. It is indeed interesting to note how the European racialist discourses of the eighteenth and nineteenth centuries, which constructed the racial hierarchies that rationalized and justified the trans-Atlantic slave trade and, later, European imperialism and colonialism, also constructed the representation of the African continent as "immobile" and "unconnected" from the world. In his posthumously published 1822–1830 *Lectures on the Philosophy of History*, Hegel, for example, declared:

> Africa proper, as far as History goes back, has remained – for all purposes of connection with the rest of the World – shut up; it is … the land of childhood, which lying beyond the day of self-conscious history, is enveloped in the dark mantle of Night. …
>
> At this point we leave Africa, not to mention it again. For it has no movement or development to exhibit. Historical movements in it – that is in its northern part – belong to the Asiatic or European World. (1837 [1956], pp. 91, 99)

Its non-factuality aside,[4] it is interesting to note how movement here was equated with humanity. Yet, as Mbembe points out, it was precisely Europe's colonizing forces that sought to restrict and control this movement:

> ... the precolonial history of African societies was a history of people in perpetual movement throughout the continent. ... The cultural history of the continent can hardly be understood outside the paradigm or itinerancy, mobility and displacement.
>   It is this very history of mobility that colonisation once endeavoured to freeze through the modern institution of borders. (2005, p. 27)

Perhaps, then, the insistence on movement in the films considered here may be understood not only as a reflection of contemporary migratory and exilic realities and Africa's internal, intercontinental questions of freedom of movement, but also, consciously or not, as an eschewing of the fetters of a long-imposed and often enduring colonial imagination. Just as the history of the continent is one of circulations, then, postcolonial sub-Saharan African and diaspora filmmaking is also a cinema of circulation, a "nomadic cinema" (Teshome Gabriel, 1988) that traces and "makes visible other cartographies" (Vergès, 2012).

While predominantly fictional, the 1960s and 1970s African films that explored the theme of exile and depicted exilic conditions focused mainly on the racial discrimination, hostile housing and working conditions, exclusion, solitude, or indifference facing African immigrants in Europe – notably, Ousmane Sembène's *Black Girl* (1966); Med Hondo's *Soleil O*; Sydney Sokhana's *Nationalité immigré* (1975), or explored the mythical lure of a European Eldorado and the dreams of an elsewhere – for example, Djibril Diop Mambety's *Touki Bouki* (1973), contemporary representations of movement in the films discussed here have tended to diversify, complexify and above all subjectivize experiences. Symptomatic perhaps of today's antinomic flows and stymying of movement, contemporary filmmakers both represent and assert a fluidity, a crossing of lines, a coming and going, a to-ing and fro-ing, a freedom of movement. Yet at the same time, their works reflect a desire for a rooting, a trace, marked as they are by a preoccupation with filiations, with family histories, often reconstructing genealogies and exploring "identities re-forged at the interface between cosmopolitanism and the values of autochthony" (Mbembe 2001, p. 4). These narratives are rooted in personal and at times autobiographical experiences – some asserting a subjective voice or viewpoint, others with directors crossing the line from behind the camera to the screen, becoming often elusive, itinerant protagonists. They incarnate a range of journeys, departures, (impossible) returns and losses that are both a quest for the self and a claiming of a shifting, polymorphous African presence in the world – a *Présence Africaine*.[5] Unveiling themselves through a variety of filmic strategies, their filmmakers thus quite literally engage with and in their narratives.

If colonization assigned colonial subjects a fixed identity and place, negating and silencing their subjectivity, and in a world today that continues often to marginalize and exclude the voices and presence of Africans, reaffirming the personal, the individual, the subjective, and the freedom to define one's own evolving and plural identities is an eminently political act of self-affirmation. Subjectivity may indeed be understood as intrinsically related to questions of time, position, and place; it is inscribed, positioned. In *Cultural Identity and Diaspora*, Stuart Hall affirms that we all speak from a particular time and place, from a "position of *enunciation*" (p. 222). The films discussed here explore and embrace these positions of enunciation as a foundation from which to construct complex fluid identities that eschew the reductive assignations and representations frequently projected upon them. This positioning, this rooting, this speaking from somewhere, does not, in these films, signify a reifying of origins, however. On the contrary, their questioning of these roots and filiations become ways in which their directors explore who they are and their journeys in the world. Or, as Mbembe fittingly writes in *Politiques de l'inimitié*:

> Traversing the world, taking the measure of the accident that our place of birth represents and its degree of arbitrariness and constraint, espousing the irreversible flow that is life's time and existence's time, learning to embrace our status of passerby in that this is perhaps the condition, in the last instance, of our humanity, the base from which we create culture. ...
>
> Becoming-a person-in-the-world is neither a question of birth nor a question of origin or race. It's a matter of journey, of circulation and of transfiguration. (pp. 175–176)[6]

Indeed, the works discussed here are films of "journeys, circulation, and transfiguration." Their forms and their questions are open, as frequently are their final shots of moving trains, or characters driving or walking off into the distance; the onus is on the continuation of these journeys, then, of life's journey, on the freedom to continue evolving.

In each of the films discussed, on each of these filmic journeys, the filmmaker assumes some form of personal presence of filmic persona in the diegesis. This crossing of lines from behind the camera is part of the quest for identify, for the "becoming-a person-in-the-world" that each of these films and the journeys they portray symbolically represent. Jean-Marie Teno, for example, in all of his documentary films over the years since *Afrique, je te plumerai* in 1992 to his most recent 2018 film, *Chosen*, crosses from behind the camera via his first-person narrative voice, now a salient and even defining characteristic of his work. This "I-voice," to borrow Michel Chion's term,[7] is a voice that guides, questions and at times provokes the spectator. It embraces subjectivity, deliberately undermining the illusion of documentary objectivity. Unlike the documentary tradition of an omniscient and supposedly neutral voice of Authority, Teno's I-voice engages directly with the screen space, with the subject matter, so that "the voice and image dance in a dynamic relationship" (Chion 1999, p. 50). While this voice undeniably assumes its own form of authority – that of the filmmaker – by speaking in the first-person, by personalizing what Teno films, and clearly stating how he relates to his subject matter, Teno both clearly announces his "position of enunciation" – we know who is speaking, and in what capacity – and directly addresses us as spectator. Distance is thus thwarted; proximity with the spectator and a point of identification are created, "such that we sense no distance between [the voice] and our ear" (Chion 1999, p. 50). A familiarity develops, drawing us into an empathetic communion; Teno speaks to us directly, intimately. It is a shared voice that does not exclude other voices. On the contrary, Teno weaves multiple voices into the narrative, creating a dialogic polyphony.

In *The Nine Muses*, Akomfrah appears as an almost spectral figure; he is present, yet deliberately anonymous. It is only in the final credits that we learn that he was one of the faceless, lone figures in the brightly-colored arctic parkas who repeatedly dot the deserted monochrome Alaskan landscapes. His on-screen presence is not personalized; his family's story is one of exile, but it is a story that he shares with countless other members of the diaspora. Akomfrah places his personal experience both within a collective diasporic one, then, but also firmly within a British one. The figure he plays is named in the credits a "Yellow Coat" (he wears a yellow parka); for anyone, like Akomfrah, familiar with 1980s quintessential popular British television culture, it is hard not to take this as a playful nod to the BBC hit comedy sitcom *Hi-de-Hi!*, set on a holiday camp and whose staff protagonists, after their uniforms, were known as the Yellow Coats.

In their very different films, Zeka Laplaine and Mati Diop both revisit their family genealogies, and the question of filiation is clearly at the heart of both works. Mati Diop is neither an on-screen nor first-person voice-over presence in *A Thousand Suns*, yet her implication in the film is implicit, as it addresses both her own family history and its inextricable ties with that of Senegalese cinema. Confronting the weighty heritage of her late uncle, Djibril Diop Mambéty, and his cult 1973 film *Touki Bouki* some 40 years on, by prolonging the trajectory of *Touki Bouki*'s fictional protagonists, French-born Mati Diop positions herself vis-à-vis this cinematic history, her own part-Senegalese heritage, and the question of cinematic transmission between uncle and niece. As she described it in a public conversation about the film with Olivier Barlet at the 2013 Festival des films d'Afrique en pays d'Apt, her film is: "A kind of letter or invisible conversation with my uncle," a way of "looking *Touki Bouki* in the eye."[8]

In *Kinshasa Palace*, Zeka Laplaine literally crosses the line from behind the camera to become a protagonist, physically inscribing himself in the film, the camera often assuming his subjective point of view. Yet, in this cinematic metalepsis, the omnipresent character that Laplaine incarnates eludes us. Named Kaze in the final credits, an anagram of Zeka, the protagonist is at once him and not him, a sort of alter-ego, a double. The shots of him are systematically back-lit so he is just a silhouette, or he is a blurry reflection in a moving train window, filmed from an oblique angle, masked, in the shadows, or filmed from behind so that we never see his face. The relentlessness of this obscuring of our vision is striking. Both a form of autofiction and an autobiographic documentary, Laplaine stages his own body and performs his subjectivity in a representation of himself and his story. While he speaks in the first-person and films real members of his family, we sense, without ever knowing precisely, that elements are fictional. The prerequisite of what literary scholar Philippe Lejeune refers to as "the autobiographical pact" – that the author and protagonist be the same person and that the author portray him/ herself as she/he truly is – is thus disrupted, Laplaine's first-person narrative voice in no way guaranteeing veracity. Here we are in the realm of what in his 1964 essay "Aragon" termed "Le mentir-vrai" (true lying).[9]

Just as the filmmakers discussed here journey in one way or another into their diegeses, actual journeys also feature of the heart of each filmic narrative. These journeys are at once a theme and a structuring device. They are often actual journeys, in cars, on trains, on foot, on boats; but they are also journeys back in time, into memory, into history, or quests to understand and/or to construct both individual and collective identities. Both concrete and symbolic, these journeys are as much about "becoming" as they are about "returning" to a place (Hall, 1989, p. 232).

A Trip to the Country opens with Jean-Marie Teno back in Yaounde, 33 years after going to school there. After visiting the now derelict Lycée General Leclerc, once Cameroon's most prestigious secondary school, he retraces the route back to his old neighborhood – now overrun with the parts of old cars that "come to die and reincarnate" as they are fixed and recycled by local mechanics – before embarking on the trip back to his grandparents' village, Bandjoun, that he used to visit once a year as a schoolboy. Given the failed promises of modernity that he points to in the city, Teno announces in his familiar, signature first-person voice-over that he wants to go to see what has become of his home village, which, when he was young, "symbolized all we had to reject if we hoped to become modern one day." Once a two-day journey, now a four-hour one, depending on the number of official and unofficial police roadblocks and tolls, Teno embarks us with him on this road trip back "to see what's left of the village" and to confront his "youthful hopes and certitudes with today's reality." The journey home is thus mediated through his eyes, but becomes our journey too as the camera, filming from inside the moving vehicle for long sequences of the journey, sutures the spectator inside the vehicle. Off, Teno characteristically shares his subjective views, his voice-over commenting and interpreting what we see, guiding us like an old friend, his often ironic reflections creating a complicity and the bond of sharing a joke.

Along the way, Teno stops off at various locations, for example, at Ebebda, a tiny hamlet that nonetheless boasts its own sub-prefect. An "important and very busy" man as Teno ironically informs us on paying a visit to his office, he is filmed imperturbably reading his newspaper; the chirpy brass-band circus music clearly lampoons him and the close-up pan from President Biya's portrait to the sub-prefect, to the latter's title and own name painted on a board speaks for itself: "Biya"; nepotism is rife! Ebebda boasts a new bridge over the river and electricity, yet, the residents tell Teno, no clean drinking water. "It'll come with time," the sub-prefect assures, before confessing that two years is too long a time ahead to plan. Teno's observing camera captures these daily scenes that one by one fall into place like a puzzle as the journey advances. Collectively, juxtaposed with Teno's incisive voice-over comments, and questions, they paint a picture of the complex-ities, contradictions, and absurdities of contemporary Cameroonian life, the emp-tiness of the ineffective and pompous politicians' promises and slogans, their inability to provide even basic infrastructures, and the impasses of an unthinkingly imposed exogenous, rather than local modernity. Teno's actual journey thus soon proves to sum up the state of the country in general, and to be a quest to under-stand how it reached its present state.

Along the actual road trip, which is filmed in long sequences rather than being suggested through ellipses, Teno's voice-over, also weaves personal childhood recollections into the present-day footage. The film also becomes a journey into memory, then, a kind of *Notebook of a Return to the Native Land*, to cite Césaire. Returning, Teno is an "insider-outsider," both intimately connected to his sub-ject matter, a member of the community that he films with such attention, yet at the same time with the critical distance of all those who have gone afar and grown elsewhere. His experience in the film brings to mind Aïssa Djebar's description of writing about Algeria from exile, of her "proche éloignement," or near distance, of "roaming in a territory where past and present respond to one another" (2000).[10] In making this *Trip to the Country*, Teno indeed (re)connects past and present, urban and rural spaces, hopes and realities, illusions and disil-lusions, seeking, as he often does in his films, to make a return that will shed new light to help to analyze and better understand the present. For, just as the character Sogbui tells the fallen and disillusioned Chamba in Teno's fiction fea-ture *Clando*, which also focuses on exiles and returns: "If you reach the point where you don't know where to go anymore, retrace your steps and start again. Come back to the source and grow." To journey, then, is to seek understanding. Or as Djebar similarly adds: "Seeking to truly know one's sites of memory is to recognize oneself, in short, to find oneself again" (2000).[11] In these works, that self is manifestly not a fixed essence, a projection of others, but "a matter of 'becoming' as well as 'being'," a positioning of oneself as subject, rather than being "subject-ed" (Hall 1989, p. 225).

The film's journey also allows Teno to identify a breakdown in transmission between the generations resulting from the colonial encounter, its promotion of a Western modernity, and denigration of ancestral beliefs, practices and village life-styles. The Western-style education that Teno received in Yaounde in the 1960s and 1970s (looping us back to the opening sequence of the Lycée General Leclerc) taught him and his generation, Teno tells us, to scorn their elders and their "archaic" values that "symbolized all we had to reject if we hoped to become modern one day." Yet, Teno asks: "The respect of our elders is one of our fundamental values ... Can you respect yourself if you despise your elders?" As Teno visits a village elder on arrival, his camera down low at the old man's level as he sits outdoors on a low stool, the elder directly addresses Teno's camera, stressing the importance of the tie between generations: "If someone passes away leaving children behind, you don't say he has died, he has just gone away." Yet, he points to the rupture in transmission, to the barrier between him and the younger generations: "Imagine that my own grandfather, our ancestor who has left this world, if he appeared today, without me, would you recognize him? No." The elder's inference is clear: The younger generations no longer know their genealogy and, by extension, their culture. Through the violent colonial encounter, they have become acculturated. While all generations construct who they are partly in opposition to their predecessors, identity is also framed by vectors of similarity and continuity (Hall 1989, pp. 226–227). Teno's trip to the country can be understood as an attempt to re-establish that continuity, that filiation, to repair the broken ties that frame identity.

In the following sequence, the camera pans around Teno's own family compound in slow motion, giving the shot an ethereal quality that is accentuated by the mysterious mood and sense of anticipation of the music's sparse cello and balafon notes. Off, Teno delivers what is undoubtedly the most personal autobiographical voice-over of all his films, revealing more about his own feelings than he is usually want to:

> It was here that I first saw my grandfather talk to a tree, thanking it for guiding me to the family home. A few years later, I remember my own embarrassment when I was left alone in a room where, in a corner stood a calabash filled with palm oil, food for my grandfather who had recently died. His skull was buried there. I was supposed to ask for his blessing before going to Europe. For a moment I stood silently, then finally murmuring, I asked his permission to go around the world. I imagine, wherever he was, my grandfather smiled, for he also loved to travel. Outside the rain began to fall.

Teno recalls, then, his young self's discomfort when confronted with belief systems and practices that reflect the conception of interpenetrating worlds of the living and dead, of "an invisible world that is omnipresent," of a flow, a connection, and a mobility between the two that his Cartesian education had taught him to separate, scorn, and reject. The sequence is deeply poignant, suggesting that Teno feels a certain loss of his heritage and culture. This *Trip to the Country* thus also symbolizes a quest to understand where he stands in relation to his conflicting autochthonous and endogenous value systems and to reconnect with a suppressed part of his identity, surpassing barriers and reconnecting the broken ties to his ancestors, their ancestral belief, and values. The very long sequence focusing on

Bandjoun's annual "Development Congress," set up in the 1970s to maintain ties between those who have left and those who remain, bridging the divides created by the rural exodus and overseas migrations, reinforces this: Once a real moment of exchange, sharing and local democracy, Teno reveals how today it has been completely rid of its substance, becoming a bonanza of advertising, consumerism and partying. Again, Teno's personal experiencing of acculturation and tussle to find some kind of harmony between these conflicting belief systems can be read as a metaphor for postcolonial Cameroon. Teno's personal experience is thus reflective of and a part of the collective, his "I" a "we."

As Teno speaks the final words of his voice-over in the family compound, the camera pans out of the compound and comes to rest on the adjacent path that disappears into the distance. The fencing along both sides of the path draws our gaze to the vanishing point, luring us into the distance too. One imagines the young Teno setting out to Europe, the call of afar. Interestingly, this shot echoes the very same shot in Teno's first short film, *Homage*, evoking the film's fictional character's – an avatar of Teno's own father, we learn – leaving Bandjoun to head for the city and abroad. Teno's own departure thus resonates with his grandfather's aforementioned love of travel and his father's departure. A kind of transmission is thus established, and such threads – *fils*, in French, whose plural resembles the word for "son" – run through and connect Jean-Marie Teno's body of films in a sort of cinematic filiation or circulation. In attempting to surpass the mental barriers of acculturation, exploring and restoring memory, and filiation, traveling back to identify where Cameroon's sham modernity went wrong, Teno appears to suggest that this is what might offer Cameroon after its "long journey to arrive at a dead end," a way out of its impasse.

John Akomfrah's polyphonic visual poem *The Nine Muses* takes us on a journey back in time to the postwar arrival in Britain of Caribbean, African, and Asian immigrants. This filmic journey echoes their voyages to Britain, and the entire work is placed under the sign of movement. Throughout the film, images of moving ships, trains, cars, and people walking, indeed incessantly repeat, their movement often echoed by the traveling camera movements. Nothing is static, least of all people.

Delving into BBC television archives from the 1950s to 1970s, Akomfrah weaves together these predominantly black-and-white, grainy extracts of news reports, documentaries, political speeches, and fiction films with starkly contrasting, sharp digital images of a mysterious figure in a contemporary British dockside landscape, and anonymous solitary figures in deserted snowy Alaska (the ends of the earth!). Together, the archive images retrace a journey of arrival, of ships pulling into docks, of West Indians and Africans landing, of their often difficult living conditions of their arduous, predominantly manual labor conditions, of their disillusions and solitude, of the angst of unfamiliarity, of racism and discrimination, and of the gradual settlement and rooting of Black and Asian communities in an unforgiving bleak, snowy, wet, cold Britain.

The archive and contemporary images are overlaid with a montage of archival voice-over testimonies of immigrants attesting to their experiences, of anti-immigrant sentiment – notably an extract of the Conservative MP Enoch Powell's notorious 1968 "Rivers of Blood" speech criticizing Commonwealth immigration and anti-discrimination legislation – and readings or intertitle citations of a staggering array of canonical literary texts, ranging from Homer to Samuel Beckett, Dylan Thomas, Nietzsche, James Joyce, William Shakespeare, John Milton, E.E. Cummings, T.S. Eliot, Emily Dickinson, Dante, and the Old Testament. These polyphonic citations, all of which evoke journeying, movement, displacement, exile and the exilic experiences of solitude, rootlessness, of motherlands and matrices, of nostalgia, of dreams, of losing and re-finding one's home and one's self, of settling and laying down new roots, of strangeness, of belonging, add layers of meaning to the images. [12] Exile in the extracts notably takes on a mythical dimension. By juxtaposing passages of Milton's *Paradise Lost* evoking the original fall and expulsion of Adam and Eve from the Garden of Eden, for example, or of Homer's *The Odyssey* hero Telemachus's epic journey into the unknown – a rite of passage, a quest – with these archive images, Akomfrah reframes these migrating populations as epic heroes, and migration as something in humankind's DNA since the beginning of time.

The film's intricate, interlacing, looping montage sets up associations and resonances between the images, sounds, and texts, linking the multiple layers of the film and its different periods and places, crossing spatiotemporal lines. The snowy, cold British archive landscapes echo with those of contemporary Alaska: A solitary figure walking in slow motion towards the fixed camera in deserted Alaska cuts directly to the slow motion movement of people trudging through the falling snow towards the camera in a 1960s busy British street as if in a continuous movement; a 1960s snowplow drives towards the camera from top right to bottom left frame; in the following shot in Alaska, a snowplow drives past, away from the camera, from bottom left to top right frame, the continuous voice-over reading linking the two. The reframed past archives thus throw light on the present, and the present offers new readings, new interpretations of the past archives.

Repeated throughout the film too are contemporary and archive images of sea-crossings, of ships, of docks. Readings of the *Odyssey*, of its sea voyage, resonate with the archive images of ships of immigrants docking in the United Kingdom and those of the sea and ships filmed in Alaska. It is tempting too, given the film's first somewhat enigmatic intertitle – "The Gold fell from very high and went very deep in the ground" – to read this as a reference both to the Asante Golden Throne[13] and to Ghana, formerly the Gold Coast, not just Akomfrah's birthplace, but also one of the major points of departure of slaves to the Americas, and thus to detect a resonance, a connection, between the different Atlantic sea-crossings in history.

The Nine Muses' sheer accumulation of the archive images of Black Britain, of faces, not only acknowledges this otherwise marginalized presence, but also actively challenges the prevailing exclusion of these populations from the official

national historiography. Akomfrah writes Britain's diaspora populations into narratives of Britishness, this black presence becoming central, and now the subject,
rather than the object of these representations. Overcoming both the excluding
boundaries that have long framed official memory and the country's collective
amnesia, Akomfrah both recontextualizes post-World War II migration and recalls
the reasons for this presence: To replenish the depleted British workforce and to
help rebuild war-torn Britain. Over beautiful grainy black-and-white archive
images of a black worker in a smelting factory, a Caribbean-accented voice-over
restores events: "If they in the first place had not come to our country and spread
fools' propaganda, we would never have come to theirs." Indeed, this first "chapter"
of the film comes under the intertitle: "Mnemosyne is the Greek Goddess of
Memory."

Not only does the film explore the identity of individuals; it explores Britain's
changing identities, then, reminding us of the imbrication of cultures, of "the
presence of the elsewhere in the here and vice versa" (Mbembe 2005, p. 28). In centering this diasporic memory, Akomfrah, gives it a value, a normality. Indeed,
speaking of his reappropriation and rearticulation of these archives from a
diasporic point of view, Akomfrah states in *Chiasmus*, a filmed interview that features on the DVD of *The Nine Muses*: "If you are a diasporic subject, the archive
acquires a special poignancy because it is one of the few tangible memorials that
attests to your existence," adding that film is one of the ways he tries to connect
who he is and where he is going. For Akomfrah, *The Nine Muses* is indubitably a
space in which to "find some answers to the question of why I am here" in the
United Kingdom, both in relation to the present and the history of the Afro-
Caribbean diaspora. Akomfrah's question indeed brings to mind and resonates
with the one that Fanon claimed colonialism forces those it dominates to ask
themselves constantly: "In reality, who am I?" (Fanon 1961, p. 250). Overcoming
the absences of the national historic narrative, then, Akomfrah not only writes his
presence, both as an individual and as a member of a community, into British
history; he simultaneously rewrites that history (Syrotinski 2002, p. 180). It is a process that recalls the words of bell hooks: "Travelling, moving into the past ... [one]
pieces together fragments ... for black folks, reconstructing an archaeology of
memory makes return possible" (1992, p. 173). For Akomfrah, the work is both an
acknowledgment of presence and a return to existence.

Zeka Laplaine's highly personal *Kinshasa Palace* opens with a low-angle shot up
at power lines rushing by, filmed through the window of a moving train. The tone
is immediately set: This is a journey, and will literally cross and recross geographic
borders from Paris to Kinshasa, to Lisbon, to Brussels and back. The power lines
may also be read as a metaphor for the lines of the scattered family that Laplaine
journeys to reconstruct throughout the film. As already seen, the French word for
these wires – *fils* – echoes the word for "son," and the film will indeed explore
father-son relations; both those of Kaze the protagonist (played by Zeka Laplaine
himself), and Laplaine's Portuguese father who features in the film, and those of
his (real? fictional?) missing brother Max and his children.

To narrate the story of Max,[14] Kaze warns us in his opening first-person narrative voice-over that he does not know where to begin. Yet the image immediately cuts to black-and-white archive images of what was then Leopoldville – now Kinshasa – the voice-over continuing: "It all started when my father and mother met," thereby introducing the journey back in time. The 1960s archive images of the city cut to old black-and-white family photos of the Laplaine couple and their seven children, of whom, we learn, only two – Max and Kaze, the narrator – will stay living with their parents. The film then proceeds unchronologically on a journey to piece together the fragments of the dislocated family's history: Family photos from the 1950s and 1960s; what appears to be "real" contemporary documentary footage of Laplaine's elderly, lonely Congo-born Portuguese father who now lives in Lisbon; "real" contemporary documentary footage of his Congolese mother surrounded by multiple members of her extended family in her Kinshasa home; "real" contemporary documentary footage of his sisters Anna in Kinshasa, Nette in Lisbon, and Fifi in Brussels; "fictionalized" (?) footage of Kaze in Paris, musing about the Max we never see and whose trace he follows to Cambodia, before losing it again; and the "home video" footage of Max's three children Iris, Gaspard, and Ambre (the real names of the three Laplaine children in the credits) that Max is supposed to have filmed before his disappearance.

The seemingly "real" documentary material, the family photos, and the archive footage that contextualizes Congolese independence in the 1960s, Patrice Lumumba's assassination, and Mobutu's ascension – the troubled post-independence period that forced Laplaine's father to leave – intertwine with the apparently fictionalized sequences of Kaze the narrator in Paris, then Cambodia, his own solitary errancy, and his many phone conversations trying to placate his sister Anna in Kinshasa and Max's children as to Max's possible whereabouts.

Adding to the blurring of the lines between the documentary and fiction is the fact that this "real" documentary footage is supposed to have been shot by Max during his trips to Kinshasa to see his mother and to Lisbon to see his father. At first, these sequences appear to be taking place in the film's present, but as we gradually understand who shot them, we come to realize that they are in fact the past tense of the film. The chronological to-ing and fro-ing continues as, in a later sequence that repeats, unfolding each time identically, almost ritualistically – Kaze's feet enter the frame descending a dark staircase; his body, obscured by the shadows, advances and exits the frame; a computer screen is seen on a desk; Kaze's feet enter a shot under the desk as he comes to sit; his hand reaches down to switch on the computer; his body leans backwards to switch off the lamp… – we see Kaze viewing these images on a computer screen, before the DV images invade the entire screen and become the film we are viewing directly, appearing again to become the present tense of the film.

The temporal confusion continues throughout the film, whose pieces only gradually fall into place like a puzzle. In Kaze's Paris apartment (the present-tense sequences of the film), we repeatedly see a red notepad alongside Max's bracelet. Yet when, in what seems to be a logical, chronological progression, Kaze journeys to Cambodia on Max's trail, he finds the red notepad abandoned in the house where Max has been living. The shots of the notebook in Paris can thus only logically be a leap forward in time, after Kaze's return, deliberately disrupting the continuity again, and again throwing us off the trail.

As the temporal and spatial boundaries blur and blur again, layering the narrative threads, images, and sequences or visual themes repeat like leitmotifs, giving a form of coherence to the otherwise fragmented ensemble and little by little guiding us in this labyrinthine journey into this family's complex history. Characters are, for example, repeatedly filmed looking out of windows – the low-angle silhouette shots of Kaze at his open window in Paris, looking up and out at the sky; his father looking out of the window of his Lisbon apartment – or gazing down from a bridge at railway tracks tracing vanishing lines – *lignes de fuite*, in French, or "lines of flight," which resonates with the father's flight from Congo, and Max's flight from Paris. These leitmotifs instill a melancholic sense of yearning, of being physically present but psychologically elsewhere, notably in the case of the Congo-born father now living in the country of his family's origin – a country that he claims not to like – before passing away, far from both homes, in Brussels. Again, any possible preconceptions of home and sentiments of belonging are thwarted; it is in Europe that the father feels in exile.

Filial ties and family boundaries and bonds are constantly questioned and challenged in the film. Kaze's relationship with his father is poor, the two men not speaking for 15 years. Despite what appears to be his good fatherly relationship in the home video footage, Max suddenly abandons his children, without a trace or word. His daughter Iris's friend, Charlotte, who accompanies them on the trip to Lisbon, no longer sees her father either. And the testimony of Nette, the sister sent at a very young age to live with the father's family in Lisbon, attests to the pain of this estrangement. Yet, the film also explores other conceptions of family ties that may not be biological. Anna, the sister who has returned to Kinshasa, has no children of her own, but is called "Maman" by several children. When Max, filming her on his trip, questions this, insisting it is strange, Anna sharply retorts: "That's white people's talk! Children you raise consider you as their real mother, and you consider them as yours!" Similarly, the French woman Kaze meets in Cambodia has forged her own Cambodian family, insisting: "Blood ties are not always so important in other cultures. They are fluid, they ravel and unravel." Other filiations, those of one's own making, the film seems to suggest, are possible. And her word "fluid" immediately echoes Max's earlier – at that point enigmatic – home video shots filmed from a moving car on the motorway and viewed by Kaze: In the dark, the neon lights of two successive motorway signs flash up, announcing, that the traffic is "FLUID."

Indeed, fluidity characterizes the whole film: The fluidity of movement between spaces and time, the fluidity of this distended family's ties, the fluid movement between documentary and fiction, reality and invention, between this family's history and Democratic Republic of the Congo's post-independence history and fragmentation. But in the meanders of this journey, Kaze (Zeka?) ultimately comes face to face not with Max, but with himself. A remarkably solitary figure, he is systematically filmed alone in his apartment, in the street, in cafés, in the train, in Cambodia. The often very low-angle shots of him in the street, or the shots that focus on just his hands, or his always obscured face give the impression of contorting, of almost fragmenting his body, just as he is initially somehow himself fragmented, incomplete. Symbolically, Max, his closest brother, his double, is lost. Much is made throughout the film of the indistinguishability of Max and Kaze: In certain childhood photos, they look so alike they could be twins. Both Max's children and the father confuse Kaze's voice on phone with Max's, and Max's voice heard occasionally in voice-over in the home video images is indeed indistinguishable from Kaze's voice. When Kaze shows people in Cambodia Max's photo, several exclaim: "It's you!" Max thus appears, like in oral literature's mirror tales, to symbolize not so much an actual person, as a facet, an alter-ego of Kaze, himself an alter-ego of Laplaine. It is not finding Max that ultimately matters – and indeed he is never found – it is the quest itself. For the first time in the film, at the remote temple in Cambodia where he finally stops looking for Max, Kaze's narrative voice addresses the absent Max directly: "I don't know if you'll find your place here. I don't even know if that's what you're looking for. You used to say we only have one life: the one we make." We sense here that Kaze has reached a point of (self-) acceptation. It is the life he chooses to make that matters, the bonds he creates, the reconfigurations, as he comes to accept his own fluidity and complexity. Ultimately it is death – that of the father, despite the very visible EVERLAST logo on the cap he wears – the death that hovers throughout the film in the newspaper headlines that Kaze reads, that reunites the members of this scattered family, Max aside, for an ultimate farewell. As the film closes on its opening images of Kaze's silhouetted reflection in the moving train window, only this time facing the opposite direction – the loop is looped, but Kaze has changed on the the journey – the famous line comes to mind: "Partir, c'est mourir un peu…," "to leave is to die a little…"[15]

Finally, Mati Diop's *A Thousand Suns*, also traces a web of journeys. The French-born daughter of musician, Wasis Diop, and niece of the legendary Senegalese filmmaker, Djibril Diop Mambéty, Mati Diop made several shorts before turning her camera to address this cinematic family heritage, connecting with it and with her Senegalese roots. The film also transgresses lines between the real and fiction, between documentary and experimental film, also linking past and present and addressing the divisions, or ties, between generations. Journeying to Dakar, Diop follows the trace of actor Magaye Niang some 40 years after he played the marginal young Mory in Djibril Diop Mambety's *Touki Bouki*. Like the character Mory, Niang has remained all his life in Dakar, whereas Myriam Niang, the actress who played Anta, like her film character, left Senegal. Both the actors' and characters' opposite paths recall the common mirroring device in oral quest tales, and their real-life journeys continue the trajectory of the fictional characters that they played. Throughout the film, confusions between the individuals and the actors, their lives and their roles arise, dissipate and arise again. References to *Touki Bouki* abound. Right from the opening sequence of the film, Niang, like Mory, drives a herd of cattle to the slaughter house. Mati Diop, like her uncle, films the blood-splattered interiors; unlike her uncle, who captured the tragic majesty of the felled zebu, she focuses on the choreographic gestures of the men who, like traditional Senegalese wrestlers, grapple with the cattle. While constantly revisiting and referencing the past classic, Mati Diop's film is firmly set in the present, creating a to-ing and fro-ing in time. If the opening shots of the aged Niang of course reso-nates with the opening shots of *Touki Bouki*, Niang and his herd are firmly posi-tioned in today's Dakar, surrounded, engulfed even, by the dense traffic and hustle and bustle.

Soon after, Niang is in his home, arguing with his wife as he gets dressed to go out, pulling on his cowboy boots and even pulling an imaginary pistol to shoot his reflection in the mirror! The reference to Westerns is not fortuitous, of course. *A Thousand Suns* also opens and closes with the theme song of *High Noon* (Fred Zinneman, 1952), reputed to have been Diop Mambety's favorite film, the influ-ences of which are patent in all his works. His wife's angry tirade brings to mind Aunt Oumy's constant berating of the "good-for-nothing" Mory in *Touki Bouki*. Indeed, Niang still lives the dissolute lifestyle of the young film character. A barfly and, like Mory, a loveable rogue, the film follows this gangly, almost disarticulated figure's long, uncertain trek from his home in the suburbs, across wasteland and into the city center, to the neighborhood where filmmaker Ben Diogaye Baye, artist and actor Joe Ouakam, and Wasis Diop – all friends and collaborators of Djibril Diop Mambéty – anxiously await him, uncertain if he will show up at the open-air screening of *Touki Bouki* that Mati Diop organizes and films to confront today's audience with the classic film. Just as *Touki Bouki* follows Mory and Anta's journey through Dakar in search of the money that will allow them to escape to France, here the camera follows Niang's voyage on foot, by taxi, his digressions en route – for example, when he stops off in a bar, where he and his drinking buddies, all in blue against the yellow walls, drunkenly philosophize and brawl – before setting off, albeit unsteadily now, on foot again. The long slow panning shots espouse his movements, capturing his loping stride and inscribing him in the land-scapes that he journeys across.

In the taxi that takes Niang into the city center, whose driver is played by the well-known Senegalese rap artist Djily Bagdad, a member of the *Y'en a marre* ("Fed Up") youth movement that began protesting government inefficiency in 2011, encouraging young people to vote, and eventually ousting President Abdoulaye Wade in 2012, gives rise to a debate between the driver and Niang over their respec-tive generation's actions and responsibilities. As soon as he gets in the taxi, Niang grumbles that the loud hip hop music is "busting [his] ears," immediately setting the tone of a classic generational divide. Filmed frontally, passenger and driver are side by side, yet ostensibly and symbolically separated by the big gold chain that hangs from the rear-view mirror between them. The young man blames the elder's generation for the country having lost its way, for having been lured by material things and the call of the West: "You fled. We shall never leave the sinking ship!" Forty years apart, the attitudes of the two generations' youth have of course changed and the different generations do not necessarily see eye-to-eye. Yet thrown together in the tight confines of this space, Mati Diop nonetheless creates a bridge between them. The scene is staged, fictional, but the discussion real, improvised;[16] elsewhere, the dialogues are fictional, written, but unfold in real settings. The fiction of *Touki Bouki* thus mingles and collides with fragments of real life, and with Mati Diop's fictional projections.

The blurring of boundaries between fiction and documentary, past and present, between Mory the character and Niang the actor, intensifies as the film progresses. There is also an increasing resonance between the themes of *Touki Bouki* – the dream of an elsewhere and the question of departure – and of *A Thousand Suns*. Niang finally reaches the open-air screening of Djibril Diop Mambety's film late, as the film draws to a close: Mati Diop's camera tracks from left to right, filming Niang in profile as he arrives; Diop Mambety's camera tracks from right to left, filming Mory in profile as he runs along the quayside away from the ship that would have taken him to France. Close-up shots of the spectators cut to a close-up shot of Mory's face on the screen, to a close-up shot of the now watching Niang's mesmerized face. Niang tells the children near him that the young man on the screen is him, but the children mock: "Wake up! You're dreaming! That's not you! You can't fool us, old man. Your hair is white!" Their incredulity bounces straight off Niang, however, the schism between reality and fiction seeming not to exist in his mind, the children's voices fading, as Niang – and we – become completely absorbed in *Touki Bouki*'s final shots of the ship, the *Ancerville*, sailing that fill the screen, leaving Mory behind, the melancholy closing music engulfing the present moment. As we watch Niang watching, we have no doubt where he is: Reliving the scene as if it were reality.

After the screening, Niang argues with Diogaye Baye and Ouakam about whether or not he wasted his talents and the "gift" that Diop Mambéty gave him, and whether or not he should have left Senegal; Diogaye Baye tells him "*Touki* means journey and you are stagnating." Niang lopes off alone into the night, the camera moving with him. We find him again, now wound up in an empty nightclub in the early hours, telling the two women with him "[his] story with Anta, [his] first love." Over shots of Anta boarding the *Ancerville*, Niang tells the *Touki Bouki* story as if it were his own, concluding: "She left. I stayed," adding that he never heard from her again. One of the young woman, her face lit only by her cellphone – phones, as in *Kinshasa Palace*, symbolizing communication and connection – looks up to directly ask the camera: "Is she still alive?" The answer comes obliquely as the following shot cuts to the Alaskan sea and shoreline filmed from a moving boat – one thinks of the *Ancerville* – the music from *Touki Bouki* creating a liaison between the two worlds. Returning to Dakar now in the daytime, Niang enters a call shop and phones Myriam Niang, who, we learn from the conversation, is now a security worker on an oil rig in Alaska. In the bright reds and yellows of the call shop, invaded by the sounds of the bustle outside, Myriam Niang's voice – actually played by an actress, but based on a real phone conversation between them – indeed seems worlds apart; her surprise at being contacted is patent and the conversation faltering. The bond is distended by time and space and Niang reproaches her for leaving without warning. Out in the street, a mysterious figure on a motorbike, his face ensconced in a red turban like Mory in a scene of *Touki Bouki*, revs the bike staring at Niang. Is he imaging himself young again in the film? The sound of the motorbike continues in transition over jerky moving shots of the deserted Alaskan landscape. A blue figure against the white, Niang struggles through the snow towards the now fixed camera. The elusive silhouette of a naked young black woman appears, and disappears in the snowy fog (an apparition? A ghost? A figment of Magaye's imagination mingling the contemporary reality of Alaska and the memory of the young Anta?). Off, the phone conversation continues – its temporal continuity disrupted – on the question of the (im)possibility of coming home. Speaking a line from James Baldwin's *Giovanni's Room*, Magaye Niang concludes: "You don't have a home until you leave it and then, when you have left it, you never can go back." The sequence ends with a close-up shot of Niang's face, back in Dakar, gazing off-screen into the distance, again crossing spatiotemporal lines in an imbrication of real and imaginary realms. The film ends, again like in *Touki Bouki*, with a return to the film's opening: Niang heads off into the distance with his herd of cattle, the loop is looped in a circularity common to initiatory quest tales.

In conclusion, the different films discussed here all strikingly question and embrace filiations and roots, exploring and asserting personal and collective memory and identity. At the same time, in an almost antinomic movement, they and their characters take flight, journey, go forth in the world, refusing to "stay in [their] place," as Fanon describes it in the lines cited at the opening of this chapter. In so doing, not only do their filmmakers assert a powerful presence in the world, but embrace their "status of passerby," to cite Mbembe again. Crossing lines of all kinds, "going beyond limits" (Fanon, 1961), they refuse to be assigned to a place, a style, an identity or an easy categorization; these are films of resonances and circulations, and their directors adopt an incredible freedom of style and themes. In a present of renewed xenophobia, closing borders, and growing demarcations, these filmmakers and their works transcend all kinds of frontiers, claiming, in what is ultimately an eminently political gesture, what Assia Djebar (2000) described as "the utmost freedom, that of movement, of journeying, the remarkable possibility of disposing of oneself to come and go." In so doing, they claim the freedom to explore and to define who they are, both rooted in and speaking from a place, yet open to the winds, to the flows. Seeking to find a place in a shifting world, they very much reflect the contemporary world's conflicting pull of both the local and the global. This is a cinema, then, that is at once situated, embedded, yet resolutely open. It is a cinema that defies constraint. It is, to cite Fanon one last time, a cinema that spans borders "in one stride."

Notes

1   "The first thing which the native learns is to stay in his place, and not to go beyond certain limits. This is why the dreams of the native are always ... of action ... I dream I am jumping, swimming, running, ... that I span a river in one stride." (Trans. Farrington 1963, p. 51).

2   In his recently published *Politiques de l'inimitié*, Achille Mbembe describes today's world as being caught in a "course vers la séparation et la *déliaison*" (my translation).

3   Mbembe continues in *Politique de l'inimitié*: "Il ne s'agit manifestement plus d'élargir le cercle, mais de faire des frontières des formes primitives de mise à distance des ennemis, des intrus et des étrangers, tous ceux qui ne sont pas des nôtres. Dans un monde plus que jamais caractérisé par une inégale redistribution des capacités de mobilité et où, pour beaucoup, se mouvoir et circuler constituent la seule chance de survie, la brutalité des frontières est désormais une donnée fondamentale de notre temps. Les frontières ne sont plus les lieux que l'on franchit, mais des lignes qui séparent." [It is manifestly no longer about widening the circle, but about turning borders into primitive forms of distancing enemies, intruders and foreigners, all those who are not one of us. In a world more than ever characterize by an unequal redistribution of capacities of mobility and where, for many, moving and circulating constitute the sole chance of survival, the brutality of borders is now a fundamental fact of our time. Frontiers are no longer the places that you cross, but lines that divide" (2016, pp. 9–10 my translation).

4   Thanks to twentieth-century archaeological discoveries, we now know of course that humanity spread from its birthplace on the African continent to Asia, Europe, and beyond, necessarily implying a long history of migration and movement, as do Africa's ancient commercial exchanges with Asia via the Silk Route as early as 500 BC, its religious exchanges (the Christianization of Ethiopia in the first century AD, or the Islamization of sub-Saharan Africa as of the eighth century AD); or its cultural and intellectual exchanges (Timbuktu was a renowned international center of Islamic scholarship in the fourteenth and fifteenth centuries), to mention a few examples.

5   The reference to the title of the journal *Présence Africaine, Revue culturelle du monde noir,* founded by Alioune Diop in Paris in 1947, is not fortuitous. The journal indeed reflected the cosmopolitanism and internationalism of black artists and intellectuals of the time.

6   "Traverser le monde, prendre la mesure de l'accident que représente notre lieu de naissance et son pesant d'arbitraire et de contrainte, épouser l'irréversible flux qu'est le temps de la vie et l'existence, apprendre à assumer notre statut de passant en tant que ceci est peut-être la condition en dernière instance de notre humanité, le socle à partir duquel nous créons la culture. ... Devenir–homme–dans–le–monde n'est ni une question de naissance ni une question d'origine ou de race. C'est une affaire de trajet, de circulation et de transfiguration" (my translation).

7   See chapter 3 of Michel Chion, *The Voice in Cinema*. Trans. Claudia Gorbman. New York: Columbia University Press, 1999, 49–58.

8   Unpublished notes taken during conversation between Mati Diop and Olivier Barlet. Festival des Films d'Afrique en pays d'Apt, France. November, 2013.

9   My thanks to Michèle Leclerc-Olive for these references cited in her unpublished article, "Evenements biographiques: des laboratoires de littérature?"

10   "Déambuler dans un territoire où passé et présent se répondent …" (my translation).

11   Seeking "vraiment à connaître ses lieux de mémoire, cela devient se re-connaître, en somme se retrouver! " (my translation). Djebar plays, in the French, on the dual meaning of "se re-connaître": "to recognize," but also "to know oneself again/anew."

12   In her article "Au-délà des épistémologies sédentaires," Michèle Leclerc-Olive (2016) aptly points to the possibility in biographic experiences of deterritoriality not only of "attachment" and "detachment," but also of a"pluri-attachment" to several places, several territories.

13   The Golden Stool is the divine Asante throne, believed to have descended from the sky into the lap of the first Asante King. It is believed to house the spirit – living, dead, and yet to be born – of the Asante nation.

14   Interestingly, in Zeka Laplaine's earlier 2001 improvisational fiction film *(Paris: XY)*, Laplaine plays a main character called Max.

15   The opening line of an 1891 poem by Edmond Haraucourt that has become a French saying unto itself.

16   During the conversation about the film with Olivier Barlet, Mati Diop described the taxi scene as "a real discussion in a purely fictional frame."

References

Chion, Michel. *The Voice in Cinema*. Trans. Claudia Gorbman. New York: Columbia University Press, 1999.

Djebar, Assia. *Idiome de l'exil et langue de l'irréductibilité*. German publishers and bookstores' "Prix pour la Paix" acceptance speech, 2000. My translation. Accessed 23 May 2016. http://remue.net/spip.php?article683

Fanon, Frantz. *Les damnés de la terre*. 1961. Paris: Gallimard, 1991. / *The Wretched of the Earth*. Trans. Constance Farrington. New York: Grove Press, 1963.

Gabriel, Teshome. "Thoughts on Nomadic Aesthetics and the Black Independent Cinema: Traces of a Journey." *Blackframes: Critical Perspectives on Black Independent Cinema*. Ed. Mbye B. Cham and Claire Andrade-Watkins. Cambridge, MA: MIT Press, 1988: 62–79.

Gilroy, Paul. *In Search of a Not Necessarily Safe Starting Point*. A conversation between Paul Gilroy and Rosemary Bechler, 1 May 2016. Accessed 26 May 2016. www.opendemocracy.net/paul–gilroy–rosemary–bechler/paul–gilroy–in–search–of–not–very–safe–starting–point

Hall, Stuart. "New Ethnicities." *Black Film British Cinema*. Ed. Kobena Mercer, Erica Carter. London: ICA Documents 7, 1988: 27–31.

Hall, Stuart. "Cultural Identity and Diaspora." 1989. *Identity: Community, Culture, Difference*. Ed. Jonathan Rutherford. London: Lawrence & Wishart, 1990: 222–237.

Hegel, G.W.F. *The Philosophy of History*. 1837. Trans. J. Sibree. New York: Dover Publications, 1956.

hooks, bell. "Representations of Whiteness." *Black Looks: Race and Representation*. Boston MA: South End Press, 1992: 165–178.

Leclerc-Olive, Michèle. "Au-delà des épistémologies sédentaires." *Parcours anthropologiques*, 10: 2015. Accessed 15 April 2016. https://pa.revues.org/443

Mbembe, Achille. "African Modes of Self-Writing." *Identity, Culture and Politics* 1, 2001: 1–39.

Mbembe, Achille. "Afropolitanism." 2005. *Africa Remix: Contemporary Art of a Continent.* Ed. S. Njami. Trans. Laurent Chauvet. Johannesburg: Jacana Media, 2007 : 26–29.

Mbembe, Achille. *Politiques de l'inimitié.* Paris: La Découverte. 2016.

Mbembe, Achille. "Evènements biographiques: des laboratoires de littérature?" unpublished.

Syrotinski, Michael. *Singular Performances: Reinscribing the Subject in Francophone African Writing.* Charlottesville and London: University of Virginia Press, 2002.

Vergès, Françoise. "The Invention of an African Fabric." *SMBA Newsletter* 130, *Hollandaise.* 2012. Accessed 23 May 2016. http://www.smba.nl/static/en/exhibitions/hollandaise/smba-newsletter-130.pdf

Filmography

Akomfrah, John. (2010). *The Nine Muses.* UK: Smoking Dogs Films.

Diop, Mati. (2013). *A Thousand Suns/Mille soleils.* France: Anna Sanders Films.

Diop Mambéty, Djibril. (1973). *Touki Bouki.* Senegal: Cinegrit / Studio Kankourama.

Hondo, Med. (1969). *Soleil O.* Mauritania / France: Grey Films / Shango Films.

Laplaine, Zeka. (2006). *Kinshasa Palace.* DRC / France: Bakia Films / Les Histoires Weba.

Lawson, David. (2012); *Chiasmus.* UK: Smoking Dogs Films.

Sembène, Ousmane. (1962). *Borom Sarret.* Senegal: Filmi Domirev.

Sembène, Ousmane. (1966). *Black Girl / La Noire de…* Senegal / France: Filmi Domirev / Les Actualités Françaises.

Sokhana, Sydney. *Nationalité immigré.* Mauritania, France, 1975.

Teno, Jean-Marie. (1985). *Homage.* Cameroon: Les Films du Raphia.

Teno, Jean-Marie. (1996). *Clando.* Cameroon: Les Films du Raphia.

Teno, Jean-Marie. (2000). *A Trip to the Country / Vacances au pays.* Cameroon: Les Films du Raphia.

Vieyra, Paulin, Mamadou Sarr and Groupe africain du cinéma. (1955). *Afrique sur Seine.* France: Groupe africain du cinéma.

Part VIII

The End of Film Criticism?
The New Beginning of Curation and Bricolage

21

Towards Alternative Histories and Herstories of African Filmmaking

From Bricolage to the "Curatorial Turn" in African Film Scholarship

Lindiwe Dovey

Introduction

Within African film studies, it has become commonplace to draw a distinction between the radical political agenda of the first African filmmakers, in the 1960s, and the more diffuse, less ideological interests of more contemporary filmmakers. Despite attempts by certain film scholars to challenge this rigid history (for example, Tcheuyap, 2011), its dominance looms over the field and has prevented more nuanced characterizations of the origins of African filmmaking, and of contemporary African filmmaking, from emerging. This chapter aims to reveal the potential for alternative histories and herstories of African filmmaking to emerge, through the incorporation of new methodologies that draw together the overlapping activities of theory and practice – revisiting archives, using film festivals and curatorial practices as heuristic devices, and attending to the work of *bricoleurs* and scholar-curators who complicate linear histories and neat boundaries and categories. At the same time, however, it emphasizes the continued importance of conventional film criticism to our methodology as African film scholars.

I take inspiration, in the first instance, from Jyoti Mistry and Antje Schuhmann's use of *bricolage* in attempting to summon herstories of African filmmaking. In their edited collection *Gaze Regimes: Film and Feminisms in Africa* (2015a), Mistry and Schuhmann aim "to collect, archive and document the very disparate stories that emerged from a unique gathering of women all working in and with film" in Johannesburg in 2010 (Mistry and Schuhmann 2015b, p. ix). Mistry and Schuhmann deliberately avoid

A Companion to African Cinema, First Edition. Edited by Kenneth W. Harrow and Carmela Garritano.
© 2019 John Wiley & Sons, Inc. Published 2019 by John Wiley & Sons, Inc.

reifying a linear history of African filmmaking, which would inevitably create "the illusion of a universal, objective representation of facts and truth" (2015b, p. xiii); rather, they bring together diverse forms of knowledge from different voices to "create a heterodox practice" (2015b, p. xiv), one that they liken to *bricolage* (2015b, p. xv). Crucial to this attempt to open African film studies to more colorful rewritings is the play between theory and practice, criticism and creativity, and they ask: "What does it mean for academics to be in conversation with creative practitioners, and how do practitioners involved in reading films as texts interpret the curatorial strategies that frame films at film festivals?" (2015b, p. xi). Adopting more fluid definitions of what constitutes theory and practice, they argue, will also help to challenge "knowledge paradigms from within patriarchal and colonial legacies" (2015b, p. xii), thereby making an approach of *bricolage* intrinsic to contemporary feminist, womanist and decolonization movements.[1]

It is important to note, however, that Mistry and Schuhmann's work as *bricoleurs* is not new; in fact, many of the pioneering figures in African film studies can be seen as *bricoleurs*. It is towards one of these pioneering *bricoleurs* – Paulin Soumanou Vieyra – that I turn first, in an attempt to revisit the archives of African film studies to provide a more nuanced and less politicized account of its origins. Thereafter I attempt to trace the influence of African film scholarship's early engagement with *bricolage* on certain key figures across African film studies up to the present day. Ultimately, I argue that through charting this lineage of *bricolage* we can better understand, contextualize, and historicize what I want to identify and call the "curatorial turn" in contemporary (African) film scholarship. This "curatorial turn" has seen many African film scholars play dual roles as academics and curators for film festivals and other live cinema events. In some cases, as I will show, African film scholars are not engaged in *literal* curation but rather adopt a curatorial voice in their scholarship, either explicitly encouraging others to screen particular films in concert, or – through vivid, performative criticism (Jayamanne, 2001) – imaginatively conjuring a film program for the reader. The "curatorial turn" could be read, somewhat cynically, as a result of the pressure on academics to create quantitative "impact" through making their research available to non-academic audiences. However, it can also be interpreted, more positively, as part of a movement towards a deeper and more diverse engagement with the object of study itself – indeed, with African films themselves. As I will argue, however, this curatorial engagement cannot be at the expense of conventional critical engagement with the films.

Rethinking the Origins of African Film Scholarship: A Glance at the Work of Paulin Soumanou Vieyra

Paulin Soumanou Vieyra is often cited as one of the collective of African filmmakers living in Paris (the African Filmmakers Group) who made *Afrique sur Seine* (1955), one of the first films by sub-Saharan Africans.[2] He is also often invoked as one of the founders of FEPACI, the Pan African Federation of Filmmakers, an organization that was founded in 1969 and that initially had a strong political vision about what African filmmaking should and should not be.[3] However, Vieyra also deserves to be acknowledged as the "father" of African film studies, for authoring the first books about African filmmaking (see Vieyra 1969, 1972, 1983). These books are rarely engaged with in African film studies, meaning that Vieyra's fascinating early reflections are lost on contemporary African film scholars. Perhaps this has to do with the relative inaccessibility of Vieyra's books. Perhaps it is partly due to the Anglophone bias in our field, which tends to ignore key texts in French and other languages. And perhaps, finally, it has something to do with the fact that we have overlooked the true extent of Vieyra's approach of *bricolage* to his work. His filmmaking and political work have been valorized over his scholarship, which was, nevertheless, groundbreaking in the ways that it documented, archived, and reflected on the early days of African filmmaking but also drew on Vieyra's intimate practical engagements with film.

Vieyra's *Le cinéma et l'Afrique* (1969) is, in my view, the book with which any conversation about the history of African filmmaking should begin. Notably, the essays within it were not written to be assembled into a book; rather, Vieyra says, they are "a testimony to [his] reflections about cinema and Africa from 1955 to 1965" (1969, p. 7).[4] The reflections are rich and nuanced and contradict the assumption that all the founding FEPACI figures made political liberation their key criterion for African filmmaking. It is also noteworthy that Vieyra does *not* use the phrase "African Cinema," thereby assuming a category that does not, and cannot, possibly exist, but rather explores the varied relationships between "cinema" and "Africa." Vieyra also reminds us, lest we overlook the imaginative dimensions of films in lieu only of their contexts of production and circulation, that "the cinema should be able to participate in its function in the creation of a new African humanism" (1969, p. 9), by which he seems to mean that African filmmaking should confidently claim its place in global history and not see itself purely as an oppositional or marginalized practice. This is a profound statement to have made in 1969, but it is also an important invitation to contemporary (African) film scholars, in a context in which African film studies continues to be marginalized within the global academy (Tsika, 2016; Dovey 2016). For Film Studies to become international will require a post-humanist perspective that is, as Chambers says, *"more human* in recognizing its own specific limits and location" (2002, p. 173); in other words, Film Studies scholars need to reckon with the insights of African film scholars to humanize their practice, and African film studies scholars need to labor to mainstream their work within Film Studies and refuse to be relegated to the margins of the discipline.

Given my interest not only in the methodological importance of using archives, but also in the possibilities of using film festivals and curatorial practices as a heuristic device (Dovey, 2015a), it is revelatory that some of Vieyra's most fascinating writing about cinema appears in two essays in *Le cinéma et l'Afrique* that concern festivals: "Notes and Reflections on the First International Conference of Cinéma d'Outre-Mer [in Lille, France]" (pp. 67–73) and "Cinema at the 6th World Festival of Youth and Students at Moscow" (pp. 74–89). Collectively these essays show how greatly these festivals, held in October 1957 and July and August 1957 respectively, shaped Vieyra's ideas – as a filmmaker, jury member, spectator, and scholar – about what cinema could and might be in diverse global contexts, from France to the Soviet Union to Africa. He speaks in euphoric terms about the Moscow festival and its impact on him, as well as on the other Africans in attendance, who were representing many different countries, such as Togo, Cameroon, Angola, and Sudan (1969, pp. 84–87).[5] Sparked by "Khruschchev's Thaw," which involved a loosening of Soviet Union policy that meant that foreigners were allowed to visit and to meet locals (although only in supervised groups), the festival was attended by a staggering 34,000 people from 130 countries. In spite of the wealth of sports and arts featured at the festival, Vieyra opens the essay by quoting Lenin that "Of all the arts, cinema is the most important" (1969, p. 74), taking inspiration herein for the development of his own passion. The film component of the festival consisted of a five-day debate amongst cinema students on the subject of "Heroes in Film" and an 11-day festival of 230 films (p. 75).[6]

Interestingly, the films that particularly impressed Vieyra, and helped him to develop his own idea of a quality cinema, were films from what was then Czechoslovakia. He praises these films for their "human qualities: youth, freshness, spontaneity" (p. 77), for the "singular power of their images" and their "psychological and emotional density" (p. 78). These criteria of judgment could not be more contradictory of assumptions that the early FEPACI members were only interested in film as a form of political liberation. It is also revealing here to make links between the nourishment and direction Vieyra found from Czechoslovakian cinema and the reflections of the current Artistic Director of the Toronto International Film Festival, Cameron Bailey, one of the most important contemporary commentators on and tastemakers of African (as well as international) filmmaking. Bailey says that he shifts "between wild optimism and utter despair when it comes to African cinema," and that what he sees as most urgent for the development of contemporary African cinema is an engagement on the part of African filmmakers with diverse global cinemas. He says:

> I think it's important if you are a filmmaker that you see other films, that you don't simply repeat tired formulas or lowest common denominator approaches to whatever film you're making. That you actually are aware of what is around you, true to the history of cinema and what's going on presently within cinema … I think in places where there is access to cinema, where people can actually see films and see the full range of what world cinema is, then I think you're going to get better films. … [F]ilmmakers such as Djo Munga [the Congolese director of *Viva Riva*], he went to Europe and trained there and he had access to seeing all of what was current in world cinema then. … I think film schools are a big part of it and I think cinematheques and cine-clubs and those kinds of environments where people can actually

sit down and watch the latest Dardenne brothers' film or watch what is coming out of China right now ... I think those are the films that African filmmakers have to see more of. (personal communication, 2011)

This view coheres with academic accounts of what is required of scholarship in African cultural studies in a context of globalization and internationalization. Eileen Julien summarizes this eloquently when she urges Africanist scholars to put "literary, film, and visual arts by Africans in dialogue with the work of artists from Asia, Europe, and the Americas"; as she goes on: "Such comparative study will require more – not less – "local" knowledge of these multiple places and will recognize both African specificities and Africa's presence in the world" (Julien 2015, p. 26).

Vieyra's pioneering openness to diverse cinemas and criteria of judgment does not mean, however, that his ability to judge the socio-political dynamics surrounding filmmaking at this time was blunted. Vieyra clearly draws on his experience of the "Soviet kindness, the Soviet hospitality, the magnificence of this extraordinary festival" (p. 89) in assessing the Lille festival several months later. For while this festival claimed – like the Moscow festival – to be "aiding the mutual understanding of civilizations, of customs, of fraternity between people" (p. 67), Vieyra notes the irony of such a claim within a context in which first, only French overseas territories (d'Outre-Mer) were allowed to participate (p. 68), and second, in which these territories were viewed as inherently in need of "education" and "elevation" by the French (p. 67). The fact that the main organizer of the festival was a priest and that the entire festival took place within a Christian humanist discourse does not escape Vieyra's sharp analysis (p. 69), nor does the fact that the organizers essentially banned any kind of political discussion (p. 68). However, Vieyra also critiques some of his countrymen (of whom there were 30 present) for whom art and especially the cinema is seen to have no value except as a weapon of liberation, and says: "One needs to remember that it is first through the spirit that a man liberates himself" (p. 70). Even when he comes to praising a handful of films for their "technical and artistic quality," he faults those that do not have enough "human warmth" (pp. 72–73), thereby making humanism his central criterion for quality aesthetics in cinema, and contradicting the long-held assumption in African film studies that the founding FEPACI members saw cinema and political liberation as a *pas de deux*.

Paulin Soumanou Vieyra was a filmmaker, a film scholar, and a member of FEPACI. He was a pre-eminent pioneer of African film, then, but what kind of pioneer was he? I would like to argue here that Vieyra's most important contribution to African film studies was a methodological one, through approaching the object of analysis from diverse angles and perspectives so as to summon it in a more intimate and nuanced way. And his contributions to African filmmaking and African film studies has had an enduring effect on the ways in which several important subsequent scholars – such as Manthia Diawara, Samba Gadjigo, and Betti Ellerson – have approached African filmmaking in their work. We can thus trace an alternative intellectual heritage and history across this work, one that has not been sufficiently highlighted in African film studies.

Old and New Intellectual Trajectories for African Film Studies: From Bricolage to the "Curatorial Turn"

Paulin Soumanou Vieyra's influence can clearly be identified in the routes that African filmmaker,[7] scholar, and curator, Manthia Diawara, has taken in his work, from producing the first major scholarly monograph on African film in English – *African Cinema: Politics and Culture* (1992) – to his most recent book, *African Film: New Forms of Aesthetics and Politics* (2010), which adopts a poetic yet conversational style and reflects as much on his experiences of curating an African Cinema programme for the Haus der Kulturen der Welt in Berlin, Germany as it does on particular African films. Ken Harrow describes the evolution of Diawara's scholarly work as follows:

> In the last chapter of Diawara's [1992] study in particular, he utilizes a few key categories, like "Return to the Sources," "Colonial Confrontation," and "Social Realist," which have been repeatedly cited over the years, and in a sense have had a detrimental effect on the level of critical commentary by enabling reductive readings of films. In his current [2010] study his work has matured ... And his readings of Sembène and others are superb, subtle, complex ... (2015, p. 14)

Indeed, Diawara's criticism is at its best when it is poetic, drawing on his filmmaker's and curator's eye, carefully following and describing the contours of particular African films rather than attempting to create rigid categories for them. Because Diawara's most recent book was published to complement the film program he curated, it is also framed quite differently from a conventional academic publication, with an attractive format and an accompanying DVD with interviews. The book is a pleasure to read, in this material sense, and also because we feel, while reading it, that we are on a curatorial voyage with Diawara, starting in Ouagadougou and ending in Lagos.

Taken as a whole, Diawara's 2010 book presents a fine example of Oscar Wilde's concept of "criticism as creation" (1993), Laleen Jayamanne's notion of "performative criticism" (2001), and Christian Keathley's evocation of the cinephile as a *flâneur* (a wanderer) (2006). In his essay "The Critic as Artist" (1890), Wilde argues: "The critic occupies the same relation to the work of art that he criticizes as the artist does to the visible world of form and color, or the unseen world of passion and of thought" (1993, p. 1623). Acknowledging that aesthetic interpretations will differ from person to person, and from critic to critic, Wilde says:

> Who cares whether Mr. Ruskin's views on Turner are sound or not? What does it matter? That mighty and majestic prose of his, so fervid and so fiery-colored in its noble eloquence, so rich in its elaborate symphonic music, so sure and certain, at its

best, in subtle choice of word and epithet, *is at least as great a work of art as any of those wonderful sunsets that bleach or rot in their corrupted canvases in England's Gallery ...* (1993, p. 1624, my emphasis)

Wilde inspires us to believe that, without having to substitute our keyboards for film cameras, we as film scholars are also capable of being artists and creators, of making things that others will decide are or are not of beauty and resonance to them. The question is not so much whether our interpretations are *correct* ("What does it matter?"); indeed, *(dis)sensus communis* will reign wherever there are diverse human beings in attendance (Dovey, 2015a). The question rather is one of form, of feeling free to express oneself through different modes.

In his 2010 book, Diawara appears to free himself from academic conventions about how films should be discussed and analyzed and allows readers to experience in a more immediate sense his passion for African films. This approach coheres with recent calls in Film Studies for a greater cinephilia in film criticism:

Christian Keathley (2006) sees the contemporary cinephile as a kind of *flâneur*. ... He would like to return to the astonishment of the early film viewers. ... In his view, most of the academic film histories lack the signs of passion for their object of study. ... His strategy is to choose an arbitrary fragment, a detail of a film which is not generally noted as important. (Bosma 2015, p. 25)

Greater creativity and cinephilia in criticism is also one of the inspirations for Sri-Lankan-Australian filmmaker and film critic Laleen Jayamanne's concept of performative criticism, which she describes as

an impulsive move toward whatever draws one to something in the object – a color, a gesture, a phrase, an edit point, a glance, a rhythm ... Enter the film through this and describe exactly what is heard and seen, and then begin to describe the film in any order whatever rather than in the order in which it unravels itself. Soon one's own description begins not only to mimic the object, as a preliminary move, but also *to redraw the object* ... (2001, p. xi, my emphasis)

In his films and curatorial work, but also in those moments when his critical work begins to redraw African films through words, Diawara brings African filmmaking to life in breathtakingly beautiful and enduring ways, continuing Vieyra's legacy of *bricolage* but also giving rise to what I will go on to theorize later as the "curatorial turn" in (African) film scholarship.

Another veteran African film scholar who, like Vieyra and Diawara, has drawn on an approach of *bricolage*, moving between the overlapping activities of theory and practice, is Samba Gadjigo. Complementing his academic research on the filmmaking of Ousmane Sembène, Gadjigo also worked as Sembène's biographer and agent for many years, and can be seen as his posthumous curator, since it is Gadjigo's archives on Sembène that will no doubt define how

Sembène's work is remembered long into the future. The image that will always remain with me from Gadjigo and co-director Jason Silverman's documentary *Sembène!* (2015) is the one of rusting film canisters encasing Sembène's films, on the rooftop of Galle Ceddo (Sembène's home), the deep blue Atlantic in the backdrop a striking symbol of how impotent humans are in the face of natural forces. That image powerfully reminds one of the symbiotic relationship between artist and scholar-curator, and of the need for scholar-curators who are also custodians, who work to keep alive what they care about. The original meaning of the word "curate" is to care (*cura*, in Latin). In my view, this involves caring not simply for the films themselves but also for the people who made them (Dovey 2015a). This is what Gadjigo has done – he has cared for the films and the person who made them, not simply written about them in scholarly publications.

The French film critic, Serge Daney, once said that the curator is the person who sets up the goal for the one who scores (Salti 2011, personal communication). Indeed, Gadjigo continues to work hard to ensure that audiences around the world see Sembène's films, and he and Silverman are currently engaged in a project to bring *Sembène!* to audiences across Africa. No artist works in a vacuum or emerges out of nowhere; artists rely on other people to recognize, value, and preserve their work. And, even once established, artists need continued and diverse forms of support. An approach of *bricolage* is displayed through the deeply collaborative nature of Gadjigo's work on Sembène, as evidenced through his documentary with Silverman, and through his co-edited volume *Ousmane Sembène: Dialogues with Critics and Writers* (1993) which brings many voices into conversation. But, like Diawara, Gadjigo has also been foundational to initiating a "curatorial turn" in (African) film scholarship, since it is difficult to isolate his curating of, and scholarship on, Sembène's work from one another.

All the scholars mentioned above have been "fathers" within African film studies in some sense. However, there are also important "mother" figures who have too often been curated out of our histories and anthologies. Betti Ellerson's approach has been nothing if not curatorial; she has produced pioneering materials that have completely transformed our field. Her book of interviews *Sisters of the Screen: Women of Africa on Film, Video and Television* (2000) with its accompanying film of the same name, her highly informative blog "African Women in Cinema" (initiated in 2009), and her two-part essay "Teaching African Women in Cinema" (*Black Camera* 7.1, Fall 2015, and 7.2, Spring 2016) are all works that make available invaluable resources about African women's filmmaking to scholars and curators. If, as I have previously argued, we need to see pedagogy itself as a form of curation subject to debate (Dovey, 2014), then Ellerson's (2015 and 2016) essay "Teaching African Women in Cinema" becomes a revolutionary call to return to our syllabi, to the ways in which we recount the history of African filmmaking, and to ensure that we do justice therein to the contributions of African women filmmakers. Indeed, it encourages us to open ourselves to alternative histories *and* herstories of African filmmaking.

I certainly have drawn on Ellerson's work while rewriting the syllabi for my African film courses at SOAS University of London, including films by pioneering African women filmmakers – such as *Saikati* (1992) by Kenyan filmmaker Anne Mungai – and using these films to motion towards previously hidden herstories of African filmmaking. I have also been inspired by Ellerson's work to attempt to put the male-dominated history of "African Cinema" into conversation with important work by African women writers and theorists, such as Obioma Nnaemeka (2004) and Montré Aza Missouri (2015). Although Nnaemeka does not write about African filmmaking, her theory of "nego-feminism" – that is, a feminism of negotiation, rather than competition, between men and women – offers an incisive way of understanding the predominance of womanist perspectives in the work of African male filmmakers (see Dovey, 2012), as well as of understanding some of the complexities of the work of African women filmmakers (Mistry and Schuhmann, 2015a). Missouri's work is crucial to fortifying the lines of analysis between the African continent and its diasporas, and reminds us of the importance, for example, of including Julie Dash's seminal film *Daughters of the Dust* (1991) in discussions of African filmmaking.[8]

The patriarchal conception of "African Cinema" as one forged by "father" figures has, in fact, been thrown into relief by the alternative narratives Ellerson has made available to us and invites further approaches of *bricolage* in which the intention is "to provide an *interruption*, to rupture classic and too often androcentric or supposedly gender-neutral approaches to academic knowledge production and publication politics" (Mistry and Schuhmann 2015b, p. xvi). Visual bricolage is also explicitly used towards such goals in *Aristotle's Plot* (1996) – one of the key films by male Cameroonian filmmaker, Jean-Pierre Bekolo (2009) – and claimed here as an intrinsically African practice. Towards the end of the film, a group of avid film fans who model themselves on their gangster heroes, build a cinema from whatever they can find. As their leader, Cinema, says: "We'll take what we can get. If it's old and it's good, fine. If it's new and it fits, excellent. … *This* is the real Africa." It seems no accident, then, that within the same film, Bekolo's narrator raises questions about why African filmmakers are always positioned either as young and emerging, or as fatherly or grandfatherly figures. The paternalism that goes hand in hand with gender bias is, in this way, revealed and critiqued by Bekolo. As Nnaemeka insists, "nego-feminism" is a mode of feminism that relies on the participation of men in order to be successful. Bekolo is one such man – and *bricoleur* – who is contributing to creating alternative ways of thinking about the histories and herstories of African filmmaking.[9]

Film Criticism, Film Curation and Contemporary Scholarship: Contextualizing and Critiquing the "Curatorial Turn" in (African) Film Studies

As I have suggested earlier in this chapter, contemporary approaches of *bricolage* have to be situated within what I want to identify and name here as "a curatorial turn" in (African) Film Studies over the past decade. Instead of simply writing about and interpreting films, many scholars have become aware of their power as gatekeepers and tastemakers and have started to explicitly foreground their curatorial aims within their scholarship – namely, their investment in helping important yet little-known (African) films to reach audiences around the world. Within African film studies, this curatorial turn is evident in recent books such as *Africa's Lost Classics* (2014), co-edited by David Murphy and Lizelle Bisschoff (one of the leading curators of African cinema, and the founder of the Africa in Motion film festival in Scotland, as well as an African film scholar), which Mark Cousins describes as follows in the Foreword:

> *Africa's Lost Classics* isn't only writing, it's a manifesto, a plea, and a call to arms. It reads like curation, as if its editors and authors have made a list of films to update and challenge our understanding of African film, and are urging cinemas, festivals, and TV stations to show the films on the list. The book's chapters are like screening notes. (Cousins 2014, p. xvi)

One has a similar feeling of curatorial intervention in Noah Tsika's introduction to his edited dossier "Teaching African Media in the Global Academy" in *Black Camera* 7.2 (2016), which is inspiring in the way that it provides a blueprint for how we might better curate Nollywood films. Just as Dina Iordanova (2013) argues that more rather than less curatorial work is needed now that the Internet has become saturated with freely available films, Tsika suggests that the fact that Nollywood films are now more "You Tube-able" than ever before (2016, p. 95) means that we need to be more creative in how we work with, teach, and present them to others – in essence, how we curate them. Tsika encourages us to pair films such as *Lady Gaga* (2012) with *Mulholland Drive* (2001) (2016, p. 99), and *Domitilla* (1997) with *The Prostitute* (2001, 2016, pp. 110–111), and also to put Nollywood films into conversation with Latin American soap operas (2016, p. 110). At this exciting moment of much greater availability not simply of Nollywood films, but all kinds of African films – for example, through video-on-demand platforms and mobile phone apps such as iROKO, AfricaFilms.tv, and Kanopy – the possibilities for using scholarship to extend curatorial practice (and vice versa) seem infinite rather than limited.

At the same time, this "curatorial turn" is also manifesting itself in less literal and more associative ways – in, for example, the tone and voice that (African) film scholars adopt in their writing. Alongside Manthia Diawara's most recent book one can situate MaryEllen Higgins' article "The Winds of African Cinema," which is exemplary for its curatorial approach and poetic tone. Higgins' article can also be seen, however, as a challenge to the logocentrism of patriarchal approaches to classifying (African) cinema movements in terms of "waves" – something that even Diawara replicates in his book (2010). Instead, Higgins argues, following Ngũgĩ's method of globalectics (2012), "for a windy decentering ... for a shifting away from habitual ways of seeing and recognizing world cinema, a wind of change in ways of speaking and writing about African cinema" (2015, p. 79). As a love letter to the many African films Higgins has watched, she reveals the cinephilia that Keathley calls for in contemporary film scholarship and she also enacts a curatorial approach through which she conjures a series of sounds and images of winds in African films that one can almost imagine playing across physical screens. Furthermore, through the poetic, performative way she invokes the films – "The wind is there in Haile Gerima's *Sankofa* (1993), rustling through cane fields, sharing the screen with the rhythms of Sankofa the Divine Drummer ..." – she breathes new life into them, bringing them to readers afresh. Her article makes one want to return to the films and watch them again and there is perhaps no better way to define a curatorial voice in scholarship than that.

The curatorial turn in African film studies is not unique but part of a global shift. We are living in a moment in which, on a global scale, the traditional role of critics is increasingly being overtaken by curators. As Jessica Morgan writes:

> Since the 1990s, the curatorial voice has to a large extent merged [with] or surpassed the critical one. No longer can we imagine a time when a critic such as Clement Greenberg might weigh heavily on the development of art. In part a result of curatorial involvement in the critical and theoretical discourse of the 1980s, the critic/curator has merged into one double-headed beast ... (2013, p. 26)

Similarly, on the important canon-making work performed by film festivals and film curators, Cameron Bailey says: "Festivals have multiplied and spread to become the single most important arbiter of taste in cinema – more important than scholars, or critics, more important even than film schools" (cited in Ruoff 2012a, p. iv). In one of the first books specifically addressing film programming as a field, Jeffrey Ruoff (2012b) points out that film curators – at their best – *become* film critics (helping us to see films in new ways), but also film historians (redefining historical narratives about cinema), film editors (bringing together and juxtaposing films in audiovisual ways), and storytellers. The merging of critical and curatorial work is also evident in another recent book which offers theoretical reflection as well as practical advice on film curating – Peter Bosma's *Film Programming: Curating for Cinemas, Festivals, Archives* (2015). It is no accident that Bosma himself is both a scholar and a curator.

The energy in contemporary African art studies has certainly emerged from scholar-curators such as Okwui Enwezor, whose multi-genre shows incorporate everything from live poetry and performance art to film and photography. As art curator and scholar Chika Okeke-Agulu points out in a curators' roundtable organized and published by *NKA: Journal of Contemporary African Art*:

> … in the field of art, especially contemporary art, curators are arguably the most powerful shapers of art's discursive horizons with their exhibitions (which can make or break artists' careers, influence values of artwork and their movement into museums) and catalogs (that have increasingly become referenced texts competing for scholarly attention with the autonomous monograph). (2008, p. 160)

Within the field of African film studies, in turn, I have attempted to explore the crucial role that curatorial practices – particularly through film festivals – have played in the very definition of African cinemas (Dovey, 2015a), building on Diawara's pioneering work on this topic (1993, 1994). In these African cinematic contexts, many prominent African filmmakers (for example, Ousmane Sembène, Pedro Pimenta, Tsitsi Dangarembga, and Martin Mhando) have *also* been film festival founders, organizers, and curators. There are also many people contributing to the circulation and redefinition of African films through regular "live cinema" events (Atkinson and Kennedy, 2016) across the continent (for example, AfricAvenir in Windhoek, Namibia; the First Wednesday Film Club in Johannesburg, South Africa; and the "Starry Nights Screenings" run by DocuBox in Nairobi, Kenya) which, because of their regularity, arguably play a more important role than rare, annual festivals, which have sometimes been accused of wasting public funds (Gibbs, 2012). These film curators allow African films to meet broad, diverse publics beyond the elite classrooms and abstruse discussions that sometimes characterize academia. Festivals and "live cinema" programmes also help to facilitate and stimulate important public debates that can impact society, although – as Litheko Modisane (2012) has shown – liveness is not a prerequisite in the creation of "publicness" through and around films, which can also develop "critical public potency" through textual forms, such as through the printed press and online social media.

The dramatic increase in online forms of criticism *and* curation has been identified as one of the key reasons behind the contemporary crisis in traditional film criticism, made abundantly clear in a new edited volume, *Film Criticism in the Digital Age* (2015). One of the editors notes that

> judging by the many journalistic articles, regular symposia and conferences, and the increasing scholarly output on the subject – which bemoan a "crisis of criticism" or mourn the "death of the critic" – it might seem safe to claim that the aims, status, and institution of arts and culture criticism in general, and film criticism in particular, are, indeed, facing possible extinction. (Frey 2015, p. 1)

This proclamation is not just a critical flight of fancy; 55 American film critics lost their jobs between 2006 and 2009 (ibid.). This crisis in criticism – most relevant to the practice of journalistic film criticism in newspapers and magazines, but also reflected through the swingeing cuts to arts and humanities funding at universities across the world – is worth dwelling on as a way of tempering any overly optimistic celebration of the "curatorial turn" in (African) film scholarship. Indeed, in the final part of this chapter I would like to reflect briefly on what might be lost through a curatorial approach without an attendant critical distance.

As Jessica Morgan warns us, the risk of a curatorial voice completely overtaking a critical one is "the loss of a critical platform, given the codependence of the curatorial world and the consequent lack of publicly voiced dissent" (2013, p. 26). Similarly, as the editors of *Cineaste* note, "In *Keywords*, Raymond Williams's classic work of cultural criticism … [he] makes clear that the term [criticism] is often synonymous with 'fault-finding'" (2016, p. 1). While curatorial work *can* offer critique, at its worst it becomes glossy and utopian, revolving around the imparting of favors, mutual backscratching, marketing, and the fear of upsetting those in power. As *Sight & Sound* editor Nick James has noted, the "culture prefers, it seems, the sponsored slogan to judicious assessment" (ibid.). The centrality of critique to academic scholarship – and, vitally, the space and prerogative to be critical – can perhaps be harnessed to ensure the necessary balance between intimacy with the object of study and distance from it. In other words, in its ideal form criticism offers us a way of not simply promoting or consuming texts, but reflecting on what is difficult or problematic about them and, thus, how we can contribute, ultimately, to a more just (re)imagining of the world.

Valuing critique as central to democratic practice can provide an antidote to those who would seek to deny the importance of academic criticism altogether, particularly in a contemporary context that is hostile to the humanities and other modes of qualitative rather than quantitative engagement. While the "passion" and "cinephilia" Keathley calls for in contemporary film scholarship is important, clearly a balance is needed between love and "fault-finding." Certain artists and scholars emphasize love at the expense of other emotions in our grappling with cultural texts. In *Letters to a Young Poet*, for example, Rilke urges the writer to

> Read as little as possible of aesthetic criticism – such things are either partisan views, petrified and grown senseless in their lifeless induration, or they are clever quibblings in which today one view wins and tomorrow the opposite. Works of art are of an infinite loneliness and with nothing so little to be reached as with criticism. Only love can grasp and hold and be just toward them. (1954, p. 29)

Similarly, the Malian filmmaker Souleymane Cissé – known for his dislike of film critics – berates African film scholar Frank Ukadike in an interview, saying "A film does not need to be commented on or you take away its universal aspects. You cannot pluck away at a film like a chicken" (Cissé cited in Ukadike 2002, p. 24). But why can filmmaking, film curation, and film criticism not co-exist?

Another statement exalting love over other emotions in our response to films comes from film curator Rasha Salti when she says: "In French we would say *coup de foudre*. I fall in love with every single film I programme" (personal communication 2011). What, then, are we to do with films that repulse us, that inspire not love but hate? As part of the 2008 London African Film Festival, I curated just such a set of films for a strand of the festival called "Early South African Cinema." Screened at the Barbican Cinema, the season included some of the first films made in South Africa, such as *De Voortrekkers* (1916) and *Siliva the Zulu* (1927). I detest *De Voortrekkers*, with its racist iconography, glorifying the murder of thousands of Zulu warriors during the Battle of Blood River. However, I felt that it was important to encourage British audiences to confront and reflect on (through post-screening discussions) these early cinematic iconographies of racism and colonialism. I had an interesting debate with a SOAS student several years ago on this topic. She argued that to screen or even teach such films re-empowers these racist discourses. I argued that it is rather a question of balance – that while such films clearly cannot appropriate too much of our time, thereby marginalizing African-made films, at the same time we cannot ban such representations outright but need to contextualize them through creating a dialogue between past and present.[10]

It is important to note here that curators have been slow to self-critique the colonial basis to their work compared to academic critics. The celebrated art curator Hans Ulrich Obrist says that curating, for him, is about two things: Love and conversation (2014, pp. 55–59). Curating, however, cannot be read innocently as *only* a positive process of lovingly nurturing artworks and creating conversations around them. Just as Susan Sontag argues that interpretation cannot be seen as an ontological presence but needs to be assessed historically (1966, p. 7), so too does curation. As I have argued (2015a), the curatorial impulse began as a violent, spectacular, imperial and racist one, and it is remarkable that Obrist, as one of the leading curators globally as well as one of the most vocal analysts and historians of curatorial work, does not acknowledge the brutal history of the "Great" Exhibitions when discussing their founder, Henry Cole (Obrist 2014, pp. 116–120). Every curatorial act, like every artwork, like every act of criticism, needs to be subject to critique itself.

In the final analysis, however, being critical should not be synonymous with being cynical. Writing about a strand of contemporary criticism in English Studies, Lisa Ruddick notes the following trend:

> Decades of antihumanist one-upmanship have left the profession with a fascination for shaking the value out of what seems human, alive, and whole. Some years ago Eve Kosofsky Sedgwick touched on this complex in her well-known essay on paranoid reading, in which she identified a strain of "hatred" in criticism (8). Also salient is a more recent piece in which Bruno Latour has described how scholars slip from "critique" into "critical barbarity," giving "cruel treatment" to experiences and ideals that non-academics treat as objects of tender concern (239–40). (Ruddick 2015, p. 72)

In conclusion, then, at this moment of a "curatorial turn" in (African) film scholarship – with scholars explicitly engaging in curatorial practice, or invoking a "curatorial voice" in their writing – I want to note and respect the history of *bricolage* out of which such a turn has emerged; but I also want to suggest the value of recognizing the symbiotic relationship between film criticism and curation, and to argue that African film critics and curators can enrich one another's work. As I hope to have shown, critical and curatorial practice overlap in significant ways: deciding which films to research or to teach is nothing if not an act of curation (Dovey, 2014). Similarly, as Ruoff argues, film curating often means engaging in a form of film criticism, in a mostly audiovisual medium and for a different kind of public. The curatorial mode can also bring in more of the performativity that is seen as central to contemporary criticism (Jayamanne, 2001) but in new forms that engage people's senses, emotions, and intellects in unorthodox ways. The "curatorial turn" also offers the possibility of more diverse, heterogeneous conversations than may happen within academic circles. Conventional scholarly film criticism, however, can introduce the necessary critique that may be lacking in the curatorial mode and – in our time of fake news, sponsored content, and anti-intellectualism – allow the necessary distance to consider, rigorously, the object of study in all its dimensions and depth.

Notes

1   In May 2015, South African students initiated the RhodesMustFall movement, thereby inspiring renewed decolonization struggles at universities around the world. In my own university – SOAS, University of London – students have initiated a "Decolonizing Our Minds" society that organizes debates, discussions and events, but that also scrutinizes the diversity of staff, students, and syllabi. Important protests in February 2017 about the lack of diversity in SOAS syllabi, and the need to contextualize any thinker or philosopher within their environment, have been grossly misinterpreted in much of the mainstream media in the United Kingdom (see www.telegraph.co.uk/education/2017/01/08/university-students-demand-philosophers-including-plato-kant/ and www.dailymail.co.uk/news/article-4098332/They-Kant-PC-students-demand-white-philosophers-including-Plato-Descartes-dropped-university-syllabus.html). As students within the decolonizing movements have emphasized, their aim is to encourage people to reflect on all kinds of privilege, and an intersectional approach that includes class, gender, and sexuality is central to their work (see https://soasunion.org/news/article/6013/Statement-on-the-recent-Press-about-Decolonising-SOAS/) (accessed June 2017).

2   *Afrique sur Seine* (1955) – made by Paulin Soumanou Vieyra, Mamadou Sarr, and Jacques Kane – can be called a "reverse ethnography," exploring Paris from the perspective of African students living there.

3   See Diawara 1992 for a historical overview of the organization. FEPACI's website is www.fepacisecretariat.org/about-us/ (accessed June 2017).

4   Translations from French to English are my own.

5   Some footage of the opening ceremony of this festival can be seen here: www. britishpathe.com/video/sixth-world-youth-festival-in-moscow-aka-6th-world (accessed June 2017).

6   See Djagalov and Salazkina (2016) for a fascinating account of a different Soviet festival during this era that also had a significant presence of African filmmakers. They call this festival a "cinematic contact zone," thereby implicitly acknowledging the importance of festivals for international exchange and as heuristic devices for scholars.

7   Manthia Diawara is an accomplished documentary filmmaker, having made films such as *Rouch in Reverse* (1995), *Conakry Kas* (2003), and *Édouard Glissant: One World in Relation* (2010).

8   As I complete this chapter (in May 2017), it is exciting to note that *Daughters of the Dust* will be screened at the BFI as part of its *Sight and Sound Deep Focus: The Black Feminine Onscreen* Season in June 2017, and also released in selected UK cinemas. The film will also be released on Blu-Ray and DVD on 19 June 2017, which will help significantly with the inclusion of this film in syllabi.

9   Bekolo can be thought of as a *bricoleur* since he is not simply a filmmaker, but also a film lecturer and a writer. See, for example, his book *Africa for the Future: Sortir un nouveau monde du cinema* (2009).

10 See Ndlovu-Gatsheni (2016) for an excellent definition of what constitutes a "decolonial" approach.

References

Atkinson, Sarah and Helen W. Kennedy. 2016. "Introduction: Inside-the-scenes – the rise of experiential cinema." *Participations* 13.1: 139–151.

Bailey, Cameron. 2011. Personal communication (audio interview). Toronto International Film Festival. 17 September.

Bekolo, Jean-Pierre Bekolo. 2009 *Africa for the Future: Sortir un nouveau monde du cinema.* Paris: Dagan.

Bisschoff, Lizelle and David Murphy, ed. 2014. *Africa's Lost Classics: New Histories of African Cinema.* London: Legenda.

Bosma, Peter. 2015. *Film Programming: Curating for Cinemas, Festivals, Archives.* New York: Columbia University Press.

Chambers, Iain. 2002. "Unrealized Democracy and a Posthumanist Art." In *Democracy Unrealized: Documenta11 Platform1,* edited by Okwui Enwezor et al., 169–176. Cantz.

Cineaste editors. 2016. "Introduction." *Cineaste* 41.1.

Cousins, Mark. 2014. "Foreword." In Bisschoff and Murphy, xv–xvi.

Diawara, Manthia. 1992. *African Cinema: Politics and Culture.* Bloomington: Indiana University Press.

Diawara, Manthia. 1993. "New York and Ouagadougou: The Homes of African Cinema." *Sight and Sound,* 3.11: 24–26.

Diawara, Manthia. 1994. "On Tracking World Cinema: African Cinema at Film Festivals." *Public Culture,* 6.2: 385–396.

Diawara, Manthia. 2010. *African Film: New Forms of Aesthetics and Politics.* Munich and Berlin: Prestel Verlag.

Djagalov, Rossen and Masha Salazkina. 2016. "Tashkent '68: A Cinematic Contact Zone." *Slavic Review* 75.2: 279–298.

Dovey, Lindiwe. 2012. "New Looks: The Rise of African Women Filmmakers." *Feminist Africa*, 16: 18–36.

Dovey, Lindiwe. 2014. "Curating Africa: Teaching African Film through the Lens of Film Festivals." *Scope: An Online Journal of Film and Television Studies*, 26: 6–9.

Dovey, Lindiwe. 2015a. *Curating Africa in the Age of Film Festivals*. New York: Palgrave Macmillan.

Dovey, Lindiwe. 2015b. "Through the Eye of a Film Festival: Toward a Curatorial and Spectator Centered Ppproach to the Study of African Screen Media." *Cinema Journal*, 54.2: 126–132.

Dovey, Lindiwe. 2015c. "'Bergman in Uganda': Ugandan Veejays, Swedish Pirates, and the Political Value of Live Adaptation." In *The Politics of Adaptation: Media Convergence and Ideology*, edited by Dan Hassler-Forest and Pascal Nicklas, 99–113. New York: Palgrave Macmillan.

Dovey, Lindiwe. 2016. "On the Matter of Fiction: An Approach to the Marginalization of African Film Studies in the Global Academy." *Black Camera*, 7.2: 159–173.

Ellerson, Betti, ed. 2000. *Sisters of the Screen: Women of African on Film, Video and Television*. Trenton, NJ: Africa World Press.

Ellerson, Betti. 2015. "Teaching African Women in Cinema Part One." *Black Camera*, 7.1: 251–261.

Ellerson, Betti. 2016. "Teaching African Women in Cinema Part Two." *Black Camera*, 7.2: 217–233.

Frey, Mattias. 2015. "Introduction: Critical Questions." In *Film Criticism in the Digital Age*, edited by Mattias Frey and Cecilia Sayad, 1–20. New Brunswick, NJ: Rutgers University Press.

Frey, Mattias and Cecilia Sayad, eds. 2015. *Film Criticism in the Digital Age*. New Brunswick, NJ: Rutgers University Press.

Gadjigo, Samba, Ralph H. Faulkingham, Thomas Cassirer, and Reinhard Sander, ed. 1993. *Ousmane Sembène: Dialogues with Critics and Writers*. Amherst: University of Massachusetts Press.

Gibbs, James, ed. 2012. *African Theatre Festivals*. Woodbridge/Rochester: James Currey.

Harrow, Kenneth. 2015. "Manthia Diawara's Waves and the Problem of the 'authentic'." *African Studies Review*, 58.3: 13–30.

Higgins, MaryEllen. 2015. "The Winds of African Cinema." *African Studies Review*, 58.3: 77–92.

Iordanova, Dina. 2013. "Instant, Abundant, and Ubiquitous." *Cineaste*, 39.1: 46–50.

Jayamanne, Laleen. 2001. *Toward Cinema and Its Double: Cross-Cultural Mimesis*. Bloomington/Indianapolis: Indiana University Press.

Julien, Eileen. 2015. "The Critical Present: Where is 'African Literature'?" In *Rethinking African Cultural Production*, edited by Frieda Ekotto and Kenneth Harrow, 17–28. Bloomington: Indiana University Press.

Keathley, Christian. 2006. *Cinephilia and History, or The Wind in the Trees*. Bloomington: Indiana University Press.

Missouri, Montré Aza. 2015. *Black Magic Woman and Narrative Film: Race, Sex, and Afro-Religiosity*. New York: Palgrave Macmillan.

Mistry, Jyoti and Antje Shuhmann, eds. 2015a. *Gaze Regimes: Film and Feminisms in Africa*. Johannesburg: Witwatersrand University Press.

Mistry, Jyoti and Antje Shuhmann. 2015b. "Introduction: By Way of Context and Content." In Mistry and Shuhmann 2015a, ix–xxxiv.

Modisane, Litheko. 2012. *South Africa's Renegade Reels: The Making and Public Lives of Black-centered Films.* New York: Palgrave Macmillan.

Morgan, Jessica. 2013. "What is a Curator?" In *Ten Fundamental Questions of Curating*, edited by Jens Hoffmann, 21–29. Milan: Mousse Publishing.

Ndlovu-Gatsheni, Sabelo. 2016. *The Decolonial Mandela: Peace, Justice, and the Politics of Life.* New York: Berghahn.

Nnaemeka, Obioma. 2004. "Nego-feminism: Theorizing, Practicing, and Pruning Africa's Way." *Signs* 29.2 (Winter): 357–385.

Obrist, Hans Ulrich. 2014. *Ways of Curating.* New York: Farrar, Straus, and Giroux.

Okeke-Agulu, Chika. 2008. "Contribution to 'The Twenty-First Century and the Mega Shows: A Curators' Roundtable'." *NKA: Journal of Contemporary African Art*, Spring/Summer: 152–188.

Rilke, Rainer Maria. 1954. *Letters to a Young Poet.* New York: W.W. Norton & Company.

Ruddick, Lisa. 2015. "When Nothing Is Cool." In *The Future of Scholarly Writing: Critical Interventions*, edited by Angelika Bammer and Ruth-Ellen Boetcher Joeres, 71–85. New York: Palgrave Macmillan.

Ruoff, Jeffrey ed. 2012a. *Coming Soon to a Festival Near You: Programming Film Festivals.* St Andrews: St Andrews Film Studies.

Ruoff, Jeffrey. 2012b."Introduction: Programming Film Festivals." In Ruoff 2012a, 1–21.

Salti, Rasha. 2011. Interview with Author. Toronto International Film Festival. 16 September.

Sontag, Susan. 1966. "Against Interpretation" [1964]. In *Against Interpretation and Other Essays*, 3–14. New York: Farrar, Straus & Giroux.

Tcheuyap, Alexie. 2011. *Postnationalist African Cinemas.* Manchester: Manchester University Press.

Tsika, Noah. 2016. "Introduction: Teaching African Media in the Global Academy." *Black Camera*, 7.2: 94–124.

Ukadike, Nwachukwu Frank, ed. 2002. *Questioning African Cinema: Conversations with Filmmakers.* Minneapolis: University of Minnesota Press.

Vieyra, Paulin Soumanou. 1969. *Le cinéma et l'Afrique.* Paris: Présence Africaine.

Vieyra, Paulin Soumanou. 1972. *Ousmane Sembène, cinéaste: première période, 1962–1971.* Paris: Présence Africaine.

Vieyra, Paulin Soumanou. 1983. *Le cinéma au Sénégal.* Brussels: OCIC and Paris: L'Harmattan.

wa Thiong'o, Ngũgĩ. 2012. *Globalectics: Theory and the Politics of Knowing.* New York: Columbia University Press.

Wilde, Oscar. 1993. Excerpt from "The Critic as Artist" [1890]. In *The Norton Anthology of English Literature*, edited by M.H. Abrams, 1620–1627. New York: W.W. Norton & Company.

Filmography

Afrique sur Seine. 1955. Dir. Paulin Soumanou Vieyra, Mamadou Sarr, and Jacques Kane. France. 22 mins.

Aristotle's Plot. 1996. Dir. Jean-Pierre Bekolo. France/UK/Zimbabwe. 70 mins.

Conakry Kas. 2003. Dir. Manthia Diawara. Guinea-Conakry / USA. 82 mins.

De Voortrekkers. 1916. Dir. Harold Shaw. South Africa. 60 mins.

Domitilla: The Story of a Prostitute. 1997. Dir. Zeb Ejiro. Nigeria. 109 mins.

Édouard Glissant: One World in Relation. 2010. Dir. Manthia Diawara. UK / USA / Martinique. 50 mins.

Lady Gaga. 2012. Ubong Bassey Nya. Nigeria. 241 mins.

Mulholland Drive. 2001. Dir. David Lynch. USA. 147 mins.

The Prostitute. 2001. Dir. Fred Amata.

Rouch in Reverse. 1995. Dir. Manthia Diawara. New York / France. 52 mins.

Saikati. 1992. Dir. Anne Mungai. Kenya / Germany. 94 mins.

Sembène! 2015. Dir. Samba Gadjigo and Jason Silverman. Senegal / USA. 90 mins.

Siliva the Zulu. 1927. Dir. Attilio Gatti. South Africa. 64 mins.

Index

A Companion to African Cinema, First Edition. Edited by Kenneth W. Harrow and Carmela Garritano.
© 2019 John Wiley & Sons, Inc. Published 2019 by John Wiley & Sons, Inc.